GUNRUNNERS
THE COVERT ARMS TRAIL TO IRELAND

SEAN BOYNE

THE O'BRIEN PRESS
DUBLIN

First published 2006 by The O'Brien Press Ltd,
12 Terenure Road East, Dublin 6, Ireland.
Tel: +353 1 4923333; Fax: +353 1 4922777
E-mail: books@obrien.ie
Website: www.obrien.ie

Hardback Edition
ISBN-10: 0-86278-908-7
ISBN-13: 978-0-86278-908-4

Paperback Edition
ISBN-10: 1-84717-014-5
ISBN-13: 978-1-84717-014-9

British Library Cataloguing-in-Publication Data
Boyne, Sean
Gunrunners : the covert arms trail to Ireland
1. Illegal arms transfers - Ireland - History - 20th century
2. Paramilitary forces - Northern Ireland - History - 20th century
3. Terrorists - Ireland - History - 20th century
4. Northern Ireland - History - 1969-1994
I. Title
941.6'0824

1 2 3 4 5 6 7 8 9 10
06 07 08 09 10 11

Layout and design: The O'Brien Press Ltd.

While every effort has been made to contact the holders of copyrights, if any omission or oversight has occurred we would welcome the copyright holder(s) to inform the publisher.

GUNRUNNERS

Sean Boyne was educated at University College, Dublin, graduating with a degree in History and Politics. He is Political Correspondent of the Dublin-based *Sunday World*. As a journalist he covered the early phase of the Troubles in Northern Ireland. One of his specialities is the arming of Irish paramilitaries. He has been interviewed widely on this topic by the BBC and other news media, and has written on the subject for *Jane's Intelligence Review*.

CONTENTS

ACKNOWLEDGEMENTS

There are many who assisted in the research for this book who do not want to be quoted by name. Some were involved in republican activity in times past; others are from the world of politics or law enforcement; some were colleagues in the world of journalism. I would like to thank them all most sincerely for giving me their trust and their assistance.

There are also those who very kindly assisted whom I can name. Taking them in alphabetical order, I would like to thank Brendan Anderson, biographer of the late Joe Cahill, for talking to me about the Canadian mercenaries who flew arms into Ireland. I am grateful to CBS 4 journalist Joe Bergantino, whom I met in Boston, for providing fascinating detail about the aftermath of the Valhalla gunrunning operation. Much thanks go to my journalist colleague and neighbour in Dublin, John Cooney, for his invaluable advice, for loaning books and newspaper clippings from his own archives and for giving me the benefit of his long experience covering Irish current affairs. In a number of interviews the late Tony Divall, who lived in Hamburg, gave a unique insight into the esoteric areas of intelligence and arms trafficking. I am grateful to him for overcoming the natural suspicion he would have of an Irish journalist, and for giving me a glimpse into his secret world.

The noted London-based playwright Sam Dowling, formerly involved with the Official republican movement, helpfully recalled events in the Border area in the early years of the Troubles. In New York, the veteran Mayo-born lawyer Frank Durkan, nephew of the legendary Paul O'Dwyer, was most generous with his time and gave me the benefits of insights from long years of experience. The Bohola man and his uncle always gave generously of their time and resources to the causes in which they believed. I am grateful to my colleague Des Ekin for agreeing to look over the manuscript – a superb journalist whose judgement I always trust.

In Dublin, Finian Fallon, son of the murdered Garda Richard Fallon, very kindly agreed to meet me and to talk of his family's campaign for justice and for closure. In Boston, movie-maker and writer Rich Farrell was most generous in steering me in the direction of the right people to talk to – again my thanks. In Brooklyn, the late George Harrison was a hugely important interviewee. He had an encyclopaedic knowledge of the subject matter. I was glad to talk to him in time – he died just three weeks after the interview. Belfast journalist Barry McCaffrey of the *Irish News* very helpfully emailed me copies of some of his stories. In Howth, County Dublin, Barney McKenna, renowned banjo player with ballad group The Dubliners, very kindly brought me up to speed on the history of his boat, a vessel formerly known as the *Marita Ann* which, under a previous owner, had engaged in a major gunrunning operation. I am very thankful to Cecilia Moore for talking to me of her memories of her partner Seamus Ruddy, who was murdered in France in 1985 and whose remains have never been found.

In Maghera, County Derry, John Kelly of Arms Trial fame gave me the benefit of his memories of some historic events. It was very important to get his perspective, and I am extremely grateful. With the death of Charles Haughey, John Kelly is the only Arms Trial defendant still alive. My colleague Hugh Jordan was very helpful whenever I needed a phone number or to clarify some obscure point. Commandant Victor Laing and Commandant Pat Brennan very kindly gave me assistance in accessing Military Archives at Cathal Brugha Barracks in Dublin. I am most grateful to Gerry McGeough for talking to me of his own memories of times past – once again I gained some extremely important insights, which I greatly appreciate. I was very glad to talk to Mrs Emily McIntyre at her home in Quincy, Massachusetts, even though she was constrained in what she could say because of a pending legal case.

In Boston, Pat Nee agreed to talk to me about his own role in the *Valhalla* gunrunning operation. This was hugely valuable and added greatly to the store of knowledge about this affair. Michael O'Brien of the O'Brien Press encouraged me to write this book – it might not have been written but for his expressions of interest in the project, and I thank him for acting as midwife. I am most grateful also to Susan Houlden and Eoin O'Brien of the O'Brien Press for their painstaking editing work, and to barrister James McGowan for a very thorough legal check. In Dublin, DR O'Connor-Lysaght talked me through the intricacies of the world of Trotskyism, and shared some of his memories of the late Peter Graham. Despite being laid low on a hospital bed in New Jersey, Lou Stephens was extremely helpful, providing valuable insights into the work that he did with the FBI – he is as passionate as ever about his core values and beliefs. Back in New York, I was very glad to meet Ken Tierney who shared some fascinating memories of the Fort Worth Five affair. My colleague Paul Williams, doyen of Irish crime journalists and Crime Editor of the *Sunday World*, was most helpful and gave me the benefit of his own vast knowledge of security matters. I would also like to thank staff at the National Library in Dublin and at the library of the Pompidou Centre in Paris for their courtesy and assistance. On a trip to the US for a journalism programme organised by Boston College, I gained new insights that were relevant to the book. I would like to thank Mary O'Herlihy and JD Myers and their colleagues at Boston College for their hard work in facilitating the visit.

Apart from the research conducted specifically for this book, I also drew on research and interviews carried out during decades in journalism. For a previous project I interviewed arms dealers around the world, and I drew on some of the information they gave me as background for this book. These include Sam Cummings, Mike Kokin and Sarkis Soghanalian. Over the years in journalism I talked to others whose comments later became relevant to the subject matter of this present work. They include Kevin Boland, Lieutenant Colonel Sean Clancy, Cleveland Cram, Rauf Denktash, Captain James Kelly, Billy McKee, Seán Mac Stíofáin and Ms Ellie Norton. Again, my thanks.

Preface

Since the Irish 'Troubles' began in the late 1960s, there were many efforts by individuals and groups on both sides of the sectarian divide to procure arms abroad and to smuggle them into Ireland, either for defensive or offensive purposes. Some efforts were successful. Others ended in failure. This is the story of those gunrunning efforts. It is a history of the arms trail to Ireland during the years of civil strife.

Gunrunners seeks to analyse how gunrunning operations were organised by groups such as the Provisional IRA. It examines the sources of the weaponry; the types and quantities of weapons involved; the manner in which arms were procured and paid for; and the way the gunrunners smuggled, or tried to smuggle, the materiel to Ireland. Also examined are the ways in which some operations were infiltrated or otherwise foiled by law enforcement and/or security/intelligence agencies. The book looks at the role of international arms dealers; the part played by 'amateur' gunrunners; the role of paramilitary members or sympathisers who became specialised in the trafficking of arms; and the important role played by Libyan leader Colonel Muammar Gadaffi, who donated large amounts of weaponry and explosives to the IRA. The book focuses on the paramilitaries' requirements in terms of war materiel – and the ways in which, in certain cases, these requirements changed and evolved over the years.

The book also deals with activities which, strictly speaking, cannot be defined as gunrunning, with its connotations of illegality. Several individuals accused of illegally trying to import arms into the Irish Republic – the affair that led to the Arms Trial of 1970 – were ultimately acquitted. These efforts to import arms may not have been illegal but they were certainly covert, and they also come within the ambit of this book.

Among those who have been interviewed, either on the record or on a non-attributable basis, are some of the gunrunners themselves, as well as individuals from the world of law enforcement and intelligence.

The book includes tables listing and analysing actual and reported arms procurement operations by the different paramilitary groups, both republican and loyalist; the outcome or likely outcome of each operation; and the types and amounts of war materiel involved, or reported/estimated to have been involved. There are also tables detailing estimates by the security forces of the inventories of arms in the possession of the Provisional IRA and loyalist paramilitaries in recent years. Also examined in detail is the process whereby IRA arms were decommissioned.

Gunrunning is a murky area and there are aspects of this secret world that may never become known. Some of the players have maintained their silence, or taken their secrets with them to the grave. Nevertheless, the author hopes that he has made a useful contribution to the study of this intriguing topic.

Prologue

The British were waiting for the signal from the elderly gunrunning ship the *Claudia*, but it never came. The spooks of the British intelligence service MI6 were getting worried. They had an informant on the inside of the IRA arms smuggling operation and he had been tutored in what to do. Gunther Leinhauser, owner of the *Claudia*, had been given a direction-finding device. He was supposed to activate it aboard the rather decrepit coaster. But the British were not picking up any signal that would allow them to locate and track the ship as it set off to ferry a consignment of weapons from Libya to Ireland. The ship could be anywhere in the Mediterranean.

The intelligence man spearheading the operation against the IRA, the late Donald Boswell Gurrey, had some inquiries made. Contact was established with Leinhauser somewhere in Europe. The bespectacled German was nervous. He had a confession to make. He had become jittery at the last minute, and admitted that he had not planted the direction-finding device on board the *Claudia*, as the ship set off on its gunrunning mission. No doubt he feared the IRA would discover that he had double-crossed them. It was a reasonable concern. Nevertheless, the British were aghast – and angry.

Leinhauser had learned of the IRA operation when he was approached by the Provos. They were looking for a vessel that could smuggle a consignment of weapons to Ireland for use against British forces in Northern Ireland. The weapons were being donated by mercurial Libyan strongman Colonel Muammar Gadaffi, who was regarded with great suspicion as a 'rogue leader' by some western governments.

Leinhauser promptly tipped off Tony Divall, an old friend and gunrunning colleague who had been a low-level employee of MI6 in West Berlin just after the Second World War. Divall, in turn, tipped off Donald Gurrey, one of his MI6 superiors from the old days in Berlin. An operation to stymie the arms smugglers was set in train. Details of this remarkable covert operation, reminiscent of a plot from a novel by John le Carre or Frederick Forsyth, emerged during research for this book.

Despite the setback caused by Leinhauser getting cold feet, the British were determined not to give up. They knew that the *Claudia*, carrying tons of mainly Eastern Bloc 'hardware', and with veteran IRA leader Joe Cahill on board, would have to sail through the 'choke point' of the Straits of Gibraltar en route to Ireland. The British have long maintained a naval base and a joint civil–military airport at the tiny UK colony of Gibraltar, and the British presence on 'The Rock' at the southern tip of Spain proved useful on this occasion. A watch was kept and the coaster was spotted as it chugged through the straits. At this period, the navy maintained a frigate and a patrol boat permanently on station at Gibraltar, but tracking the *Claudia* called for more subtle measures. A Royal Navy submarine was assigned to follow the *Claudia* as it sailed to Ireland. The RAF kept a squadron of seven Nimrod maritime surveillance aircraft at Luqa in Malta, and it is possible that an aircraft from this squadron was also deployed.

When it was confirmed that the gunrunning ship was on its way, the British government passed the word to the Irish authorities. Taoiseach Liam Cosgrave was very determined indeed to intercept the arms. The Irish naval service seized the vessel off the County Waterford coast on 28 March 1973, and commandeered its cargo. It was one of the first major international gunrunning operations mounted by the IRA as the Troubles escalated. Joe Cahill, whose record in the IRA went back to the 1940s, was one of those who went to jail.

As a reporter, I covered aspects of the *Claudia* drama, and it was one of the events that stirred my interest in the shadowy world of gunrunning and that helped to inspire this book. There were to be many other gunrunning operations, some of which ended in failure. But the IRA was to prove extremely resourceful in procuring weapons abroad, and in smuggling them to Ireland.

Leinhauser and Divall were not acting solely out of principle in undermining the IRA operation. When all the fuss had died down, there remained one final duty for Donald Gurrey to perform. According to an informed source, he travelled to Germany for a rendezvous with Divall and Leinhauser. The British were angry with Leinhauser for failing to carry out instructions. But the arms cargo had been seized, and it was a question of 'all's well that ends well'. Gurrey met the two wheeler-dealers in that classic location for furtive, spy-novel meetings – an underground car park. And there, away from prying eyes, he handed over an envelope to each man, containing a generous 'gratuity'. There was nothing so indiscreet as a few drinks or a meal to celebrate. It was the first time that Gurrey had actually come face to face with Leinhauser. Having pocketed their pay-offs from Her Majesty's government, Divall and Leinhauser thanked their benefactor, shook hands, made their excuses and left.

Introduction

My journalistic interest in paramilitary weapons goes back a long way, to 1972. That was the year I saw firearms being carried openly on the streets of the mainly Catholic enclave known as Free Derry. Back in that far-off era, journalists reporting on Free Derry could see, at first hand, weapons being carried by members of two rival organisations, each claiming to be the genuine Irish Republican Army (IRA) – the Provisional IRA (PIRA), linked to Provisional Sinn Féin, and the Official IRA (OIRA), linked to Official Sinn Féin. Masked men from both organisations, with their guns, were out on the streets mounting checkpoints, night and day. Various classes of weapons were regularly on public show. I had a journalist's curiosity about the history behind those weapons – how they were acquired and how they made their way to Ireland. It was one of the factors that eventually gave rise to this book. Back in the early 1970s, one could not ask too many questions about where the guns came from. In more recent years, however, with the dying down of the Troubles, some of the players have been more prepared to talk about arms trafficking and other things that happened during those long years of conflict.

I visited Free Derry as a reporter during the month of April, 1972. It was an extraordinary place – a region of a Northern Ireland city, officially part of the United Kingdom, where the writ of Queen Elizabeth did not run.

Back in those early days, the Provos mainly operated in the Bogside area, while the Officials' power base was in the nearby Creggan housing estate.

Looking back on it now, neither wing of the IRA in Derry in 1972 seemed to have terribly advanced weaponry, at least to judge by the arms carried in public. A PIRA roadblock at Lecky Road in the Bogside that I encountered was manned by three men carrying M-1 carbines – Second World War-vintage weapons. Up the road in Creggan, an OIRA checkpoint was manned by two men, one carrying an ancient-looking Lee Enfield .303 rifle and the other sporting an equally venerable Thompson sub-machine gun. There was no sign of the more modern Armalites or M-16 rifles that were being smuggled into Ireland around that time.

The weapons brandished in public were not just for show, as a number of chilling incidents illustrated. A Catholic driving a bus in Free Derry was dragged screaming from his vehicle by masked Provisional gunmen and shot dead on the street – it had been discovered that he was a part-time member of the Ulster Defence Regiment. Extreme elements in the Officials shot dead Marcus McCausland, a local landowner, for alleged spying, even though the 'evidence' was very scant indeed. I remember meeting a senior figure in the Officials, the late Malachy McGurran, and he was clearly embarrassed by the murder.

There was also a range of handguns in use in Free Derry – I myself encountered one senior Provo in the enclave carrying a .45 Colt automatic in the inside breast pocket of his jacket and a snub-nosed .38 Smith and Wesson shoved inside his belt. One of the reasons I remember the man so well is that, despite being virtually a walking armoury, he made the Sign of the Cross devoutly as I travelled with him in a car by the Catholic church in Creggan.

Apart from M-1s and Thompson sub-machine guns, the Provos in Free Derry also had a few Sterling sub-machine guns, and a few Lee Enfield .303s, mainly used for sniping. At one stage they were even said to have acquired a Bren gun. In the North generally at this period, the Provos had a ragtag collection of weapons, with types ranging reportedly from the American Springfield rifle to the .223 Remington, with Armalites also making their debut.

Free Derry was set up as a 'no-go' area following the internment swoops of August 1971. During my visit the following year, the youthful Martin

McGuinness was generally seen as *de facto* chief of the IRA in the enclave. He had his headquarters in an industrial-type building in the Bogside. Attired in his trademark anorak and jeans, he was frequently to be found there, conferring discreetly with his followers. My guide, an IRA supporter, pointed to a number of modern cars parked outside the Provo HQ. With a hint of pride, he explained that they had all been hijacked. In an era when many cars were of the modest two-door variety, these vehicles were all sleek, four-door models. 'It makes it easier for the boys to get in and out during an operation,' my guide explained helpfully.

I recall meeting McGuinness himself during my visit. He didn't have a great deal to say. He didn't talk much to journalists in those days. That was to change in later decades, however, as he came to international prominence as Sinn Féin's chief negotiator in the Peace Process.

Free Derry came to an end in late July 1972, in an incursion mounted by the British Army called Operation Motorman. It marked the end of a period when paramilitary weapons were on daily show on the streets of a Northern Ireland city. In the years that followed there would be occasional displays of weapons by the Provisionals, for propaganda purposes, but never on the same scale as occurred in Free Derry.

The start of the Troubles in the late 1960s in Northern Ireland had marked the beginning of a scramble for weapons, especially on the part of the republican element which became the Provisional IRA. The Provos were looking not only for more firearms; they also wanted to upgrade the quality of their arsenal.

The trouble had begun to boil up as hardline loyalists reacted angrily to civil rights demonstrations by Catholics protesting against discrimination under a Unionist-dominated Stormont government, especially in the areas of housing allocation and voting procedures for local government. Vivid TV imagery went around the world of members of the Royal Ulster Constabulary (RUC) batoning civil rights demonstrators off the streets in Derry, adding to the sense of resentment against the northern state. Reforms that were to be introduced to deal with Catholic grievances failed to stem the rising levels of violence. Tension escalated in 1969 with attacks by loyalist mobs on Catholic areas. There were fears of a full-scale 'pogrom' against Catholics, and refugees from nationalist areas fled south to the Irish Republic.

The events of 1969 brought about a crisis within the IRA, a mainly Catholic, nationalist guerrilla force that was outlawed on both sides of the Border. The organisation had waged a spasmodic paramilitary campaign for some years up to 1962, when hostilities fizzled out. It was a relatively chivalrous campaign. One of those active in the republican movement at this period, Tomás Mac Giolla, who later became President of Official Sinn Féin and an outspoken critic of the Provos, has pointed out that in order to avoid inflaming sectarian passions the North's part-time police, the B-Specials, were never targeted during the Border campaign. This was in contrast with the later, more extreme, Provo campaign that got under way in the 1970s, when, in effect, there was a potential death sentence on anybody joining the security forces in the North, either on a full-time or part-time basis.

The traditional aim of the IRA was to secure a British withdrawal from Northern Ireland, and the reunification of the country under a native Irish government. During the 1960s, a left-leaning leadership under chief of staff Cathal Goulding was increasingly moving away from traditional republican militarism. It has even been claimed that in 1968 some of the IRA's weapons were sold to a tiny group of Welsh nationalist extremists who called themselves the Free Wales Army. It has also been said that in the same year the IRA sold arms to the underground Basque separatist group ETA.

Some key supporters of the Goulding wing at the time increasingly saw paramilitary violence as a negative force, driving a wedge between the two communities in the North and fomenting sectarian strife between the Catholic minority and the approximately one million Protestants who saw themselves as British. They wanted to break out of what they saw as the blinkered thinking of those who sought to reproduce the 'physical force' republicanism of the past. In the bitter war of words that followed the formation in late 1969 of the breakaway Provisional IRA, which aimed to follow in the traditional path of republican 'armed struggle', some of Goulding's followers liked to refer to their Provo rivals as 'green fascists', accusing them of extreme nationalism, authoritarianism and the glorification of violence, and comparing them to the German Nazis of the 1930s.

Many Northern Ireland Protestants, for their part, saw little future for themselves in a united Ireland. The economy of the South was quite weak at the time, and Unionists resented the idea of being bombed into a

Catholic-oriented state ruled from Dublin. Many northern Protestants saw the Republic, where divorce was forbidden and even condoms were outlawed, as a state that reflected conservative Catholic values. They feared that such a state would not respect their civil liberties and traditions. Constitutional nationalists North and South developed their own criticisms of the Provisionals as the IRA began to take human life in pursuit of a united Ireland. The Provo movement was seen as being dominated by middle-aged or elderly men in love with the romance of violent rebellion, who were irresponsibly sending out impressionable young people to put their lives on the line in a war that could never be won; men who were intolerant of the majority view in favour of peace, who were politically immature and lacked the imagination to see a way forward other than through traditional 'physical force' militarism, and who lacked respect for the most fundamental civil liberty of all – the sanctity of human life.

The Provisionals, for their part, saw the British as having no right to rule any part of Ireland, and saw themselves as inheritors of a long tradition of 'armed struggle', martyrdom and self-sacrifice in the separatist cause. The movement exercised a powerful emotional attraction for young Catholics, who felt themselves to be second-class citizens in a Unionist-dominated state. Many of those who were interned or who went to jail for the cause found a great sense of comradeship and camaraderie as they shared life 'inside' with other republicans, further enhancing loyalty to the movement. Major reforms that were carried out to make the Northern state a warmer house for Catholics did not meet the basic Provo demand of a British withdrawal.

The Provisional strategy, as enunciated in the handbook for its members known as the Green Book, was to carry out a war of attrition against enemy personnel 'aimed at causing as many casualties and deaths as possible'. While Sinn Féin politicians frequently talked in public of the IRA's defensive role in protecting the nationalist people, the internal IRA handbook was privately sending out a very different message to the Volunteers – the emphasis was on taking offensive action and on killing the 'enemy', not on defence. The Green Book talked of the importance of luring the enemy into situations where they could be shot. 'If the Brits don't make themselves available to be shot when and where it suits us we attempt to get them to an area where we can operate against them on some bogus pretext or other, bomb scare, body found, reported robbery etc.'

It was also part of the strategy outlined in the Green Book to defend the war of liberation 'by punishing criminals, collaborators and informers'. In line with this principle, punishment attacks and kneecappings were carried out on youths and young men alleged to have been involved in petty crime and anti-social behaviour. Some criminal offences were punished by death – that was the fate meted out to a number of alleged cannabis dealers during the 1990s, although the IRA did not claim formal responsibility for these murders.

Over the years, there were regular killings of those judged to be collaborators or informers. From the 1980s, the IRA waged an assassination campaign against workmen carrying out repair work on British Army and RUC bases. In January 1992, the IRA detonated a 500lb roadside bomb at Teebane, County Tyrone, as a bus carrying fourteen employees of a construction firm passed. Eight workers, all Protestants, were killed. The firm had been carrying out work at Lisanelly military base in Omagh.

Some individuals were targeted for other reasons. In 1990, a man called Patsy Gillespie seems to have been singled out because he worked in the canteen of a British Army base. In an area of high unemployment such as Derry, many nationalists would not have seen such work as deserving of punishment of any kind – certainly not capital punishment. Nevertheless, Mr Gillespie was abducted and used in a 'human bomb' attack. IRA Volunteers tied him into a car containing a bomb and he was forced to drive the vehicle to a British Army checkpoint. The bomb was then detonated, blowing Mr Gillespie and five soldiers to pieces.

In addition, the IRA waged war on the Northern economy, mounting bomb attacks on office blocks, luxury hotels, department stores, factories and the like. Often the preferred weapon was the car bomb left on a city street, which could cause carnage among members of the public. During a left-wing phase of the struggle, a number of English businessmen with links to Northern Ireland were assassinated by the IRA, apparently because they were seen as members of the 'employer class'. The IRA also carried out some random killings of Protestants in retaliation for loyalist terrorism.

Sometimes, during the years of conflict, the British Army acted as a recruiting sergeant for the Provos by, for instance, shooting dead thirteen unarmed civilians during a civil rights march in Derry on 'Bloody Sunday',

30 January 1972. Internment without trial had been introduced the previous year, with hundreds of republican suspects 'lifted' – just one of a series of events that was to alienate nationalists.

The IRA had an increasing tally of members killed during the conflict and the powerful, emotional weapon of martyrdom enhanced support for the organisation. The ranks of the republican dead were later to be swelled by those who starved themselves to death in the H-Blocks at the Maze Prison in 1981 in a campaign for political status as prisoners. Among them was Bobby Sands, who was elected a Westminster MP while on hunger strike. It emerged that there was collusion between some elements in the security forces and loyalist death squads – another factor that disgusted and alienated nationalists.[1]

In the midst of all this turmoil were the moderate Northern nationalists like John Hume, leader of the Social Democratic and Labour Party (SDLP). These nationalists campaigned vigorously for civil rights and assailed the abuses of the security forces. They favoured a united Ireland, but sought to achieve their aims by peaceful, democratic means. Hume took the view that murder and mayhem was not the best way to build bridges between communities and develop a just, pluralist society. He and other like-minded activists favoured peaceful co-existence between Catholics and Protestants, but sometimes the voice of moderation was drowned out as the conflict escalated.

The vast majority of nationalists on the island of Ireland voted for parties that rejected violence, even though those parties may have originated in the 'armed struggle' of the 1920s. Many nationalists refused to accept that the IRA had a moral or legal right to wage war and take life in the name of the Irish people.

In the South, in the early 1970s, the Fianna Fáil party was in power. The party had evolved from those who had fought on the republican side in the Civil War of 1922–23, and was founded by one of the leaders of the 1916 Rising, Éamon de Valera, after he broke with the IRA in 1926. As the Troubles started, Taoiseach Jack Lynch, who led the Fianna Fáil government, enunciated the policy of the party – it aimed to achieve the unity of Ireland, but by consent.

The ranks of the Provisional IRA were swelled in the early 1970s by republicans who were deeply dissatisfied with the move away from the physical force tradition, and who considered that not enough was being done to provide armed protection to Catholic areas. Those who stayed with the Goulding wing of the movement, which became known as the Official IRA (OIRA), also engaged in violence and killings but were to call a cease-fire in 1972. There was sporadic ongoing violence on the part of the OIRA, and throughout the 1970s OIRA gunmen carried out unclaimed armed robberies for fund-raising purposes. There was a significant development in the middle of the decade when a militant element broke away from the OIRA to form the ruthless Irish National Liberation Army (INLA).

As the Provisionals moved from purely defensive to offensive operations, they saw an opportunity, as they perceived it, to finally push the British out of Northern Ireland. In line with the Provos' militant nationalist ideology, attacks were mounted on the security forces in the North, as part of a wide-ranging paramilitary campaign. Personnel from the British Army; the largely part-time locally recruited force, the Ulster Defence Regiment (UDR); the Royal Ulster Constabulary (RUC); and the RUC Reserve were all targeted, as were loyalist paramilitaries. The targeting of locally-recruited members of these forces provided the IRA with many opportunities for assassinations. In a rural area, for instance, republicans generally knew which of their Protestant neighbours had joined the security forces. Such men could be killed with comparative ease while off duty in their homes, on their farms, at their places of work, or on their way to church. The killing could be by means of shooting, or by the under-car booby-trap bomb, which usually blew off the victim's legs – a device known in Provo parlance as an 'up and over'.

Critics of the IRA campaign argued that republican violence only helped to fuel loyalist paramilitary violence, and resulted in further retaliatory attacks on Catholics. Many Protestants, appalled by the murders of their co-religionists, saw the IRA campaign as a ruthless, inhuman attempt to oppress, intimidate and terrorise their community. Some talked of a republican attempt at 'ethnic cleansing'. The moderate Archbishop Robin Eames, Church of Ireland Primate of All Ireland, was an outspoken critic of the horrific violence perpetrated by loyalist paramilitaries, but he also focused on one of the key dilemmas posed by the IRA campaign: 'To argue that its violence is a consequence of injustices perpetrated on the community it claims to defend seems to ignore the real injustice the IRA inflicts on its victims.'[2]

To pursue the strategy outlined in the Green Book of killing as many 'enemy personnel' as possible, the Provos needed weaponry. They became adept at manufacturing mortars and explosives, especially in South Armagh where they had strong support and where the movements of security forces were hampered due to the threat posed by roadside bombs and snipers. However, the IRA also needed more advanced arms and ammunition, and this need gave rise to a series of gunrunning operations from the late 1960s to the 1990s. Some were successful; others ended in failure.

Generally it can be said that the Provisionals were the most active of the Irish paramilitary groups in terms of procuring arms from foreign sources. Despite some failures, they were to show considerable resourcefulness in importing arms. By the mid-1990s, security sources in the Republic estimated that the organisation had accumulated enough weaponry, mainly from Libya, to equip about 800 men – the equivalent of a full-strength infantry battalion in a conventional army.

In the PIRA structure, the senior figure ultimately responsible for procuring and storing war materiel, the Quartermaster General (QMG), had a particular status. He was always a member of the Army Council, the seven-person body that runs the IRA on a day-to-day basis.[3]

In their drive to procure arms in the early years of the Troubles, Irish nationalists turned on a number of occasions to international arms dealers or gunrunners. These operations, employing the professional services of men from the 'grey' area of the arms trade, mostly ended in failure. One of the first attempts to procure arms for the defence of nationalist areas in the North was spearheaded by an Irish Army intelligence officer. He attempted to buy weaponry covertly through a German arms dealer using Irish government funds that had been allocated for the 'relief of distress' in the North but which, a parliamentary inquiry later found, had been improperly diverted to the procurement of arms. Two government ministers were sacked over the affair. In the ensuing furore, the arms were never delivered.

A senior IRA figure travelled to the Eastern Bloc in the same era to buy a consignment of arms from a Czech state company, again with the aid of an arms dealer. Once again, the operation was detected by the authorities, and the arms seized. In 1973, another arms dealer provided a ship to transport a cargo of arms from Libya to Ireland, and here again the operation failed, with the arms being captured. During research for this book, details emerged as to how British intelligence infiltrated both the Czech and Libyan operations.

The IRA fared best at this period when it relied on its own die-hard supporters, especially in America, to acquire arms and to smuggle them, often in very small quantities, to Ireland. The IRA's most reliable asset in New York at this period was the veteran gunrunner George Harrison, a life-long supporter of the republican campaign to drive the British out of Ireland, who ran guns not for money but for the cause. The USA, with its large Irish ethnic population and liberal gun laws, was for many years an important source of weaponry for the IRA.

Apart from the Harrison network, other groups and individuals in the US also became involved in the procurement and/or smuggling of arms; some operations were successful, others were detected by the authorities. Arms procurement was centred mainly, but not exclusively, on the east coast – there was also some activity in San Francisco, for instance. There was also republican gunrunning activity in Canada. Throughout the 1970s, groups of republican sympathisers in various cities in the US came together to buy arms, such as Armalites and pistols, in gun shops, and sent them to Ireland. By the 1980s, arms procurement in the US had come under the tighter control of the IRA leadership in Belfast. Now gunrunning operations tended to be overseen by members of the IRA, rather than by local sympathisers, although the latter continued to play a role.

The Middle East was another area explored in the 1970s as a source of weapons. There was at least one attempt to import arms provided by Palestinian elements in Lebanon.

Meanwhile the FBI, with the advantage of new anti-terrorism laws, became more proactive in tackling Irish gunrunning. By the mid-1980s, it had become more difficult for Provo gunrunners to operate effectively in the US. In the 1980s and early 1990s, several attempts by republicans to acquire arms in the US, or to smuggle them to Ireland, were foiled, partly due to 'sting' operations mounted by the FBI. Nevertheless, there were gunrunning operations that were never detected, with arms coming from unknown locations, and by the 1980s the IRA had managed to equip its members with advanced assault rifles such as the Heckler & Koch 7.62mm G3.

In the mid-1980s a major source of arms opened up. The IRA experienced massive good fortune when Libya's Colonel Gadaffi donated several boatloads of weaponry, greatly boosting the IRA arsenal. These deliveries ensured that by the latter part of the 1980s, the IRA was by far the best armed of the paramilitary groups operating in Ireland.

With their need for infantry and support weapons and deadly Semtex explosive largely satisfied by the Libyan shipments (although modern automatic pistols may have remained in relatively short supply), IRA bosses were able to concentrate on special requirements. They began developing high-tech bomb equipment, and the means to counter the electronic countermeasures employed by the British Army. Efforts were also redoubled to procure high-powered sniper rifles and surface-to-air missiles.

The Good Friday Agreement of 1998 heralded, it was hoped by many, a move away from paramilitarism and an end to arms smuggling. However, in 1999, an IRA gunrunning operation was uncovered in Florida – another setback for the Peace Process.

The smaller Irish republican paramilitary group, the INLA, also sought to import weaponry from the US, but relied more on supplies from sources in Lebanon and, later, from Palestinian sources in Eastern Europe. Surface-to-air missiles were on the INLA shopping list, but the organisation failed to secure such weapons.

When dissident republicans broke away from the IRA in the late 1990s in protest at the latter's ceasefire, and formed the Real IRA (RIRA), the new group's quest for weapons took them to a region that had not previously been explored by Irish paramilitaries in search of arms – the former Yugoslavia, where, following years of warfare and turmoil, everything from hand grenades to anti-tank weapons was available on the black market. In regions such as Bosnia, gunrunners could get heavier equipment such as Soviet-designed rocket launchers that were not available 'over the counter' in US gun stores.

On the other side of the sectarian divide, the loyalist paramilitary organisations became increasingly militant and ruthless – they would claim it was in response to republican terrorism – and they were also in the market for arms. The Ulster-Scots Protestant diaspora proved useful in this regard. Guns and detonators were smuggled in from Canada, and explosives were procured in Scotland. Loyalists also looked further afield, and through a

South African-linked intermediary, a large shipment of arms was imported in the 1980s. There was also an abortive attempt to import a major arms shipment from Poland in the 1990s.

The loyalist paramilitaries did not need large quantities of weapons to carry on a campaign of sectarian terror. Very often their targets were ordinary Catholics with no paramilitary links who were chosen at random for death. The murder gang known as the Shankill Butchers showed that spreading terror does not require a large arsenal of firearms. Members of this depraved gang used knives to torture and slaughter Catholics abducted at random on the streets. The RUC, in one of its better performances, cracked down on the gang and put its key players behind bars.

For anyone studying gunrunning operations of recent decades, it is useful to bear in mind that the tradition of gunrunning on both sides of the political divide in Ireland goes back several generations. I was reminded by John Cooney, Director of the Humbert Summer School, that when France's General Humbert landed with his forces in County Mayo in August 1798, he brought with him a consignment of cannon, muskets and other materiel to be distributed among the Irish insurgents.

Some gunrunning episodes have entered the annals of Irish folk history. One of the best-known loyalist gunrunning operations took place on 25 April 1914, when the *Clyde Valley* landed 30,000 rifles and five million rounds of ammunition at Larne for the Ulster Volunteer Force, whose members were opposed to Home Rule – they wanted to keep the connection with Britain. In the mid-1970s a British Army patrol found about fifty of these rifles, in their original grease and packing material, walled up in a house in Belfast – the Mausers had been there for more than sixty years. The Catholic occupants of the house had been blissfully unaware of the arsenal under their noses.

In July 1914, the English-born spy thriller writer Erskine Childers sailed his yacht *Asgard* into Howth harbour, near Dublin. The vessel was crammed with 1,500 rifles destined for the Irish Volunteers, who, a couple of years later, would take part in the 1916 Rising. In August 1914, another consignment of rifles for the Volunteers was landed at Kilcoole, County Wicklow. A German ship, the *Aud*, which had sailed from Lübeck, tried to land arms in County Kerry for the 1916 Rising, but was scuttled by its crew after capture.

Other operations are less well-known – for instance, during the War of Independence there was a steady stream of arms coming to the Volunteers from republican sympathisers in Scotland.[4]

Returning to more recent times, in 1998, after decades of conflict, the people of Ireland, North and South, voted for the Good Friday Agreement, heralding, it was hoped, a new era of peace in Ireland. The decommissioning of IRA arms in September 2005 marked a major landmark on the long road to normal politics, and the ending of the rule of the gun. Dissident republicans have held on to their arms and, at the time of writing, efforts are being made to persuade loyalist paramilitaries to decommission their weapons.

The path to peace has been long and difficult. Guns were just one symptom of a deeper malaise. There will be many who hope that the ongoing peace process will ensure not only the removal of all paramilitary weapons from the equation, but also the mindset that led to their procurement and use in the first place.

CHAPTER 1

Saor Éire and the Haughey Connection

It started out as a quiet, uneventful morning. It was Friday, 3 April 1970, and I was a reporter in the newsroom of the *Irish Press* on Burgh Quay, Dublin. There was the usual clatter of typewriters. Reporters sat around the big table at the heart of the newsroom, writing news stories, reading newspapers or talking into phones. There were no major stories breaking.

A colleague had somehow managed to tune a transistor radio into the Garda communications network. There were routine calls, as Gardaí went about their work of policing the city. And then, on the crackling radio link, we heard the words that would always be seared into my memory. An anguished voice was sending an urgent message to the officers manning the Garda control centre in Dublin Castle, and it was a message that shocked and electrified us all: 'Garda Fallon has been shot.'

A distraught colleague of the severely injured Garda was on the radio seeking assistance. The call sparked a major manhunt and stunned the nation. Forty-two-year-old Garda Richard Fallon had been gunned down by a gang robbing the Bank of Ireland on Arran Quay, in Dublin's city centre. Fallon and two colleagues, all unarmed, had gone to the bank in a patrol car to check out an alarm. Three bank robbers, all carrying firearms, emerged from the bank as the Gardaí arrived. A fourth gang member was acting as driver of the getaway car. The courageous Fallon tried to grab one of the raiders. The gunmen opened fire. Dick Fallon, a father of five, was hit in the shoulder by a .22 bullet. Another bullet, from a 9mm pistol, hit him in the neck and he fell, mortally wounded. Garda Fallon's two colleagues, Paul Firth and Patrick Hunter, were lucky to escape with their lives.

Like most of my colleagues on duty that day, I worked on the story. I recall talking to shocked colleagues of the dead Garda at Mountjoy Garda station, where he had been based. The following evening, I was one of the journalists covering the removal of the remains of Richard Fallon from the morgue at Jervis Street Hospital. One of my abiding memories is of seeing Garda Fallon laid out in an open coffin, with what appeared to be a dark bruise on his temple. The minister for justice at the time, Micheál Ó Móráin, seemed in shock as he approached the coffin to pay his respects. The removal was the prelude to a huge funeral, attended by thousands of members of the Garda Síochána, with crowds respectfully lining the streets. Members of the North's police force, the Royal Ulster Constabulary (RUC), also took part.

In the Dublin of 1970, murders were comparatively unusual, and the murder of a Garda was extremely rare. The last member of the force to be murdered had been Garda George Mordant, shot dead in Donnycarney, Dublin, in 1942. He had been trying to arrest Harry White, a prominent IRA man and uncle of the prominent Sinn Féin activist and writer Danny Morrison.

The ruthless killing of Garda Fallon made a deep impact on the Irish people at the time. The murder was committed by a small republican para-military group called Saor Éire, which had been carrying out a series of bank robberies. The group had smuggled in pistols from abroad, and there were rumours that it was carrying out robberies in order to buy arms for the nationalist community in the North.

Garda Fallon was the first policeman to die in the Irish Republic in the Troubles that began in the late 1960s. It could also be said that he was the first victim in the Republic of gunrunning linked to the Troubles of that era. Gardaí have never found the 9mm murder weapon and, at the time of writing, some official files relating to the case still have not been released. Nobody has ever been convicted of the murder.

At the time the killing happened, secret contacts were being made between figures in the ruling Fianna Fáil party and members of the IRA. There had also been contact, to a more limited extent, between at least one Fianna Fáil activist and an individual linked to Saor Éire. Arrangements were being finalised to covertly import arms for the defence of Northern nationalists who were under threat from loyalist mobs. Only about a month after the murder, the secret attempt to import arms led to one of the biggest sensations in the history of the State – the sacking of two government ministers, Charlie Haughey and Neil Blaney. They were dismissed on suspicion of seeking to import arms illegally from the Continent, with the aid of finance from Irish State funds. This was the saga known as the Arms Crisis, which led to what some called the court case of the century, the Arms Trial.

In the aftermath of the Fallon murder, questions were asked as to whether political figures had also been involved in, or turned a blind eye to, a previous operation involving the importation of arms. There was a suspicion that some of these weapons may have ended up in the hands of Saor Éire, and that one of them may even have been used to murder Garda Fallon. There were also rumours that the killers of Garda Fallon may have been helped to escape by people in high places in the world of politics.

Around the time of the Fallon murder, members of the Special Branch were aware of contacts between Neil Blaney and republicans. John Kelly, one of the republicans Blaney was in touch with, and who was later to be cleared in the Arms Trial, recalls clearly the day that Garda Fallon was murdered, and an incident later that night. He was coming out of Leinster House with Neil Blaney and Paddy Kennedy, the Republican Labour MP at Stormont, when they encountered some members of Special Branch. 'The Special Branch were all over the place and I detected a certain hostility coming from them against Neil Blaney. You could almost feel it ...'

Within days of the Fallon murder, the Gardaí took the unprecedented step of publishing the names of seven individuals whom they wanted to interview. Addresses were also given, but at least two of them were incorrect – one turned out to be the address of a senior journalist at the *Irish Times*.

The murder of Garda Fallon focused attention like never before on Saor Éire, one of the more unusual paramilitary groups of that era. Founded in the late 1960s, it was a loose alliance of former IRA men and young radicals from the extreme left. A couple of individuals associated with the group, or with members of the group, went on to become prominent in the Dublin criminal underworld. One of these was Christy 'Bronco' Dunne, a well-known armed robber.

In some ways, the group had a strongly Trotskyist flavour. One of its leading members, Peter Graham, was also a member of Trotskyist alliance the Fourth International. Another member, Máirín Keegan, had been in Paris during the student 'uprising' in May 1968. A former Saor Éire member told me that Ms Keegan was 'very active' in Saor Eire and that two other women were also involved. This source claimed that at the height of its activity, Saor Éire had 'a few dozen' members. One of the founding members was Liam Walsh, who had been active in the IRA in the 1950s.

Some ex-IRA men were attracted to Saor Éire because they were disillusioned with the failure of the Border Campaign, which petered out in 1962. Ernest Mandel, Marxist economist and leading theoretician of the Fourth International, was said to have met leading members of Saor Éire during a visit to Dublin in 1972.[1] However, a source said they would not have been presented to him as Saor Éire members.

Saor Éire purported to draw its inspiration from both the Irish republican tradition and international revolutionary movements like the Tupamaros urban guerrilla group in Uruguay. It saw itself as an urban guerrilla force, seeking to promote revolution among the working class.

In fact, the group was best known at this period for robbing banks, mostly in the Republic but also in the North, beginning in the late 1960s. In December 1970, it was calculated that the group had been involved in seventeen bank robberies over the previous three years, with £60,000 to £70,000 taken – a sizeable sum in those days. Saor Éire achieved particular notoriety in February 1970, when members virtually took over the village of Rathdrum, County Wicklow. The gunmen cut phone wires and held up traffic while they robbed the local Hibernian Bank.

At least one member of the group was reputed to be a student at Trinity College, Dublin. According to Dublin legend at the time, which may or may not be true, he managed to avoid capture after taking part in an armed robbery by strolling casually through a Garda cordon with his university textbooks tucked primly under his arm – he had apparently brought his books with him as a 'prop'.

SAOR ÉIRE AND THE HAUGHEY CONNECTION

A problem for Saor Éire was that as well as left-wing idealists like the late Peter Graham, there were some more opportunistic elements involved who wanted to line their own pockets, according to a source who was close to Graham. While the IRA long had a rule that its personnel were not to attack members of the security forces in the Republic, Saor Éire took a more aggressive line. A former member of Saor Éire explained it thus: 'Our attitude was that if we were attacked, we would attack back – in other words we would defend ourselves.' This more hardline approach was to have tragic consequences when Garda Fallon confronted members of the group – even though he was unarmed, he was shot dead.

The authorities threw their net wide as they sought to track down the killers of Garda Fallon. Ironically, one of the people with a republican background checked out by the Special Branch at this period was a man called Con Ahern, who lived in Drumcondra on the north side of Dublin. He was not exactly a prime suspect, or an urban guerrilla in the Tupamaros tradition. Con was a hard-working employee of the All Hallowes centre for the training of students for the Catholic priesthood – he ran the seminary farm. Con had an eighteen-year-old son, Bertie, who was interested in politics – he is currently Taoiseach. Con Ahern was a republican in County Cork during the Civil War of the 1920s and was interned. He remained on Garda intelligence files after his release from the Curragh internment camp in 1924, even though he led an absolutely blameless life. As Bertie Ahern told the authors of a 1998 biography, after Special Branch had visited his father following the Fallon murder, they decided to take his name off intelligence records – he was, after all, aged sixty-six at the time.[2]

The shooting of Garda Fallon happened well over three decades ago, but his family are still looking for answers to many questions. In their quest for closure, they have been seeking a government inquiry into the callous murder of a devoted family man. Dick Fallon's youngest son Finian, who was only three when his father was murdered, has been leading the campaign for an inquiry. His mother Deirdre died in 1994, aged only fifty-seven, and his brother Joe passed away in 2004. An accountant by profession, Finian said that some Department of Justice files on the murder had still not been released, even after the thirty-year deadline when government files normally become available. 'We think the whole thing needs to be examined,' he told me when we met.[3] 'We see a whole spectrum of unanswered questions.'

He professed himself unhappy with the response of the government to his calls for an inquiry. A former member of the Progressive Democrat party (PDs), he ran for the party in the Dublin North constituency in the 1997 general election, and in the subsequent by-election called after the resignation from the Dáil of controversial TD Ray Burke. Now he describes himself as a former member of the PDs.

In July 2001, the demand for answers was fuelled when former PD leader Des O'Malley made a statement in the Dáil concerning the Arms Crisis. He said there was reason to believe that Garda Fallon had been murdered with a weapon that had been part of earlier illegal arms shipments into the State (before the attempted importation of arms that led to the Arms Trial). Mr O'Malley went on: 'There is also reason to suppose that some senior Gardaí suspected that a prominent politician was fully aware of this earlier importation and had turned a blind eye to it. These same Gardaí became aware through intelligence reports that by December 1969 certain politicians were funding illegal organisations … Such was the depth of the crisis which confronted Mr Berry[4] [secretary of the Department of Justice] in April 1970 and which – following my appointment as Minister for Justice in May 1970 – I in turn confronted. Had Jack Lynch, Peter Berry and various ministers been less than steadfast in their determination to preserve democracy and the rule of law, heaven knows what catastrophe would have befallen this State and the people of the entire island.'

One of the rumours that circulated at the time was that one or more members of the gang responsible for the murder of Garda Fallon had been driven away in a State car and helped to disappear. Fine Gael TD Gerry L'Estrange raised this matter in the Dáil. On 4 November 1971 he declared: 'One of those men who murdered Garda Fallon was brought down to the Greenore [County Louth] ferryboat in a State car and if you want to know who owned the car I can also tell you.' The following 16 December he returned to the same topic in the Dáil, declaring: 'The Government did nothing about the murderers of Garda Fallon. One of them was brought in a State car to get away on a boat to Ostend.'

Another Fine Gael TD, John Bruton, who was later to serve as taoiseach, referred to the murder of Garda Fallon in the course of a debate on 13 May 1970, stating: 'It is well known that the Garda Síochána are of the opinion that they are not getting support in pursuing these killers. This might again suggest that there is some tie up between elements of the Government and the people responsible for this killing.'

In some of the rumours that were circulating about links between government figures and members of Saor Éire, the finger was pointed at the late Neil Blaney, the Donegal man who was prominent among the more republican element in Fianna Fáil, and who became one of the central figures in the 1970 Arms Crisis, when he was sacked as agriculture minister. Blaney himself was well aware of the rumours, and during the Arms Crisis debate in the Dáil on 8 May 1970 went on the offensive to tackle the innuendo head-on. He vehemently denied any collaboration with the group, and spoke of Saor Éire with contempt as 'this lousy outfit'.

In his impassioned speech, in which he denied he had ever been involved in gunrunning, Blaney also attacked those who sought to link him or his associates with Saor Éire. 'I want to say that I have nothing but the utmost contempt for that outfit [Saor Éire] and any association with them would be as repugnant to me as it would be to any other member of this House. The blackening operation was the suggestion of a tie-up between this organisation and certain government ministers who are said to have intervened and used their influence to try to cover up and to allow to escape from this country, as it is said they have escaped, the murderers of Dick Fallon. These are the sort of things that those who are peddling them should be ashamed of. These are the things that those who unwittingly are merely repeating what others have said should try to retract as fast as they can, because this is not the case, never has been the case, never would be the case in so far as I or any of the people with whom I have associations and friendship are concerned, whether they be north or south.'

A former member of Saor Éire told me that any suggestion that members of the group were helped to flee by elements in Fianna Fáil was a 'fairytale'. 'It just never happened,' he said. This man, who was close to the late Liam Walsh, one of the founders of Saor Éire, also expressed scepticism about reports that there was a friendship between Walsh and Blaney.

Following the shooting of Garda Fallon, a man from Finglas, north Dublin, was extradited from the UK and went on trial for the capital murder of the policeman. He was acquitted. Subsequently, in 1972, two other men, Joe Dillon and Sean Morrissey, went on trial for the murder of the Garda, and were also acquitted. However, they were jailed for eighteen months for possession of firearms.

Saor Éire began to disintegrate following the murder of Garda Fallon. The group came under enormous pressure as Gardaí mounted a major hunt for those who shot the policeman. In December 1970, Jack Lynch's government came close to introducing internment, after Justice Department secretary Peter Berry reported that some fifteen Saor Éire activists were planning to kidnap him for ransom. The internment plans were ultimately scrapped.

But Saor Éire-linked bloodletting was not over. In October 1971 one of the group's political ideologues, Peter Graham, was found shot dead at an apartment on St Stephen's Green, Dublin, where he had been staying. It was not generally known at the time that he was a member of Saor Éire – this connection only emerged later. Graham was known in left-wing circles as a very dedicated chairman of the Young Socialists, who were affiliated to the Labour party. The Young Socialists were an entirely legitimate political grouping that attracted young left-wing idealists. Graham (twenty-six) had managed to keep his 'other life', his involvement with Saor Éire, very secret indeed. Even close political associates were unaware of his involvement.

Born in 1945, Peter Graham had grown up in a terraced house just off Meath Street, in the Liberties area of Dublin. He worked for a time as an electrician with the State transport company, CIÉ. He belonged to a range of left-wing groups in Dublin, starting off with the Connolly Youth Movement. He developed an interest in Trotskyism, which brought him to the Irish Workers Group. He played a role in the founding of the League for a Workers Republic and the Young Socialists. He spent some time in London where he was a member of the International Marxist Group (IMG), the British section of the Trotskyist organisation, the Fourth International, and was a member of the editorial board of the magazine *Red Mole*. He returned to Dublin to found an Irish branch of the Fourth International, and met his death shortly afterwards.

Soon after his murder, associates of Graham, who were among the last to see him, told me about his final hours. He had been drinking with a woman friend in a pub on South King Street. He later linked up with two of his Young Socialist colleagues at the group's HQ in a basement in Hume Street. He parted from them around 11pm on Molesworth Street. At about

12.50am, two men called to the building on St Stephen's Green where Graham was staying alone, in a flat rented by DR O'Connor-Lysaght, a member of the Young Socialists. The two callers inquired of the elderly woman caretaker about the location of the flat. Shortly afterwards, neighbours heard a commotion and a sound like a shot. A man was seen running from the house with blood on his hands. Graham was found to have been killed by a .45 bullet in the head.

O'Connor-Lysaght was on his way back from Galway when he heard of the murder of a young man through a radio playing in the carriage. On arrival in Dublin he saw a headline in the *Evening Press* – the story revealed the identity of the young man who had been murdered. O'Connor-Lysaght was shocked. 'I tried to get in touch with the various comrades to find out what was up,' he told me. He contacted a solicitor and went around to the Gardaí at Harcourt Terrace to make a statement. He told me there was a rumour that the two individuals who confronted Graham may not have meant to kill him, that they pointed a gun at his head to intimidate him and that the gun went off. After the killing, the landlady became unhappy with the idea of O'Connor-Lysaght remaining in the flat, so he left and took up residence in the home of Máirín Keegan, who lived on Parnell Road overlooking the Grand Canal. She had become a kind of publicity officer for Saor Éire. Like Peter Graham, she was a member of the Young Socialists, and she succeeded Graham as the Irish representative of the Fourth International.

O'Connor-Lysaght, who was brought up in Wales in a family of Irish background, was never a member of Saor Éire and confined his activities to the purely political sphere. He had moved to Dublin in 1959 at age eighteen, taking a BA degree at Trinity College and an MA degree at UCD. A well-known Trotskyist activist, he went on to become a writer and historian, and has remained involved in Trotskyist activities to this day, as a member of the group Socialist Democracy.

Bernadette McAliskey, the firebrand civil rights leader who had been elected a Westminster MP, was one of those who attended the funeral. Graham's friends in the Young Socialists turned out in force for the obsequies. According to an IRA statement, four officers from the Northern Command of the IRA attended. Even though, as a Trotskyist, Graham would have been an atheist, he nevertheless had the benefit of a Requiem Mass in St Catherine's Church, Meath Street, close by his family home.

Graham was buried at Dean's Grange cemetery in south Dublin. The Pakistani-born left-wing activist Tariq Ali, a leading figure in the Fourth International, led the mourners, marching in formation to the graveside, preceded by a young man carrying the flag of the left, the Starry Plough. Tariq Ali gave an oration, pledging that they would find out who had 'done this deed'. The comrades sang the left-wing hymn 'The Internationale', and gave the clenched-fist salute.

Tariq Ali told me, during a visit to Dublin in February 2006, that they never did find out who killed Graham: 'It remains a mystery. There was talk that people from within some splinter group had done it. It was not the State. But more than that we never got. It is such a long time ago, one would imagine that somebody would come out and admit it.'

O'Connor-Lysaght left the funeral early for an urgent meeting with the security officer of Official Sinn Féin, as part of the quest to find out who might have killed Graham, and found him 'quite helpful'. O'Connor-Lysaght recalled: 'There was some loose talk that the Officials might have done it. I wanted to make it clear that I did not think, and still don't, that the Sticks [Officials] did it.'

After Graham's funeral, the Provisional IRA issued a statement which spoke of the dead man in eulogistic terms, and said that his death had come 'as a severe blow to the national resurgence'. The statement said that Peter Graham was 'instrumental in providing aid of all forms to the besieged people of the North'. This led to speculation that the aid included arms, or the money to buy arms. According to at least one source, when the trouble erupted in the North in 1969, Saor Éire supplied 'some weapons' to the nationalists in the North, gave 'military training' to a number of them, and 'provided funds expropriated in bank raids'.[5]

A former Saor Éire member, whom I shall call Mr A, gave the impression in an interview in February 2005 that it was more than just 'some weapons' that were supplied. He said the main purpose of the bank raids was to finance the purchase of arms for political purposes, and that after the Troubles broke out in 1969, it was decided that arms would be sent to Belfast and Derry. He also said that one of the first outsiders to go into Derry in 1969 to assist with the local defences was a Saor Éire member, the late Sean 'Ructions' Doyle. In October 1968, Doyle was one of two men arrested after a shooting incident with Special Branch, following an attempt to burn down the headquarters of the Fianna Fáil party on Upper Mount Street, Dublin. The men were freed in January 1970 when the State entered a *nolle prosequi* after it found that two of its witnesses were indisposed.

Doyle was one of the more colourful members of Saor Éire. Mr A recalled that Doyle was in Dublin's St James' Hospital when told he had only three months to live. Doyle and his friends came up with a novel idea. It was decided that wakes would be held for him before he died rather than after, so that he himself could take part in the festivities. As a result, three highly enjoyable 'advance' wakes took place in pubs, attended by large numbers of his friends, with Doyle himself as the guest of honour, before he finally succumbed.

Nobody was ever brought to book for the murder of Peter Graham, and there was much speculation at the time about the motive for the murder, some of it very wild indeed. Some leftists wondered if sinister State forces were involved. However, the indications are that the killers came from much closer to home. A man who had been a close friend and political colleague of Graham's has told me that he believes two members of Saor Éire were involved in the killing. The source said that Graham had been involved in channelling funds from Saor Éire bank robberies to republicans in the North who emerged as the Provisional IRA. There was speculation that some of this money was earmarked for buying arms. The source alleged that two of the more opportunistic elements in Saor Éire were demanding 'legitimate expenses', and a bitter dispute arose which culminated in the fatal shooting when the two men went to confront Graham.

Mr A said members of the group considered taking revenge against the two Saor Éire 'renegades' who allegedly attacked Graham, but decided against it as it would have led to internecine violence, as later happened with the Irish National Liberation Army (INLA), many of whose members died through internal feuds. He said that he believes the dispute which ended the life of Peter Graham was over the control of arms caches, rather than money. (Another source familiar with individuals who were active in Saor Éire told me that Peter Graham's father, a highly principled man, was horrified when he heard rumours that there might be retaliation, and made it clear to friends of his son that he wanted no bloodshed.)

The Graham murder represented another violent episode in the turbulent history of the gang that gunned down Dick Fallon. Did Graham have prior knowledge of, or any connection with, the robbery that resulted in the Fallon murder? After all, he was described by one source[6] as the 'head of the Dublin Brigade' of Saor Éire, a rather elaborate title for a very small group. However, Mr A refuted the suggestion that Graham held this position, and said there was no basis for any rumour that Graham was linked to the Arran Quay robbery. He said that Graham was not involved on the 'military' side of the organisation at all, but was a purely 'political' member. Security sources are also satisfied that Graham was not one of the Arran Quay gang.

The death of Peter Graham was one of the events that disrupted Saor Éire during this period. The previous year, Liam Walsh had died in a premature bomb explosion on a railway embankment at the rear of McKee army barracks, off Blackhorse Avenue, Dublin.[7] Liam Dalton, who was also associated with Saor Éire, was found dead on a railway line in London. A native of County Offaly, in the 1950s he had been a member of a breakaway republican paramilitary group headed by Joe Christle. In January 1972 Máirín Keegan died of cancer. Despite a large Garda presence, shots were fired over her coffin. Just like Peter Graham, she was given a Catholic funeral, with a Requiem Mass at her local church, St Bernadette's on Clogher Road, Dublin. As one observer remarked: 'They may have been Trots, but they were Irish Trots.' In both cases, the comrades showed full respect for the wishes of the families for their loved ones to be buried with the rites of the church.

In May 1973, eight Saor Éire prisoners in Portlaoise Prison announced that they were resigning from the organisation. They complained that Saor Éire had ceased to play a progressive role, and that during the previous two years 'undesirable elements have been able to operate around its fringes and carry out actions'. It is understood that the remaining members of Saor Éire wound up the group around 1975. By then, of course, republicans who wanted 'action' had the choice of the Provisional IRA or the emerging INLA. One of those who signed the letter, Danny McOwen, went on to become a prominent member of the Dublin criminal underworld and was shot dead in a gangland feud outside Dublin's Cumberland Street labour exchange on 14 June 1983.

Saor Éire may now be consigned to history, but the murder of a Garda carried out by the group has continued to have repercussions. In 2001, questions were asked in the Dáil about the possibility of releasing papers relating to the case of Garda Fallon. Socialist TD Joe Higgins recalled that the justice minister had stated that there was a departmental file relating to the Fallon case that was not released. Fine Gael's Michael Noonan pointed out that the family of the late Garda Fallon 'is concerned that his murder may have been connected in some way with the importation of arms into the country'. Taoiseach Bertie Ahern replied: 'I am aware of what has been requested by the Fallon family. Deputy Noonan has made a few requests and I will bring them to the attention of the Minister. He will have to seek advice in that matter. The Deputy knows that there were court cases about the issue and the people acquitted are still alive. I will raise the issue and ask for it to be examined ...'

When I met him, Finian Fallon was still pressing ahead with his campaign for answers to questions arising out of his father's death, and for access to official papers. He was also hoping to talk to people who were members of Saor Éire, to see if they could cast any light into dark corners. He said he would like to see an All-Ireland peace and reconciliation commission to look into murders and related issues.

He was clearly still angry over a statement issued by Saor Éire following his father's murder, which added insult to injury. The statement did not claim responsibility for the shooting, but sought to deny that the Garda was killed 'in the course of protecting the public'. The statement, which showed little concern for the feelings of a bereaved family, said: 'He died protecting the property of the ruling class, who are too cowardly and clever to do their own dirty work.' Finian Fallon could not understand how any group who had claimed the life of an innocent man could come out with a crassly insensitive statement like that. 'It was a shocking thing to say.'

Who brought in the gun that killed Garda Fallon?

So, what is the real story behind Saor Éire and the covert importation of arms into Ireland? What was the connection with Fianna Fáil? What, if any, was the link with the murder of Garda Fallon?

The late Pádraig 'Jock' Haughey, a brother of the then finance minister Charles J Haughey, figures in the story. Like other nationalists in the South, Jock was concerned about the plight of Northern nationalists, and wanted to assist. His older brother, the charismatic Charlie, one of the most powerful figures in the ruling Fianna Fáil party at the time, was also seen as sympathetic to the plight of Northern nationalists, despite his image as a hard-living man-about-town.

Charlie, who had gone to live on a magnificent country estate at Kinsealy, County Dublin, had a lifestyle that some saw as not being in tune with the traditional culture of Fianna Fáil, or with the ascetic image of the party's founding father, Éamon de Valera. Haughey, known to his admiring followers as 'The Boss', rode to hounds, loved fine wine and collected works of art. He acquired an ocean-going yacht and also bought Inishvickillaune, one of the Blasket Islands off the Kerry coast, where he built a luxurious holiday home. An English journalist said of him once: 'Somehow, he managed to combine the streetwise look of an Irish bookie, with the grand manner of a medieval pope.'

As justice minister in the early 1960s, Haughey had cracked down on the IRA. Nevertheless, he and Jock were conscious of their family roots in Swatragh, County Derry. Their father, Sean 'Johnnie' Haughey, had been a leader of the IRA in South Derry during the War of Independence. It was said that Johnnie's later ill health was due to living rough in a hillside bunker with IRA comrades while on the run.[8] He went on to serve as an officer with the Free State Army during the Civil War.[9] According to a former comrade from that era, Lt Colonel Sean Clancy, whom I interviewed in 2001, Haughey senior was always extremely loyal to the Free State and to its leader, Michael Collins. The family retained strong nationalist leanings. A brother of Johnnie Haughey remained on in the IRA after independence, and was interned in the North decades later.[10]

In his earlier years, Jock Haughey was famous more for his GAA prowess than for politics – he won an All-Ireland football medal with Dublin in 1958, and there is a theory that his fame as a footballer was a factor in his brother winning a Dáil seat for the first time the previous year.

Jock became involved in the relief effort for nationalists who had been forced to flee their homes, and in August 1969 he visited London to contact organisations and Irish businessmen who might be able to help with the relief of distress.

His relief mission had the blessing of his brother Charlie, who arranged the Aer Lingus tickets. On the first trip, departing on 17 August, Jock was accompanied by a number of friends from the northside of Dublin, including the brothers Desmond and Eamonn Francis from Collins Avenue West, who have both passed on, and an old Fianna Fáil colleague, Joe Teeling. They were all back in Dublin by the following day. Then, in the third week in August, on the twenty-second of the month, Jock made another visit to London, this time in the company of Joe Teeling only. It has been alleged that during this trip Jock was also pursuing a more covert way of assisting Northern nationalists – by helping in the procurement of arms.

While in London, he met with Cathal Goulding, chief of staff of the IRA. The meeting was set up with the help of an Irish priest based in London. According to evidence that would later be given to the Dáil Public Accounts Committee (PAC) in February 1971 by Chief Superintendent John Fleming, head of Special Branch, Jock handed over £1,500 to Goulding. The PAC was inquiring into the spending of the government's grant for the relief of distress in the North.

According to another account, in a pamphlet published in the 1970s called 'Fianna Fáil and the IRA Connection', written from a pro-Goulding standpoint, the money was meant for the purchase of arms, and more money was promised.

According to this pamphlet, which appears to be based, directly or indirectly, on Goulding's account, the priest had contacted the IRA chief, and said he could put him in touch with an unlimited supply of money which was available for the purchase of arms if it was guaranteed that these would be sent directly to the Six Counties. The priest said it would be necessary for a leading member of the IRA to travel to London to meet the man who was offering the money. Next morning, Monday, 18 August, Goulding flew to London and met the priest, who introduced him to the IRA's new benefactor, Jock Haughey. Haughey asked, if Goulding was supplied with money, could he supply the Northern people with arms? Goulding said that this would be no problem, if the money was forthcoming. He said that the amount would have to be at least £50,000, in order to get the co-operation of an arms dealer. Jock Haughey handed him £1,500, promising more within days. Goulding returned to Ireland with the £1,500, which he put in the 'standing arms fund'.

Special Branch came to suspect that some arms consignments bound for the IRA came into Ireland in the following weeks. Chief Superintendent Fleming told the PAC inquiry that at least one consignment of arms came into Dublin Airport in October 1969 and was passed on to the IRA. He said there might have been two or three other shipments. John Kelly said, during my interview with him, that he understood that four cases of handguns came in through Dublin Airport, and that they went to Cathal Goulding.

All arrangements to take the known consignment through the airport in October had been made by Pádraig 'Jock' Haughey, Superintendent Fleming told the PAC. The arms could have come from England or the Continent. Fleming said he had no idea of the size of the consignment. Two prominent IRA men spoke to Pádraig Haughey at the airport and as far as the Superintendent was aware, the consignment was taken away in a truck. The head of Special Branch also said that Pádraig Haughey met IRA leaders in Dublin in August 1969 – shortly after the outbreak of trouble in Northern Ireland. Fleming said that as far as he knew, the money for the shipment through Dublin Airport could have come from 'private sources'.

Details of Special Branch intelligence on a number of small arms shipments allegedly smuggled into Dublin in September and October 1969 were outlined in a document drawn up by Peter Berry, in his role as secretary of the Department of Justice. The four-part, unpublished document was prepared by Berry for the benefit of the attorney general in advance of the 1970 Arms Trial. The twelve-page document was mentioned in the Berry Papers – a diary compiled by Berry and published, after his death, in the June 1980 edition of *Magill* magazine. Because of the sensitive nature of some of the material, the four-part document itself has not been released to the State archives. However, during research for this book, I learned reliably about some of the contentious material in the document. Berry explains in his memo how Special Branch were receiving information from confidential sources that small consignments of arms were being imported by the IRA, without customs checks, into Dublin Airport and at Dún Laoghaire sea port. Berry said the Gardaí had information that one such consignment went to the gang involved in robbing banks which later, on 3 April 1970, shot Garda Fallon – a reference to Saor Éire. Berry did not say where this consignment had entered the country, or was suspected of entering.

According to the Berry document, the importations were said to be coupled with, *inter alia*, Jock Haughey. Berry commented: 'It was freely said in Special Branch circles that Mr Charles J Haughey was aware of what was going on.' At another point in the document, Berry said that Garda Fallon was shot dead by bank robbers, one of whom had been reported some months earlier to have received guns which were imported without undergoing any customs checks, through general arrangements in which Jock Haughey was playing an active part and of which Charles Haughey was alleged to have a 'general awareness'.

There was an implication in Berry's remarks that the killer of Garda Fallon may have been armed with a gun imported with the connivance of Jock Haughey. Such an allegation, if true, would be sensational. However, it should be pointed out that, again during research for this book, and as will later be explained in more detail, I was told by senior sources in the security establishment in early 2005 that the Gardaí are now satisfied that there was absolutely no Haughey link to the arming of Saor Éire, or to the gun that killed Garda Fallon. It would appear that better intelligence helped to clarify the matter, and led to the earlier view being revised. Nevertheless, suspicions had persisted over the years in various quarters that the importation of the Fallon murder weapon was somehow linked to people in high places.

If a link to Jock Haughey had been proven, an appalling vista would have opened up. The brother of the minister for finance would have been implicated in the supply of a weapon that was ultimately used in a shocking crime, the murder of a Garda. Jock was always considered very close to his brother Charlie, and also had a connection at this period with another powerful minister, Neil Blaney, in the moves to supply aid to Northern nationalists. There would have been much collateral damage. Both Charlie Haughey and Neil Blaney would have been caught up in a scandal that would have put even the Arms Crisis in the shade. Nevertheless, as we shall see, Jock Haughey did indeed have dealings with an individual linked to Saor Éire. This individual's only role was to introduce Jock to an arms dealer. Nevertheless, this may have been one of the factors that contributed to the rumours.

It is unclear why Peter Berry or his Special Branch sources thought that arms smuggled into the country for the IRA might have ended up in the hands of Saor Éire. No evidence is presented to back up this rather unlikely theory. It is highly unlikely that the IRA would have given away guns to a smaller, rival paramilitary group. Also, one has to bear in mind ideological differences, which might seem very obscure and pedantic to outsiders but, to activists immersed in the doctrinally sensitive world of the hard-left, were very real. The Trotskyist element in Saor Éire would have seen themselves as philosophically poles apart from the Goulding element of the pre-split IRA, and the latter's successors the Official IRA, as they would have been seen as 'Stalinist'. In these circumstances, transfers of arms between the two groups seem highly unlikely.

It is even more unlikely that Jock Haughey, a dyed-in-the-wool Fianna Fáiler, would have had anything to do, directly or indirectly, with facilitating the delivery of guns to a group like Saor Éire, which was virulently opposed to Fianna Fáil and sought to destabilise the Fianna Fáil government. The implication that Charlie Haughey had a 'general knowledge' of guns that ended up in the hands of Saor Éire, a group that wanted to destroy him, his party and his government, is just not credible, and there is no evidence for it.

Peter Berry has given an insight into the manner in which arms were allegedly smuggled through Dublin Airport in the early 1970s. In the Berry Papers published in *Magill*, Berry refers to 'confidential information' coming through to the Special Branch in February 1970 of arms being brought in through the airport. One consignment was labelled 'agricultural machinery' and had been invoiced to a company in Walkinstown, Dublin, where staff were puzzled to receive notification from customs of a cargo for them. When they sent a representative to the airport, the cargo had disappeared. Another cargo, weighing three-and-a-half cwts, labelled 'machine parts' and invoiced to an engineering firm, disappeared in similar fashion. Berry says that Special Branch had information about the IRA members involved and other details, but to protect a confidential source the importations had not been reported on in writing.

There was yet another twist in the saga when a Fine Gael TD, Patrick Hogan, asked a Dáil question on 14 May 1970. He inquired if arms had got through Dublin Airport in crates labelled for the Red Cross, and if these crates had got through without customs examination after a minister intervened. Finance minister George Colley replied that he knew of no foundation for such allegations.

Jock Haughey never went public with the full story of his link to arms procurement attempts or the alleged importation of arms. When he went to the grave in October 2003, aged seventy-one, he took his secrets with him. Like his older brother Charlie, he was not in the habit of sharing his innermost thoughts with the media. Jock's devotion to the code of silence was apparent when he was called before the PAC inquiry in February 1971. His appearance followed the allegations made to the inquiry by Supt Fleming that Jock had overseen the importation of arms destined for the IRA through Dublin Airport. Jock refused to answer questions. But he did make a statement, in the course of which he clearly sought to distance his brother Charlie from any alleged importation of arms, and to dispel any suspicion that Charlie, as finance minister, could have used his legal authority over customs to clear an arms shipment through the airport.

In his statement to the PAC, Jock said he had never, directly or indirectly, got in touch with Charles Haughey about authorisation for customs clearance of any guns, ammunition or materiel of any nature. He also stated that no moneys from the grant-in-aid for relief in the North were paid to him, nor did he have any control of these moneys. Because of his failure to co-operate with the inquiry, the PAC referred the matter to the High Court, which sentenced him to six months' imprisonment. He was given bail, and appealed the verdict to the Supreme Court, which, in a landmark decision, allowed his appeal on the grounds that the legislation empowering the Dáil committee to find him in contempt was unconstitutional.

The rumour of a Haughey link to the gun that killed Garda Fallon was to persist, as was to be made clear in the Dáil debate following the publication of the Berry Papers in *Magill*. Extrapolating from comments made in the Berry Papers, left-wing TD Dr Noel Browne said in the Dáil on 25 November 1980: 'Mr Berry apparently had the greatest respect for the efficiency of the present taoiseach [Charlie Haughey] as minister but he came round to the conclusion that the present taoiseach was fully aware almost at all times of a conspiracy to import arms for the use of the IRA and Saor Éire, as mentioned by Deputy FitzGerald, in the murder of a Garda.'

For his part, Dr Garret FitzGerald, the Fine Gael leader, said in the course of a lengthy speech during the same debate: 'There is one other fresh allegation, and a very serious one, with which any or all of the four people I have named might be in a position to deal, that is the allegation in the June 1980 issue of *Magill* that the Berry Papers contain a statement by Mr Berry that the gun that shot Garda Fallon was imported through Dublin Airport in September 1969 with the knowledge of a member of the then government. The seriousness of this allegation needs no emphasis from me. The Garda Síochána, who have recently lost three members as a result of armed attacks similar to those on Garda Fallon, are entitled to know whatever can be known about this allegation.'

The full story of the arms being smuggled into Ireland at this period may never be known. Some of the main players have died or have been reluctant to talk. An important point emerging from the saga is that Saor Éire had its own independent supply of weapons. The arms were being smuggled in from Birmingham, and Gardaí now believe that one of these guns was used to kill Garda Fallon. They are satisfied that he was not killed by a weapon imported through another route, or by a weapon linked to Jock Haughey.

Saor Éire had been building up a small arsenal of weapons for some time in the late 1960s. A former Saor Éire member confirmed reports that the group had a contact working in the British Small Arms factory in Birmingham. The factory proofed 9mm Star pistols for the Star munitions factory in Spain. The contact was able to set aside perfectly working pistols as 'rejects' and later smuggle them out of the factory. They were then sent to Ireland, being brought in through Dublin Airport. Security sources believed that .38 handguns were also smuggled in. These guns are believed to have formed the bulk of the weaponry held by Saor Éire, although weapons from other sources also formed part of the arsenal. Former Saor Éire member Mr A said that arms were also brought in from the Continent, likewise through Dublin Airport. 'It was easier to get stuff through the airport in those days,' he said.

According to Mr A, an arms dealer in London made contact with a person linked to Saor Éire in the UK in the late 1960s. The 'arms dealer' was a small man with a goatee beard who indicated he could supply weaponry. He is said to have given his name as Randall, although other versions of the name were also reported. The Saor Éire-linked individual in the UK, in good faith, passed on this contact to his friends in the organisation back in Ireland, who were equally unsuspecting. In retrospect, the possibility opens up that British intelligence somehow detected Saor Éire activities in the UK and decided to attempt to infiltrate the subversive group by using an agent or a 'front' man, the mysterious Mr Randall. If this is the case, then the fishing expedition led to a far bigger catch than the small-time gunrunners of a fringe paramilitary group.

For his part, Jock Haughey, in his quest for arms for the defence of Northern nationalists, was at a disadvantage. He was unfamiliar with the murky world of the arms trade. A surveyor by profession, his leisure activities centred on golf, GAA and soccer, not on matters to do with arms or international intrigue. Through a series of contacts he was put in touch, around the end of October 1969, with a man who has been described as a socialist republican and who, it was said, could introduce him to an arms dealer in London able to supply weapons. This man was, in fact, involved with Saor Éire, but it is not clear whether Jock Haughey was aware of this connection at the time. Even though the murder of Garda Fallon was in the future, the average Fianna Fáiler, as already indicated, would not have had any sympathy with Saor Éire, in light of its armed robbery activities and its desire to subvert not only Northern Ireland but the twenty-six-county state as well.

Informed sources indicated to me that the contact between Jock Haughey and the man linked to Saor Eire came about in the following way: Jock and Charlie Haughey had a close friend, long-time Fianna Fáil activist Joe Teeling, who lived in Clontarf, Dublin. As outlined above, Teeling had accompanied Jock on two visits to London in August 1969. Teeling, who was in the fruit business, had acted as a kind of 'father figure' to the youthful Charlie when the latter joined Teeling's Fianna Fáil Cumann in the Amiens Street/Fairview area in the late 1940s. Charlie Haughey had been encouraged to join the cumann by Harry Boland, a school friend from a notable Fianna Fáil family and later business partner with Charlie in an accountancy practice. Another school friend of Haughey's, George Colley, later to be a minister, was also a member.

Joe Teeling was very impressed by the eager, bright young Haughey. He took him under his wing and gave him encouragement, according to a source close to the late Mr Teeling. Boland and Colley proposed Charlie as Cumann secretary and by all accounts he took to the work with gusto, showing great aptitude in handling Cumann business. It appears that Teeling was impressed, and became a kind of mentor to one of the future stars of Fianna Fáil. The two men were to remain life-long friends, and Teeling campaigned for Charlie as the youthful politician began his meteoric rise in Irish politics. Both were active in the part-time defence force Fórsa Cosanta Áitiuil (FCA).

Teeling, in turn, had a friend called Richard 'Dick' Timmins, who had a strongly republican background. Originally from the Capel Street area of Dublin's north inner city, he was a boy when the 1916 Rising took place. In the late 1930s he was the head of the IRA in London and, on the instructions of IRA chief of staff Sean Russell, took part in the bombing campaign in England masterminded by Russell. Russell himself was to die aboard a German submarine in 1941, en route to Ireland. The colourful and very mercurial Brendan Behan, who later won fame as a playwright, also took part in the bombing campaign. Behan was arrested, but because of his tender years got just three years in borstal – an experience that later gave rise to the classic *Borstal Boy*.

Timmins, who became a close friend of Brendan Behan and his brother Dominick, a writer and ballad singer, was also arrested. He appeared at Carmarthen Assizes on 17 November 1939, and was sentenced to fourteen years in prison for possession of explosives. Aged thirty at the time, he had appeared in court under the name Richard Coen, alias Michael O'Farrell, but asked that he be sentenced under his real name, Richard Timmins. A twenty-two-year-old associate, Barbara Jones, alias Rita McSweeney (her real name), from a republican family in Waterford, got five years for being an accessory and for possession of explosives. She had been acting as a courier for the IRA bombers in Britain.

After about ten years in Wakefield Prison, Timmins escaped and went on the run in England, during which time he met up with his old friend Brendan Behan, and finally made his way to Galway in a coal ship. By 1969 he was living with his wife and six children (five daughters and a son) in a corporation house in Coolock, north Dublin. Like other republicans, Timmins felt the call to return to the cause when the Troubles in the North exploded in 1969. He was later to be jailed for five years at Portlaoise Prison for arms offences. He died of cancer in the early 1980s.

Timmins had a close friend, another former IRA man who had joined the movement in the late 1940s and who went on to join Saor Éire in the latter part of the 1960s. Through this contact Timmins got to know people in Saor Éire, and as a result of this chain of contacts Timmins introduced Jock Haughey to a republican associated with the group. It was indicated that this man could point Haughey in the right direction in terms of procuring arms, and would act as 'The Intermediary'.

According to one account, Timmins introduced Jock to The Intermediary at a meeting in the Holybrook Hotel, Clontarf. Haughey was told that The Intermediary had already been to London and seen the arms they wanted at a factory in Eltham, south London. It was agreed that Haughey and The Intermediary should go to London so that Haughey could try to arrange a deal with the 'arms merchant' Randall and his colleague, a businessman named, or using the name, Godfrey. The Intermediary had already been introduced to Mr Godfrey. The Intermediary was unemployed and had little money, so on 1 November he and a friend called to Jock Haughey's house on Foxfield Avenue, Raheny, where Haughey handed him an envelope containing £12 to cover his boat fare to and from London. The Intermediary departed by ferry the following night, and Haughey flew to London on the morning of 3 November. They met at midday at Marble Arch and made their way immediately to Godfrey's office on bustling Oxford Street, in a building that housed a number of business concerns.

The two Irishmen took a creaking lift to Godfrey's office on the sixth floor, past offices, a model agency and the workroom of a skirt manufacturer. Godfrey's office was located next to a model academy and agency. Godfrey was smartly dressed and well-spoken, and gave the impression that he considered himself immensely attractive to women. A meeting was held between the two Irishmen and Godfrey. Also present was a ship's navigator, whose role would be to transport the arms by sea, aboard Godfrey's yacht, from a point on the Welsh coast to a port on the northwestern coast of Ireland – presumably a harbour in County Donegal, near the border with Northern Ireland.

A list was produced of the arms that The Intermediary had been shown. Godfrey phoned his colleague, the 'arms dealer' Mr Randall, and got the price list from him. Prices seemed surprisingly low. Sten guns were going at

£11 each, self-loading rifles at £30, and machine guns at between £40 and £60. It is understood that the inventory of weapons to be supplied also included Bren guns. It is presumed that ammunition would also have been part of the deal. Godfrey said that as middleman in the transaction, he would add on £1 to each of the lower-priced weapons in the deal, and bigger sums to the prices of the more expensive weapons. He would be in line for a sizeable profit.

A deal was worked out for an initial shipment of arms, worth about £10,000. If all went well, the next shipment would be worth £50,000 and a third worth £40,000. Weather permitting, the navigator reckoned he could do the voyage to Ireland with the first consignment in five or six days. He was promised a bonus for fast delivery, and Haughey was willing to sail on the yacht with the arms. The weapons were destined for the Catholic community in Northern Ireland. Haughey was said to have paid a deposit of £3,300 for the first shipment. Other payments were to be made – when the arms left the factory; when the consignment was put aboard the vessel; and when the cargo finally reached the Irish coast.

Haughey and The Intermediary were back in Ireland by 4 November. The Intermediary appears to have had no further role in the affair.[11] According to Mr A, this was Jock Haughey's only encounter with anybody linked to Saor Éire, and Haughey had nothing whatsoever to do with procuring arms for the group. Haughey made a further trip to London in mid-November to see the 'arms dealer' Randall, this time accompanied by Northern republican John Kelly. This was the first trip abroad in connection with an arms deal by a person who was later to be one of the defendants in the Arms Trial.

As will become clear in the following chapter, there is reason to believe that this arms deal, from the start, was a set-up by British intelligence, who would thus have known from an early stage about the moves to acquire arms for the North, and the involvement of a member of the Haughey family. Needless to say, the arms never arrived. Ironically, the initial link that brought about this first contact with an 'arms dealer' abroad came through Saor Éire. This may have been one of the factors that fuelled the belief in some security circles that Jock Haughey had some link to the arming of Saor Éire – a belief that has now been discredited.

Nevertheless, there are intriguing questions that remain unanswered. Is it true, as suggested in Peter Berry's unpublished memo, that Charlie Haughey had a 'general knowledge' of arms allegedly supplied by his brother Jock to the IRA in 1969? What was the origin of the arms and who supplied them for shipment to Ireland? What knowledge, if any, did Charlie have of the money reportedly given by Jock to IRA chief Cathal Goulding that same year, for the purchase of arms? (Charlie himself met Goulding in Dublin in September 1969.) Why was Jock Haughey never charged in connection with the alleged provision of arms and money to the IRA? Did Special Branch fear that a high-ranking informer, or informers, in the IRA might be exposed if Jock were to face prosecution?

What knowledge, if any, did Charlie have of the gunrunning to Northern Ireland, albeit on a small scale (*see* Chapter 2), reportedly carried out by his friend and Fianna Fáil colleague Joe Teeling? Following Charlie Haughey's death in June 2006, there was speculation about the content and ultimate fate of his private papers. In the event of the papers becoming available to historians and researchers, will the records solve any of the riddles related to the turbulent career of Charles J Haughey? Time will tell. In the meantime, in pondering aspects of Charlie Haughey's role during a tempestuous period in Irish history, a quote from Winston Churchill comes to mind: 'It is a riddle, wrapped in a mystery, inside an enigma.'

CHAPTER 2

The Gun Dealer and the Arms Crisis

Otto Schlüter was a wily German arms dealer with a reputation for cheating clients. He worked out of a well-secured apartment in Hamburg and tended to be careful about his personal security. Schlüter had good reason to be wary – he had made some enemies over the years. While he had an arms dealing licence issued by the West German government, he had a history of operating in the 'grey' area of the arms trade and had supplied arms to Algerian insurgents fighting the French during the rebellion of 1954–62. As a result, during the Algerian war, French secret agents made two attempts to kill him.

It was the late Otto Schlüter who was chosen as the middleman to provide arms for the defence of Northern nationalists in the 1969–70 period, with the finance coming covertly from Irish government funds. These funds had been voted for the relief of distress in Northern Ireland and a Dáil inquiry was later to find that some of the funds had been improperly diverted to the purchase of arms. In light of his background, he was, perhaps, an unfortunate choice as a middleman. The arms were never delivered and Schlüter, who liked to demand cash up front, never gave the money back.

The operation turned out to be the most sensational of the covert attempts at gunrunning during the period of the Troubles, for one of the key figures involved was a highly respected Irish Army intelligence officer, Captain James Kelly. The affair, which became known as the Arms Crisis, shook the Irish State to its foundations, and resulted in the sacking by Taoiseach Jack Lynch of two government ministers, Charles Haughey and Neil Blaney, on suspicion of conspiring to import arms illegally. The sackings were followed by a sensational Dublin court case in 1970, which has gone down in contemporary Irish history as the Arms Trial.

Charges of attempting to import arms illegally were brought against ex-ministers Haughey and Blaney, Captain Kelly, militant Belfast republican John Kelly and businessman Albert Luykx. Luykx had been sentenced to death in his native Belgium just after the Second World War for alleged collaboration with the Nazis, but had always protested his innocence.[1] The charges against Blaney were subsequently thrown out, but the others appeared at the Central Criminal Court amid a welter of publicity. The first attempt at a trial was aborted, and this was followed by a second trial. Haughey denied all knowledge of any illegal shipment of arms and was acquitted. The others agreed they were involved in an attempt to import arms but said they considered they were acting in accordance with government instructions and in accordance with the law, and that they had done nothing illegal. They also were found not guilty

Requests for arms had come from members of defence committees which had been set up to protect nationalist areas in the North. The arms were meant for defensive purposes in a 'doomsday' situation. There were fears that loyalist attacks on Catholic districts could escalate into a full-scale pogrom. The worst atrocities of republican paramilitary groups were still in the future and, seen in the context of the times, procuring arms for purely defensive purposes carried a certain respectability in the eyes of some nationalists North and South – including those opposed to terrorism.

The purchasers obviously wished to have 'deniability' – so that if any arms sent to the North were captured, they could not be traced back to Dublin. Firearms carry serial numbers and this system of identification markings provides a 'numbers trail' through which the origin and transfer of weapons can be traced, from the point of manufacture to the final 'end user'. Some analysts believe that if the arms had been brought into Dublin, they would have been commandeered by the IRA and taken out of Captain Kelly's control.[2] However, according to evidence given by Army intelligence chief Colonel Michael Hefferon during one of the arms trials, the plan was that the arms would be stored at a monastery in Cavan, under the control of Captain Kelly in his capacity as an Army officer.

In retrospect, if the arms had been handed over to Northern activists, there is no doubt but that they would have come under the control of the fledgling Provisional IRA, which was establishing itself in early 1970 in nationalist areas in the North, especially Belfast and Derry. This was the group to which John Kelly, the Northern representative in the arms procurement group, was aligned. Said John Kelly: 'The expectation was that the weapons were intended for the defence of Northern nationalists, and the people who were defending Northern nationalists at that time were the Provisional IRA.' Had weapons been handed over by Captain Kelly, they would have gone to the Provisionals, not to the Officials, according to John Kelly. 'That was the plan.'

There was media speculation that the monastery in which the arms were to be hidden was Kilnacrott Abbey in County Cavan, run by the Norbertine order. In recent years a priest, Father Cataldus McKiernan, who was based at the monastery at the time and who died in October 2002, talked to a journalist about the matter. The journalist gave me an outline of what the priest said. According to Father McKiernan, he was approached by Captain Kelly and another man and asked to hide arms in outbuildings or sheds at the monastery. It was indicated to the priest that the matter had something to do with the government. The priest was horrified – one of his concerns was for the students in a school run by the order at Kilnacrott at the time. He refused point-blank to have anything to do with storing arms.

It was unusual for Irish Army intelligence to become embroiled in public controversy. The intelligence wing of the Irish military had always adopted an extremely low profile. Colonel Hefferon was a highly respected officer who had been appointed director of intelligence at Army HQ in October 1962. Neither he nor Captain Kelly was used to the glare of publicity.[3] The spotlight was also turned on John Kelly, a member of the embryonic General Headquarters (GHQ) staff of the emerging Provisionals, who was reporting directly to Seán Mac Stíofáin, the first chief of staff of the Provisional IRA.

Despite his reservations about the involvement of some individuals linked to Fianna Fáil, Mac Stíofáin was prepared to go along with the idea of buying arms with the aid of money being covertly channelled from the state fund for the relief of distress, as at that time he had few other resources. John Kelly, who believed there was government approval for the operation in the light of the involvement of a prominent Cabinet minister, Neil Blaney, said: 'Mac Stíofáin agreed that we would do this … There were certainly people with misgivings about it. I had misgivings about it. I had my doubts and concerns about it, but you must remember that given the circumstances in which we were living, no one else was offering the kind of assistance that was being offered through the mediation of [Captain] Jim Kelly.'

The crisis which led to the gunrunning had begun to escalate the previous August. That month saw the first deaths of the Troubles, and the rioting which became known as the 'Battle of the Bogside'. Taoiseach Jack Lynch went on television to make his famous statement that the government would no longer 'stand by'. The phrase was rendered in popular folklore as: 'We will not stand idly by.' Lynch's Cabinet, meeting in almost continuous emergency session, voted to set up a fund for the relief of distress in the North. The idea was that the fund, amounting to £100,000, would be administered by a subcommittee of Haughey, Blaney and two other ministers.

Even moderate Catholics had been appealing for aid – including guns – to protect their lives in a doomsday situation. The IRA had virtually gone out of business as a paramilitary force by early 1969. Under left-wing chief of staff Cathal Goulding, the organisation had turned towards social agitation in the South, and civil rights campaigning in Northern Ireland. The British Army had not yet arrived on the streets of the North to keep loyalist mobs in check, and there was much distrust in nationalist areas of the RUC, and especially of the auxiliary police force, the B-Specials.

At this period, there was a certain amount of small-scale gunrunning to the North as Southern nationalists sought to supply defensive 'hardware' to their Northern brethren. I recall a Fianna Fáil activist telling me in 1972 how a number of his fellow party members on the northside of Dublin had been involved in shipments of small quantities of arms to nationalists in Northern Ireland in the 1969–70 period. I was not told the nature of these weapons, but I assume that many of them were legally-held firearms such as shotguns, that were probably reported as 'stolen' to the Gardaí. According to my source, the guns were hidden below the floorboards of a van, which made a number of runs to the nationalist Unity Flats in Belfast.

More recently, I learned that one of those involved in bringing guns to the North was Joe Teeling who, as will be recalled from the last chapter, was a long-time Fianna Fáil activist and a friend of Charlie Haughey and his brother Jock. It is unclear if he was involved in the runs to Unity Flats referred to by my source in 1972. A source who was close to the late Mr Teeling told me that at the start of the Troubles the Fianna Fáil man made a number of trips to the North at the wheel of a vehicle with arms hidden on board.

Teeling was also involved in transporting relief supplies such as food. Dick Timmins, who had been imprisoned for IRA activities in England (*see* last chapter) also travelled with Teeling on these trips, I was told. The source said that like others in the South involved in supporting the nationalist people in the North, Joe Teeling became sickened and disillusioned by the campaign of the IRA, as it went from defensive to offensive operations, and began to engage in 'thuggery' and to carry out atrocities.

There was a certain amount of virtually obsolete weaponry stashed away around the country from conflicts in previous generations, and anecdotal evidence suggests that some of this materiel was also sent north. (At the end of the Civil War in 1923, the order went out from Frank Aiken, the IRA chief of staff, to 'dump arms'. Weapons were not formally surrendered and there was no decommissioning, so quantities of arms remained hidden in arms dumps, while some individuals hid away their own personal weapons.) I recall a former member of Sinn Féin telling me how, in the 1969–70 period, he had gone to the home of an elderly, life-long Fianna Fáil activist, a man in his nineties, after getting word that he still had a weapon hidden away from his involvement in the conflict of the 1920s. The man retrieved from its hiding place a .45 revolver and five bullets, and handed them over. John Kelly told me that people all around the Twentysix Counties contributed weapons at this period, and it was not just Fianna Fáil supporters – people aligned to Fine Gael, traditionally seen as strongly anti-IRA, also helped out. 'Whatever they had, shotguns, old rifles, Mausers going back to the First World War, were handed over.'

When Seán Mac Stíofáin took over as chief of the fledgling Provisional IRA, one of the first things he did was to set up a Supply Department, under a quartermaster general, with the role of channelling whatever supplies of war materiel were available into the movement.[4] A big man with an imposing presence, Mac Stíofáin was an unusual figure in the IRA. He was, in fact, a Londoner who had reinvented himself as an Irish guerrilla fighter. Born John Edward Drayton Stephenson in Leytonstone, London, in 1928, he had tenuous Irish family connections. His father, a solicitor's clerk, was English. Mac Stíofáin believed his mother, who died when he was ten, was from Belfast. According to another report, she was English-born, granddaughter of an Irish woman.[5] Mac Stíofáin, who worked on the railways in his younger days, retained the London accent of his youth, even while speaking Irish, in which he was fluent. In my encounters with him as a journalist, I had the impression of a man who was fanatically devoted to the cause, and who could also be volatile and intimidating. He was very conscious of the dignity of his rank as commander of the Provisionals, but a former IRA man who knew him said he could also be 'unassuming'.

Mac Stíofáin related in his memoirs how he and his people took over three arms dumps that were supposed to be under the control of the 'National Liberation Front' – the term then used by the Provisionals for the Official IRA. A few dozen sub-machine guns and many rifles and pistols were removed from the dumps and distributed in Belfast and elsewhere.

Mac Stíofáin set about renewing contacts with businessmen who had promised contributions towards Northern defence before the Provisional/Official split, and donations began to flow. One could speculate that some of these funds were used for buying war materiel.[6]

Mac Stíofáin and the IRA were ruthless in their campaign to kill British soldiers and RUC men. His great rival in the republican movement, Cathal Goulding, the chief of the Official IRA, was quoted once as saying that Seán was always trying to prove to everybody that he was as Irish as they were, and that in the IRA he had to show that he was more violent than the rest. 'He's too narrow, doesn't understand politics as such, and believes physical force is the only answer.'[7]

A former IRA man who knew Mac Stíofáin at this period said he brought a considerable degree of military discipline to the organisation.

Mac Stíofáin had done his national service in the Royal Air Force, becoming a corporal. In addition to this personal experience of life 'in the ranks', he was a keen student of guerrilla tactics. He was involved in one pioneering project – the introduction in 1972 of the car bomb, set with a timer to explode after being left on a city street. He seemed to take a child-like pride in this development. The tactic was to cause considerable carnage and material damage over the years. On 21 July 1972, known as 'Bloody Friday', the use of the car bomb brought terror to Belfast, when a number of IRA devices exploded in the busy city centre, killing nine people and injuring 130 others.

Mac Stíofáin, a non-drinker and devoted family man who was strongly anti-communist, managed to combine an old-fashioned Catholic religious faith with a marked enthusiasm for killing soldiers and policemen. Taking human life did not seem to bother him. At times, in his memoirs, he seemed to take delight in the infliction of death. On the other hand, he told me once of his shock and revulsion that a Dublin politician had broken up with his wife and remarried after getting a foreign divorce.

As the Troubles got under way in late 1969 and early 1970, there were freelance attempts, or suspected attempts, by community activists to procure arms in London for *ad hoc* defence groups in Catholic areas. In 1969 two Belfast men were arrested in England in connection with an alleged attempt to procure arms for a defence committee in the Short Strand area, a small Catholic neighbourhood in East Belfast. They were held for six months at Brixton Prison and released after charges were dropped.[8] In December 1970, two Belfast men were jailed at the Old Bailey, one for two years and the other for three years, over an attempt to procure arms in London for Catholics in Northern Ireland. The arms were said to consist of revolvers, rifles, Bren guns and ammunition. Judge Mervyn Griffith-Jones accepted that the two men were of the highest character and were motivated by a desire to defend their community rather than by any idea of attack. A part-time arms dealer from Hampshire was jailed for five years for supplying the arms. Two other men with addresses in London were jailed for two and four years.

In a follow-up case at the Old Bailey in March 1971, a Belfast-born Catholic was jailed for two years after the court heard that arms had been found in his business premises in Hammersmith. The court also heard evidence from a Scotland Yard detective that several consignments of arms were taken to Northern Ireland by hand in a grip [ie. a bag], and that one consignment was smuggled over in the boot of a car. The court heard that the arms were bound for Catholic defence committees in Belfast.

According to a source linked to an individual who took part in these gunrunning activities, a number of those involved were Northern Ireland trade unionists, who in turn were linked to the trade union movement in Dublin. Some money may have come from sources in Dublin to help pay for the arms. The source said the operation had nothing to do with the IRA. 'People were worried at the time about their security in view of loyalist activity. The arms were for defensive purposes, and those concerned were trade unionists who would have been involved with the defence committees.' This source believed that some arms did get through before the operation was blown – a view that tallies with the evidence given in the case by the Scotland Yard detective.

One of those suspected of smuggling arms to the IRA from the UK in the early 1970s was the heiress Bridget Rose Dugdale. According to media reports, the former debutante fled to Ireland from her home in England after learning that Scotland Yard was preparing to bring gunrunning charges against her. An Oxford graduate with a doctorate in economics who was dubbed 'Red Rosie' by the media, Dugdale received a nine-year sentence in Ireland for the 1974 robbery of art treasures worth millions from Russborough House, the County Wicklow mansion home of South African diamond magnate Sir Alfred Beit, and for hijacking a helicopter to drop home-made bombs on an RUC station at Strabane in Northern Ireland.

In March 1973, there was a sensation after an allegation surfaced that 630 sticks of gelignite and 150 detonators had been stored at a Catholic priest's house in Glasgow. The occupant of the house moved to Ireland and escaped extradition after a year-long legal struggle. The High Court in Dublin decided that the charge the priest faced in Scotland had to do with an alleged political offence. In a newspaper interview the priest said he was not a member of the IRA, nor did he have sympathy with the IRA. Two others appeared in court following the seizure of the explosives cache. A twenty-three-year-old woman with an address at Maryhill, Glasgow, got five years, while a twenty-eight-year-old Donegal man got seven years.

Genesis of the moves to procure arms

John Kelly recalled the origins of the attempt to procure arms with Irish State funds. He was introduced to Captain Kelly through Paddy Kennedy, a Republican Labour MP in Stormont. The meeting took place in September 1969 at the home of another Republican Labour MP, Gerry Fitt, on the Antrim Road, Belfast.

'At that meeting, in attendance were the representatives of a cross section of the nationalist community in Belfast, professionals, middle-class people, including people who had been involved in the IRA's 1956 campaign and who had become members of the embryonic Provisional IRA. It went on from there. Captain Kelly was telling us he was acting on behalf of the Irish government, that he was their emissary, and his sole function was to ascertain the extent to which Northern nationalists needed defending and who would defend them. Following that, [Captain] Jim Kelly arranged meetings and contacts with the Irish government, and that began the delegations that went down to meet the various Cabinet ministers in Dublin, including Taoiseach Jack Lynch. We met Lynch, Blaney, Haughey; there was no one we did not meet. Ironically there was nobody in the Irish government who did not want to meet us.'

On 4 October 1969, a meeting took place in Bailieboro, County Cavan, which some analysts see as the genesis of the plan to import arms from the Continent. Among those present were Captain Kelly and members of Northern defence committees, including people with IRA connections.

Later that month, as outlined in the last chapter, Jock Haughey, according to Special Branch, oversaw the importation of arms through Dublin Airport, that were handed over to the IRA. Money had also been given to IRA chief of staff Cathal Goulding. Any such activities were not financed from Irish government funds, John Kelly said. He did not know where the finance came from.

Around 16 or 17 November, Jock Haughey travelled to London to pursue the discussions on arms procurement that, in the company of a Saor Éire-linked intermediary, had earlier that month been opened with the businessman called Mr Godfrey and, indirectly, with the latter's 'arms dealer' colleague, Mr Randall. This time, Haughey was accompanied by John Kelly, and they were to deal directly with Randall. Captain Kelly was suspicious and feared it was all a set-up. In advance of the trip, he met Jock Haughey and advised him not to go.[9]

When I spoke to him in early 2005, John Kelly indicated that the trip to London to see Randall was organised under the auspices of Neil Blaney. The then agriculture minister was described by Kelly as the driving force behind the move to procure arms. Blaney was an unflappable, pipe-smoking Donegal politician who grew up near the Border and who came from the more republican element in Fianna Fáil. He was the son of a Fianna Fáil TD who had fought in the War of Independence and on the republican side in the Civil War. Neil Blaney was one of the most powerful figures in Fianna Fáil, and ran a superbly effective political machine in his Donegal bailiwick. According to John Kelly, it was Blaney who introduced Jock Haughey into the arms buying mission. Jock was 'a very sound individual, a very honest, reliable guy,' Kelly added.

After arriving in London, Kelly and Haughey made their way to the office at Oxford Street where the encounter with Mr Godfrey had taken place. Randall was waiting to meet them. The 'arms dealer' claimed to have done arms deals in the Middle East. The three left the office and walked to another venue to discuss business. Kelly had the distinct impression that he and Haughey were under surveillance as they walked along the street. He noticed a man and a woman, both with what appeared to be radio ear pieces, who seemed to be following them.

Kelly and Haughey made an appointment to see the arms dealer the following day. However, the two Irishmen became suspicious and decided to return to Dublin. Randall came to Dublin to pursue the matter further, staying at the Gresham Hotel and, it would appear, other city-centre hotels as well. He met John Kelly at Buswell's Hotel for further talks and inquired about visiting IRA camps. Kelly became even more suspicious. The Englishman was advised, for his own safety, to return to Britain, which he did around early December.

During his visit or visits to Dublin, I learned that Randall also had contact with Saor Éire, the conduit through which he first became involved in the arms deal talks. He met Liam Walsh and another member of the group at the Shelbourne Hotel. I also learned that as the Saor Éire people became suspicious of Randall, Liam Walsh contemplated taking action against him. A source indicated to me that Dick Timmins persuaded

Walsh not to move against the dealer. For his part, Captain Kelly has indicated that he intervened with some Belfast republicans to prevent Randall being killed.[10]

John Kelly's suspicions about being under surveillance were later confirmed. He discovered that he and Jock Haughey had been surreptitiously photographed by British Special Branch as they emerged from the underground in Oxford Street. Some time after their return to Dublin, Captain Kelly showed them a copy of one of the surveillance pictures. British Special Branch had sent the photo to Irish Special Branch in order to identify Kelly – apparently they recognised Jock Haughey, perhaps from his previous trip to London. Irish Special Branch had in turn asked Irish Army intelligence if they knew the identity of the second man in the photo. 'The British Special Branch obviously knew through Randall that two people were arriving from Ireland,' said John Kelly, who concluded that Randall was probably linked to British intelligence. The photograph was proof, if proof were needed, that British security/intelligence people were taking very seriously indeed the possibility of arms being covertly transferred to Northern nationalists. Captain Kelly subsequently stated that he reported Randall's activities to Irish military intelligence.

John Kelly recalled that he argued that instead of dealing with dubious characters in London, they should be looking to the Irish in the US. 'I said we should be dealing with those who have been traditionally involved in our hour of need – the Irish-American diaspora.' He considered that these were the people who understood the Irish national question, and who could be trusted. And so it was that Captain Kelly decided to send John Kelly and veteran Derry republican Sean Keenan to the US in December 1969, on an arms procurement mission. The trip was financed from the State funds that had been voted for the relief of distress in the North. They were both representing defence committees, but they also wore another hat – they were both linked to the IRA.

Keenan was a respected figure among republicans. First jailed in 1935, he was interned by the Northern authorities in the 1940s and also the 1950s. His wife, the former Nancy Ward, was herself interned at Armagh Prison in the early 1940s. Their son Colm, a member of the IRA, would be shot dead in the Bogside area of Derry by the British Army in March 1972.

John Kelly also had a long background in republican activity. His mother had worked for James Connolly, one of the leaders to be executed after the 1916 Rising, when he was building up the trade union movement in Belfast. In the 1920s she helped Éamon de Valera and Frank Aiken, who were to become two of the icons of the Fianna Fáil party, after they were jailed in Belfast's Crumlin Road Prison. They had been accused of entering the North illegally. Mrs Kelly would bring in their lunch and wash their shirts. Born in Belfast in 1936, John Kelly joined the IRA as a teenager, and led a flying column in County Tyrone during the Border Campaign that started in 1956. He and other members of his group were surrounded at a barn near Donaghmoyne in the foothills of the Sperrins by a force of RUC and B-Specials. He spent six-and-a-half years in jail.

As soon as they arrived in New York, Kelly and Keenan had a meeting with a group of Irish republicans. These included men who had been on the republican side in the Civil War and who had moved to America after the conflict – Michael Flannery from County Tipperary, John McGowan from County Clare and Jack McCarthy from County Cork, all of whom have since passed away. The tall, rake-thin Flannery was typical of a certain type of republican of a former era – ascetic, deeply religious, and with an almost fanatical devotion to the cause. These men were strongly anti-Fianna Fáil, and were suspicious of the involvement of the Irish 'Free State' government in arms procurement. Those who had founded Fianna Fáil had also been on the republican side in the Civil War but had later taken the constitutional route and entered the Dáil, much to the disgust of hardliners.

The visitors from Ireland also met Liam Kelly, a Tyrone-born republican who, in 1951, was expelled from the IRA for carrying out an unauthorised operation. In 1953 Kelly set up his own short-lived paramilitary group, Saor Uladh (Free Ulster). Kelly further annoyed his former colleagues in the IRA by breaking the abstentionist rule and taking a seat in the Senate in the Irish Republic. He then emigrated to America. Kelly was once quoted as saying: 'I do not believe in constitutional methods. I believe in the use of force, the more the better, the sooner the better. That may be treason or sedition: call it whatever you like.'

Of the republicans encountered by Kelly and Keenan, Mike Flannery was particularly suspicious of the use of Irish State funds to buy arms. Kelly recalled: 'Flannery was the man who was adamant about not dealing with the Free State.' Nevertheless, the emissaries from Ireland pointed out that there was money available from Irish State coffers for arms, up to £100,000, and who else had that kind of money to provide for the purchase of guns?

John Kelly saw this meeting, which took place in a room below a launderette in the Bronx, as extremely crucial and indeed historic. He recalled that the men attending the meeting were to form the nucleus of the group that would later become Irish Northern Aid, or Noraid. The declared purpose of the organisation was to raise money for the families of republican prisoners in Northern Ireland. Through its branches all over America, it was to raise millions of dollars. The authorities in the US, Ireland and the UK believed that some of the money raised was used to buy arms for the IRA, though this was always denied by Noraid. Nevertheless, money raised by the organisation would have freed up other funds to go towards the purchase of arms and the support of IRA activity.

It could also be said that the meeting helped to set the scene for Irish-American support for the Provisional movement back in Ireland, rather than the Official wing, which never received the same degree of support in the US.

Mike Flannery's close friend in the republican movement, George Harrison, was not at this meeting in the Bronx, but Harrison was to become a major organiser of arms shipments to the Provisionals. (Flannery and Harrison had met in the mid-1950s through groups such as the National Graves Association, which looks after IRA graves and memorials, and remained friends ever since.) Other small groups of activists set up gunrunning operations in cities such as Philadelphia and Baltimore. Indeed, through Harrison and other activists, America was to become a primary source of arms for the Provos during the 1970s.

Kelly said that major progress was made during that trip. 'We set in motion the arrangements for importing a sizeable consignment of arms into Dublin. The arrangements were very thorough and very meticulous.' They had in America a man from the North of Ireland, who was very familiar with the acquisition of weapons, and who had the necessary contacts. 'He made the arrangements for the buying and supplying of the arms. We had made the arrangements for the shipping of the arms from New York and we also made the arrangements for the arrival of the weapons in

Dublin, through a contact that we had at Dublin port.' The weapons would be cleared through the port in New York with the aid of the late Teddy Gleason, the influential Irish-American head of the powerful dockers' trade union the International Longshoremen's Association. The arms consignment was to consist of M-1 rifles, machine pistols and pistols, as well as ammunition. The weapons were to be paid for from the fund back in Ireland, and money would also be raised independently in the US.

Kelly went on: 'We put all those things in train and had been informing [Captain] Jim Kelly at home and we were happy with the way things were going. Then out of the blue we got a message from Jim Kelly to come back to Ireland.' John Kelly was extremely disappointed when he got his instructions to cut short the arms transaction and come home. 'We got a call from Jim Kelly to say he had arranged a fresh contact on the Continent and we had to return. We had to put the deal on hold in New York, much to our own discomfiture, because we had utter confidence in the people in New York. On arriving back we were told of this arms contact on the Continent, and when I argued against that, I was told that these people [on the Continent] were nearer, [the arms] more readily available, there was less transportation time, and that was how the Schlüter debacle began.' (Another source indicated during research for this book that an arms shipment arising out of the New York talks was subsequently delivered to Ireland.)[11]

John Kelly recalled that in arguing against cutting short the New York arms deal, he tried to convince Neil Blaney that they could trust the people in New York, but Blaney was not to be turned on the issue. 'When I argued against [cutting short the New York deal] at the time, and pointed out that we were dealing with our own people in America, dealing with Irish and Irish-Americans, and that we could trust them, Blaney argued against that, saying that these things [arms] were readily available [on the Continent].

'Looking at it in retrospect, I can only conclude that Blaney felt that by going the route that we were going, the Irish-American route, that they would not have had the same kind of control as they would have had over the arms coming from the Continent. It further reinforces my view that the Irish government was involved. There was this anxiety to keep the weapons under control. It was not to say that the weapons would not have been under their control if they had come from America, they would still have been under Jim Kelly's control, that was our trust, that was the arrangement that we had made. But I think the anxiety on Blaney's part was that they would not have had the same control over arms coming from America.'

The contact on the Continent was arms dealer Otto Schlüter. Blaney had found him through the Belgian-born businessman Albert Luykx, who lived in the pleasant seaside suburb of Sutton, the area where Blaney had his Dublin residence. Luykx in turn had got to hear about Schlüter through a contact of his own on the Continent. Blaney and Luykx were friendly – they had known each other about twenty years. Luykx was a guest at Blaney's wedding reception in Dublin's upmarket Shelbourne Hotel, attended also by Sean Lemass, one of Ireland's most significant political leaders, who served as taoiseach in the 1960s. It was through his friendship with Blaney that Luykx became caught up in the drama.

Luykx had himself been put in touch with Schlüter through an intermediary on the Continent called Bill Regnoriers. John Kelly, who met Regnoriers, said he was a flamboyant character, who was given the nickname 'Bill the Baron'. Schlüter ran his business from his plush apartment home on a tree-lined avenue called Loogestieg, in Hamburg's Eppendorf district. Schlüter had been in the arms business all his adult life and was also a skilled gunsmith, capable of making firearms himself.

John Kelly, Captain Kelly and Albert Luykx made trips to the Continent in connection with the deal. There were meetings with Schlüter in various locations, including Hamburg and Vienna. John Kelly was suspicious of Schlüter, and had a very low opinion of the arms dealer from the first time he met him. He said he shared his suspicions with Captain Kelly.

'I felt Schlüter was untrustworthy, dishonest and shifty.' He felt that Schlüter was informing the German authorities of what was going on. He had no direct evidence of this, but had no doubt that it was happening. Looking back on it now, he felt it was possible that the German authorities informed the British about the attempt to buy arms, and that they in turn tipped off Irish Special Branch. Kelly accepted that this may have been one of the ways in which Irish Special Branch kept tabs on their activities, apart from the information that Branch detectives were getting from their own sources in Dublin.[12] He suspected that Schlüter's real agenda was to keep the money paid for the weapons, without actually delivering them. He reckoned that Schlüter had an arrangement that if arms were handed over to the clients, the authorities would give them back to the arms dealer, 'so that he would have his money and the arms that he supplied'.

Reflecting on the dealings with Schlüter, John Kelly said: 'It was in many ways a wild goose chase, running all over the place and getting nothing. Things were supposed to be on their way and then did not arrive. There was always an excuse for things not happening. In a very short time I came to the conclusion that this was a dead end. I could not convince Luykx, or Blaney or Jim Kelly of that. They got stuck on this rail and they were staying on it.'

After convoluted dealings with Schlüter, a consignment of arms was finally to be sent by ship from the Belgian port of Antwerp to Dublin on 25 March 1970, but the paperwork was not in order, and the arms were not transported because of the lack of an 'end-user's certificate'. Captain Kelly took Albert Luykx with him as an interpreter on a trip to the Continent as he tried to sort out the problem. They flew to Brussels and travelled on to Antwerp. They continued on to Dortmund and travelled by taxi to Hamburg, where they met Schlüter. Captain Kelly made arrangements with Schlüter to fly in arms from Vienna to Dublin straight away.

Meanwhile, Luykx talked to Schlüter about the possibility of becoming an agent for him in Ireland. Schlüter told Captain Kelly he had 400 extra sub-machine guns and a lot of ammunition available. Captain Kelly agreed to buy the lot. As Luykx was to learn to his cost, Schlüter liked to have the money up front, and he wanted immediate payment for the materiel. Kelly did not have the money on him. The captain asked Luykx if he could oblige for a few days, so Luykx gave a cheque for £8,500 to cover the goods and the carriage on the aircraft. Captain Kelly later gave him a cheque for the same amount, drawn on one of the bank accounts set up for northern relief, and signed by 'Ann O'Brien' – the pseudonym/code name under which the account was operated. On 17 April, Luykx again went to the Continent with Captain Kelly. They stayed in the Intercontinental Hotel in Vienna, met Schlüter and saw more arms.

When the Irish banks reopened after a strike, Luykx found to his horror that the cheque made out to his firm Welux had bounced. Doubtless, Captain Kelly had given him the cheque in good faith, but fate had intervened. Luykx said rather plaintively in a letter to the Dáil Public Accounts Committee, which was later to investigate how State funds had been spent: 'I never would have had anything to do with the whole affair if I had known that everything was not above board – but why should I have had any doubts as I was introduced to it by a senior minister?' He enclosed a copy of the bounced cheque. Captain Kelly was later to tell the PAC that the total cost of the arms was £42,750, including the £8,500 advanced by Luykx.

It is surprising the number of articles written about the arms controversy that omit to mention the quantities and types of weapons that Captain Kelly sought to procure. According to Captain Kelly's testimony at the PAC, they consisted of the following:

400 x sub-machine guns @ £16 each

25 x heavy machine guns @ about £30 each

40 bulletproof vests @ about £70 each

about 250,000 x rounds of ammunition @ 9d each

about 400 x pistols @ £23 each

According to another source,[13] the consignment included a quantity of 9mm Browning pistols, Sterling sub-machine guns and Italian Beretta automatic rifles, with the ammunition being a mixture of 9mm and 7.62mm. However, during the Arms Trial itself, the materiel at the centre of the charges were said in court to consist of 500 pistols and 180,000 rounds of ammunition. Some observers have remarked that the inclusion of heavy machine guns in Captain Kelly's 'wish list' did not fit with the idea of arms for purely defensive purposes.

The final attempt to transport arms to Ireland by air from Vienna was to end in disarray. The plan was that the arms cargo would be flown to Dublin Airport on an Aer Lingus flight on Sunday, 21 April 1970. An Aer Lingus cargo transport official, concerned about the legal paperwork required for the transport of arms, and realising that no clearance had been obtained from the International Air Transport Association (IATA) for the transport on a passenger plane of guns and ammunition, contacted the Department of Transport and Power, which in turn contacted the Department of Justice, the matter ending up on the desk of the Department's formidable secretary, Peter Berry. As a result of the information filtering through, members of Garda Special Branch were standing by to seize the cargo unless told otherwise.

As Berry remembered it, he received a phone call at his home from finance minister Charlie Haughey on 18 April, asking if a cargo arriving at

Dublin Airport on Sunday would be allowed through, on a guarantee that it would go direct to the North. According to his evidence given during the Arms Trial, Berry made it clear that the cargo would be grabbed if it came into Dublin Airport. Berry quoted Haughey as saying: 'I had better have it called off.' In his evidence in court, Haughey disagreed with Berry's recollection of the conversation. His version was: 'It had better be called off – whatever it is.'

Haughey always denied knowing that a consignment of arms was involved, and stuck with that position throughout the Arms Trial. However, in 1997, I talked to the late Kevin Boland and he said he was very surprised indeed when Haughey gave this evidence. Boland said that at the time of the attempted importation, Haughey had come to him and told him the exact content of the cargo – arms.

This was an extraordinary situation, whereby two elements of the State security apparatus were working against each other. Captain Kelly, working with the approval of the head of military intelligence, Colonel Michael Hefferon, was seeking to bring in a cargo of arms covertly, while Garda Special Branch and Peter Berry, secretary of the Department of Justice, were seeking to block the importation.

Peter Berry, who was in effect the security supremo in the Department of Justice, personally informed Taoiseach Jack Lynch about the involvement of Haughey and Blaney in the arms importation attempt. Lynch confronted the two ministers, and Berry formed the view that Lynch was willing to let them continue in office, on the basis that there would be no repetition[14] – an Irish solution to an Irish problem.

One theory is that Lynch decided to sack the ministers only after it emerged that the leader of the opposition, Fine Gael chief Liam Cosgrave, received information about the gunrunning attempt – a version of events denied by Lynch. Cosgrave had gained his information in a note from an anonymous Garda and also, according to an informed source, from a man who had been a senior figure in Special Branch for many years. Why did these men from the State's security services become politically involved in this way? Had they been motivated, in part, by the rumours of collusion on the part of people in high places with Saor Éire, the gang that killed one of their own, Garda Fallon?

The spy and the arms dealer

In retrospect, if those behind the purchase of the weapons wanted to do so covertly, there was little prospect of keeping a transaction such as this under wraps. Irishmen seeking to buy arms on the Continent at a time of great turmoil in Ireland would be bound to attract attention, even if they considered that they were acting with the lawful authority of the Irish government. In 2000 I asked Tony Divall, a former member of British intelligence, for his comments on this matter. I thought he might have some interesting insights, in light of his career as a gunrunner after leaving MI6 in the 1950s, going on to be a whistleblower in the 1980s after falling out with his former bosses in MI6. Divall knew Schlüter well, and they lived close to each other in Hamburg. The two had done business together in the 1950s when both were involved in supplying arms to the Algerian rebels of the Front de libération nationale (FLN) who were fighting French colonial rule at the time.

Divall, in effect, backed up John Kelly's suspicions. He said that Schlüter, who operated as an arms dealer under a licence issued by the federal German government, would have been at pains to keep the German authorities informed on any business he was transacting with his Irish clients. Divall explained that Schlüter, under the terms of his licence, would routinely report transactions to the German authorities in order to abide by regulations and protect his own back. If he hadn't done so, it is unlikely he would have been allowed to stay in business for long.

Divall had good reason to remember his dealings with Schlüter – getting involved with the German in the Algerian business was a life-threatening experience. Agents of the SDECE, the French secret service, were given a licence to kill in their pursuit of arms dealers and gunrunners. Some of those providing arms to the rebels were murdered, and gunrunning ships and boats were blown up and sunk. The campaign of assassination carried out by death squads from a special unit of the SDECE called Action Service targeted not only arms dealers but others supporting the Algerian rebels of the FLN – it has been reported that scores were killed by France's clandestine and highly efficient killing machine. To disguise the identity of the real culprits behind the attacks, they were claimed by fictitious groups such as the Red Hand.

There had been two attempts on Schlüter's life. The first attack was made on 28 September 1956, when a powerful bomb consisting of five kilos of explosives was set off at Schlüter's Hamburg office. Schlüter suffered only superficial injuries but an assistant, a man called Lorenzen, was killed. Assassins tried again to eliminate Schlüter on 3 June the following year, when secret service agents planted a bomb in his Mercedes 220. When he started the engine the bomb exploded, killing his mother and injuring his four-year-old daughter Ingeborg. Once again Schlüter survived, but this time he had learned his lesson. He decided to cancel his arms contracts with the FLN.

Another German arms dealer, who had done business with the Algerian rebels, also survived a bomb attack during this era. Others involved in the traffic were not so lucky. An arms merchant who happened also to be a former SS officer was seriously injured when a bomb blew him through the roof of his car in Munich – he lost both legs. Leningrad-born George Puchert, who operated out of Hamburg and who had also lived in Tangier for ten years, had three of his ships blown up. Puchert himself was killed in Frankfurt in April 1959 when he pressed the starter of his Mercedes, detonating a bomb containing ball bearings that had been planted under the seat. A Swiss arms dealer, Marcel Leopold, who had supplied explosives to the FLN, was assassinated in truly bizarre fashion – he was hit by a poisoned arrow in the lobby of a Geneva hotel.

A former high-ranking French official, Constantin Melnik, gave a unique insight into the Mafia-style killings carried out by French secret service death squads in the 1950s and early 1960s, when he talked to the media in 1996. He was publicising a novel he had written based on his experiences. Melnik, who oversaw the secret services during the period in office of prime minister Michel Debré, told how in 1960 alone, 135 people were assassinated. A committee comprising himself, Debré and another senior official, the formidable Jacques Foccart who was close to General de Gaulle, met regularly to draw up lists of names to be passed on to the SDECE for assassination. The first meeting of the committee dealt with the arms dealers supplying the rebels. A dozen of these men were marked down for death, a cross marked beside each name. One of those condemned was Otto Schlüter. Melnik told how the Action Service unit planted a bomb in Schlüter's car, but it failed to kill him. 'Nevertheless, after failed attempts [to assassinate him], the man dropped out [of supplying arms to the rebels].' Melnik described how another arms trafficker was kidnapped and then executed in a secret SDECE house in a Paris suburb. The body was encased in concrete and dumped at sea from an aircraft. Melnik also recalled how SDECE sank vessels that were involved in transporting arms to the rebels.[15]

The French went after Tony Divall's gunrunning operation also. Like Schlüter, Divall had a lucky escape after he began transporting arms to the Algerians. Divall had learned how to operate boats in the Royal Marines, and as a gunrunner was using a former German wartime E-Boat for his clandestine activities. Divall received a very severe warning from the French when they blew up his boat in Tangier. Divall, a hint of lofty disdain in his voice, told me he considered it a typically nasty reaction from French intelligence, and wasn't in the least surprised many years later when French secret agents were exposed as the culprits behind the bombing of the Greenpeace ship *Rainbow Warrior* in New Zealand.

Tony Divall had a low opinion of Schlüter. In the light of Divall's own gunrunning activities over the years, this might be seen by some as a case of the kettle calling the pot black. Nevertheless, as somebody who knew Schlüter well and had done business with him, his opinion of the German arms dealer is relevant. Divall considered that Schlüter would have sought to squeeze as much money as he could out of his Irish clients, without delivering the weapons.

Divall told me that as well as the French, he thought the Algerian rebels would have been gunning for Schlüter in the old days as he allegedly defrauded them of about $400,000. It has also emerged that Schlüter had his own brushes with the law. In 1964 he was charged with defrauding three customers, two of them from small Arab countries, of a total of almost £11,000 in connection with an arms deal. In 1968 Schlüter was sentenced to six months and heavily fined for selling 2,500 pistols and 150,000 rounds of ammunition to people who had no proper licence. The sentence was quashed on appeal.

Said Divall: 'Schlüter was an unpleasant character, a dodgy individual. He was a small man, tubby, with a round, bald head. When he was dealing with the people from Ireland he would have been looking for a way of ensuring that the arms did not go through while holding onto the money.

He was known in our nefarious trade as Uncle Otto. But despite the kind of work he did he was very domesticated. He liked nothing better than to sit at home in his carpet slippers and watch TV.' Divall, of course, in light of his intelligence background, would have been more than happy to have stymied Captain Kelly's transaction by tipping off his friends in MI6, but he never gave any indication that Schlüter informed him about the deal, or that he [Divall] personally played any role in undermining this particular arms procurement operation.

One cannot rule out the possibility, as John Kelly suspected, that the German security services learned quite early on of the deal, perhaps through Schlüter complying with the normal arms deal reporting procedures, and that they passed on word to their counterparts in Britain, who in that case would certainly have tipped off Irish Special Branch. The magazine *This Week*, which provided some well-informed coverage at this period, claimed that it was British Special Branch that passed on information about the arms deal to their Irish counterparts. An article in the magazine stated: 'The bubble burst when the British Special Branch passed on details about the arms deal to the Garda Special Branch in Dublin Castle.'[16] The magazine claimed that inquiries were carried out, and reports sent to the Department of Justice, ultimately reaching the desk of the then minister, Micheál Ó Móráin. As indicated above, some of the activity connected with the arms deal took place in Vienna, and the London *Times* reported that Austrian police conducted inquiries into the arms shipment at the request of the British Embassy in Vienna.

Irish Special Branch may have had other sources closer to home on the activities of Haughey and Blaney. According to one report, Special Branch at this period was getting information from two members of the IRA Army Council.[17] A source who was part of the Provisional wing in the early days told me that he and others in the movement suspected that a particular man, a senior figure in the Goulding wing, was giving information to the Gardaí at this period, in order to discredit those on the embryonic Provisional wing by highlighting their contacts with elements in Fianna Fáil. The Goulding wing considered that Fianna Fáil was trying to split the republican movement by helping to form a breakaway IRA that would operate only in the North, by supplying arms and support to those traditional physical force elements who went on to form the Provisionals, while seeking to sideline the Gouldingites, who were against the 'capitalist' twenty-six-county State and were seeking a 'workers' republic'.

On 10 April 1970, in the final stages of the attempt to import arms, a new head of Irish military intelligence took over. Colonel Patrick Delaney replaced Colonel Michael Hefferon, who retired. Intelligence files in the Military Archives show that in communications with the chief of staff, Lieutenant General Sean MacEoin, and defence minister Gibbons, Colonel Delaney was highly critical of Captain Kelly's activities. Colonel Delaney gave a verbal briefing to the defence minister on 22 April, a written account of which was given to the chief of staff. According to the file, Colonel Delaney said that, from November 1969, Captain Kelly 'ceased to have any contact with the Security Sub-Section and no reports from him are on record in the Intelligence Security Sub-Section'.

Colonel Delaney also reported in his memo on the 22 April briefing that it was apparent that there was an attempt to import arms illegally for subversive groups on both sides of the Border. 'The purchase of arms in this fashion has grave implications for military and state security. Weapons should be purchased only for the forces of the state NOT for illegal groups. The giving of arms to untrained people is a most serious matter. John Hume expressed the view that such action would be "suicide".'

Colonel Delaney warned that such weapons could be used not only against the British, 'but against our own forces'. He also warned that if any of the weapons were subsequently captured, 'it will be possible to trace their origin'. He said that Captain Kelly had made no attempt to conceal his identity, which was utterly irresponsible and must seriously compromise the Intelligence Section. His open contact with illegal groups was also a serious security matter.

Colonel Delaney went on: 'It must be accepted that British intelligence, now operating in a big way in Northern Ireland, will get onto it. They have their own international links with European security agencies and with the CIA, so the likelihood of these activities going undetected is small. As well as the intelligence implications, there is the political reaction of the British government to be considered.' He warned that if the arms eventually ended up in IRA hands, 'they constitute a threat to army security ...' Colonel Delaney recorded that An tAire [the minister for defence, Mr Gibbons] 'agrees that (a) arms could be turned against us (b) untrained people in NI [Northern Ireland] should not get arms (c) British Intelligence and CIA could know.' In another document, Colonel Delaney referred to Captain Kelly's 'emotional reaction to events in Northern Ireland', which pointed to 'his having lost that cool behaviour so necessary in an intelligence officer'. On 1 May, Captain Kelly retired from the Army, and was arrested by Special Branch.

Drama in the Dáil

When Jack Lynch confronted Blaney and Haughey, both denied any wrong-doing. Lynch's tense meeting with Haughey took place in the Mater Hospital. Haughey had been injured and there were wild rumours he had been beaten up at a public house. In fact the truth was far more mundane – he had fallen off a horse at the stables at his country estate.

Haughey, with his hooded eyes and commanding presence, often displayed a tough, macho attitude to the world. But he could also be sensitive, and it is said that he broke down and cried when confronted by Lynch. No doubt the extremely ambitious finance minister feared that his career in politics, that had looked so promising, had come to a shuddering halt. Lynch was later quoted as saying: 'Charlie Haughey was in tears … It was a deeply distressing and very trying occasion.'[18]

The soft-spoken Jack Lynch, despite his record as a tough, determined player on the hurling field, was often seen as a consensus politician, who shied away from confrontation. Nevertheless, he bit the bullet and when Blaney and Haughey refused to resign, he sacked them.

The Arms Crisis, of course, threw the ruling Fianna Fáil party into turmoil, with elements in the party lining up behind what was called the Haughey wing, and others, the majority, supporting the line taken by Lynch. As a reporter with the *Irish Press*, I was on the press gallery in Leinster House on the night that Lynch made his formal statement in the Dáil announcing the sacking of the ministers. It was an event of high drama that will forever be etched in my memory. The tension almost crackled in the air as a packed, hushed House heard Lynch announce that he had dismissed Haughey and Blaney, after being informed by the security forces of an alleged attempt to import arms illegally from the Continent. Since the two ministers had not resigned when asked to do so, he advised President de Valera to remove them from office.

On that fateful night, Wednesday, 6 May 1970, Lynch also announced that a third minister, Kevin Boland, had resigned. Boland, as it turned out, was not implicated in any gunrunning allegations, but had walked out in protest following the sacking of his colleagues.

Everyone knew the gist of what Lynch was going to say before he said it. The dismissal of the ministers had been announced by the Government Information Bureau at three o'clock that morning. But the formal announcement made by the former Cork GAA star still sent shockwaves around the country.

It was a short, ten-minute statement, but it ended with the careers of three ministers in shreds on the floor, and a nation in turmoil. As Lynch sat down, the hush over Leinster House was palpable. The distinguished visitors' gallery was packed, as were the public galleries. The government and opposition benches were full to capacity. Everyone, from public to politicians to VIPs, seemed stunned. For once, the Dáil, which like any parliamentary chamber was no stranger to verbosity, had been shocked into silence. After what seemed like an eternity, but which was probably no more than a few moments, the opposition leader, Liam Cosgrave, rose to his feet to reply.

Journalist John Healy, writing next day in the *Irish Times*, described vividly how the Dáil was so hushed by the taoiseach's statement that the thump-thump of an engine [which apparently ran the heating system] in the bowels of the building reached into the assembly and 'sounded like the communal heartbeat of the crowded Chamber'.

I recall Neil Blaney around Leinster House that night, a sardonic smile playing around his lips. He may have been in the eye of the storm, but he came across as laid back and utterly calm. He stood in the lobby overlooking the chamber, gazing down at the packed benches, as relaxed as if he were checking out calves at a mart somewhere in the far reaches of his native Donegal.

Haughey, who was still in hospital, issued a statement categorically denying being involved 'in any illegal importation or attempted importation of arms into this country'. During the subsequent debate, Blaney also issued a vehement denial of involvement in gunrunning. 'I have run no guns,' he said. 'I have procured no guns. I have provided no money to buy guns, and anybody who says otherwise is not telling the truth.'

One Fianna Fáil TD was so carried away that he used the 'f...' word on a number of occasions as he hurled insults at the Fine Gael benches opposite – I could hear him clearly from the press gallery. There is no record of this particular four-letter world being used in Dáil debates – either on that memorable night or since, or indeed on any other occasion since the foundation of the State. Some of the Deputy's more outrageous interjections were probably recorded in the official record as 'interruptions'. Nowadays, there would be a storm of controversy over the use of such language in the Dáil, but in those far-off days political correctness had not yet taken hold in Ireland.

As I hurried out of Leinster House that night on my way back to the *Irish Press* newsroom, there were small groups of people gathered outside the gates on Kildare Street, staring in at the building. There was an air of tension about them, almost as if they were expecting the government to be overthrown. It is bizarre to look back on it now, but there were even some people who wondered if a *coup d'état* designed to overthrow the government had been nipped in the bud. The marathon Dáil debate on the Arms Crisis began on Friday, 8 May, and continued non-stop for more than thirty-seven hours, until late on Saturday night.

During the long Dáil debate there was at least one moment of farce, as I was to learn many years later from an eye witness. A man who was not a TD, who was believed to have been 'under the influence', somehow wandered into the actual Dáil chamber, nodded politely towards the ceann chomhairle [chairperson], and sat down to listen intently to the debate. I presume this happened in the early hours of the morning when there were few people around. The tipsy intruder was quickly spotted and removed by an usher before there was a major commotion.

There were many conflicting opinions in the country at the time on Lynch's actions in sacking the ministers, and on the question of supplying guns for self-defence to Northern nationalists. There were those who held that in a doomsday situation in the North, with a total breakdown of law and order, Catholic communities would need guns to defend themselves. Others took the view that sending arms to the North was irresponsible; that it would only fuel sectarian tensions, driving a greater wedge between the two communities and leading to even greater bloodshed.

There was further shock throughout the land when the suspects were arrested and charged, and were put on trial. Jack Lynch had turned the files on the case over to the attorney general, Colm Condon, and it was he who decided that the prosecutions should take place.

Meanwhile, in Germany, inquiries were also being carried out. Indications have emerged that German security services became suspicious after learning of Schlüter's dealings with his Irish customers, and the types of weapons involved in the deal. The German authorities considered that some of the pistols being sold by Schlüter were of inferior East European manufacture, not up to the standards of those produced by, say, Colt or Browning. The authorities considered that Schlüter, as an experienced arms dealer, would know that no national defence force would buy them; that only illegal paramilitary organisations would be foolish enough to want them. These suspicions were voiced in a German document dated 20 May 1970, which surfaced in Irish State papers released in early 2003.[19]

Because of his republican background, John Kelly was used to appearing in court and to clashes with authority. In that respect, he was probably more mentally prepared for coping with the trial than the others. Blaney, of course, was cleared at an early stage in the process, but Haughey, Captain Kelly and Albert Luykx had to endure lengthy hearings. To add to the agony, the first Arms Trial was aborted, and the defendants had to go through a second trial. For Haughey and Captain Kelly, both of whom had done the State some service in their respective careers, the experience of facing criminal charges was particularly stressful and painful. For Albert Luykx, being hauled before the courts must have been a very bitter experience indeed. He had been through some very traumatic times in his earlier life in war-torn Belgium, but had put all that behind him and had prospered in Ireland. He pointed out that he had been brought into the arms-buying operation by a prominent government minister, Neil Blaney, and that he had no reason to believe that the operation was illegal.

Ironically, Luykx was always sensitive about his reputation as an upright citizen. In 1969 he heard 'malicious accusations' in Belgium that he had engaged in neo-Nazi activity in Ireland. He contacted Peter Berry, secretary of the Department of Justice, who gave him a letter confirming that since arriving in Ireland in 1948 he had not offended against the criminal law and had not engaged in any subversive political activities. But now, with the arms conspiracy charges, he was accused, in effect, of subverting the authority of the State that had given him refuge.

John Kelly considers that the Arms Trial was a betrayal of the nationalist people of the Six Counties. 'From the time of partition, Northern nationalists had looked to the Southern government as their first guarantor in times of trouble. Here we had, for the first time since partition, an opportunity for an Irish government to show its sincerity and resolve, and what do they do? They betray Northern nationalists and throw them back into the arms of the British government and more particularly of Unionism.'

Kelly believes that, had the Irish government taken a firm hand at the time, the following thirty years of carnage would not have happened. 'It was the betrayal and the sense of abandonment that Northern nationalists felt, that fuelled the rise of the Provisional IRA. It drew Northern nationalists to recognise that the only people who were going to defend them, if the British and the Irish could not do so, were their own people on the ground, which was the emerging Provisional IRA.'

Much has been written about the rights and wrongs of the Arms Trial, and the topic can still excite lively debate. On the occasions I met Captain Kelly I was always struck by his conviction that he had never done anything wrong or illegal. He suffered grievously for his actions, and his military career was ruined. I had the impression of a man who had acted out of a sense of idealism. He probably had become emotionally involved, and somebody more calculating might have avoided this risky venture that was to destroy his career. He certainly had nothing to gain personally by his actions, either materially or in terms of career advancement.

For his part, defence minister Jim Gibbons always insisted he did not authorise any arms importation, but he did concede in evidence during the Arms Trial that he had been informed of the attempted importation of arms through Dublin port in March, and had allowed Captain Kelly to stay in place. It was put to Gibbons that by his acquiescence in Captain Kelly's continued duties in the Army, the minister had led the captain to believe that he, Gibbons, was authorising what he did. Gibbons insisted again that he gave no authorisation. For their part, members of Gibbons' own family have been deeply hurt by the allegations made against the former minister.

When I interviewed Captain Kelly in 1980, ten years after the Arms Trial, he told me that he had made a complaint of perjury against Gibbons, and that the Gardaí launched an investigation. However, no prosecution for perjury took place. The interview took place in Captain Kelly's home, over the pub he was running at the time in his native Bailieborough. Des O'Malley, who was appointed by Jack Lynch as justice minister in 1970 in succession to Micheál Ó Móráin, stood up for Gibbons' integrity in a statement in 2001: 'I cannot imagine anyone less likely to commit perjury than the late Jim Gibbons. He was a man of considerable religious scruples, obsessed with the truth, and possessed of a deep and genuine private morality, often expressed to me and indeed expressed publicly and visibly from his voting record in Dáil Éireann on other matters.'[20]

Some still question the legality of the attempt to import arms – but it has to be remembered that all the accused were found not guilty. The operation was certainly covert. Arms were not being procured through 'open' procedures. There was no public tendering process. No details were entered into the appropriate register kept at the Department of Defence, which recorded authorisations given on behalf of the defence minister for the importation of arms and ammunition. None of this, however, means that the attempted importation was necessarily illegal. A covert operation does not necessarily imply illegality. But the absence of documentation was to disrupt the transfer of the weapons both by ship and by air.

In his memoirs published in 2005, Pádraig Faulkner, who was education minister at the time of the Arms Crisis, and who was a member of the Cabinet Sub-Committee on Northern Ireland, states that 'at no time did the Government agree to, sanction, or involve itself with the procurement of arms, other than for the legitimate forces of the Irish State'. He also states that if any individuals were led to believe that they were acting on behalf of, or in accordance with orders from the Government, or of the Sub-Committee, in procuring arms for any other purpose, 'then they are mistaken in that belief'. Faulkner makes the point, incidentally, that the Sub-Committee met only once. Neil Blaney, Charlie Haughey, Joe Brennan from County Donegal and himself had been appointed to the Sub-Committee by Jack Lynch in August 1969, and it had its first meeting shortly afterwards. Brennan and Faulkner turned up for the second meeting and were both annoyed when the others failed to show. The Sub-Committee never met again.[21]

One of the great ironies of the Arms Crisis, in John Kelly's view, is that Neil Blaney was cleared in the early stages of legal proceedings, during the deposition stage in the Dublin District Court, even though he was the moving force behind the drive to import weapons. Blaney was represented by prominent barrister Liam Hamilton, later to become Chief Justice. The State pressed ahead with the case against Charlie Haughey, even though he had a much more peripheral role. Said John Kelly: 'We met Charlie Haughey only twice, in August and September 1969, but as soon as the government Sub-Committee [on the North] was set up, and Blaney took control, we never met Haughey again at this period. It was Neil Blaney who was the engine room behind this quest for arms, it was he who was directing it. When we were in America, it was he who gave the order to call us back again. It was he who directed the Randall thing in England, it was he who directed the Schlüter thing, so Blaney was at the centre and was the engine room of the whole arms importation thing, he was directing it and it was very hands-on direction.'

Kelly, like others, was surprised at Haughey's defence during the trial that he did not know what was in the consignment that was coming in from the Continent, and for which he tried to arrange customs clearance. 'I find that difficult to understand. As time goes by, I think that what motivated Charlie in taking that line, and it's the only conclusion I can come to, is Blaney's stance ... Blaney was the whole driving force, but he gets himself off at the depositions stage. Charlie would have felt that Blaney, who was the mastermind, had engineered his way out of it and was free, in spite of his deep involvement. Charlie had a much more peripheral role. I think maybe Charlie's attitude was influenced by that. Maybe he felt a sense of betrayal by Blaney. I think that Blaney regretted he himself did not go the full distance [in the Arms Trial].'

Kelly said that to this day he feels sorry for Albert Luykx. 'This was a man who was a non-national by origin, who believed, because he was meeting with Neil Blaney, that he was acting on behalf of the Irish government. He had no reason to believe otherwise. He suffered socially and economically in the fall-out.'

During the huge celebrations that took place when the four Arms Trial defendants were cleared, John Kelly found out something that astonished him. There were some republicans from Belfast present in court during the trial, and had he been found guilty and sentenced to a prison term, they were ready to mount a rescue attempt. 'They told me they would have sprung me from the Four Courts.' He believed they had a 'safe house' prepared in Dublin where he could lie low.

The Arms Trial had repercussions on domestic Irish politics. After Charlie Haughey was acquitted, he gave a press conference and threw down the gauntlet, angrily demanding the resignation of Taoiseach Jack Lynch. Blaney and Boland also demanded that Lynch step down. Lynch was in New York at the time, where he addressed the General Assembly of the United Nations, and he flew back into Dublin Airport on the night of 26 October 1970 to meet the challenge head-on. Members of the government and of the Fianna Fáil parliamentary party turned out in force to greet their leader and to show their support. I was one of the reporters covering the event, and was struck by the massed ranks of Fianna Fáilers assembled in a solid phalanx behind a very determined Lynch as he gave a press conference at the airport. It became clear that there was not going to be any heave that would overthrow Jack Lynch. Despite all the turmoil, he remained in control of the party.

I cannot recall all the politicians who were there that night, but it has been recorded that Frank Aiken and Sean McEntee, of the 1916–23 generation, were present.[22] Looking back on it now, Aiken's presence would have had particular symbolic resonance. As already indicated, he was the last IRA chief of staff at the time of the Civil War, and had very strong republican credentials. But he had gone the constitutional route, and had served in senior ministerial posts in Fianna Fáil governments, notably as minister for external affairs. Even as the war drums began to beat in the North in 1969–70, he was still taking the constitutional line, and throwing his weight behind Jack Lynch.

Also at the airport was another man who carried significant symbolic weight – Máirtín Ó Flathartaigh, secretary to president de Valera, and a native Irish speaker from Connemara. His presence seemed to indicate that Dev himself, one of the leaders of the 1916 Rising, was giving his imprimatur to Jack Lynch and his constitutional approach.

By a curious coincidence, as well as Aiken there was another former IRA chief of staff at Dublin Airport that night. Security was more relaxed in those far-off, pre-9/11 days, and reporters were allowed out onto the tarmac to meet Lynch as he came off the aircraft. I spotted Sean McBride among the passengers entering the terminal building. I spoke to him briefly and he was courteous and friendly. McBride had served as IRA chief for a short period in the 1930s. He also had a place in the history of Irish gun-running. In the 1920s he had been sent on a mission to Hamburg by nationalist leader Michael Collins to rescue a consignment of arms destined for Ireland that had been seized by the authorities.[23] However, like Frank Aiken, McBride had taken the constitutional route. He became prominent as a barrister, government minister and human rights campaigner, winning both the Nobel and Lenin peace prizes.

Taking up the gun has been a familiar theme in recent Irish history, but so has the idea of walking away from the gun and abandoning violence and 'armed struggle' for peaceful, constitutional means – one of the key concepts behind the current Peace Process.

The State tries to get its money back

The Dáil Public Accounts Committee held a special inquiry into how the money voted by the government for the relief of distress in the North had been spent. The first sittings were in January 1971. During one of the hearings, Captain Kelly said that moneys drawn from one of the bank accounts that had been set up, the George Dixon account, were used mainly in connection with the purchase of arms. (George Dixon was a pseudonym.) Of the £38,249.13.9 accounted for directly through this account, Captain Kelly indicated that sums totalling £32,500 were used for the purchase of arms in Germany, of which £26,000 to £28,000 had been paid for arms, the balance being for expenses. Captain Kelly also said that £849.13.9 was used to finance a trip to the US seeking general assistance and arms, and £1,600 for an abortive arms purchase in Britain.

The PAC took a poor view of the use of State funds to buy arms, and considered that this amounted to misappropriation. A report issued by the PAC chairman Patrick Hogan on 13 July 1972, found that of the £105,766.5.9 spent, £29,166.12.0 was spent on the relief of distress; £34,850 was possibly spent in Belfast but for undetermined purposes; £250 was spent on purposes possibly related to the relief of distress; and £41,499.13.9 was not spent on the relief of distress.

The report spread its criticism wide. It found that if Colonel Hefferon had taken appropriate action when he learned from Captain Kelly about the proposed arms importation and his drawings from the account, 'much of the money might not have been misappropriated'. The report continued: 'Had the then Minister for Agriculture and Fisheries, Deputy Blaney and the then Minister for Finance Deputy Haughey and the then Minister for Defence, Deputy Gibbons passed on to the Taoiseach their suspicion or knowledge of the proposed arms importation, the misappropriation of part of the money which is now known to have been spent on arms might have been avoided.' I do not recall if Colonel Hefferon made any public comment about the criticism of him voiced in the PAC report. About ten years after the Arms Trial, I spoke briefly by phone to Colonel Hefferon. He admitted that he felt 'hard done by' as a result of certain things that happened during the Arms Crisis saga, but added with a touch of humour that it only happened if he allowed himself to think about the past.

The Department of Finance made various attempts to recover the money that had been paid to Otto Schlüter, but to no avail. Irish officials made several visits to Hamburg to meet Schlüter, but in the end the arms dealer failed to return the money. Initially, the wily Schlüter took the view that he had not transacted any business with the Department, so why should he cough up money to a body that had not been his client? He told a court hearing in 1977 that his business was with a Dublin-registered company called Welux Ltd – he had agreed to send £40,000 worth of arms and ammunition to this company. This was the company associated with Albert Luykx.

During one visit by Irish officials to Hamburg in 1971, Schlüter showed them a cargo of arms in Hamburg docks that, he said, was destined for Welux. Schlüter offered to transfer the arms to Dublin but the officials told him the government had no wish to obtain arms – the government wanted its money back.

Ireland's consul general in Hamburg, Aidan Mulloy, had meetings with Schlüter and was initially told by the arms dealer that so far as he was concerned, the Irish business was closed. State papers released in January 2003 show that Mulloy had a meeting with Schlüter on 11 February 1971. In his report, Mulloy outlined the arms dealer's dismissive attitude: 'The Irish customers had ordered certain goods, made a payment and failed to collect.

It was no concern of his what had happened to his customers subsequently, nor was it his concern whether the money with which this payment was made was their own or belonged to the Irish State.' Mulloy also reported how Schlüter talked dismissively of the 'inexperience' of the Irish people with whom he had dealt.[24]

Mulloy told Schlüter that Captain Kelly did not have the authority of the Irish government to enter into an arms contract.[25] Schlüter, who did not deny receiving £40,000 from his Irish clients, claimed he had entered into a commercial deal and denied having had any connection with the Dublin government. He asked the consul general for a letter stating that the money in question was government money and that Captain Kelly had no authorisation to use it for an arms deal. Schlüter insisted that with such a letter he could approach Captain Kelly.

On 27 March 1971, Mulloy again met Schlüter. This time he was accompanied by Tony Fagan, principal officer in the Department of Finance, and formerly personal secretary to Charlie Haughey during his period as finance minister. Schlüter was given the letter he requested. Meanwhile, it emerged that Schlüter was involved in moves to sell the arms at the centre of the Arms Crisis to the Philippines. It is unclear if the deal was finalised.

Schlüter made the intriguing claim that some of the arms did indeed get through to Ireland, by charter boat from Spain, for which he had paid. He said that this was a separate transaction involving an agent in Spain, and that Irish government money was not involved. The money for this particular arms purchase came out of the money provided by Mr Luykx, which amounted to £8,500.[26] I am not aware of any other report to back up Schlüter's claim, and it does not tally with a later claim by the arms dealer that he refunded the £8,500. Schlüter may simply have been trying to muddy the waters, to frustrate attempts by the Irish to get the money back. John Kelly is convinced there is no truth to Schlüter's claim that arms came in from Spain.

The Irish government brought legal proceedings against Schlüter and there was a hearing in Hamburg on 25 May 1977, at which Albert Luykx was present. Two Irish reporters covered the proceedings, John Cooney of the *Irish Times* and John McAleese of RTÉ.

Tony Fagan was among the Irish officials who gave evidence. He told how, at a meeting in Hamburg in October 1971, Schlüter promised Irish officials, including Fagan, that he would pay back £20,000. This figure was apparently based on what Schlüter was deemed to owe after storage and other expenses had been deducted.

A year later, when no money had been paid, Fagan, accompanied by secretary of the Department of Finance Michael Murphy, again met Schlüter in Hamburg. Both gave evidence that Schlüter once again promised to refund £20,000. However, Murphy testified that Schlüter refused to put the promise in writing. Schlüter, for his part, denied that he had given any such undertaking. During his evidence, he claimed that he gave back £8,500 to the purchasing company Welux, as a gesture of good will – apparently the money that had been advanced by Luykx. He also claimed that the original deal had been made with his Hamburg business firm and not himself personally.

The case was adjourned to the following 22 June, but there is no indication that the hearing was resumed. The Dublin government may have decided that it had little chance of success, and that there was no point in throwing good money after bad.

Haughey the survivor

The most high-profile of the Arms Trial defendants was Charlie Haughey. He stayed within the Fianna Fáil fold and showed himself to be the survivor of the seventies by, Lazarus-like, eventually returning to the Cabinet and, ultimately, becoming taoiseach.[27]

Haughey always declined to discuss the events of the Arms Crisis. As he passed his final years in the seclusion of his Abbeville estate at Kinsealy, he never broke his silence. His faithful aide PJ Mara, who served him as government press secretary, once remarked in his inimitable way to a journalist who was about to be shown into Haughey's presence for an interview: 'None of that oul' Arms Trial shite now.' That remark summarises The Boss's *omerta* attitude towards certain events in his past, an attitude that he maintained up to his death.

John Kelly, who now lives in Maghera, County Derry, kept in touch with fellow Arms Trial defendants Captain James Kelly and Charlie Haughey over the years. 'Jim was a very decent, honourable man. We would meet up in Dublin or if he was up here [in County Derry] he would call ... Jim would have been your typical Fianna Fáil County Cavan republican. His father was Fianna Fáil. Coming from Cavan, he would have grown up in a very Ulster environment, and would have been very aware of partition, and had a sense of history about it.' He said the Arms Trial had become an obsession with Captain Kelly: 'It was a cancer, it just ate away at him, he would never give up on it. I used to say to him: "Jim, for Christ's sake, put it to one side," and he'd say, "Yeah, I will," but ten minutes later he always went back to what happened.'

John Kelly supports the Peace Process in the North and the Good Friday Agreement, and became a Sinn Féin member of the North's power-sharing Assembly. He was still a member of the Assembly in July 2003 when James Kelly died, aged seventy-three. In an oration during the funeral Mass in Our Lady of Refuge Church, Rathmines, Dublin, he said that Captain Kelly had come to them as a beacon of hope in their hour of darkness. He told the packed church there was a 'deep sense of betrayal' when Captain Kelly was arrested, along with former members of the cabinet.

John Kelly has since dropped out of politics and has severed his links with Sinn Féin because of differences with the party leadership. He was critical of the way that decommissioning had been dragged out, and was being used as a bargaining tool. He said that republicans should have done what was done in the early 1960s – IRA units were stood down, arms were dumped and people embarked on a political course. Unionists accepted this in good faith at that time, and he believed it would have been acceptable to them in more recent times. (These comments were made in early 2005, when the final act of IRA decommissioning was still some time in the future.) He alleged some senior figures were using the latter-day IRA as a militia to 'impose their will'.

In media comments in 2005 he was particularly scathing about the republicans who murdered Robert McCartney after a Belfast pub row, and who were involved in the subsequent cover-up. He wondered if the 'Orange jackboot' had been shaken off, only to be replaced by the 'green jackboot'.

Even though he was acquitted in the Arms Trial, a shadow remains over Captain Kelly, and a campaign has been in progress for some years to clear his name. John Kelly was a regular visitor to Charlie Haughey at his home in Kinsealy. The two men remained friends. Talking in 2005, about eighteen months before Haughey's death in June 2006, John Kelly recalled that they did not talk much about the old days. 'We talk about current affairs, how things are ...' Kelly said that he did not think there would be a resolution to the petition to have Jim Kelly vindicated, so long as Charlie Haughey was still around. He added that this was Charlie's opinion too: 'Charlie believes that people do not want to clear Jim Kelly while he himself is alive, as it would vindicate Charlie as well.' There were too many people out there who did not want to see Charlie vindicated. 'If they vindicate Jim Kelly, how could they not vindicate the rest of us?'

The failure of the attempt to import arms with the aid of the funds voted for the relief of Northern distress had an important sequel – key members of the emerging Provisional IRA such as Daithí Ó Conaill and Sean Keenan redoubled their efforts to procure weaponry from other sources. Ó Conaill had already taken steps to reactivate a 1950s arms supply network in New York (*see* Chapter 3). Keenan and Joe Cahill were also to visit America, inspiring ad hoc groups of Irish-Americans to procure and send arms to Ireland. The US was to emerge as a major source of arms, but potential sources in other areas of the world were also checked out. Captain Kelly may not have succeeded in getting arms into Ireland, but there were others who would follow in a similar role, and in the following years the floodgates would open.

CHAPTER 3

The IRA and the Harrison Network

George Harrison had a very clear memory of the first guns he ever supplied to the IRA. A native of County Mayo, he had emigrated to the US just before the Second World War, but retained an almost religious devotion to the Irish republican cause. He mixed in republican circles in the US, and one day a County Kerry-born republican who lived in the Bronx, and who was a member of an Irish republican support group, had a proposition for him: 'Now, lad, if you ever come across a few pieces we can always use them.' Harrison recalled: 'I brought him four or five Colt .45 automatics. When I gave him the guns he said: "Now, I am not going to say thanks, because it's only your duty." That's the way it was. He was a great guy.'

This was in the early 1950s, and it was the start of a remarkable clandestine career. Over a period spanning four decades, Harrison was to become one of the most important gunrunners in the history of the IRA. In what was to be the last interview he ever gave, three weeks before his death in 2004, he told me that he reckoned he supplied up to 3,000 firearms to the IRA. His gunrunning career stretched from the 1950s to the early 1980s, when the FBI broke up his gunrunning network.

Small in stature but feisty and full of energy, Harrison never married – all his spare time was devoted to the causes that he espoused. His modestly-furnished apartment at Prospect Park Southwest, Brooklyn, was like a shrine, the walls decorated with political posters. Pride of place was given to a 'Free Róisín McAliskey' poster. Ms McAliskey, who was in prison in the UK for a period in the 1990s, is the daughter of firebrand republican Bernadette McAliskey, a former Westminster MP who became a friend of Harrison's in the 1960s, and was a character witness for him during his trial on gunrunning charges in 1981.[1]

There were also photos of relatives, and friends such as lawyer Paul O'Dwyer. It was the time of the US presidential campaign, and Harrison had a John Kerry poster in his front window. Somehow, I suspected that for Harrison it was more a question of being anti-George W Bush than pro-John Kerry.

Harrison was born on 2 May 1915, in Shammer, near Kilkelly in County Mayo, one of a family of ten children. His father Tom, known as 'Tom Yank' because he had spent some time in America, was a stonemason and his mother, the former Winnie McDermott from the nearby village of Bar-nacogue, ran a small shop. One of his earliest memories was of a banner commemorating Thomas Ashe, a republican who died in 1917 after being force-fed during a hunger strike. The banner, with the inscription 'United We Stand', belonged to the local Thomas Ashe Cumann of Sinn Féin. Harrison was about six at the time. He was later to become a close friend and ally of the republican Paddy McLogan who had been on hunger strike with Ashe and who remembered Ashe being wheeled down a corridor, in agony, at Mountjoy Prison in Dublin.

Harrison remembered the Troubles of the 1920s, and recalled the members of paramilitary police force the 'Black and Tans', who were despised by many nationalists, coming into his mother's shop and taking eggs away in their caps. During this period the Black and Tans were active in the Kilkelly area because the IRA had burned down the local barracks of the Royal Irish Constabulary (RIC). The house of local IRA leader Martin Casey was burned by the Black and Tans. According to Harrison, the Tans also abused Casey's mother, who died a short time later. 'Martin never forgave them for that,' Harrison said. Casey took the republican side in the Civil War, and it was he who brought the youthful Harrison into the movement in the latter part of the 1920s. Casey was the officer commanding the local company of the East Mayo Battalion of the IRA. Harrison was only thirteen or fourteen when he became a courier for the IRA, carrying messages between Casey and the latter's superior officer Pat Finn, who lived a few miles away near Charlestown. 'Going to see Finn was like going to see God,' Harrison said.

Harrison was given training in arms as part of his youthful apprenticeship as an IRA man. He and other volunteers would engage in target practice in a field on a Sunday afternoon, taking turns with a solitary Lee Enfield rifle. Harrison said he was considered quite a good shot. Then, one day in the 1930s, a man who was to make a lasting impression on Harrison arrived in Shammer on a bicycle. Bob Bradshaw came from the Lower Falls area of Belfast and had joined the IRA at an early age. In February 1932, aged twenty, he fled south to the Republic after a Belfast gun battle with police in which he shot dead an RUC man, County Tipperary-born Constable John Ryan. The incident happened after Bradshaw had, under IRA orders, opened fire on lorries breaking a strike. In 1934 the IRA appointed Bradshaw as training officer for units in the west of Ireland.

Harrison recalled: 'Bob Bradshaw was as good a man with small arms as I ever met, and I met quite a few. He was as good an instructor as I ever came across. He could take the Thompson sub-machine gun apart blindfolded. I benefited in particular from his instruction as he was staying in my family home in Shammer. We used to train in a disused farmhouse.' Bradshaw had left-wing views, and Harrison was to take the leftist path as well. 'At the time, the Soviet Union was growing, and Bob said to me: "It's a new way of life. We'll see if it lasts."' When the training sessions were over, Bradshaw mounted his bicycle and departed. The two men never met again.

The authorities in the Republic interned Bradshaw in the 1940s at the Curragh and when he was released he left the IRA, joining the Irish Labour party instead. He was later to leave the party and abandon political activity altogether, becoming a building contractor in Dublin.

I met Bradshaw about 1972, long after he had abandoned republican activity. I recall being introduced to him in McDaid's, a renowned Dublin literary pub which had over the years counted among its clientele such major Irishmen of letters as Patrick Kavanagh and Brendan Behan. Bob

Bradshaw, who had been a close friend of Behan's, was a colourful character, a dashing figure with a flowing mane of white hair, extremely argumentative and very pugnacious in debate. He was interested in literature and the arts, and knew many figures in that world.

Bradshaw was one of the influences that confirmed Harrison in what might be described as the republican faith. In such manner is the Irish republican 'creed' with its associated cult of violence handed on from generation to generation. It is intriguing to think that the 'faith' which Bradshaw helped to impart after cycling one day into Harrison's home village of Shammer in the far-off 1930s continued to live on in Harrison long after the 'missionary' himself had moved away from it. Harrison never deviated one iota from that old-style republican faith – he had little time for electoral politics in the Irish context, seeing physical force as the means to drive the 'Brits' out of the Six Counties. When I first talked to Harrison on the phone in 1990, I mentioned that I had known Bob Bradshaw. He immediately inquired about his old arms instructor, saying: 'He was a very able man, a very efficient man. I had a great admiration for him.'

Another notable republican who influenced Harrison was Sean Russell, chief of staff of the IRA in the 1930s, who oversaw a bombing campaign in England in that period that claimed a number of civilian lives. There was a flirtation between the German Nazis and the IRA during the Second World War, and Russell spent some time in Germany during the early part of that conflict.[2] In August 1940 a German submarine was bringing Russell and Frank Ryan, an Irish republican who had fought against Franco in the Spanish Civil War, to Ireland, with the intention of landing them secretly on the west coast. Russell became ill on board the U-Boat and died in Ryan's arms. He was buried at sea.[3]

Harrison was an admirer of Russell: 'I had great time for him. The first time I heard him speak was at a Manchester Martyrs memorial ceremony in Ballaghadereen in 1931. He was speaking before a hostile crowd, and he impressed me so much.' Harrison recalled Russell attending an IRA battalion convention in East Mayo in the 1930s. Harrison was standing guard at the hall where the event was being held. About midnight, some of the girls and wives came in with pots of tea and sandwiches. Russell made sure that it was not just the delegates that were fed – Harrison and his friends were looked after as well.

Harrison went to England in the mid-1930s and worked on farms in Yorkshire and Lincolnshire. He returned briefly to Ireland before emigrating with his family to America in 1938. They had very little land in County Mayo and there seemed little future for them in Ireland. 'Martin Casey backed me up. He said I could do as much [for the cause] in America as in Ireland.' He would never return to Ireland. Harrison worked at a variety of jobs in New York City, and served in the US military in the Pacific towards the end of the Second World War. He was in the Army from April 1944 to February 1946, and became a corporal in an artillery unit.

In 1947 he became a Brinks security guard, a job he would hold for thirty-six years. He was involved in left-wing activity, but also remained a committed republican, which led him to supply arms for the IRA's 1956–62 Border Campaign, also known as the Fifties Campaign.

Harrison, along with another ex-IRA man, County Kerry-born Liam Cotter, became involved in gunrunning for the campaign after being contacted by Paddy McLogan, a leading member of the movement in Dublin, who was later to become president of the IRA's political wing, Sinn Féin. Harrison had met Cotter through the James Connolly Club and the two became firm friends. Like Harrison, Cotter worked as a security guard. He had been been active in the IRA back in Ireland in the 1930s, and was interned at the Curragh in the 1940s. He was a friend of George Plant, who was executed at Portlaoise Prison in March 1942 for the murder of an IRA man accused of being an informer. Cotter emigrated to America in 1949 but retained his republican sympathies.

Harrison obtained much of his arms supplies through George DeMeo, a friendly Brooklyn neighbour of Corsican background who ran a gun shop. The guns, which included M-1 rifles and Thompson sub-machine guns, were mostly smuggled through the Brooklyn docks and onto ships bound for Europe. The arms helped the IRA to conduct its intermittent Border Campaign which petered out after a few years.

Harrison recalled: 'It wasn't easy getting the stuff to Ireland; you had to depend on people going over.' He had a contact on the docks, an Irish-American longshoreman, the late Pat Malone, who would help out. Harrison would give him a few dollars. 'Pat would get stuff aboard a ship; he was an ace in the hole. I met him at the docks once, and had a couple of trunks going onto a ship. A customs man walked by and Pat must have looked worried. The customs man said to him: 'Jesus Christ, Pat, don't worry.' At the time, the customs thought it might be sweepstake tickets in the trunks. They would let the stuff go through.'

Harrison told how the hell-raising writer and former IRA man Brendan Behan, whom he met in New York around 1960, agreed to assist in smuggling some arms to Ireland. The consignment consisted of a few Thompson sub-machine guns and some handguns, as well as ammunition, hidden in two trunks. The hard-drinking Behan provided Harrison with an address to which the trunks should be sent, but the address turned out to be fictitious. Eventually, after much confusion, the IRA in Dublin learned of the existence of the trunks and had them picked up.

Cathal Goulding, a member of the IRA's Army Council and quartermaster general at the time, was personally involved in sorting out the mess. Goulding's people in Dublin were angry about the mix-up. Said Harrison: 'They came down on me. I told Brendan that they chewed me out good. Brendan said: "F*** Goulding, don't worry about Goulding, I will take care of him. I got them 3,000 miles for them, if they can't get them the rest of the way, f*** them."' Harrison recalled that, of course, Behan was very close to Goulding. 'They grew up together.' He also recalled with some amusement how Behan pronounced 'Goulding' – it came out as 'Gowlding'.

Procuring weapons in the US was not too difficult. Harrison said: 'It was not hard to get the Thompson [sub-machine gun] in the US. The old Thompson had a drum magazine which would jam, so we had to get a straight magazine. We also got a few German Schmeissers captured during World War Two – these were very good weapons. You could buy them in gun shops.'

Two Schmeisser sub-machine guns that may well have been supplied by Harrison were seized by Garda officers in County Wicklow in 1983, when they intercepted members of an IRA gang who were about to kidnap wealthy Canadian businessman Galen Weston. Among the other weapons recovered at this time was a Gustav sub-machine gun, a type of firearm that had been procured for the Irish defence forces in times past, but was not commonly associated with the IRA.

Veteran County Tyrone-born republican Eoin McNamee, who was based in Chicago but made trips to Ireland, was Harrison's contact man in the IRA. McNamee, who had been involved in the IRA's bombing campaign in England in the late 1930s, would relay details of the IRA's arms requirements, and also supply money from IRA coffers for the purchase of arms. 'Eoin was more or less a Trotskyist,' Harrison said. 'Myself and Liam Cotter would have been more with the Soviet Union, we would have been more Stalinist at that time.'

One of the senior IRA figures with whom he had contact during the 1950s was Tomás Mac Curtain, who was prominent in the movement in the run-in to the Border Campaign but who was interned during the campaign itself. Mac Curtain, who was a son of the Lord Mayor of Cork shot dead by State forces in front of his family during the War of Independence, clearly made a deep impression on Harrison. Mac Curtain was in Portlaoise Prison at the time of the execution by firing squad of the republican George Plant. 'Mac Curtain told me they knew there was an execution because they heard the volley ...' According to Harrison, Mac Curtain was very interested in the 'hardware' that was being supplied, and was involved in the arms pipeline to Ireland during this period. 'He would be my role model as a revolutionary,' said Harrison, who expressed the belief that, if circumstances had been a little different, Mac Curtain might have become the Fidel Castro of the movement. Coming from Harrison, this was praise indeed, as he was an enthusiastic admirer of Castro and of his regime. 'I think Mac Curtain thought the Fifties Campaign was going on too long. He said you had to have the element of surprise, and when you call a cease-fire, you don't give up the guns, you hide them.'

After the end of the Border Campaign, there was friction in republican ranks. The Harrison–Cotter group cut their links with the movement because of fears that it was going 'political'. Harrison also considered that his great ally, Paddy McLogan, who had become president of Sinn Féin, was being blamed wrongly for the failure of the campaign. The dispute was a forerunner of the schism in 1969–70 which saw the IRA split into the physical force Provisionals, and the more political, Marxist-leaning Officials. The dispute led to McLogan resigning from Sinn Féin.

McLogan was to die in mysterious circumstances in Dublin in 1964, found dead at his home with a gunshot wound to the head and a German-made P38 pistol in his hand. The weapon was believed to be one of a batch of pistols left over from the Border Campaign and sent to Ireland by

Harrison for safekeeping by McLogan. While the death had the hallmarks of suicide, Harrison remained convinced to the end of his days that his friend was murdered by the 'revisionists' within the movement – the people who were later to follow the Goulding line, and move away from the 'armed struggle'. Harrison claimed that one of the 'revisionists' privately admitted that McLogan had been murdered. 'An old friend of mine challenged one of them and he said: "Yeah, we got him, and we will get everybody else as well."' However, there would have been no question of Harrison or his friends calling in the Irish police. 'The oldtimers said: "We have to be careful, or the State will come into it," and you could not have that happening,' said Harrison. 'McLogan would not want that, he would not want the State getting involved.'

The gunrunning network is revived

When civil strife flared in Northern Ireland in the late 1960s, leading to a revival of the IRA's paramilitary campaign against the security forces in the North, and against those deemed to be 'collaborating' with them, Harrison returned to his gunrunning activities. He was approached in early 1969 by his friend of long standing, Eoin McNamee, who had been visiting Derry, one of the main centres of civil strife. McNamee's message was simple – the movement needed weapons. 'Whatever the hell you have, let's have it.' Harrison still had about seventy weapons stashed away that had been collected in the late 1950s or early 1960s for the abortive Border Campaign, and these were quickly dispatched to Ireland, with sympathisers smuggling them over in small quantities. It is believed they reached Ireland in mid-1969, along with about 60,000 rounds of ammunition. There were about sixty M-1 rifles, including twenty carbines with folding stocks, as well as some handguns and some M3 sub-machine guns of Second World War/Korean War vintage known as 'grease guns'. 'I don't think I ever came across one of those carbines with folding stocks again, but they were top shelf,' said Harrison.

This first shipment of arms went to the pre-split IRA, and Harrison believed that a small proportion ended up in the hands of the faction that would go with the Officials when the split occurred in December 1969. 'It would be wrong for me to say that none of it went to the Officials because I know that some of it did.' In 1972 a Dublin-based magazine, *This Week*, published photographs of members of the Official IRA (OIRA) training in a remote mountain area in the Border region with M-1 rifles. When I mentioned this to Harrison, he said it was possible that these came from the batch that he sent over in 1969.

Despite his left-wing views, when the split in the IRA came, Harrison threw his weight behind the physical-force Provos rather than the Marxist-leaning Officials. The ideology of the 'armed struggle' was deeply ingrained in Harrison and there was no doubt as to which faction he would support – he would back the group with the best prospects of killing soldiers and policemen. Although the Official IRA was also involved in acts of violence, it tended to move away from the simplistic physical force tradition, a tendency that resulted in the OIRA cease-fire called in 1972.

Harrison hinted that he might have supplied the Officials with arms if they had continued with the 'armed struggle'. He remarked: 'We kept an open faith with the Officials until 1972, and then they pulled out of the struggle. I had nothing to do with them after that … After 1972, the Officials did not need any more guns.' He added: 'I didn't consider them leftists. In my view, they were opportunists.'

Eoin McNamee took steps to ensure that the Harrison supply line was revived, and he liaised with the IRA leadership in Ireland to arrange for the proper co-ordination links to be set up. McNamee informed Dáithí Ó Conaill, one of the leaders of the emerging Provisional IRA, that Harrison and Tom Falvey, another trusted republican, would be willing to start supplying guns again on a regular basis. Falvey had been active with Harrison in the network that supplied arms to the IRA for the Border Campaign. As a result of McNamee's intervention, Harrison was contacted by Ó Conaill, who travelled over to New York in early 1970 for a meeting with the Mayoman. Ó Conaill was a member of the IRA Army Council, with special responsibility for arms procurement. Harrison and Falvey had a lengthy meeting with Ó Conaill at the Horn and Hardart automat near Columbus Circle on Manhattan's West Side. They agreed to revive the gunrunning network, using trusted helpers from the Border Campaign era like Liam Cotter.

'Some of the oldtimers I was involved with, I told them to turn over whatever they had to the new campaign,' said Harrison. Harrison managed to get some firearms to Ireland in 1970 – about forty, mainly handguns.

The following year, Harrison and Cotter acquired their first Armalites for transfer to the IRA, weapons that were to greatly push up the body-count. Later in 1971, the Harrison network began to acquire M-16s. According to one account, the IRA in Belfast decided in late 1971 to send a senior member, Brendan 'The Dark' Hughes, to New York to ensure the delivery of Armalites rather than the Second World War-vintage weapons such as the M-1 rifle that had previously been sent over.[4] Hughes told in an interview how, after reading a brochure about the injury-inflicting capabilities of the Armalite, as well as its lightness and reliability, he was very impressed and decided the IRA would have to have it. 'The brochure said that if a person was shot in the arm, it would break every bone in his body.'[5]

It is believed that some bolt-action Mauser rifles of First World War vintage were also smuggled to Ireland for sniping purposes. It is reckoned that from about 1973, the Harrison network supplied 200 to 300 firearms a year to the IRA until it all began to go wrong in 1979, when a major shipment was seized in Dublin. McNamee continued to act as a contact man between the Harrison network and the IRA leadership. McNamee was to die in August 1986. His ashes were brought back to Broughdearg, his native place in County Tyrone.

Ó Conaill also met the elderly County Tipperary-born republican Mike Flannery in early 1970 to discuss the founding of Irish Northern Aid, or Noraid, an organisation that would help the families of republican prisoners. Flannery, who was in the IRA during the Troubles of the early 1920s, would become one of the figureheads of Noraid. Meanwhile Sean Keenan, the Derry republican who had accompanied John Kelly on the abortive arms acquisition trip to New York in December 1969, made return trips to America, visiting cities such as Boston and Philadelphia. Keenan and Joe Cahill, both important figures in the emerging Provisional IRA, became trustees of the fledgling Noraid organisation.

Keenan, who became head of the IRA in Derry, is also believed to have been involved in the setting up of secret committees to send money and arms to the IRA. Arms procurement groups were set up in cities such as Philadelphia and Baltimore, which were separate from the Harrison network. Some of the activists who were subsequently arrested for gunrunning were also active in Noraid.

The arms were generally bought over the counter in gun shops. An informed source, a New York-based republican familiar with arms procurement activities during this era, told me that in order to increase the numbers of guns purchased, sympathisers would 'lend' their driver's licences as identification to those doing the buying.

As the IRA campaign got under way, some of the acts of violence perpetrated by republicans were condemned as particularly savage and callous. Civilians were being killed or 'disappeared' on very flimsy grounds. There was also a sectarian element in some killings. A number of Protestants found in Catholic areas of Belfast at night were abducted and murdered.

One of the most horrifying incidents concerned the abduction and murder of widowed mother-of-ten Jean McConville in Belfast in 1972. She was a Protestant who had married a Catholic, and was living in a Catholic area. A large group of republicans abducted her on suspicion, never substantiated and almost certainly groundless, that she was an informer. She was never seen alive again. Her children ended up in care and her secret grave near a beach remained hidden for almost thirty years. An autopsy showed she had been shot in the head.

Even Harrison, with his wholehearted support for the 'armed struggle', seemed taken aback by certain killings of civilians and by the sectarian nature of some IRA actions, and feared they might affect support in the US for the republican movement. According to one account, he raised queries with McNamee about the murder by the IRA of a number of Belfast Catholics who were alleged to be criminals.[6] McNamee made inquiries and assured Harrison that the killings had been 'spontaneous' and had not been sanctioned by the IRA command.

Harrison also queried the massacre of ten Protestant workers who were taken from a bus on their way home from work in January 1976 by gunmen and mown down with sub-machine guns and Armalite rifles – possibly rifles that were supplied by Harrison's own network. The only Catholic on the bus was spared. The massacre, at Kingsmill, South Armagh, was in response to a murder campaign by loyalist gunmen – the UVF had murdered five Catholics the night before, including two brothers, members of the Reavey family. (A third brother, who was wounded, later died.) While the IRA did not claim responsibility for the Kingsmill massacre, it was widely assumed that the organisation was responsible – an assumption shared by Harrison. Harrison and Cotter told McNamee that the massacre would hurt their fund-raising and their position in the US.[7]

Nevertheless, Harrison was not deterred from continuing to supply weapons that must have been responsible for considerable carnage in Ireland. His aim was to provide the means to escalate the death rate among British soldiers, so as to force the British to withdraw from the North, just as he believed the Americans were forced to pull out of Vietnam by a rising death toll among US soldiers. Between 1970 and 1974, 285 members of the British Army and the Northern Ireland police force, the Royal Ulster Constabulary (RUC), were killed, mainly by the IRA. One can only guess at how many of those killings were carried out with weapons supplied by the Harrison network.

The first British soldier to be shot dead by the IRA during the Troubles was twenty-year-old Gunner Robert Curtis, killed in the Ardoyne area of Belfast on 6 February 1971. As the death toll mounted during the 1970s, the British reportedly sent members of the elite special operations force, the Special Air Service (SAS), to find the sources of loyalist and IRA gunrunning. It is unclear what success, if any, they had. At one stage, SAS troopers raided a fishing boat in County Down in search of arms, but nothing was found.[8]

While Harrison preferred the IRA to concentrate on killing soldiers and policemen, he did express full support for the assassination of the elderly Lord Mountbatten, a cousin of Queen Elizabeth II, blown up on his boat while on holiday in Ireland in 1979. In an interview in 2000[9] Harrison declared: 'Well, he [Mountbatten] was an imperialist of the purest type. He knew there was a war between Ireland and England. He shouldn't have been vacationing in enemy waters.' It is unclear from the interview whether Harrison also condoned the murders of the three others who were blown up when the watching IRA men on shore detonated the bomb after seeing the party set off in their boat. These were Lady Brabourne, an eighty-three-year-old grandmother, and two schoolboys, Mountbatten's grandson Nicholas Knatchbull (fourteen), and Paul Maxwell (fifteen), who was helping out on the boat.

As Harrison revived his network, once again George DeMeo, the Yonkers gun shop owner, was to play a vital role in supplying arms. Harrison recalled that there was an indirect connection between DeMeo and

Dáithí Ó Conaill going back to the Fifties Campaign. Harrison said: 'In the 1956 campaign, Liam Cotter had a bazooka and George DeMeo taught Liam how to use it, and Liam in turn taught Dáithí Ó Conaill.' While other individuals and groups in America also became involved in gunrunning operations, Harrison's network remained the most effective and security-conscious during the 1970s.

Harrison reckoned that the Provos could do with more sophisticated hardware – hence the concentration on procuring Armalite and M-16 rifles. Some time previously, through his job as a security guard, he had had a chance to examine an M-16 rifle, the standard assault rifle of the US Army. His close encounter with the M-16 occurred while he was helping to load a gold consignment from Fort Knox onto an aircraft at the airport in New Jersey. He became friendly with a US Army sergeant during the operation, and the sergeant showed him his M-16 and told him all about it. For Harrison, it was part of the process of keeping up to date with 'hardware' that might be of interest to the IRA. 'Oh my God,' he said to himself as he examined the M-16, 'we are going to be hearing more about this.'

George DeMeo came up with a regular supply of Armalites and M-16s for Harrison, some of the M-16s having been stolen from the US Army. Such weapons were to transform the campaign of the Provisionals, giving them effective firepower, and helping to escalate the death rate among 'enemy personnel'.

DeMeo was taking a risk getting involved again in Harrison's gunrunning activities, as he had already come to the attention of the authorities. In 1965 he was arrested along with two others on suspicion of having amassed an illegal arms shipment in Brooklyn for shipment to Cuban anti-Castro rebels. The outcome of this case is unclear. In 1969 he was arrested again, this time in connection with a suspected plot to smuggle arms to rebels trying to overthrow the Duvalier regime in Haiti. Also arrested was an arms dealer from Fayetteville, North Carolina, on whose farm DeMeo had stored five tons of weapons. This man had once served as a US Army intelligence officer. A lawyer for the North Carolina arms dealer said the arms were, in fact, destined for Chad. Charges against the men were dropped amid suggestions that the CIA was behind the arms deal. The alleged CIA connection was to have an important bearing years later when Harrison and some of his friends were to end up in court on arms charges.

How the arms were smuggled

Harrison's main role was to procure weapons – it was the responsibility of others to get the guns to Ireland. 'We got a regular [supply] line going, through contacts in the shipping world,' he said. It is known that during the early 1970s guns were smuggled to the UK port of Southampton aboard the Queen Elizabeth II (QE2) liner. The arms would be picked up in the port and taken by car to Northern Ireland – sometimes hidden in the door panels. In November 1975 police, military and customs personnel carried out a major search of the QE2 at Southampton, even to the extent of tearing panelling from cabin walls. Also searched was a car ferry operating between Southampton and San Sebastian in Spain. There were no reports of any explosives or illegal arms being found.

In the latter part of the 1970s, a more common way was to conceal the arms in cargo containers being shipped across the Atlantic. This method meant that greater numbers of weapons could be smuggled in one operation. Harrison said that individuals also took over small amounts of weaponry. Some women helped out. Hardly anybody said 'no'. 'A few priests took them over in their baggage. Usually customs do not bother a reverend father.'

Arms were also hidden in the infrastructure of aircraft, and transported as aircraft cargo. Two separate shipments of guns were found at Kennedy Airport, in the holds of jumbo jets bound for Ireland, in the 1979–81 period. Firearms were also sent by post, or smuggled over in coffins, hidden with the bodies of exiles being returned home for burial in the old country.[10] Specially designed cargo containers with false panels were also used to get guns to Ireland.

One of the first smuggling operations to be uncovered came to light in October 1971, and it involved the QE2. The liner made a stopover at Cobh, County Cork, dropping anchor to allow a party of New York teachers to disembark. The ship was en route from New York to Le Havre and Southampton. Six large suitcases were left unclaimed in the customs shed. When examined they were found to be crammed with weapons. There were seven rifles, including three Armalites, thirty-seven hand grenades and 6,458 rounds of ammunition.[11]

The suitcases were in the name of a person called Walsh, whose first-class cabin had remained unoccupied on the voyage from New York.

Inquiries were carried out, and Walsh turned out to be a venerable lady of eighty-three years, called Mrs Catherine Walsh, who lived in Greenwich, New York, and who was on holiday in County Cork. The gray-haired grandmother assured police: 'I am no gunrunner.' Mrs Walsh was eliminated from inquiries, the authorities accepting that she had nothing to do with the guns. As a result of the investigation into gunrunning aboard the QE2, two members of the crew were arrested in the UK and went on trial at Winchester Crown Court in April 1972 charged with illegal possession of firearms. They were acquitted.

In the US, the trail led to a licensed gun dealer based in Yonkers, New York State. It was alleged he had supplied some of the weapons that had been discovered in the suitcases. He was indicted for violating firearms laws, and jailed for a year. An Irish-born New York City bus driver was indicted for alleged involvement in the QE2 smuggling operation. He was acquitted of conspiracy charges, but found guilty of using false identification in regard to four different purchases of weapons in New York, and in 1973 was given a suspended sentence. The man, from County Roscommon, was reported to be a member of Noraid, the group set up to raise funds for the dependants of republican prisoners.

The authorities in the US believed that money raised by Noraid was also going towards the purchase of arms for the IRA – this was always denied by Noraid. Nevertheless the fact that a number of Noraid activists were to be indicted, or came under suspicion in regard to the procurement of arms for the IRA, bolstered suspicions as to how some of the money was being used. As the death toll in the Troubles mounted, there was an increasing focus by the authorities on the funds raised by Noraid. In the mid-1970s Irish foreign affairs minister Garret FitzGerald claimed that every dollar contributed to Noraid 'contributed to the deaths of Irish people'.

Harrison said that as well as himself, there were other people in North America procuring and smuggling arms to the IRA, some of whom were never detected. There was activity in Canada, for instance, that was entirely separate from him. 'There were some good men there,' he said. On one occasion he received a number of deactivated Sten guns through a contact in Canada. He had to get one part to make each weapon operational again. DeMeo came up with the parts. 'The Sten guns went to Ireland,' said Harrison.

Not all of the activists seeking to procure arms for the IRA in North America were of Irish background. One rather eccentric individual, Larry Gladstone, decided he wanted to help the cause of Irish freedom by personally procuring arms for the IRA, even though he had no discernible Irish connections. This was in the late 1960s, quite early on in the Troubles. Gladstone, who resided in Norwich, New York State, travelled to the southern state of Georgia and made contact with some locals in an attempt to buy guns. The authorities were quickly tipped off. Gladstone, who was apparently using his own money to buy the guns, was arrested, went on trial and was jailed. He was in the news subsequently in 1983 when he and his wife Christine were arrested after a bizarre hostage-taking incident at the Chenango County Office Building in New York state. The couple took about twenty people hostage in an eight-hour siege, during which they assured the hostages that nobody would be harmed. They demanded the return of their dogs – forty-three had been seized in 1981 following a complaint.[12] Nobody was, in fact, harmed and the couple surrendered to the authorities.

The Fort Worth Five go to jail

As the US authorities sought to move against those suspected of running guns to the IRA, five Irish-born men from the east coast region were summoned before a grand jury in Forth Worth, Texas, in 1972. They faced questions about an alleged plot to import arms from Mexico to Ireland, via New York. There is no reason to believe the five were involved in any such plot, or had any knowledge whatsoever of it. They were all respectable, hard-working citizens, and were jailed for contempt after refusing to cooperate with the inquiry. Their plight aroused much controversy in political circles. The men were finally freed in August 1973.

The men, who became known as the Fort Worth Five, were Ken Tierney, who had been born in Glasnevin, Dublin, the son of one of the first members of the Irish police force, the Garda Síochána, and lived in Tuam, County Galway, before emigrating to the US; Mattie Reilly, a native of County Fermanagh; Paschal Morahan, from County Roscommon; Tom Laffey, a native of County Galway; and Danny Crawford, from Belfast. They were represented with much skill and tenacity by Mayo-born lawyer Frank Durkan.

Ken Tierney told me in an interview in New York in September 2004 that he knew absolutely nothing about any plot to run guns from Mexico to Ireland. In fact he did not even know most of the other men who were summoned before the Grand Jury in Texas – he knew Danny Crawford slightly, but not the others. 'Yet we would be accused of being part of a conspiracy to smuggle guns to Northern Ireland.'

Tierney believed he himself had been singled out because he took part in a weekly radio programme, and had spoken out about events in Northern Ireland. He believed that he and the other four had been summoned before the jury so they would give information about others – in other words, to become informers. He saw the decision to hold the hearings in Fort Worth, more than a thousand miles from their homes, as part of an attempt to rail-road them. On legal advice, he pleaded the Fifth Amendment all the way through. At one stage an exasperated lawyer asked him: 'Mr Tierney, what time does that clock on the wall say?' There was laughter as the witness replied after a pause: 'I'd like to talk to my lawyer about that, too.'

Senator Ted Kennedy and other leading politicians took up the men's cases. They were eventually released by order of the liberal Supreme Court justice William O Douglas, on the grounds that the US government had illegally eavesdropped on a telephone conversation between Frank Durkan and a witness who had been served with a subpoena to appear before the inquiry.

Frank Durkan believes that the Fort Worth Five case had far-reaching effects. It got US politicians involved in issues to do with Northern Ireland, and he believes that from this case one can trace the chain of events that led to the later involvement in Irish issues of President Clinton, the decision to give Sinn Féin President Gerry Adams a US visa, and ultimately the Good Friday Agreement. 'Politicians got involved and became cognisant of what the issues were.'

One of the Fort Worth Five, Mattie Reilly, prior to being summoned before the grand jury, had filed his application to become a US citizen, and received notice to report for his induction as a citizen while he was being held for contempt in jail in Texas. When the government got wind of the fact that he was in prison, his admission to citizenship was revoked. This sparked a legal challenge by Frank Durkan's uncle, the formidable civil rights lawyer Paul O'Dwyer. He argued that Reilly should not be denied citizenship as a result of exercising his constitutional right not to co-operate with the grand jury. O'Dwyer brought a court action to compel the government to admit Reilly to citizenship, which it duly did. It was a notable legal victory for the veteran campaigning lawyer.

The authorities clamp down

The authorities in Ireland seized illegal arms on a regular basis, which made it necessary for George Harrison and other gunrunners to send a steady supply of arms across the Atlantic, partly to replace those weapons that had been captured. While smugglers usually filed off the serial numbers of weapons to stop them being traced back to their origins, some weapons were found in Ireland with serial numbers still intact or not sufficiently erased. As a result, by the mid-1970s, the authorities in the US had identified at least nine licensed gun dealers from whom weapons had been bought which had then been sent to Ireland. During the decade there was a steady stream of court cases involving attempts or alleged attempts to smuggle arms from north America to the IRA.

The US Justice Department saw Philadelphia as an important source of weaponry for the IRA in the earlier part of the 1970s. Among those who came under scrutiny were a number of men of Irish background living in Philadelphia. One of those was Daniel Cahalane, a middle-aged building contractor and member of Noraid. In 1973 he was subpoenaed to appear before a grand jury in Philadelphia to answer questions. In June 1976 he was convicted of conspiracy to illegally export arms, as was fellow Noraid member Neil Byrne. It was alleged in court that between 1970 and 1973, in one year they bought 366 firearms, at a cost of more than $30,000, and 100,000 rounds of ammunition. The weapons were said to consist of Armalite, Lee-Enfield and Springfield rifles as well as M-1 carbines. Also procured was armour-piercing ammunition, according to court records. It was stated that about fifty percent of the weapons were seized by the authorities in Northern Ireland.

In 1977 the two men lost an appeal. Judge Weis, of the US Appeal Court, said in his written judgement that Byrne negotiated with a government informant for the purchase of rifles, machine guns, armour piercing ammunition, rocket launchers and mortars. Byrne told the informant that the arms would be shipped directly to Ireland from New York. The informant quoted another Noraid member as saying that the arms were sent to Ireland 'crated as plumbing stuff'. Judge Weis said a Noraid member told a government witness that a member of the organisation once disguised himself as a priest to get two trunks past customs and aboard a ship bound for Ireland.

Among others indicted by the grand jury in this case was Vincent Conlon, who was active in the 1950s campaign, and who had returned to Ireland in the earlier part of the 1970s. He had won fame in republican circles as the driver of the truck which transported the IRA team that attacked Brookeborough RUC barracks in January 1957. Despite being wounded, he managed to drive the gunfire-damaged truck away from the scene with the IRA party on board. Two of the raiders, Sean South and Fergal O'Hanlon, died from gunshot wounds. Dáithí Ó Conaill also took part in this raid.

Conlon had lived in the US before the 1950s campaign, and he returned to America after two escapes from the Curragh camp where he was interned. The lawyer Paul O'Dwyer mounted a successful legal case in the US courts to prevent him being deported back to Ireland. Conlon, a native of Benburb, north of Armagh city, died in Monaghan in 1995, aged sixty-six. Sean Keenan, who visited Irish republicans in Philadelphia, and stayed with Vincent Conlon, is believed to have played a key role in setting up the arms pipeline from the city.

In September 1974, a forty-one-year-old Irish-born New York City bus driver was arrested at his Pearl River home by agents of the Bureau of Alcohol, Tobacco and Firearms (BATF). He was charged in an indictment, returned by a federal grand jury, with inducing a gun dealer to sell him firearms without maintaining the proper records that were required by law. It was alleged that the Irishman had purchased fifty-six firearms from a dealer in Manhattan. The weapons consisted of eleven M-1 carbines, nineteen Lee Enfield .303 rifles, four AR-180 Armalite rifles and twenty-two FN semi-automatic rifles. The arms were alleged to have been purchased between 1 December 1971 and 1 June 1972. The licensed gun dealer was indicted for selling weapons without properly recording information about those purchasing the weapons. He was subsequently convicted and put on probation. Frank Durkan, who represented the Irish bus driver at his trial, recalled the case well. The jury's sympathies were with the defendant rather than the prosecutor, and the judge was liberal. The man was convicted on one count of conspiracy and walked free from the court with a suspended sentence.

There were US gunrunning investigations in other regions beyond the east coast as well. One investigation centred on San Francisco and Butte, Montana, where many people of Irish descent worked in the copper mines. It was launched after a trunk broke open in the Aer Lingus freight shed at Heathrow Airport, London, on 1 June 1972. Packed inside were two rifles, three pistols and 350 rounds of ammunition. The battered sea chest, accompanied by two suitcases, had begun its journey in San Francisco, from where it was flown on an American Airlines flight to New York, and from there on an El Al flight to London.

The trunk was repacked and flown on to Shannon Airport. It was consigned to an address in Lettermore, in the Irish-speaking Connemara area of County Galway. Surveillance was kept on the trunk at Shannon, but nobody came to pick it up. However, one of the rifles, a .44 Luger carbine, was traced to a forty-seven-year-old San Francisco resident called Charles 'Chuck' Malone. The father of seven, who worked as a pest exterminator, had bought the rifle on 23 May. Malone had been a visitor to Butte, Montana, and an investigation was launched into a suspected conspiracy by law enforcement officials and others to aid in illegal shipments of arms to the IRA. One individual was jailed for refusing to talk to the San Franscisco Grand Jury. In January 1973 Malone, dubbed the Golden Gate Gunrunner by the media, pleaded guilty to illegally exporting rifles and ammunition to the IRA. He was given a one-year suspended sentence and put on two years' probation. In the 1980s he was to figure in another gunrunning case (*see* Chapter 8).

Canada also figured in investigations into republican gunrunning. This was underlined in July 1973 when Gardaí seized a cache of arms which had been smuggled into Dublin port aboard a British freighter that had sailed from Montreal, Canada. The consignment consisted of eight cases containing seventeen rifles, 29,000 rounds of ammunition and about sixty pounds of gunpowder. One rifle was an Armalite – others included Winchesters and Springfields. The cargo had been hidden in a container marked 'machinery' and had been shipped by an unsuspecting freight company in Toronto, bound for what turned out to be a 'dummy' company in Dublin.

Shortly after the seizure, the Gardaí, acting on information received, arrested an Irish-born Canadian immigrant as he arrived in Dublin Airport on a flight from Canada. He was charged with illegally importing firearms destined for the IRA, and conspiring with others to import the arms. An unusual aspect of this case is that there was a report that the arms were, in fact, destined for the Official, rather than the Provisional, IRA, even though the Officials were on cease-fire at this stage.[13] As part of the investigation, police and members of the Royal Canadian Mounted Police (RCMP) raided the suspect's home in the Scarborough area of Toronto and seized five Sten sub-machine guns, eleven handguns and 10,000 rounds of ammunition. The weapons were packed into wooden crates in the attic, and seemed ready for shipping. The swoops were the culmination of a three-month investigation by Gardaí and the RCMP.

Evidence also emerged that republican activists were trying to smuggle arms across the border from Canada into the US for onward transfer to Ireland. In 1974 the authorities in Canada became aware of a group of activists trying to smuggle modern assault rifles along this pipeline. Officers found that two Toronto residents had received a shipment of rifles and packed them into boxes. Later they would find that the arms were handed over to another Toronto resident, who in turn supplied them to a Michigan resident described by police as a Noraid activist.

A three-month investigation culminated in July 1974 with the arrest by Canadian police of this man, as he tried to cross from Canada into the US with arms hidden in his car. He was stopped on the Ambassador Bridge travelling from Windsor in Canada to Detroit in the USA. He was found to have, hidden in his car, fifteen FN rifles and a .50 calibre machine gun barrel. The 7.62mm FN rifle was in use by troops of NATO. It was one of the quite advanced modern weapons that kept cropping up in the Provo arsenal until the AK-47 became the dominant assault rifle used by the organisation, following the delivery of large quantities of these weapons from Libya in the mid-1980s.

After the arrest, three other suspects were rounded up who lived in the Toronto area. They were charged and went on trial in June 1975. All four pleaded guilty to various charges and were jailed for periods ranging from seventeen months to two years.

Arrest of the Baltimore Four

Among the Irish gunrunning cases to come before the American courts in the mid-1970s was one concerning a group of citizens of Irish background who became known as the Baltimore Four. The case first hit the headlines in February 1974, when Treasury agents stopped a truck in Woodside, in the Queens borough of New York, and arrested two men. Seventy Armalite AR-15 rifles were found in their hired truck. It was reported at the time that the agents had been keeping the men under surveillance since the arms were allegedly bought at a Maryland gun shop some time previously.

One of those arrested was thirty-four-year-old James Conlon, an Irish citizen who owned a bar in Woodside. The authorities concluded that the arms were destined for the IRA. This was one of the biggest Irish-linked gunrunning cases in the US at this period. Two other men were picked up, one of them former amateur boxer and ex-seaman Harry Hillick, who worked at the time in an Irish bar in Washington DC. In later years he became well known in Manhattan as a barman in the Beaten Path bar on Warren Street. The owner of a gun shop in Baltimore was also arrested.

It was reported in the media at the time that the gunrunning group had large amounts of money, and had placed a standing order for 100 AR-15s a month with the dealer. According to Jeffrey White, United States attorney for the District of Maryland, the guns were going to be sent through New York to Ireland in crates labelled as machine parts. He quoted Hillick as saying they were going to be used to 'pot the dummies' – a reference to killing British soldiers. White claimed that the case was broken after Hillick talked about the weapons to an undercover agent with the Washington metropolitan police force who was posing as an artist in Irish bars.[14] A grand jury in Baltimore indicted the five men on charges of conspiring to smuggle 175 semi-automatic rifles and 23,000 rounds of ammunition to the IRA. All were jailed, although an appeal was to succeed on a major point. Conlon, who had been in poor health, died soon after getting out of prison.

Hillick, nicknamed Manhattan Harry, was born in north Belfast in 1943, one of a family of fourteen. In his youth he emigrated, joining the Cunard Line in Southampton, and becoming a crew member aboard the QE2 liner.

In the mid-1960s he give up the life of a seaman and settled in New York, going on to win an award, 'The Best Bartender in New York'. When the Troubles began in Northern Ireland he became involved in raising money for the republican cause and sending arms to the IRA. After being convicted on arms conspiracy charges, Hillick did his time in a succession of federal prisons – Lewisburg, Terre Haute and Danbury.

It was in Danbury that he became friendly with the tough-minded and very resilient G Gordon Liddy of Watergate fame who, it transpired, was quite a clever jailhouse lawyer. Hillick said in a newspaper interview in 1999 that Liddy gave him the legal advice that helped him defeat an attempt by the Immigration and Naturalisation Service (INS) to deport him back to Ireland.[15] According to the article, it was said that Hillick had smuggled guns back to Ireland in the cargo hold of the QE2, and that Hillick never denied it. Hillick, who contracted lung cancer, went to live in Belfast in 2000 but early in 2005 returned in a wheelchair to New York, where his health deteriorated further. He died at St John's Hospital, Queens, on 14 October that year, and his ashes were scattered at the republican plot in Milltown Cemetery, Belfast, eleven days later.[16] Like other individuals implicated in gunrunning to the IRA in the 1970s, Hillick was active in Noraid.

In May 1975 Frank Grady, founder and first chairman of the Yonkers chapter of Noraid, was indicted on arms charges following the discovery of a number of rifles in Northern Ireland. Also indicted was a licensed Yonkers gun dealer, John Jankowski. The following April, in federal District Court in Manhattan, Grady was given a two-year sentence, suspended except for four months, Judge Brieant saying that Grady had acted out of 'mistaken idealism'. Jankowski got a heavier sentence of three years, the judge having decided that he was 'motivated by greed'. Both were found guilty of conspiracy and of falsifying federal firearm control records. In addition, Grady was convicted of unlawfully exporting firearms. The court heard that Grady had bought twenty semi-automatic rifles in 1970 from Jankowski at his J & J Bait Shop in Yonkers, and that twelve of these weapons were later seized in Ireland. An appeal by the men was rejected by the US Court of Appeals in October 1976.

A close shave for Harrison

As George Harrison pressed ahead with his arms procurement activities, he sometimes bought guns directly from suppliers. He had a close shave in 1975 after making a purchase in New Hampshire. The transaction came to the attention of the Bureau of Alcohol, Tobacco and Firearms. He was apparently traced as a result of a cheque made out to a New Hampshire gun shop. Two agents visited his home in Brooklyn, at East 9th Street, to tell him he would be required to appear before a Grand Jury in New Hampshire. At that very moment, Harrison had a significant collection of arms stashed away in the back of the house – 200 rifles and 150,000 rounds of ammunition. 'I asked the agents if they would like a cup of tea and they said "yes".' Harrison served the tea, hoping against hope that the agents would not ask to look around the house. They eventually departed without detecting the arms cache. 'The whole thing was right in front of them,' said Harrison. 'I got it moved a few days later.'

When he appeared before the Grand Jury in Concord, New Hampshire, he only answered two questions, giving his name and his address when he was asked for these details. He never faced any charges arising out of his activities in New Hampshire. Oddly, the Grand Jury hearing never led to further investigations.

Harrison was not the only person to come under investigation from the authorities in New Hampshire at this period. J Herbert Quinn, a flamboyant former mayor of Concord, was the focus of an arms investigation in the mid-1970s. Quinn was no stranger to controversy. While serving as mayor, the Irish-American politician had been suspended by the Board of Aldermen in 1967 for allegedly abusing his authority, but was later reinstated. In the autumn of 1975 he was asked to explain certain arms purchases to a federal Grand Jury. It was alleged that he had bought 218 rifles and handguns at a gun dealership in Concord. Quinn claimed that he had bought the guns 'for a little hunting trip in Alaska'. It was alleged by the Justice Department that some of the arms had turned up in Northern Ireland. Quinn was offered immunity but still refused to answer questions before the Grand Jury. He made it clear to the media that he had no intention of talking. 'They think I know quite a bit,' Quinn snapped. 'But I'm not saying a word.'[17] In December 1975 Quinn was jailed for refusing to answer questions. His jailing had been postponed earlier in the month to allow him to have a hernia operation. Before entering the prison, a Federal Marshal brought him to hospital for the removal of surgical stitches.

The Harrison network suffered a major setback in April 1976 when one of the main players, Liam Cotter, was shot dead in New York in the course of his work as a Purolator security guard. Along with another security man he had gone to a cinema on Times Square to collect the takings for the week, when they were confronted by armed robbers. Cotter opened fire and was felled by a shotgun blast. His remains were taken back to his native County Kerry and buried near Tralee. Harrison was devastated. Cotter's death was not only a blow to the gunrunning network and to the cause – it meant the loss of a good friend.

Harrison and the M-60 machine guns

Harrison's arms dealer sidekick George DeMeo had a particularly good source of weaponry in North Carolina, where he had once lived. Security at the US Marine base there, Camp Lejeune, was very slack at the time, and for a period in the 1970s, arms and ammunition went missing from the base on a regular basis and could be bought on the black market. DeMeo bought weapons, including M-16 rifles, directly from serving members of the US Marines, and passed them on to the Harrison group. Quantities of ammunition were also acquired on the black market and passed on to the Harrison network. Harrison went along with DeMeo a couple of times when he was doing deals with Marines from Camp Lejeune. Harrison recalled: 'We used to meet the Marines at a gas station in New Jersey. George would make the deal with them there. There would be two or three of them on each occasion. They were not gang-sters, just guys making a couple of bucks.' Harrison said that the prices being charged gradually went up.

DeMeo had an important contact in the region, a gun store owner named Howard Barnes Bruton Jnr, who ran a firm called B & B Guns in Wilson, North Carolina. DeMeo would buy guns 'off the books' from Bruton. Over a three-year period DeMeo made regular, twice-monthly trips from New York to Wilson, on each occasion filling up the boot of his Cadillac with high-powered rifles to be ferried back to New York and handed over to the

Harrison group. On one occasion Bruton casually inquired where the guns were going. 'Some place cool and green,' said DeMeo.

For the Harrison network, DeMeo was to prove an important source of Armalites. The Armalite is a high-velocity semi-automatic hunting version of the military assault rifle, the M-16. Both the version known as the AR-15, and another version, the AR-180, were ideal for the type of offensive being mounted by the Provos in Northern Ireland. Used to fire single shots or in semi-automatic mode, the Armalite was less likely to suffer blockages or to waste ammunition. The Armalite fired a .233 calibre bullet that could penetrate British Army flak jackets, creating a tumble shock wave and extensive injuries. The Armalite could be bought freely in a number of American states as a hunting rifle.

The Armalite gave the IRA a taste of lethal, modern firepower and it became a potent symbol of Provo violence. The weapon figured in a phrase coined by senior Sinn Féin man Danny Morrison, in which he talked of 'an Armalite in one hand and a ballot box in the other ...' At one stage IRA supporters inscribed on a wall in Derry's Bogside area: 'God made the Catholics, but the Armalite made them equal.'

One of Harrison's coups was to acquire a number of M-60 heavy machine guns, which were to prove not only of military but of publicity value to the movement back in Ireland. The M-60s were among weapons stolen from the National Guard armoury at Danvers, Massachusetts, in August 1976. Also stolen in the break-in were about 100 M-16 rifles and two grenade launchers. Some time after the break-in, Harrison got word through a contact that some hardware might be available. 'This guy says: "Would you come up to Boston?" and I said: "No problem," so I went up to Boston.' Harrison took a bus to Boston, where he was picked up at the bus station and taken, so far as he could recall, to a room at a gas station. He met about six men, a mixture of Irish underworld and Italian Mafia. They had some samples of what was on offer. 'The funny thing about it was, the people up there, the underworld, did not know beans about guns,' Harrison said. He had to teach them some basic safety rules while handling firearms. He told them the first thing you do with the gun, you make sure it's empty before you start handling it. You keep it pointing at the wall. If it's pointing towards you and it goes off, 'it will go right through you, it won't bypass you.'

One of the men asked Harrison, was there no other way of dealing with the problems in Northern Ireland other than violence? According to Harrison, he replied: 'I wish to hell there was, but it's the only language they [the British] know.' Harrison was asked what would happen if he were caught by the authorities – would he talk? He told them if he talked he would talk no more. In other words, if he turned informer his own people would kill him. And if anybody betrayed him [Harrison], somebody else would go after the informant.

Harrison reckoned he bought about a half-dozen M-60s and about fifty M-16 rifles. He had to pay very little, 'almost nothing'. He made a couple of trips to Boston in connection with the transaction. 'We had a safe house in Boston and I picked up the M-60s there,' said Harrison. He also collected the M-16s. 'I had a good safe driver with me – you can put a lot in the back trunk.' The first thing he did after taking delivery was to examine, clean and oil the weapons. 'I always believed in putting plenty of oil on them to preserve them. Then they would be taken from us and they would be on their way.' It is believed that six M-60s reached Ireland in the summer of 1977, concealed in a consignment of industrial equipment that arrived by ship from Brooklyn docks, and that an additional M-60 was kept in storage and sent to Ireland in 1979. (In April 1980, fire authorities responding to a fire in a house in Walpole, Massachusetts, found part of the collection of weapons stolen from the Danvers armoury. The weapons recovered from the burning garage included forty-six M-16 rifles, seventeen assorted handguns and rifles and thousands of rounds of ammunition.)

There appears to have been considerable excitement in the upper echelons of the IRA at the prospect of getting the M-60. The weapon enjoyed a good reputation in military circles, and was in general use by the US Army. Developed in the 1950s, with a design that owes much to the German MG42 and FG42, it fires 600 7.62mm rounds per minute and, properly employed, can be used to bring down a helicopter. Using the M-60 for this purpose was of major interest to the IRA since the British Army used helicopters extensively in Northern Ireland, especially in areas where travel by road was considered too dangerous. On a heavy tripod, the M-60 can provide sustained fire – a useful feature for attacks on police stations and military outposts.

Another item from the Danvers armoury that reportedly ended up in the hands of the IRA was a pair of US Army electronic AN-PAS-5 night-sight binoculars. This was said in the 1980s to have allowed the IRA to spot infra-red beams, invisible to the naked eye, used by the British Army at night to detect movement around security installations.[18]

Disaster for DeMeo

It was an indiscreet phone call to Ireland, picked up on a phone tap, that was to mark the beginning of the end of the Harrison gunrunning network. The call was made by one of a number of activists fresh from Ireland who were seeking to bring the arms pipeline more directly under the control of the IRA leadership in Belfast. This was part of the general take-over of the movement by the Northern element, while the traditional Southern leadership, including Dáithí Ó Conaill, was being sidelined. Harrison may have been regarded by the emerging Northern leadership as too independent. Even though he was a major gunrunner, he had distanced himself from the IRA following the McLogan affair, and memories are long in the republican movement.

Although the phone call that caused all the problems did not refer specifically to arms – the reference was apparently to a frigidaire – it would have been easy for any sleuth listening in on the line to realise that an arms shipment was on its way to Ireland. The cargo arrived at the docks in Dublin in October 1979 and was under surveillance by plain-clothes detectives from the time of its arrival. The IRA obviously realised that something was wrong and nobody arrived to claim the cargo, which was listed as industrial equipment. The cargo was one of the biggest single shipments ever sent by Harrison and had been assembled with the aid of George DeMeo. It amounted to more than 150 firearms and 60,000 rounds of ammunition. The guns included fifteen M-16s, a large number of M-14s and an AK-47. There were also two M-60 machine guns. Apart from the M-60 that was part of the batch picked up in Boston, the Harrison group had apparently managed to come up with an additional M-60.

A major investigation into the IRA arms pipeline from America was launched, involving police and other agencies in Ireland, Britain and the US. The arms shipment seized in Dublin docks was traced back to a small

Brooklyn shipping company run by County Leitrim-born Bernard 'Barney' McKeon, who resided with his family in Queens. In November 1979 he was summoned to appear before a federal Grand Jury in Brooklyn and questioned about gunrunning to Ireland. He refused to answer questions and was jailed for contempt, serving five months in the Metropolitan Correctional Centre in Manhattan. In August 1982 he faced a nine-count indictment, charging him with numerous violations of the Arms Export Control Act. The prosecution dragged on for quite some time. The first two trials ended in mistrials. He was finally convicted in a third trial in the federal District Court in Brooklyn in June 1983, and the following September was sent to jail for three years. He died in 1998, shortly after attending the funeral in Bohola, County Mayo, of his friend, the lawyer Paul O'Dwyer.

Evidence given during the proceedings underlined the involvement of British intelligence in international moves against the IRA. A US Customs officer, Stephen Rogers, was sacked from the service after naming in court a British secret service agent involved in the case. Rogers also testified that the information that led to McKeon's arrest in New York came from a tap on a trans-Atlantic phone conversation. Another customs officer had earlier testified that there were no phone taps, legal or illegal, in the operation that led to McKeon's arrest. Following an appeal in May 1985, Rogers was reinstated, with back pay. The Federal Merit Systems Protection Board concluded that Rogers' naming of the British agent was 'inadvertent rather than a result of IRA sympathy'. Rogers himself stated that he had no links to the Irish republican movement, and that he knew nobody in the US Customs service who was in favour of the IRA.[19] (However, it has been claimed that there was another customs officer who did assist IRA gunrunners, as will become apparent in Chapter 8.)

Through an oversight, the IRA gunrunners had failed to remove the serial numbers from a few of the weapons seized in Dublin. This was to herald major trouble for DeMeo. There would also be far-reaching implications for the Harrison network. The trail led to Camp Lejeune, to the illegal arms activity linked to the camp, and to a gun dealership, B & B Guns. Investigators established that B & B boss Howard Bruton Jr had sold weapons to DeMeo, and that the sale had not been recorded, contrary to law. DeMeo and Bruton were charged with a range of arms offences.

During their trial a number of the recovered rifles, which had allegedly been supplied to the IRA, were shown in the courtroom. They were mostly Armalites – AR-15s and AR-180s.

During the trial, prosecutors sought to link the defendants to firearms that had turned up in Ireland and Britain from 1975 to 1979. The court heard of one AR-180 rifle that was recovered by detectives following a six-day siege in 1975 of a house in Balcombe Street, Marylebone, London, where members of an IRA gang had held a middle-aged couple hostage. Federal prosecutor Julian Greenspun said the rifle was identified by a man called William Redding as one of eighteen stolen from his house in Wilson, North Carolina, in July 1974. Greenspun said that these guns were sold to B & B Guns, most of them being sent to Ireland via New York. The four-man IRA gang, known as the Balcombe Street Four, was responsible for a series of bombings and assassinations that caused mayhem in London. The four – Martin O'Connell, Eddie Butler, Harry Duggan and Hugh Doherty – faced a range of charges at the Old Bailey in 1977, including seven murders and conspiring to cause explosions. They received multiple life sentences. The judge recommended that each should serve at least thirty years, but the four were released in 1999 under the terms of the Good Friday Agreement.

In October 1980, DeMeo and Bruton were found guilty by a jury at a court in Raleigh, North Carolina, on federal arms charges, and given heavy jail sentences by Judge Franklin Dupree Jr. The charges against DeMeo and Bruton included conspiracy to smuggle eighty to 100 guns and up to one million rounds of ammunition to the IRA; the smuggling of specific weapons; and falsifying sales records. DeMeo got ten years in prison and a $20,000 fine, while Bruton got five years and a $20,000 fine. Most of the charges against a third man were dismissed by the judge, except for a conspiracy count. He was sentenced to five years and a $5,000 fine, but became eligible immediately for parole. DeMeo could not stomach the prospect of a ten-year sentence, so in August 1980 his lawyer offered a deal to the Justice Department. In return for a lighter sentence, his client would give them the IRA's top gunrunner in America.

CHAPTER 4

The Spooks and the Arms Deal in Prague

In 1971 an American climbed up the narrow stairs to the cramped top-floor offices of Provisional Sinn Féin at Kevin Street, in Dublin city centre. He gave his name as Freeman. He had a proposition. For a comparatively modest fee, he offered to organise an arms deal that would procure the IRA some badly-needed weaponry.[1] The people manning the office were used to odd-ball individuals like would-be mercenaries calling in to offer their services. The overtures were normally rejected. Freeman must have been unusually persuasive, for the IRA leadership decided to take him up on his offer.

By now the IRA's campaign was well under way. Arms were being smuggled in from America in dribs and drabs, and there were often problems finding the correct ammunition for a range of weapons. The IRA leadership considered that in order to boost the war effort, and increase the 'body count' of British soldiers killed, they needed a substantial consignment of modern weapons and ammunition that would radically improve the IRA arsenal, and improve the efficiency of the 'killing machine'. These considerations may have persuaded them to do business with Freeman.

It has been suggested that Freeman learned of the quest for arms as a result of the arms procurement activities in the US of Dáithí Ó Conaill, a member of the IRA Army Council with special responsibility for obtaining guns for the campaign. Freeman may have had some republican sympathies, but it appears that his main aim was to make some money. He may also have been attracted by the cloak-and-dagger aspect of doing a covert international arms deal. He does not appear to have had much experience in the arms world. Information that came to light during research for this book indicates how the gaffe was blown on the operation.

Freeman went to London to make contact with arms dealers in the quest for a middle-man who could broker a deal. It was, in retrospect, an ill-judged move. British arms dealers were unlikely to want to supply arms to be used against British forces. It is not unusual for arms dealers to have police or security contacts. It emerged that one of the arms dealers contacted by Freeman tipped off the British intelligence service MI6. An MI6 operative, Donald Gurrey, began working on the case. British intelligence spooks had apparently become concerned about Irish-related gunrunning in the wake of the attempt to procure arms on the Continent in 1970, the affair that led to the Arms Trial, and were anxious to stymie any further gunrunning attempts.

Gurrey was a wily MI6 man of long experience. Born in London in 1919, he had dropped out of university to join the forces after the start of the Second World War. He served as a lowly gunnery officer in Algeria, Tunisia and Italy before finding a more intriguing outlet for his talents – as an intelligence officer. Promoted to captain and later major, he served with British Army counter-intelligence in Italy from 1943, operating against the German intelligence services.[2]

Having found his true vocation as an intelligence man, he joined MI6 after the war, and served from 1946 to 1949 in war-ravaged Germany. He was based in that hotbed of espionage activity, Berlin, from where MI6 kept a wary eye on the Soviet forces which had occupied a sector of the city and the eastern part of Germany. It was in Berlin that he got to know low-level MI6 driver and 'fixer' Tony Divall who, as we shall see, figures along with Gurrey in another IRA gunrunning drama, the *Claudia* operation (*see* Chapter 5). After Germany, Gurrey went on to serve in other regions around the world, including Communist-dominated Eastern Europe, the Far East and the Caribbean.

By 1971 the intelligence man, who was under cover of working as an official with the Foreign and Commonwealth Office, was based in London. At this period MI6 operated from a building called Century House in Lambeth. He was in his early fifties and his globe-trotting days were largely over. But he was still very much active as a 'spook'.

After getting the tip about Freeman's quest for arms, Gurrey set about organising a 'sting' operation against the IRA. Gurrey recruited an arms dealer of his acquaintance who was not British but was based in London, and could be trusted. This dealer was put in touch with Freeman and man-aged to 'infiltrate' himself into the IRA arms-buying operation, coming to an arrangement with Freeman to procure arms for the Provos in Eastern Europe. Freeman and the arms dealer travelled to the Continent to set up the weapons deal. The IRA arms procurement operation was 'blown' almost from the start.

In September 1971 an unsuspecting Dáithí Ó Conaill, aged thirty-three at the time, travelled to the Continent to liaise with Freeman and the dealer. Ó Conaill was accompanied by a twenty-three-year-old middle-class Dublin university graduate, Maria McGuire. She was a recent con-vert to the republican cause. Like a number of other young women of her class and education in that era, she may have been influenced by the romantic idea of mixing with men involved in the 'armed struggle'. During her flirtation with the republican movement, she even took to carrying a small pistol in her handbag. She had been an actress for a short period at Dublin's famed Abbey Theatre, and after taking a degree at Uni-versity College Dublin (UCD), she had studied for a period at Madrid University. She had been married briefly to an Englishman while living in Spain. It has been reported that she did a short stint as a go-go dancer, and that she once played the girlfriend in an undergraduate production of *Billy Liar.*

Some republicans had reservations about her from the start, though others thought she was good for the image of the movement. The Provi-sionals had a blue-collar, proletarian image and some considered that it did them no harm to have a well-spoken, sophisticated, university-educated young woman with a cosmopolitan background among their ranks. Even-tually, partly because of her facility with languages, she ended up on the arms-buying mission in Europe with Dáithí Ó Conaill. It was also reckoned that she could provide 'cover' for Ó Conaill – a 'couple' would be less likely to attract attention than a man operating alone.

Ó Conaill was taking a risk by going personally on the mission, which took him to a number of countries on the Continent. There was a reasonable chance that, during a time of great turmoil in Ireland, the movements of a senior republican across international borders would be noted by police and security agencies. Ó Conaill's name was known to the authorities – he had a long and very public record of involvement in the IRA, and had done time for the cause.

Dáithí Ó Conaill (sometimes known by the English version of his name, David O'Connell) joined the republican movement in 1955, aged seventeen. He was still in school at the time. When the IRA launched its Border Campaign in 1956, he was one of the new generation of guerrilla fighters who took part. It has been said that he was extraordinarily courageous and audacious during operations. He was involved in one of the best-known raids during this era – the attack on an RUC barracks in the small village of Brookeborough, County Fermanagh, on New Year's Day 1957. Another participant was Sean Garland, who was later to become prominent in the Workers Party.

The raiders planted two mines at the station, which failed to go off. There was an exchange of fire between the IRA men and an RUC man shooting from a window on the upper floor of the station. The policeman, Sergeant Kenneth Cordner, got the upper hand in the shootout, firing bursts from a Sten gun. As the raiders prepared to make their getaway, he emptied a magazine into the men who had scrambled into the back of their dumper truck. Several were injured and two men, Sean South and Fergal O'Hanlon, later died of their wounds. As a schoolboy, I recall seeing South's coffin being brought through the streets of Dublin and laid before the Municipal Art Gallery on Parnell Square, escorted by a republican guard of honour. Crowds turned out to line the streets and pay their respects. It was a time of high emotion for many.

After the disastrous raid, Ó Conaill made his way with the other survivors into the Republic, where he was arrested. He got six months under the Offences Against the State Act for refusing to answer questions. When he emerged from prison in the summer of 1957, he was rearrested and interned. He became a close friend of fellow inmate Ruairí Ó Brádaigh, who was to become leader of the Sinn Féin wing allied to the Provisionals following the 1970 split in the movement.

The two men escaped together from the Curragh internment camp in October 1958. Ó Conaill returned to the fray, taking part in a number of operations. His luck as a guerrilla fighter ran out in 1960, when the IRA tried to ambush an RUC patrol in County Tyrone. As the RUC returned fire, he was hit six times. Bleeding heavily from stomach, leg and hand wounds, he sought help at a house near the shores of Lough Neagh. He feared he was dying, and asked for a priest and a doctor. The people in the house were loyalists and they called the RUC instead. Two officers arrived. One held a gun to his head, but the other summoned medical help. Ó Conaill was sentenced to eight years in Crumlin Road Prison but got out after three, after the IRA campaign fizzled out in the early 1960s.

Shortly after coming out of prison he married his sweetheart, Deirdre. He returned to his native Cork to take up a post in education – he was a woodwork teacher. He retained his interest in republicanism, becoming a member of the Wolfe Tone Society in Cork. When the Troubles flared up in 1969, Ó Conaill joined with other militants, like his old friend Ruairí Ó Brádaigh and Seán Mac Stíofáin, to set up the Provisional republican movement.

As a member of the Provisional IRA's Army Council, with the role of raising funds and procuring arms, Ó Conaill's travels took him to the US, Eastern and Western Europe, and, according to security sources, Libya. He was also to become a key political strategist for the Provisional republican movement, until he was overshadowed by the rise of the Northern element in the movement, and the advent of new figures like Gerry Adams. While Ó Conaill played a key role in reactivating George Harrison's gunrunning network in New York, he also took a hands-on approach to arms procurement.

As outlined in Maria McGuire's book *To Take Arms*,[3] in autumn 1971 Ó Conaill was involved in a series of cloak-and-dagger meetings around the Continent. It is understood that at a meeting in Paris, Freeman introduced the arms dealer to Ó Conaill, and they discussed the transaction. Ó Conaill also travelled to Switzerland, and got a Czech visa in Berne. McGuire joined him later in Zurich, and they had a meeting in the city with Freeman. There were further meetings in Brussels and Amsterdam between Ó Conaill, the dealer and Freeman. Ó Conaill travelled to Prague with the dealer, and they visited the offices of Omnipol, the State export firm supplying the weapons. They were taken to a depot and shown the merchandise, and Ó Conaill was impressed. Ó Conaill paid over a large sum of money from a cache of large-denomination Swiss currency crammed into a briefcase.

Arms flight to Schiphol

Ernest Koenig, an American of German background, was called in to make air freight arrangements to ship the weapons from Prague to Schiphol Airport in the Netherlands. Based in Luxembourg, he worked in the air transport business but has also been described as an arms dealer. He was a friend of former MI6 man Tony Divall, Donald Gurrey's colleague from the old days in West Berlin. Despite these connections, there is no indication that Koenig was involved in blowing the lid on the operation. Neither is there any indication that Divall was involved. Nevertheless, Divall, who remained a freelance MI6 operative when he turned to gunrunning after leaving the service, potentially had an informant at the heart of the operation to transport the IRA weapons. When I interviewed him, Divall said that Koenig 'did some jobs for him' from time to time.

Divall had another potential informant who might have been in a position to know about the Ó Conaill shipment – the late George Strakaty, an arms dealer in Vienna who had dealings with Omnipol. Strakaty had defected from Czechoslovakia for a new life in Canada but returned to Europe, re-establishing links with MI6 through Divall.[4] When I interviewed Divall about his gunrunning career, he made a number of references to Strakaty. He said that he and Strakaty had worked together on putting together a collection of arms for an MI6-linked attempt to overthrow the Libyan leader Colonel Gadaffi, often referred to as 'The Hilton Assignment' after a book of the same name about the affair.[5] One writer has claimed that it was Strakaty who exposed the Ó Conaill shipment.[6] Divall himself never made such a claim for his friend when I spoke to him, even though, towards the end of his life, he appeared willing enough to acknowledge any intelligence coups with which he was connected, directly or indirectly.

Like Divall, Koenig had taken part in the Biafran airlift during the Nigerian civil war. Koenig, something of an adventurer, was just one of a number of mercenary aviators who flew transport aircraft for the Biafrans.

It was a very dangerous occupation, involving flying into an improvised jungle airstrip at Uli under hazardous conditions.

For the Ó Conaill shipment, Koenig chartered an aircraft from a Belgian-based company called Pomair. He walked into the company's office in Ostend on 11 October, and made the arrangements. Koenig made it clear from the outset that the cargo would consist of 'military equipment'. As the company had not done business with him before, they asked for the money up front, which he paid – $3,000. Pomair was also supplied with an import certificate, which purported to have been issued by the UK Board of Trade, indicating that the arms were being bought by Wendamond Ltd, City Road, London. The British authorities later indicated that the reference number on the certificate did not correspond with any of their official documents.

Koenig personally supervised the loading of the arms at Prague. He travelled with the arms cargo on the flight to Schiphol. The only other person on board the DC 6, call sign Charlie Tango Kilo, was the pilot, Jean Honweghen. Pomair was a recently formed air transport company and it was the first time they had transported arms. They had no reason to believe there was anything dubious about the operation, and they went to great lengths to comply with air transport regulations concerning arms cargoes. The firm received the relevant permissions from the Dutch, Belgian and German aviation authorities for the transport of the cargo, consisting of four tons of arms in 166 boxes. Meanwhile, it has to be presumed that the arms dealer involved in setting up the 'sting' was keeping spymaster Donald Gurrey informed about developments.

As they waited in a hotel in Amsterdam for the arrival of the arms cargo, due in on Saturday 16 October, Ó Conaill and McGuire had the feeling that they were under surveillance. McGuire recalls in her book how they both felt uneasy. Then an astonishing thing happened. The arms dealer showed Ó Conaill a brief item in the *Daily Telegraph* newspaper. The item reported that Ó Conaill was on the Continent to buy arms for the IRA! The only inaccuracy in the story was that Ó Conaill was described as chief of staff of the IRA, a post that had, of course, been taken by Seán Mac Stíofáin, a prickly, difficult man who was very jealous indeed of his authority. Both Ó Conaill and McGuire were shocked and dismayed, and immediately checked out of their hotel, hoping to lie low and throw any police on their trail off the scent. It is believed that the item was leaked by MI6 to the *Daily Telegraph* to distract attention away from the arms dealer who was working for them. That evening Ó Conaill and Maguire suffered a further blow. They heard a news flash that told of the discovery of the arms consignment at Schiphol. It was time to cut their losses and head home to Ireland.

The British, through Scotland Yard, had informed Dutch authorities about the illicit nature of the arms shipment, and police were waiting for the aircraft when it arrived. Ernest Koenig was about to supervise the unloading of the aircraft when he and the aircraft captain were arrested. The weapons were impounded in a special strong room with anti-theft devices, pending further clarification.

Chief Inspector Winslow of Scotland Yard travelled to the Netherlands to assist Dutch police in the questioning of Koenig. There was a media report that police found documents in Koenig's possession indicating that the arms formed only part of the IRA's shopping list. It appears that Koenig told police that the arms bought by the Wendamond company were ultimately bound for a bona fide customer in West Africa, and that his responsibility for the arms ended as soon as they were delivered to Schiphol. A Mr Dougan was then to take over the consignment for onward delivery to the client.

Koenig had with him a large, yellow envelope marked incongruously 'Operation Patriot'. The envelope contained a number of documents. One of them was from Wendamond, giving power of attorney to a 'Mr M Dougan' of the firm's 'export department' to take delivery of the arms and ammunition at Schiphol and to act on its behalf. Inquiries indicated that Wendamond had been incorporated just a couple of weeks before and did not exist except on paper. A man using the name of Warrington had incorporated the firm, claiming an address at Chapel Street in London SW1. The address happened to coincide with the entrance to the Irish Embassy, around the corner from Grosvenor Place. It may have been a touch of dry humour by whoever set up the firm. Nobody at the embassy had ever heard of anyone called Warrington based at the address.

Meanwhile Ó Conaill and McGuire crossed the frontier into France by taxi and took a scheduled flight from Paris back to Ireland, disembarking at Cork Airport. The original plan had been to take the arms to Ireland by sea after transfer from Schiphol. A vessel – probably a fishing boat skippered by an Irish sympathiser – was said to have been standing by in Rotterdam for this purpose.

The consignment, apparently earmarked for the IRA in Derry, included forty carbines with cartridge belts and bayonets; twenty rifles; six machine pistols; four anti-tank rocket launchers with 200 rocket-propelled grenades; 520 detonators; 7,040 NATO-type rounds of ammunition for the carbines and rifles; 2,640 other rounds; and 500 fragmentation grenades. The IRA held a court of inquiry to find out how the operation went wrong, but its findings were inconclusive. The outcome of the operation must have been quite satisfactory from the British point of view. A significant arms shipment to the Provos had been seized, and the IRA's coffers had been depleted.

Ironically, even if MI6 had not infiltrated the operation, it is possible that the shipment might have been uncovered anyway. A cargo handling firm had been contacted by a woman with an upper-class Dutch accent, who gave her name as Miss Van Leeuwen. She said she was acting on behalf of a gentleman from Wendamond. They were expecting a consignment of arms and wanted the cargo firm to handle storage and transhipment. The mysterious Miss Van Leeuwen also contacted Sabena Airlines and said she had a shipment of arms for 'West Africa'. When the cargo handling company could find no trace in London of Wendamond, the police were alerted.[7]

Following questioning, the pilot was allowed to proceed on his way, and flew the DC-6 back home to Belgium. The aircraft had been released in time for its next scheduled mission – the rather more mundane task of transporting pilgrims and invalids to that renowned religious centre in southwestern France, the shrine at Lourdes.

Koenig was held for ten days in what was described as pre-trial detention. The public prosecutor applied to Haarlem District Court for a thirty-day extension of the period of detention, but the court ordered his release. Koenig was freed on 26 October and wisely hopped on a flight to Brussels. The public prosecutor was unhappy with his release, and on 19 November brought an appeal to the Appeals Court of Amsterdam, which ruled that the Luxembourg resident had been wrongly released. By then, of course, Koenig had flown the coop. It would have been open to the public prosecutor to ask for Koenig's extradition, but his whereabouts at that time were unknown. His name was placed on the register of people wanted by the police. So far as is known, he was never subsequently arrested by the Dutch authorities. The Dutch also wanted to question Ó Conaill, McGuire and Freeman, but they were also unavailable to them.

As for the mysterious arms dealer who had infiltrated the operation on behalf of the spooks, he seemed to simply disappear. It is safe to assume that he received a sizeable pay-off from Donald Gurrey for 'services rendered'. Presumably, he also pocketed a hefty commission from Ó Conaill for arranging the arms deal. The year after Gurrey oversaw the 'sting' operation, the veteran spy figured in Queen Elizabeth's honours list. On 3 June 1972, he was made an OBE (Officer of the British Empire). Of course there would have been no mention of MI6 in any official citation. Gurrey's cover was that of a mere civil servant. One could speculate that the spoiling of Ó Conaill's gunrunning operation was one of the exploits that led to the intelligence man being honoured by the Queen of England.

Tony Divall had an intriguing story to relate about Ernest Koenig – he said that Koenig's father had been a member of the German navy, and had a role in the naval operation that brought Irish patriot Roger Casement, on board a German submarine, into Banna Strand, County Kerry in the prelude to the Easter Rising of 1916. There was, of course, a gunrunning connection as well – the submarine was preceded by the German ship, the *Aud*, with a cargo of arms for the Rising. The *Aud* was scuttled by the crew after being captured by British warships. It appears that Koenig senior was on board the *Aud*. The old saying comes to mind: 'There is nothing new under the sun.' Divall was an unsentimental man, but he did betray some emotion when he reflected on the passing away of his friend. 'Koenig is gone – they're all gone,' he said. Divall and Ó Conaill are also deceased, making it all the more difficult to find the answers to outstanding questions about the Omnipol affair.

Following the arms seizure at Schiphol, British authorities made representations to the Czech government. In November, secretary of state for foreign and commonwealth affairs Sir Alec Douglas-Home told the House of Commons he had been informed by the Czech government that, according to their information, the arms seized at Schiphol were definitely not intended for Northern Ireland, but for a completely different part of the world. 'They have assured us that it is not their policy to get involved in the affairs of Northern Ireland ...'

In the early 1990s, while researching another book, I called to the Omnipol office in Prague's downtown commercial district. The company operated from a modern building with a black glass facade on Neka-zanka Street. In the communist era, Eastern Europe had a reputation for being a region where one could buy weaponry on a clandestine basis, with few questions asked. However, we were now in a different era. Communism had collapsed and Omnipol was now under a democratic government. The Omnipol official delegated to see me was Zdenek Burian, a youthful, soft-spoken man who was in the happy position of not having been with the company in the old days, when some rather dubious transactions had taken place.

One of the topics we touched on was the Ó Conaill/IRA arms shipment. It quickly became clear that Burian had no startling insights into the affair. He had not even heard of the matter, and went on to state that if Omnipol arms were found to have been used by illegal organisations, then these arms must have been supplied by a third party, without the knowledge or the permission of the company. All arms sold by Omnipol were supplied on condition that the customer was the end-user.

Maria McGuire tells in her book how the IRA leadership was eager to push up the body-count of British soldiers killed. Ó Conaill and other members of the Army Council believed that once eighty soldiers had been killed, the pressure on the British to negotiate would be immense. 'I remember the feeling of satisfaction we had at hearing another one had died,' she wrote.[8] This was the culture that had developed among the Provisionals and their supporters at the time. I remember as a reporter covering a Sinn Féin rally outside the General Post Office (GPO) on O'Connell Street, Dublin, in the same era. The building had enormous historical symbolism for republicans of all hues. The rebels had occupied the GPO during the 1916 Rising and Pádraig Pearse, the deeply idealistic rebel leader, had read the Proclamation of the Irish Republic to a small crowd outside the building. By the early 1970s, the mood of republicans who still followed the physical force tradition was more vengeful. During the rally, I recall one republican on the platform, with a transistor radio, relaying a news bulletin through the public address system to the crowd. When the newsreader announced that a young British soldier wounded in Northern Ireland had died, there was a loud cheer from the crowd.

Ultimately, Maria McGuire became disillusioned by what she saw as the simplistic militarism of some of the IRA leaders, especially Seán Mac Stíofáin, and by the collapse of the truce of summer 1972. She defected from the movement in August that year and left Ireland. In her book about her experiences, *To Take Arms*,[9] she claimed that the Basque separatist group ETA had supplied the IRA with fifty revolvers in return for training in the use of explosives. I remember her from the Dublin of the early 1970s, a diminutive figure, self-confident, solemn and rather aloof. I recall her attending a Sinn Féin press conference in a hotel on the Dublin quays – she was handing out the press releases. Ó Conaill was also there. There is no report of her ever returning to Ireland, and her present whereabouts are unknown.

Seán Mac Stíofáin was enraged by derogatory comments made about him by McGuire in newspaper articles and in her book. He angrily denied that he had made the bigoted, anti-Protestant comments that she attributed to him. He was also furious that she had been brought on a sensitive arms-buying mission abroad, in light of the fact that she was a total newcomer to the movement and, according to him, was not even a member of the IRA. Mac Stíofáin believed in delegating responsibilities to his subordinates, and had clearly left the fine detail of the Omnipol operation to Ó Conaill – a decision that he came to bitterly regret.

Mac Stíofáin was forming the view that the secret services of at least three countries – Britain, the US and the Soviet Union – were trying to prevent the purchase of arms by the IRA in Europe. He also believed that the police and intelligence agencies of the NATO powers were assisting the British in every way to prevent the IRA procuring new equipment.[10] While it was obvious that Britain's NATO allies would seek to prevent the IRA procuring arms to kill British soldiers, it is unclear why Mac Stíofáin came to the conclusion that the spooks of Russia's KGB were also proactive in this field. Did the strongly anti-Communist Mac Stíofáin suspect that the IRA had somehow been set up by the KGB, working through their subordinates in communist-era Czech intelligence, when Daithí Ó Conaill did an arms deal with Omnipol? Was he blaming Moscow, instead of the real culprits, MI6?

Some years after the Omnipol affair, in April 1976, a Czech diplomat serving in Ireland died suddenly after receiving a mysterious visitor. It was reported that he had planned to defect to marry his Irish girlfriend. Some

British newspapers suggested that he was about to give a detailed account of his government's dealings with the IRA. It was pointed out that Czech intelligence had once managed to get into a closely guarded Austrian police station and kill a defector with a poison that had no known antidote. The newspaper reports were recalled in a book about Carlos 'The Jackal' by English journalist Colin Smith, who first told McGuire's story in a series of articles in the *Observer* – the prelude to McGuire's book. However, the suggestion of dirty work in the case of the Dublin-based diplomat remains very much in the realm of speculation.[11]

The Official IRA and the KGB arms

According to some accounts, the Provisionals may not have been the only republicans to have an arms procurement link with the communist bloc in the early 1970s. It has been claimed that the Official IRA received arms from the Russian intelligence service, the KGB, in 1972. Details of the alleged delivery are contained in KGB documents smuggled out of Russia by defector Vasili Mitrokhin, and reported in a book co-written by himself.[12] According to the documents, an intermediary for OIRA chief of staff Cathal Goulding and his colleague Seamus Costello made contact with Moscow with regard to buying arms in November 1969. This would have been shortly before the formal split in the IRA into Provisional and Official wings.

Costello later broke away from the OIRA to launch the Irish National Liberation Army (INLA). The alleged intermediary was named as Michael O'Riordan, who was then general secretary of the Irish Communist Party, and who had fought in the International Brigade against Franco during the Spanish Civil War. O'Riordan, who was to die at age eighty-eight in May 2006, denied involvement.

According to the KGB documents, KGB chairman Yuri Andropov, who later became Soviet leader, approved a plan in 1972 for the supply of arms to the OIRA. 'Operation Splash' was said to have involved the delivery of two machine guns, seventy automatic rifles, ten Walther pistols and 41,600 rounds of ammunition. In order to disguise their origin, all the weapons were of non-Soviet manufacture. It was said that an intelligence-gathering vessel, the *Reduktor*, disguised as a trawler, transported the arms cargo to the Irish Sea. The weapons, in waterproof wrapping, were attached to a marker buoy and submerged to a depth of about forty metres on the Stanton sandbank, ninety kilometres from the coast of Northern Ireland, for later recovery. The KGB documents also state that other arms deliveries were made to the OIRA.

Cathal Goulding denied to the media that any arms ever arrived from Russia. During research for this book, I spoke to two individuals who were active in the Official republican movement at this period, and they were unable to confirm the gunrunning claims in the KGB archives. One former OIRA man said the organisation at this period would have been more interested in financial support than in arms. The other former OIRA activist also had no knowledge of arms coming from Russia. However, he did disclose an intriguing piece of information – he said that the OIRA at this period had its own trawler. 'If they wanted to get stuff into the country they would have used it,' he said. It appears that the OIRA kept the trawler for only a short period, before deciding that it was a waste of money. A decision was made to dispose of the trawler, and the OIRA 'navy' was no more, according to this source.

A former Russian journalist, Boris Shtern, has given an account of how Soviet fishing trawlers were often used by the KGB for intelligence and operational purposes. He claimed that he was on board a Soviet trawler off the Irish coast one night in 1971 when a secret cargo was unloaded to Irish boats. He said a KGB officer on board the trawler transferred a crate to two Irishmen. Shtern, who later settled in Canada, gave an account in 1981 of the incident.[13] He said that he and others on board formed the opinion that the crate contained arms.

In 1969 a leading figure on the left of the republican movement, who was to go with the Officials after the split, was accused of an attempt to buy arms covertly. This was Dublin-born Eamon Smullen, whose involvement in the movement went back to the 1940s. In fact, in Dublin in 1943, he had been sentenced to fourteen years in prison for trying to murder another IRA man suspected of being an informer.

When the Northern Troubles flared in the late 1960s, Smullen, who was living in the UK, found himself in trouble once again. He was arrested in 1969 when it was alleged that he had tried to incite a Huddersfield gun dealer to transfer arms. Smullen, who was described as a carpenter, with an address in Leeds, appeared before Leeds Assizes in February 1970. He was convicted of conspiring with persons unknown to buy firearms in contravention of the Firearms Act, and was sentenced to eight years. Another man, with an address in Glasgow, got four years. The judge told the jury to find both men not guilty on the charge of inciting the gun dealer to provide arms. A third man was acquitted on arms charges. A court of appeal later reduced the sentences on the two convicted men, Smullen's sentence being reduced from eight to five years, and the other man's sentence being cut by a year. On his release, Smullen returned to Ireland and went on to work full-time for the Workers Party. He resigned from the party in April 1990 following an internal dispute, and died some months later.

Fianna Fáil and the Official IRA

Just a couple of weeks after the close of the Arms Trial, there was an intriguing Garda investigation in the Border region. On 8 November 1970 Sam Dowling, a member of the civil rights movement, was arrested by Gardaí at Kilcloney, County Louth. Dowling, a surveyor by profession, was associated with Official Sinn Féin, political wing of the Official IRA. He had an address at Francis Street, Dundalk, and another address in Newry, just north of the Border in County Down.[14] It was alleged later in court that he was in possession of 3.5lbs of gelignite, three sub-machine guns, a .303 rifle, a revolver, two pistols and 175 rounds of ammunition at the time of his arrest.

During his trial at Dundalk Circuit Court in January 1971, Dowling stated that Captain James Kelly and the agents of the Irish government gave the beleaguered citizens of Northern Ireland money for arms for community defence purposes, but they were not given any licences for the arms. He insisted he was not guilty of any crime if Captain Kelly was not guilty and the Irish government was not guilty. Captain Kelly was present in court for the hearing, but was not called as a witness. Dowling was acquitted by the jury on arms charges and walked free from the court.

It was believed that the arms that were seized belonged to the Official IRA. The court case gave rise to some speculation. Did Dowling's remarks mean that the arms at the centre of the case had been supplied by Captain Kelly, or been acquired with the aid of State funds? When I spoke to

Dowling by phone more than thirty-five years later, in February 2006, he said that this was not the case – neither Captain Kelly nor the Irish government was involved in providing the materiel. Dowling, a prominent playwright living in London and now in his mid-seventies, said he did not know the origin of the weapons and explosives. 'It was pretty ancient stuff – I did not ask where it came from.' He wanted to convey in court that there were parallels between his case and that of Captain Kelly, and they decided to call Kelly as a witness. Kelly came along to the court but was reluctant to testify, and did not give evidence. But Dowling felt that Kelly's presence in court helped to underline the message they were trying to get across.

Dowling went on to reveal that he had had contacts during the period not with the Irish government *per se*, but with elements in the ruling Fianna Fáil party. He was approached in Dundalk by people in Fianna Fáil who wanted to meet the Official IRA. 'I was involved as a go-between between the Belfast Command of the Officials and some Fianna Fáil people.' He set up a meeting in a room over a pub in Dundalk between the two elements, but was not present himself. He could not say if this meeting was directly linked to the meeting in London between IRA chief Cathal Goulding and Fianna Fáil-linked Jock Haughey, brother of the then finance minister Charlie Haughey, when Jock apparently passed over money for arms, but it was 'part of the same syndrome'.

It was believed that following the Goulding–Haughey meeting, arms were brought into Dublin and handed over to Goulding (*see* Chapter 1). Dowling recalled that there was some suggestion at the time from Fianna Fáil people of sidelining some of the Officials, like Billy McMillan, who were considered too radical. (McMillan, a leading Belfast Official IRA man, was assassinated by the INLA in a feud in 1975.)

Dowling said that the pre-split IRA did not have much of an arsenal. 'They did not have a lot – enough to do a bit of damage, I suppose. The IRA had been run down prior to the Troubles. They had been moving away from militarism.' When the Troubles started, and as the Provos began to split away, the Officials developed a renewed interest in getting weapons. 'I think the Officials had to compete for the high ground of republicanism, and go against their policy in a way,' said Dowling. 'I was active in Official Sinn Féin, later the Workers Party. The split between the Officials and the Provisionals was already happening when I came into the movement. I was not really involved in the split. I was only on the periphery when that was happening.' Dowling was, of course, pleased to be acquitted. 'I could have got fifteen years.' He believed that his case was one of the last arms-related trials to be held with a jury. Soon afterwards the non-jury Special Criminal Court was brought in, featuring three judges, for subversive-linked cases.

After his acquittal, Dowling resumed his work as a surveyor, but later decided to change career. He went back to college, took a degree in philosophy, and became a writer. 'I have been writing professionally ever since. I have written twenty or twenty-five plays, and have been living in London, safe in the arms of Britannia.'

After 1972, the year that the Official IRA declared a cease-fire, the organisation had little use for major imports of arms. Nevertheless, it maintained a small arsenal of weapons which it never gave up or decommissioned. The arsenal in the early 1970s included some rather elderly M-1 rifles of Second World War vintage and Luger pistols. These were the weapons on show when, in early 1972, a photographer colleague working for *This Week* magazine was brought to an Official IRA training camp in a remote mountain area in the Border region, and produced a photo feature for the magazine.[15] The trainees included a woman. It is possible that the rifles used in the training exercise came from the batch that George Harrison had collected in the late 1950s and which he sent to the 'pre-split' IRA in mid-1969.

Members of the Official IRA also somehow managed to get their hands on a small quantity of obsolete German-manufactured Mauser rifles, part of the big consignment smuggled into Ulster in 1914 on the *Clyde Valley* for the Ulster Volunteer Force.

One former member of the Officials recalled that in the early 1970s he was driving on a little-used road across the Border from County Derry into County Donegal, with six Mauser rifles hidden under a blanket in the boot of the car. To his great dismay he was stopped at a Garda checkpoint. A Garda glanced casually into the boot of the car, but it was very dark and he did not notice the rifles underneath the blanket. The Garda remarked to the superintendent in charge of the checkpoint: 'Nothing here, Super.' The driver, breathing a very deep sigh of relief, was allowed to proceed. It was a close shave. 'The rifles were single-shot but still useable and very accurate,' he added.

Another individual, who was a member of the Official IRA in the 1970s, said that they did not engage in any large-scale arms smuggling during that period. 'If a mate was going to America you might ask him to try to get you a particular type of handgun – that was the extent of it.' Another former Official told of an ingenious method used to smuggle small quantities of pistols from America in the early 1970s. 'The pistol would be disassembled and the parts concealed in a canteen of cutlery, which would then be sent by post, with the usual customs declaration filled in. Sympathisers would be alerted to expect packages in the post. The re-assembled handguns would then be hidden in a tank of sump oil at a service station. What Garda is going to put his hand into a tank of oil at a garage to search for guns? The oil did not do any harm to the weapons.'

An arms shipment from Canada intercepted at Dublin port in 1973 was, according to one report, destined for the Official IRA, although this was not confirmed (see Chapter 3).[16] Later in the 1970s, one of the reasons for the Officials maintaining an arsenal was to carry out unclaimed fund-raising robberies. Another was to retain means of defence and retaliation in feuds with other paramilitary organisations. There was, for instance, a feud in the mid-1970s with the breakaway INLA.

A former Provisional told me that the PIRA seized an Official IRA arms dump in County Tyrone in the early 1980s. It consisted of a few AK-47 rifles, packed in grease, which looked like they had never been used before. They were of East European origin. The source said that the person holding the cache was told the arms were being commandeered and that he had no choice in the matter. How the weapons made their way to Ireland, or ended up in the hands of the Officials, remains a mystery.

By the latter part of the 1980s, the Official IRA appeared dormant, although security sources during that period believed the organisation was still in existence. This belief was boosted in February 1990, when a woman appeared in court in Belfast in connection with an arms cache found in the garden of her home in the Turf Lodge area of the city the previous year. The court heard that the woman had told police that she had been asked in 1984 to store the weapons by a member of the Workers Party (successor party to Official Sinn Féin), acting on behalf of the Official IRA. The cache consisted of an M-1 carbine, a sub-machine gun and almost 400 rounds of ammunition. The M-1 was, of course, a type of weapon known to have previously been in the arsenal of the

Officials. Following the court case, the Workers Party issued its routine denial of any link with any armed organisation. In any case, by now, the gunrunning days of the Official IRA seemed definitely over.

British intelligence try to trace the source of IRA weaponry

Intelligence services and police forces have always taken a particular interest in the origins of weapons seized from paramilitaries – it can provide valuable intelligence on the sources of illegal weaponry and provide insights into paramilitary activity and thinking. In 1972, the British secret intelligence service MI6 had an agent operating in Dublin. He visited the city from time to time, having recruited as an informant a Garda in C3, the Garda Crime and Security Branch, which has a particular role in monitoring the activities of subversives. The British agent was seeking to build up information on the IRA and on the smuggling of arms from various foreign locations. The agent and his Garda contact were arrested in December 1972, and in February 1973 appeared at the Special Criminal Court in Dublin. The Garda was found guilty of unauthorised possession of official documents and the agent was convicted of unlawfully attempting to obtain information from a public official. They were sentenced to three months' imprisonment, dating from the time of their arrest, meaning that they would walk free immediately. It is believed the two men immediately flew to the UK.

It was reported that the agent, when arrested, had notes containing the intriguing reference 'RL'. This was believed to stand for 'rocket launchers'. One theory is that he was trying to check the origins of the RPG-7 rocket launchers that the IRA had begun deploying against security forces in the North during 1972. It is now known that a consignment of these Russian-designed weapons had been flown into Ireland from Libya earlier that year (*see* Chapter 5). In his memoirs, Seán Mac Stíofáin recalled that while he was being held in the Curragh military prison in 1972, the IRA began to use the RPG-7. He said the weapon had been used in the course of one day in a 'co-ordinated wave of IRA attacks', in which two British soldiers and an RUC man had been killed. According to Mac Stíofáin, the British were 'flabbergasted' by the sudden appearance of these weapons in numbers.[17]

Just a few months later the *Claudia*, with arms from Libya on board, would be captured, proving that Colonel Gadaffi had begun supplying weaponry to the Provisionals. However, this particular cargo contained no RPG-7 rocket launchers or rockets. The British continued to seek to identify the source of the RPG-7s in the Provo arsenal, although Libya became a prime suspect. It was reported that after capturing one of these RPG-7s, British intelligence sent samples of the dust and sand found inside the launcher to experts from leading petroleum companies in an attempt to identify the geographical origin of the weapon, but the scientists were unable to do so.[18]

The RPG-7 was probably the first Russian-designed weapon recovered in Northern Ireland during the Troubles. The next Soviet-designed weapon to turn up was a 7.62mm SKS carbine, seized in a raid on Bally-murphy housing estate, Belfast, in 1974.[19] It was the first Eastern Bloc-type rifle to be seized in the North, even though IRA gunmen had been spotted in possession of Soviet-designed AK-47-type rifles about 1973.

There was some mystery as to how the SKS carbine had reached Belfast. The weapon bore Chinese characters, indicating that it might have been one of a large number of SKS rifles supplied by the Soviet Union to China's People's Army before the Sino-Soviet split in the mid-1960s. Some of these rifles might then have been transferred from China to North Korea or to Albania. There was speculation that the rifle might have come to Ireland from Eastern Europe.

Another weapon of mysterious origin to turn up in Northern Ireland at this period was the .22 Lanedesmann rifle, a number of which were cap-tured. The weapon had been designed for German shooting clubs, but their sale was subsequently banned under federal German legislation. Stocks of the rifles had been sold off to arms dealers in Europe, and there was speculation that an IRA 'front' person may have bought some weap-ons from one of these dealers.

In 1977, Soviet-designed hand grenades were reported as being in use by the IRA – once again there was much speculation as to their origin.[20]

The Eastern Bloc-origin weapons discovered during the 1970s were harbingers of future deliveries. By the end of the 1980s, the IRA had come into possession of large quantities of Kalashnikov rifles and other Soviet-designed arms. By then, of course, British intelligence and other services had established the answer to the question of who was supplying RPG-7s to the IRA – it was Libyan leader Colonel Muammar Gadaffi.

CHAPTER 5

The Infiltration of the *Claudia* Operation

Tony Divall, a professional gunrunner and former British intelligence man, had a bright but very dangerous idea back in the early 1970s. According to his own account, he decided to mount a 'sting' operation against the Provisional IRA which was urgently seeking to acquire arms on the international black market. Divall, based in Hamburg, had a long history of involvement in gunrunning and dangerous escapades. And there is evidence to back up his claim that he played the key role in disrupting one of the most significant IRA arms procurement operations of the early 1970s, when a consignment of Libyan arms was seized en route to the IRA aboard the freighter *Claudia*.

The murky world of intelligence and arms trafficking has produced a myriad of remarkable characters, but English-born Anthony Divall has to be one of the most remarkable of them all. It is not unusual for those who operate in the grey area of the arms business to have contacts in the intelligence world. In the case of Tony Divall, however, he had worked in that world, as a member of the British intelligence service MI6, before becoming a gunrunner in various trouble spots around the globe. Somehow one is not terribly taken aback when former CIA men crop up in the arms business, but it is a little more surprising in the case of that far more straight-laced and secretive organisation, MI6.

A native of Kent, Divall was a captain in the Royal Marines. He saw action in the Normandy landings in June 1944 and in other engagements during the Second World War. After the war he settled in West Berlin, that hotbed of espionage activity, as a member of a sizeable MI6 station. He started off as a low-level operative. He was a driver, 'fixer' and general factotum. He worked for a station that controlled agents and informants based 'on the other side' as Divall, in his laconic way, liked to describe it – ie. the other side of what became known in the post-war era as the Iron Curtain.

In those days it was often a simple matter of gathering 'human intelligence' or 'humint' – information from contacts on the ground in Soviet-dominated East Germany and Eastern Europe. These sources reported on such mundane matters as troop movements or the types of weapons being used by Eastern Bloc soldiers, while better-placed individuals reported on more high-level strategic matters. According to Divall, MI6 'contacts' ranged from cleaning ladies working in government offices to civil servants to members of armed forces, of both low and high rank.

For a period, Divall worked from an MI6 house in West Berlin. This was a rather pleasant villa, surrounded by trees, at 20 Winklerstrasse. In order to get a ready supply of roubles to finance the work of British agents in the Soviet Union, Divall came up with the ingenious idea of smuggling gold Swiss watches into Russia, where they were sold at a good profit on the black market. Divall used East German railwaymen working on trains travelling to Russia to smuggle these treasured items – heavy, gold watches produced by the International Watch Company in Schaffhausen, Switzerland. The smugglers got a rake-off and Divall got his roubles – the whole operation was self-financing.

All worked well for seven years, until the double-agent George Blake took charge of the scheme on joining British intelligence headquarters in Berlin in 1955. The operation was one of those allegedly 'blown' to the Russians by Blake, who, incidentally, had learned some of his Russian in Ireland, from a Russian *émigré*. For many years Divall had a treasured relic of his time as a master smuggler based in Berlin – an IWC watch which, greatly to his regret, was stolen by a burglar who broke into his home.

However, after the Berlin Wall fell, the IWC published an account in the company magazine of Divall's smuggling activities, and in return for his co-operation presented him with one of their most valuable watches, worth about £1,000. Divall was wearing it when I met him in Hamburg in the early 1990s.

Towards the end of his time with MI6, Divall had a close shave while infiltrating an agent into Estonia from the sea. He was in a motorboat off the coast, having put the agent into a dinghy, when two patrol vessels made a sudden appearance, opening fire. Divall just managed to escape into international waters. He later learned that the operation had been betrayed by a double-agent. Appalled by how close he had come to being sacrificed, he left MI6.[1] He had been a full-time employee of MI6 from 1946 to 1955, but after he resigned he continued to work for the agency on a freelance basis in his travels around the world.

After a stint as a Berlin racing driver (which in old age he regarded as one of the most enjoyable episodes in his long career), Divall moved on to pastures new, establishing a base in Hamburg from where he engaged in a series of international adventures, many linked to the arms trade. He received a retainer from MI6 until his links with the agency, also known as the Secret Intelligence Service (SIS), were cut in acrimonious circumstances in 1987.

Having come from a long line of smugglers of French descent operating along the Kent coast, it was perhaps inevitable that Divall himself would turn to the same line of business, having left the full-time service with 'The Firm', as he sometimes referred to MI6. In the latter part of the 1950s he surfaced in Tangier, a traditional hotbed of clandestine activity, running guns to the Algerian insurgents who were in rebellion at the time against French rule – and also keeping his old friends in MI6 informed as to the Algerian situation.

One of the dealers who supplied him with arms for transfer to the Algerian rebels was Hamburg-based Otto Schlüter – the arms dealer who figured in the renowned Arms Trial (*see* Chapter 2). The link between Divall and Schlüter was a typical example of the network of personal connections that often exists in the covert arms trafficking world. Divall went on to launch a small air transport company specialising in assignments in Africa, and was involved in gunrunning operations on that continent during the

1960s. He was one of the blockade-breaking aircraft operators involved in the Biafran airlift during the Nigerian civil war.

One of the clandestine adventures in which Divall became involved was a 1970–71 operation known, in true Hollywood style, as the 'Hilton Assignment'.[2] This was an operation mounted by Libyan exiles to overthrow the regime of Colonel Gadaffi, who had seized power in 1969 while Libya's King Idris was on holiday abroad. The plan was hatched by a former MI6 man who had turned freelance, and appears to have had the blessing, at least for a time, of MI6 and of their American counterparts the CIA. The idea was that a party of French mercenaries would storm ashore in Zodiac inflatables from a former German patrol boat, blow a hole in the wall of the prison which was known with a touch of irony as 'the Hilton', and liberate about 150 supporters of the King. The former inmates would then carry out an improvised coup, overthrow Gadaffi, and restore the monarchy. Divall's role was to assist in providing the arms for the operation. A consignment of arms was procured from the Czech state company Omnipol, and stored at Ploce, Yugoslavia. According to Divall, the CIA decided it did not want the operation to go ahead. The British also decided they did not want to see the coup take place. Italian authorities moved to impound the plotters' boat, which was docked in Trieste, before it could collect the arms from Ploce.

When the operation was called off in March 1971, the conspirators were left with access to a consignment of arms and, according to his own account when I interviewed him, Divall decided to use the arms to conduct a 'coat-trailing' exercise in regard to the IRA. It was a ploy of intelligence/security services and, perhaps, of their freelance operatives, to lure a 'target' group or organisation into an arms deal, in order to exhaust the opponent's funds without delivering the equipment. The arms dealer operating the sting would try to pocket any money handed over by the arms buyers. The arrest of the would-be arms buyers would be an additional bonus. There would also be a handsome pay-off from the intelligence service behind the 'sting'.

Divall had previously been reluctant to talk about his operations against the IRA, but towards the end of his life he agreed to give me at least some of the details of his version of events. Divall sometimes operated through 'front' men and this occasion was an example of this arrangement. Divall claimed that he arranged for one of his close colleagues, an arms dealer called Gunther Leinhauser, who was based in West Germany, to develop contacts with the republican movement. It is unclear exactly how this was done. It is doubtful that Leinhauser used the unsubtle method of simply making a phone call to Dáithí Ó Conaill. It is more likely that Leinhauser made use of contacts in the murkier area of the arms dealing world to attract the attention of the Provos.

Ironically the arms, stored in a warehouse at Ploce, that were to be used as a lure, did not actually belong to Leinhauser, or indeed to Divall. The purchase of the weapons from Omnipol in Prague had been reportedly financed by a wealthy Libyan exile. The weaponry never did end up in the hands of the IRA. According to the authors of the *The Hilton Assignment*, in October 1971 the arms were shipped to Morocco where a senior official in the royal court, Mohammed Oufkir, was considering taking charge of the operation to overthrow Colonel Gadaffi.[3]

The powerful and much-feared Oufkir never got the chance to move against the Libyan leader. Oufkir, a former defence minister, was accused of masterminding a plot to assassinate his own monarch, King Hassan II. Moroccan air force F-5 jets tried to shoot down the king's Boeing airliner on its way home from France on 10 August 1972. The airliner was hit but still managed to land safely, and the king survived. The following night Oufkir was shot dead at the king's seaside palace at Skhirat, near Rabat. He was hit in the back by several bullets. The official story was that he committed suicide.

Presumably, as a result of using the Ploce weapons as a lure, Leinhauser, who was the effective owner of a 298-ton coaster called the *Claudia*, was now 'on the radar' so far as people linked to the IRA were concerned. It would appear that he had an acquaintance, an Italian arms dealer who was trying to buy arms for the IRA in the early 1970s through another dealer based in Geneva. Apparently, the latter was not reliable and the deal did not work out. The Italian, in turn, appears to have been operating at the behest of a man of German background who had links to the IRA, and who was working for Dáithí Ó Conaill. According to one account, Leinhauser entered the arms procurement circle when he was introduced by the Italian to The German.[4] According to another account, the introduction took place in May 1972.[5]

It appears that after the deal with the Geneva dealer flopped, Leinhauser was brought in to get another deal off the ground. It has been reported that Leinhauser tried to conclude a deal with Omnipol in Prague for the supply of weapons to the IRA, presenting the company with a phoney End User's Certificate (EUC) from Zaire, but that Omnipol refused to do business.[6] Perhaps the Omnipol people had their suspicions in regard to the EUC. Also, they had received much unwelcome publicity as a result of the deal some time previously with Dáithí Ó Conaill which resulted in an IRA arms consignment being seized at Schiphol Airport, and may have been wary as a result (*see* Chapter 4).

Leinhauser may have failed to conclude an arms deal for the IRA, but his contacts with the gunrunning circle had one important result – when the IRA found it needed a ship in early 1973 to bring a consignment of arms from Libya to Ireland, Leinhauser was chosen to lay on the transport. The materiel was being donated by Libyan leader Colonel Gadaffi, but it was down to the IRA to arrange the shipping. There was even a rumour that Leinhauser himself had suggested getting arms from Libya, since his own efforts at buying weaponry from Omnipol had failed. According to IRA chief Joe Cahill, the chartering of a ship to bring the weapons to Ireland was left to a German IRA volunteer.[7] This man (clearly one and the same as The German referred to above) lined up Leinhauser, whose Cyprus-registered vessel, the *Claudia*, just happened to be available. At some stage in the proceedings, Leinhauser came face-to-face with the main man himself, Dáithí Ó Conaill. So far as Divall could recall, they had a meeting in Switzerland. According to another account, the two met in Hamburg in January 1973.[8]

Tony Divall was obviously very interested indeed in getting information from Leinhauser about the Provo gunrunning plan. After Divall tipped off Donald Gurrey, his handler who had been superior to him in the old post-war days when they had both served in the MI6 station in West Berlin, Gurrey worked out how the 'sting' should proceed. Leinhauser was promised a handsome pay-off for his assistance in blocking the shipment, as was Divall. For Donald Gurrey, it would be a good follow-up to the ruining of Ó Conaill's Omnipol operation a couple of years before. The clandestine IRA operation to import arms from Libya was blown from the start.

Leinhauser was taking his life in his hands by cheating the Provos – but he was used to operating in the danger zone, and had a habit of turning up in trouble spots around the world. Like Divall, he was said to have his own connections in the intelligence world. As an arms dealer, he had been involved in a transaction to supply arms to Kurdish forces in Iraq during trouble in that region back in the 1960s. He had been convicted in 1967 of attempting to smuggle arms from Czechoslovakia to the rebels, having been apprehended on the French-German border with a consignment of pistols and revolvers of US, German, Italian and Yugoslav origin. He got a nine-month suspended sentence and was fined 5,000 DMs, equivalent at that time to about £730 sterling. He was to claim later in comments to the media that he got involved in running guns to the Kurds because he supported their cause, while his deal with the IRA was just 'business'.

It is known that Leinhauser visited Beirut in the mid-1970s, where civil war was raging, to check out the arms dealing possibilities there. There were reports that he visited the turbulent arms-dealing town of Darra in Pakistan's tribal area in the 1980s during the insurrection in neighbouring Afghanistan against the Russian occupation – presumably with the aim, once again, of checking out the business possibilities. Also during the 1980s, he had business links with an Iranian wheeler-dealer immersed in the Iran–Contra affair – the *cause celebre* that involved senior US officials covertly supplying arms to Iran. It emerged that towards the end of 1985, Leinhauser represented the Iranian in a deal for the delivery from China to Iran of 1,000 12.7mm machine guns and twenty-five million cartridges.

Divall told me that in the early 1990s Leinhauser also turned up in the former Yugoslavia after that country began to disintegrate. According to Divall, Leinhauser visited the Slovenian capital Ljubliana, and also the Croatian capital Zagreb, to discuss possible weapons deals. In fact, as is indicated below in this chapter, he was later to come under scrutiny for suspected involvement in breaking a UN arms embargo on the former Yugoslavia. But one of his most remarkable exploits must be his involvement in the *Claudia* operation, which came about after Libya's Colonel Gadaffi decided to donate a sizeable consignment of weapons to the IRA.

Gadaffi had decided to help the IRA after being impressed by the performance of the senior Provo figure Joe Cahill at an extraordinary press conference in Belfast held in the wake of the internment swoops of 9 August 1971, when more than 300 republican suspects were arrested (or 'lifted' in Belfast parlance) in early-morning raids. Cahill had succeeded Billy McKee, who was among those 'lifted', as Officer Commanding (OC) of the IRA's Belfast Brigade.

Even though Cahill was high on the wanted list, he managed to appear at the press conference, held at St Peter's School in the Whiterock Road area of nationalist West Belfast, on 13 August. The area was heavily patrolled by British troops and nobody in the media knew that Cahill was going to be at the press conference, which had been called by Stormont MP Paddy Kennedy and members of the local Citizens' Defence Committee. The conference followed several days and nights of rioting and fighting sparked off by the internment swoops.

I was one of the reporters who attended the event, travelling to the venue by taxi with a colleague from the *Irish Independent*, Máirtín Mac Cormaic. At the event itself, I recall seeing a small, unidentified, bespectacled man with a cap pulled down over his head, sitting silently at the table with the main speakers. These included John Kelly, the Belfast republican who was acquitted in the Arms Trial.

In reply to a question from one of the reporters, Paddy Kennedy, of the now-defunct Republican Labour Party, said he could not answer the question himself but perhaps the OC of the Belfast Brigade of the IRA could answer it, pointing to Cahill, who was sitting beside him. One could feel the ripple of excitement run through the international press corps – nobody had realised the little man with the cap and the dark-rimmed spectacles was a paramilitary, let alone a senior IRA figure. Cahill, who looked tired and unshaven, addressed the press conference, but was not identified by name during the event. He said the losses suffered by the IRA were very slight. The IRA had lost thirty men who were arrested, with two being killed and eight wounded. 'We had advance notice of the round-up,' he said. As a result, people were not sleeping in their own beds. 'They did not get near the leaders at all.' He said they would 'have to go deeper underground'. I also recall Cahill admitting that his men were 'running out of ammunition'.

As Cahill's comments were being eagerly recorded by the television crews, some of the older reporters recognised him, now that they were taking a closer look at him. As the press conference came to a close, I remember that the name of Joe Cahill spread like wildfire among the journalists. Within a short time, Cahill was to be a household name. Back in the 1940s, he had been one of a number of IRA men sentenced to death for the murder of a policeman. One IRA man, Tom Williams, was hanged, while Cahill and the others were reprieved.

The fact that Cahill was able to appear before the world's press in spite of the internment swoops was a huge morale booster for the IRA. With the help of scouts keeping watch around the school, Cahill slipped away quietly when the press conference was brought abruptly to a close for security reasons. A British journalist, who had left the conference early to phone a story through to his newspaper, was seen talking to a nearby military patrol.

Cahill has described how, some time after the press conference, a Libyan emissary made contact through the late Yann Goulet, a Breton nationalist and sculptor living in Ireland.[9] It was to be the beginning of the IRA's involvement with Libya. A Libyan emissary later arrived in Ireland to talk with the Provisionals. The relationship was to continue into the mid-1980s, when the IRA received the biggest consignments of arms in its history, courtesy of the Libyan strongman. Cahill and other members of the IRA visited Tripoli, and Cahill had personal meetings with Gadaffi.

The first concrete example of Gadaffi's largesse came in 1972, when a consignment of RPG-7 rocket launchers was sent to Ireland. The IRA hired two Canadian mercenaries to fly the consignment in a small plane to Ireland – the intended destination was Farranfore, a local airport in County Kerry. Weather conditions forced the pilot to make instead for the much larger facility, Shannon Airport, a short flying time away. The weapons were smuggled out of the airport. There were rumours in media circles at the time that arms had been transported covertly through Shannon, but nothing could be confirmed. The two mercenaries set off for Canada in the small aircraft but word came through that the plane went down in the Atlantic and that the two men were lost.[10] Belfast journalist Brendan Anderson, who wrote Cahill's authorised biography, recalled that Cahill told him an intriguing detail about the two mercenaries – they were Jewish. This made their trip to Libya all the more remarkable, given the anti-Israel and anti-Zionist policies being pursued at that time by Colonel Gadaffi.

The arrival of the RPG-7 rocket launchers allowed the IRA to step up their attacks on the security forces in the North. The Soviet-designed weapon, which consists of a tube-style launcher that fires a grenade with large knife-like fins, was the standard man-portable short-range anti-tank weapon of the former Warsaw Pact countries, and was widely distributed in the developing world. Of course the weapon could also be used against targets other than tanks. By the end of 1972, IRA members were using the RPG-7 with lethal effect in the North. One of the tragic early victims of an RPG-7 attack by the IRA was Eva Martin, a part-time member of the Ulster Defence Regiment (UDR). Ms Martin (twenty-eight) was killed in an IRA assault on a UDR base in Clogher, County Tyrone in May 1974. One of the IRA men who took part in this operation was Sean O'Callaghan, later to become an informant for the authorities.[11]

Gadaffi agreed to supply a wider range of weaponry required by the IRA, and arrangements were set in train in 1973 to ship the arms to Ireland. Final arrangements for the deployment of the *Claudia* were made early in March in Tunis. Those involved stayed at the Hotel Africa (also known as the Hotel Afrique). It is believed that they included Leinhauser, Ó Conaill and The German. The *Claudia* docked at Tunis on 12 March and the German skipper, Hans Ludwig Fleugel, was instructed by Leinhauser to proceed to Tripoli to pick up the arms. Joe Cahill was also reportedly at the Hotel Africa at this period, but the account he gives of his itinerary in his biography makes no mention of a trip to Tunis.

Presumably, Leinhauser would have had an opportunity in Tunis to deploy on board the *Claudia* the direction-finding bug given to him by British intelligence to facilitate the tracking of the ship's movements. Perhaps for fear of the Provos finding out, he failed to do so (*see* Prologue). In an interview, Leinhauser said he travelled to Libya 'and arranged things with the IRA men', but was not present when the ship was being loaded.[12] It is thought that Leinhauser sailed on the *Claudia* to Tripoli, rather than travelling by air as the members of the IRA group did. When the *Claudia* arrived off Tripoli, it was guided by a pilot into the harbour area.

Dáithí Ó Conaill, travelling on a false passport, flew from Tunis to Rome and from there to Tripoli. It is believed that The German also travelled from Tunis to Tripoli. Joe Cahill and two other republicans, Sean Garvey and Denis McInerney, also arrived in Tripoli by air from Rome. Members of the Irish party were brought to meet Colonel Gadaffi in a military barracks, and Cahill presented the list of arms required by the Provisionals.[13]

According to Cahill's account in his biography, he was to learn some years later why the Libyans loaded a smaller quantity of arms than the IRA had expected. When it emerged that it was the *Claudia* that was to transfer the weapons, the Libyans began to have their doubts – the vessel had a notorious international reputation for being involved in smuggling. According to another source, Leinhauser had a small fleet of vessels trading in cigarettes in the Mediterranean and the Black Sea region, and the *Claudia* was just one of them. Because of their doubts, the Libyans loaded five tonnes of weaponry on board the *Claudia* in Tripoli harbour – only one eighth of what had been expected by the IRA, according to Cahill.[14] Prior to loading, the *Claudia* was guided by a Libyan naval patrol boat to an isolated quayside in the port of Tripoli. The cases of arms were loaded during the hours of darkness by about ten uniformed members of the Libyan armed services, supervised by two officers, in the light of the headlamps of three Libyan Army lorries. Cahill and at least one of his travelling companions oversaw the loading of the ship, as did the skipper, Fleugel.

The *Claudia*, with Cahill and other republicans on board, set sail for Ireland under the hot north African afternoon sun. They were escorted out of the harbour by Libyan naval vessels. There were reports that Daithí Ó Conaill was also on board the ship. However, Cahill in his biography does not mention him as having sailed on the *Claudia*. During research for this book a friend of Ó Conaill's assured me that the IRA man was not on the ship for the voyage to Ireland. According to this source, Ó Conaill spent some of the period of the *Claudia* voyage to Ireland at a house in Coolock on the north side of Dublin, a couple of miles from the Ó Conaill family home in Raheny, and the rest of the time at a house on the south side, in the Rathfarnham area. Apart from the skipper, it has been reported that the crew included a Yugoslav, a Belgian and a German cook. There was also apparently an Italian crew member, but some trouble arose with him, and he left the ship, using a small boat with an outboard engine to go ashore during the voyage.

Despite the setback caused by Leinhauser's failure to activate an MI6 direction-finding device on board the *Claudia*, the British managed to keep very close tabs on the movements of the ship, after it had been detected off Gibraltar. It can be presumed that the Royal Navy submarine that tailed the *Claudia* to Ireland kept the British authorities informed as to the vessel's every move. Meanwhile, MI6 informed their masters in the Foreign Office of what was afoot. The information was relayed by the British to the Irish government at the highest level. The British ambassador in Dublin at the time, Sir Arthur Galsworthy, went to see the taoiseach, Liam Cosgrave, who in turn informed defence minister Paddy Donegan. Senior Gardaí were alerted. A major security operation was put in place to grab the ship, the arms cargo and those on board.

As the *Claudia* came close to Helvick Head on the County Waterford coast towards the end of March, the skipper spotted the periscope of a submarine. He also spotted a number of objects on his radar – probably Irish naval vessels lying in wait. According to an interview given by Fleugel, he decided to turn around and lie off about fifteen miles from the Irish coast.[15] It appears that the original plan was to offload the arms onto a smaller boat that would land the arms at Muggles Bay, but that the weather proved too rough to transfer the cargo on the high seas. In the meantime, the Irish Navy and RAF surveillance aircraft from St Mawgan in Cornwall were observing the *Claudia*.[16]

At night, the *Claudia* crept shorewards as weather improved, and about 9pm a boat came out to the ship and a number of men went on board. According to the skipper Fleugel, one of the IRA men who had travelled from Tripoli fetched a briefcase from his cabin and went ashore with the men on the boat. (If the story is correct, then this IRA man evaded capture. It has been suggested that this was Dáithí Ó Conaill. However, as indicated above, a friend of Ó Conaill's insisted he was not on board.) Once again, the skipper spotted objects on his radar, and was instructed by an IRA man on board (probably Joe Cahill) to move further offshore again.

A launch approached the *Claudia* and went alongside the ship; one of the IRA men, Denis McInerney, embarked on the boat to go ashore and arrange for the reception of the arms. Meanwhile, the skipper was ordered to move closer to the shore, perhaps having received reassurance from the men on the launch that there was no sign of activity by the security forces. However, as the skipper steered the ship closer into Dungarvan Bay, he noticed three or four objects on his radar and concluded, correctly, that they were ships of the Irish Navy. The small boat heading towards shore was intercepted by the navy. McInerney and local men on board were detained. The *Claudia* itself was boarded by Irish naval personnel. The boarding party was led by Sub-Lieutenant Brian Farrell of the naval vessel *Deirdre*, armed with a Browning automatic pistol. Also taking part in the operation were the Irish naval vessels *Fola* and *Gráinne*.

According to evidence that would later emerge in court, the *Claudia*, identified by the codeword Dandoline, had been marked on an Irish naval chart about thirty miles off the Irish coast, on the basis of information supplied by a person 'who was not a member of the Irish Naval Service'. It was thought the information was relayed from an RAF Nimrod aircraft which reportedly alerted the Irish Navy as the *Claudia* approached Irish territorial waters.[17] During the court hearing the question of co-operation between a Royal Navy submarine and the Irish authorities was also raised by Joe Cahill. The court heard that the *Deirdre* established radar contact with the *Claudia* on 27 March, the day before the ship was seized.

After Cahill and his Irish friends had been taken into custody, the *Claudia* was escorted to Haulbowline naval base in Cork harbour, where soldiers from the local Collins Barracks unloaded the cargo. Army ordnance experts examined the weaponry and drew up an inventory, as well as listing serial numbers of the weapons. Photographs (black & white) were taken of the captured equipment – they are still preserved in the Military Archives. As soon as the unloading was completed, the skipper and crew were allowed to sail away on the *Claudia*, about twelve hours after they had first been arrested.

Questions were raised in the Dáil by the Opposition as to why the ship was allowed to depart. Taoiseach Liam Cosgrave replied: 'The decision to let the MV *Claudia* resume her voyage was taken by me. I had considered the facts reported to me as well as confidential reports which it would not be in the public interest for me to disclose.' One can only speculate as to the nature of the 'confidential reports' – presumably Cosgrave had been informed of the 'sting' operation that had taken place. No doubt, as part of his arrangement with MI6, Leinhauser would have sought and been given a guarantee that his ship, called after his daughter Claudia, would not be impounded, and that the captain and crew would not face charges, but would be allowed to continue on their way.

The *Claudia* docked in the port of Hamburg on Monday, 2 April, at 6.40pm, and an anxious Leinhauser went on board. Both he and his vessel became the focus of unwelcome attention from the German authorities and also from the dreaded media. In unusually frank comments to reporters, Leinhauser, a small, bespectacled man aged about forty, said the IRA had approached him to do the delivery, and the plan was that the ship would deliver the arms to the IRA outside of Irish territorial waters, and the IRA would then take them ashore. Payment was on the basis of fifty percent in advance and the balance after delivery. Leinhauser believed that 100 tonnes of arms had been loaded, and that ninety-five tonnes of arms must have been jettisoned. However, the skipper of the vessel told reporters that no cargo had been thrown overboard. Leinhauser was never to face charges in connection with the *Claudia* affair, although German police did search his home in the Saarbrücken area.

It emerged that the *Claudia* was owned by a Cyprus-based company called Giromar, of which Leinhauser was managing director. His wife Marlene held ninety percent of the shares, the remainder being held by a businessman based at that time in Frankfurt. This man told the media he had no idea the ship was engaged in a gunrunning operation – he had been informed the *Claudia* was undergoing repairs in Tunis.

Shortly after the capture of the *Claudia*, Irish military intelligence drew up a memo giving details of the two individuals considered to have been the prime movers behind the effort to import arms – Daithí Ó Conaill (referred to in the memo as Daithí O'Connell) and the man referred to above as The German. According to the document, dated 29 March 1973, which was declassified in recent years, Ó Conaill was seen in Rome and Tunis in early March and visited Tripoli at least twice. The memo states that Ó Conaill used a passport in a false name, Kenneth Browne, that was issued in Dublin in October 1970. The German was using a passport issued in Dublin on 9 February 1972. The memo stated that Ó Conaill and The German were in Tunis on 6 March, and stayed in the Hotel Africa for two days. Then they travelled from Tunis to Tripoli.

In the wake of the *Claudia* capture, Irish military intelligence produced an analysis of the gunrunning operation for the chief of staff of the Defence Forces. In a document dated April 1973, the intelligence section, designated G2, found that the organisers of the operation were 'rash and unsubtle' on a number of counts. The document pointed out that it was rash to send a well-known person – a reference to Joe Cahill – on the mission in the first place; 'a person who had no particular talents in this field'.

G2 also found it was rash to bring a ship into territorial waters, 'when they could have offloaded out to sea, out of sight of possible observers on shore'. The memo found that the IRA had also neglected security surveillance in the hinterland, 'which could have detected Army and Garda movements in the Dungarvan area ...' The G2 analysis found that the organisers failed to react to information available to them when a submarine was spotted close to the *Claudia* off the Irish coast, and when the captain informed the IRA that he had picked up three ships on his radar. 'They should have been sufficiently suspicious to remain outside territorial waters.'

On the other hand, the analysis found that the IRA had been 'very discreet with their preparations for reception of the cargo' and had been careful not to use any well-known IRA personalities from the local area.

Some of the items seized were accompanied by documents containing technical detail in Russian cyrillic script – they are still preserved in the Military Archives at Cathal Brugha Barracks in Dublin. Military intelligence arranged for them to be translated soon after they were seized. One document related to a quantity of TM 46 anti-tank mines, recording that they had been manufactured in 1957. Much of the equipment seized, such as AKM rifles, was of Soviet design.

There are indications in the archives that information was requested from the US authorities in relation to the US-manufactured equipment found on board – eg. Smith & Wesson revolvers. The cargo did not include surface-to-air missiles, even though Libya would probably have been in a position to supply short-range Soviet-designed SAM-7 missiles. It appears that in the early phase of the Troubles, in the early 1970s, the IRA did not regard surface-to-air missiles as a priority. That was to change in the 1980s, as the Provisionals increasingly felt the need to acquire the means to shoot down British Army helicopters. Another omission from the *Claudia* cargo was the RPG-7 rocket launcher. As already indicated, this had been supplied in 1972, and was later to feature in arms supplied by Libya in the mid-1980s.

Suspects sentenced to death by the IRA

At the Special Criminal Court in Dublin in May 1973, Joe Cahill got three years for his role in the gunrunning operation, while his two travelling companions, Denis McInerney from County Clare and Sean Garvey from County Kerry, each got two years. Donal Whelan and Gerard Murphy, both from County Waterford, who had gone in a small boat to rendezvous with the *Claudia*, were each given suspended sentences of two years. Cahill told the court his only crime was in not 'getting the contents of the *Claudia* into the hands of the freedom fighters in this country'.

The court hearing was told that the authorities had recovered five tonnes of arms. It emerged that the arms cargo included 247 AKM rifles, 246 bayonets and scabbards, 243 revolvers (mostly Smith & Wesson and Webley), close on 100 anti-tank mines, 24,000 rounds of ammunition, 850 magazines and 500 grenades, as well as 300kgs of gelignite and 48lbs of high explosive.[18]

Donal Whelan, a native of Abbeyside, Dungarvan, had a high profile as a GAA star. Nicknamed 'Duck', he was on the Waterford team that won the All-Ireland hurling final in 1959, having defeated Kilkenny in a replay. He remained a highly influential figure in the GAA, and represented Waterford on the GAA Central Council. He was the headmaster of St Declan's Community College, Kilmacthomas, and passed away in 1995. There was a strong republican tradition in his family. His father, Pax Whelan, was an officer with the 3rd Battalion, West Waterford Brigade of the IRA during the War of Independence, and later took the republican side in the Civil War. Pax Whelan was also said to have been involved in moves to import arms 'for the cause', this time from Germany, during the early years of the Civil War.

The other defendant who got a suspended sentence, Gerard Murphy, was sacked from his job as an engineer with Waterford County Council after the court hearing. The Department of Local Government had written to the council notifying the authority of the 'forfeiture' by Mr Murphy of his position, under the terms of the Offences Against the State Act. Mr Murphy found other employment and in 1993 brought a case against the State for damages for alleged breach of constitutional rights. In 1996 the High Court found against him, deciding that he was not entitled to damages.

For a period, there were lingering suspicions that the Irish security forces had failed to get all the arms cargo from Libya, and that some of the consignment may have been off-loaded before the *Claudia* reached Helvick Head, or dumped at sea. It was thought unlikely that the Libyans would have supplied only five tonnes of arms, when the vessel would have been able to accommodate a much bigger consignment. There was speculation that the *Claudia* may, in effect, have been part of a decoy operation, that about ninety-five tonnes of arms had been unloaded onto other vessels and smuggled into Ireland at various points, while the security forces concentrated on grabbing the *Claudia* with just a small quantity of arms on board.

This theory is not supported by Joe Cahill's account of the arms consignment being reduced by the Libyans. It is interesting that the British were expecting the *Claudia* to have a much bigger quantity of armaments on board, indicating that they had good intelligence about what the Libyans were originally expected to supply to the Provos. British State papers released in early 2004 indicated that in 1973 the British ambassador, Sir Arthur Galsworthy, had informed Taoiseach Liam Cosgrave that the *Claudia* might be carrying up to 100 tonnes of war materiel. Sir John, reporting on a meeting with the then Irish defence minister, Mr Donegan, said: '[What] interested me was the obviously genuine surprise when I mentioned that my original report to the Taoiseach had spoken of the possibility that the *Claudia* might be carrying up to 100 tonnes of arms. He [Mr Donegan] explained that the Taoiseach had given him only verbal instructions, and had not mentioned the figure of 100 tonnes, only that *Claudia* was believed to be carrying arms.'[19] It also emerged in the State papers that the Cosgrave government arranged for samples of the arms seized to be handed over by the Irish Army to the British military attaché, for transfer to British military HQ in Lisburn, Northern Ireland.

The uncovering of the operation made the IRA deeply suspicious. How had the Irish authorities been lying in wait for the *Claudia*? How could the Irish Navy and the Gardaí have had such good intelligence on the movements of the gunrunning ship? Following the seizure of the *Claudia*, Seamus Twomey, the hardline IRA chief of staff at the time, stated that he was in no doubt but that his organisation had been double-crossed. Twomey was convinced he knew who to blame. He and two other senior Provisionals, Kevin Mallon and JB O'Hagan, had staged a daring escape by helicopter from Dublin's Mountjoy Prison in October 1973. Less than a month later, Twomey surfaced in the city to give an interview to a journalist from the West German magazine, *Der Spiegel*. Twomey declared that death sentences had been passed on two people arising out of the 'betrayal' of the arms cargo. They were Gunther Leinhauser and 'a second person involved'. Twomey, who was himself to die peacefully in a hospital bed in Dublin in 1989, went on: 'We shall carry out the sentence at a time and place of our choice.' Leinhauser denied to reporters at the time that the IRA had been double-crossed. He was, of course, being economical with the truth. Twomey had accurately identified him as one of the culprits. There is no evidence that the organisation made any attempt to kill Leinhauser or the other person who, according to Twomey, had been marked down for death. This person has never been identified.

In search of Exocets

Following the *Claudia* operation, Gunther Leinhauser apparently moved, for a period, from his home in the German state of Saarland to Paris. His wife Marlene continued to run a small stationery and toy shop in St Ingbert, near Saarbrücken, the main city in Saarland. Leinhauser had a small office behind the shop. It was from this office, later to be equipped with a fax machine, that he conducted some of his rather mysterious business affairs. For 'sensitive' calls, he would use a public phone near the shop. Perhaps Leinhauser figured that, in view of the IRA threat, it was safer to go to ground in the French capital, at least for a while.

According to one account, he had good connections to the French security service, the Direction de la Surveillance du Territoire (DST), which provided him with a rent-free apartment in Paris. He was also said to have connections with the French external intelligence organisation, Direction Generale de la Securité Exterieure (DGSE), with Colonel Massimo Pugliese, head of the Italian security service, SID, and with the Italian intelligence service, SISMI.[20]

Divall continued with his rather mysterious activities. Probably the most remarkable operation of Divall's varied career took place in 1982. It had to do with the Falklands War and directly involved his old employers MI6, who found they had a need for Divall's 'unofficial' services. Having scored a success against the IRA in the *Claudia* operation, Divall's controllers were apparently hoping that he would score a similar success against the Argentinians who had invaded the British-controlled Falklands. According to Divall, he was summoned to London in May 1982, at the height of the Falklands conflict, for a meeting with his MI6 case officer, whom he identified only by the pseudonym Tommy Balham. Argentina had used its French-made Exocet missiles to lethal effect on ships of the British task force. The Argentines were running out of Exocets and were seeking ways of beating various embargoes to buy more. The British, badly shaken by the effectiveness of the Exocets used against them, were determined that the Argentines would not get fresh supplies anywhere. And this is where Divall came in. MI6 wanted him, or an associate, to pose as an underworld arms dealer who would offer to sell the Argentines the Exocets they required, thus diverting them from black market dealers who might, in fact, be able to provide the missiles.

Divall lined up his old friend from the *Claudia* operation, Gunther Leinhauser, to assist in the Falklands 'sting'. One of Leinhauser's roles was to scour the international arms market for Exocets that could be used as part of a 'coat-trailing' exercise. This was reminiscent of Divall's account of how he had used Leinhauser in the early 1970s to lure the IRA by using an arms cache in Ploce, Yugoslavia. Leinhauser had by now acquired a new cargo ship, registered this time in Panama. Owning your own ship was a useful asset for any gunrunner.

The man chosen by Divall to actually approach the Argentines was John Dutcher, who also had a colourful background, and who was partly of Irish descent. Dutcher, who had fought in Vietnam with the elite Green Berets, was a martial arts expert who used to run a karate school in Washington. At one stage he worked in Libya for Ed Wilson, a former CIA man who had developed close links with the Gadaffi regime, and who was later to be jailed in America for smuggling arms and explosives to Libya.

Dutcher phoned the Argentine Military Sub-Commission in Paris and made contact with a senior official there. They arranged to meet. Dutcher received details of the Argentines' military shopping list, which was in itself of interest to British intelligence. The most important item on the list was, of course, the Exocet. Dutcher and Divall found an Italian company which claimed to have thirty Exocets available – and backed up its claim by providing serial numbers. It transpired that the Italian company was acting for a Swiss arms dealer who demanded proof that Dutcher had the funds to buy the missiles. In order to keep the 'sting' in operation, MI6 arranged for the transfer of £16 million from Williams and Glyn's Bank in London to Divall's bank in Hamburg. The Hamburg bank then telexed the Swiss dealer's bank in Lugano, to say the money had arrived and was available. Divall and Dutcher planned to buy the thirty missiles from the Swiss arms dealer at $1 million each; to sell them to the Argentines for a higher price; and to divert the Exocets to the UK while returning the $30 million dollars to the British – and keep the profits themselves.

Ultimately the Swiss arms dealer got cold feet and the Exocets, said to have been stored at a location in France, were never delivered. But by then the Falklands War was over and, according to Divall, the Argentines, by concentrating on his bogus offer, lost the chance to get fresh supplies of the lethal missile. Dutcher, incidentally, seemed to disappear without trace. Divall believed he was killed during some adventure in Africa.

Divall was later to come under the scrutiny of the German authorities for his role in the Exocet affair. It happened almost by chance, due to a hitch that had arisen in another operation. Divall had taken on the task of arranging to fly a consignment of arms from East Berlin to Seoul. The job was on behalf of a British-based arms concern and when an American lawyer later became involved it emerged that the ten-ton arms shipment, which included SAM-7 missiles, was being financed by the CIA and ultimately destined for the Afghan rebels. This was in the early stages of the Afghan conflict, when the CIA was supplying 'untraceable' Eastern Bloc weaponry to the insurgents fighting Soviet occupation forces.

The Caravelle aircraft transporting the cargo developed engine trouble and had to land at Saloniki, Greece. Following a mysterious telephone tip-off from New York, the Greek authorities began investigating the arms shipment, and found discrepancies in the paperwork. The Greek police asked Interpol to assist and as a result the West German Federal Office of Criminal Investigation (BKA) raided the Frankfurt offices of Divall's German aviator colleague. There they found telexes relating to the Exocet deal, for the German was to have transported the Exocets had the need arisen.

Following the discovery of the telexes, BKA officers swooped on Divall's penthouse apartment in Hamburg. MI6 arranged for Divall and his German-born wife Sigrid to come to London where they stayed for a month at the Waldorf, all expenses paid. Ultimately, the British authorities managed to sort out the matter with the BKA and also with the Hamburg police, who had also begun taking an interest. (With the benefit of hindsight, Divall later came to the conclusion that the British may have been seeking to protect not so much himself as a respected member of the British establishment who had a link with the procuring of the arms from East Germany – Lord Winterbottom, who had served in Labour governments in the 1960s and who had later gone over to the Tories. Lord Winterbottom died in July 1992 and, oddly, none of the obituaries that I read mention his involvement in the arms trade.)

By 1987 certain individuals in MI6 were apparently beginning to tire of the hassle with the German authorities over the Divall affair. The service had made very good use indeed of Divall's unusual talents and connections. But the Falklands War was now over and MI6 seems to have taken the cynical view that Divall had outlived his usefulness, at least so far as Argentina was concerned. His old pal Donald Gurrey, who had overseen the *Claudia* 'sting', was no longer his handler. Gurrey had retired from MI6 in the 1970s.[21] He and Divall exchanged Christmas cards for many years. But the good old days when they worked as a team were gone forever.

Divall now had a case officer who was not very sympathetic towards him. In December 1987, this officer paid a visit to Divall in Hamburg, gave him an envelope containing £2,500 and informed him coldly that the Firm was cutting him off for good. Divall was very bitter. In his view, after his long years of loyalty to MI6 and the risks he had taken, he had been cut off without a pension, without proper compensation for his services, without even being reimbursed his expenses.

There was a report that Divall was planning to sue the British government for more than £200,000 on the basis that he had not been reimbursed for money spent running his spy operations around the world. Divall told me later, however, that he had no intention of suing. He considered it would be a very expensive undertaking and that the chances of winning would be very slight. 'Nobody in their right minds, unless their fortune is counted in multiples of millions, would attempt it,' he said.

Ironically, it was the media coverage which resulted from Divall's decision to go public about his differences with MI6 over the Falklands operation, that focused attention once more on his involvement in the *Claudia* episode. It was in 1988 that he began talking on-the-record to journalists. The *Claudia* affair figured in a couple of the stories that were generated at this period. One newspaper reported that Divall planted a direction-finding bug on the *Claudia* after convincing the IRA of his credentials as a gunrunner, and that the bug enabled the British authorities to monitor the vessel's movements. I was interested to read about the *Claudia* connection and, some time later, I made my first contact with Divall, after getting a phone number for him in Hamburg.

Even though he was now a whistleblower, he appeared wary about getting a call from an Irish journalist whom he had never met before. He was willing to talk about some aspects of his career – with the exception of the *Claudia* operation. When I asked Divall about the story that he had planted a direction finding bug on the ship, he said the report was 'exaggerated'. He refused, at that particular time, to elaborate on the exact nature of his role in the affair. All he would do was to make the rather mysterious comment that he was the only person who had the full story of exactly what happened. He preferred to leave it at that, and to maintain his silence on the matter. In the summer of 1992, a French independent television company tried to persuade Divall to talk about the *Claudia* affair, but without success.

Divall was a useful source on gunrunning around the world – a topic I was researching at the time for a book. He had an encyclopaedic knowledge of the subject and of the characters involved. Although unprepared to discuss the *Claudia* affair, he was ready to talk about other adventures and to share some of his insights. During interviews with him, one of the factors that struck me was how he was close to a number of the shadowy individuals who figured, or were alleged to have figured, in a number of the covert arms procurement operations to do with the Irish Troubles in the early 1970s. He had done business with Otto Schlüter, the arms dealer involved in the affair that led to the Arms Trial. He was close to Ernest Koenig, who arranged air transport for the arms bought by Dáithí Ó Conaill from Omnipol. He was close also to George Strakaty, the arms dealing figure who was alleged by one author to have been involved in blowing the

Left: Garda Richard Fallon and wife Deirdre. Garda Fallon, who was unarmed, was shot dead in 1970 in Dublin when he confronted a gang of bank robbers from the Saor Éire group. *Photo: courtesy of Finian Fallon.*

Above: Finian Fallon, who has been seeking answers to questions about the murder of his father, Garda Richard Fallon.
Photo: Sean Boyne.

Left: John Kelly, one of the defendants cleared in the Arms Trial, pictured at his home in Maghera, County Derry, in January 2005. *Photo: Sean Boyne.*

Right: US gunshops have long been a source of weaponry for the IRA. These handguns, on sale in a California dealership, are Mauser 'Peter the Painter' weapons, of a type used by the Old IRA in the War of Independence of the 1920s. *Photo: Sean Boyne.*

Left: Charles Haughey, who was acquitted of gunrunning charges in the Arms Trial of 1970, went on to serve three terms as Taoiseach. *Photo: Colman Doyle.*

Right: A victim of Dublin bombing, 1974. The attack by loyalist paramilitaries was one of the worst atrocities of the Troubles. *Photo: Colman Doyle.*

Above: These IRA men in action near Crossmaglen, County Armagh, appear to be armed with a Sten gun and an Armalite rifle. *Photo: Colman Doyle.*

A female member of the IRA with a handgun, June 1975.
Photo: Brendan Murphy.

Above left: George Harrison, the IRA's leading gunrunner in the US during the 1970s, pictured at his apartment in Brooklyn, New York, in September 2004. This is one of the last pictures ever taken of him – he died three weeks later. *Photo: Sean Boyne.*

Above right: Liam Cotter, a member of George Harrison's IRA gunrunning network in New York. Born in County Kerry, Cotter worked as a security guard and was shot dead in New York in 1976 while trying to foil a robbery. *Photo: courtesy of George Harrison.*

Below left: Members of the Fort Worth Five group pictured at a function in the Irish-American Centre, Mineola, New York, in 1989. *Left to Right*: Tom Laffey, Ken Tierney and Mattie Reilly. *Photo: courtesy of Ken Tierney.*

Below right: Frank Durkan, of the law firm O'Dywer and Bernstien, who represented Irish defendants in gunrunning cases in the US, pictured at his office in New York, September 2004. *Photo: Sean Boyne.*

Above: IRA men armed with weapons of types used in the earlier stages of the Troubles – M1 carbines, a Thompson sub-machine gun and a Stirling sub-machine gun. *Photo: Colman Doyle.*

Right: Despite becoming a whistleblower, Tony Divall, a former member of the British intelligence service MI6, remained camera-shy. When the author met him in Hamburg, he would only consent to a photo that did not show his face.

Below left: Former IRA gunrunner and republican activist Gerry McGeough, pictured in Dublin, 2005.

Below right: Louis Stephens, former head of the FBI's PIRA Squad agreed to be interviewed for this book while in hospital in New Jersey, September 2004. *Photos: Sean Boyne.*

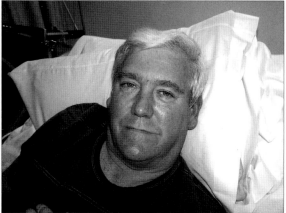

Joe Cahill, the leading IRA man arrested by the Irish authorities on board the *Claudia*, off the County Waterford coast in 1973, while trying to land a cargo of Libyan-supplied arms. *Photo: Colman Doyle.*

Above: A female IRA member aims her AR-18 Armalite rifle on a west Belfast street corner during the Troubles. *Photo: Colman Doyle.*

Below: An IRA man takes aim with an RPG-7 rocket launcher. Another man (*left*) has a grenade for reloading; the third IRA man keeps watch with an Armalite rifle. *Photo: Colman Doyle.*

IRA men loading an RPG-7 rocket launcher. *Photo: Colman Doyle.*

gaffe on the IRA/Omnipol operation; and of course he was a long-standing friend of Gunther Leinhauser, effective owner of the *Claudia*, the vessel at the centre of the Libyan arms drama. With contacts such as these, it is easy to see why British intelligence would have kept him on a retainer after he left the full-time service of MI6. Incidentally, all the arms procurement operations outlined above had a couple of factors in common – they all involved professional arms dealers or gunrunners with a background in covert activity; and they all ended in failure.

Meeting a former spook

After some phone conversations with Tony Divall, I finally met the ex-spy in Hamburg in the early 1990s. Divall told me in advance how I would recognise him – he would be carrying a copy of the *Financial Times*. It wasn't difficult to make him out as he came to meet me on the terrace of the Europaischer Hotel, just opposite the main railway station in Hamburg, with a copy of the relevant newspaper under his arm. Although aged seventy at the time, he looked a lot younger. A fit, dapper figure, he strode along purposefully, reminding me a little of the veteran television presenter of former years, Alan Whicker. At the same time, Divall, on the surface, was an unlikely James Bond character – despite his background as a Royal Marines officer, secret service agent and gunrunner. In appearance he could have passed for a retired accountant or a former bank manager. But then again, it is said that the best intelligence agents never look like spies.

My mind went back to my initial impression of him during our first phone conversation – he came across like one of those much-travelled old Fleet Street correspondents that one sometimes meets in foreign hotel bars – cynical, laconic, worldly wise, and convinced that modern civilisation is going swiftly downhill. I suppose that remained largely my impression after we met, although it was supplemented by a very healthy regard for Divall's exceptional knowledge of the 'grey' arms world and those who figure in it, as well as the world of intelligence.

It emerged that the author Frederick Forsyth, in his bestseller *The Dogs of War*, had based the character of freelance gunrunner Alan Baker on the former MI6 man. Divall and Forsyth knew each other. They had both been in Biafra during the civil war – Divall as a gunrunner and

Forsyth as a journalist. In writing his thriller, Forsyth had drawn heavily on his experiences of mercenaries during the conflict. Forsyth had, in fact, travelled to Hamburg to consult Divall on various details so that his fiction would have that sense of authenticity that is one of his trademarks as a bestselling writer.

Divall was at pains to reject the description that had been applied to him in the past of 'arms dealer'. He emphasised to me that he did not sell arms to people – he simply delivered them. He preferred the more accurate term 'gunrunner'. During my contacts with Divall, he talked about the highlights of his career. He told me how he had operated a small air company in Africa which provided him with the means to transport 'sensitive' cargoes from A to B. His philosophy was simple – so long as he did not have a conscientious objection to what a client was doing, he would provide the transport for whatever they wanted delivered, 'whether it was tins of corned beef or boxes of bullets'. With his air transport operation, Divall had many adventures in a range of African conflict zones, including the Congo, Biafra, Uganda and Angola.[22]

As I carried out my researches into international gunrunning, I thought it would be useful to speak to Divall's sidekick Gunther Leinhauser. I was in Paris at the time, in 1990, and I phoned Divall and asked him if he would set up an interview for me with Leinhauser. Leinhauser was still resident in the city and maintained an office there, dividing his time between the French capital and his family home near Saarbrücken in Germany. Divall said he would get Leinhauser to phone me. Divall told me that Leinhauser was checking out the possibilities of selling gas masks to the Israelis for the looming 1991 Gulf War – there were fears at the time that Iraq might fire poison gas missiles at Israel. Leinhauser had spotted a potentially lucrative business opportunity. Somehow, one was reminded of Arthur Daly, the wheeler-dealer character in the British 1980s-era television series 'Minder'. Divall explained that Leinhauser was essentially a general trader, and arms just happened to be one of the things that he dealt in: 'Leinhauser would just as easily trade in potatoes or garden furniture if he thought there was going to be a good financial return from it.'

I asked Divall if he thought that the publicity-shy Leinhauser would get in touch with me. 'He will phone you if I tell him to do so,' said Divall, underlining the close working relationship that existed between the two gunrunners. Divall said that he and Leinhauser went back so far they could never remember where it was they had first met – it might have been Beirut, but then again it might have been Morocco.

Some days later, I received a phone call from Leinhauser at the apartment in Paris where I was staying. To my dismay and indeed my surprise, this globetrotting wheeler-dealer insisted that he could not speak English. He indicated that, apart from German, he spoke only French. We would have to talk in French, and I was not very fluent in the language. The soft-spoken gunrunner told me he was still in the arms business, but did not wish to discuss work in progress. He did not really have very much else to say. Perhaps in light of the sentence of death pronounced by IRA chief Seamus Twomey, he was wary of talking to an Irish journalist. The conversation came to a close.

Subsequent events indicated that Leinhauser was telling the truth when he told me he was still in the arms business. In December 1991, an eleven-ton cargo of Chilean-supplied arms was seized at the airport in Budapest, Hungary, on suspicion of being destined for Croatian forces immersed in the Yugoslav conflict. Any such arms shipment to Croatia would have been in contravention of a UN embargo on the sale of weapons to either side in the fighting. The discovery sparked off investigations around the world. It was reported that the shipment was taken to the airport at Santiago, Chile, with a supposed destination of Sri Lanka, but that the papers were changed, redirecting the shipment to a company in Budapest belonging to Gunther Leinhauser. Some high-ranking Chilean military officers were suspected of complicity in the deal. In 2006 the affair was still stirring up controversy in Chile. However, Leinhauser is not around to clarify matters, as he died in the mid-1990s.

In a phone conversation in September 2002, I asked Divall once again about the *Claudia*. This time, he agreed to talk, and the essence of what he told me is included in this chapter. Leinhauser was dead at this stage, and perhaps Divall felt free to talk about the involvement of his late friend, and the way, according to himself, he used Leinhauser to 'sting' the IRA. Perhaps as he approached the end of his life, he figured it was safer to reveal the broad outline of the story. The question arises: To what extent can Divall be believed? After all, he had spent much of his life operating in a very murky world, sometimes involving deceit.

Another individual, the late Leslie Aspin, also claimed credit for inform-ing the authorities about the *Claudia* operation. Aspin, an English adven-turer with links to the mercenary world, claimed he was recruited by MI6 in 1970, and that his first success was to learn of the *Claudia* shipment.[23] Aspin also claimed that, on behalf of his MI6 controller, 'Homer', he set up a sting operation against the IRA in the wake of the *Claudia* affair. With the aid of an intermediary who liaised with the IRA, he arranged an arms deal between a Libyan diplomat based in Malta and the Provos. A consignment of seven tons of automatic weapons and six Soviet rocket launchers was sent by ship to Killala Bay, off the west coast of Ireland, where fishing boats were standing by to take the arms on board. According to Aspin, the 'sting' went wrong when an Irish naval vessel arrived too late to prevent most of the arms being spirited away by the fishing boats.

I am not aware of any evidence to back up these claims by Aspin, who died in 1989. Divall's claim to have 'blown' the *Claudia* shipment has credi-bility, in my view – the evidence is on his side. During research for this book, an informed source confirmed that Divall played a key role in under-mining the operation, and provided additional detail. There is also the fact that running a sting operation came naturally to the former spook, as dem-onstrated by Divall's Falklands operation.

After speaking to Divall in 2002, there were still some gaps in the story. However, I reckoned it should be possible to meet up with Divall again and tie up some loose ends. Divall was occupying his time in retirement at this period, writing a novel based on his real-life experiences. The book included a story from his days with MI6 in post-war West Berlin. He had fallen in love with a beautiful young Polish exile. Then one day she broke his heart by telling him that there was somebody else that she loved – a Russian KGB man on the 'other side'. The Soviet spook wanted to defect. Would Divall help him to 'come across' to the West? Despite his broken heart, Divall saw an opportunity. The Russian spook might be his love rival, but he could still be useful to 'the Firm'. Divall said to the young woman: 'Tell him to stay in place for a year, to feed us all the intelligence he can, and then I will bring him over.' I never found out how the story ended.

In April 2004, I was heading off to the Continent for a working holiday, during which I planned to do research for this book. I phoned Divall's home in Hamburg, to see if I could set up another interview with him.

Divall's wife Sigrid answered the phone. I asked for Divall. She sounded upset. 'Tony died last November,' she said. I was taken aback. I sympathised with her. She said he had been ill for some time. Somehow, Tony Divall, veteran of so many adventures around the world, who had survived so many close shaves, had seemed indestructible. Typical of a man who had lived much of his life in the shadows, Tony Divall had taken at least some of his secrets with him to the grave.

Frank Terpil and the Vietnam rifles

In its quest for arms, the IRA spread the net wide, if we are to believe some of the allegations that emerged in the latter part of the 1970s. It has been claimed that IRA emissaries made a discreet approach to an American arms dealer called Frank Terpil at a trade fair in Brighton, England, in the summer of 1976, to inquire about the possibility of procuring M-16 rifles.[24] It seems odd that the IRA would have sought to use international arms dealers to procure arms, in light of their previous bad experiences in the Omnipol and *Claudia* affairs. Nevertheless, an account was given by Kevin Mulcahy, a former business associate of Terpil, of contacts between the arms dealer and the IRA.

According to Mulcahy, Terpil told the Irish he was willing to do business with them. He said that huge stocks were available, explaining how the North Vietnamese had captured enormous quantities of the US-supplied assault rifles when they overran Saigon. The North Vietnamese had agreed to sell the M-16s to legendary arms dealer Sam Cummings, who had in turn agreed to sell Terpil as many as he required, Terpil claimed.

There was only one problem with the story – the part about the Vietnamese agreeing to sell the rifles to Cummings was untrue. Cummings himself told me, about twelve years after the reported contact between the Irish emissaries and Terpil, that he was indeed interested in buying the stocks from the North Vietnamese, but Hanoi had not wanted to do business. Also, there is no indication that Cummings ever met Terpil, and Cummings would never have considered doing anything illegal like selling arms, directly or indirectly, to the IRA.

It is now clear that in the mid-1970s the Garda Síochána had been concerned about the prospect of arms coming to the IRA from Vietnam.

A secret Garda report written in June 1975 for the then justice minister Patrick Cooney, and declassified in 2005, stated that the IRA had already received 'a considerable consignment of small arms' from abroad, and that a supply of similar weapons, 'emanating from Vietnam', was en route to Ireland. It is unclear if the latter arms reached the IRA. The report also claimed that the IRA had acquired considerable financial resources – $50,000 – which it planned to spend on procuring arms.[25]

Samuel Cummings was, incidentally, familiar with IRA weapons but only through his legitimate dealings with governments. In the 1950s he bought Thompson sub-machine guns from the Irish government that had been seized from the IRA – some may have dated back to the Civil War of the 1920s. Cummings sold these weapons to the Batista regime in Cuba, which was to be overthrown by the forces led by Fidel Castro.[26] Cummings was also a noted collector of weapons – in his premises in Manchester his colleague Hamilton Spence showed me an RPG-7 rocket launcher which had been seized from the IRA in Northern Ireland, part of a batch which the Provos had received from Libya. Cummings' firm Interarms obtained it for his collection in a swap with the UK Ministry of Defence.

The late Sam Cummings, who had served as a youthful weapons expert with the US Central Intelligence Agency was the biggest dealer in small arms in the world in the 1980s. The affable, globetrotting weapons merchant resided in the millionaire's playground of Monaco, and his firm had premises in the US and the UK. I met him in the late 1980s at his extraordinary private arsenal in Manchester, a ten-storey redbrick building, fortified like Fort Knox, crammed with crates of countless thousands of weapons. The IRA had procured arms stolen from military armouries in the US, but I am not aware of any attempt by paramilitaries to beat the state-of-the-art security systems that were installed at this cavernous warehouse, which housed the biggest privately-owned arsenal in Europe. Cummings, whose paternal grandfather came from Dublin, confirmed to me that he was still interested in the materiel in Vietnam. In fact he said he had talked to the US State Department about buying US equipment captured by the Vietnamese even before the US pulled out in 1975. He said he accurately foresaw that the Americans were going to lose the war and that they would soon have to withdraw from Vietnam, leaving large stocks of weaponry behind. But the Vietnamese had never agreed to sell to him.

Cummings could not understand why the Vietnamese, with their impoverished economy, did not try to cash in on the vast amounts of war booty seized from the US by selling it off on the international market. 'Why didn't the Vietnamese sell the American weaponry just after the war? Look, I talked in Paris to Le Duc Tho, a senior member of the Hanoi politburo, the year after the catastrophic collapse of South Vietnam. In effect he said, we have not made a decision on what we will do with this materiel – don't call us, we'll call you. And the phone didn't ring for all those years.' Cummings said he had recently received an indication that there was some movement. I never did find out if Cummings did any kind of a deal with the Vietnamese – I suspect he may have had second thoughts in view of the downturn in the international small arms trade that was occurring at that time.

If Mulcahy's account of what passed between Terpil and the IRA emissaries is correct, then one possible explanation is that Terpil was planning to cheat his Irish contacts, taking the money upfront and failing to supply the weapons. However, there is no indication that Terpil ever clinched an arms deal with the Provos.

The late Mulcahy eventually went to the authorities in the US, alleging that Terpil and his business partner Ed Wilson were supplying explosives and other materiel illegally to the Gadaffi regime in Libya. Wilson was jailed for fifty-two years but, in 2003, after he had served twenty years, a federal judge overturned his conviction for trafficking high explosives to Libya. Terpil went on the run and has remained a fugitive for decades – he is believed to have been residing in Cuba.

Mulcahy, Terpil and Wilson all had one thing in common – they had all worked previously for the CIA. The fact that one of Wilson's associates, John Dutcher, was also associated with Tony Divall is yet another example of the interconnecting relationships in this mysterious world of spooks and arms dealers.

CHAPTER 6

The Liverpudlian, the Greek Cypriots and Arms from Lebanon

During the 1970s the IRA engaged in at least one operation to import arms from the Middle East – apparently supplied by elements in Al Fatah, part of the Palestinian Liberation Organisation (PLO). It has been suggested that contacts between the Provos and the Palestinians went back to the early 1970s when contact was made in Libya, at a time when Libya's Colonel Gadaffi was supporting both the IRA and the Palestinians. But there are indications that a 1977 arms shipment may have been arranged by the IRA through Greek Cypriot intermediaries, rather than through direct contact with the Palestinians.[1] A veteran republican, Seamus McCollum, was at the centre of an ingenious but ultimately unsuccessful plot to smuggle a consignment of arms and explosives provided by Palestinian elements in Lebanon into Ireland.

McCollum was one of those IRA men who came from the Irish diaspora. He was born in Fleetwood in Lancashire, England, in 1922. His mother died as a young woman and his father remarried. McCollum was brought up by a maternal aunt in Liverpool. He developed an early interest in Irish republicanism. In 1954, before the start of the Border Campaign, he was arrested in possession of a suitcase full of explosives at Lime Street railway station in Liverpool. He was given a six-year sentence, which he served at Wakefield Prison, where members of the Greek Cypriot insurgent organisation, EOKA, were also imprisoned.

McCollum and the Cypriots had something in common. Just as the IRA was trying to expel the British from Northern Ireland, EOKA's campaign was designed to force them out of Cyprus. Through these prisoners McCollum was to establish contacts in the world of Greek Cypriot nationalism who were apparently to prove useful to him in later years. Also locked up at Wakefield were three other IRA men – James Murphy, Joe Doyle and future chief of staff Cathal Goulding.

In 1956 the IRA hatched an ambitious plan to 'spring' Goulding, McCollum and the others from prison. To assist with the jailbreak, a large party of IRA men and women travelled to the UK on an airliner hired at considerable expense from Aer Lingus, under the guise of being a drama group, the Skellig Players. However, Goulding and the others could not get over the wall, and the operation was aborted.[2] On his release, McCollum moved to Ireland where the Border Campaign was under way. He came to the attention of the Irish authorities, and in 1958 was interned at the Curragh. He stood out among the internees with his strong Liverpool accent. When released, he stayed on in Ireland, working as an insurance agent, before returning in 1965 to Liverpool, where he took a job as a shipping clerk. This was an occupation that was to prove useful for a subsequent IRA arms plot. He gradually dropped under the radar so far as the Special Branch was concerned.

When the new IRA campaign got going in the early 1970s, McCollum felt drawn again to the cause. Despite having been imprisoned with Cathal Goulding, who went on to become chief of the Official IRA, he decided to go with the rival Provisionals when the split in the movement occurred. It is understood that McCollum offered his services to the Provos and that he was told to bide his time and to lie low. The call on his particular type of expertise came around 1976, as the IRA felt the need to step up deliveries of arms and explosives. Supplies were still coming from America but, with ongoing seizures by the security forces, it was decided to look in another direction also – the Middle East.

When McCollum embarked on a gunrunning operation, his *modus operandi* might have been drawn from the pages of a spy novel. He appeared in Dublin, under a false identity, using a ploy described in Frederick Forsyth's thriller *The Day of the Jackal*, which had been published earlier in the 1970s. He 'borrowed' the identity of a dead man, John O'Neill, and managed to get a passport in that name. To muddy the waters further, he used yet another name for business purposes – Robin Kingsley. The name sounded quintessentially English, and fitted with McCollum's English accent. Under his Kingsley identity, he set up a business concern called the Progress Electro Company, in April 1977. The firm was based in a dingy, upstairs office on Middle Abbey Street, Dublin. This was a 'shell' company, set up to facilitate the importation of a clandestine arms cargo.

For reasons of security, it is understood that he dealt with just one person in the IRA, who supplied him with whatever finance or other assistance he needed. This was believed to be the chief of staff himself, Seamus Twomey. To enhance his image as a respectable businessman, McCollum rented a flat at Martello Terrace, in the pleasant and rather upmarket seaside suburb of Sandycove, not far from the Martello Tower associated with the writer James Joyce and his classic novel *Ulysses*.

It appears that at some time in 1977, McCollum got in touch with some old Greek Cypriot contacts in Nicosia. His purpose was to arrange a consignment of arms and explosives from Lebanon, a comparatively short distance by sea from Cyprus. Individuals linked to EOKA had experience of smuggling arms into Cyprus from the time of the insurgency against the British. Palestinians in Lebanon in the 1970s had a plentiful supply of war materiel, and were clearly willing to do a deal to sell off a small part of their military supplies in return for cash to finance their cause.

During the years of the Lebanese Civil War, ships that did not wish to risk entering strife-torn Lebanese ports would offload cargo in Cyprus for onward transfer by rust-caked Lebanese coasters which were used to taking risks. In some cases arms were smuggled into Cypriot ports such as Limassol for onward shipment to Palestinian and other armed factions in Lebanon. Some arms cargoes were intercepted by the Greek Cypriot authorities, and others at sea by Israeli patrol boats. The Turkish Cypriot leader Rauf Denktash used to allege that the Greek Cypriots turned a blind eye to some gunrunning operations – allegations always denied by the Greek Cypriots.[3] But in the light of smuggling patterns in the region at this period, it would not be a huge surprise if some arms travelled along the usual route but in the opposite direction, from Lebanon to Cyprus.

In Dublin, McCollum arranged, through his Irish company, to purchase two three-ton electrical transformers. The deal involved a sizeable outlay, more than £30,000. He arranged for the large, grey-coloured transformers to be shipped to Antwerp and from there to the Cypriot port of Limassol 'for repair'. While in Cyprus, one of McCollum's Nicosia contacts removed the insides of the transformers and filled them with a cache of five tons of war materiel that had been smuggled over from Lebanon. Then the transformers were securely rivetted closed and enclosed in slatted wooden packing cases.

The war materiel included twenty-nine AK-47 rifles; twenty-nine French-made sub-machine guns; seven RPG-7 rocket launchers with almost sixty rocket-propelled grenades; two bren guns; eighteen boxes of grenades, each holding a half dozen; 11,000 rounds of SLR ammunition and thirty-six kilograms of 9mm ammunition. There were also mortars, a light machine gun, empty magazines and other items of military kit. The explosives component of the cargo was particularly significant and would have given a serious boost to the Provo bombing campaign. This included 168 x 1lb sticks of trinitrotoluene; 264lbs of TNT in 44lb blocks; and plastic explosive in fourteen 1¼lb packs and seventy-four 5½lb packs.

McCollum's Cypriot contact marked the transformers 'defective' and transferred them to the port area of Limassol where they were loaded onto a 1,599-ton British freighter, the *Tower Stream*. The unsuspecting captain and crew had no reason to have any doubts when the transformers were put on board. Word was sent to McCollum that the transformers were on their way back to him. It is unclear when, or how, the authorities learned of the illicit arms cargo, but the gaffe had been blown by the time the ship docked at Antwerp in late November 1977. A theory has been put forward that the operation may have been uncovered by the Israeli intelligence service Mossad, which has always closely monitored activities in Cyprus because of its strategic location close to Middle-East hotspots. In addition, Mossad has always taken a keen interest in transfers of arms linked to the Palestinians.

Police services from a range of countries were following the progress of the hidden arms cargo as it made its way to Antwerp, with information from naval services and port authorities being co-ordinated by the West

German police intelligence computer in Wiesbaden. It was not apparent at this stage for whom the arms were destined. The West German and Italian authorities feared the arms might be bound for terrorist groups in their own countries. The Dutch were concerned that the arms might be earmarked for a South Moluccan insurgent group.

When the ship docked in Antwerp the authorities had to make a decision. They could allow the shipment to proceed further so that those who took delivery could be arrested. But there was always a danger that the plan could go wrong and that the arms would end up in the wrong hands. They decided to play safe and to grab the shipment. Customs officers moved in to open up the crates containing the transformers, claiming that the ship's manifest was not in order. The illegal cargo was discovered. Some of the boxes were marked 'Fatah'. There were labels on the crates marking them as being consigned to the Progress Electro Company in Dublin. The Belgian Army moved in to take possession of the ammunition and explosives, while customs impounded the arms in a warehouse.

The focus of the probe moved swiftly to Dublin. Special Branch visited the offices of the Progress Electro Company, and from there the trail led them to McCollum's flat in Sandycove where, on 2 December 1977, he was arrested. While detectives were on their way to pick up McCollum, they spotted a car containing IRA chief of staff Seamus Twomey, who had escaped from Mountjoy Prison by helicopter in 1973. Twomey was also arrested. There was speculation that Twomey may have been coming from a meeting with McCollum when he was spotted. I well remember being present along with other reporters in the quaint, historic precincts of Dublin's Special Criminal Court at Green Street when Twomey was escorted in following his arrest. He looked dishevelled but was full of anger and defiance, and gave cheek to the three judges in his broad, Belfast accent.

The grey-haired McCollum was said to have appeared quite calm when he subsequently went on trial in the same court. In July 1978 he was found guilty of conspiring with others unknown to import arms and explosives, and with being a member of the Provisional IRA. He was jailed for ten years on the conspiracy charge and for three years on the IRA membership charge, both to run concurrently. McCollum had pleaded not guilty. Estimates of the amounts of money invested by the IRA in the shipment ranged from £200,000 upwards. It was a serious setback for the Provos.

According to prominent Irish politician Dr Garret FitzGerald of Fine Gael, who served as foreign affairs minister during the 1970s and as taoiseach in the 1980s, it was possible that the PLO did not fully understand the nature of the IRA.[4] As part of his official duties during Ireland's presidency of the European Community, Dr FitzGerald visited the countries of the Maghreb, during which he had talks with a PLO representative in Algiers. He gained the impression that the PLO man regarded the IRA as the 'underground army' of the Irish government, and that condemnations of their activities by the government were no more than 'pro forma' statements designed to placate the British government. FitzGerald tried to persuade the PLO man that this was not the case.

The mercenary and the Sinn Féiner

In the latter part of the 1970s, there was another strange case of an alleged IRA gunrunning attempt, this time involving the mercenary recruiter John Banks, later to be described by Labour MP Chris Mullin in the British House of Commons as 'an extreme rogue'. Banks, a former British Army paratrooper, was the star witness in a court case at the Old Bailey in 1977 in which a Sinn Féin activist in the UK and three other individuals were charged with an alleged conspiracy to procure arms. Special Branch arrested the men in May 1976, after they were shadowed to a meeting with Banks in London. Banks had reported that a proposal had been put to him about an arms deal.

Banks was no stranger to controversy. In early 1976, the former paratrooper had begun recruiting mercenaries to fight in the civil war in Angola, against the Marxist MPLA. The Angola adventure proved disastrous. About 180 mercenaries went to war, and fourteen of them were 'executed' by their own side. Others were killed, or captured by the victorious MPLA, which executed two of the 'soldiers of fortune'.

During the hearing at the Old Bailey, Banks was accused by defence lawyer Rock Tansey of being an *agent provocateur* on behalf of the Special Branch. Tansey said Banks had been the prime mover behind the abortive deal, inciting the defendants to buy weapons they had not wanted. Banks denied that he was an *agent provocateur*. In evidence, he said he suspected the weapons deal was being put to him on behalf of the IRA. Meanwhile, it emerged that one of the defendants had been active in organising Provisional Sinn Féin on the UK 'mainland'. Banks denied that he had tried to incite this man to buy 1,000 M-1 carbines and ammunition. The arms were supposed to be stored in Belgium.

The Sinn Féin man, who lived in Luton, was given a particularly heavy sentence. He received two consecutive five-year sentences for receiving six walkie talkie sets for use in connection with acts of terrorism in the UK in connection with Irish affairs, and for soliciting John Banks and others to provide 1,000 M-1 carbines, ammunition and accessories, intending that they should be used for the same purpose.

Another Sinn Féin man, who denied lending the defendant £500 knowing or suspecting that the money would be used in connection with acts of terrorism, was found not guilty and discharged. Two other men, Glaswegians living in London, were also jailed on arms charges. Banks, who was immersed in controversy as a result of the ill-fated mercenary expedition to Angola, went on to achieve even more notoriety. In 1980, he was convicted and jailed for two years for blackmail and threats to kill. The following year, he absconded from Coldingley open prison, and was on the run for eight months.

Some gunrunning mysteries still unsolved

There has been some speculation that the IRA, in the latter part of the 1970s, received some assistance from elements in southern Africa – possibly linked to one of the radical insurgent groups active in the region at the time. The speculation arose after explosives and bomb-making equipment were found in luggage unloaded from a ship which docked in Dublin port in April 1978 after a voyage from Capetown, South Africa. Gardaí seized the materiel, which had been hidden in a trunk left in a customs shed. Gardaí said they were seeking a Dublin man in connection with the find. This appears to have been a one-off shipment, and the full story behind it has never been clarified.

Mystery also surrounds another effort to procure arms that allegedly occurred in 1982 on the Continent. A writer on security matters has reported that British intelligence kept tabs on a three-man IRA team with £1 million in cash who travelled around Europe trying to buy arms on the black market. It was claimed that the men visited France, Belgium, West Germany and Italy, and at each stop were defrauded by crooked arms dealers who took hefty deposits from them without delivering any weapons. According to the story, the men returned home empty-handed, and minus the £1 million.[5]

In his book *The Informer*, former IRA man Sean O'Callaghan also refers to an IRA arms-buying group operating on the Continent at this period. He claims the group acquired arms and explosives worth more than £2 million from Middle Eastern sources, and stored them near Milan in northern Italy, but gives no indication as to whether or not the materiel eventually made its way to Ireland.

The Belgian and the arms deals

In the early 1980s, a wily arms trafficker based in Belgium was suspected of arranging arms supplies to a range of extremist groups, including the IRA. He was believed to be primarily a supplier of arms to the Basque separatist group ETA. But he was also believed to have links to both IRA and INLA activists living on the Continent. In addition, he was believed to have contacts with the group of international terrorists headed by the notorious Carlos 'The Jackal' (real name Ilich Ramirez Sanchez), as well as with extremist Palestinians.

The French were particularly concerned about the activities of The Belgian. They believed he had contact with James Kerr, an INLA man based in Basle, Switzerland, as well as with members of a small coterie of activists based in France who were linked to Irish paramilitary organisations. One was an Irishman linked to the Provisionals who, the French authorities believed, had spent time at a Palestinian training camp in Lebanon.

In the earlier part of the 1980s, French security services were keeping surveillance on Irish republican activists in France – both those aligned to the IRA and others linked to the INLA. Also under surveillance were French left-wing activists believed to be in sympathy with Irish republican causes. The French security service, Direction de la Surveillance du Territoire (DST), was getting information from the British authorities on Irish suspects located in France, who were acting as a conduit for arms shipments en route to Ireland. As regards the arms pipeline through France, the INLA was the more significant operator, but there was also some IRA gunrunning activity. The French kept watch on a particular Paris bar frequented by Irish people suspected of being linked to paramilitary groups, and surveillance photos were snatched of the suspects.

In 1983 the French somehow learned that a shipment of illegal arms was coming from Belgium into France. The Belgian was believed to be involved. DST agents tracked the arms truck after it crossed the border into France, but then lost sight of it. With the aid of information from the British, the DST began pursuing certain lines of inquiry. Ultimately, the French focused on the activities of an Irish truck driver in France, Michael Christopher McDonald, from County Louth. He was suspected of being an IRA sympathiser. He made regular trips to the meat market at Rungis, near Paris, in his thirty-two-ton Volvo truck. Apart from beef, he also transported other cargo. On his way back to Ireland with a load of electrical goods, McDonald missed the ferry at Le Havre, and parked his truck to wait several days for the next sailing to Rosslare. The authorities closed in before he could catch the next ferry. The swoop occurred on 12 August 1983. A search uncovered what the French security people had been looking for – quite a significant cache of paramilitary arms and explosives, destined, they believed, for the IRA.

It was the culmination of a two-month French investigation into an IRA arms pipeline that went through France. The searchers uncovered, hidden among the electrical goods, twenty-five handguns of US, Belgian and West German origin; 12,000 rounds of ammunition; 100 magazines for Russian-made assault rifles; two hand grenades; 22lbs of explosives; 200 detonators; and 500 yards of detonator wire.

McDonald was detained in prison at Rouen. He was in custody until he went on trial in Le Havre the following year. Also arrested in connection with the arms find was a French journalist who worked for a Paris-based newspaper. He had taken a keen interest in Irish affairs and had visited Northern Ireland. Police questioned more than a dozen other people. It was suspected that the arms had been bought elsewhere, possibly in Belgium, transported to France and hidden in the Paris region before being taken to Le Havre for onward shipping to Ireland.

A month after the men's arrest, there was an unusual development. A young Irishwoman travelled to France, and made contact with a French lawyer. She claimed to be a representative of the IRA, and wanted to make certain representations to the French government. The lawyer in question passed on her remarks to a senior French official working for Prime Minister Pierre Mauroy. The woman said the IRA was 'astonished' at the recent arrest of Mr McDonald. The IRA had assumed that there was a tacit agreement with the French that they would not interfere with the transport of weapons to Ireland. In return, the IRA had given a number of instructions to its members. These included orders not to carry out attacks on British targets on French soil; to avoid contact, on the military level at least, with Corsican and Basque separatists seeking autonomy from France; and to avoid assisting international terrorist groups with logistics bases in France, such as those linked to the Palestinians. The woman wanted to know if they should deduce from the McDonald arrest that the French government had decided to end the tacit agreement. In that case, the IRA would have to review its position.

The French official checked with Gilles Ménage, President Mitterand's chief of staff, who assured him that there was no agreement with the IRA on arms trafficking. If arms had been smuggled successfully through France and on to Ireland in the past, it was because the French authorities had not known about them. Ménage emphasised there was no way that the French government would tolerate illegal arms trafficking on its territory.[6] Apparently, the French official, in checking with Ménage about policy in regard to the IRA, pointed to the Donaldson affair as possible evidence of an 'ambiguous' attitude to Irish republicans on the part of the French: Denis Donaldson, a personable, diminutive Belfast man who had served time for explosives offences in the 1970s and who went on to become active in Sinn Féin, had been arrested at Orly Airport on 25 August 1981, along with another Irish republican. They were travelling from Beirut on false passports. The two were held briefly and released. According to Ménage, who had no personal role in the Donaldson case, the two men were in possession of rolls of film showing Palestinian training camps in Lebanon.[7] It was reported in the media at the time that the two men told French security officials they had spent 'several months' in such a camp.

Despite the lenient approach taken to Donaldson and his travelling companion, it was clear that the French were becoming more concerned about Irish paramilitary activities in France. This is shown by the arrest in

Paris on terrorism-related charges on 28 August 1982 of three Irish people known as the Vincennes Three, who were later cleared (*see* Chapter 12).

Donaldson went on to become notorious in republican circles when he confessed, in December 2005, to having been a paid informer of the British since the 1980s. In April 2006, he was shot dead at the remote cottage in County Donegal where he had been lying low. There was some speculation that he may have been 'turned' when he was arrested in France, but this was never proven. A bizarre aspect to this saga is that when he was arrested at Orly, the French found a photograph of the security system used by the Israeli airline El Al at the airport. This gave rise to speculation that he may have been spying on the Israelis for the Palestinians before he ever began spying on the IRA for the British.

Incidentally, the young woman who purported to make representations on behalf of the IRA to the French government was not the only person who assumed there was a 'special relationship' between the French and Irish republicans. I recall a former member of the IRA saying to me in the 1970s, 'The French don't bother Irish republicans much – if you don't interfere with them, they won't interfere with you.'

There was another Irish-linked investigation in August 1982, which received much less attention than the case of the Vincennes Three. On 17 August, a French activist with Irish republican sympathies was detained by French customs while about to drive his Renault 16 onto an Irish-bound ferry at Cherbourg. A search of the vehicle revealed 432 metres of detonating cord, hidden in the doors. The twenty-eight-year-old suspect came up with the classic 'man I met in a pub' explanation. He told the authorities that he had been asked to transport the explosive substance by an Irishman he met in a Paris bar, called John. He did not know for which movement in Ireland the detonating cord was destined.

According to a French police file, dated 25 January 1983, the authorities were unable to identify the man called John, or even establish that he existed.[8] Nor was it possible to establish who was involved with the Frenchman in the smuggling operation, or which paramilitary organisation in Ireland was to receive the detonating cord. Police interviewed the Vincennes Three, who were being held at different prisons in the Paris region, in connection with the Cherbourg find. However, it appears that they were unable to provide any additional information. According to the police file on the Cherbourg operation, the suspect's address book included contact details in Belfast for a member of the Irish Republican Socialist Party (IRSP), the political wing of the INLA, and also contact details for Sinn Féin's Denis Donaldson.

As for twenty-six-year-old Michael Christopher McDonald, when he went on trial in March 1984, he pleaded guilty to possessing and transporting 'weapons of war' and was sentenced to a year in prison. He was banned from visiting France for five years – a significant penalty for a European truck driver. In addition, he was fined 61,666 francs, the estimated value of the arms and explosives he was transporting. He told the court that he did not know the ultimate destination of the materiel. The other man who was arrested, the French journalist, pleaded not guilty, but was sentenced to a year in prison. However, the court rejected a charge of importing prohibited arms on the grounds that it had not been proven that he was involved in the importation of the arms from Belgium in May the previous year, or that any such arms were found in McDonald's truck. Media reports quoted the journalist's strong denials of guilt, and his comments that he supported Irish unity, but only within the limits of legality. McDonald was to find himself in the headlines in later years for another attempted arms trafficking operation. He went with the Real IRA (RIRA) after it split away from the Provisional IRA, and in 2001 was arrested in Slovakia in connection with an attempt to buy arms (*see* Chapter 14).

Much to the frustration of the French, the arms trafficker known as The Belgian was never brought to book. Belgian authorities carried out their own follow-up investigations and interviewed a number of individuals believed to be involved in the Flemish separatist movement about alleged gunrunning links to the IRA. In December 1983 three men, including a lawyer, were arrested in Brussels in connection with this probe. It was reported that two Irishmen were also being sought following the break-up of an IRA gunrunning ring in Brussels. The lawyer appeared in court, charged in connection with the 1983 gunrunning operation, but the verdict was that the case against him had not been proven. The public prosecutor appealed against this verdict, and in 1988 the lawyer was convicted and given a one-year prison sentence, suspended for five years. It was stated that the arms in question had been found by French police at Le Havre.

The raid in the Netherlands

In 1985 the Dáil passed an emergency law, an amendment to the Offences Against the State Act, enabling the Irish government to seize almost 1.75 million Irish punts held in a bank account in Navan, County Meath. The funds had been transferred from the US to the Navan branch of the Bank of Ireland, and the Dáil heard that the Gardaí believed it was IRA money.

On 19 February 1985, the then justice minister Michael Noonan told the Dáil that information had been conveyed to him by the Garda authorities that 'a large sum of money which is the proceeds of criminal activity by the IRA, specifically extortion under threat of kidnap and murder, has found its way into a bank in this country and is being held to the use of and for the purposes of the IRA.' Mr Noonan went on: 'In recent days it became apparent that those who are the custodians of this money would find it necessary to make a very early move to transfer it. This necessitated urgent action by the government to prevent the money becoming available to the IRA to fund its campaign of murder and destruction ...'

A businessman, originally from County Louth, who owned pubs in Ireland and the US, Alan Clancy, launched a legal challenge along with another man, claiming that the money was legitimate and was earmarked for developing a business exporting pork from Ireland to the US. 'I have no connection with the Provisional IRA, Sinn Féin or any agent or support group of theirs such as Noraid,' Mr Clancy said in the statement. 'I believe in and aspire to the unification of Ireland by peaceful means. I condemn political violence for that or any other purpose.' In May 1988, the High Court in Dublin upheld the right of the Irish government to seize money it believed was destined for or belonged to the IRA, and ruled that the law passed in 1985 was constitutional. Alan Clancy died in 1995.

Files kept by the East German secret police, the Stasi, which came to light in 1996, indicate that the Stasi believed that the money that was seized was earmarked for financing an arms deal. The document, dated 20 October 1986, identified an Austrian citizen as the IRA's contact for the weapons transaction, and indicated that information on this person's movements had come from a Stasi mole in the Austrian Interior Ministry.[9] There has been no independent confirmation of the Stasi mole's assessment, and it should be borne in mind that the Stasi were not always well-informed about the activities of the IRA. In the document referred to above, a twenty-page analysis of the IRA, the Stasi concluded that arms shipments from the US to the IRA were controlled and supervised by the CIA.[10]

Even though the IRA was not a major target of the Stasi for intelligence-gathering purposes, the agency was clearly interested in gathering information on certain paramilitary activities. The document cited above, for instance, records that a Stasi agent within the West German embassy in the Netherlands passed on a list of IRA weapons found by the Dutch authorities, complete with serial numbers. It is unclear why the Stasi would have had a particular interest in this information. The weapons list probably refers to arms seized in a swoop by Dutch police in January 1986 on an apartment in Amsterdam, which netted three Irishmen, two of them prominent IRA members, as well as a cache of weapons that had been collected by the Provisionals.

The two senior IRA men were identified as Brendan 'Bic' McFarlane and Gerry Kelly, both of whom had taken part in a mass breakout from Northern Ireland's top security Maze prison in September 1983. McFarlane, who had an extrovert, outgoing manner, had been jailed for life for leading a gun and bomb attack on a Protestant-owned pub, the Bayardo Bar, in Belfast's Shankill Road area in August 1976. Five Protestants died in the sectarian attack, which was said to have been in retaliation for a loyalist attack on a Catholic bar. Four of the victims died almost immediately while the fifth, nineteen-year-old Linda Boyle, died just over a week later of her injuries.

Known as 'Bic' after a popular brand of ballpoint pen, because of his note-taking skills at IRA meetings in prison, McFarlane came to prominence during the 1981 hunger strikes. He succeeded Bobby Sands as Officer Commanding (OC) of the IRA prisoners in the Maze prison, following Sands' death on hunger strike. McFarlane led the 1983 prison breakout, when thirty-eight prisoners escaped. A prison officer died from a heart attack after being stabbed with a screwdriver.

Gerry Kelly had been a member of the first IRA active service unit to target London during the Troubles. He was involved in planting car bombs on London streets in 1973 which injured 180 civilians, one of whom later died of a heart attack. He was caught and received two life sentences. He was later transferred to the Maze prison in Northern Ireland, and helped organise the 1983 mass escape. In more recent years he became a senior member of the Sinn Féin leadership.

Dutch police let it be known that when they swooped on the IRA men they were acting on information provided by the Dutch secret service and the British police. In front of the flat police found a rented container holding some forty weapons, including thirteen FN FAL rifles, an AK-47 rifle, two hand grenades and 70,000 rounds of ammunition. Also recovered were four oil drums containing nitrobenzene. Police in Amsterdam said the arsenal was ready for dispatch to Northern Ireland when intercepted. The origin of the firearms is uncertain, but it was thought the ammunition was taken from NATO bases in Europe.

Nitrobenzene is a chemical which the IRA used to manufacture bombs. It is mixed with other substances, usually fertilisers, to produce a fairly unsophisticated type of explosive. Unlike the odourless plastic explosive Semtex, nitrobenzene emits a pungent odour, and this was considered a disadvantage from a bomb-making point of view.

Nevertheless, the IRA continued to import nitrobenzene, as demonstrated by one particular incident in November 1988. A truck was intercepted by Gardaí near Kells, County Meath, and was found to contain more than 380 gallons of nitrobenzene, packed into thirty drums. Once again, there was an Amsterdam connection. The truck driver told police he had picked up the cargo in Amsterdam. He had been approached by a man in Dundalk who asked him to go to Amsterdam where two men would meet him in a cafe near Schiphol Airport. The trucker duly met his two contacts, who took his truck away and loaded it with drums of nitrobenzene.

The man admitted to Garda officers that he had taken part in the operation for money and in February 1989 he was jailed for six years for his role in the affair. It was estimated that the value of the nitrobenzene involved was Ir£1 million, and it would have been sufficient to make 800 mortar bombs. It was the biggest seizure of explosives materiel ever made by police in the Irish Republic. The IRA had evidently established a major black market source of nitrobenzene in the Netherlands, where there is a sizeable chemicals industry.

The strange case of the Norwegian rifles

The IRA has never put all its eggs in one basket as regards procuring arms. It has always believed in having a diversity of sources for its war materiel. Even as the Provos were stocking up with Semtex and arms from Libya in the mid-1980s, they had men on the Continent acquiring arms and other types of explosive materiel on the black market. The IRA had cells operating on the Continent over many years. Some specialised in attacks on British servicemen and other targets, while others concentrated on acquiring war materiel for the campaign back home.

Modern assault rifles stolen from the Norwegian armed forces were among the items acquired by the IRA on the black market in Continental Europe during the 1980s, and smuggled to Ireland. Evidence of the traffic emerged after the seizure of an IRA arms cache at a farmhouse in Craughan, County Roscommon, in January 1986. Some of the weapons recovered had been stolen from an army base in Norway. Ten captured Heckler and Koch G3 rifles were thought to have been part of more than 100 such rifles taken from a Norwegian Reserve Force arms depot at Vestbygd, near Oslo, in May 1984. A number of Norwegian nationals had been charged in connection with the theft, but until the discovery of the arms cache in County Roscommon, none of the rifles had been recovered. Similar rifles were later to be recovered in Northern Ireland. The G3 had been the standard assault rifle of the Norwegian Army since 1968.

It was reported that the IRA had taken delivery of a range of weapons stolen from the Norwegian arsenal – more than fifty G3 rifles, along with four sub-machine guns, a machine gun and two cannons.[11] The arms had apparently been acquired by the IRA from an arms dealer in Belgium, which had long been a centre for covert dealings in weaponry. G3 rifles carried by masked IRA men featured in images used for publicity purposes by the organisation. The Craughan swoop was just one of three seizures of arms and ammunition by police in the general area of County Roscommon and County Sligo during January 1986, in which a total of more than 120 German and Eastern Bloc firearms were captured.

An MG3 machine gun of Norwegian origin acquired by the IRA was among weaponry seized by Gardaí after six men were arrested near the Border at St Johnstone, County Donegal, in September 1992. Gardaí suspected that the men were on an operation to shoot down a British Army helicopter. Also recovered was a GPMG machine gun, three AKM rifles (probably part of the Libyan shipments) and 700 rounds of ammunition. At a hearing in the Special Criminal Court in Dublin in February 1994, a detective from the Garda ballistics department said the MG3, of German design and manufactured in 1969, was the first to be recovered in the state.

A republican source told me that some of the Norwegian rifles were used to fire a volley in a salute to prominent IRA man Jim Lynagh, during his funeral in County Monaghan in May 1987. Lynagh was one of eight IRA men killed when they were ambushed by members of the British Army's elite Special Air Service (SAS) as they tried to bomb an RUC station in the County Armagh village of Loughall. It was the biggest single loss of life suffered by the IRA during the Troubles. The source said that some of the weapons misfired on the day of the funeral. The G3 rifle is highly regarded and lack of maintenance seems to have caused the malfunction. 'It was embarrassing,' the source said.

The British were anxious to close down IRA sources of arms, and they took a particular interest in the case of the Norwegian rifles. In August 1991 a British diplomat, who was also a member of MI6, approached a former Norwegian military intelligence officer, Espen Lie, to discuss undercover ways of finding out how the rifles were getting to the IRA, and the identity of those involved in the traffic. The MI6 man was introduced to Mr Lie by a serving member of Norwegian military intelligence, who knew the MI6 man well. Mr Lie reported the approach to the Norwegian secret police. Meanwhile, a local newspaper, *VG*, got wind of the story and published some of the details.

The intelligence man who introduced the MI6 man to Mr Lie and who held the rank of lieutenant colonel, was subsequently sacked because he had allegedly failed to keep his superiors informed of the matter. In more recent years, Mr Lie was reported to be heading a group of Norwegian security contractors working on an extremely hazardous contract to protect oil pipelines in Iraq. It is not known if the British ever did find out how the IRA acquired the rifles.

It emerged that the IRA had also considered the possibility of acquiring arms in Sweden during the 1980s. A republican source told me that among the arms procurement measures that were considered at this period was a break-in at a Swedish military arsenal at Skane, in the southern part of the country. The idea would have been to clear out the arsenal and spirit the contents away to the Provos back in Ireland. It was an ambitious plan, but there were too many potential difficulties and the operation never got off the drawing board.

The French connection

Paramilitaries continued to try to use, from time to time, the ferries from France to Ireland to smuggle in arms. On 12 July 1989, customs officers at the County Wexford ferry port of Rosslare stopped and searched a vehicle that had arrived on the car ferry *St Patrick* from the French port of Cherbourg. Customs found a suspicious substance, which later turned out to be sodium chlorate, wrapped in black plastic in a case belonging to a young man called Leonard Hardy. Hardy (twenty-eight), attempted to run away but was apprehended. A later search revealed ten mercury-tilt switches in his case, of the type used in booby-trap bombs. Hardy's girlfriend Donna Maguire (twenty-two), from Newry, County Down, was arrested in a car park outside the ferry terminal.

A couple of days later, the couple appeared at the Special Criminal Court in Dublin charged with possession of explosive substances. They both denied the charges when they went on trial in February 1990.

Hardy's defence counsel, Rex Mackey, said Hardy had asked him to tell the court that he had gone to the Continent to bring money to people who were on the run there, and had been asked by them to deliver a parcel of explosives back to Ireland. Hardy, a native of Belfast but with an address at Coolock, Dublin, was found guilty and sentenced to five years. Donna Maguire was acquitted. The presiding judge, Mr Justice Liam Hamilton, said it might well be that Hardy and Maguire were engaged in a joint enterprise of some kind. However, the court was not satisfied beyond a reasonable doubt with regard to Maguire, and she was allowed to walk free.

In June 1995, Maguire was given a nine-year sentence in Germany for her role in a bomb attack on a British Army barracks at Osnabrück. She was freed almost immediately, on the basis that she had already spent almost five years and eight months in custody on remand. It was estimated that she had served almost the two-thirds of the sentence she would have had to serve before being entitled to parole. In freeing her, the judge said he was taking into account the Peace Process in Ireland. In 1996 Maguire married Leonard Hardy. The couple, who lived in County Louth in the Irish Republic, were on holiday in Spain in August 2005 when Hardy was arrested. He was extradited to Germany the following January, and went on trial at Celle, in Lower Saxony. In March 2006 he pleaded guilty to charges arising out of the 1989 attack on the British military base at Osnabrück, and was subsequently sentenced to six years in prison.

CHAPTER 7

The FBI Man and the Mayo Gunrunner

When he was head of the FBI PIRA Squad, Louis Stephens was relentless in his pursuit of Irish republican gunrunners. He is of Irish descent – his grandfather Patrick Stephens came from Cork – and he values his Irish heritage, but he hated what the IRA were doing. He hated the idea of bombs going off in London, killing people innocently doing their shopping or having a drink in a pub. He hated the idea of teenage soldiers, sent to Northern Ireland to keep the peace, being gunned down. These soldiers had, after all, originally been sent to the North at the start of the Troubles to protect the Catholic population.

Stephens hated the maimings, the murders and the terror perpetrated by paramilitaries. He hated what he saw as the intolerance of the IRA, the way a small group of paramilitary godfathers could decide, without any democratic mandate, to impose death and destruction on their fellow citizens, or sentence individuals to death. He said: 'I did not like Oliver Cromwell any more than the next guy, I don't think he did right, and I think there were an awful lot of abuses and injustices, but I don't think that this [terrorism] is the way you solve a problem.'

One of the atrocities that angered him was the assassination of Lord Mountbatten. The elderly Mountbatten was blown up in his boat by the IRA while sailing near his Irish holiday home in County Sligo in 1979. An elderly grandmother and two schoolboys also died. What threat did they pose to anybody? What harm had they done to any Irish person? How did two elderly people and two kids deserve a horrible death like that? To Stephens, this was an unspeakably cruel, senseless attack. He could not understand how anyone could justify it, or turn a blind eye to it. The IRA called itself an army, and armies were supposed to spare non-combatants, especially the very old and the very young. 'What the IRA were doing really pissed me off,' he said.

He also despised what loyalist extremists were doing, and in later years could not understand how Catholic children could be intimidated and harassed by loyalists on their way to Holy Cross School in Belfast. 'You can't have a situation like that, it's unacceptable, it just can't happen,' he fumed. He hated the idea of people being murdered over tribal 'bullshit' on either side of the sectarian divide. But the immediate challenge on his own patch was posed by those who were running guns to the IRA. He saw it as part of his job to stem the flow. The FBI man was to become an implacable enemy of IRA gunrunners in the US. And he was to prove a very tough and formidable opponent indeed.

In the late 1970s, Stephens was a supervisor in the FBI's Foreign Counter-Intelligence-Terrorism (FCI-T) unit in Washington DC. Much of his work was to do with Middle Eastern terrorism. Part of his role was to liaise with representatives of the British security service MI5, who were based at the British Embassy. At this period there were two MI5 men running a liaison office in Washington. One dealt with the communist threat – the Cold War was still on, and the Soviet Union was some years away from collapse. The other agent dealt with everything else, including Irish terrorism. He was a shrewd operator, and was anxious to get the Americans to become more proactive against the IRA.

Stephens recalled how he became friendly with this MI5 man – they used to socialise together. The MI5 man thought the US was not doing enough to counter the activities of IRA supporters who were sending guns to the paramilitaries. The MI5 man had examined recent US legislation designed to crack down on the activities of agents of foreign-based terrorist groups and he pointed out that it was not just Middle Eastern groups who could be targeted under this legislation, but IRA activists as well. Stephens said: 'I remember having a conversation with the MI5 guy. He talked about what the IRA were doing. He asked me why we were not doing something about this? He said: "Why are you applying a different set of guidelines to these [IRA] investigations than you apply to Middle East terrorism – Palestinian groups, bombings, aircraft hijackings and so forth? Look at your guidelines, read what your guidelines say." When I did that, I found he was right on point.'

Stephens said there was a mindset among some elements in the FBI and the New York Police Department (NYPD) which considered that the Irish could do no wrong. History was romanticised; the Black and Tans were remembered as the bad guys; other stuff was forgotten. The result was that some law enforcement people were reluctant to move against Irish activists. 'There were FBI men who were Irish who did not want to see action taken,' he said. 'There was pressure in the agency not to touch the Irish, to look the other way. There was a mindset to let other agencies tackle the Irish cases, like the Bureau of Alcohol, Tobacco and Firearms [BATF], the customs or the immigration people.'

To Stephens, it was a lot simpler. He considered he had taken an oath as an FBI man to enforce *all* the laws. He considered his oath did not allow the turning of a blind eye to certain aspects of terrorism, while concentrating on others. 'My badge said: "Special Agent, Federal Bureau of Investigation". It did not say: "FBI except for Irish cases", it did not say that.' When he was transferred to New York in the summer of 1980, he became the head of a new PIRA Squad, which pulled out all the stops in the pursuit of gunrunners linked to the IRA and the smaller paramilitary group, the INLA.

His superior was Donald McGorty. McGorty told Stephens he wanted him to make New York the premier FBI office so far as the investigation of terrorism was concerned. Stephens said that McGorty left him alone to do his job and gave him any resources he needed. 'McGorty would say to me: "What do you need?" and the next day I had it.' Stephens went on: 'McGorty is a true-blue Irishman, a fine fellow, a graduate of Manhattan College, a former Marine, just a class guy.'

The squad was to score some notable successes. From the early 1980s on, it became far more difficult for Irish gunrunners to operate effectively in New York City, because of the relentless determination of Lou Stephens and his men.

Despite the misgivings of some of his colleagues, nobody in the FBI ever tried to mount a serious effort to stop him doing his job and going after the gunrunners. On the rare occasions when somebody in the agency would approach him and say, 'You're not doing the right thing,' there was a no-compromise reaction from Stephens. 'I would back 'em down, I would say, "I don't want to hear it, I am not going to have this discussion with you. If you think I am violating a rule or a law or a regulation, you write me up, and we will go to the mats on this, but I'm telling you, you are going to lose. This is the right thing to do. Not because it's the Irish, but because they are violating our laws."'

He recalled the emotion that prevailed in some circles during the H-Block hunger strikes of the early 1980s, as the PIRA Squad began operating. He revealed that some elements in the NYPD were causing problems for his squad as it targeted suspected gunrunners. 'They were overturning our surveillance vans because they did not want us to investigate these guys. It happened two or three times. The agents would be inside the vans when they were overturned. They were warning [former IRA leader] Joe Cahill; he would come in wearing his wig. They would surround you and harass you. I would have to get on to the police brass and say: "Gentlemen, it's time to look to your badges, it's time for you to make some decisions here, it's time for you to fish or cut bait, because I will have every one of you standing post at the Israeli embassy for the rest of your careers, if this ever happens again."'

Stephens made it a matter of principle not to share information with the police on his gunrunning investigations. 'The police knew our faces; they would know we were around this bar or that; they knew something was up, but they did not know exactly what.' The police also knew the vehicles being used by the squad, and in order to tighten security even further, the squad began renting vehicles which the police would not recognise. 'Since my work was always highly classified, I made a conscious decision, which the bosses supported, that there would be no policemen assigned to a joint terrorism task force working for us, and there were none. And that is the reason there were no leaks. We did not share any information with them. Even when we went and made the arrests and carried out raids, we did not invite the police along. We would invite customs; they were a very good service and had some experience in dealing with low-level IRA stuff, and knew some of the personalities.'[1]

In times past, FBI men were known as 'G-Men', a term popularised in Hollywood movies about the exploits of crime-busting federal agents. Stephens was a traditional G-Man to his fingertips – tough-minded, resourceful and streetwise. He has long since left the FBI and now runs a highly-successful private detective agency with offices in New Jersey and Manhattan. When I interviewed him in September 2004 at a New Jersey hospital, where he was recuperating after treatment for back trouble, he came across as somebody who could be an extremely loyal, generous colleague and friend. But I also got the impression that if Lou Stephens reckoned you were one of the bad guys, he could be your worst nightmare. He talked with great warmth of former colleagues in the agency who worked with him on Irish gunrunning cases – people like John Winslow, Greg Auld, John Schulte and others. He talked of them as men whom you could trust with your life. 'These are the salt of the earth; they don't come any better in the world; these are the best, the cream of the crop; I could not have accomplished any of what we did without them.'

Stephens came from St Louis, Missouri. His father was a surgeon, and wanted his son to follow him into medicine or the professions. But when Lou, aged fifteen, saw the movie *The FBI Story*, starring James Stewart, his mind was made up – he wanted to join the agency. When he was eighteen, he attended a wake with his father and broke the news that his ambition was to be an FBI man. His father would hardly speak to him for six months.

Stephens graduated from St Louis University and married his sweetheart, Eileen Concannon, who had strong Irish connections. He had to drop out of law school as she was expecting a baby. He joined the local police in 1967, and struggled to make ends meet on a meagre salary. His boyhood dream finally came true when he was accepted into the FBI in 1971, after the agency director, the legendary J Edgar Hoover, got authorisation from the US Congress to recruit 1,000 agents. There were still concerns at the time about the communist threat – a 'threat' that appears very slight by today's standards, in the light of 9/11, the Iraq War and Al Qaeda.

After graduating from the FBI's Quantico academy, he was sent to work in the southern state of Georgia, gaining experience in a wide range of law enforcement work. He operated for a time out of Atlanta, and then Savannah, where he became a senior agent. He investigated organised crime, such as bank robberies, illegal gambling and truck hijackings. Some of the work was dangerous. He had a close shave one dark night when dealing with a hijacked truck. A guy jumped out of the truck and pointed a gun at him. Stephens opened fire, bullets hit the tarmac and a ricochet killed the hijacker.

Because he had had bomb-disposal training as a policeman, Stephens was transferred to Washington, to the terrorism section. He was assigned to domestic terrorism and managed some old investigations, like the bomb attack by the Weather Underground on the Capitol Building in 1971. He found the work very unsatisfying, as trails had gone cold and the investigations were going nowhere. But the work got more interesting. There was a reorganisation within the FBI. The terrorism section, which had formerly operated within the Intelligence Division, was transferred to the Criminal Investigation Division. Stephens began working for a unit dealing with international terrorism, the Foreign Counter-Intelligence Unit, and this appealed to him. It was formed at a time when the FBI was concerned about Middle Eastern terrorism and extremist Palestinian groups. There were incidents that led to a greater focus on international terrorism – such as the 1972 massacre of Israeli athletes at the Olympic Games in Munich, and the 1976 Entebbe hostage affair, which led to a spectacular operation by Israeli special forces.

Stephens took on assignments largely to do with the Middle East. His duties included the management of FBI resources in relation to investigations, making applications for wire taps, and co-ordination with foreign and local police agencies and other foreign services. He was involved in running criminal cases, and also in building up systems to collect, categorise and analyse intelligence. He had to give regular briefings to his bosses on the seventh floor of FBI headquarters. The FBI director at the time, Judge Webster, was always calling down, asking for information. 'It was at that time that we had the Iran hostage crisis, so I was the person responsible for kicking the Iranians out of the US embassy in Washington DC,' said Stephens. 'I was also responsible for kicking the Libyans out of their embassy in Washington. It was an exciting time.'

Stephens was transferred to the New York office of the FBI, and continued his work in international terrorism, focused mainly on Middle Eastern targets. A sub-unit was formed in May 1980, the PIRA Squad, and he was to direct its activities. This squad had the role of tackling gunrunning and other illegal activity linked to the IRA and other Irish paramilitaries. There is a saying that Napoleon wanted generals who were lucky. In Lou Stephens, Judge Webster had an agent who was lucky, and indeed who helped to make his own luck. Within a short time Stephens had made a breakthrough. He came face to face with the man who would help the FBI infiltrate the inner circle of Irish republican gunrunners in New York. Underworld arms dealer George DeMeo, who had been supplying guns to George Harrison for the IRA since the 1950s, had run into problems with the law. He was facing ten years in prison, and wanted a way out.

Reminiscing on his first major probe into Irish gunrunning, Stephens remarked, 'I was in the right place at the right time.' He recalled: 'I no sooner got up to New York, than I was introduced to George DeMeo, a small-time La Cosa Nostra wannabe hood who dealt in automatic weapons. He would go out to what was then these legal, weekend gun club shows, and he would buy automatic weapons right off the table. Then he would sell them to the highest bidder, and they would use them for robberies, for stick-ups, for murders. He would also sell them to the IRA. At the time, the main IRA arms-buying people in New York were George Harrison and his friend Tommy Falvey. DeMeo looked like he was Mafia, and talked and acted as if he was Mafia. In fact he was not a made member of La Cosa Nostra or anything like that. He was not mobbed up. I believe he is of Corsican background. But he would do business with the mob. He had gotten himself arrested in North Carolina, and he was represented by this little Jewish lawyer who had the common sense to say: "Maybe I can do a deal for George."'

And so it was that the lawyer called the squad and a deal was made. DeMeo would help the FBI set up a 'sting' operation against the Harrison network, in return for getting his sentence halved. It seemed to the 'Feds' like a very good trade indeed. It was agreed that DeMeo would introduce an undercover agent to the Harrison people, so that they would buy guns from the agent and thus provide the basis for being arrested and charged. It was arranged for DeMeo to get bail so that he could make the approach to Harrison and launch the 'sting' operation.

Stephens had his first conversation with DeMeo at the FBI man's office on Federal Plaza. He got the names of the main players in the gunrunning operations and, upon checking out the FBI's own files, discovered something that astonished and delighted him. There was already a huge, untapped reservoir of intelligence available about the suspects and other Irish republican activists. 'When DeMeo and I had our first conversation in my office, and he told me what information he had, the very first thing that I did was to check our Bureau files, our Bureau indices. The Bureau are great historians. When they write it down it stays written; it's in the record.

'I would ask the girls to run the indices on the names and information DeMeo had given me, and there were reports on all the players that DeMeo was talking about and others associated with them – in some cases going back twenty-five years. Some were dead, and most of those alive were still active. It was all right there in the files – their names, their social security numbers, their birth dates, their addresses, their girlfriends, the bars they hung out in – it was all there. All I had to do was write a summary memo and I had the predicate for my case. All of that was just lying there – photos, surveillance pictures, the whole thing. All you had to do was plant the garden.

'What a wonderful tool that was – reports on all these people. There was information going back years on people like George Harrison, Tommy Falvey, Mike Flannery and others. The Bureau were writing intelligence reports on people like Harrison, but they did not know what to do with the information because at the time the only thing the Bureau had in terms of jurisdiction was a lousy neutrality violation – that was not going to go anywhere. We had to have something with some teeth in it, we had to have something with some sex in it, we really had to put some meat in it.'

And what had put 'teeth' into the FBI investigations? Stephens considered that what made a huge difference was a law passed in 1978 called the Foreign Intelligence Surveillance Act (FISA), which gave the FBI greater powers to investigate agents of foreign-based terrorist organisations. Under the Act, FBI agents could apply to a judge at a special court sitting behind closed doors in Washington, to get a warrant to wire-tap suspects, whether the group they represented was sponsored by a foreign state or foreign terrorist organisation. Stephens explained that the other law under which wire-taps were carried out, the Crime Control and Safe Streets Act passed in 1968, authorised wire-taps only for fifteen-day periods. Authorisation could then be renewed for additional fifteen-day periods. This statute also required 'real time' monitoring – in other words, an agent had to monitor the microphone and, if he heard an incriminating conversation, turn the recorder on. If he heard the subject talking to his wife about buying bread on the way home, he turned the recorder off. 'That's a very labour-intensive situation,' said Stephens. On the other hand, the FISA wiretap authorisation was for ninety days, which could be renewed, and there was no requirement for real-time recording. 'You could turn the recorder on, and listen to the conversation afterwards, and ignore the conversations that were not necessary to the case.'

Stephens immediately set about instituting wiretaps on the Irish gunrunning suspects, and setting up surveillance. As they pored over the recordings, the agents began to learn a lot about the targets, over and above what was already in the archives. Said Stephens: 'We began to learn about the different players, the terminology being used, their codes, their tradecraft, where they would hang out, who they would meet, what discussions they were having. We also set up surveillance and saw all this activity taking place.' The FBI agents were able to assess the kinds of weaponry that the suspects were collecting for transfer to Ireland – apart from rifles and other firearms, they wanted ammunition for a 20mm cannon. The FBI also learned that the gunrunners were particularly interested in devices for the construction of bombs.

All this intelligence was useful by way of background information. But the FBI agents needed harder evidence and the key to getting that evidence was George DeMeo. For his part, IRA gunrunner George Harrison was very concerned when DeMeo went down for ten years. Many may abhor Harrison's support for the 'armed struggle' that resulted in so many families being bereaved, but he could never be faulted in terms of loyalty to his friends. The Mayoman wanted to do all he could to help DeMeo in his hour of need. They had worked together for a long time, and had become very close. Harrison considered there was a strong mutual trust between them. He also admired DeMeo's other qualities – his skills as a gunsmith and his capacity for hard work. 'We became very friendly,' Harrison told me. 'I would go to his wakes and he would come to mine. At wakes, he would be the man with the bow tie who took charge. He was as good a gunsmith as I ever came across. He could actually manufacture guns. He was a hard worker, too. A workaholic. He had no use for a guy that wouldn't work.'

DeMeo approached Harrison and said he would like to introduce him to another arms dealer who would be able to provide weapons while he, DeMeo, was in jail. In the light of the shipment that had been seized in Dublin and the conviction of DeMeo and Barnes, Harrison was wary. He did not distrust DeMeo in the least, but feared that in the light of recent set-backs his arms network was falling apart. Still, it was the time of the H-Block hunger strikes. Emotions were running high, and he was under pressure from senior republicans for more weaponry. Besides, DeMeo was holding out the possibility of some really lethal firepower, in the form of MAC-10 machine pistols, noted for their rapid rate of fire. Such weaponry would really enhance the capabilities of the IRA.

On 17 May 1981, DeMeo introduced Harrison to his contact, a bearded man in his thirties who purported to be an underworld arms dealer called John White. In reality, 'White' was undercover FBI agent John Winslow. The meeting took place at a house DeMeo had built for himself in Pelham, New York. Both DeMeo and Winslow were wired for sound. Everything that was said was recorded by the FBI. The agent offered to supply Harrison with 350 stolen MAC-10s and twelve AK-47 rifles. A deal was worked out, and subsequent meetings were held. Harrison also needed ammunition for a 20mm cannon which he had procured. It was capable of bringing down a British Army helicopter. White supplied twenty-four rounds for the 20mm cannon – Harrison was not to know that the rounds had been rendered inert before being handed over. Meanwhile, Harrison informed the IRA that a big deal was pending and the organisation sent over a senior figure to oversee the transaction. The IRA was also getting wary and appears to have decided that this should be the last operation carried out by the Harrison network.

The FBI monitored a conversation between the IRA boss, Harrison and his gunrunning colleague Tom Falvey, at the Harrison residence. The two elderly republicans had been involved in gunrunning to the IRA from as far back as the Fifties Campaign, but they were now coming to the end of the road. Falvey, who worked as a labourer, was a native of County Kerry. Said Stephens: 'What we heard was the senior IRA guy retiring Harrison and

Falvey. He told them it was over, that they had to do this in a more careful, quiet way.' Stephens went on: 'The IRA boss chose another man, and we knew that man to be Gabriel Megahey.'

The IRA had chosen a man who had already come to the attention of the authorities in the UK. MI5 knew all about his background. Megahey had moved to the US in the mid-1970s after being excluded from the UK because of suspected IRA activities. The British had suspected Megahey, who had been based in Southampton, of involvement in the arms pipeline that operated through the port in the early 1970s, with the aid of people linked to the Harrison network. Unlike Harrison, who was essentially a sympathiser doing his bit 'for the cause', the authorities in the US were to conclude that Megahey was a senior member of the IRA, in charge of arms procurement operations in North America, and under the control of the IRA back in Belfast.

Harrison and the sting

When I interviewed him in 2004, Harrison said he did not recall anybody coming over from Ireland to tell him he had to give up his gunrunning role. 'I have no recollection of anybody saying to me, "You have to step down." No recollection whatsoever. If they had told me, I would not have stepped down anyways, if I had my hands on weapons ...' Harrison did indicate that there were some younger elements who were 'vocal in the bars' and who poured scorn on the older people involved in arms procurement – Harrison and Falvey were in their sixties when they were busted. Harrison recalled that after he himself was arrested, Gabriel Megahey took over his gunrunning role. Harrison stressed that there was a very good relationship between himself and Megahey. 'When Gabe was arrested I stuck with him all the way through ... I have nothing but respect for him.'

Agents watching the Harrison home noted the comings and goings of the IRA boss who had come over from Ireland. The agents took surveillance pictures of the IRA man and showed them to MI5, who identified him as a senior player. According to Stephens, the MI5 people were extremely excited at the detection of this man: 'They could not stop shitting for a week.' The IRA man was picked up, held for a period, and then deported. Stephens could not remember the man's name, but he was almost certainly the late

Eamonn Doherty (sometimes referred to as O'Doherty), who at this period was reputed to be a senior figure in the movement, with special responsibility for procuring arms from sources abroad.

Doherty, born in Carrick-on-Suir, County Tipperary, in 1940, joined the IRA in the early 1960s and rose to a high rank in the organisation, serving as chief of staff for about a year from June 1973.[2] At one stage in his youth, in furtherance of the republican cause, he even joined the Parachute Regiment of the British Army. In 1981, after he was detected visiting the home of George Harrison, he was arrested at the Port Authority Bus Station in New York. He was held in federal prison and deported late that year. While in jail, Doherty was befriended by Mafia member Jimmy 'The Gent' Conway, the inspiration for the character played by Robert de Niro in the film *Goodfellas*.[3] Doherty died in 1999.

Another senior republican figure, Joe Cahill, who had slipped across the border from Canada and who was involved in fundraising, was also noted at Harrison's home during this period. It was believed that Cahill was the 'money man' who would collect funds raised in the US for the IRA, and hand the money over to Harrison for arms purchases.[4]

Meanwhile, the deal with 'John White' was progressing. On 19 June, Harrison collected more than $16,800 from Noraid founder Michael Flannery to pay for an initial consignment of weapons. It was arranged that White would meet Harrison and Falvey at Falvey's home in the Hollis area of Queens, and hand over weapons there. White delivered forty-seven MAC-10s, some AK-47 rifles and an Uzi sub-machine gun. He collected the cash and departed in his pickup truck. Later that night, Falvey and Harrison came out of the house and got into Falvey's Buick. Falvey planned to drive Harrison to the subway station. Harrison was carrying a bag with him.

When the waiting FBI agents saw Harrison with a bag, they feared that it might contain at least one of the firearms that had been handed over. They did not want to let any weapon disappear and end up in Ireland, where it would be a threat to life. Agents moved in and intercepted the car, arresting Harrison and Falvey. Stephens said the Bureau was paranoid about making 'controlled' sales of arms to the Irish paramilitaries. 'They were so afraid that one of the guns was going to get out of our control and the next thing it was going to do was to kill some poor British non-commissioned officer in Northern Ireland whose mother would hate us for the rest of her life.'

The result was, in the various Irish cases they investigated involving the controlled transfer of arms to the gunrunners, twenty-four-hour surveillance had to be laid on – sometimes for months. It was very labour-intensive. 'One time I had seventy-two people a day working on surveillance,' recalled Stephens.

The FBI agents looked in Harrison's bag, but it was found to contain nothing more lethal than a couple of cans of beer. The agents had search warrants for the homes of the two men, and the home of one of their associates, Paddy Mullin. A thin, gray-haired man no longer in the first flush of youth, Mullin was arrested at his residence early the following morning. Officers who searched the garage at Mullin's home at Ridgewood Avenue, Brooklyn, found a cache of weapons including seven automatic rifles, a machine pistol, a pre-Second World War 20mm cannon and a flame-thrower. Records found at Harrison's home showed he had been smuggling weapons for the IRA for at least twenty years. The traffic appeared to involve more than 1,000 weapons and close to one million rounds of ammunition – with a value of more than $1 million. In fact the records told only part of the story – the real figure supplied by Harrison to the IRA over the decades was probably well over 2,000 weapons – Harrison himself reckoned the real figure could be closer to 3,000 (*see* Chapter 3).

Harrison was brought to the FBI building at Federal Plaza, and came face to face with Lou Stephens. There was a rather tense confrontation. Stephens' recollection is that Harrison said to him, 'You know, I am not doing anything different from what your forefathers did when they fought against the British in the colonial war.' Stephens shot back, 'Listen to me, I'm the one wearing the badge tonight, don't you cite the Constitution of the United States to me. I'm the one who is the expert on the Constitution of the United States tonight. Not you.'

The following October Mike Flannery, who lived at Jackson Heights, Queens, was arrested on his return from a trip to Ireland. A prominent figure in the Gaelic Athletic Association (GAA) in New York, he went over to Dublin every year for the All-Ireland football and hurling finals held at Croke Park in September. A native of Knockshegowna, County Tipperary, the venerable white-haired figure had joined the IRA at age fourteen – he was tall for his age and could pass for being older. He fought with an IRA flying column in his native county during the Troubles of the

1920s. He took the republican side in the Civil War that followed, as a member of the Tipperary No. 1 Brigade of the IRA.

Harrison recalled that Flannery was in Mountjoy Prison, Dublin, on the day in 1922, during the Civil War, when a Free State army firing squad carried out the reprisal executions of four republican prisoners – Rory O'Connor, Liam Mellowes, Joseph McKelvey and Richard Barrett. They were shot on 8 December, the Feast of the Immaculate Conception. These events left a deep impression on the Tipperary man. Flannery told friends of seeing the dust and the grit rising up past his cell window as the bullets hit the sandbags.

Many years later, Flannery told an Irish journalist that he had never knowingly killed anyone during the Civil War, but he had once put a gun to the head of a Free State soldier and it had misfired. 'To this day I regret that it misfired,' he said.[5] Flannery emigrated to America in 1927, and worked as an insurance agent. A few years after arriving in New York he married Dr Margaret Mary 'Pearl' Egan, a native of Mullinahone, County Tipperary, who had been a member of the republican women's group, Cumann na mBan. They had no children. Flannery was active in Catholic Church activities, and was a life-long teetotaller as a member of the Church's Pioneer Total Abstinence Association.

When the FBI swooped on 2 October, Flannery, a daily communicant, was arrested coming from early morning Mass at his local church, the Church of the Blessed Sacrament, in Jackson Heights. He and his wife had just returned from Ireland the night before. Stephens recalled that he assigned a female agent to carry out the arrest. Flannery was detained by the agent, accompanied by three male colleagues. He was allowed to call in to his nearby home to tell his wife Pearl that he was under arrest. He was then taken to FBI headquarters in downtown Manhattan. Shortly afterwards, he was given bail. In April 1982 another suspect, Leitrim-born Danny Gormley, was picked up. The curly-headed Gormley was one of the younger suspects.

Harrison, who idolised Flannery, resented the way his friend was arrested. 'Michael Flannery was a very distinguished and honoured man. They tried to diminish him, you know. They arrested him near the church. Michael was a church-going man. I think he went to church daily. They let him go to Ireland and when he came back they arrested him in front of his neighbours. They said, in effect, "This is what we think of Flannery."'

The five men, known as the Brooklyn Five, went on trial on arms trafficking charges in federal court in Brooklyn on 23 September, 1982.
George Harrison, Thomas Falvey, Patrick Mullin, Michael Flannery and
Daniel Gormley were defended by O'Dwyer & Bernstien, the firm of the
formidable Irish-born lawyer Paul O'Dwyer, who had been active in many
political causes. O'Dwyer's nephew and law firm colleague Frank Durkan
took a prominent role in the case.[6] The defence lawyers devised a most
ingenious and courageous defence: the argument was advanced in court
that George DeMeo was a CIA agent and that the defendants assumed
they were working for the US government at the time of their arrest. Flannery was the only one of the defendants to take the stand. He said he would
not have got involved in an arms procurement scheme with George Harrison had he not known that DeMeo had connections to the government.

'Because you did not intend to violate the laws of the United States, correct?' his lawyer asked him.

'Exactly,' the octogenarian Flannery promptly replied.[7]

The jury accepted the argument and the men were acquitted on 5
November, after a nine-week trial, even though DeMeo went on the stand
and denied a connection with the CIA. The claim that DeMeo had CIA
links was bolstered by the 1969 incident in which he and an arms dealer
from North Carolina had had gunrunning charges against them withdrawn
amid reports that they were acting on behalf of the CIA (*see* Chapter 3). It
was not unknown for the CIA to use arms dealers as a 'front' in covert
transactions. Defence lawyers tracked down the North Carolina businessman in Paraguay and he testified for the defendants, saying he believed
DeMeo was an agent of the CIA.

The accused Irishmen and their friends and supporters were jubilant at
the outcome of the case. Celebrations were held. O'Dwyer's firm had given
their legal services free, earning the undying gratitude of the defendants.
Harrison told me: 'Paul O'Dwyer was the mastermind behind the defence.
There was no charge. It would have cost us at least $1 million otherwise.
All the attorneys like Frank Durkan worked pro bono. One of them was
Barry Scheck, who later defended OJ Simpson.'

When I spoke to him towards the end of his life, Harrison appeared to
make some allowances for the action of his former friend George DeMeo
in informing on him to the authorities. He saw DeMeo as acting out of

weakness rather than malice. 'He turned us in. But he was not a professional plant. He weakened at the end. There is a difference between somebody who weakens and somebody who comes in deliberately to blow you apart. He weakened; he could not face the ten years. I tell you the truth, he surprised me. I had so much going with him. We had so much confidence in each other.' Harrison said that his friend Tom Falvey had even begun working for DeMeo in construction. Harrison was hoping to get some work also. 'If things had gone on okay, DeMeo had something in mind for me in that line too.'

In 1986, Harrison and his friend Mike Flannery went with the small group that broke away from Sinn Féin to form Republican Sinn Féin (RSF). RSF virulently opposed the Sinn Féin decision to end the policy of abstention from the Irish parliament, the Dáil. One of the leading lights in RSF was Harrison's old gunrunning colleague, Dáithí Ó Conaill. In an interview in 1990, Harrison told me of his reasons for going with RSF and his support for the abstentionist policy: 'That's the way we started out in my youth and I did not see how we could advance on the road to the Republic by any participation in the institutions that we were set up to overturn in the first place.'

In my interview with Harrison in 2004, he rejected the Peace Process and the Good Friday Agreement. The latter had been endorsed by the Irish people, North and South, but Harrison was still not for turning on the issue. He appeared to follow the traditional view that the Irish people do not have the right to reject the Republic. Referring to the Good Friday Agreement, he said, 'I would like to know what's "good" about it ... The problem is the Brits. They are the problem in Ireland. They have tried everything but leave. They are the main problem and they will be the problem until they leave.'

During the 1970s, Harrison kept open house for any senior republicans visiting New York. Joe Cahill, Martin McGuinness and Ruairí Ó Brádaigh were among those who stayed in his home. However, after the 1986 split, people like Cahill, McGuinness and of course Gerry Adams, now part of 'mainstream' Sinn Féin, were regarded as political opponents by Harrison. He virulently disagreed with the path they had taken.

He had no regrets about his own political decisions. 'I have no doubts about it now,' he told me in his last interview. 'Gerry [Adams] has taken the wrong turn. I don't want nobody to hurt him in any way. If he is waiting for me to hurt him he will live forever. They are doing what they're doing, and let them go. History will judge them.' Nevertheless he had some good memories of former colleagues. He remembered Martin McGuinness as a 'real gentleman', adding: 'I don't think he took a drink.' He had many memories also of Joe Cahill, the former senior IRA man who died in July 2004, and who backed the Adams line on the Peace Process. 'Joe Cahill, poor fella, my house was his house for a long time, and he is gone now. He went the wrong way at the end. I had great time for Joe and great time for his wife Annie. She was a good singer. They gave him a good send-off in Ireland and here, but history will judge them, like it will judge us.'

The fact that Mike Flannery, the founder of Noraid, came up with $16,800 in cash for the purchase of the weapons involved in Harrison's last arms deal bolstered long-standing suspicions that Noraid money was being used to finance arms and to further IRA activity. However, looking back on his gunrunning career, Harrison insisted that no money from Noraid was used to buy guns. 'None of the Noraid money went to purchase arms. Not one dollar. We had our own sources. When push came to shove we would take out a loan from a bank. And we would pay back. We always had people who would come up with a few thousand when it was needed.' During his trial, Flannery was also insistent that no Noraid money went on arms. He said that people donated money for the specific purpose of assisting the IRA, especially at the time of the H-Block hunger strikes, and he kept this money separately, at his home, while the money donated to Noraid was placed in a bank account. Flannery was to die, at age ninety-three, on 30 September 1994.

According to Harrison, after he himself was busted and put on trial, he ceased his involvement in gunrunning, although he was available to give advice. 'The only way you could do it then was to advise.' Nevertheless, in my 1990 interview with him, he said that he had to assume that he was still under surveillance by the authorities. The Harrison network, undoubtedly the most successful and most enduring gunrunning group of its kind to be associated with the IRA, was no more. Harrison and his small circle of friends had supplied thousands of firearms and unquantifiable amounts of ammunition 'for the cause'. For the PIRA Squad, it was just the beginning of a blitz against IRA gunrunning, and the Feds were to make further breakthroughs in the campaign to disrupt the arms trail to Ireland.

CHAPTER 8

A Quest for Missiles

IRA gunrunner Gerry McGeough was in Florida in the summer of 1982 when he got an urgent phone call. It was from another member of a Provo gunrunning circle operating on the east coast of the United States. McGeough was told to travel to New York immediately for a very important meeting. For security reasons, the purpose of the meeting was not mentioned over the phone. When he met his gunrunning colleague at an apartment in the Bronx, McGeough was given some disturbing news – the authorities had intercepted one of their arms shipments. A contact in US customs had tipped off the IRA group that an arms consignment going through Newark port in a cargo container, en route to Ireland, had been seized. McGeough had contributed arms to the shipment. He knew he would be a target for the FBI's PIRA Squad, led by the relentless Lou Stephens.

McGeough immediately went to ground. He crossed America, sometimes living rough, sometimes taking low-paying casual jobs like picking fruit. At one stage he made his way to Hawaii and slept on the beach there. He had his own contacts in the US, but for security reasons avoided Irish bars and other centres where people of Irish background hung out. He eventually made his way to Europe.

It appears that McGeough's friends were unaware that the FBI had allowed some arms to proceed to Ireland in the container, to ensnare whoever turned up to collect them. No warning got through, and two people were arrested and charged after collecting the container in Ireland. The perception seems to have been that McGeough was the person most at risk – the gunrunners seemingly did not realise, at the time, the extent of FBI surveillance on members of the group. Other activists were to be rounded up in New York.

It was in the early 1980s that Gerry McGeough became an IRA gunrunner in the USA. He belonged to the new breed of younger operators who took over arms procurement activities following the break-up of the Harrison network. McGeough, from the Dungannon area of County Tyrone, was an experienced IRA operator. He had gone to school at St Patrick's Academy, where one of his teachers was Father Denis Faul. Father Faul was prominent in the campaign against human rights abuses by the security forces, and was a chaplain who tended the spiritual needs of republican prisoners at the Maze prison. But Father Faul also went on to become an outspoken critic of the IRA's campaign of violence. He persistently demanded that the IRA stop the killing. Because of this, he became a reviled figure for many in the republican movement but other republicans, like Gerry McGeough, retained a soft spot for the courageous, outspoken cleric.

It was not just a secular education that Fr Faul provided to his charges in St Patrick's – he also sought to inculcate a strong Catholic religious faith, including an abhorrence of abortion. In the case of McGeough, Father Faul was pushing an open door. Despite pursuing the paramilitary path, McGeough was to remain a dedicated, traditional, practising Catholic. The idea of the strongly Catholic IRA man was common enough in the 1920s, and later during the 1950s Border Campaign. During the more recent Troubles, with increasing secularism taking hold in Ireland, it was, perhaps, a little more unusual among the younger generation of IRA men.

McGeough joined Sinn Féin in 1975, at age sixteen, and became a member of the Tyrone IRA later that year, having reached the age of seventeen. With little or no training, he was soon engaged in operations against the security forces, and had some very close shaves. He was later to recall how the IRA men were using ancient, bolt-action .303 rifles against the far better-equipped British Army and RUC. (A former IRA man told the author that in one particular area of Tyrone in the mid-1970s, the local

IRA unit had just one modern weapon – a rather battered AK-47 rifle. It bore Chinese characters, and had been brought back from Vietnam by a US soldier. The source recalled how he had to figure out for himself how to fire the rifle, and how to change the weapon from single shot to automatic mode. Such experiences gave an added impetus to efforts to procure modern weapons for the IRA. The former Provo added that he and his colleagues were seasoned operators, with three years' experience behind them, before they were sent to a training camp.)

McGeough was arrested in London in 1978 and served with an exclusion order, preventing him from entering the UK 'mainland'. He was sent back to Northern Ireland. Subsequently, he was seriously wounded in a shoot-out on the Border. He ended up in hospital in the Irish Republic, under heavy guard. He slipped out of the hospital and in 1981, relying on his own resources and initiative, made his way via Iceland to the USA. His main role now would be in procuring arms for the IRA.

McGeough recalled later how, during a stopover in the airport at Reykjavik, a large contingent of British soldiers came into the lounge. He was afraid that some of them might have served in Northern Ireland, and might recognise him from mugshots of IRA men distributed to soldiers on the ground. But nobody 'sussed' McGeough and the moment of danger passed. (Despite media reports that McGeough was once arrested on the Border farm of the republican Thomas 'Slab' Murphy and taken away by British Army helicopter, McGeough is at pains to state that this is untrue – he says he has never met Murphy. He is also at pains to refute a media report that he was trained in Libya – he states that he has never been to that country.)

McGeough based himself in New York, making regular forays to Florida and other locations to acquire weapons for transfer to the Provos. He would operate essentially independently, but in liaison with the arms trafficking network headed by New York-based Gabriel Megahey, who had succeeded George Harrison in this role. It is believed McGeough was assisted by a small Irish-American republican support group based in the US.

Different states had different gun laws, and he learned quickly about the best ways of acquiring firearms. Some weapons were acquired by the simple stratagem of going into a gun shop, showing a driver's licence and making the purchase. In those days, with no closed circuit cameras and little in the way of computerised records, it was possible for an individual to buy a multiplicity of guns without arousing too much suspicion. Another method was to check out the 'Guns For Sale' ads in local newspapers, and buy direct from private individuals.

McGeough transported small quantities of weapons back to New York by taking them with him in his baggage as he travelled by Greyhound bus. At one stage, McGeough received word that somebody had a small collection of AK-47 rifles in the San Francisco area. He was bringing them back in his baggage aboard a Greyhound bus when police boarded the vehicle en route. He feared the worst. How had the cops got onto him? In fact they ignored him. Their focus was on a teenage couple who had run away from home together, and whose parents were worried.

Megahey's network would arrange to transport the weaponry McGeough had sourced to Ireland. A type of 'cell' system operated. McGeough considered it was good for security to keep his own operations in Florida and elsewhere separate from whatever the people in New York were doing.

Gabriel Megahey, a Belfast-born former seaman, had settled in New York after his exclusion from 'mainland' UK as a terrorism suspect in the mid-1970s. He worked for a time as a barman in the Queens area, and also worked in construction. One of Megahey's priorities was to secure surface-to-air missiles to bring down British Army helicopters operating in Northern Ireland – especially in the strongly republican of South Armagh. Because of the threat from roadside bombs and landmines, the British forces preferred to operate by helicopter in areas such as Crossmaglen. The military base there was supplied by air. Procuring missiles that would threaten the British command of the air was an ambitious project.

By early 1982 the FBI had identified Megahey as the man who had succeeded George Harrison as head of the IRA's New York-based arms procurement drive. The FBI estimated that he had a group of about ten men working with him on arms procurement and smuggling. Megahey was unaware that he was now a major focus of attention for the very determined agents of the FBI's new PIRA Squad. Lou Stephens recalled: 'Megahey was very coy, very cagey, very well disciplined in his tradecraft. He had a crew around him who were very, very dedicated.'

In June 1981, just as the FBI was closing down the Harrison network, the PIRA Squad had a stroke of luck, which led to the penetration of the Megahey network that had replaced the Harrison group. That was the month that Andrew Duggan, an Irish-American member of the Megahey group, who was also active in the Irish republican fundraising group Noraid, approached a New York electronics surveillance and counter-surveillance expert, Michael Hanratty. Duggan had been put in touch with Hanratty by an acquaintance.

Accompanied by a Belfast man called Brendan, Duggan met Hanratty. The two men identified themselves as members of the IRA and said they wanted to buy equipment for use against the British in Northern Ireland. They met again the same evening and Duggan, accompanied by Brendan and another associate, explained in more detail the IRA's requirements. They enquired about a variety of equipment – including bulletproof vests, electronic tracking systems and devices to detect the presence of electronic surveillance. But their main interest was in acquiring sophisticated remote-control detonators for remote-control bombs – items that Hanratty could not supply.

Hanratty immediately tipped off the FBI. Members of the PIRA Squad were ecstatic. They could not believe their luck. It was the kind of opening into the IRA's inner circle in New York that they were hoping for. Hanratty agreed to co-operate with FBI agent Enrique Ghimenti in a 'sting' operation. Wiretap surveillance was to prove a vital part of the investigation.

Stephens explained: 'We not only had the wiretaps, we had an informant, Hanratty, and the arms buying people went to that informant because they were so afraid to go into Radio Shack [a chain of US electronics stores]. This was because at the time they made you sign a receipt for whatever you purchased and give an address so they could send you a marketing brochure. So they had my guy go in and do that stuff for them and he would report back to us and he would wear wires at the various meetings they would have.'

It was a slow-burn investigation. Over the next six months, Duggan and Brendan made a number of contacts with Hanratty concerning the purchase of a variety of items that could be used as fusing mechanisms for bombs. According to a court document, Brendan also asked Hanratty if he could supply surface-to-air missiles (SAMs) to shoot down British Army helicopters. Hanratty claimed that Duggan told him the IRA 'wanted to make larger strikes – rather than shooting down one man with one gun, they wanted to shoot down a whole plane-load'.

During his meetings with Hanratty, Duggan apparently often spoke of the 'money man' who would arrange the supply of finance for IRA purchases. In January 1982, Duggan summoned Hanratty for his first meeting with this 'money man', who turned out to be Gabriel Megahey. The Belfast man introduced himself as the head of IRA operations in the US, and indicated that he was meeting Hanratty because he had become an important asset to the organisation. He also reminded Hanratty of the need to deliver certain devices that had been ordered – safety mechanisms for the making of remote-controlled bombs.

After Megahey's debut on the scene, the FBI immediately applied to a judge, in a special court set up under the Foreign Intelligence Surveillance Act (FISA), for an order allowing agents to tap Megahey's home phone. The phone surveillance began on 10 February 1982, and soon bore fruit for the listening agents.

Some days before, on 6 February, US authorities in Buffalo had detained five men with Irish republican links as they crossed the border from Canada. One of them was Dessie Ellis, who had jumped bail on explosives charges in Dublin. (On 3 March 1983, Ellis was deported to Dublin where, on 19 April, he was convicted of possession of explosive substances and sentenced to eight years. In more recent years he entered politics, and in June 2004 was re-elected as a Sinn Féin member of Dublin City Council.) A search produced what appeared to be a shopping list for war materiel – 200,000 rounds of ammunition and electronic bomb-making equipment. A list of contacts was also uncovered, including the name and phone number of Gabriel Megahey. The FBI wiretap on Megahey's phone recorded him on 14 May expressing dismay to another man about the fact that the men arrested had his contact details on them. 'Every time somebody comes down, there is a problem,' Megahey fumed. 'You know what they had on them? My name!'

The wiretap also intercepted several conversations between Megahey and Duggan regarding IRA activities. Information from the wiretap led agents to place the home of Eamon Meehan, an associate of Megahey's, under surveillance. Agents also tried to keep surveillance on Megahey but found it difficult to keep track of him – he proved to be an expert in counter-surveillance techniques.

In March 1982, Hanratty obtained the safety devices he had been asked to secure, and FBI agents kept watch as he delivered them to Duggan. FBI technical experts had already microscopically marked the devices to facilitate identification at a later stage. Hanratty was again asked by two associates of Duggan about the possibility of acquiring SAMs. Hanratty said he knew a possible source, a Miami-based wheeler-dealer called Luis who supplied arms to countries in Central America and elsewhere. Duggan and Megahey were eager for Hanratty to make contact with Luis.

On 2 May 1982 Hanratty, at the instigation of the FBI, finally introduced Duggan to one of Luis's lieutenants, an Hispanic-looking man called Enrique. This was, in fact, FBI special agent Enrique Ghimenti. The FBI secretly videotaped the meeting in New York as Duggan explained that, while he was interested in buying grenades and automatic weapons, his main priority was SAMs. The FBI agents monitoring the meeting were frustrated when Duggan did not sit where they had expected him to sit. As a result, they failed to get the anticipated video footage but they did manage to record his voice. Duggan agreed with Enrique that a further meeting would be held, to be attended by IRA representatives who were more experienced in arms and their prices. When word was relayed back to Megahey that arms dealers with a Latin American connection might be able to supply missiles that could shoot down helicopters, the Belfast man was very interested indeed.

Stephens had a way of getting missiles or other weapons that might be needed for a controlled delivery to suspects as part of a 'sting' operation. 'We would go to the Brooklyn naval yard – the Marine Corps had a naval criminal investigation service there. There was a place where we could get all of this stuff. It was readily available. We would just pick it up.' Missiles were deactivated before being used in a controlled delivery situation. Nevertheless, the downside of making a controlled delivery was that the FBI then had to mount intense surveillance to keep track of the weaponry involved. 'That's what ate up all our manpower,' said Stephens.

The next meeting to discuss the missile deal was to be held in New Orleans. Megahey had to find somebody to travel to New Orleans with another operative called Sean to make further inquiries into the deal. He made contact with Gerry McGeough and asked him to travel to Louisiana to check out what was on offer. McGeough was being asked to fill in for somebody else who could not go on the trip. McGeough has said he felt he was not fully up to speed on what was to be discussed.

Deception in New Orleans

McGeough and his colleague Sean, along with Duggan, met the 'arms dealers' at an upstairs office in a warehouse in the New Orleans docklands area. Duggan made the introductions and then absented himself from the meeting. 'Enrique' was accompanied by two undercover FBI agents, one posing as 'Luis', the other posing as Luis's 'technical adviser'. McGeough was given to understand that the shadowy figures he was dealing with had been engaged in gunrunning in Central America. The story was plausible enough. There was armed conflict in Central America at that time, and New Orleans would have been a convenient base for arms traffickers seeking to supply that market. No doubt New Orleans was chosen as a venue to give an additional element of credibility to the 'dealers'.

The Irishmen described themselves as being from the 'Provisionals – the Irish Republican Army'. The 'dealers', who looked Hispanic, said they could supply Redeye missiles at $10,000 a go. (The FIM-43 Redeye is a short-range, man-portable, surface-to-air missile that was produced by the US concern General Dynamics. It incorporated 1960s-era technology that would have been considered outmoded by contemporary military standards – nevertheless it would have been extremely useful to the IRA.) The IRA negotiators indicated that they would be interested in five Redeyes at that price. They were also interested in automatic rifles and sub-machine guns. The 'gunrunners' showed off a Heckler and Koch MP5 sub-machine gun. It was agreed that another meeting would be held two weeks later to further discuss the transaction.

The New Orleans meeting was secretly videotaped by the PIRA Squad. It was too soon, however, for the FBI to spring the trap, and McGeough and his colleague were allowed to go on their way. McGeough reported back to Megahey. Unfortunately for McGeough, having previously operated discreetly and undetected, he was now very much in the frame and a major focus of FBI attention.

McGeough made a subsequent visit to New Orleans, driving from Florida in a camper van with the intention of picking up the missiles, but the meeting with the 'suppliers' failed to take place. McGeough was to bitterly regret being drawn into the New Orleans affair, as it was to compromise not only his own Florida arms procurement operation, but was to make him personally a target of the FBI, having previously never come to the notice of the US authorities.

Meanwhile, the PIRA Squad found out that the Megahey group was preparing to send a consignment of weaponry to the IRA back home. Said Stephens: 'We knew that Megahey had been given the signal to move any missiles and weapons he had purchased to Ireland. Megahey's people rented a Red Barn [rental company] truck, and in the middle of the night they went out to all these places where the stuff had been stored – a guy's house, the cellar of a bar in Queen's, and other places.'

The agents watched as the truck, with all the collected arms on board, travelled to a building on West 40th Street in Manhattan. The date was 27 May. The gunrunners parked the truck, and took eleven boxes of arms and ammunition out of it. They went upstairs to a second- or third-floor warehouse, and came out with comforters, roller skates and all kinds of toys. The arms and ammunition were loaded into the back of a shipping container, and all the 'innocuous' cargo was loaded into the front, hiding the lethal part of the shipment. Stephens outlined how the FBI agents tailed the truck transporting the container as two men from Northern Ireland, Eamon Meehan and an associate, drove it to the docks in the New Jersey port of Newark.

The agents did not move in straight away. They observed the unsuspecting Irishmen drive off after delivering the container for shipment to Ireland. Stephens recalled: 'Later that night we called in the US customs. They have extraordinary search authority without benefit of a warrant for a cargo like that.' When the customs opened the shipping container, labelled 'roller skates and comforters', they found an arms cache that included fifty-one rifles (including twenty-five Armalite AR-15s and a number of HK91s), fifty-five blasting caps and remote-control devices. The FBI recovered from the container the switches that had been marked by the agency's laboratory personnel before being handed over by Hanratty to Duggan.

The FBI removed most of the arms, but allowed a few sample weapons to travel to Ireland in the container with the roller skates and comforters, tipping off the Gardaí to keep a lookout for whoever collected the container on the other side. Just to be on the safe side, the weapons were decommissioned before being allowed to proceed to Ireland. Said Stephens: 'We sawed off the firing pins of the weapons and put them back on the container. They were no good except to be used as clubs.' Some time later, John Moloney and Patrick McVeigh, who arrived to pick up the container, were to be arrested in Limerick by the Gardaí.

Having dispatched the arms cargo to Ireland, the unsuspecting members of the Megahey group pressed on with efforts to procure surface-to-air missiles. A further meeting was set up with the 'arms dealers' who were to supply the weapons. It was to be held on 11 June 1982, at the St Regis hotel in New York. Megahey himself decided to go along this time, to put the finishing touches on the deal. The Feds could not believe their luck when Megahey walked in. Lou Stephens was outside the venue in a car, monitoring events. 'We had the room all wired up. We had briefcases on the bed with cameras, we had microphones, and lo and behold, who walks in but Megahey … My back teeth were clacking I was so nervous.'

The agents secretly videotaped Megahey as he affirmed the order for the Redeye missiles. He boasted that he had $1 million available for missiles and automatic weapons. He was also filmed proposing a hostage exchange arrangement to ensure that neither side was betrayed. 'One thing's sure, that if any of my men get nicked, you're dead. If any of your men get nicked, the guy you've got is dead,' Megahey said on the FBI tape. The 'dealers' did not want to go along with the proposed exchange of hostages, and the SAM 'deal' was cancelled. Megahey walked out of the venue, apparently still not suspecting a 'sting'. Stephens decided that they had enough evidence, and that they would start wrapping up the case, although they would not arrest Megahey straight away. Recalled Stephens: 'It was at this point I decided we can't take this any further.'

At some stage members of the Megahey group learned, to their great consternation, that the arms shipment sent through Newark had been intercepted. It is unclear exactly when the tip came through to the group. It would appear that the gunrunners were unaware of the extent of FBI surveillance, and that they judged that McGeough was the person most at risk, as there was a danger that weapons in the consignment could be traced to him. He had gone on the run by the time the FBI began to make arrests.

On 21 June 1982, the FBI swooped in New York, arresting Gabriel Megahey and Andrew Duggan. The arrests took place just ten days after Megahey's meeting with the undercover agents in the St Regis Hotel. Megahey was grabbed on the construction site in Manhattan where he was working as a crane and elevator operator. Agents with guns drawn pushed the stunned IRA man over the bonnet of a car to frisk him, before taking him to FBI Central Headquarters. The PIRA Squad were jubilant. Megahey and Duggan were charged with conspiracy to violate the National Firearms Act. Also rounded up were Eamonn Meehan and his sidekick. They were charged with trying to smuggle firearms, ammunition and bulletproof vests to Ireland.

Some time after Gerry McGeough went to ground, a member of the IRA's General Headquarters (GHQ) staff travelled to the US and made contact with him. I have been given to understand that the arms procurement effort was revived, and a new gunrunning group set up that was not detected during the period in which it operated. According to a republican source, lessons had been learned from the debacle that the IRA had suffered, and stringent new security precautions were put in place. The source said that a major shipment of arms was assembled, including G3 rifles, sub-machine guns and high explosives, and successfully shipped to Ireland via France in 1983.

According to the source, an IRA man travelled from the US to the port of Cherbourg to expedite the onward shipping of the container to Ireland. The operation was almost aborted when a difficult French official raised a query about the date on the shipping documents. The confusion arose over differences in the US and European methods of giving a date in numerals – the Americans put the month first and the day second, while in Europe it's the other way around. The IRA man was in a sweat. Having brought the consignment so far, he did not want to lose it now. He managed to mollify the official and clarify the matter. The container continued on its way to Ireland. For the IRA, the successful delivery of this consignment must have provided some consolation after its arms procurement drive had suffered major setbacks in the US, with the Harrison and Megahey networks being broken up.

The source said he often wondered whether high explosives that were delivered in this consignment were used in the attack in Brighton, England, in October 1984, aimed at assassinating British prime minister Margaret Thatcher and her entire cabinet. It has been widely reported that Semtex explosive was used in this atrocity, which killed five people but failed to kill the main target, Mrs Thatcher.[1] If so, this Semtex would not have been part of the sizeable load of Semtex delivered from Libya in the mid-1980s – those deliveries did not begin until 1986. So what was the origin of the high explosive used in the Brighton operation? Could it have been delivered from the US, via France, in 1983?

While most Irish-related arms procurement activity during this period was centred on the eastern seaboard of the US, especially in the cities with large Irish communities like New York and Boston, there was also some suspected activity in the west. In 1983 the FBI arrested an Irish-born man at Timnath, Colorado, after he allegedly tried to buy explosives in Wyoming. He was arrested again in Fort Collins, Colorado, in June 1985, and charged with attempting to buy arms illegally. He pleaded guilty to a charge of conspiracy to purchase firearms and was deported to Ireland in November 1985. However, no information emerged about the man's paramilitary connections, if any.

For Gabriel Megahey and the three others who were rounded up in New York in June 1982, it was to be the end of their arms trafficking activities. During the ensuing trial, lawyers for Eamonn Meehan and the other man who helped take the weapons to the port said they had been detained as internees at Long Kesh camp, and suffered post-traumatic stress. A plea of not guilty because of insanity was entered. This was rejected by the judge after hearing psychiatric evidence. (Eamonn Meehan's legal team included up-and-coming lawyer Barry Scheck, of OJ Simpson defence team fame, who was also part of the legal team that defended George Harrison and his co-accused.)

Lawyers for the accused men also tried the 'CIA defence' that had worked so well in the Harrison/Flannery case. They argued that the defendants thought that Michael Hanratty was a CIA agent and that they therefore thought that the US government had given approval to the gunrunning scheme. The 'CIA defence' failed to work this time. The prosecution produced CIA affidavits stating that Hanratty was not one of the agency's operatives.

Megahey would later be described in an appeal court judgement as 'the leader and financier' of IRA operations in the US. He and the other defendants were said to be 'part of a network of men working clandestinely on behalf of PIRA to acquire explosives, weapons, ammunition and remote-controlled detonation devices in the United States to be exported to Northern Ireland to be used in terrorist activities'.

Duggan, an American citizen, was described as 'Megahey's assistant in contacting sellers of electronic equipment to be used in remote-controlled bombs and other sophisticated weaponry'. It was stated that Eamon Meehan, under the direction of Megahey, 'gathered and stored firearms and explosives', and that Eamon and his associate, 'both aliens living illegally in the United States, secreted these materials in a shipment of goods bound for Northern Ireland'.[2]

During the trial Frank Schulte, from the FBI PIRA Squad, told the court that he had contact with the British authorities in connection with the case, but refused to elaborate. One could speculate that this contact was in relation to Megahey, who had come to the attention of the UK authorities in the 1970s.

After a nine-week hearing, the men were found guilty on 13 May 1983 on most of the charges against them. Megahey, who was considered the ringleader of the conspiracy, was sentenced to seven years' imprisonment. Andrew Duggan and Eamon Meehan were each given three years, while the fourth defendant was jailed for two years, having been acquitted on some of the conspiracy charges. Another man who was sought by the FBI in relation to the investigation had moved to Ireland, but decided voluntarily to return for trial. His lawyers successfully argued that he did not know that the boxes that he transported for Eamonn Meehan contained arms. He was finally cleared of all charges in November 1983.

Megahey and the other three convicted men all appealed against their convictions, their lawyers arguing in particular that the District Court erred in refusing to suppress evidence obtained through a wiretap pursuant to the Foreign Intelligence Surveillance Act (FISA). It was argued that the FISA was unconstitutionally broad, and violated the 'probable cause' requirement of the Fourth Amendment.[3] The Appeal Court decided in August 1984 to reject the appeal.

Closer ties between US and UK agents

Back in Ireland, John Moloney and Belfast-born Patrick McVeigh, who were arrested when they tried to pick up the container with the weapons sent by the Megahey group, went on trial. It was stated that the container had been shipped to Dublin port and then shadowed by detectives as it was transported by road to Limerick. Stephens and other members of the FBI PIRA Squad travelled to Dublin to give evidence in the Special Criminal Court. Stephens liaised with his opposite number in Dublin at the time, assistant garda commissioner Ned O'Dea, whom he described as a good friend.

While in Ireland, Stephens availed of the opportunity to travel up to Belfast, where he met with his RUC counterpart, assistant chief constable Brian Fitzsimmons, head of RUC Special Branch, who also became a close friend, and other senior RUC officers. Stephens was introduced to the RUC men by Bob Moore, who was then the FBI's UK representative, or legal attaché, based at the US Embassy in London. 'We met with some very fine people and established some great lines of communication,' said Stephens. He stayed at the upmarket Europa hotel in Belfast, which had been the target of IRA bomb attacks, and saw at first hand the security situation on the ground – the British Army patrols, the fortified police stations, the security at banks and business premises.

He was greatly saddened when Fitzsimmons was killed in the RAF Chinook helicopter crash in June 1994, along with more than two dozen of Northern Ireland's most prominent security and intelligence people. Fitzsimmons was the most senior of the police officers to die, and among those who attended his funeral was Stella Rimington, the then director general of MI5.

As Stephens and his squad made headway against the IRA and its gunrunners in the earlier part of the 1980s, Stephens sensed that the British security people, traditionally very reserved and secretive, were becoming more open towards the FBI, and more co-operative with the agency. In the security world, British intelligence culture was far more secretive than that of the Americans, but in Stephens' view the British began to loosen up a little. 'When we started the IRA cases, and had those successes, things opened up for our legal attaché in London, Bob Moore, who was a good friend of mine, things that had previously not been opened. It was because we were having such success.'

According to Stephens, he had some shouting matches at one stage with the British to convince them to share their information with the FBI. 'You have to understand that back then, the British mentality was that everything had to be held very close to the vest. The natural British tendency to keep things very close and not share things was a very real hindrance to our cases, because they had real critical, crucial information that we had to get entered into our criminal cases if we were going to win. If we were not going to win a case, what the hell was the sense of the exercise?' Stephens said he had to make the British understand that 'things are different in our country, we don't have the same tradition of secrecy – things don't get done that way'.

Stephens took part in a number of anti-terrorism conferences, involving a range of police and security agencies from the US, UK, Northern Ireland and the Irish Republic. He hosted the first such conference in New York, in one of the big hotels on Central Park West. Representatives of the FBI, New Scotland Yard, the Gardaí and MI5 attended. There was a social side to the conference, with delegates going for meals and for drinks together. He found the conference particularly helpful in establishing a rapport with his opposite numbers in other agencies and forces.

In early 1983, John Moloney and Patrick McVeigh were sentenced. Moloney got three years, while McVeigh got seven years for IRA membership and possession of an Armalite rifle. When McVeigh was released from Portlaoise Prison in May 1988 after serving five years and four months of his seven-year sentence, he was rearrested by Gardaí. The British were seeking his extradition on explosives charges. He was accused of having control of explosive substances between August 1981 and October 1983, and conspiring with others to cause an explosion in the UK. As his lawyers were to point out, he was in Irish custody for some of that period.

There was drama as detectives tried to serve McVeigh with the extradition warrants. Troops fired warning shots in the air as Sinn Féin demonstrators tried to impede his arrest. McVeigh was taken into custody and more drama was to follow. A district justice in Portlaoise ordered his release, ruling that he had not been identified in court as the man sought by Scotland Yard and named in two extradition warrants. British prime minister Margaret Thatcher was said to be 'utterly dismayed'. This was the first test of a new extradition agreement between Ireland and the UK and, so far as the British were concerned, it had failed miserably.

John Moloney's brother Patrick, a Melkite Catholic priest based in New York city, was also arrested in Limerick when the Gardaí swooped on the container, but was later released. In February 1995 Father Moloney, who had emigrated from Ireland in the 1950s and who ran a New York city shelter for troubled teenagers and illegal immigrants, was to end up in prison after being convicted in another case. He was sentenced to four years and three months for conspiracy, after a US federal court heard he had been caught with some of the proceeds from a $7.4 million Brinks armoured car robbery. The authorities suspected that the heist was IRA-related, but could produce no hard evidence that this was the case.

Also jailed for the same incident was Samuel I Millar who did time in prison in Northern Ireland on explosives and firearms charges and for membership of the IRA. (Millar has said that he carried out the robbery on his own initiative and that it had nothing to do with the IRA.) A Brinks guard, who described how he was kidnapped by the robbers, was cleared of taking part in the robbery. A fourth man was acquitted of conspiracy.

Clinton lets Megahey stay

Gabriel Megahey's troubles were not over when he emerged from prison in June 1988. He was one of a number of Irish republican aliens whom the authorities wished to deport. A major publicity and lobbying campaign was launched in support of the men being allowed to remain in the US, and protest demonstrations were held. The men had been living in the US for some time, and did not want to go back to Ireland, either Northern Ireland or the Irish Republic. In support of Megahey's case, it was pointed out that he had lived in America for many years, his wife Patricia is a US citizen and that they had a daughter, also a US citizen.

In a television interview in August 1998, Megahey talked about his motivation in running guns. He claimed he was justified in what he did, because he had seen his people suffer – they were attacked and had their houses burned out. He had also seen ten men die on hunger strike. He claimed he was justified in seeking missiles to shoot down British Army helicopters, as they were being used to terrorise people – 'dropping in a field, and letting the troops out'.[4] Finally, in December 2000, the Clinton administration attorney general, Janet Reno, terminated deportation proceedings against Megahey and five other men. Ms Reno also ordered that no further proceedings be taken against three other Irishmen who were facing likely deportation orders.

The Peace Process and the Good Friday Agreement played a key role in saving the men from deportation. Ms Reno said, 'I have been advised by the secretary of state that terminating deportation proceedings against six aliens who have engaged in activity on behalf of the Irish Republican Army (IRA) and foregoing proceedings against three others would serve the interests of United States foreign policy by contributing to the course of reconciliation reflected in the Good Friday Accord.' President Clinton said that while in no way approving or condoning past acts by the nine, he believed that 'removing the threat of deportation for these individuals will contribute to the Peace Process in Northern Ireland'.

The PIRA Squad moves against the INLA

Lou Stephens and his squad came to grips not only with gunrunners acting for the IRA but with arms buyers trying to procure weaponry for the smaller paramilitary group, the Marxist-leaning INLA. Stephens recalled that it was through a wire-tap that the Squad got onto Colm Murphy and a gunrunning associate in New York in 1982. They were both from Northern Ireland, natives of County Armagh. The Squad learned that the two men were looking for a range of weapons, including surface-to-air missiles (SAMs). Murphy was friendly with George Harrison and was in touch with him, but it is unclear whether it was this connection that brought Murphy to the attention of the FBI. The INLA made some attempts to procure arms in the US, but the group's main sources of weaponry were in the Middle East and Eastern Europe.

At one stage, Murphy was in contact with FBI undercover informant Michael Hanratty, who figured in the Megahey case outlined above. According to court papers, Hanratty told Murphy a story which, in hindsight, sounds very familiar indeed – he had a 'friend' who was an arms dealer and who would probably be able to supply Murphy with a variety of arms. Hanratty suggested that the arms dealer could meet with Murphy in New Orleans [where Gerry McGeough had his fateful encounter with undercover agents] to discuss a deal. Hanratty even offered to pay Murphy's expenses. The meeting did not go ahead, apparently because Murphy did not have funds at the time to buy weapons.

Later, in March 1982, Murphy was introduced to a man called Sydney Kail in a Manhattan bar. Murphy was not to know that Kail was an undercover FBI informant. According to court papers, Murphy told Kail he was a member of the INLA, and interested in buying heavy military equipment. Murphy was alleged to have mentioned missiles, mortars and machine guns. Kail explained that he did not sell arms – he was only a middleman, but would take Murphy to meet his 'partner', a member of the Mafia who dealt in arms. This 'Mafia contact' was in fact Lindley DeVecchio, an FBI undercover agent with considerable experience in firearms.

On 21 April 1982, Murphy, Kail and DeVecchio held a meeting. The encounter took place in DeVecchio's car, and the agent had a hidden tape recorder running. Once again, Murphy outlined his arms requirements, especially heavier equipment such as SAM-7 missiles or 'something that has the capability of taking down a helicopter'. When DeVecchio explained that he could not procure such items, the discussion turned to M-16 rifles and Ingrams MAC-10 sub-machine guns. Murphy explained that he was interested in developing a weapons 'connection' on the east coast and stated that if he got a 'decent deal' he would 'be back with $180,000'. The M-16s were for use 'on the streets of Belfast', he said.

Murphy had a second meeting with DeVecchio on 2 June, during which there was further discussion of an arms deal. Once again, the conversation was secretly taped. It was during a third meeting, a month later, that a deal was worked out. It was agreed that Murphy would buy twenty M-16 rifles for $11,000. The two men arranged to meet in Astoria, Queens, on the evening of 21 July, for the hand-over of the weapons. Murphy said he would use travellers' cheques in payment.

DeVecchio met Murphy on the arranged date, at a McDonald's restaurant in Queens. An FBI agent, Bruce Stephens, accompanied DeVecchio, posing as a Mafia bodyguard. Over a dozen FBI agents had the encounter under surveillance. Lou Stephens recalled how a couple of agents were in a surveillance van opposite the McDonald's. And then the operation came close to being blown in a moment of high farce. Recalled Stephens: 'Some stupid sonofabitch decided he wanted to steal the surveillance van. He thought there was nobody inside. So he broke into the van, only to be confronted immediately by my good friend Marty Robbins, who was a short agent, with a gun of about eight foot long and he brought it out and shoved it in that guy's nose and he just shit himself literally, right on the spot. Just lost it.' There was quite a commotion as the would-be car thief was taken into custody. The cops arrived on the scene and Murphy inevitably noticed the rumpus.

To the great concern of the FBI agents, Murphy left the McDonald's with DeVecchio and Bruce Stephens. This was not part of the plan. The agents keeping watch were afraid that Murphy had been spooked and had decided to abort the deal. It transpired that Murphy just wanted a quieter venue, away from all the police activity. Said Stephens: 'We all thought that was the end of the case, that we would not be able to make the case.' But he was not ready to give up. 'I said, we are not going to break this off, we have too much invested in this.'

A member of the PIRA Squad, Frank Schulte, was operating on a motorbike that night and was able to trail the three men as they moved to a White Castle restaurant a few blocks away. Through the radio in his motorcycle helmet, he was able to keep Lou Stephens updated on the movements of the trio. At the restaurant another man, Murphy's gunrunning associate, eventually joined the company, and Murphy introduced him to the FBI agents as the man who would inspect the weapons.

The man then went with DeVecchio to his car, as the agent had the M-16s stashed in the trunk. He counted and inspected the weapons, and then loaded them into a car he had borrowed for the evening. He took a package from the wheel well of his car from which Murphy extracted travellers' cheques, as well as some thousands of dollars in cash. Murphy handed the money to DeVecchio and Murphy's accomplice drove off. Murphy was arrested as he signed over his last traveller's cheque. He was shocked to find himself in custody.

One of Lou Stephens' agents was eager to arrest the second man, but the plan did not work out, and it fell to Lou Stephens to make the actual arrest. The suspect had only driven about half a block when Stephens moved in. He smashed the windscreen of the suspect's car with the butt of his gun, hauled him out of the car and put him on the ground, face down. Later, Stephens personally interrogated Murphy.

In June 1983, after a four-week trial in a US District Court in Brooklyn, Murphy (thirty-one), an illegal alien, and his associate, a legal resident of the US, were convicted on illegal weapons charges. Murphy got five years in prison and was fined $10,000, while the other man was sentenced to eighteen months and was fined $7,500. Both men appealed unsuccessfully against their convictions.[5]

George Harrison came to the aid of his friend Murphy after he was arrested. Harrison recalled that some people in republican circles were reluctant to give support to Murphy, because he was INLA rather than IRA. They wanted to separate him from other prisoners. Harrison threatened to sever his own connections with the movement if Murphy was not looked after. 'I went up to them and said, if you separate Colm from anybody you separate me too.' Harrison went on: 'I wanted Colm to be supported and we did support him; we were there at his trial, and there was fundraising.'

Murphy got early release and left jail in November 1985. He returned to Ireland the following month. A determined paramilitary, he had 'form' prior to his arrest in the US. His first brush with the law had come in March 1972 when Gardaí found a loaded revolver in his car. The discovery was made after police arrested him in Dundalk, County Louth, just south of the Border, for questioning in connection with an assault. He was jailed for two years. He was held at the Curragh military prison but escaped a few months later, in October. He was recaptured in May 1973, but after release continued his involvement in paramilitary activities. In June 1976 he was back before the Special Criminal Court, which jailed him for three years for firearms offences. He was given a one-year concurrent sentence for IRA membership.

In January 2002, Murphy notched up the conviction that was to bring him the most notoriety. He became the first person to be found guilty in relation to the worst single atrocity of the Irish Troubles, the 1998 Omagh bombing, which claimed the lives of twenty-nine people, including a woman pregnant with twins. The attack was carried out by the Real IRA (RIRA), which had broken away from the IRA in disgust at the latter's cease-fire. Murphy was found guilty of conspiracy to cause an explosion, and was sentenced to fourteen years. However, in January 2005, the Court of Criminal Appeal overturned the conviction, and Murphy was released from prison. He showed flashes of anger towards the photographers who pursued him as he walked down a street near the courthouse.

Stephens was intrigued when he originally heard the news of Murphy's arrest in connection with Omagh. The name rang bells immediately – his mind went back to the time he had interrogated the South Armagh man all those years before. 'When that guy Murphy was arrested after Omagh, my mind went back in a heartbeat.'

George Harrison always remained well-disposed towards Murphy. He spoke of the Armagh man with great warmth, and said he had sent books to him in Portlaoise prison. He described Murphy as 'very nice and friendly'. Harrison retained a deep-seated loyalty to Murphy, and complained bitterly that the press, 'the bastards', had taken a dislike to him.

It was not just Irish paramilitary gunrunners who were targeted by Stephens' PIRA Squad. The unit also went after wanted republicans who were on the run in the US. The PIRA Squad was responsible for tracking down Belfast IRA man Joe Doherty, who had escaped from prison in Belfast. Doherty had been jailed for life for the murder of an SAS officer, Captain Herbert Richard Westmacott, in a gun battle. Doherty and three other IRA men had been captured after the shootout in Belfast in May 1980. The group were known as the M-60 Squad because they were armed with an M-60 machine gun. The weapon provided a link to one of George Harrison's more notable gunrunning operations. The US Army-issue machine gun, which can fire 600 rounds a minute, was one of seven M-60s stolen from the National Guard Armoury in Danvers, Massachusetts, in August 1976; the machine guns were acquired subsequently by the Harrison network and smuggled to Ireland (*see* Chapter 3).

A year after being captured, Doherty was one of a number of IRA men who escaped from Belfast's Crumlin Road prison. He was subsequently sentenced, in his absence, to life for murder. Doherty made his way to New York, where he went to ground and worked at various jobs, under the assumed name of Henry J O'Reilly. Lou Stephens recalled how, one Saturday, he was helping a neighbour paint his house when he got a phone call from colleague Frank Schulte to say that he thought they had Joe Doherty identified, working in a bar on Third Avenue, Manhattan. Schulte was wondering about the basis on which to arrest him – there was apparently some grey area to do with an extradition warrant. Stephens said: 'I said to Frank that this guy was an illegal alien, and I told him to get somebody from immigration, and go up there and arrest him.' On 18 June 1983, Schulte and two other FBI special agents from the PIRA Squad, Greg Auld and John Winslow, all armed, went to the bar. They were accompanied by four agents from the Immigration and Naturalisation Service (INS). Doherty was arrested under an INS warrant and taken to FBI headquarters at Federal Plaza, Manhattan.

It was to be the beginning of a remarkable legal saga. Doherty spent the next nine years in prison in Manhattan, fighting an extradition warrant. He won a series of court battles on the grounds that his offences were political in nature, but was ultimately deported back to Belfast in February 1992, for entering the US illegally. He was jailed at the Maze prison, but was later freed under the Good Friday Agreement.

Lou Stephens left the FBI in 1987, but others associated with the PIRA Squad went on to have interesting careers with the agency. Frank Schulte continued to work on Irish cases. Enrique Ghimenti, who took part in the 'sting' operation against the Megahey group, became an FBI representative, or legal attaché, in the US Embassy in Madrid and later in Paris, where he played an important role in liaising with French intelligence in the moves to track down Al Qaeda operatives.

Looking back on his time with the PIRA Squad, Lou Stephens considers that he and his people made a contribution to the Peace Process in Ireland. In his view, their disruption of the flow of arms helped to put the Irish issue on the agenda, so that politicians and decision-makers could make progress towards peace. 'We had one small accomplishment – for quite a period of time, we stopped the flow of guns. We were able to penetrate [the gunrunning groups]. They knew we were out there. They were not the best at what they did, and they knew that they were capable of being penetrated; that we could prosecute them and really make a dent and cause them problems. The second thing that happened was something that my people had just a little to do with, because it was beyond our scope, but we did help to put the problem on the map, so that there were points of discussion for guys like Bill Clinton and his aide Sandy Berger, who came to power, who could make decisions, who could say: "This has got to end, there has to be a way to take this forward."' Stephens asked himself a rhetorical question: 'Am I proud of that?' He went on, 'You're goddamn right I'm proud of that. I'll take it to my grave any damn day.'

He is glad that the US played a big role in the Peace Process. 'I knew that the only way that this problem was going to be resolved was the way it is now being resolved. We had to get [US special envoy] Senator George Mitchell over there, we had to get everyone on board, we had to go through all those tough negotiations, we had to run all that money in there. But what is money, what is a thousand stinking farthings when it's compared to those poor kids in Omagh who were just walking down the street when they were blown up?'

There are some in the Irish community in New York who still resent the activities of Lou Stephens and the PIRA Squad. Said Stephens: 'Even to this day, I would walk into a pub in New York and people would recognise me and it's just silence. It's as if Matt Dillon from *Gunsmoke* walked into a room and you knew there was going to be a gunfight. Unbelievable.' He has remained on good terms with one of the men he helped to put behind bars, and who has now put paramilitary activity behind him. Stephens and the other agents clubbed together and helped out the man's wife and family while he was 'inside'. Stephens said, 'To this day when he sees me on the street he will come up and say: "Lou, how are you? When you were doing all of this I hated you so much, but I will never forget the kindness you people showed to my family." The guy was a devoted terrorist, but a class act.'

Other North American arms plots

During the early to mid-1980s, the IRA explored a number of unusual arms procurement possibilities on the North American continent, according to a republican source. The source stated that at one stage a member of GHQ travelled to Mexico City to discuss arms procurement possibilities with individuals from Castro's Cuba and from a Peruvian left-wing movement. Nothing came of these talks. Contact was also made with militant right-wing Cuban exiles in Miami who had experience in paramilitary activities and in training to overthrow Castro – again nothing came of these contacts.

The source said that at one stage, an ingenious plan was under considera-tion, whereby the IRA would, in effect, through a 'front', set up its own licensed gun shop in the US and then arrange for a 'break-in', to seize the stock. The plan would have involved an IRA sympathiser, perhaps a former member of law enforcement, with no criminal record and with a respectable image, establishing a licensed gun dealership, and then ordering all the types of weapons in which the IRA had an interest, in the required quantities. Then, one weekend, an unfortunate 'burglary' would occur, the entire stock would be cleared out and spirited away to boost the arsenals of the IRA. Ultimately, the IRA did not go ahead with the plot.

Murder by the shores of Lough Neagh

The fallout from the smashing of the Megahey operation was to continue. FBI agents working on the case established that some of the weapons seized at the port of Newark had been acquired by a man using the fictitious name 'Robert Power'. The FBI had a sample of fingerprints belonging to 'Power', from a form that he had completed. They also had 'Power's' fingerprints taken from three Armalite rifles in the batch found at Newark. As a result of further fingerprint analysis, the FBI decided that the prints belonging to 'Power' matched those of a man called Liam Ryan, who had been born in Northern Ireland but had been residing in the US. He was a prominent member of the IRA in New York, and indeed was reputed to be the Officer Commanding the Provos in the city. According to a republican source, Ryan was a 'money man', involved in transferring funds to the IRA back in Ire-land. 'He would make trips to Ireland carrying $10,000 in cash with him at a time,' the source said.

Ryan was in Ireland in early 1985, but returned to the US on 14 April that year. Ten days later he was arrested at the Bronx apartment where he was visiting his girlfriend. Ryan (thirty-five), who had become a US citizen in 1984 and worked as a meter reader for an electricity company, was released on an unsecured bond of $750,000. At his trial he pleaded guilty to making fraudulent statements in purchasing the rifles from a New York gun dealer in 1982, and walked free after receiving a four-year suspended sentence.

Ryan returned to his native County Tyrone and, with the aid of savings accumulated from his years in the US, took over ownership of the Battery bar in Ardboe. It has been reported that he was the IRA's Tyrone Brigade intelligence officer when the Loughall ambush happened, and that he gathered the intelligence for the operation.[6] Loughall was a major disaster for the IRA. Eight IRA men died when they were ambushed by the British Army's elite Special Air Service (SAS) after they tried to bomb an RUC station in the County Armagh village in May 1987. In the close-knit republican community of County Tyrone, Ryan would have known these men well and the wiping out of a key IRA unit must have been come as a severe blow to him.

Ryan married in 1988 and his wife gave birth to a son the following year. By now, he had become a marked man, and was receiving death threats. In November 1989, loyalist gunmen burst into the pub and opened fire. Ryan was killed, along with one of his customers. The Ulster Volunteer Force (UVF) claimed responsibility, saying that Ryan was their main target. Ironically, the murder of Ryan, as well as evidence of collaboration between some elements in the Northern Ireland security forces and loyalist paramilitaries, boosted the ability of some republicans to fight deportation from America, by arguing that their lives would be in danger if sent back to Northern Ireland.

Trials of Gerry McGeough

The 1982 FBI swoop at Newark was to cast a long shadow and to have repercussions into the next decade. In addition to the arms and ammunition seized, the FBI also intercepted a consignment of electronic 'tone frequency' switches bound for the Provos. By 1984 the FBI had traced the purchase of about fifty of these items to an Irish-American electronics genius called Richard Clark Johnson. As explained in Chapter 11, the FBI discovery was ultimately to lead to the jailing in 1990 of Johnson and others for conspiring to provide the IRA with a guided missile system.

Gerry McGeough, on the run from the FBI, travelled to Sweden in August 1983 to seek political asylum. It was to be the start of a remarkable odyssey. Having failed to be granted asylum, he left Sweden in early 1987. He was back in the news the following year. On the night of 30 August 1988, he and Gerard Hanratty were arrested by German border guards as they crossed the German/Dutch border by a back road. It was believed they had received orders from Provo chiefs back in Ireland to move a cache of arms as a security precaution – in fact it led to the capture of the two Provos and the seizure of the weapons. The border guards found two AK-47 rifles, three pistols and an assortment of ammunition in the car in which they were travelling. The two men were eventually charged with two bomb attacks in Germany against British military targets – at Muncheng-ladbach in March 1987 and Duisberg in July 1988. They were also charged with illegal possession of weapons, possession of false passports and ille-gally hiring cars with false documents.

McGeough was to spend nearly four years in jail in Germany. He was held in the grim surroundings of the punishment block of Frankenthal Prison. For the first few months he was not allowed to go Mass. After he took legal action, he was allowed to attend Mass every two weeks. The two men went on trial in a bunker-style court that was specially built within the confines of a major police base. But the probe into the gunrunning opera-tion in America back in the early 1980s was still hanging over McGeough. In January 1990, US authorities made a formal request for the extradition of McGeough, based on the 1982 warrant for his arrest. A year later, before the end of his trial, the German authorities granted the extradition request. It has been suggested that the Germans feared that the major charges against McGeough in the German court would not stick. McGeough's co-defendant, Gerard Hanratty, was eventually found guilty solely on the weapons possession charges, and given a two-and-a-half year sentence.

On 20 May 1992, McGeough was taken in chains, and wearing two sets of handcuffs, under very heavy escort from his prison cell to be flown back to the US. The convoy sped to Frankfurt Airport, but there was consterna-tion among the security guards when they could not find the US marshals who were to take charge of McGeough. The penny dropped – the guards realised they were at the wrong airport. There was then a frantic dash to the military air base in Frankfurt. The guards were in a panic as they tried des-perately to locate the US marshals. McGeough said he learned later that if he had not been handed over to the custody of the US authorities by 11 o'clock that day, the Germans would have had to release him. He was eventually taken in charge by grim-faced US marshals and strapped into a US Air Force C-141 cargo aircraft for the nine-hour flight in freezing con-ditions to Dover air base in Delaware. He found the Air Force crew to be friendly but the US marshals unpleasant. After a gruelling four-hour car journey, the exhausted prisoner was placed in the maximum security section of the Metropolitan Correctional Centre in Lower Manhattan.

After ten days in prison, McGeough was released on bail. He eventually appeared in court, charged with conspiracy to purchase and export Redeye surface-to-air missiles for the Provisional IRA. He was advised that a plea bargain would be in his best interests. As a result, in June 1993, a federal judge sentenced McGeough, aged thirty-four at the time, to three years in prison. He was freed on bail pending an appeal, which he lost at a hearing in December 1993. He began his sentence on Easter Monday, 4 April 1994, and was to do his time in a number of penitentiaries, enjoying the novel experience of flying on aircraft operated by the Justice Prisoner and Alien Transportation System (J-Pats), more colourfully known as 'ConAir'.

On release from prison on 14 March 1996, McGeough was escorted by two US Marshals on a flight to Shannon Airport. Ultimately, he went to live in Dublin. As he settled back into life as an ordinary citizen, progress was being made in the Peace Process, culminating in the Good Friday Agreement of 1998. Gunrunning had been just one of McGeough's activities as a republican – he had been an active IRA man in County Tyrone, had taken part in the H-Blocks campaign in the early 1980s, and was to become active in Sinn Féin at a high level. But his paramilitary days, and his activities as a gunrunner, were over.

As a fragile peace took hold, he learned that the British had even lifted the exclusion order which prevented him from visiting 'mainland' UK. He pursued higher level studies in Dublin, taking an honours history degree at Trinity College, Dublin, and a higher diploma in education (HDE) at University College, Dublin (UCD). The latter qualification prepared him for a teaching career. He found work, teaching in a second-level school in Dublin, and had risen to the position of vice-principal, but was sacked after the parent of one of the pupils complained to the principal about the Tyrone man's paramilitary background. In the meantime, he had become a member of the Sinn Féin Árd Chomhairle (national executive), but resigned because of differences with the organisation.

In the run-up to the elections for the European Parliament in June 2004, McGeough voiced criticism of Sinn Féin. He told a journalist during the election campaign: 'Like hundreds of republicans, I'm very disillusioned with the current [Sinn Féin] leadership. They have betrayed the ideal of a united Ireland. I don't believe the ordinary decent rank-and-file supports the radical pro-abortion stance Sinn Féin now adopts.' He went on to say that there was a large disenfranchised community out there: 'It's Catholic, extremely nationalist, pro-life, EU-sceptic, and disgusted by the sleaze in Irish politics.'[7] As I interviewed McGeough in a Dublin hotel, he told me that he and his Spanish-born wife had two children, and were expecting a third – a son was subsequently born. He had been earning a living working on building sites, but later went on to become a teacher of English as a foreign language. He also began to work in Catholic journalism.

During one of my meetings with him, he gave me a written statement setting out the reasons for his activities: 'All my actions in relation to the Irish political situation have been and are motivated by patriotism. My credo is that it is a man's duty to worship God, protect his family and defend his country to the best of his ability. Failure to do so is the mark of cowardice. Those who avoid their patriotic duty or misuse it for self-gain and/or self-promotion lack moral fibre and are utterly contemptible.' He went on to express disappointment in the current Sinn Féin leadership: 'They have squandered the heroism of a generation in pursuit of narrow political gain, which will prove fleeting. How can they endorse policy that will inexorably lead to abortion, the destruction of "generations yet unborn" as declared in the 1916 Proclamation, and dare pose as Irish patriots? God help Ireland should their day ever come, which I suspect it never shall.'

The Boston 'sting'

In Boston in the mid-1980s, the FBI sent out an undercover agent to tour Irish bars, posing as a black market arms dealer who could supply arms discreetly, no questions asked. It was part of the FBI offensive against IRA gunrunning, which sometimes involved 'sting' operations. The agent, known as 'Bill', finally found a man called John 'Jackie' McDonald who expressed an interest in buying guns for the IRA. McDonald, in his late thirties, introduced Bill to Irish-born Noel Murphy, who had come to the US a few years earlier. Murphy, a native of County Kerry, had gone to study at Trinity College, Dublin, in 1980. He began a relationship with an American woman and moved with her to Boston. Their daughter was born in 1982. Meanwhile, he opened a variety store in the Brighton area of Boston, and made a modest living.

The agent had a number of meetings with Murphy over a period of months. Murphy was not himself a member of the IRA. It appears that following the approach from the undercover agent, he made contact with the Provisionals in New York and Belfast. Murphy told 'Bill' that the IRA wanted M-16 rifles, MP-5 sub-machine guns and M-60 heavy machine guns. But the most significant item on the shopping list was a Redeye surface-to-air missile. As usual, the IRA was on the lookout for a weapon that would bring down the helicopters that were of such crucial importance to British Army operations in Northern Ireland.

In March 1986, at a meeting in Boston, Murphy finally introduced the undercover agent to his contact man in the IRA, Ciaran Hughes from Belfast. The agent, Joseph W Butchka, secretly taped conversations with Murphy and Hughes. In one conversation, Murphy told of his ambitions to gain advancement in the IRA. 'I got political ambition within the organisation,' Murphy said on the tape. 'I want to put a deal together. I want to offer them something other than what the average guy would offer them.' In another conversation, Murphy indicated that the IRA had become very wary of 'sting' operations mounted by federal agents posing as black market arms dealers, because they had been stung badly in this way. As a result, he had to fall back on a more secure way of acquiring arms for the IRA – he claimed he was buying firearms stolen during break-ins in private houses.

A price was agreed for a consignment of weapons – according to subsequent court testimony, the figure was $73,000. The consignment was to consist of 100 M-16 rifles, two MP-5 sub-machine guns and 100 rounds of ammunition for each weapon, the total cost for these items to be $60,000. A Redeye missile was to cost an additional $13,000. The arms suppliers arranged to lay on an executive jet to fly the weapons to Ireland. It should have sounded too good to be true to the conspirators – the undercover agent must have been really convincing. Murphy lined up six Boston residents, two of them Irish-born, to travel on the jet and to help with the unloading of the cargo when it reached Shannon Airport.

On 20 May 1986, the FBI swooped. Murphy and Hughes were arrested on board the executive jet as they loaded the firearms, the ammunition and the Redeye missile onto the aircraft. The location was an airfield about ten miles northwest of Boston, Hanscom Field in Bedford. It turned out that the FBI agents involved in the sting were using an aircraft normally assigned to Ed Meese, the US Attorney General. Five other members of the gunrunning group, low-level 'helpers', were arrested at a nearby hotel, while a sixth, John 'Jackie' McDonald, the original contact man, was arrested at his home.

In October 1986, the two main players in the gunrunning drama, Noel Murphy (twenty-six), an alien living illegally in Boston, and Ciaran Hughes (twenty-four), from Belfast, were found guilty on a range of charges. They were convicted in US District Court of conspiracy to export arms without a licence, conspiracy to export a missile without a licence and dealing in firearms. The following month Murphy was sentenced to nine years, while Hughes got eight years. Jackie McDonald subsequently got eighteen months for his role in the affair. The judge described McDonald as the 'go--between' who introduced an FBI undercover agent to IRA-linked operators.

The helpers got softer sentences, ranging from six months to a year. Each man had been charged with one count of conspiracy to violate the federal Arms Export Control Act. William Brown, a lawyer for one of the men, said that the plot to send arms to the IRA had been hatched in a bar 'over free mugs of beer'. He declared that the men were 'the Budweiser Brigade of the Irish Republican Army'.

After serving six years, the prison sentence imposed on Noel Murphy (also known by the Irish version of his name, Noel Ó Murchú) was deemed to have come to an end, in 1992. However, he now faced deportation as a security risk, and opted to stay voluntarily in jail to mount a legal challenge to the attempt to send him back to Ireland. He and his partner had broken up and he was particularly anxious to stay in the US so that he could see his daughter, aged ten at the time, who was living in Massachusetts with her mother. He knew that if he stepped out of prison he would be put on the next plane to Shannon. After close on two years of an ultimately unsuccessful legal battle, Murphy was judged to have exhausted his legal remedies. He was taken from his cell at New Hampshire State Prison and sent back to Ireland in 1994. Shortly after arriving in Ireland, he told a journalist that he would never give up trying to get back into the United States, because his daughter is there.[8]

The series of coups pulled off by the FBI against IRA gunrunners meant that the US was no longer an easy source of weaponry for the movement. The smooth workings of the Harrison network were very much a thing of the past. An FBI expert on terrorism, writing in a Bureau bulletin in October 1987, recorded with evident pride and satisfaction how, as a result of the agency's 'aggressive investigative effort', they had been successful 'in a number of Irish terrorism investigations by obtaining indictments and convictions'.[9]

JL Stone, a supervisory intelligence research specialist with the FBI's Terrorist Research and Analytical Centre in Washington, explained how FBI investigations into Irish terrorist activity were focused on three principal areas of activity: first on the list was weapons procurement in the US and illegal transport of these weapons to Northern Ireland or the Republic of Ireland. The second area of investigation concerned fundraising efforts in the US 'with illegal transfer of this funding to Northern Ireland to directly support Irish terrorist elements operating there'; while the third was the identification of 'Irish terrorists who are in the US illegally'.

Stone outlined some of the methods used to pursue such investigations: 'Lawful intelligence gathering techniques, such as use of informants, undercover operations, and court-ordered electronic surveillance, are instrumental tools in this effort. Also of benefit are good working relationships with intelligence and law enforcement agencies at all levels, both in the United States and internationally.'

The Golden Gate gunrunner arrested again

In 1988 Brian Joseph Fleming, a young Irish-American living in Alabama, approached JR Cambron, a gun dealer in Daleville, and asked about purchasing an Armalite AR-15 rifle and leather Sam Browne belts for members of a junior Irish republican organisation, Fianna Éireann. Cambron felt obliged to inform the federal authorities. As a result, US customs agent James Duff, posing as an arms dealer, joined the talks with Fleming. Conversations with Fleming and an associate, Charles Farrell Malone, were secretly taped as they discussed an arms deal. After a thirty-three-month investigation, Fleming and Malone were arrested.

'Chuck' Malone, from San Francisco, was a prominent activist in Irish republican causes in his home city for many years, providing support to different groups, including the Irish Republican Socialist Party (IRSP). He also had 'form' – he had been convicted in 1973 in relation to IRA gunrunning charges (*see* also Chapter 3). For many years he had headed the US support group for Fianna Éireann, and in that capacity had often led the group's adult and child members in the St Patrick's Day parade, marching in military formation in green woollen uniforms.

Fleming and Malone went on trial before a jury in a federal court in Montgomery, Alabama. Testimony was given that they were officers in Fianna Éireann. An RUC officer told the court that Fianna Éireann was the youth brigade of the illegal IRA, and that Fianna Éireann itself had been outlawed by parliament in 1978. Fleming said it was an Irish scouting organisation. In April 1990, Fleming (thirty-two), of Enterprise, Alabama, and Malone (sixty-three) were convicted of conspiring to export rifles, including AR-15s and M-16s. Fleming, who ran a print shop, was also convicted of unlawful interstate transportation of a firearm, arising out of the mailing of a handgun to a friend in New York. The following July, Fleming was sentenced to three years in prison, while Malone got two years with three years probation.

Federal investigators concluded that the men had been planning to send between fifty and 100 M-16 and Armalite rifles, as well as night vision goggles, to the IRA, using trans-shipment points in Panama and Africa. However, Malone had, in fact, thrown his weight behind a dissident, breakaway group, Republican Sinn Féin, launched in 1986 in protest at the decision by the 'mainstream' Sinn Féin to end its policy of abstention from parliamentary bodies.

Malone's name surfaced in phone-tap transcripts in 1989, as the FBI investigated an IRA plot to develop a radar-guided missile capable of shooting down British Army helicopters in Northern Ireland. Several arrests were made, and in court papers the FBI alleged that one of the accused, Richard Clark Johnson, had been in touch with a number of Irish republican activists since 1978, including Charles Malone. Another person who was arrested, Christina Leigh Reid from Sunnyvale, California, was described as an associate of Malone's. Malone was not charged in connection with the missile case. Malone, who suffered from Parkinson's disease, died in March 1998.

CHAPTER 9

The Curse of the *Valhalla*

Patrick J Nee, a member of the Boston-Irish underworld, flew to Ireland with a number of friends on 21 September 1984. He had some vital information stored away in his memory, data so sensitive that he did not even write the details on a piece of paper. Neither phone lines nor the postal services from the US to Ireland could be trusted. It was decided that the safest way for Nee to pass on the information, relating to an important operation, was verbally, when he met his IRA contacts in Ireland. The data that Nee had memorised consisted of longitude and latitude co-ordinates, marking the spot on the high seas where two vessels would meet for an important rendezvous.

A vessel called the *Valhalla* had set sail a week earlier from a port in Massachusetts with a significant load of weapons on board, bound for the IRA. The plan was that a County Kerry fishing trawler, the *Marita Ann*, would sail out from the Irish coast to meet the *Valhalla* in the Atlantic fishing grounds known as the Porcupine Bank, close on 200 miles off the Irish coast. The cargo, seven tons of weaponry, would be transferred to the trawler, and then smuggled by the *Marita Ann* into the Irish Republic, where bunkers had been prepared to receive it. That was the plan. Those involved were not to know that the operation had been betrayed to the authorities. 'I flew over with the co-ordinates in my head – it would not have been wise to write them down, with X marks the spot,' Nee told me.[1] Nee felt excited and buoyed up as he travelled with his five companions on the Aer Lingus flight from Boston to Dublin. He and others had put a lot of time and effort into assembling the arms cargo. He was looking forward to the final act in an operation that would provide significant extra fire-power to the IRA.

Patrick Nee was born in the Irish-speaking Rosmuc area of Connemara, County Galway, a few days before Christmas of 1944. As a boy, he emigrated with his family to the US in April 1952, sailing on board the passenger liner *Britannia* – he still has the dinner menu from the last night of their voyage. When I met him, I spoke to him in Irish, assuming he was still a native speaker. He looked at me blankly. He knew what language I was speaking, but that was all. He explained that while he spoke Irish as a young boy, he had gradually lost his facility with the language while growing up in Boston. 'I'm sorry I lost the language,' he told me.

As a young teenager, he was a tearaway, becoming involved in small-time thieving as a member of the Mullen gang in Boston. He joined the US Marines, served from 1962 to 1966, and fought in Vietnam, where he was stationed for nine months in 1965. He was given an honourable discharge, and is still proud of his Vietnam service – he considered the Americans were fighting a war of liberation, and still believes the war could have been won.

After leaving the Army, he embarked on a career as a professional criminal and an active member of the Boston underworld. His activities included breaking into warehouses and robbing consignments of ciga-rettes. 'I started young – I saw it all around me growing up on the water-front.' His father was a labourer and Patrick wanted a more adventurous and exciting life. Nee always kept fit, was as tough as nails physically and mentally, but had an Irish charm and made friends easily.

He was on the opposite side to the notorious Irish-American gangster James 'Whitey' Bulger during a Boston gangland feud that flared up in 1969. The war was between the Killeen gang, with whom the much-feared Bulger was associated, and the Mullen gang to which Nee was aligned. During one incident Bulger, carrying a firearm, popped up at the window of Nee's ground-floor apartment, with the obvious intention of shooting the former marine. Nee reached for his .45 handgun. Then Nee's girl-friend's young daughter came in and got in the way. Even a sadistic serial killer like Bulger did not shoot children, and he held his fire. As Bulger ran off, Nee grabbed a hunting rifle from a closet and tried to get the fleeing gangster in the crosshairs, but he got away.[2] At one stage during the feud, Whitey Bulger and two henchmen tried to kill Nee by opening fire on himself and a friend in their car. The assailants' aim was not very good. Nee managed to duck, and escaped with some scratches from broken glass, although the car was a write-off.

The gang war came to an end after about three years. Nee and Bulger made up, with the Connemara man joining forces with Bulger. Reflecting on those days with a wry smile, Nee told me he reckoned he is one of the few underworld types who opposed Bulger in a feud, lived to tell the tale, and then formed an alliance with the crime boss.

When the Troubles got under way in Northern Ireland in the late 1960s and early 1970s, Nee found a cause. He wanted to help out his fellow nationalists in Northern Ireland. He might have been a robber by profession, but when it came to Ireland, he was an idealist. He told how he gradually became more deeply involved. At first, he helped with fundraising for Noraid in the Boston area, then graduated in the 1970s to supplying arms to the IRA.

For a couple of years, with the help of a contact linked to the undertaking business, arms were smuggled in coffins containing the bodies of elderly Irish exiles being returned home for burial in the 'auld sod'. Nee found he could hide five rifles, a couple of handguns and some ammunition under a corpse.[3] The downside of this system was the lack of flexibility – Nee had to wait for exiles to die in order to avail of space in their coffins.

Whitey Bulger gave his blessing to Nee's attempts to help the IRA, although Nee felt this was just lip service.[4] At one stage, in the early 1970s, he and Bulger met socially with legendary IRA leader Joe Cahill at a bar on Broadway in South Boston.[5] According to his own account, Nee's arms shipments to the IRA were small to begin with. 'As the 1970s went into the 1980s, the shipments were getting larger.'

He travelled to Ireland in connection with the arms deliveries, and recalled one time when he was brought to meet people from the IRA. The meeting took place in a house somewhere near Dundalk in the Irish Republic, close to the Border with Northern Ireland. With another car leading the way, he drove along narrow country roads at night to the meeting place. It was possible they crossed the border, into the nearby strongly republican area of South Armagh. He met IRA people, whose real names he never found out. He dealt with people from South Armagh and from Belfast, and ascertained their requirements in terms of arms. He also met republicans in Paris in connection with an arms shipment. Now that it was all part of history, he felt he could talk about some aspects of what he did, without breaching anyone's security.

When I met him in September 2004 in an upstairs room at his terraced home in the predominantly-Irish area known as Southie, or South Boston, Nee told me that he had got a significant arms consignment through to Ireland before the *Valhalla/Marita Ann* operation. In his book he gives more detail. A consignment of thirty automatic rifles, twenty-five handguns, ten blocks of C-4 explosive, 2,500 rounds of ammunition and fifteen electric detonators was hidden in a secret compartment in a van shipped from Newark, New Jersey, to Ireland via the French port of Le Havre.[6]

Nee said Whitey Bulger donated some arms for the *Valhalla* shipment to the IRA, and had also done so previously. But in Nee's view, Bulger was not totally enthusiastic about the *Valhalla* project. The crime boss was enthusiastic in the beginning about the gunrunning, but when he saw it growing he wanted to derail it, according to Nee. Bulger came to see the gunrunning as a distraction from the serious business of making money.

Bulger was a Jekyll-and-Hyde character. He could be nice to old ladies, and would contribute generously to worthy causes and to people in need. But he was also feared among the Boston underworld as a ruthless killer who would not hesitate to murder anyone who caused him offence or threatened his interests. He had a streak of sadism, and evidence emerged in court hearings that he had strangled some of his victims, including two young women.

Born on 3 September 1929 in South Boston, he is the older brother of William Bulger, former president of the Massachusetts State Senate who also served as president of the University of Massachusetts. In the earlier part of his career, Whitey Bulger spent close on ten years in prison for bank robbery. Part of his sentence was spent at Alcatraz, the forbidding maximum-security prison on an island off San Francisco. When he emerged from jail in 1965, he took steps to ensure that he would never do time again. As he became the leading crime boss in Boston, he was noted as a careful, clever operator, who rarely made a mistake. He kept physically fit and was abstemious in his habits, neither smoking nor taking drugs. Bulger was involved in rackets that ranged from extortion to money laundering.

One of the small crew of 'enforcers' Bulger gathered around him was Kevin Weeks, a tough, fearless street fighter with black curly hair from South Boston. Born in March 1956, Weeks was working part-time as a bouncer at the Triple O's bar on West Broadway, South Boston, in the mid-1970s, when he attracted the notice of Bulger. The crime boss was impressed by Weeks' ability to handle himself in a fight. He also had a licence to carry a gun. Eventually Weeks would become a full-time member of the Bulger gang, with his own interests in loan sharking and extortion. Weeks was the gang member called in to dig secret graves to bury, or rebury, the remains of individuals murdered by Bulger.

Weeks and Bulger were both of Irish descent and had IRA sympathies. Weeks has told in his autobiography how, in the couple of years prior to the *Valhalla* shipment, he and Bulger put together consignments of arms that were transported by various methods to the IRA. Sometimes the arms were hidden in hides built inside pieces of furniture. On one occasion they sent arms inside a hide built into a van.[7] This may be the same operation referred to by Patrick Nee above, when a van was transported via France to Ireland with arms hidden on board.

Nee played a key role in setting up the *Valhalla* shipment, working in close collaboration with another former US Marine, Sean (also known as John) Crawley. Nee had met Crawley through republican circles in Boston. Crawley, an Irish-American, was not part of the criminal underworld. He was the only member of the gunrunning group on the American side of the operation who was actually a member of the IRA. In that capacity, he had a general supervisory role.

Crawley lived in Nee's home for about two years before the *Valhalla* operation, and the two became firm friends. Crawley was born in New York in 1957 and lived for a period in Chicago. As a teenager he moved to Dublin with his family. In 1975 he moved back to the US and joined the armed forces. After four years service in the US Marines, which ended in 1979, he returned to Dublin and became active in the IRA. He was one of the few Americans to be recruited into the ranks of the IRA and was a useful addition because of his military background and specialised training.

During his service as a US Marine, Crawley rose to the rank of sergeant, and worked as an instructor, training troops in reconnaissance. He was a member of an elite 'Force Recon' unit, with training in special operations. His diligence and professionalism earned him the high grading 'average to excellent' on his military record. He spent some time serving with a battalion in Japan, where he was trained to read maps, to handle explosives and to carry out demolition work behind enemy lines. He had particular expertise in deploying bombs to destroy key installations such as power stations – a particularly useful skill for an IRA man. In Boston, his role as a paramilitary was in the procurement and shipping of arms on behalf of the IRA. Through Nee, Crawley got to know Whitey Bulger.

One of the most important players in the *Valhalla* affair was the Boston-Irish drug smuggler Joe Murray, a dynamic, forceful marijuana merchant with a big ego and an even bigger bank account. According to Nee, the drug trafficker, who had made millions from the drugs trade, put up the money for the arms cargo, and also laid on the boat. Murray personally bought arms for the shipment, and stored weapons at properties that he owned while awaiting the departure of the *Valhalla* on its trip to Ireland.

An investigation by authorities was to show that much of the war materiel assembled for the *Valhalla* voyage was acquired by mail order; some items were bought over the counter in gun shops; other items had been stolen. Nee, using the fictitious name 'Patrick Mullen', ordered a range of defence items from assorted suppliers in a variety of states, as far apart as Colorado, Maryland and California. He specified that the items be delivered to a yacht club in the Boston area, of which he was a member. He would pay by money order, and personally collect the packages after they arrived at the yacht club. In April 1984, he even ordered three rocket warheads from a firm in Ohio and had them delivered to the club.

Joe Murray helped out by buying rifles at a number of gun shops in the Boston area. He acquired a collection that included Colt AR-15s (Armalites), HK91s and one Steyr .308 SSG sniper rifle. The authorities would later state that he made purchases on six separate occasions, and was accompanied by Pat Nee on two of those occasions. It was also alleged that Nee, Murray and Crawley arranged for the purchase of ten bulletproof vests by two Boston policemen, which were also to form part of the *Valhalla* shipment.

According to Nee, Joe Murray, with the huge wealth he had made in the drugs trade, could easily afford to finance the arms-supply operation. Murray was another ally of Whitey Bulger and in the early 1980s was probably one the most significant smugglers of hash into the Boston region, shipping the drug in by sea. Nee told me that by bankrolling the *Valhalla* shipment, Murray was 'buying friendship and good will', the implication being that Murray was acquiring 'protection' for his own criminal activities.

Murray may have had good reason to seek the good will and a guarantee of 'no interference' from the Bulger network. An allegation was reported in court pleadings that on at least one previous occasion, in 1983, the year before the *Valhalla* arms shipment, Bulger extorted $60,000 to $90,000 from Murray because Murray was storing marijuana in South Boston, which was part of Bulger's territory.[8] Other reports suggest that the sum paid over was at the higher end of that estimate – $90,000. For Bulger, the extortion of money from marijuana and cocaine traffickers in return for permission to operate on his territory was always a lucrative part of his crime business. Murray had no choice but to pay. He did not have a gang capable of taking on Bulger's gang. He needed the good will and 'protection' of people like Bulger and Nee to operate his drugs business without interference. Helping to finance the *Valhalla* arms shipment was one way of currying favour, although Murray also appears to have had republican sympathies.

Nee said that they had approached Murray and asked him to help out with the gunrunning operation. The fact that Murray was of Irish descent was a factor: 'We appealed to his Irish heritage.' Nee reckoned that if you wanted to carry out a smuggling operation, it made sense to enlist the aid of a professional smuggler.

There has been speculation that Murray received payment from the IRA for his role in the *Valhalla* shipment and that he made a healthy profit, but Nee insisted that this was not the case – those involved did not make money from the operation, he said. Far from being paid for the *Valhalla* guns, the operation actually cost Murray a lot of money, according to Nee. 'It cost him about a million dollars – he could afford it.' Nee denied a report that the leading New England Mafia family, the Patriarcas, were involved in the supply of the illegal weapons.[9] 'The Patriarca family had nothing to do with it,' said Nee. 'It was kept tight in the Irish-American community. I have nothing against the Italians, but I would never let them know my business.'

Nee recalled that it was very hard work assembling the arms cargo. It would later be established that the consignment included 163 firearms, 71,000 rounds of ammunition, eleven bulletproof vests and a variety of related items, such as ammunition pouches, gun cases, and weapons manuals. The firearms consisted of ninety-one rifles (many of them Armalites; others included HK91s), eight sub-machine guns, thirteen shotguns and fifty-one handguns. There were three Browning heavy machine gun barrels with 1,000 rounds of armour-piercing ammunition. The consignment also included North Korean-made hand grenades, night sights and electronic debugging equipment. Estimates of the value of the consignment ranged from $1 million to $1.7 million.

Some weapons included in the shipment were donated by republican sympathisers or support groups. Also included in the shipment were pistols, revolvers and shotguns that had been stolen in burglaries in the Boston area, going back to the early 1970s. These weapons were collected with the aid of Nee's underworld contacts.

According to Nee, the IRA back in Ireland was anxious that a boat associated with drugs would not be used for shipping the cargo. He assured them that the *Valhalla*, an eighty-two-foot fishing trawler, was 'clean'. It took some time to get the *Valhalla* in shape for the demanding voyage across the Atlantic. The boat was in dry dock in the New England port of Gloucester during the summer of 1984, undergoing repairs and renovation. The work was completed in mid-August, and the boat was judged to be seaworthy. On 12 and 13 September, the skipper, Robert Andersen, arranged for crushed ice and 7,899 gallons of fuel to be loaded on board. He told staff at the Gloucester Marine Railway, where the boat was serviced, that he was going on a trip to the Grand Banks, off Newfoundland, to catch swordfish. A tall, rugged individual, Andersen was an intrepid and highly experienced mariner of Danish descent, and also an IRA sympathiser.

Whitey Bulger turned up to see the *Valhalla* off on its trip to Ireland. According to testimony that his sidekick Kevin Weeks would later give to the authorities, Bulger and he were at the pier in Gloucester to provide security as the guns were loaded onto the boat. Weeks, one of Bulger's top lieutenants, sat with the crime boss in a car keeping watch, and using a radio scanner to check any nearby police calls. There was an air of urgency about the loading operation. Weapons were gathered up by Patrick Nee and Joe Murray from the houses where they had been hidden. Several vehicles with weapons on board drove through the quaint, eighteenth-century streets of the central area of Gloucester, and down to the docklands area where the *Valhalla* was berthed. One of the vehicles was driven by Joe Murray himself. The loading was done in the hours of darkness. Taking part were Nee, Murray, Crawley, Andersen and the others who would soon sail across the Atlantic.

It took about an hour to load the crates and duffle bags containing the materiel onto the *Valhalla*. It took longer to stow everything safely on board for the long voyage.

The vessel finally set sail at about one o'clock on the morning of 14 September 1984. Instead of looking for swordfish, the vessel headed east into the Atlantic in the direction of Ireland. In addition to the captain, Bob Andersen, those on board included a tall, wiry thirty-two-year-old Massachusetts native, John McIntyre, a skilled mechanic and experienced mariner who would act as engineer on the voyage; IRA man Sean Crawley, whose role was to oversee the delivery of the weapons; and some others. (John McIntyre would later tell police that the 'others' consisted of three men who were not mariners and who went by the names of Hughie, Charlie and Jimmy. In his view, they just seemed to be along for the ride, rather than mariners who could make a useful contribution to the sailing of the boat. In his own memoir,[10] Pat Nee refers to only two men, who were both part of his circle of friends.)

A week after the departure of the *Valhalla*, Nee flew to Ireland as one of a six-person party. He brought with him his then girlfriend Mary. Also on the flight were the operation's 'money man' Joe Murray and his wife Susan, and another couple. This couple stayed with friends while the others booked into a Dublin hotel. Nee met with his IRA contacts in Dublin. He confirmed that the *Valhalla* was on its way, and gave the co-ordinates for the rendezvous with the *Marita Ann*. The rendezvous had been the subject of advance discussions and Nee was simply confirming what had previously been agreed. The confirmed details were passed to the *Marita Ann* skipper. Nee said that on this trip to Ireland he did not meet the senior County Kerry republican Martin Ferris, who was to sail on the *Marita Ann* during the arms operation, and who was reputed to be the head of the IRA in southwestern Ireland at the time.

Ferris, a fisherman, was later to become well known in Ireland as a Sinn Féin politician, both at local and national level. Tall, bearded and with an athletic build, he had a reputation locally as a rebel who was involved in constant run-ins with authority. There was a republican tradition in his family, and he joined the Munster organisation of the IRA in 1970 at age eighteen. The IRA in Munster, part of the IRA's Southern Command, had the role of providing back-up and support to the Northern Command units who were at the 'cutting edge' of the conflict. The Munster section of the IRA carried out 'fundraising' robberies, and was involved in the procurement and storage of arms and in the manufacture of home-made explosives, as well as the provision of personnel for the 'armed struggle'.

Ferris had quickly come to the attention of the Garda authorities for his IRA activities. In 1975 he was jailed for a year for IRA membership and a year later convicted again of the same offence, receiving another twelve-month sentence. In 1977 he was fined and received a suspended sentence for assaulting a Garda. As a fisherman in the 1980s he was involved in a number of confrontations with naval and Garda authorities seeking to clamp down on illegal salmon fishing along the coast.

Ferris, a charismatic character with the whiff of sulphur about him, was also an accomplished GAA footballer in his youth. He played on the Kerry County Minor team – a useful accomplishment for anyone seeking a political career in this region. Kerry has a long, glorious GAA history, and there has always been a fanatical following for the County team. Ferris took the lead role in the operation to receive the *Valhalla* arms and to ensure that they were safely spirited away to the bunkers and hides that had been prepared to receive them.

Joe Murray and his wife, who was three months pregnant and feeling unwell, returned early to the US via Dublin Airport. It is believed that Murray was annoyed when the IRA decided that, for security reasons, the American visitors should stay away from the *Marita Ann* and from the area where the guns were to be landed. One could speculate that the Provos were concerned about the adverse publicity that would ensue if two members of the Boston criminal underworld, one of them a major drugs trafficker, were arrested in Ireland in connection with an attempt to import arms for the IRA. Nee did not feel the need to be around the *Marita Ann*, or to be on the coast to watch the guns being brought ashore. He decided to relax and await developments. He and the others availed of the chance to do some touring in a rented car. They went to the west of Ireland to explore the beauty of the countryside.

The *Valhalla* encountered horrendous weather on its two-week voyage across the Atlantic. The vessel took a mauling from hurricane-force winds and suffered considerable damage. After the epic voyage, the *Valhalla* was late for its rendezvous with the *Marita Ann*, which had set out from its home harbour of Fenit, County Kerry. Some time before the boats met, the crews of both vessels, much to their dismay, spotted an aircraft from Britain's Royal Air Force (RAF) flying low overhead. Were they under sur-veillance? On the *Valhalla*, Andersen was particularly worried. He was to confide later that he remarked to Crawley, 'The jig is up.' They had various options: they could dump the weapons at sea, or return to the US with the cargo, to try another day. Crawley decided to take a chance and proceed with the delivery.

Tension on both boats was running high. The two vessels kept radio silence as far as possible. But when the *Valhalla* was just a few hours' sailing from the meeting point, it was necessary to make radio contact. In the radio exchanges, Andersen detected impatience and frustration on the *Marita Ann* – the *Valhalla* was nearly two days late, forcing the *Marita Ann* to steam around in circles, thus running the risk of attracting unwanted attention. Andersen was not in the mood for making apologies – he had brought the *Valhalla* through hurricane storms which had almost destroyed the boat. The skippers were not to know that their comments were being recorded by an RAF aircraft flying overhead. Andersen decided to wait until the hours of darkness before transferring the weapons.

When the two boats came together, the seas were running high. The boats crashed into each other. There were fears that if the steel hull of the *Valhalla* continued to collide with the wooden hull of the *Marita Ann* in the Atlantic swell, severe damage could be caused to the latter vessel. The two vessels therefore lay off from each other, and crewmen secured a rope between them. The skippers kept their vessels in position by steering with just enough power to avert a crash. *Valhalla* engineer John McIntyre used the rope to haul himself along in a punt, making more than a dozen trips to transfer the crates of arms from the *Valhalla* to the Irish trawler. It was a difficult, physically demanding and indeed hazardous manoeuvre, which took several hours. On the punt's last trip, Sean Crawley transferred from the *Valhalla* to the *Marita Ann*, to accompany the arms cargo on the last leg of its long voyage to Ireland. The two boats parted company, the *Valhalla* sailing south at first to take a circuitous route back to the US, while the *Marita Ann* headed for a point on the County Kerry coast where republicans were waiting to unload the arms. It is believed that the trawler's destination was somewhere along the Kenmare River, a long inlet, flanked by mountains and featuring a number of small harbours.

Surveillance from the sky

The *Marita Ann* was inside Irish territorial waters, only about two miles from the Skellig Islands off the County Kerry coast, when the trap was sprung. The trawler was intercepted at about 1.30am on 29 September by two patrol vessels of the Irish Navy, the *Emer* and the *Aisling*, which had been hiding behind the vast bulk of Skellig Michael, and which could not therefore be detected by the radar equipment aboard the *Marita Ann*. They had set out from Haulbowline Naval Base on 25 September, on a mission to intercept the illicit cargo.

Powerful searchlights lit up the *Marita Ann* and naval personnel sent a message over the radio and by means of a loudhailer to 'cut the engines'. When the *Marita Ann* failed to stop, the 972-ton *Emer* fired four tracer rounds across the trawler's bow. The trawler came to a halt. It never got as far as the point where it could turn into the mouth of the Kenmare River.

Two boarding parties used fast-moving Gemini craft to approach the trawler. The Irish Naval Service, because of its fishery protection role, has long experience in boarding vessels on the high seas, and personnel are well trained for such a mission. The naval officer in charge of the boarding party was armed only with a pistol, a 9mm Browning, but he never had to cock it. His men were armed with the standard assault rifle of the Irish defence forces at the time, the 7.62mm FN. Armed Gardaí also went on board. There was no resistance from anyone on the trawler. The cargo of about seven tons of firearms, ammunition and explosives was seized, and those on board were handcuffed. Detained aboard the *Marita Ann* were the skipper, Michael Browne; republican activist Martin Ferris; crewmen Gavin Mortimer and John McCarthy; and, of course, Sean Crawley, the IRA man who had transferred from the *Valhalla*. Garda inspector Eric Ryan, who had boarded the boat with the naval personnel, placed the five men under arrest.

The skipper was left on the *Marita Ann*, under guard, for the 100-mile voyage to Haulbowline naval base in Cork harbour. His companions were transferred to the naval vessels, two to each boat. The vessels sailed in convoy, the trawler being taken in tow after developing engine trouble. The vessels docked that night at the base, and detectives with Uzi sub-machine guns kept guard on the dockside. Searchers went into the hold to check out the weapons and ammunition, packed into kit bags, trunks and wooden crates. The searchers also found Sean Crawley's wire-bound note-book with a detailed inventory of the arms, and equipment.

The gunrunners had made sure to obliterate the serial numbers on the firearms that had been bought from gun shops – including a Steyr sniper rifle. However, the Gardaí found a hidden serial number on the barrel of the Steyr that had escaped the notice of the gunrunners, and authorities in the US would later establish that the weapon had been bought by Joe Murray at a gun shop in Boston.

Meanwhile, on land, Gardaí sought to round up those waiting to receive the arms. Three men were arrested travelling in a car near Bantry, County Cork, but they were later released without charge. Some months later, on 11 December 1984, at the Special Criminal Court in Dublin, Browne, Ferris and Crawley were to receive ten years apiece for their roles in the affair, while Mortimer and McCarthy got suspended sentences of five years each.

The RAF had played an important role in the operation, keeping surveil-lance on the gunrunning boats, and providing details of the movements of the *Marita Ann* to the Irish Navy and Gardaí prior to the interception of the vessel. The RAF had presumably been asked for assistance when the Gardaí learned in advance of the gunrunning plot. The RAF had more advanced maritime surveillance capabilities than the Irish Air Corps, and had deployed two Nimrod maritime surveillance aircraft as part of the operation. Bob Andersen's hunch that his boat was under surveillance proved to be correct.

Details of the RAF role were given in a memorandum prepared for the US courts by the prosecution in a case that would be brought against some of those involved on the US side of the gunrunning affair.[11] According to the document, RAF personnel established that the *Valhalla* and the *Marita Ann* met in international waters in the late night and early morning of 27/28 September 1984. The RAF taped a radio conversation between the two boats, suggesting that items were being moved from one vessel to the other. As investigations developed on both sides of the Atlantic, the taped conversation was reviewed by law enforcement officers in Ireland and the US. Garda officers recognised one voice as that of Michael Browne, the captain of the *Marita Ann*, while US agents identified the other voice as that of Robert Andersen, captain of the *Valhalla*.

The RAF Nimrod crews stated that the *Valhalla* sailed from the area immediately after meeting with the *Marita Ann*, without any stops for fishing, while the *Marita Ann* sailed towards the Irish coast, where it was intercepted. According to the RAF, surveillance was conducted constantly by radar, with an additional two visual sightings, and at no time during the rendezvous did the surveillance aircraft lose radar contact with the two vessels. The memo recorded a significant fact – one of the Nimrods took a picture of the *Valhalla* several hours after its meeting with the *Marita Ann*, and about thirty miles from the meeting point. This may have been the first clear evidence identifying the *Valhalla* as the 'mother ship' in the gunrunning operation.

Nee told me he was touring in the Charlestown area of County Mayo when he heard that it had all 'gone bad', that the *Marita Ann* had been caught. He found out through a news bulletin on the car radio. He was devastated, in a state of utter shock. But he also had to act quickly. It was time for him and his friends to get out of Ireland. They had been scheduled to return to the US from Shannon Airport, but Nee decided there had to be a change of plan.

The party drove immediately to the County Wexford port of Rosslare and took a ferry to Le Havre in France. From here they travelled by taxi to Paris and checked into a hotel. Nee made an urgent phone call from the hotel to the Charlestown, Boston, home of Joe Murray, seeking assistance. Murray went straight to the TWA desk at Logan airport, Boston, and paid cash for four air tickets to enable the group to travel home the next day,

2 October. Murray then used a pay phone at the TWA terminal at Logan to call Nee's hotel in Paris to confirm the travel arrangements. The party duly flew out the following day. Recalled Nee: 'They were waiting for us at Logan.' Nee was detained by US customs and questioned for about two hours about his activities in Ireland and France. He didn't give anything away. His companions were also quizzed.

The customs agents were unaware of Nee's role in the gunrunning plot at this stage, and had targeted him because of his contact with drugs trafficker Joe Murray. Apparently, a court-authorised tap on Murray's phone had picked up the conversation with Nee. Nee's name was placed on a watch list, and customs were alerted to his impending arrival at Logan. Customs agents suspected that Nee might have become involved with Murray in some international drug smuggling operation. Nee's baggage was searched thoroughly, but nothing incriminating was found. Nee told me that when the gunrunning probe eventually got under way, the US customs was the lead agency in the investigation until the FBI took over. As regards the unused tickets from Shannon, Nee did not believe in wasting money. He sought, and received, a cash refund.

On 3 October, the assistant customs attaché based at the US Embassy in London alerted the assistant special agent in charge (ASAC), US customs, Boston, that the *Valhalla* was the mother ship that had transferred the weapons to the *Marita Ann*. US customs began inquiries into the ownership and background of the *Valhalla*. It was established that the boat, then known as the *Kristen Lee*, had been seized by US customs in 1981 from its owner, Robert Andersen, for swordfish smuggling. The boat was sold at a US Marshals' auction in July 1984, and was bought by a Massachusetts businessman who formed a company to register the ownership. As he was legally entitled to do, the businessman arranged for Andersen to operate the boat he (Anderson) had formerly owned, and the name was changed to *Valhalla*. The customs service now figured that the *Valhalla* would return to a port in the northeastern United States, and personnel were instructed to keep a lookout. The Coast Guard was also alerted.

When the *Valhalla* slipped back into US waters, Bob Andersen reckoned it would be wise not to dock in Gloucester, where the boat had begun its gunrunning voyage. He steered the craft into Pier 7 in Boston Harbour, around eleven o'clock on the night of 13 October. It was about a month since they had set out on their remarkable trans-Atlantic adventure. To the great relief of all on board, there was no sign of any law enforcement people lying in wait for them when the vessel docked at the Boston Fish Harbour. The crew dispersed into the night. Some would never face prosecution.

It was not long before the vessel came to the attention of the authorities. At 12.30pm on 16 October, two US customs patrol officers noted the *Valhalla* among other fishing boats at Pier 7. They alerted their supervisors. Quite independently of US customs, agents of the Organised Crime Drug Enforcement Task Force (OCDETF) had been keeping Joe Murray under surveillance. On 16 October, the agents observed Murray and Pat Nee driving from Murray's home to Pier 7, where they met with Bob Andersen and John McIntyre, and delivered a brown paper bag to them. When this meeting broke up, Andersen and McIntyre returned to the *Valhalla*. A short time later, US Customs agents arrived on the dockside at Pier 7. As they did so, they noticed Andersen and McIntyre walking away from the *Valhalla*. The two men were stopped and it was later alleged that they initially denied any connection with the boat.

The agents questioned the two men about their links to the *Valhalla* and their activities in recent months. The two suspects made no admission of any lawbreaking, although Andersen noted with disquiet that McIntyre was extremely nervous and agitated. (It would only emerge later that McIntyre was already providing confidential assistance to the authorities.) Agents recovered the brown paper bag, which was found to contain $10,000. According to some reports, Andersen was paid this amount for the gun-running trip. It is unclear if the cash represented this payment, or if it was meant also to cover repairs to the boat. There was a danger that the collision with the *Marita Ann* might have provided forensic evidence of contact with the trawler – an incentive for speedy repairs to be carried out.

The two men were allowed to go free but they would remain under investigation, and the *Valhalla* was seized. The vessel was detained for an alleged violation of the US Neutrality Act, which forbids arms exports without a licence, and for failure to report to customs. The businessman who owned the Valhalla told the media he knew nothing of any gunrunning operation, and thought the vessel was on a swordfishing trip.

The boat was moved to Boston Fuel Docks, a private facility rented by the government, where it was held under twenty-four-hour guard. A thorough bow-to-stern search and examination of the vessel was carried out by agents and forensic experts. Agents seized the vessel's charts, and a 1984 calendar with handwritten notations of longitude and latitude, set out on dates from 14 to 30 September. While the charts found on board were said to be sufficient only for navigation to the Flemish Cap, a fishing area east of the Grand Banks, a review of the written notations by a US Coast Guard navigator was said to indicate that the *Valhalla* had sailed much further afield. The navigator found that the longitude and latitude plotting by date would put the *Valhalla* in a position about 250 miles off the Irish coast on 24 September.

Some copies of magazines were found – *Guns and Ammo*, and *Soldier of Fortune*. One of the latter was found to contain two fingerprints belonging to Pat Nee. He read such magazines to keep track of developments in the arms world, and to check the mail order ads when he was procuring arms for the IRA. Agents also found two volumes of a three-volume set of *The Green Flag* by Robert Kee, a work about Irish nationalism. These had belonged to John McIntyre who, in his spare time during the long voyage across the Atlantic, liked to read up on Irish history. Among the other items found on board the *Valhalla* was a drill press and bit. According to the authorities, an examination of the equipment indicated that it was consistent with equipment used to obliterate the serial numbers on guns seized aboard the *Marita Ann*.

Nee was not indicted until some months later, and then went to ground for almost a year before being caught. He spent some of the time hiding out at a property in Mexico owned by Joe Murray. Ultimately, Nee and others went on trial in the summer of 1987. Joe Murray was jailed for ten years, and Bob Andersen, the *Valhalla* skipper, got four years. The sentences imposed on Murray and Andersen were for the gunrunning operation and also for smuggling marijuana into the US on board the vessel *Ramsland*. Nee was jailed for four years on the arms charges. John McIntyre disappeared and was never brought to trial. The US authorities believed that Whitey Bulger had a role in the *Valhalla* operation, or at the very least had given it his blessing, but he never faced charges in connection with the affair.

There was consternation in the IRA and among the Boston gunrunners in the immediate aftermath of the seizure of the *Marita Ann*. How had the Irish authorities known about the shipment? Was there an informer at work? The immediate suspect after the capture of the arms was John McIntyre. It would later emerge that after McIntyre and Andersen were initially questioned by Customs agents at Pier 7, Bulger heard that one of the men was co-operating with the authorities. Bulger did not know at that time which one was the informer. However, subsequent information pointed the finger firmly at John McIntyre.

McIntyre went missing on 30 November 1984, some weeks after the *Marita Ann* seizure. There was speculation that he had betrayed the operation; that his disloyalty had been discovered; that he had been kidnapped and murdered, his body buried in a secret location. Early on in the saga, McIntyre's distraught parents were convinced their son had been killed by British agents. Another, more plausible, theory was that McIntyre had been murdered by the Bulger gang after they found out he was talking to the police.

The media had begun covering the gunrunning saga and the American connection. One day Boston journalist Joe Bergantino, who was working on the story, got a call from a young man who had some important information to impart. The caller, who did not give his name and never called again, said that Whitey Bulger was linked to the arms cargo that was sent to Ireland. Bergantino was working for an NBC affiliate at the time. To this day he remembers the call, although he cannot remember if it came through while he and his colleagues were working on the story or after it aired. He believes he knows who was on the line. 'I'm almost certain it was John McIntyre who called,' said Bergantino, currently a prominent investigative reporter with CBS 4 in Boston. In the weeks before he disappeared, had McIntyre decided to tell all, not only to the authorities but to the media as well?

The full story of what happened to McIntyre took years to emerge. All the indications are that McIntyre talked *after* the *Valhalla/Marita Ann* operation, and that he was not the source of the advance tip-off that led to the capture of the arms. It all began to go wrong for McIntyre over a relatively minor incident on 14 October 1984, shortly after he returned to his parents' home from the *Valhalla* voyage. It appears that McIntyre left his baggage at the house and decided later that night to go out to visit his estranged wife in his home area of Quincy. His parents dropped him off in their car. He seemed certain that the woman would be at home. His parents drove off in good faith, without waiting to see if he found anyone at home.

Had they waited, the disaster that was to befall their son might have been averted. McIntyre rang the doorbell and, when there was no reply, he climbed onto a balcony. He had been drinking. Police arrested him as a suspected burglar. Police records showed that a warrant had been issued for his arrest after he failed to show up in court on a drunk driving charge. He was detained on the basis of the outstanding warrant.

McIntyre had dropped out of Boston's Northeastern University to join the US Army. He followed in his father's footsteps, serving in military intelligence. At one stage he was posted to NATO's Strategic Command Communications Centre in Karlsruhe, West Germany.[12] He had been doing well when his military career suffered a setback after marijuana was allegedly found in his locker, leading to a court martial in July 1971. He was sentenced to three months, but the conviction was overturned on appeal. When he left the Army he went on to work in underwater construction and acquired a small fishing boat, which he used for lobster fishing.

In a docklands bar he came into contact with Joe Murray, one of the major drugs traffickers in the region at the time, whose gang merged with the gang headed by Whitey Bulger. McIntyre became involved as a low-level worker, or 'lumper', in Murray's drug smuggling empire, helping to unload bails of marijuana from freighters in the Atlantic onto smaller boats for transfer to Murray's drug warehouses in Charlestown and Southie. But apart from the drink driving charge, McIntyre had never come to the notice of the authorities in relation to any significant offence – police records showed he had once been involved in a minor incident, when he assaulted some youths who had stolen car wheels and equipment from him, and there had also been a charge of disorderly conduct in a bar. According to his mother, he and a friend had taken on a gang of racist thugs who had been picking on two black Marines. It was all very minor stuff – the record did not indicate a hardened career criminal.

In an apparent attempt to sort out his problems with the local cops, and to escape from the criminal underworld in which he had become immersed, McIntyre made a serious error of judgement, from the point of view of his own security and safety. He began telling the police officers an amazing story about a voyage to deliver weapons, some of them stolen, to the IRA, and also tales of huge quantities of marijuana being smuggled into Boston harbour. McIntyre began naming names in relation to the gunrunning – among those identified were Whitey Bulger, Bulger's lieutenant Kevin Weeks and Pat Nee.

The officers called in Detective Richard Bergeron, of Quincy's Organised Crime Unit. McIntyre repeated his story to Bergeron. According to McIntyre's family, Bergeron realised that the information McIntyre was providing would be significant to several law enforcement agencies and he immediately arranged for agents of the Drug Enforcement Agency (DEA) and the US customs service to take part in the debriefing of McIntyre. Bergeron also informed the FBI, and McIntyre was interviewed jointly by an FBI agent and a US customs agent on or around 17 October.[13] McIntyre's relatives have claimed he told police that he was willing to co-operate with law enforcement, but was 'petrified' of the people that he was discussing. He was fearful that his identity would be disclosed. He knew that if Bulger or Flemmi learned of his willingness to co-operate with law enforcement officials, his life would be in danger.[14]

During his interviews with law enforcement officers, McIntyre provided an advance tip-off – he warned that Joe Murray's people had a major shipment of marijuana coming into Boston harbour on board a vessel called the *Ramsland* the following month, November. The drugs shipment was supposed to pay for the guns donated to the IRA, McIntyre was said to have told the authorities.[15] The DEA agents were excited. McIntyre appeared to have excellent information, and the agents were delighted to get such an important source within the Bulger crime empire. They had been working on an operation against the Bulger gang and this was the kind of inside information they needed.

On 14 November, federal agents seized the *Ramsland* as it entered Boston harbour. As McIntyre had predicted, it was carrying a cargo of marijuana – thirty-six tons of the drug – which it had taken on board at sea from another ship. Several arrests were made. Murray apparently suspected the shipment had been betrayed by one of those on board the ship, who included McIntyre.

Whitey Bulger discovered at some stage that McIntyre was talking to the FBI and his fate was sealed. When McIntyre was last seen alive, on 30 November, he was talking of running away on a ship to South America. But first, there were some domestic tasks to attend to. As he left the family home, he told his parents he was going out to cash his army veteran's cheque. They never saw him again. His pick-up truck was found a few days later, abandoned on the Boston waterfront, less than a mile from where his body would be discovered many years later. His uncashed cheque for $1,200 was still in the vehicle. According to evidence that would later be given in court, Bulger personally killed McIntyre after confronting him and accusing him of informing to the FBI. How did Bulger find out?

John Connolly, Bulger's 'rogue agent' contact in the FBI, has strenuously denied tipping off the crime boss. Connolly, who retired from the FBI in 1990 and was later jailed over his collusion with Bulger, has said he never even heard McIntyre's name before he vanished, and had no recollection of ever being told that McIntyre was a source.[16] Connolly had recruited Whitey Bulger and his sidekick, Stephen 'The Rifleman' Flemmi, as informants in operations against the Boston-based Italian Mafia, but was also secretly protecting them. Bulger and Connolly went back a long way – they had grown up together in the Irish-American neighbourhood of South Boston.

During the 1990s, former IRA man Sean O'Callaghan revealed that it was he who had tipped off the Irish authorities on the *Valhalla/Marita Ann* operation. The gaunt, heavy-smoking O'Callaghan was probably the most important informer to emerge from the Southern Command of the IRA. From a republican family in County Kerry, O'Callaghan rose to a senior level in the organisation. After secretly turning against the movement, he gave Gardaí a series of important tip-offs on IRA activities. O'Callaghan wrote a best-selling book chronicling his time in the Provos and outlining the reasons why he became disillusioned. He describes in his book how he pumped eight bullets into a Catholic RUC man, and portrays some members of the movement as sectarian bigots. He tells how one senior IRA man expressed the hope that a murdered policewoman had been pregnant, 'as this would mean two for the price of one'. One of the most valuable services he performed for the Garda authorities was to provide the tip about the *Marita Ann* gunrunning affair. O'Callaghan gives a detailed description in his memoirs of how he found out about the operation, and passed the information to the Gardaí.[17]

There is no indication that O'Callaghan had advance information about the identity of the vessel bringing the arms across the Atlantic. It seems that it was an RAF Nimrod surveillance aircraft that first identified the *Valhalla* as the 'mother ship', with John McIntyre later confirming the role of the *Valhalla* and filling in details as to the identities of those involved on the US side of the operation.

Another theory has emerged about the detection of the *Valhalla* – that Whitey Bulger himself had blown the gaffe to the FBI in advance of the *Valhalla* operation, in order to avoid criminal charges, while pocketing whatever profit he made from providing the arms to the IRA. He had, after all, been a long-time FBI informant. It would not have been the first time that an arms trafficker had informed on an arms shipment to which he was connected. In 1997 the *Boston Globe* newspaper reported that authorities believed that Bulger had compromised his own operation – after taking a hefty profit for selling many of the guns on board. According to the newspaper, Bulger was one of three men suspected of putting up the money for the gunrunning operation. A law enforcement official familiar with the case was quoted as saying: 'Whitey waved goodbye to the *Valhalla*, then made a phone call. He got most of the money for the guns up front.'[18]

Nee strongly rejected these claims when I met him. He pronounced himself no friend of Bulger, but was at pains to emphasise that he did not believe that Bulger betrayed the *Valhalla* operation. And, of course, he reiterated that none of the participants made money from the *Valhalla* arms run. He took the view that it was Sean O'Callaghan, not Bulger, who betrayed the *Valhalla* and the *Marita Ann*. 'O'Callaghan knew a lot more than he should have known.' Nee said that when he linked up with Bulger, he didn't realise that the crime boss was leaking information to the FBI. 'We did not know we had formed an alliance with a rat. He was the biggest Irish informant ever.' Nevertheless, Nee remained confident that the *Valhalla* gunrunning voyage was one operation that was not betrayed by Bulger.

Other information gleaned during research for this book tends to support the contention that it was O'Callaghan, not Bulger, who provided the vital tip that led to the interception of the arms shipment. According to one source, Gardaí actually planted an eavesdropping device and a direction-finding device on board the *Marita Ann* after getting the tip from O'Callaghan. It was also said that some time before the *Marita Ann* set out on its gunrunning voyage, a Special Branch detective went on board the vessel in its dock in Fenit when no members of the crew were around, and renewed the batteries in the listening and direction-finding devices. It is also understood that there is no record of Bulger passing information on the *Valhalla* to the person in the FBI most likely to receive it – Bulger's long-time contact John Connolly.

The eleven bulletproof vests found on board the *Marita Ann* were traced to three Boston police officers. No action was taken against any of the officers. Two Metropolitan Police officers confirmed they had bought ten of the vests, but said they were not acquired with any illegal purpose in mind. The officers told police authorities they understood the vests were meant for the personal protection of Sean Crawley and some friends, who were making a trip to Northern Ireland as tourists.

The eleventh vest was traced to Michael Flemmi, a member of the Boston Police Department's bomb disposal squad, who said the vest had been stolen from his car. Flemmi, a brother of Stephen Flemmi, Whitey Bulger's lieutenant, was to be jailed in 2002 for ten years in relation to another matter. He was convicted in US District Court in Boston of perjury, obstruction of justice and illegal possession of firearms. The court heard that he had moved an arsenal of firearms from its hiding place to another location because his jailed brother Stephen feared that Kevin Weeks, who was co-operating with the authorities, would lead police to the arsenal.

The end of the Bulger empire

In the latter part of the 1990s, there was a major drive by the authorities against the Bulger crime empire and the law enforcement officers alleged to be in league with him. A number of gangsters agreed to testify against Bulger, including former New England Mafia chief Frank Salemme, self-confessed mob hitman John Martorano and Kevin Weeks, who was particularly trusted by Bulger.

Whitey Bulger received a tip from John Connolly that he was about to be indicted, and he went on the run in late 1995. At the time of writing he is still at large, wanted for involvement in nineteen murders and other crimes. The FBI, as it sought information on his whereabouts, described him as 'the long-time head of Boston's Irish mob following his release from Alcatraz where he served a federal sentence for bank robbery in the

1960s'. The FBI statement goes on: 'Whitey Bulger became the chieftain of Boston's Winter Hill Gang after its leader, Howard 'Howie' Winter, went to prison on charges of fixing horse races at Suffolk Downs. Bulger was a crime boss in South Boston and ran his criminal organisation for thirty years in that area.'

As various individuals went on trial following the crackdown on the Bulger organisation, information emerged in relation to the aftermath of the *Valhalla* gunrunning operation. Kevin Weeks was a particularly important witness. Weeks agreed to testify against his former mob friends in return for a more lenient sentence. The barrel-chested former boxer who, along with Bulger, had kept a lookout when the *Valhalla* was being loaded with arms, helped the authorities to uncover the secret graves of six mob victims. One grave, uncovered in January 2000, contained the bodies of three victims, including that of John McIntyre. He had been missing for fifteen years. The discovery of his body was the culmination of a long quest for his remains on the part of his family. His grieving mother had always assumed he was murdered.

Weeks said in court that Bulger confronted McIntyre, who admitted to being an informant. After giving up on a plan to send McIntyre into hiding in South America, Bulger killed him. Weeks, whose testimony helped bring indictments against a number of mob figures, ultimately got six years in prison. Had he not cut a deal with federal prosecutors, he could have faced a life sentence. Weeks was released in February 2005. He refused to enter the FBI's Witness Protection Programme. It emerged later in the year that he had teamed up with a writer to produce a book about his adventures as a member of the Bulger mob.

Pat Nee, in his memoirs published in 2006, revealed that it was he who brought McIntyre to see Bulger at a house in South Boston, believing that the crime boss was going to arrange for McIntyre to flee to Spain. Bulger had asked Nee to set up the meeting. Nee left McIntyre with Bulger, Steve Flemmi and Kevin Weeks. When he came back to the house some time later, he was shocked to find McIntyre dead, with a rope around his neck and a bullet through his head.[19]

Steve Flemmi, Bulger's lieutenant, was finally brought to book in early 2004. He was sentenced to life imprisonment for his role in the murder of John McIntyre, and nine other murders, including the gruesome killing of an ex-girlfriend, and the daughter of another girlfriend.[20] In some cases Flemmi had removed the teeth of his victims to make it more difficult for police to identify them. McIntyre was one of the victims whose teeth had been torn out. Flemmi told investigators that he and Whitey Bulger found out that McIntyre was talking to the police about a marijuana shipment and an IRA gunrunning operation.

Detailed and very disturbing accounts have emerged of the final moments in McIntyre's life, after he was lured to a house in South Boston. Waiting to confront him were Flemmi and Bulger, backed up by Kevin Weeks. An account of what happened was given by Flemmi in June 2006 in court testimony.[21] Flemmi (seventy-two) said in his evidence that he and Bulger had 'flushed out' McIntyre by devising a phoney investment scheme related to a drugs deal. McIntyre had offered to invest $20,000 which had been given him by the 'Feds' to allow him to play along with the Bulger gang. Once they had McIntyre in the house in Southie, he was chained to a chair and a sub-machine gun pointed at his head. McIntyre was frightened and caved in within seconds, admitting he was an informer, and that he had told the authorities about the IRA gun-running operation involving the *Valhalla*. He apologised, saying: 'Sorry, I was weak.'

Flemmi and Bulger questioned him at length about what he had told the authorities. One can only imagine the terror that McIntyre must have experienced during the interrogation. After some deliberation, Bulger decided to kill him. The manacled captive was led to the basement where he was put sitting on a chair. Bulger tried to strangle McIntyre with a rope but did not have much success. McIntyre was still alive and was vomiting. Bulger said to him: 'Do you want one in the head?' McIntyre replied: 'Yes, please.' Bulger shot him in the back of the head. Flemmi felt McIntyre's pulse and he still seemed to be alive. Flemmi propped him up and Bulger shot him again in the head. Flemmi ripped out McIntyre's teeth and also part of his tongue. The body was stripped naked, and the clothes and pulverised teeth were later to be dumped in the sea from a pier in South Boston.

Kevin Weeks has admitted that he dug a grave in the basement, and that McIntyre was buried alongside the remains of a bank robber called Arthur 'Bucky' Barrett who, according to Weeks, had been murdered by Bulger in 1983. Also to be buried in the grave was another murder victim, Deborah

Hussey, a daughter of Flemmi's long-time girlfriend Marion Hussey. At a later stage, the Bulger gang became concerned that the remains of McIntyre, Hussey and Barrett might be discovered. The bodies were exhumed and reburied in October 1985 in a shallow, makeshift grave in a gully on a highway embankment along the Southeast Expressway in Dorchester, Massachusetts. This was where the remains lay until exhumed by the authorities, on the basis of information supplied by Kevin Weeks. Of the three gangsters who oversaw the traumatic final hours in the life of John McIntyre at the house in Southie, only Bulger has remained unpunished, although it can be said that Weeks got off lightly.

As for Bulger's FBI handler John Connolly, the suave former agent got ten years imprisonment in May 2002 for racketeering and obstruction of justice. He was accused of helping Bulger to evade arrest by warning him to flee before his indictment in 1995.

In May 2000, the family of John McIntyre filed a lawsuit against the federal government, claiming that a corrupt relationship between elements of the FBI in the Boston office and informants Whitey Bulger and Steve Flemmi had contributed to McIntyre's death. It was claimed that the FBI was responsible for his murder, because the two gangsters were given free rein to commit crimes while they also acted as federal informants. The law suit alleged that John Connolly, while serving as a special agent of the FBI, 'alerted Bulger and Flemmi to the identity of confidential law enforcement informants in order to protect Bulger's and Flemmi's ongoing criminal activities'. Bulger, Flemmi and Weeks were also sued as part of the case. A federal judge originally dismissed the suit in 2003, claiming the family had waited too long to file their case. However, in May 2004, The First US Circuit Court of Appeals overturned the dismissal of the case, and the McIntyre family were allowed to continue with the lawsuit. It was a matter of great relief to McIntyre's aged mother, German-born Emily McIntyre.

The hearing of the case opened in the US District Court in Boston in June 2006, and a star witness was Stephen Flemmi. Mrs McIntyre did not attend the court on the opening day. The McIntyre family counsel, Steven Gordon, indicated that Mrs McIntyre did not want to see the face of the man who was involved in her son's death, and who had ripped out his teeth.

Joe Murray and the missing millions

One of the main players in the *Valhalla* drama, Joe Murray, was shot dead in September 1992 by his estranged wife Susan at a lakeside house he owned at Belgrade Lakes, Maine. (This is believed to be one of the locations where part of the *Valhalla* arms cargo was stored before the voyage.) Police said Mrs Murray acted in self-defence, and no charges were brought. Patrick Nee recalled how Murray had told him that he was teaching his wife to shoot, and in particular how to fire the powerful .357 Magnum revolver. Nee thought this was a bad idea and told Murray so. The Murrays were not getting on and Nee thought, under the circumstances, that it was tempting fate for Mrs Murray to be shown how to use a firearm. You never know what might happen, he reasoned. His caution proved to be justified. Mrs Murray is now also deceased.

In his autobiography, Kevin Weeks claims that Murray offered money to himself, Bulger and Stephen Flemmi to murder Susan and another person. Murray feared Susan was going to 'out' him as a police informer, and wanted her out of the way. Bulger and his two associates demanded $1 million for the 'hit'. Murray thought the price too steep and the deal fell through.[22]

Speculation has persisted that Murray made money from providing guns to the IRA. There has also been a theory that some or all of this alleged income may have been hidden away in the Caribbean. On the other hand, as outlined already, Patrick Nee has said that nobody made money from the *Valhalla* operation. Certainly, Murray had millions of dollars to hide away in a safe haven, and it appears he had good connections among the international money laundering fraternity. In May 1987 a senior diplomat from the Caribbean state of St Kitts & Nevis resigned after FBI allegations that he had laundered drugs money for Joe Murray. Dr William Herbert, who served as ambassador to the US and the United Nations, protested his innocence.

In addition to the alleged use of Dr Herbert's services, it emerged that Murray used an Irish-American money-laundering expert called John ('Jack') Fitzgerald to salt away about $7 million in bank accounts in Antigua between 1985 and 1987. Because the money was suspected of being the proceeds of drugs and/or arms trafficking, the US authorities moved to freeze the funds. Investigators believed the money was under the control of Joe Murray and his brother Michael. The latter was jailed in the US in 1994 for thirty years and fined $10 million for marijuana trafficking.

Murray's money was deposited in Antigua in the Swiss American Bank (SAB) and the Swiss American National Bank (SANB), both part of the Swiss American Banking Group (SABG). US Senate investigators referred in a report to the sale of weapons to 'IRA terrorists' and said it was reported to them that some, or even all, of the Murray/Fitzgerald funds deposited into accounts at the SAB and SANB 'were associated with the IRA'.[23] Despite the best efforts of the US authorities, the money has never been recovered.[24]

Joe Murray, gunrunner for the IRA, was to figure after his death in another extraordinary saga. In March 2004, allegations surfaced that thirteen paintings stolen in America's biggest-ever arts theft had ended up in the hands of the drugs/guns trafficker. The claims were made in an ABC television interview with an antiques dealer called William P Youthworth III, and gave rise to speculation about an IRA connection. The Manet, Rembrandt, Vermeer and Degas works, worth hundreds of millions of dollars, were taken on St Patrick's night in March 1990, when two men posing as policemen persuaded security guards at Boston's Isabella Stewart Gardner Museum to open the side doors. Murray's involvement in the affair has never been confirmed.

As for some of the others on board the *Valhalla*, Patrick Nee was jailed in 1991 after being convicted of a scheme the previous year to hold up an armoured car carrying cash in Abington, Massachusetts. He told me that he had been donating a proportion of the proceeds of robberies he carried out to the republican cause. In his memoirs, he states that he had agreed with other members of the gang planning the Abington heist that the IRA could have twenty percent of the take – out of roughly $2 million, the IRA would get $400,000 and each member of the gang would pocket over $260,000.[25] But everything fell apart when the FBI moved in before the gang could even attempt to hold up the armoured car.

While in prison in 1995, Nee suffered a personal tragedy that still haunts him – his son Patrick Junior was stabbed to death in the Charleston, Boston, area by gangster Jimmy 'Jimma' Houlihan, in retaliation for the victim's mother and sister testifying in criminal cases against individuals linked to Houlihan. In 1997 Houlihan got fourteen years for second-degree murder.

Nee was finally released in 2000, and has gone 'straight' since then, working at an ordinary job for a wage. He has been leading a peaceful life, and does not have the hassle of police or gangsters on his trail. As he expressed it himself: 'Nobody is knocking at the door.'

Sean Crawley served his time in Ireland for the *Valhalla* gunrunning operation, and returned to the fray after he was released. He was one of a number of IRA men arrested in London in 1996 and charged with conspiracy to cause explosions at London electricity substations. This was during the period when the IRA was off cease-fire. He and five others were convicted the following year, and sentenced to thirty-five years each. One of Crawley's fellow conspirators was Gerard Hanratty, who had been convicted in Germany on weapons possession charges after being arrested in 1988 with Gerry McGeough, who was involved in IRA arms procurement in the US (*see* Chapter 8).

According to a republican source, while he was held in British custody, Crawley was approached by two American 'spooks', who tried to recruit him as an intelligence source – he refused to co-operate with them. Crawley was later transferred to Portlaoise prison in the Irish Republic, and was given early release under the terms of the Good Friday Agreement. He has since been living in Northern Ireland, where he is involved in running a programme for republican ex-prisoners.

As for others who sailed on the *Marita Ann*, the best-known remains Martin Ferris, who was elected for Sinn Féin to the Dáil (Irish parliament) in the general election of 2002, for the Kerry North constituency. The father of six had always stressed that he was strongly anti-drugs. Indeed his role as a determined and committed anti-drugs crusader is emphasised in his authorised biography. The book describes how, despite 'harassment' by the Gardaí, he confronted drugs barons and dealers personally, 'stretching the rule of law, but gathering massive public support'. The book states: 'Ferris defends vigorously his aggressive attitude towards the drug pushers and drug bosses.' He is also quoted as saying that drug dealers would never be tolerated in the IRA or Sinn Féin.[26]

In comments made on RTÉ radio on 13 February 2005, Ferris made a brief reference to the arms cargo that he tried to import into Ireland more than twenty years before. 'It was to be used against Crown forces in the six occupied counties,' he said. In his radio comments, Ferris was at pains to deny he was a member of the IRA Army Council – he also denied he was currently a member of the IRA. Ferris had been named some years previously in the House of Commons in London and in the North's Assembly at Stormont as a member of the Army Council. The naming had been done by Peter Robinson of the Democratic Unionist Party. Ferris was also accused by Irish Justice Minister Michael McDowell of being a member of the IRA's seven-person ruling body, in comments made in the Dáil in April 2005. The following July, the minister said he understood that Ferris had now left the Army Council, along with Sinn Féin leaders Gerry Adams and Martin McGuinness.

Some time after the seizure of the *Marita Ann* on the high seas, the trawler changed hands. It was bought by the noted banjo player Barney McKenna, of the renowned ballad group the Dubliners. The boat's name was changed to *Daragh Liam*. McKenna had no connection with the previous owners. There was a clean break with the past – the vessel's law-breaking days were over. For some years McKenna had a skipper and crew operating the boat out of the County Kerry harbour of Fenit, mainly drift netting for salmon. Then, about 1990, he decided to base the trawler in picturesque Howth harbour, near Dublin, where it is located to this day. Barney, who lives beside the seafront in Howth, told me: 'I don't use her as a trawler any more. She can be used for diving or angling. She is in good fettle and she is taken up every year for an overhaul.' The *Valhalla* also survives, although its name has also been changed.

Whitey Bulger is thought to have been travelling extensively, always staying a step ahead of the FBI. According to the Bureau, he has been visiting such countries as Italy, Ireland and Canada. The FBI states that he has 'exhibited a violent temper and is in possession of a knife at all times'. He was said to be travelling with Catherine Elizabeth Greig, described in some media reports as a 'bottle blonde', who is also wanted by federal authorities. Greig has been charged with harbouring a fugitive.

According to the FBI, apart from nineteen counts of murder, Bulger is being sought for conspiracy to commit murder, conspiracy to commit extortion, narcotics distribution, extortion and money laundering. He is also wanted for RICO (racketeering influenced and corrupt organisations) offences. The FBI states that he is being sought for his role in murders that were committed from the early 1970s to the mid-1980s in connection with his leadership of an organised crime group 'that allegedly controlled extortion, drugs deals and other illegal activities in the Boston, Massachusetts, area'. The FBI has offered a reward of $1 million for information leading to his arrest.

One theory that has been checked out by the FBI is that, in return for assistance with gunrunning, Irish republicans may have helped Bulger go to ground, perhaps by providing him with a false Irish passport. It is not known if there is any basis for such a theory. Patrick Nee reckoned that Bulger would be difficult to catch. 'Whitey Bulger is not your normal seventy-five-year-old guy. He tries to stay in shape. He is very crafty. He stays ten steps ahead of everybody else.'

The *Valhalla/Marita Ann* gunrunning operation was unusual at the time in that it involved an alliance between Irish nationalist militants on the one hand, and a coterie of criminals and drug smugglers on the other. The older, more traditional of the IRA leaders never liked the idea of their men consorting with criminals. They considered themselves patriots fighting for a cause, and regarded themselves as morally superior to professional criminals who broke the law to line their own pockets. I remember one elderly former IRA leader, Billy McKee, telling me of concerns he had in the early years of the Troubles, that some of the younger volunteers might be 'corrupted' if they were forced to mix with 'ordinary' criminals in prison. This was one of the reasons he wanted 'special category' status for IRA prisoners.[27]

As regards the drugs trade, the IRA has been accused by sources in the security forces in Ireland of benefiting indirectly from drugs by extracting 'tribute' from some drug dealers. In addition, three Irish republicans, James Monaghan, Martin McCauley and Niall Connolly, travelling on false passports, were arrested in Colombia in August 2001 after visiting the region held by the FARC rebel group, which funds its activities with the aid of money from the cocaine trade. Speaking in the Dáil in December 2005, Justice Minister Michael McDowell said that on the basis of intelligence reports furnished to him, the visit of the men to Colombia appeared to be connected to a deal whereby the Provisional IRA furnished know-how in the use of explosives, in return for the payment of a large amount of money to the organisation by FARC, 'which finances its activities by its control of the cocaine trade in the area of

Colombia which it controls'. (The three men, who returned to Ireland in 2005, denied being involved in any paramilitary activity in Colombia.)

On the other hand, back in Ireland, the IRA has taken an anti-drugs stance, and indeed murdered a number of alleged dealers in 'soft' drugs in Northern Ireland in the 1990s, using as a cover name Direct Action Against Drugs (DAAD). However, in regard to the *Valhalla/Marita Ann* operation, it is presumed that Provo bosses took the pragmatic view that if it helped them to procure arms, they had no problem working with drug traffickers and figures from the criminal underworld.

For his part, John McIntyre seems to have convinced his mother Emily that he did not like the marijuana smuggling business, but went along with it because of a promise made by Joe Murray that the proceeds would go towards arming the IRA. Mrs McIntyre said in an interview that John saw 'little harm in making money selling grass to college kids in exchange for what he saw at the time as the greater glory – arming the Provisional IRA'.[28]

A mother's search for her son

A number of those linked directly or indirectly to the *Valhalla* operation, or to those who took part, suffered misfortune in the aftermath of the affair. It was almost as if they were victims of a *Valhalla* curse. Joe Murray was shot dead by his wife, who herself passed away. One of Murray's alleged money laundering contacts, Dr William Herbert, disappeared on a fishing trip in the Caribbean in June 1994. Neither he nor his boat, nor his five companions, have been seen since, and there has been speculation about foul play. Patrick Nee's son Patrick Junior was stabbed to death. And, of course, there was the tragedy of John McIntyre – murdered, his body dumped in a secret grave, with teeth pulled out and limbs cut off.

McIntyre's parents originally believed that their son had been murdered by members of the SAS at the behest of British intelligence, in order to protect a high-ranking mole within the IRA. By an odd twist of fate, both parents had first-hand knowledge of the shadowy world of intelligence. John McIntyre senior, a Boston Catholic whose father was Irish-born, had served with the US Army's Counterintelligence Corps in Germany in the late 1940s and early 1950s, taking part in covert 'Cold War' operations against the Eastern Bloc.

Emily McIntyre (*née* Beider), who came from near Munich, had gone to work as a clerk in 1948 for fledgling German intelligence agency the Gehlen Organisation, headed by Major General Reinhard Gehlen. The wily spy chief, who headed German army intelligence for the eastern front during the Second World War, had built up a detailed knowledge of the Soviet Union and its military doctrine and tactics. He persuaded the Americans that they needed his expert services, and the services of his Nazi-era agents, to confront the Soviet threat. Emily met John at the Gehlen Organisation's sprawling twenty-five-acre compound near Pullach, south of Munich. They married, and their first son, also called John, was born in Germany in October 1952.

Although long retired from the intelligence business, the heartbroken John McIntyre senior used his intelligence contacts in a desperate attempt to find out what happened to his son. Apparently, shortly before his death from heart disease in June 1985, an intelligence source told him that John was killed by the British – it appears that an IRA source backed up that story in a meeting with a lawyer friend of the McIntyres, John Loftus. This is the gist of the story told in a book written by Emily McIntyre in co-operation with Loftus. The book put the blame squarely on the British for killing John.[29] However, subsequent events pointed the finger in a much different direction.

On a rainy day in September 2004, I spoke to Emily McIntyre at her detached colonial-type house in the quiet Squantum area of Quincy, close by the sea. For the frail widow in her seventies, the loss of her son is a heartache that never goes away. After John disappeared, she was told by US customs agents that they believed he had been murdered. In a desperate attempt to find her boy, she would frantically tour Charlestown and other areas of Boston in the hope of finding some trace of him. The eventual discovery of his mutilated remains gave her some degree of closure, but it also turned the knife viciously in an old wound.

'John was one of the nicest sons a mother could ever have, believe me,' said Mrs McIntyre. It was noticeable that she still spoke with a German accent despite decades in the US. It was December 1953 when she moved to America with her husband and baby son John, travelling by US troopship. The couple went on to have two other children, Chris and Patricia. As we spoke, Mrs McIntyre admitted she was not in the best of health, but said she was determined to pursue her legal case against the US government over John's death. The suit was being taken by herself and her son Chris. 'If I get too tired or too ill, Chris will continue,' she told me. She said she had been advised by her lawyers not to discuss the case in detail with the media.

Mrs McIntyre blamed the early death of her husband on the trauma caused by her son going missing. Recalling his disappearance, Mrs McIntyre said: 'My husband died soon afterwards – he was so upset. He was a very great patriot. He did things that nobody ever knew about. I can't speak on behalf of that.' She said the FBI had a very nice man in the Boston area with whom she had dealt, but was almost speechless with anger and disgust when she referred to former FBI agent John Connolly, jailed for ten years for breaking the law to protect his notorious gangland informants Bulger and Flemmi. 'Connolly should not have been at the FBI. If my husband had known all about John Connolly, he would have dropped dead immediately.'

Mrs McIntyre spoke of her pain to think of what was done to her son before Whitey Bulger and his sidekick Stephen 'The Rifleman' Flemmi killed him. Although evidence emerged to the contrary, she still believed that her son had been mutilated before, rather than after, death. 'What makes me physically sick is that they disassembled him before they killed him. He had thirty-two beautiful teeth – I am sure they pulled them out before they killed him. When his body was found it had no hands. He was tortured for many hours ...' Mrs McIntyre broke down in tears at the thought of what had been done to her son.

CHAPTER 10

The *Eksund* and the Spy in the Sky

In mid-October 1987, a US spy satellite recorded some intriguing images following a sweep over the port in Tripoli, Libya. The surveillance photos showed a small ship being loaded by members of the Libyan navy with crates and other items of cargo, at an armed forces dockyard. Perhaps to disguise the sensitive nature of that cargo, the loading took place during the hours of darkness, over two nights.

The Libyans may not have realised that the US National Reconnaissance Office (NRO) had begun deploying satellites that could take well-defined pictures even at night. The NRO designs, builds and operates the US network of spy satellites. What the satellites observe is determined by other US agencies, like the CIA, the National Security Agency and the Defence Department. On this occasion, a satellite, probably a highly manoeuvrable KH-12 with imaging power for night and all-weather observation, had been specially tasked to carry out the operation over Tripoli.

Intelligence about what was happening in Tripoli was quickly shared with the Garda authorities in Ireland. They were to learn that the images recorded were of extremely good quality. There was some amazement in security circles in Ireland at the strides made by the Americans in terms of satellite technology, developments that would transform the international gathering of intelligence. Officers from C3, the Garda Crime and Security Branch (CSB), the top intelligence wing of the Gardaí, were involved in formulating plans for a major security operation. The vessel that was spotted in Tripoli was called the *Eksund*, and the cargo, bound for Ireland, was a deadly consignment of arms and explosives being donated by Libyan strongman Colonel Gadaffi to the IRA.

The fact that the vessel had been spotted in a military dockyard in Tripoli by a US reconnaissance satellite remained unpublicised for many years. However, while researching this book, a person who had been a senior figure in the Irish security establishment in the 1980s confirmed a rumour I had heard – that the IRA's *Eksund* operation had been uncovered with the aid of satellite surveillance. I received further confirmation when I interviewed Lou Stephens, the former head of the FBI's New York-based PIRA Squad. He said he was familiar with the matter, and confirmed that the satellite had been specially tasked for the operation over Libya. He did not know how the authorities found out about the *Eksund*'s visit to Tripoli but he knew that the satellite was deployed to gather intelligence on the ship's activities. 'I am familiar with the fact that it happened, and that the satellite was tasked to go over Libya to take those pictures.'

Stephens believed the CIA was involved in having the satellite carry out the surveillance, but also believed that the operation would have been organised at the highest levels of intelligence, even higher than the CIA. He believed a White House emissary would have been involved, and thought it likely that the British would also have had an involvement. He had not seen the images that resulted from the Tripoli satellite operation, but had seen similar images from satellite surveillance during this period, and said the images were extremely clear and detailed. 'Let me tell you, it's something to see, you can almost count the hairs on the face ...'

At first glance, it seems unlikely that the intelligence that blew the IRA's *Eksund* operation derived solely from the images gained by satellite. It may have been that the *Eksund* came under suspicion for some other reason, that it was shadowed on its voyage to Tripoli, and that the satellite images then helped to confirm that it was engaged in gunrunning. On the other hand, a security source pointed out during research for this book that the

Eksund may simply have been picked up through the intense surveillance that the US was maintaining on Libya at this period, especially on vessels entering Libyan ports.

After the Irish authorities received news of the images showing the *Eksund* loading a cargo in Tripoli, Garda bosses drew up an elaborate plan to disrupt a highly significant IRA gunrunning operation. According to the plan, the *Eksund* would be kept under constant surveillance, but it would be allowed to land its cargo in Ireland. Then the arms would be followed as they were transported to their ultimate destinations, so that Gardaí could establish the locations of secret IRA arms bunkers. The aim was to widen the net as far as possible, and to grab not only the weapons and the gunrunning ship, but all those involved in the importation, unloading, transport and storage of the arms.

The Gardaí, as it turned out, never got to mount that ambitious operation. The French moved in first, with customs officers intercepting the *Eksund* off the coast of Brittany. The *Eksund* had drifted into French territorial waters and had, in effect, committed an offence under French law, by bringing prohibited goods into France. The *Eksund*, its cargo and its crew ended up in French hands, on 31 October 1987.[1]

A search of the vessel's hold revealed a real prize – a lethal cargo comprising 150 crates of arms. The consignment included at least twenty SAM-7 surface-to-air missiles; approximately 1,000 AK-47 rifles; at least 600 Soviet F1 grenades; approximately ten Soviet 12.7mm heavy machine guns with anti-aircraft gun mounts; a quantity of anti-tank recoilless rifles, and ammunition for them; a quantity of Beretta 9mm M-12 machine guns; a quantity of RPG-7 rocket-propelled grenade launchers and ammunition; a quantity of mortars; and fifty tons of ammunition. There were also explosives on board. In fact, one of the most significant finds was the discovery of two tons of the powerful Czech-made explosive Semtex, which has no smell and is very difficult to detect as a result. The Semtex came with detonators and fuses. Justice minister Gerry Collins told the Dáil on 5 January that it was estimated the arms cargo weighed between 100 and 150 tons, and was worth between £15 million and £20 million.

The taoiseach of the day, Charles J Haughey, who had himself been acquitted on gunrunning conspiracy charges in 1970, conveyed the congratulations of the Irish government to the French government on the seizure of the arms cargo. Justice minister Collins also thanked the French and extended congratulations. However, on a private level, there was also some regret in the Irish security establishment that an opportunity had been lost to strike a blow against those in Ireland who were part of the IRA's arms procurement network, or who were involved in moving and storing the weapons. The Irish did not blame the French – it later emerged that the *Eksund* would have been scuttled, with all the evidence going to the bottom of the sea, had the French not moved in to seize the vessel.

The Garda Síochána sent two senior officers to France to liaise with authorities there. One was Assistant Commissioner Eugene Crowley, who had special responsibility in the security area. He was accompanied by a Chief Superintendent. Some disturbing facts emerged. Prior to the *Eksund*, there had been four shipments of arms that had been landed successfully, giving an enormous boost to the IRA arsenal. It represented a major intelligence failure by the Irish and British authorities. The *Eksund* cargo was the biggest of the five shipments sent from Libya and was a major loss to the IRA, but the other arms consignments had already been hidden away in IRA bunkers.

There was some surprise in Ireland when the identity of the *Eksund* skipper emerged. He was Adrian Hopkins, a businessman from Bray, County Wicklow. He had no record of previous subversive activity, and got involved in gunrunning because he was short of money. A court was to be told that the IRA paid him a total of £150,000 to undertake the first two missions in 1985. He had once been a seaman in the British merchant navy, and was well known in Ireland in the travel trade. He had operated a company, Bray Travel, which had collapsed some years earlier, leaving many clients out of pocket. One of the other men found on board was said to be one of the IRA's leading technical experts.

As police inquiries continued, a fuller picture of Hopkins's gunrunning activities emerged. He had ferried the four 'pre-*Eksund*' shipments of arms into Ireland over a two-year period. The shipments began in August 1985 and on each occasion the arms were picked up from a Libyan 'mother ship' at sea – three off the Maltese island of Gozo and the fourth off the Libyan coast. The fifth cargo was loaded at the docks in Tripoli. The four shipments that got through successfully were landed on the County Wicklow coast south of Arklow, the first three being taken ashore at Clogga Strand, and the fourth at a jetty further along the coast.

For the first three shipments, Hopkins used a sixty-five-foot fishing boat, the *Casamara*, which he bought in July 1985 for £45,000, and which he later renamed the *Kula*. For the fourth trip he used a bigger vessel called the *Villa*. His fifth arms voyage, aboard the *Eksund*, was to prove his undoing. A Libyan intelligence officer acted as liaison man between the Libyans and the IRA on the gunrunning operation. The French authorities believed they established his identity, and also the identities of other Libyans implicated in the affair.

The arms that were smuggled successfully into Ireland in the earlier four shipments were to form the bulk of the IRA arsenal. Inquiries by security forces came up with figures for the types and quantities of materiel supplied by the Libyans. The quantities were astounding, in the context of a paramilitary organisation. It was estimated that weapons imported included 1,200 AKM assault rifles (a more advanced version of the AK-47), as well as RPG-7 rocket launchers and dozens of machine guns. (For the full estimated list, see Appendix A.)

It was a matter of great concern to security forces that ten SAM-7B surface-to-air missiles were included on the list – however, the IRA failed to use these to any effect. The Soviet-designed SAM-7 is an easily concealed weapon, operated from the shoulder. It fires a heat-seeking warhead that locks onto an aircraft's engines, tracking it until it scores a hit. The weapon is widely available in eastern Europe and in the developing world. Gardaí believed that the missiles delivered to Ireland became degraded through damp storage.

One of the most dangerous items supplied was an astonishingly large quantity of Semtex explosive, which was to prove vital to the IRA in its bombing campaign. (More than 4.5 tonnes of Semtex is believed to have been given to the IRA – of this amount a consignment of two tonnes was seized on the *Eksund*, but other quantities survived and by 1998 the security forces estimated that the Provisionals still had more than 2.5 tonnes of the explosive in their arsenal.) This was bleak news for the authorities north and south of the Border.

The IRA began to use Semtex explosive to lethal effect in the latter part of the 1980s. In fact, just days after the capture of the *Eksund*, on 8 November 1987, a bomb planted by the IRA blew up during an annual Remembrance Day ceremony at Enniskillen, County Fermanagh, killing eleven people and injuring another sixty-three. It emerged that Semtex had been used in the bomb. The IRA blamed the British Army for setting off the device prematurely, by using a high frequency scanning device. But the question was asked – why had the Provos planted the bomb in the first place? The IRA was widely condemned as sectarian for targeting an event which involved a largely Protestant crowd commemorating their war dead.

The IRA was angrily denounced in the Dáil. On 10 November, during an adjournment debate, Fine Gael leader Alan Dukes said the Enniskillen outrage appeared to have been carried out with the same kind of explosives as were found on the *Eksund*. He said there may now be on this island 'arms, ammunition and explosives which have come from the same source and by a similar route'. He went on: 'Our feelings of outrage, sorrow and sympathy for the bereaved and injured are sincere and deeply felt but even that sincerity is not enough because it is up to us to make it a positive force in supporting action in every possible way to bring an end to this violence. The President of Sinn Féin, Gerry Adams, had the effrontery to extend sympathy and condolences to the families and friends of those killed and injured in Enniskillen. That is a hollow, meaningless and shameful state-ment from a man who has played and continues to play a major role in advocating and perpetuating violence.'

For close on two years before the capture of the *Eksund*, security forces in Ireland, North and South, had indications that Libya might be involved in renewed gunrunning to the IRA. In arms raids, police found crates with Libyan markings. For instance, in January 1986, Gardaí swooped on a farm at Gurteen, County Sligo, and uncovered a cache of thirty semi-automatic rifles, some made in East Germany and others in Romania. They were par-ticularly interested in boxes containing more than 7,000 rounds of Yugoslav-made ammunition, for the crates bore the words 'Libyan Armed Forces' and 'Destination Tripoli'.

As one police source pointed out at the time, this in itself was no proof that Gadaffi was sending arms once more to the IRA, for, in the labyrin-thine world of arms dealing, weapons can change hands many times before finding a permanent home. However, the discovery of such boxes with Libyan markings was enough to arouse suspicion about Gadaffi's possible involvement, a suspicion that was not confirmed until the *Eksund* opera-tion came to light.

Voyage of the *Eksund*

Adrian Hopkins had located the *Eksund* through a ship-broking company in Sweden. He told the brokers he wanted a 250-tonne, shallow-draft boat to transport cargo on the rivers of Nigeria. The agent came up with the *Eksund* and, in May 1986, Hopkins flew to Stockholm to finalise the purchase, for £50,000. He hired a professional delivery crew to take the vessel to Malta. The vessel suffered mechanical problems on the way and had to undergo repairs, arriving finally in Valetta in late August. The delivery crew returned home.

Hopkins flew out to inspect the boat and to arrange for further repairs. He departed but reappeared in early October, with an Irish crew. On 12 October, the vessel set sail again, purporting to head for Kiel in West Germany. In reality the *Eksund* sailed to Tripoli where a large consignment of arms was taken on board. The *Eksund* sailed out of the Mediterranean and then north, through the Bay of Biscay. On the evening of Tuesday, 27 October, a French customs aircraft flew low over the vessel to check out its identity. The presence of the elderly ship was reported back to the customs operation centre in Nantes.

A senior French customs official was later quoted as saying that he consulted a nautical register and, becoming suspicious that an elderly coaster would be making such a long voyage, decided to keep it under surveillance. There was an implication that this was the type of vessel that might be used for drug smuggling. In fact, it is likely that the French, on the basis of international security co-operation, would have been alerted by the Americans and/or the British to the *Eksund*'s gunrunning activities. Customs aircraft continued to monitor the progress of the *Eksund*, and on the afternoon of Friday, 30 October, an aircraft spotted some odd activity on board, as if the crew were preparing to launch a dinghy. Were the crew trying to head for the shore? Were they trying to rendezvous with another vessel? Or were they going to scuttle the vessel?

When the *Eksund* entered French territorial waters, the customs authorities decided to board the vessel. A party aboard a customs cutter headed out from its base at Lezardrieux, and three officers, armed with handguns, slipped on board the *Eksund*, meeting with no resistance from the skipper and the four other Irishmen on board. The vessel was about five miles off the Roscoff coast. Three of the Irish crew were in survival suits and were clearly preparing to leave the vessel onboard the dinghy. The customs officers asked to see the ship's cargo manifest and logbook. When the skipper was unable to show these, he was ordered to head for Roscoff.

Customs began a detailed search of the ship that night, and twelve bundles of plastic explosive were found, connected to a detonator, in the hold. It appeared that the crew was preparing to scuttle the ship. On the bridge, hidden below lifejackets, searchers found five loaded AK-47 rifles and a machine gun. It later emerged that the gunrunners had been 'spooked' after being tracked by surveillance aircraft. They were also concerned about mechanical faults that had developed with the steering of the elderly vessel. A decision had been made that the skipper and crew would take to an inflatable dinghy, and that the vessel and its cargo would be blown up with the aid of a timing device – hence the explosives connected to the detonator. However, according to evidence that would later be presented in a Paris court, it was decided instead to simply scuttle the vessel and its cargo. It may have been thought that this would be a more discreet way of getting rid of the vessel and destroying the 'evidence' than an explosion, which could be heard and seen for miles around.

In order to scuttle the ship, it was necessary to enter more sheltered waters, out of the way of the gales that were blowing, to allow emergency repairs to be carried out to the steering system, so that the vessel could reach a suitable location where it could be sunk. It was planned that the five men on board would head for the French coast in their dinghy, slip quietly ashore, and then make their way back to Ireland. However, in heading for shelter, the *Eksund* entered French territorial waters, and thereby became of additional interest to the French authorities. According to one report, a British nuclear submarine had shadowed the *Eksund* all the way from Libya up to the point of capture, never surfacing during the operation, and relying on its 'active-passive' sonar system.[2]

How had the authorities got wind of the *Eksund* operation? Hopkins may have unwittingly attracted attention to himself by using large sums of money to buy ramshackle boats, of the type sometimes used by drug smugglers, and having repairs and renovations carried out with no expense spared, despite the fact that his travel business had gone bust and he was short of money. In addition, Irish customs and Gardaí in County Wicklow had heard of suspicious activity at Clogga Strand, with dinghies moving back and forth from ship to shore. In October 1985, Garda and customs officers actually searched Hopkins' boat the *Kula*, but nothing was found. The suspicion at this period was that Hopkins was involved in drug smuggling – a suspicion that was to prove unfounded.

There has been speculation that a British intelligence 'mole' in the higher echelons of the IRA may have blown the gaffe on the *Eksund*, but there is no conclusive proof of this. A source close to individuals in the republican movement told me that in the mid-1990s a man, who had been on the IRA Executive, the body that appoints the Army Council, came forward to the leadership and admitted that he had been providing information to the British. He had somehow been 'turned' while on a trip abroad. As he had voluntarily come forward and admitted his role, he was given an amnesty by the Provos. He had been active in Sinn Féin at a local level, but was told he could no longer have any role in republican activities. It may be that the information he supplied to the British was more in the nature of guidance on thinking within the movement in the moves leading to the Peace Process, rather than information that led to the seizure of weapons or the arrest of individuals. In December 2005, another high-level informant for the British was unmasked – senior Sinn Féin official Denis Donaldson. But there is no indication that he informed on the *Eksund* plot, or that he knew anything at the time about arms coming from Libya.

A republican source with a South Armagh background could not rule out the possibility that there had been a leak of information which led to the operation being uncovered. He considered that if the operation had been kept within the South Armagh element, security would have been much tighter. Shared with the people in Belfast, he appeared to think that the possibility of information leaking out was much greater. His attitude was, perhaps, an indication of the 'superior' attitude among some of those from the South Armagh republican enclave towards republicans from other sectors of the movement. Despite the suspicions about a 'mole' in the IRA, it is always possible that the *Eksund* was detected primarily as a result of US intelligence-gathering related to Libya – satellite surveillance and perhaps other methods, including eavesdropping on communications. By entering the port of Tripoli, the *Eksund* ran the risk of attracting unwanted attention – the previous four arms shipments had been transferred at sea from a Libyan 'mother ship'. This may have been an important factor in the detection of the vessel's gunrunning activities.

Apart from Hopkins, the other men arrested aboard the *Eksund* were Henry Cairns, a bookseller who also came from Hopkins' home town of Bray; James Doherty and James Coll, both from County Donegal; and Gabriel Cleary, from the Dublin area, who was thought to be one of the IRA's top technical experts. He was reported to be one of several IRA men who were trained in Libya, with the aid of a simulator, to fire surface-to-air missiles. (Cleary would later deny a French prosecution claim that he had undergone a three-month training programme in Libya, followed by further training in Lebanon.)[3] A French court was to hear that Hopkins claimed that he was introduced to the IRA by Cairns. Doherty and Coll were fishermen and is thought that their role was simply to act as crew on the voyage.

After the story broke, journalists approached the men's families. I recall meeting James Coll's wife in November 1988, at her bungalow near the sleepy village of Rosnakill, in a scenic area of northern County Donegal. A close neighbour was the politician Neil Blaney, of Arms Crisis fame. Mrs Coll was smiling and polite, but all she would say about her husband was: 'I have been to see him and he is fine.' At the bungalow home of fisherman James Doherty on scenic Cruit Island, on the west coast of County Donegal, it was a similar story. Mrs Doherty was away, apparently visiting her husband in jail in Paris, but daughter Rosie was at home. All she had to say was a very definite, 'No comment.'

The examining magistrate appointed to investigate the *Eksund* affair was Jean-Louis Bruguière, the most celebrated of France's several hundred *juges d'instruction*. The office of *juge d'instruction* dates back to Napoleon, and combines the role of a judge with that of a crusading, American-style district attorney. Just like the brooding Inspector Maigret of detective fiction fame, Bruguière smoked a pipe and liked to rely on his instincts. But Bruguière was rather more colourful than the old-fashioned policeman invented by writer Georges Simenon. Bruguière was extraordinarily gung-ho, prepared to travel the lengths of the world in his quest for evidence while investigating a case. All he had to do was to tell the Justice Ministry that he needed airline tickets and advance expenses. He did not have to explain to anybody why he needed to travel.

Bruguière was France's best-known investigator of terrorist activities. He had cut his teeth investigating domestic crime, and was particularly knowledgeable of the Paris underworld. Among the high-profile cases he had handled were those concerning Madame Claude, the refined lady who ran a high-society brothel; and an upper-class Japanese student, Issei Sagawa, who killed and ate his Dutch girlfriend. He had interrogated every type of undesirable, from pimps to assassins. The office of *juge d'instruction* gave him extraordinary powers – apart from interrogating witnesses and suspects, he can order searches, and issue instructions for phones to be tapped. He can call for assistance from France's security and intelligence agencies, as well as its police forces and diplomats.

Bruguière's reputation for unorthodox methods was enhanced while investigating suspected Libyan involvement in the bombing of a French DC10 airliner in September 1989. During his probe he piloted a military transport aircraft over the Sahara and after, handing over the controls, parachuted into the desert to hunt for clues.

He began specialising in terrorism cases in 1981, and from 1982 to 1987 led the investigation into Action Directe, a home-grown French terrorist organisation which had links with the INLA. Key members of the group ended up in jail, serving life sentences. Bruguière clearly became unpopular in some quarters – in 1987 a booby-trap grenade bomb was planted at his apartment. His police bodyguards managed to disarm the device. Bruguière began carrying a personal firearm – a powerful .357 Magnum revolver of the type made famous in the 'Dirty Harry' movies – and earned the nickname 'The Sheriff'. He worked on an investigation into the 1988 bombing of Pan Am Flight 103 over Lockerbie, Scotland. In 1994 he spearheaded the probe into the world's most wanted terrorist, Ilich Ramirez Sanchez, better known as Carlos 'The Jackal', who had been grabbed by the French in Sudan and, trussed up like a chicken, flown to France.

Bruguière developed a special expertise in Irish paramilitary activities. It was he who spearheaded the investigation into INLA members who, along with a most unlikely accomplice, a middle-aged Hollywood scriptwriter called Bill Norton, were arrested at Le Havre in 1986 with a consignment of weapons bound for Ireland (*see* Chapter 12).

Then, the following year, another Irish gunrunning case landed on his desk. This time, however, there was a much more significant international dimension – it involved the Libyans, and their mercurial leader Colonel Gadaffi. Bruguière conducted an exhaustive investigation into the *Eksund* affair over more than two-and-a-half years, compiling an enormous dossier stretching to more than 4,000 pages. As usual, he worked from a cramped, fourth-floor office, behind a bulletproof glass door at the Palais de Justice on the Quai des Orfevres, situated on the Ile de la Cité in downtown Paris. Suspects would regularly be taken from the various Paris prisons in which they were held to Bruguière's office for interrogation. The prisoners would arrive in heavily guarded vehicle convoys, with blue lights flashing and motorcycle outriders.

Bruguière made an unpublicised visit to Malta in June 1989, as part of the probe. The Malta connection was important, and Bruguière was anxious to interview a number of Libyans who had been based in this small, island state. However, there were bureaucratic delays, and the Libyans in question had returned to Tripoli before Bruguière could interview them. In November 1989, a group of French investigators again visited Malta, and Bruguière issued international arrest warrants for six Libyans.

A court hearing arising out of the *Eksund* affair heard that one of those sought was Colonel Nasser Ashour, a member of Libyan intelligence, who travelled on a diplomatic passport. He was alleged in court to be the liaison man between Libya and the IRA gunrunners. Ashour was reputed to be one of Colonel Gadaffi's most astute operatives, working in the foreign intelligence field. In 1976 he graduated from the Tripoli police college and, during the period 1979–80, went on training programmes to East Germany and Bulgaria. He joined Libya's Foreign Security organisation, rising to head of Special Operations section. Among the other Libyans sought by Bruguière was a Libyan businessman who had been based in Valetta, the Maltese capital.

In the weeks following the capture of the *Eksund*, security forces in the Republic and in Northern Ireland carried out major search operations. The result was the discovery of sophisticated underground bunkers, some of which seemed designed to hold large quantities of weapons – another theory was that they were designed as underground firing ranges. Security forces on both sides of the Border also made a number of major arms finds. Some of the containers used to pack the weapons bore clear Libyan markings. In Belfast in 1988, security forces seized a flame thrower – the first weapon of its kind to be found in paramilitary hands in the North. A senior RUC officer said it was of 'Warsaw Pact' origin and was thought to have been supplied by Libya.

So why did Colonel Gadaffi resume arms supplies to the IRA at this period in the 1980s? The Libyan leader and the Provos had a kind of love–hate relationship over the years. Having sent arms to the IRA aboard the *Claudia* in 1973, Gadaffi went on the following year to express admiration for the general strike organised by the Ulster Workers Council. It is possible that he did not realise that the strike was organised by loyalists, sworn enemies of the IRA for whom he had also expressed support. However, in November 1974, there was a very real rapprochement between the Libyans and the loyalists when the main loyalist paramilitary organisation, the Ulster Defence Association, sent four of its leaders to Tripoli.

Gadaffi was away but the delegation, which included Glen Barr and Tommy Lyttle, persuaded Libyan officials that arms supplied to the IRA resulted in the killing of ordinary working-class people in Northern Ireland. The Libyans cooled towards the IRA, but in the following decade Gadaffi found new reasons to resume gunrunning to the Provos.

In 1984 the British expelled all Libyan diplomats after fire was opened from the Libyan People's Bureau in London on a crowd of demonstrators, killing a young policewoman, Yvonne Fletcher. Ironically, the Libyan official who negotiated the departure of the diplomats from the Bureau was Nasser Ashour, who, it was later alleged during a court hearing in Paris, was the link man between the Libyans and the IRA. In 1985, Britain supported the US air raid on Tripoli. From Gadaffi's point of view, helping the IRA was an effective way of taking revenge on the British. And so the guns began flowing again, culminating in the *Eksund* cargo, the biggest single Libyan arms shipment ever sent to the Provos.

In importing these huge quantities of arms, it appears that the IRA was planning to dramatically escalate its level of violence and the scale of its operations, in what some have referred to as a 'Tet offensive', after the Vietnam War-era offensive by the Viet Cong. An ambitious plan had been formed to carry out 'spectaculars'. Surface-to-air missiles would be used to exclude British Army helicopters from South Armagh, extending control by the IRA of the republican 'enclave' beside the border. According to evidence that was to be given in court in Paris, the IRA also planned to launch a major attack on the Maze and Armagh prisons.

The seizure of the *Eksund* may have taken the wind out of the Provos' sails so far as the 'Tet offensive' was concerned. The element of surprise was gone. But the materiel that had been imported thus far gave the IRA an impressive arsenal. The organisation no longer had to worry about securing supplies of rifles and ammunition from abroad in the wake of the break-up of the Harrison network and the disruption of other US-based gunrunning operations. The organisation now had a plentiful supply of assault rifles, ammunition and heavier equipment, and was better armed than at any time since the start of the Troubles. There was also a change in 'weapons culture', with the Libyan-supplied Kalashnikov succeeding the US-origin Armalite as the assault rifle most often used by the Provos. There was a report that a sixth shipment of arms may have been sent from Libya to Ireland after the seizure of the *Eksund*, but this was never confirmed and in retrospect seems unlikely.

Probably the most important single item imported was a sizeable quantity of Semtex. The plastic explosive gave the Provos a new capability in the production and deployment of a variety of bombs, such as improvised grenades and mortar bombs, car bombs and roadside bombs. Semtex was particularly useful in the under-car booby trap, which could blow the legs off a victim. A comparatively small quantity of Semtex would form the core of the device, packed into a plastic lunch box, and, with the aid of a magnet, attached unobtrusively to the underside of a vehicle. One such device placed under a van killed seven soldiers in June 1988 at Lisburn, County Antrim, after they had taken part in a run in aid of charity.

The Unkindest Cut

In July 1990, Adrian Hopkins was given bail and promptly fled to Ireland where he was arrested and held in custody. In March 1991, a French court sentenced him to seven years in his absence. Cleary, Coll and Doherty got five years each and Cairns got five with two suspended. The following July, Hopkins pleaded guilty before the Special Criminal Court in Dublin to charges arising out of the *Eksund* affair. He got eight years, with five suspended.

As he picked up the pieces of his life after his release from jail, Adrian Hopkins harboured a sense of grievance over the way he was treated by the French and Irish authorities. He had spent almost three years in prison in France, and when he fled back to Ireland after being given bail, he was apparently under the mistaken impression that the Gardaí had promised him immunity. Instead, he was arrested, tried and jailed. He had already been tried *in absentia* in France, and he saw this as a breach of his human rights. When I met him at his home in early 2000, he also complained about 'double jeopardy' – being tried twice for the same offence. He talked of taking a case to the Court of Human Rights in Strasbourg. A spokesperson for the court confirmed that Hopkins had lodged a case against the French government in 1993, but it was found to be inadmissible. She could find no record of subsequent proceedings.

In recent years he has been living quietly in a modern, detached house in the picturesque County Wicklow village of Delgany. He did not want to discuss the events that landed him in prison. 'I have knowledge of things that I would prefer not to have,' he told me when I called to see him. He added that he had received approaches to write a book, but had turned down all offers. Hopkins used to be a pillar of society around his home area of Bray, County Wicklow, and served as a rugby referee with the Leinster Branch of the Irish Rugby Football Union. One of the unkindest cuts of all must have been when some members of Greystones Rugby Club told him, after he emerged from jail, that they would prefer if he did not remain a member.

CHAPTER 11

High-Tech Operators of the IRA

Shortly after flying into the small South African airport, Peter Eamon Maguire sensed that there was something wrong. The middle-aged Irishman had been living a secret life close to the edge for a couple of decades, and his instincts for survival were well honed. He had been working in Africa for several years, and as he moved around the continent in the early 1990s he had to be careful. He had to avoid those countries with an extradition agreement with the US. The mild-mannered, highly-trained electronics expert and aircraft engineer was in his fifties at the time.

For a man of his years and background, it could not have been an easy way to live life, constantly looking over one's shoulder. However, the alternative was not very attractive either – he could give himself up to the US authorities, who had warrants out for his arrest, which meant he would almost certainly face jail time. One of his pals, who faced similar charges, had been given a hefty sentence of ten years, with no parole. The FBI regarded Maguire as one of the IRA's top technical experts, who had been immersed in a US-based plot to supply or develop the missile equipment that would help shoot down British Army helicopters in Northern Ireland. He was a man the FBI and the British dearly wanted to see captured.

In his years on the run, Maguire worked for a time for Nigerian Airways in Lagos. Then he moved to Mozambique, taking up a job in the capital

Maputo as an aircraft engineer. Life in Maputo had its own stresses and he decided he needed a break for a couple of days. It was coming close to Christmas. He reckoned he would take a short flight from Maputo to South Africa, to unwind and relax. Since going on the run, it would be the first time that Maguire set foot in a country that had an extradition treaty with the US. He may have figured that his name would not come up on a watch list in the small South African airstrip with the impressive name of Nelspruit International Airport, located close to the Kruger National Park and the Mozambique border. But soon after disembarking from the aircraft, he knew he had made a terrible mistake.

One can only guess at the sinking feeling he must have experienced as the security police approached him. They knew exactly who he was, and the fact that he was a fugitive. A senior officer addressed him by his name and told him that he had a warrant for his arrest from the US authorities. It was pointless to resist or to protest. Maguire was taken on an aircraft, under escort, to Pretoria, where he was interviewed by a senior police officer, with the rank of general. Maguire was soon to face court hearings, as US authorities sought to get him back to America to face serious charges in federal court.

An informed source said that as Maguire reflected on how the cops had been ready and waiting for him, he could not help feeling that somebody had betrayed him. The suspicion was that prior to his arrival at Nelspruit, the police had his travel itinerary, and were expecting him, and that he had not been detected simply as a result of a routine immigration check.

Maguire was not a typical IRA volunteer. While many IRA members came from working-class or small-farm backgrounds, Maguire was middle-class and college-educated, and lived with his wife in a respectable Dublin suburb. He was the type of person who, like the majority of people in the Irish Republic, one would expect to be opposed to paramilitary violence. However, for years Maguire had been leading a remarkable double life. To his neighbours and colleagues, Maguire was a man with a well-paid job as a senior aircraft engineer with the Irish national airline, Aer Lingus, a job that involved an interesting globe-trotting lifestyle.

In his hidden life, he was using his professional expertise to help the IRA develop technologies to further their deadly war against Britain. Maguire became involved in assisting the IRA as far back as the 1970s. He was driven by a sense of grievance over what he saw as the repressive regime in Northern Ireland. He was also resentful of what he regarded as the failure of successive Irish governments to bring pressure to bear on the British for a better deal for the Catholic minority in the Six Counties.

The shaping of a rebel

Peter Eamon Maguire grew up in Churchill, County Monaghan, close to the border with Northern Ireland. He was known to friends and colleagues as Eamon, but would be referred to in press reports and in court documents as Peter. He was born in December 1936, one of a large family. His family home was not far from Crossmaglen, across the Border in South Armagh. As was often the case in this frontier area, his family straddled the border – he had relatives on both sides. He was distantly related by marriage to Frank Aiken, who came from County Armagh and who was the last chief of the IRA during the Civil War of the 1920s, before entering constitutional politics, going on to become a senior figure in successive Fianna Fáil governments. Maguire himself may have been from County Monaghan, but his republican attitudes were very much those of South Armagh, often dubbed 'Bandit Country' by the British media.

Ironically, he did not come from a traditional republican family background, to the extent that he had an uncle who was a member of the Royal Ulster Constabulary (RUC), the Northern Ireland police force despised by republicans. Nevertheless, Eamon Maguire felt driven to throw in his lot with the Provos. Sources say his role was as a kind of boffin, advising on high-tech measures to beat the enemy, using easily available components and devices. 'Cowshed technology' was how one republican source described it to me.

The foundations of his technical expertise went back to the mid-1950s when, after leaving school in Carrickmacross, County Monaghan, he joined the Irish Army Air Corps as a teenager. He began his service with six months basic military training at the Curragh Camp in County Kildare. At the time, the Air Corps, which had its main base at Baldonnel, near Dublin, was still flying Spitfire fighters of World War Two RAF vintage, and the youthful airman technician enjoyed trips with a pilot in the two-seater training version of the aircraft. The Spitfire, with its distinctive swept-back wings and droning engine sound, became a familiar phenomenon to locals as the aircraft went through aerobatic exercises over Blessington Lake and the mountains of West Wicklow.

Maguire developed his technical expertise during studies at the College of Technology in Kevin Street, Dublin. In 1962, after six years in the Air Corps, he left and did some more training in London. In 1964 he married his fiancée Caroline, and they went on to have a son and a daughter.

From 1964 he worked abroad as an aircraft engineer, residing in Kenya, Singapore, the Persian Gulf region, Peru and Malaysia. During the period that he worked in Nairobi, he met Jomo Kenyatta, the man who was accused of leading Kenya's Mau Mau insurgency against British colonial rule.

There was a lively social scene among the ex-pats in Kenya, which included horse racing. On a social occasion he was introduced to two of the senior colonial security figures who had played key roles in suppressing the Mau Mau rebellion – General Frank Kitson and Colonel Ian Henderson. Kitson went on to become one of the British Army's main counter-insurgency experts and was based in Northern Ireland for a period in the early 1970s. Scottish-born Colonel Henderson went on to become the director of the Bahrain Security and Intelligence Service, a post he held from the mid-1960s up to his retirement in 1998, when he became an adviser to Bahrain's Ministry of the Interior. Little did these two security experts realise that they were meeting a man who was later to become a stalwart in the struggle against British forces in Ireland. Ironically, in the course of his globetrotting, Maguire worked for a period in Bahrain, at a time when Henderson was the head of security and intelligence in the emirate.

In the latter half of the 1970s, Maguire returned to Ireland. Maguire and his family settled down to suburban life in Dublin – their house in Clondalkin was bought in 1977. From the following year, Maguire worked as an aircraft engineer with Aer Lingus. He specialised in avionics, the care and maintenance of the electronic instrumentation and control equipment used in aircraft. According to a former colleague, Maguire was a 'brilliant' avionics man, working on a range of aircraft types. 'On the courses that we did, he always picked things up immediately. He was extremely bright. He was top class at what he did.' The source added: 'At the same time, many of

Above: IRA volunteers posing with Kalashnikov rifles. These rifles are Romanian-made AKMs, a more advanced version of the AK-47. Libya dispatched more than 2,000 to the IRA during the 1980s. Many were seized, but by 1998 the IRA still possessed close on 600.
Photo: An Phoblacht.

Below: Bob Andersen, skipper of the gunrunning vessel the *Valhalla*, in 2005 in his home port of Gloucester, Massachusetts.
Photo courtesy of Rich Farrell.

Above: The offices of Omnipol in Prague, early 1990s. It was from this Czech state company that IRA man Dáithí Ó Conaill bought a consignment of arms. The Czechs said that they did not know the arms were for an illegal organisation. *Photo: Sean Boyne.*

Above: An IRA man, with M1 carbine, keeping watch in Free Derry.
Photo: Colman Doyle.

Right: Barney McKenna, a member of the folk group The Dubliners, with his boat the *Daragh Liam* in Howth harbour, County Dublin. Under a previous ownership the boat was known as the *Marita Ann*, and figured in a gunrunning operation in 1984. Barney subsequently bought the trawler for fishing purposes, and changed the boat's name, marking a clean break with her controversial past. *Photo: Sean Boyne.*

Left: Clogga Strand, County Wicklow, where IRA arms shipments from Libya were landed in the mid-1980s. *Photo: Sean Boyne.*

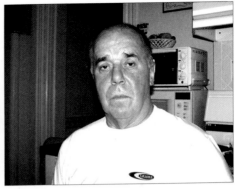

Above left: Naquora harbour, South Lebanon, in the early 1990s. A major arms cargo bound for loyalists in Northern Ireland is believed to have left this port in 1988. At the time the picture was taken, the harbour was in the Israeli-controlled sector of South Lebanon. *Photo: Sean Boyne.*

Above right: Patrick Nee, a former member of the Boston-Irish underworld, was jailed for his role in the *Valhalla* gunrunning operation. He is pictured at his home in South Boston, Massachusetts, September 2004. *Photo: Sean Boyne.*

Below: The FBI 'wanted' notice for James 'Whitey' Bulger, the Boston-Irish crime boss who has been on the run since 1995. He is wanted for a range of crimes, including murder. He provided arms for the IRA, and kept a lookout when the *Valhalla* was about to sail for Ireland with a consignment of arms for the Provos.

FBI TEN MOST WANTED FUGITIVE

RACKETEERING INFLUENCED AND CORRUPT ORGANIZATIONS (RICO) - MURDER (18 COUNTS), CONSPIRACY TO COMMIT MURDER, CONSPIRACY TO COMMIT EXTORTION, NARCOTICS DISTRIBUTION, CONSPIRACY TO COMMIT MONEY LAUNDERING; EXTORTION; MONEY LAUNDERING

JAMES J. BULGER

Photograph taken in 1994   Photograph taken in 1994   Photograph retouched in 2000

Aliases: Thomas F. Baxter, Mark Shapeton, Jimmy Bulger, James Joseph Bulger, James J. Bulger, Jr., James Joseph Bulger, Jr., Tom Harris, Tom Marshall, "Whitey"

DESCRIPTION

Date of Birth:	September 3, 1929	Hair:	White/Silver
Place of Birth:	Boston, Massachusetts	Eyes:	Blue
Height:	5' 7" to 5' 9"	Complexion:	Light
Weight:	150 to 160 pounds	Sex:	Male
Build:	Medium	Race:	White
Occupation:	Unknown	Nationality:	American
Scars and Marks:	None known		

Remarks: Bulger is an avid reader with an interest in history. He is known to frequent libraries and historic sites. Bulger is currently on the heart medication Atenolol (50 mg) and maintains his physical fitness by walking on beaches and in parks with his female companion, Catherine Elizabeth Greig. Bulger and Greig love animals and may frequent animal shelters. Bulger has been known to alter his appearance through the use of disguises. He has traveled extensively throughout the United States, Europe, Canada, and Mexico.

CAUTION

JAMES J. BULGER IS BEING SOUGHT FOR HIS ROLE IN NUMEROUS MURDERS COMMITTED FROM THE EARLY 1970s THROUGH THE MID-1980s IN CONNECTION WITH HIS LEADERSHIP OF AN ORGANIZED CRIME GROUP THAT ALLEGEDLY CONTROLLED EXTORTION, DRUG DEALS, AND OTHER ILLEGAL ACTIVITIES IN THE BOSTON, MASSACHUSETTS, AREA. HE HAS A VIOLENT TEMPER AND IS KNOWN TO CARRY A KNIFE AT ALL TIMES.

CONSIDERED ARMED AND EXTREMELY DANGEROUS

IF YOU HAVE ANY INFORMATION CONCERNING THIS PERSON, PLEASE CONTACT YOUR LOCAL FBI OFFICE OR THE NEAREST U.S. EMBASSY OR CONSULATE.

REWARD

The FBI is offering a $1,000,000 reward for information leading directly to the arrest of James J. Bulger.

RUC Chief Constable Sir John Hermon (*centre*) presides over a press conference featuring a display of captured paramilitary weaponry and ammunition, found in both loyalist and republican areas. *Photo: Brendan Murphy.*

Right: The aftermath of a republican car bomb, Enniskillen, 1983. A UDR man sustained serious leg and abdominal injuries in this attack. *Photo: An Phoblacht.*

Below left: Seamus Ruddy, who ran arms from Lebanon for the INLA, was later murdered in France by members of the organisation. His body was never found. *Photo: courtesy of Cecilia Moore.*

Below right: The apartment block at 82 rue Diderot in Vincennes, a suburb of Paris, where three Irish republicans were arrested in 1982. It was later shown that arms found in their apartment had been planted by the Gendarmerie. *Photo: Sean Boyne.*

Above: IRA men pictured in 1991 with a range of weapons. The man in front is armed with a Heckler & Koch G3 rifle. (In the 1980s the IRA took delivery of a number of such weapons, which had been stolen from the Norwegian military.) The second man appears to be armed with an Armalite rifle, while the third is carrying an RPG-7 rocket launcher.

Below: Masked IRA gunmen make a brief appearance at a 1916 Rising commemoration ceremony in Ardoyne, Belfast, in March 1996. The man in front is carrying an AKM rifle.
Photo: Brendan Murphy.

IRA gunmen show up at a 'Troops Out' rally in Andersonstown, Belfast, August 1980.
Photo: Brendan Murphy.

Above: One of the last photographs taken of a gunman in Belfast. *Photo: Brendan Murphy.*

Below: IRA patrolling the streets of North Derry in the 1970s. *Photo: Colman Doyle.*

us felt we never really got to know him. There was always a very private aspect to him. Of course as we later were to discover, he was leading a double life.'

After his return to Ireland, Maguire soon came to the notice of Garda Special Branch. In 1981, he was one of seven suspected IRA members arrested by Gardaí. The Irish police suspected the men of making remote-control bombs. There was not enough evidence against Maguire and he was allowed to go free. However, he continued to be a person 'of interest' to Special Branch. He took great care as regards security when he was working for the movement. He preferred to travel alone, was careful what he said over the phone, and was always aware of the possibility of being under surveillance.

In June 1981, he travelled to New York to meet up with two of the movement's main figures in the city – veteran gunrunner George Harrison, and Noraid founder Mike Flannery (see Chapters 3 and 7). When he arrived to meet them, he discovered that Harrison had been arrested the day before. He may well have breathed a sigh of relief – he could well have been caught up in the swoop had he arrived a day earlier. However, it later emerged that the FBI had noted his presence in New York, and his contacts with Irish republicans. While he may have been under surveillance during his visit, Maguire generally had the advantage of being somebody who did not attract attention. Of slight build and medium height and with a low-key manner, he could blend into any crowd.

Maguire was suspected of being one of the IRA's senior technical people, involved in the development of remote-controlled bomb techniques and, later, the development of missiles to target British Army helicopters. The FBI had been given a strong indication of the IRA's attempts to move into the high-tech arena when, in 1982, the authorities swooped on an IRA arms consignment being smuggled through the port of Newark, New Jersey. Included in the cargo was a number of electronic 'tone frequency' switches, devices that can be used to detonate explosives. As indicated in Chapter 8, by 1984 the FBI had traced the purchase of about fifty of these items to an Irish-American electronics expert, Richard Clark Johnson. The FX-401 frequency selector switches had been bought in California. The IRA had begun using such switches after it found that the British Army could detonate the older type of remote-controlled device by transmitting a signal on open radio frequencies. An integrated circuit decoder, the FX-401 tone frequency selector switch represented a major technological advance as, when 'teamed' with a particular transmitter, it would respond only to that transmitter's demands.

Johnson was interviewed by FBI agents in 1984 about his reasons for acquiring the switches. He said he had bought them in connection with a part-time security business he had been running. The FBI agents were told by Johnson's attorney that his client did not wish to answer further questions about the matter. It was later to emerge that Johnson had been in close touch with Eamon Maguire for some years. The US authorities have alleged that Johnson had been active in the research and development of bomb techniques for the IRA from as far back as 1978.

According to prosecution evidence that would later be presented in court, based on correspondence seized from Maguire, Johnson sent a series of letters to Maguire between 1981 and 1986, regarding the procurement and development of remote-controlled bombs. The letters described Johnson's efforts to perfect the remote-control devices that were used by the IRA in its bombing campaign since the early 1970s. In the letters, Johnson referred to the acquisition of 27- and 72-megahertz radio transmitters, the type typically used by the IRA to set off bombs. The letters also outlined Johnson's efforts to improve the detonation mechanism of the bombs through the use of laser technology, which would shield the system from jamming attempts. According to court documents, the FBI was to seize most of the components of this laser-based system from Johnson's workshop.

The seized letters described Johnson's attempts to enhance the detonator system by using the Weather Alert radio frequency. This was a satellite-activated system used in North America to warn mariners and mountaineers of severe weather. It had a frequency of 162.55 MHz unique to North America, and was therefore a clear channel that could be used by the IRA. According to evidence that would emerge in court, from 1983 on, the authorities in Northern Ireland began to recover the remains of what were described as 'Weather-Alert bombs' in the wake of IRA bomb attacks. Johnson's letters also detailed his procurement of model FX-401 frequency selector switches which, as outlined above, were used by the IRA as decoders in its remote-control bombs. Also described were Johnson's efforts to develop a time-delayed fuse controlled by a digital wrist watch.

Christina Leigh Reid, a dark-haired young American with radical political views, assisted Johnson as a courier. She was an electrical engineer from Sunnyvale, California. The letters outlined how Reid carried a component for a bomb in June 1983, to 'Sean' in Northern Ireland, and referred to her delivering a message from 'Sean' to Johnson that 'Sean' was in need of handguns. The letters also stated that Reid was 'doing a fine job', 'really taking to electronics' and becoming a 'real asset'. She was often referred to in the letters as 'the bird', 'the girl' or 'our young friend'. According to evidence that would later be presented in court, in 1983 Reid gave a false address and social security number in order to secure a post office box in her name. The idea was that the post office box would ensure the security of letters being sent to Johnson, and also to an Irishman, Martin P Quigley, who was also to become active in high-tech procurement for the IRA.

In recruiting Richard Johnson, the IRA could hardly have chosen a more technically qualified expert. Johnson graduated with a degree in electrical engineering from the Catholic University of Washington in 1970, and two years later took a master's degree from the University of California, Berkeley. He went on to occupy a number of sensitive posts with a range of major defence concerns in California. His first job was with the Hughes Aircraft corporation in Fullerton, where his work involved the development of radar and electronic equipment for electronic warfare devices and systems. In January 1975 he left Hughes Aircraft and went to work for TRW in Redondo Beach, where he developed expertise in radio-frequency receiver design and micro-processing. He left TRW in February 1979, going to work later that year for the Jet Propulsion Laboratory in Pasadena. In 1983 he was employed by the Northrop Corporation at their B-2 'stealth bomber' division in Pico Rivera, specialising in radar-related work. The programme to develop a 'stealth bomber' that could operate undetected by enemy radar was one of the most sophisticated and most expensive defence projects in the US, and involved a dramatic leap forward in technology.

In late 1986 he moved from California to the east coast, taking up a post with another defence concern, the Mitre Corporation in Bedford, Massachusetts, just fifteen miles east of Boston, where he specialised in work on radar technology and imaging transmission, and had access to projects in electronic countermeasures and counter-countermeasures. The Mitre Corporation has been described as one of the world's most significant developers of computer systems to control tanks, submarines – and missiles. It was learned that Johnson was given secret security clearance in 1978, which was upgraded to top secret clearance in 1986, giving him access to the most sensitive US government classified information.

Johnson's mother Ann was the daughter of Irish immigrants and his father Roy was an American with no apparent Irish background. Johnson, who was born on 6 July 1948, grew up in Rocky Hill, a suburb near Hartford, Connecticut. From the early 1970s on, he had become interested in the conflict in Northern Ireland. He was studying at Berkeley when, on 30 January 1972, British paratroopers shot dead thirteen unarmed civilians during a civil rights demonstration in Derry. The atrocity, which became known as Bloody Sunday, is believed to have had an impact on Johnson. In 1976 he visited Northern Ireland and on his return to California became active in a group called Friends of Ireland, which sometimes held protest demonstrations outside the British Consulate in Los Angeles. In the latter part of the 1980s, Johnson, a bachelor, was living at Nashua, New Hampshire, but spent many of his weekends at his parents' home in Harwich, Massachusetts, where he made use of a basement workshop. His unsuspecting parents were blithely unaware of his 'extra-curricular' activities.

The FBI remained interested in Johnson's reasons for acquiring the electronic switches and, in February 1986, he agreed to be interviewed at his home by an FBI agent. He elaborated on the reasons he needed the electronic switches for his security business. He also said he might have sent some of the switches to his friends in Ireland.

It appears that by this time Johnson had broken off contact with Provo activists in the US because of the security risks involved – he had, after all, come to the attention of the FBI. However, in November 1987, Johnson was on one of his regular trips to Ireland and, unfortunately for him, was noticed consorting with subversive elements. Gardaí stopped a car in which he was being driven by a man described in FBI documents as an 'active recruiter for the PIRA'. During that same month detectives raided the home of Eamon Maguire in Clondalkin, Dublin, and discovered a cache of letters in a lock-up garage, letters that were later to play a key role in the FBI investigation into the activities of Maguire, Johnson and others. They were later to be referred to in court hearings in the US as the 'Clondalkin Letters'.

There were about forty letters in all. According to testimony given in court in Boston in July 1989, the letters 'related to the construction of explosive devices, the procurement of parts and the jamming of radio interference with detonators'. Johnson was the main letter writer. A source said that Special Branch also searched Maguire's locker at Dublin Airport.

Johnson returned to America and the FBI kept him under surveillance. In July 1988, FBI agents took out a court order to tap the phones of suspects in the case, under the Foreign Intelligence Surveillance Act. They went on to mount a major surveillance operation, using not only phone-taps but bugs planted in suspects' cars and homes. Aircraft were to be used to shadow suspects as they drove their cars. Johnson's phones, his car, his Nashua apartment and his parents' Harwich home were all bugged.

After Johnson's important contributions to IRA bomb technology, he was asked by the organisation to help out in a rather more ambitious project – the development of a missile system to attack British Army helicopters. The request was made by Martin Quigley, a native of Dundalk, County Louth. Aged in his mid-twenties, he had come to the US to study computing at Lehigh University in Pennsylvania. He was put in touch with Johnson by Christina Reid in late 1988. She phoned Johnson and said a friend of 'Ed's' was in San Francisco and would like to talk to him. It was arranged that Quigley would call Johnson at a pay phone on 13 December.

The FBI bugged the pay phone, and observed Johnson as he took the call. The FBI taped the conversation as Quigley asked Johnson to help him in developing a system 'to counteract low-flying helicopters'. Quigley referred to Johnson's previous work perfecting IRA weaponry, including a laser-detonation mechanism for remote-control bombs, and to his ongoing efforts. Johnson was very willing to help.

According to a transcript quoted in court documents, Quigley said, 'As you probably guessed by now, I kind of, we're experiencing a slight technical problem, and you kinda helped us out of these situations before and ah, we're looking to you once again.' Johnson replied, 'Sure, name it.' Quigley related how they were developing a new system. 'It's a much different system. But it's what's available to us as you well knew so some of these use radar, infra-red, acoustic magnetic, et cetera. So we're kinda looking to you if, if possible, could you look into that field for us? As [Maguire] said to me, yourself and him, we're always about ten years ahead of everybody else.'

The components necessary to develop such an anti-aircraft capability were tightly controlled in Ireland. However, some were easily available in the USA, and so work on the project was to be centred in America. A republican source told me of one of the reasons it was so important for the IRA during this period to develop an anti-helicopter system – helicopters gave the authorities a formidable 'rapid reaction' capability. The IRA had calculated that the British could have a helicopter at the scene of any incident in Northern Ireland within four minutes of it happening. IRA operations had to be designed so that volunteers were well away from the scene of an attack within that four-minute time span. The main helicopter base in Northern Ireland was at the RAF air base at Aldergrove, and all parts of the North were within easy flying distance from there.

According to the FBI, Reid began acting as an intermediary between Johnson and Quigley. FBI agents were later to state in court that they believed Quigley was an IRA technical expert who was acting under the instructions of Peter Eamon Maguire, whom they came to regard as the brains behind the drive to develop an anti-helicopter missile system for the IRA. The FBI also believed that Quigley was being groomed to succeed Maguire as head of the missile procurement group.

In February 1989, Maguire visited the US and spent three days at Johnson's Nashua apartment, where agents had planted bugs in the kitchen ceiling and living room. Maguire was clearly being careful in what he said to Johnson inside the apartment, but eventually let down his guard. Agents monitoring the bugs heard the two discussing methods of defeating radio jamming techniques used by the British Army to disrupt remote-controlled bombs. A source said that Maguire was later to see these conversations, with great regret, as his only security lapse in twenty-two years as an operator. Agents also recorded some key conversations between Johnson and Quigley. The investigation was greatly assisted by the contents of the Clondalkin Letters.

In April 1989 Quigley travelled to Nashua for a meeting with Johnson, and they travelled on to Johnson's parents' home in Cape Cod. They worked on equipment that Johnson had set up in the basement there. Later the two men met up at a picnic spot, and the FBI listened in as the two men talked in Johnson's Subaru station wagon. The FBI was gradually building up a detailed picture of the project being worked on by the two men.

FBI agents were ultimately obliged to swoop on the conspirators earlier than they would have liked. On 12 July 1989, two agents were working surreptitiously to replace a battery in a listening device that had been planted below the dashboard of Johnson's Subaru. The vehicle was parked in the car park at the suspect's place of employment. Johnson caught the agents in the act.

The FBI had no choice but to make their move. Johnson was arrested on the spot, and Quigley and Reid were quickly rounded up. Also arrested was an associate of Quigley's, Gerald V Hoy. When she was arrested, Reid was working for an electronics company in Cupertino, California. It was reported that she had tried to get a job with a major defence concern in the state, but was turned down on security grounds because of her background in radical politics.

At Reid's apartment, the authorities seized a note requesting her to ship 'as soon as possible' a PRO 30 scanner, a variant of which was recovered from an IRA car bomb detonated in Northern Ireland in 1985. The note stated that 'the rest of the gifts can follow at intervals as usual'. In addition, seized from Reid's apartment was a letter from a man called 'Liam', asking Reid to warn Johnson that the Irish authorities had seized his letters to Maguire and to urge him not to respond to any letter without being certain of its authenticity.

All those arrested were duly indicted. Hoy was described in court documents as a university lecturer and computer scientist from Easton, Pennsylvania, whose help was sought 'to develop, test, and export a missile and rocket system to be used against British Army helicopters in Northern Ireland'. Hoy was a graduate student and research assistant at Lehigh University and an instructor at the Allentown Campus of Pennsylvania State University. According to the indictment, Hoy and Quigley had acquired a .50-inch calibre rifle, and were planning to export it. According to evidence at their trial, the rifle was to be used against British helicopters.

With the aid of wire-taps, surveillance and eavesdropping devices, FBI agents had effectively penetrated the IRA-linked cell, but they wanted to continue to garner valuable intelligence. One of the downsides of the agents making their move earlier than they wished was that Eamon Maguire was out of their reach. He had returned to Ireland and apparently went to ground as soon as he received word of the arrests. By the time the

Special Branch called around to his Dublin home he had disappeared. In the US, the Justice Department prepared the relevant papers to have Maguire arrested in Ireland, but he was now beyond the reach of the law. It was the beginning of an odyssey for Maguire as he moved around Africa, seeking to evade capture.

An investigation co-ordinated by the Boston office of the FBI concluded that the group associated with Maguire was trying to develop a missile that would be radar- and computer-guided to within twenty or thirty feet of its target. A radar 'trigger' would then detonate the warhead. FBI agents found that it was this 'proximity' triggering device that was being designed by Johnson in his basement workshop. It was believed that the IRA aimed to produce a missile capable of overcoming electronic counter-measures and shooting down British Army helicopters, and possibly other low-flying military aircraft. It was feared that armoured vehicles and military installations might also have been targeted.

Agents believed that Quigley was in charge of developing the missiles' propulsion and guidance system. When the FBI searched Quigley's apartment in Bethlehem, Pennsylvania, they found amateur videos showing Quigley and another man experimenting with the firing of computer-guided, short-range, unarmed missiles in the Appalachian mountains. Some of the launches failed, but others were successful.

Indications are that the FBI had the co-operation of British intelligence in their investigations. An FBI affidavit filed in federal courts showed that the surveillance of the suspects involved 'foreign intelligence wire-taps' – almost certainly a reference to Britain's Government Communications Headquarters (GCHQ), the Cheltenham-based agency that specialises in the interception of electronic communications, and which works in close liaison with its US counterpart, the National Security Agency (NSA).

Those arrested in connection with the affair duly went on trial. During the hearings, the prosecution alleged that Johnson was involved in the construction of an unexploded IRA bomb found outside a police station in Armagh in March 1985. A British bomb expert testified that a circuit board he found in the bomb was similar to a part seized by the FBI from Johnson's home. An FBI agent testified that they had compared the Armagh detonator with devices found in Johnson's workshop in Massachusetts – and concluded that he had assembled it.

During the court hearings, testimony was given by an RUC bomb expert about the increasingly sophisticated methods used by the IRA to detonate bombs. As far back as January 1972, the authorities discovered that the IRA was using a device made from a guidance system for a model aircraft to set off explosive devices. By the mid-1970s, the IRA had moved on to the use of sophisticated electronic switches, in an attempt to counteract the efforts of British Army radio operators to jam the airwaves, and to prevent bombs being detonated prematurely. In the early 1980s, the authorities discovered that IRA bomb-makers were using detonators adapted from the Weather Radio system. In 1988, the authorities seized the first radar detector device adapted to set off a bomb; two more were subsequently discovered. The bomber would use a radar gun of the type used to detect speeding cars, and aim it at an explosive device up to a half-mile away. When the signal was picked up by the radar detector, which had been rewired to convert it into a detonator, the bomb would be set off.

Apart from the evidence given by the RUC expert, there were other indications that the IRA had been developing its high-tech capabilities back in Ireland. The organisation had been making use of a new breed of volunteer: the university-educated computer expert who can construct sophisticated timing and remote-control mechanisms for use in bombs and mortars. In 1993, Gardaí uncovered an IRA workshop at Kilcock, County Kildare, which was producing a wide range of advanced electronic detonators, underlining the advances made by the organisation in this field.

Endgame for the Provo boffins

In June 1990, Johnson, Quigley and Reid were convicted in a Boston court on a range of charges, including aiding an insurgent group in violation of US laws; conspiracy to violate the federal Arms Export Act and to destroy or injure property belonging to the UK; and possession of property to aid foreign insurgents. Hoy had earlier pleaded guilty. In August, a Boston court handed down some heavy sentences. Johnson (forty-one) got ten years; Quigley (twenty-seven), eight; Reid (twenty-five), three-and-a-half years; and Hoy (forty), two years. It had been thought that Johnson, who had no previous criminal record, might get five years. However, in view of the top-secret security clearance that gave him access to some of the US government's most sensitive defence data, he was seen as a 'threat to national security' and got a very heavy sentence, double the suggested five years. Moreover, he was to serve his time in a federal prison, where parole was not available. (Johnson, Quigley and Reid appealed against their convictions, but the appeals were rejected by the US Court of Appeals in December 1991.)[1]

During proceedings against Johnson, there was some adverse comment by the defence on the electronic eavesdropping carried out by the FBI under the Foreign Intelligence Surveillance Act (FISA). According to an FBI affidavit, both the bug planted in Johnson's car and the wire-taps of Johnson's payphone conversations were authorised by the Foreign Intelligence Surveillance Court, the special court sitting privately in Washington that was set up under FISA. Kevin O'Dea, a lawyer for Johnson, was quoted as saying that he was disturbed by the use of the FISA wire-taps in the case, particularly the length of time that wire-taps occurred.[2]

Meanwhile, a warrant was issued for the arrest of Eamon Maguire. Ahead of the long arm of the law, he moved to Africa. He apparently had little difficulty getting a job in Lagos, Nigeria, doing the same kind of aircraft engineering work he had done with Aer Lingus. Having previously lived in Lagos with his wife, on secondment from Aer Lingus, the city was not entirely unknown territory to him. When he went on to work in Maputo, Mozambique, the big attraction was that the country did not have an extradition arrangement with the US.

Then, on 13 December 1992, Maguire took a chance, travelling to South Africa. Having evaded capture for three years, had he been lulled into a false sense of security? It must have been a severe shock to him to end up in a prison cell in South Africa, but it was to prove a very temporary sojourn. The month following his arrest, a South African magistrate refused to extradite Maguire to the US, ruling that the alleged offences specified in the US indictment were not offences under South African law. In other words, a plot to shoot down British Army helicopters in Northern Ireland was not a specific offence under the laws of South Africa. Maguire was freed by the court in Nelspruit.

His dilemma then was – where to go? Maguire could have found work in another African country, but he did not want to run the risk of being arrested again and held in some African hell-hole of a jail. He knew enough about Africa to know that jail conditions could be very unpleasant indeed. Your life could be at risk from disease and other dangers. He decided it was time to return home to Dublin. At least from then on, if arrested, he would be in a western-style jail with basic facilities. He had virtually run out of places to hide.

The US Justice Department pressed ahead with its pursuit of Maguire, perhaps in order to demonstrate its determination that it would not tolerate the use of US territory as a base for foreign insurgency. Having come so close to getting their man, FBI agents were determined to keep track of him. It is likely that Maguire's movements were monitored on his long journey back to Ireland. He was home for just two weeks when Special Branch came for him, arresting him in February 1993.

There followed a series of court hearings on foot of US moves to have him extradited. FBI agent Frank Schulte, who had been a prominent member of the PIRA Squad under Lou Stephens, gave evidence in the Dublin District Court. He told the court that he had been involved in surveillance on Maguire in 1989. The agent gave evidence of items that were found in Maguire's luggage during a covert search at JFK Airport in New York. The items included diagrams 'to be used for bomb-making applications'; catalogues of radar guns and photocopies of microchips or micro-circuit boards.

Maguire was finally extradited to the US in February 1994. He was sent to Boston on the basis of three US warrants alleging conspiracy to export weapons without a licence, conspiracy to destroy helicopters, the property of the British Government, and possession of property in aid of foreign insurgents. He was not given bail. A pre-trial services report gave details of his family, his employment record and property that he owned in Ireland. The report noted that Maguire had been a fugitive since 1989 and had lived in a number of countries throughout the world. The report also noted that the offences for which he was charged constituted 'a serious danger'. On this basis the report assessed that Maguire should be considered 'both a risk of flight and danger to the community' and found that detention was warranted.

Maguire appeared in a US federal court in Boston and, after a plea bargain, pleaded guilty in April 1994 to the charges against him. Assistant US Attorney Alexandra Leake told the court that if the case went to trial, evidence would be produced to show that Maguire, back in November 1978, had begun to recruit people to supply hardware and technology for IRA use. She said that in order to prove Maguire's involvement, the prosecution was prepared to play tapes of conversations between Maguire and his four co-defendants, that had been secretly recorded by the FBI.

In June 1994, Maguire was sentenced to seventy months in prison. Judge David Mazzone referred to a letter sent to him by Maguire saying he supported the Peace Process in Ireland, abhorred violence and hoped for the success of the peace talks. The judge told him: 'I urge you to pursue any means you know to make that come true.' The judge ordered that he be given credit for time served in South Africa. The Irishman became a federal prisoner with the inmate register number 19986-038.

Maguire, who was described in some US media reports as the IRA's top technician, was, in a way, fortunate. It is reckoned that the judge took into account the fact that the Peace Process had begun in Ireland. The sentence handed down was comparatively lenient – just under six years, in comparison with the ten-year sentence imposed on Johnson. There was speculation that Maguire might have been sent away for as long as twelve years if the Provos had still been at war. The US Justice Department announced in January 1997 that Maguire would be allowed to finish the last year of his sentence in Ireland.

Sniper rifles and the IRA

As the FBI investigated the IRA missiles case, evidence emerged that a high-powered sniper rifle may have been successfully delivered to Ireland. According to the US government prosecution case, Martin Quigley and Gerald Hoy acquired the .50-calibre rifle in the summer of 1989. Correspondence found at Quigley's home suggested that the rifle was a powerful Barrett 'Light Fifty' and that it had already been sent to Ireland. When the FBI arrested Quigley on 12 July, they found a letter he had just written to unidentified friends to say that 'the 50 has arrived'. An FBI agent told a court hearing that he considered this was a reference to a Barrett .50-calibre rifle, which fires a heavy, half-inch round. Such is its impact that it can be used not only against human targets, but also against aircraft. The Barrett was believed to be part of the IRA quest to procure weaponry that could threaten British Army helicopters.

In South Armagh, the IRA made particular use of the Barrett in sniping attacks on members of the security forces. From the mid-1980s, the IRA had been making particular efforts to procure such powerful rifles with telescopic sights, so as to overcome any improvements that might be made to body armour issued to soldiers on the ground. Another reason for the procurement of sniper rifles was that the security forces in South Armagh had effectively denied the IRA many potential targets, by largely withdrawing ground transport from the area. There was much reliance on helicopter transport. In addition, the British Army had built a line of observation posts from Newry to the region where County Monaghan juts into Northern Ireland, known as the 'Monaghan salient'. However, the security forces still had to leave their fortified bases to patrol and to mount checkpoints, and the IRA sought to exploit this situation by sniper attacks.

Since the start of the Troubles, the IRA placed particular importance on sniping. A successful sniper operation had a double effect – it led to the death or wounding of a member of the security forces, and it also spread apprehension and fear among other security force personnel. The tactic as used in South Armagh during the 1990s claimed a number of lives and helped to restrict the movements of British Army personnel in the danger zone. IRA sniping operations went back to the early 1970s, when the then IRA chief of staff Seán Mac Stíofáin devised sniping tactics for the organisation. He implemented the concept of the two-man sniping team, who would receive specialised training. The better marksman of the two would be the 'lead' sniper – the other was his number two, who observed for him and acted as back-up. The idea was to fire only one shot, after which, successful or not, the team would immediately go to ground, making it difficult for enemy personnel to locate their position. Weapons used at this period included the Garand, the .303 Lee Enfield and hunting rifles with telescopic sights.[3]

In South Armagh during the 1990s, there was a further development in tactics. The local Provos devised a sniping system involving the use of an ordinary family hatchback car. The vehicle would have an armour-plated shield fitted into the rear area, and the sniper fired through a foot-square hole cut in the shield, after the tailgate had been propped open with a piece of wood. The sniper then tugged on a string, dislodging the piece of wood and closing the tailgate. Apart from the marksman, the team comprised a back-up gunman/observer and a driver, whose role was to make a quick getaway after the sniper had fired his single shot at the target.

Rifles and other equipment seized in the 1980s gave an indication of the IRA's desire to boost sniping capabilities. In 1984 the arms cargo seized aboard the *Marita Ann* off the Kerry coast included, significantly, a .308 Steyr SSG sniper rifle, as well as rifle night-vision sights that would have enabled snipers to pick off British soldiers or RUC men almost as easily at night as in daylight. In 1985 Gardaí found a sniper rifle at Dublin Airport, concealed behind a panel in a cargo aircraft that had flown from New York. It was believed to be destined for the IRA.

In 1986 an arms find underlined the fact that the IRA had moved to acquire one of the world's most sophisticated and most lethal sniper rifles – the US-manufactured Barrett M82. Gardaí in Dublin seized a number of packages containing firearms at a Dublin postal sorting office. Detectives found a Barrett M82 broken down into various components, as well as 200 rounds of .50 calibre ammunition and three magazines for the rifle. The haul also included seven revolvers, four pistols and 550 rounds of ammunition for the handguns. The packages had been posted in Chicago and the firearms were believed destined for the IRA.

The finding of the Barrett M82 was a disturbing development so far as the security forces were concerned. The M82, built by the Barrett company in Murfreesboro, Tennessee, was marketed as the ideal weapon for use not only against human targets, but against armoured personnel carriers and even aircraft. With its heavy .50-calibre round, it has achieved 'hits' at 1,800 metres, well over a mile, and has a maximum range of 6,800 metres.

There were indications that the Provisionals were also in the market for other types of sniper rifle. In the latter part of the 1980s, the FBI's PIRA Squad played a role in disrupting one particular attempt to smuggle a sniper rifle to Ireland, which was believed to be destined for the IRA. The individual at the centre of the importation attempt was an Irish customs officer, Frank Sutcliffe. Sutcliffe was arrested by Gardaí in Dublin in August 1988, after a package was intercepted at a post office in Finglas, in the north of the city. It contained a .308 Ruger hunting rifle with telescopic sights.

The package had been sent to a post office box number that had been opened in the name of a dead man. It had been posted in New York State by an individual using the name Jackson, which turned out to be a false name. The previous month Gardaí had intercepted, at the same post office, a package posted from Amsterdam containing radio transmitters, including encoders and decoders, capable of detonating explosives and of protecting signals from the type of radio scanners used by the British Army in Northern Ireland to find and set off bombs prematurely.

Twenty-nine-year-old Sutcliffe, of Donnycarney, Dublin, appeared in the Special Criminal Court in April 1989, on a charge of importing a Ruger rifle between 1 July and 6 August 1988. He pleaded guilty and was jailed for a year. The State dropped another charge of IRA membership.

Evidence that emerged during the investigation into the IRA arms procurement activities in Florida in 1989–90 of Kevin McKinley indicated that he was looking for .50 calibre sniping rifles (see below). In August 1993, security forces uncovered an arms cache at a house in Belfast, which included a Tejas .50-calibre rifle, the first of its kind found in Northern Ireland. The Barrett-type weapon had been made by a gunsmith in Texas, a former employee of Barrett, and sold legitimately by him. It eventually ended up in the hands of the IRA. In a separate development, republicans also managed to import at least one Belgian-made FN sniper rifle – such a firearm was found, along with other weapons, in September 1998, in a hide near Inniskeen, County Monaghan. There was speculation locally that these were IRA arms that had fallen into the hands of dissident republicans.

The IRA in South Armagh made particular use of the sniping tactic during the 1990s. In February 1997, Lance Bombardier Stephen Restorick was shot dead by a sniper while on checkpoint duty at Bessbrook. He was the ninth member of the security forces to be killed since 1992 in South Armagh by a single high-velocity bullet. The following April, SAS troops made a major breakthrough in South Armagh when they raided a farm and arrested members of an IRA unit, one of whom, Bernard McGinn, was later to be convicted of the Restorick murder. Seized in the raid was a Barrett 90, a lighter and shorter variant of the Barrett 'Light Fifty'. According to one report, the serial number identified it as one of a pair that had been sold by the manufacturer to a firearms dealer in January 1995.[4] A week later the dealer sold the two rifles to a Cuban living in Oregon, who had in turn passed them on to an unknown Irishman.

Soon afterwards, and less than six months into the IRA's 1994 ceasefire, the weapons had been smuggled into Ireland, with a quantity of ammunition. Each of the guns had been fitted with a Vari-X III telescopic sight, made by Leupold & Stevens in Beaverton, Oregon. On the basis of this report, it was believed that the IRA had at least one other Barrett 90 in its armoury at this period.

As late as 1999, the Provos still appeared to be in the market for sniping rifles and heavy calibre ammunition when a Belfast IRA man spearheaded an arms procurement operation in Florida (*see* below). Meanwhile, the Real IRA (RIRA) was also showing an interest in sniper rifles. These weapons were among the items being sought when RIRA arms buyers were lured to Slovakia in 2000, as part of an MI5 'sting' (*see* Chapter 14). It was reported that sniper rifles were also on the 'wish list' when the RIRA allegedly tried to buy arms in France in 2006 (*see* also Chapter 14).

The IRA quest for missiles goes on

Just as the FBI were closing in on Richard Clark Johnson and the other members of the IRA-linked group developing an anti-helicopter missile capability, the IRA was launching a separate operation in the US to secure surface-to-air missiles. Republican activist Kevin McKinley arrived in Florida in July 1989, seeking to fulfil this long-standing IRA requirement.

McKinley, a Belfast IRA man, had spent several years living in Dundalk, just south of the Border in the Irish Republic. He rented a holiday home at Riviera Beach, south Florida, and quickly began the search for specialised war equipment for the IRA. This particular procurement operation was masterminded by senior Provos in the republican stronghold of South Armagh.

The IRA had more than enough assault rifles, thanks to the generosity of Libya's Colonel Gadaffi, and was now in the market for more specialised equipment. Among the items on McKinley's shopping list were high-powered .50 sniper rifles, and detonators for use in bombs and landmines. The US authorities would later allege that McKinley was also seeking grenade launchers and plastic explosive.

The IRA were also still in the market for surface-to-air missiles (SAMs). Various attempts had been made to procure Redeye missiles, but they had all ended in failure. Now the Provos had moved their sights to a more sophisticated type of missile, the Stinger, a successor to the Redeye. The

Stinger had proven its worth in the hands of the Afghan Mujahideen rebels fighting the Soviet occupation forces during the 1980s.

Through phone-taps, the FBI concluded that a leading figure in the IRA conspiracy to acquire a Stinger missile was a man from a prominent republican family who remained at his base in South Armagh.

In Florida, Kevin McKinley made contact with a Vietnam veteran who worked on a diving boat at a marina and who also operated a gold mine in Arizona part of the year. The contact was made in light of a particular item on the IRA shopping list – detonators. Because of his mining work, the former soldier had a legitimate reason to buy detonators.

McKinley drank regularly in the Chateau bar, next door to the trailer park where he lived. It was at this bar that he met Michael Burdof, a thirty-one-year-old gun enthusiast, in November 1989. McKinley asked him about the possibility of getting arms for the IRA, and Burdof tipped off the FBI. Burdof was later to testify that McKinley had asked him about getting a .50 calibre rifle that he had seen in a gun magazine and that would be useful to the Provos.

Two undercover federal agents, posing as arms dealers, held an initial meeting with the unsuspecting McKinley at Big Daddy's Lounge. The agents – John Fields, of the Bureau of Alcohol, Tobacco and Firearms, using the name 'Greg'; and Larry O'Donnell, of the US Customs Service, using the name 'LJ Connelly' – discussed a deal with McKinley for .50-calibre rifles and a Stinger missile. The agents secretly recorded the conversation. When the tapes were later played in court, the music of ZZ Top and Lynyrd Skynyrd could be heard blaring loudly and rather incongruously in the background.

FBI inquiries and phone-taps soon threw up another list of suspects. Agents concluded that McKinley was liaising on his arms-procurement activities with two Irishmen living in Toronto, Canada. One was Seamus Moley, from a prominent republican family in South Armagh, and the other was Cork-born Denis Leyne, a senior bank executive. At the request of the FBI, the Royal Canadian Mounted Police (RCMP) began keeping surveillance on the two men, assisted by Canada's spy agency, the Canadian Security and Intelligence Service (CSIS).[5]

Shortly after McKinley's meeting with the undercover agents, the Irishman, using an assumed name, flew from West Palm Beach to Tucson, where he had another meeting with the Vietnam vet. Moley also arrived in

Tucson, having travelled from Toronto via New York where, it is believed, he picked up the money to pay for a consignment of detonators. Moley then returned to Toronto.

Despite having come to the attention of the FBI, McKinley was able, with the assistance of the Vietnam vet, to procure a large quantity of Ireco detonators – 2,500 electrical detonators and 400 fuse detonators. The detonators were packed into boxes marked 'clothes' and sent by Greyhound bus to New York. They were picked up six days later by a man using a fictitious name. The FBI concluded that some of the detonators were stored by a republican sympathiser in New York, while others were kept by Denis Leyne in Toronto.

The FBI believed that the detonators were moved to Ireland, into the hands of the IRA, over a period of time. Agents reckoned that Leyne got his consignment of detonators to Ireland by posting them to an individual in County Donegal. The successful delivery of the majority of the detonators gave a major boost to the IRA's bombing campaign in Northern Ireland and 'mainland' UK. In 1993 the authorities in the Irish Republic recovered a package containing 140 detonators that had been posted from Yonkers, New York. It was believed that these were among the detonators that had been acquired in Tucson.

As McKinley made progress, as he thought, in clinching a deal for other materiel, including a Stinger missile, Seamus Moley travelled to Florida to take part in the talks with the 'arms dealers'. McKinley introduced him to the two men in December. Moley, as the money man, had been involved in raising the cash for the Stinger. He also had a shopping list of other equipment needed by the IRA, including night-vision equipment. Moley made a phone call to Northern Ireland on 24 December 1989, which, it later emerged in court testimony in the UK by FBI agent Frank Schulte, was intercepted by the FBI.

It was decided that a third man, Joe McColgan, a weapons expert who had married the sister of senior republican Martin McGuinness, would travel over from Ireland in January to take part in the final stages of the deal. McColgan, who had been living in Dundalk, County Louth, arrived in Florida just days before the transaction was to be finalised for the purchase of the Stinger missile for a mere $50,000 – estimated to be one-third of its black-market value.

On 9 January, the two undercover agents met McColgan and McKinney at a restaurant in North Palm Beach, Florida. To whet the appetite of the IRA men, one of the agents showed them two polaroid photos of the Stinger that was to be supplied. McColgan gave details of other materiel in which he was interested – M-203 and M-79 grenade launchers that could be used to penetrate British armour. It was also alleged that the conspirators were interested in acquiring C-4 plastic explosive. Following the meeting, the agents noticed that they were being followed by an associate of McKinley's, driving a Lincoln that had previously been driven by McKinley. The agents drove evasively and lost the 'tail'.

After further contacts, the final meeting to clinch the deal was held on 12 January. McColgan met the 'arms dealers' at a warehouse in West Palm Beach. He seems to have been wary, insisting on frisking the two men. Agent Fields asked him jokingly if he always went this far 'on a first date'. The agents produced a Stinger missile, which had been loaned by the US Defence Department, but with vital parts removed. The agents gave a quick demonstration of how the missile could be fired. The deal was finalised. The IRA men had already arranged to place $47,500 in a joint-access safe deposit box at a local bank to pay for the weapon. McColgan tried to stash the Stinger, wrapped in a blanket, in the boot of his hire car. It would not fit, so he wedged it behind the driver's seat. Before he could drive away, he was arrested. Moley and McKinley, who were nearby, were arrested minutes later.

With the three men under arrest, the FBI backtracked and looked into the detonator aspect of the case. During his contacts with the 'arms dealers', McKinley had let slip about the detonators. FBI inquiries led agents to the Vietnam vet with the gold mine. He agreed to co-operate, and to testify against McKinley and Moley. But by then it was too late to stop the transfer of the detonators to Ireland.

The three Irishmen, McKinley, Moley and McColgan, were ultimately convicted in December 1990 of purchasing and attempting to receive a US Army Stinger missile with intent to kill. They were each given four years in prison after a court hearing in Fort Lauderdale, Florida, in June 1991. During the hearing, prosecutors claimed the trio had continued to try to acquire missiles for the IRA while detained in a federal prison outside Miami. Subsequently, in June 1995, McKinley and Moley got an extra nineteen months in a court hearing at Tucson, Arizona, in connection with the detonators aspect of the investigation. After a plea bargain, the two men agreed to plead guilty to wilful possession of 2,900 detonators in aid of the IRA, and shipping the devices on a vehicle engaged in interstate commerce.

After his release from prison, Kevin McKinley was to find himself in the news once again. In May 1998, he was arrested in Portugal, after a major consignment of smuggled tobacco worth £1.7 million sterling was tracked from South Africa to a warehouse in Cascais. He had arrived in the Portuguese resort with his Texan girlfriend the previous September.

Meanwhile, investigations were also carried out in Northern Ireland. A man from South Armagh was extradited to the US where, in June 1995 at a court hearing in Tucson, he was given sixteen months after pleading guilty to one count of conspiracy to obtain munitions and weapons illegally.

As part of the investigation into the supply of detonators to the IRA, FBI agents arrested Denis Leyne and three other Irish-born males in co-ordinated swoops in New York on 11 November 1992. The catalyst for the swoops was Leyne's arrival at La Guardia Airport on a flight from Canada. These four men, along with two Americans, were to go on trial in Tucson in relation to the detonators. Ultimately, in 1994, all six were acquitted.

Denis Leyne, who died of a heart attack in February 1995, aged fifty-seven, was an unusual republican activist – senior bankers are not normally found in the ranks of those who support the IRA. Canadian police kept him under surveillance from at least January 1990, at the request of the FBI. A father of five, he had emigrated to Canada in his youth, getting a job with the Imperial Bank of Canada in Montreal in 1958. He rose steadily through the ranks in the banking world. He studied at the Graduate School of Business at the University of Toronto, and was a member of the Montreal Golf Club and the Montreal Amateur Athletic Association.

In 1991, Leyne was fired from his job as senior vice-president of the Canadian Imperial Bank of Commerce. The bank said he did not fit into their future plans. Leyne told the media he suspected his dismissal was prompted by the international police probe that had already begun. Leyne always denied involvement in the supply of detonators and the attempted supply of a Stinger missile to the IRA, but never made any secret of his support for the Provos. As a supporter of the republican cause, he had been questioned by police as far back as 1973.

While the FBI prevented the delivery of a deadly Stinger missile to the IRA, the successful transfer of close on 3,000 detonators was to prove a valuable coup for the Provos. Law enforcement officials became very concerned at indications that the IRA was using the detonators supplied from Tucson in a stream of bombings. From 1991 detonators similar to the Tucson devices were figuring in improvised grenades, home-made mortar bombs and other bomb devices deployed by the IRA.[6]

Brought to book

In 1997, another Irish-linked gunrunning case came to light in Florida, but by comparison with the attempt to obtain a Stinger missile, it was a small-scale operation. The suspect was an unlikely gunrunner – a middle-aged professional woman who was a pillar of the community. Margaret Bannon, a medical doctor and qualified lawyer, had been born in Derry, Northern Ireland. She was arrested after a container containing guns and ammunition was discovered in a Dublin postal sorting office.

The discovery was made after some of the bullets spilled out of the package. The container was found to contain three handguns and 500 rounds of ammunition, and was addressed to a house in Derry that Dr Bannon owned. The weapons and ammunition had been placed inside a metal device designed to hide them from customs X-ray examination. An attempt had been made to delete the serial numbers of the weapons, but Gardaí were still able to decipher them. The best clue as to who had posted the weapons was provided inadvertently by Dr Bannon herself. She had written her name on one of a number of books found lying on top of the guns.

It took some time to bring the case to court. A US customs officer, testifying in court, claimed there was a delay on the part of the Irish authorities in sending the guns to the US for use as evidence. In early 2003, Dr Bannon admitted that she bought the firearms in Orlando gun shops and posted them to Derry. When Dr Bannon (fifty-two) appeared in court in Orlando the following May, the court was told she suffered from epilepsy and had other health problems. The delay in bringing the case to trial may have worked in favour of Dr Bannon, as the Good Friday Agreement was signed the year after the gunrunning episode and may have been a mitigating factor when it came to sentencing. Judge Ann Conway sentenced

Dr Bannon to six months' house arrest for trying to ship weapons to the IRA, and placed her on two-and-a-half years' probation. The 1997 Bannon smuggling case was to be followed by a much more controversial Irish-linked gunrunning case, also in Florida, just a couple of years later.

The IRA and the Florida guns affair

Regina Lombardo, an agent with the US Bureau of Alcohol, Tobacco and Firearms, was suspicious. Returns from gun dealers in South Florida showed that a woman called Siobhan Browne was making multiple purchases of firearms. Her shopping spree had begun in late March 1999. Who was she and why did she need the guns? It was not against the law to buy arms, but Ms Lombardo decided to make some further checks, just to make sure there was nothing sinister behind the purchases.

To an outside observer, it might have seemed unlikely that the IRA was involved. After all, they were on cease-fire, the Peace Process was well under way, the Good Friday Agreement had been signed in 1998, and a decommissioning body had been set up to oversee the disarming of para-military bodies. Surely the IRA was not looking for fresh supplies of arms at a time when many were hoping that the organisation was going to decommission its existing weapons and go out of business?

Locating Siobhan Browne presented its own challenges. Her only known address was a post office box number on Las Olas Boulevard in Fort Lauderdale. Ms Lombardo got a court order and checked the mailbox. She found that a man called Conor Claxton was getting his mail there as well. Ms Lombardo's probe threw up a third name – that of Anthony Smyth. He appeared to be a constant companion of Ms Browne, and he made purchases of guns himself. Ms Lombardo forwarded the names to the BATF HQ in Washington for background checks. The bureau contacted Interpol, the international police organisation. And then the probe began to take on a whole new dimension. Interpol reported that Claxton had suspected links with the IRA, and tipped off Scotland Yard. Alarm bells began to ring, metaphorically speaking.

Meanwhile, authorities in England and the Irish Republic had begun intercepting guns that had been sent through the post from the US, sparking off investigations by Scotland Yard, the Gardaí and the FBI. The probes began on 6 July, when an English Special Branch officer, Steve Norman, was wakened by a phone call to say that a package containing a .357 Magnum pistol was found in the post, passing through West Midlands International Airport at Coventry. An X-ray check had shown up the unmistakable outline of the powerful handgun, in a package marked as containing toys, computers and baby clothes. The package was addressed to a person in Dublin. Further checks uncovered other arms shipments at the airport, in parcels marked as containing various types of innocuous consumer goods. At a postal sorting office on the Naas Road, Dublin, two suspicious packages were discovered, the contents of which were found to include a pistol, a revolver, about thirty rounds of ammunition and about forty .5-inch bullets suitable for a high-powered sniper rifle. Four more boxes containing guns were posted in Philadelphia, and intercepted in New York.

Surprisingly, the smugglers had failed to obliterate the serial number on the Magnum revolver found at Coventry airport. It had been posted in Fort Lauderdale, and was traced back to South Florida gun dealer Ed Bluestein, who ran a business called Big Shot Firearms. FBI agents, who were trying to trace the origins of the guns being mailed to Europe from the US, heard about the investigation being carried out by Ms Lombardo. The result was a meeting in Miami in July of personnel from the BATF, the FBI's terrorism task force and Scotland Yard. The FBI and Scotland Yard were interested in the globe-trotting Claxton, but did not know which country he was lying low in. There was no record of him entering America. Ms Lombardo was able to help them, producing surveillance pictures of Claxton taken at the post office box in Florida. It later transpired that he had used a false passport to slip into the US.

Round-the-clock surveillance was mounted on Claxton, Browne and Smyth. In the early hours of 26 July 1999, FBI and BATF agents swooped on Smyth's residence at Weston, a suburb of Fort Lauderdale, and arrested him and his partner Browne. Regina Lombardo took part in the swoop. On the same morning, agents arrested Claxton at the Buccaneer motel in Deerfield Beach. Surveillance of Claxton had led investigators to a fourth suspect, Martin Mullan, a native of Northern Ireland, who had stayed in a motel near Claxton in mid-July. Mullan, from Dunloy, County Antrim, was arrested in Philadelphia. Security video cameras at post offices in Fort Lauderdale, Boca Raton and Deerfield Beach showed the two men mailing packages to Ireland that were believed to contain guns and ammunition. The boxes were labelled as various types of consumer goods.

In Ireland, police raided a holiday home at Inverin, County Galway, after a 'controlled' delivery of an intercepted weapon had been made, and seized a cache of weapons which had come from Florida – three Ruger .357 Magnum revolvers, three Glock semi-automatic pistols and 120 rounds of ammunition. A woman in her thirties, the mother of a young baby, was arrested but charges against her were later dropped.

Gunrunning for Love

Some run guns for a cause. Others do it for money. Siobhan Browne would argue that she did it for love, after being drawn in by her partner. For Browne, it all began to go wrong after she started a relationship in 1998 with Belfast-born Anthony Smyth, whom she met at Waxy O'Connor's Irish pub in Fort Lauderdale. He had emigrated from Northern Ireland about twenty years earlier, but retained strong Irish republican sympathies. He made a modest living as a used-car salesman. He liked pub social life and was said to be very good at darts.

Siobhan Browne was a native of Youghal, County Cork, one of a family of thirteen brothers and sisters, and had never been to Northern Ireland. She was later to insist that she had little interest in politics. At age twenty-one, in the mid-1980s, she emigrated to the US. While working in a deli in Brooklyn, she met a globe-trotting Israeli businessman, Meir Rapaport. In 1987 they married in Las Vegas, where he liked to gamble. They bought property in Fort Lauderdale and began spending winters there. They eventually separated, although they remained friends and kept in touch.

Browne, hard-working and ambitious, set about building a career. She took out a real-estate licence, and ran a bar with a business partner for a period. She became a stockbroker, with an expensive apartment in Boca Raton and a silver Mercedes. Life was good. It was some years after her marriage break-up that she met Anthony Smyth. He moved into her home, and about a month after they met he introduced her to a visitor from Belfast, a brash young man called Conor Claxton. Early the following year, Claxton moved into a spare room in her apartment, and lived there for some time before moving out to a motel. Like Smyth, Claxton was an enthusiastic supporter of the Irish republican cause. Browne developed a strong dislike for Claxton who, like Smyth, liked to party. Browne found Claxton obnoxious. Browne eventually went to live with Smyth at his residence in Weston.

Browne has stated that Smyth began acquiring guns at the behest of Claxton. At first, Smyth could not buy the firearms directly, as he did not yet have a green card. So he got Browne to buy the guns in her name. In early March 1999, in the company of Smyth, she began buying guns designated by Smyth at pawn shops and gun shows. On 25 April, she arranged to buy her biggest single batch of guns at a gun show in Fort Lauderdale – ironically on the day that Smyth got his green card and became eligible to buy guns directly himself, which he proceeded to do. Browne ordered two Ruger .357 magnums, two Smith and Wesson .40-caliber semiautomatic pistols, and a .38 revolver. These weapons were bought from Boynton Beach gun dealer Ed Bluestein. It later emerged that, in return for an additional payment of $50 a gun, Bluestein agreed to sell weapons 'off the books' – without informing the authorities. However, he had previously made returns to do with purchases by Browne, and he had received a call from the BATF about the paperwork. This made Browne uneasy. She probably did not realise that when she embarked on the purchase of guns, she would come to the attention of the BATF.

Court papers later indicated that between 29 April and 6 May, the couple bought at least thirty-eight guns from Bluestein, in addition to at least a dozen weapons bought from other dealers and private citizens. A handwritten list drawn up by Claxton and faxed to Bluestein by Smyth gave an insight into some of the materiel apparently being sought by the IRA at the time. (Claxton would later claim that the list was meant to check if Bluestein could be trusted. If he claimed to be able to supply those arms, he would have to be an informant. Claxton insisted the weapons were not supplied.) The list included sniper rifles, including a Robar SR90; large-calibre ammunition; 'anything silenced .25 and up; any small concealable .25 and up; any full auto sub-machine gun ... the smaller the better; H&K MP5 Auto [Heckler & Koch MP5 sub-machine gun] in briefcase if possible'.

There was an international sensation when news broke that an apparent IRA gunrunning operation had been uncovered in Florida, and that four suspects had been arrested. The fact that the arrests occurred just months after the 1998 Good Friday Agreement was signed was of particular concern. There had been high hopes that the IRA would decommission its sizeable arsenal of weapons after its political wing, Sinn Féin, signed up to the Peace Process. Now, far from getting rid of weaponry, the IRA, or elements in the IRA, had apparently decided to augment and modernise its arsenal by setting up an operation to acquire up-to-date, high-powered handguns and other weaponry in South Florida. The arrests served to further undermine Unionist confidence in the Agreement, and raised questions about the commitment of some senior figures in the republican movement to the Peace Process.

On the other hand, the inept nature of the gunrunning operation led to questions being asked as to whether this was really an IRA operation. The man seen as the ringleader of the group, Conor Claxton, had failed to ensure that the serial number was obliterated from the first weapon to be intercepted by the authorities – the Magnum revolver found at Coventry airport. Transferring weapons using parcel post, in packages that were quite easily detected, was another major flaw in the operation. Nobody seemed to have warned Siobhan Browne, who had no previous experience in buying firearms, that purchasing several guns at a time would bring her to the attention of the BATF. Also, discretion does not seem to have been Claxton's strong point – he was noted for singing rebel songs during drinking sessions, and he had a keyring marked 'Provisional IRA'. Claxton was not the most competent of gunrunners.

At an initial court hearing, prosecutor Richard Scruggs stated that Claxton had told FBI agents that he was taking part in an IRA procurement operation and acting under IRA orders. He had been told by his superiors in the IRA to buy arms, because the Peace Process had failed. The weapons would be used against British troops, members of Northern Ireland's police force the RUC, and members of loyalist paramilitary organisations.

The IRA issued a statement that it had not authorised any arms-buying operation. Nevertheless, prosecutor Scruggs remained convinced that there was an IRA connection, that the arms-buying spree had either been authorised by the IRA Army Council or allowed to go ahead by senior figures in the organisation. The aim may have been to appease hardliners unhappy with the cease-fire, and/or to 'tool up' in the event of the Peace

Process breaking down. There was also speculation that IRA activists may have been seeking to fill certain gaps in the IRA arsenal. There was a suspicion that in the event of IRA weaponry being decommissioned as part of the Peace Process, republicans wanted to retain 'untraceable' weapons for emergencies and for 'policing' operations involving punishment beatings or kneecappings.

Faced with the threat of a range of serious charges, Siobhan Browne decided to accept a government offer, and plead guilty to a single arms violation. However, she decided that she would not testify against the three others accused. In March 2000, Browne pleaded guilty to conspiring to buying nineteen handguns for transfer to Ireland. The guilty plea meant that she would not be tried with the other three suspects, Claxton, Smyth and Mullan, who were facing terrorism charges that could carry a life sentence. The following August, a federal judge sentenced her to twenty months' imprisonment and a $25,000 fine.

Prison came as a shock to the young woman, who was used to a comfortable lifestyle. Inmate number 55004-004 left prison in January 2001, and was sent to a halfway house, finally gaining full release in March 2002. After leaving jail, she was appalled to find that because of her felony conviction she could no longer work as a stockbroker. Instead, she took a humble $6-an-hour job in a video store. She began paying off her $25,000 fine at the rate of $25 a week. Browne gave newspaper interviews, saying how foolish and naive she had been, and describing her resentment at having been 'used' by others. She talked of how she despised Conor Claxton in particular.

In June 2000, Claxton (twenty-eight), Smyth (forty-three) and Mullan (thirty) were convicted on charges relating to the shipping of the weapons to Ireland. However, the three Irishmen were cleared on the most serious charges against them – shipping weapons to terrorists and conspiracy to maim or murder persons in a foreign country. The court heard that 118 weapons had been ordered and eighty-six purchased before the three were arrested. Of these, fifty-seven were seized and twenty-nine were never located.

The following September, sentences were handed down and all three went to jail. Claxton, who had been convicted on thirty-nine counts, including arms smuggling, using a false passport to facilitate terrorism and conspiracy, was jailed for four years. Judge Wilkie Ferguson said he regretted he could not impose a heavier sentence, stating that if a person could get life for possessing $400 worth of cocaine, this kind of offence ought to merit the death penalty.

Smyth had been convicted on thirty-one counts, including firearms smuggling, making false statements to a firearms dealer and unlawful sale of firearms. The car salesman got three years and was ordered to pay fines and assessments totalling $6,100. Mullan, who worked as a handyman in Philadelphia, had been convicted on ten counts, including arms smuggling and possession of a weapon by an illegal alien. He was jailed for three years and ordered to pay $1,000 in fines and assessments. It emerged that the US authorities were seeking at least one other Irishman in connection with the investigation. Ed Bluestein, the arms dealer who supplied the group with some of the weapons, was given two years' probation, including six months' house arrest, and fined $25,000.

Following the case, there were further developments in Ireland, both in the Republic and in Northern Ireland. In January 2001, Sinn Féin activist Sean Kind and three other men were arrested in County Cork after their car was stopped by Gardaí near Mitchelstown. Three pistols found in the possession of the men had come from a batch of weapons smuggled into Ireland from Florida, according to security sources quoted in the media. Also recovered were ammunition, balaclavas, a baseball bat and an iron bar. The discovery of this equipment led Gardaí to suspect that the men were about to carry out a punishment attack. Indeed the Special Criminal Court heard Garda evidence that one of the men admitted during questioning that they were on their way to carry out a punishment beating.

Kind, who was described in court as an anti-drugs activist, and the three others were jailed in October 2002 at the Special Criminal Court in Dublin on arms charges. They were found guilty of having three pistols and eighteen rounds of ammunition without a firearms certificate, and of having the pistols and ammunition for an unlawful purpose. Kind, of Passage West, County Cork, was jailed for six years, while the others received lesser sentences. All four also got three years to run concurrently for possession of firearms without a certificate. The court was told that Kind had been previously sentenced to seven years, in 1980, for possession of explosives with intent to endanger life. He had been arrested at an IRA training camp in Kerry.

Meanwhile in Northern Ireland, police pursued their own investigation into the Florida gunrunning, focusing in particular on the financing of the arms purchases, and the transfer of funds. A number of people were arrested in late 2002 in connection with the probe. Two men and a woman were charged with a number of offences, including helping the IRA buy arms and import them into the UK, and conspiring to make available money or other property for the IRA's use. A fourth person, a woman, was charged only with conspiracy. All were acquitted at Belfast Crown Court in summer 2005.

The alleged role in the Florida gunrunning of a man called Robert Flint was referred to under parliamentary privilege in the British House of Commons on 22 January 2004. The MP who raised the matter, Roy Beggs of the Ulster Unionist Party, also talked in the House of other alleged plots to run arms to the IRA from Colombia and even from Poland, although hard evidence was not presented. The East Antrim MP referred to the arrest in Colombia of Martin McAuley, James Monaghan and Niall Connolly, remarking that it was 'not an unreasonable assumption that the republican movement was teaching FARC how to launch urban bomb attacks in exchange for fixing up a lucrative drug and weapons connection'.

Mr Beggs went on: 'The case of the Bogota Three is not the first time the IRA has been linked to drugs. In 2000 Neil Mackay in the *Sunday Herald* uncovered the fact that during the trial of another three IRA men in Florida, details emerged of a huge arms cache in Colombia, which the IRA wanted to ship to Ireland. That was linked to a convicted American drug dealer, Robert Flint, who had flown cocaine out of Colombia for organised crime gangs. When he was arrested in Galway, Mr Flint – who incidentally was also a major contributor to Noraid, one of Sinn Féin's big US donors – claimed that Seamus Moley, a senior IRA man, was also involved in a complex plot to transport five tonnes of cocaine to Iran, where it was going to be used to pay for weapons from Poland, which would be shipped to Ireland via Rotterdam in Holland. Yet Sinn Féin–IRA still insist on portraying a public image, through groups such as Direct Action Against Drugs, that is firmly against drugs and therefore not involved in drug dealing …'

The Florida gunrunning case caused much concern among senior government figures in the US, UK and Irish Republic who were charged with copperfastening the Peace Process. The gunrunning scandal could not be allowed to jeopardise moves to achieve a lasting peace. Many lives would be at stake if there were to be a return to a full-scale guerrilla war.

In an interview with the US edition of *GQ* magazine in the summer of 2001, prosecutor Richard Scruggs said that officials in the Clinton administration brought pressure to bear on him to retract a statement he had made blaming the IRA's senior command for organising the arms smuggling operation from Florida. He said that 'everyone went ape-shit' after he gave an interview on Ulster Television in 2000, in which he blamed the IRA leadership for setting up the arms procurement network in Florida. He told the magazine that a senior official in the FBI in Washington phoned him on behalf of senior White House staff, and put pressure on him to retract his statement. He said a press release was issued the next day by the FBI in Washington stating that the FBI did not believe the gunrunning operation had been sanctioned by the IRA leadership.

In January 2004, Scruggs' story was essentially confirmed by Hector Pesquera, who gave a media interview as he retired from his post as head of the FBI in Miami. Pesquera told the *Irish Voice* that there was 'serious tension' between the White House and the FBI on whether to prosecute the three gunrunners in the wake of the signing of the Good Friday Agreement.[7] Pesquera said it was 'touch and go' whether the FBI would be allowed to press ahead with the case against the three Irishmen, because the Clinton administration had policy objectives that might be derailed by the prosecutions.

The mystery of Mr Meli

In November 2001, the FBI made another arrest in an Irish-linked arms probe, but this time investigators could find no clear link to paramilitaries. It was a curious and baffling case. Bernard Maserati Joseph Meli (fifty-eight), a Catholic Italian-Irishman, was detained in Florida on suspicion of dealing illegally in firearms. Meli, a car dealer from West Belfast, had moved to London about twelve years earlier with his only son. His parents had emigrated from Sicily after the Second World War and had gone into the fish and chip business in Belfast.

Meli's Protestant wife Sandra had been murdered by loyalists in Belfast in December 1972. The twenty-six-year-old woman was shot dead in the kitchen of her home at Flora Street, in the east of the city. Paramilitary group the Ulster Defence Association was suspected of being responsible. The assassins had probably singled out the couple because they were in a mixed marriage. Meli himself may have been the main target of the killers.

A small, balding man with an unassuming manner, Meli arrived in Miami on 10 July 2001, and the following day visited a Miami gun shop and bought a .38-calibre Charter Arms revolver with a credit card. The transaction came to the attention of the FBI. Meli had claimed on the federal firearms form that he was a resident of Cocoa Beach on the east coast of Florida, while he was, in fact, resident in London. He returned to the shop on 26 November, buying another revolver and 1,000 rounds of ammunition. He also paid over $4,000 as a deposit on a $15,000 order to purchase twenty handguns and 1,000 rounds of ammunition.

Meli was arrested by the FBI as he emerged from the store. According to the FBI, Meli told agents that he planned to conceal the guns in motorcycles or cars and ship them to Northern Ireland, where he hoped to sell them to associates for $1,000 each for self-defence purposes. He denied any links with paramilitaries, and expressed horror at the very idea of anybody being killed through terrorism. The authorities in Ireland had no record of Meli being involved in subversive activities. The following January, he pleaded guilty to dealing illegally in firearms and making false statements on federal gun forms. When he appeared in federal court in Miami in March 2002, US District Judge Federico Moreno sentenced him to one year in prison.

CHAPTER 12

Arms and the INLA

As they watched the van crossing the border from Turkey, Greek frontier police moved in to take a closer look. Two Irishmen were ordered out of the van. The police carried out a detailed search and found a secret compartment in the vehicle, containing a cache of AK-47 rifles, hand grenades and explosives. It has never been made clear whether it was a routine search or whether the police had advance information. On 2 February 1979, shortly after the discovery of the weapons, the police chief in the northern frontier town of Alexandroupolis, Colonel Nikos Stathopoulos, told the media that two men from Northern Ireland had been arrested and charged with arms smuggling. One of the men held was Seamus Ruddy, aged twenty-seven. The police chief said that on being questioned, the men said they had bought the weapons in Lebanon and Syria, and were taking them back to Northern Ireland.

Some news reports at the time mistakenly described the men as being members of the IRA. Ruddy was, in fact, a senior figure in the more extreme, Marxist-orientated Irish National Liberation Army (INLA). For keen observers of the Irish paramilitary scene, Ruddy's arrest was one of the first public indications that the INLA had established an arms pipeline from the Middle East. In fact Ruddy had acquired the weapons from Palestinian sources in Beirut. It emerged that Ruddy, who was held for a time before being released, was one of the more important gunrunners for the INLA. A native of Newry, County Down, he was reputed to have been, for a period, the organisation's quartermaster general, in charge of procuring weapons and looking after arms dumps.

It was a risky venture, travelling overland to Beirut at this period. The city had been in turmoil since the start of the Lebanese Civil War in 1975. Beirut was divided between the Christian eastern sector and the Moslem west, by a *de facto* border known as the Green Line. Many of the buildings on both sides of the line had been ruined in the fighting. When I visited the Green Line in 1994, the sector was still in a state of devastation. In some of the bullet-scarred buildings that were damaged but still standing, families had established a semblance of normal living, clothes lines hanging incongruously from bomb-damaged balconies.

In 1978, the year before Ruddy made the marathon road journey to Lebanon that resulted in his arrest, Syrian forces had unleashed a devastating artillery barrage on the Christian sector of the city. There was little of what would normally pass for law and order in Beirut at this period. Sectors of the city were held by militias who were a law unto themselves. After Ruddy and his friend picked up the weapons and stored them in their vehicle, the road home led through Syria and Turkey, before passing into Greece. The journey to and from Lebanon must have been a logistical nightmare.

Law enforcement officials believed that Ruddy had got a consignment of weapons through to Ireland along this route the previous year, before he fell foul of the Greek border police. The French became aware of the shipment, and it is referred to in the memoirs of Paul Barril, formerly a senior figure in an elite counterterrorism unit of the French Gendarmerie.[1] According to another report, the materiel involved in the 1978 operation consisted of thirteen AK-47 rifles and Soviet-made explosive.[2] Information given to the French authorities by an informant, Bernard Jegat, a French left-wing activist who had become involved in helping the INLA in Paris, indicates that the INLA had come to an agreement with the Palestine Liberation Organisation (PLO) whereby the INLA would have access to PLO arms dumps in Lebanon, but it would be down to the INLA to arrange transport of weapons to Ireland.[3]

After the 1979 arms shipment was intercepted by the Greeks, it was decided to abandon this particular method of delivery, Jegat claimed in his comments to the police. It was considered that the high risks involved were out of proportion to the small amounts of weaponry that could be concealed in a small vehicle. (However, the indications are that German sympathisers were also heavily involved in transporting arms by car from PLO elements in the Middle East to Europe for the INLA and, after the PLO left Beirut in 1982, deliveries were to continue from PLO elements in Prague.) Jegat claimed he was asked to check out the possible purchase of small sailing craft that could cross the Mediterranean – he supposed that delivery by sea was being considered to replace the hazardous road-transport method. Nothing appears to have come of the idea of acquiring a boat for arms-smuggling purposes.

Ruddy was fortunate in the lenient treatment he received from the Greeks. The authorities would have probably taken a more serious view had it been drugs rather than arms that he was smuggling. The downside was that, having been arrested by the Greeks, it became more difficult for him to operate as a gunrunner across international borders – he was now on the records of police forces and intelligence agencies. But there were to be other regular deliveries by operators who had not come to the attention of the authorities.

Birth of the INLA

Defectors from the Official IRA (OIRA), impatient with the latter's cease-fire which had been in operation since 1972, were the main movers behind the foundation of the INLA in the mid-1970s. The INLA was organised along lines broadly similar to the IRA. A ruling body was set up, an Army Council, a member of which was the chief of staff. There was also a General Headquarters Staff; a Belfast Brigade and a Derry Brigade were set up, with other units based in other parts of Northern Ireland. There were also personnel in the Border area and the Irish Republic. The new force was to develop a reputation as one of the most ruthless of Irish paramilitary groups. When the INLA faction broke away from the Officials, they took with them some arms from OIRA dumps, and this was one of the reasons for a feud with the Officials that claimed a number of lives. It was to be the first of a series of inter-republican feuds involving the INLA. In fact the INLA became notorious for internal feuds that resulted in a spate of killings.

The INLA's first 'spectacular' was the assassination of prominent British Conservative MP Airey Neave in London in 1979. He was killed when a bomb, activated by a mercury tilt switch, exploded under his Vauxhall Cavalier car as he drove up a ramp from the car park at the House of Commons. Neave was close to Tory leader Margaret Thatcher, and was the party's spokesperson on Northern Ireland. He was on the hard right of the party, a determined opponent of republican paramilitaries and an outspoken advocate of tougher security measures. He had won fame as the first British officer to escape successfully from the high-security German prisoner-of-war detention centre at Colditz Castle during the Second World War. He absconded in 1942, and made his way back to Britain. He was assassinated a few weeks before the 1979 general election that brought Mrs Thatcher to power as prime minister.

A senior INLA figure, Ronnie Bunting, is believed to have been involved in planning the murder of Airey Neave. Bunting was an unusual figure in the INLA. He came from a middle-class, Methodist background in Belfast, and studied at Queen's University. His father was Major Ronald Bunting, a former officer in the British Army who became a top aide to the North's anti-republican firebrand, the Reverend Ian Paisley. Major Bunting, with his trademark bowler hat, was a familiar figure around Belfast in the early 1970s, as he accompanied Paisley to press conferences and other events.

Bunting junior, who had developed a reputation among family and friends of being a rebel, joined the Official IRA in the early years of the Troubles, becoming a friend of a noted Official IRA gunman, Joe McCann. Bunting was interned, and continued with paramilitary activity after he was released. He joined the INLA at its inception. He was assassinated at his home in a strongly republican area of Belfast in 1980, along with another Protestant republican, Noel Lyttle, who had joined the INLA's political wing, the Irish Republican Socialist Party (IRSP). No organisation claimed responsibility for the murders. The killers, who struck in the early morning, operated with clinical efficiency, giving rise to the suspicion in INLA and IRSP circles that members of the Special Air Service (SAS) had taken revenge for Airey Neave.

A few weeks after the killing of Airey Neave, the INLA followed up on this widely-publicised assassination with an operation demonstrating that it was prepared to break a taboo by murdering women. Members of the INLA opened fire on a group of four unarmed female prison officers as they emerged from Armagh Prison to go to lunch. As the women lay wounded and moaning in agony on the ground, one of the INLA men threw a hand grenade into their midst, in an apparent attempt to finish them off. Surprisingly, only one woman died in the onslaught, forty-year-old mother-of-six Agnes Jane Wallace. Her husband said later that normally she brought a packed lunch, but on this particular day had decided to go to lunch 'with the girls'.

The attempted massacre was widely condemned and, being an organisation of the left, INLA supporters drew on an argument from the world of feminism and political correctness to answer the critics. An INLA-linked publication published a letter arguing that it was sexist to condemn the killing of a 'female screw'; that women should be seen as the equals of men, not only in life but in death.[4]

Other notable INLA attacks included the bombing of the Droppin' Well disco in County Derry in 1982, which killed eleven off-duty soldiers and six women civilians. This was the year the INLA managed to kill more people than the Provisionals. The following year, gunmen opened fire on Protestants as they sang hymns during a prayer service at the Mountain Lodge Pentecostal Church at Darkley, near Keady, South Armagh. The service was being audio-taped at the time. On the tape, one can hear the congregation singing, and then the sound of gunfire, and the cries of the victims. Three of the congregation were killed and seven injured.

The INLA rejected responsibility for the atrocity, and INLA chief Dominic McGlinchey condemned it. However, he admitted that the organisation was 'indirectly' involved. While the leadership apparently did not authorise the attack, it was believed that it was carried out by INLA members, using INLA weapons. A spokesman for the INLA's allied group, the IRSP, initially blamed the attack on British Intelligence.

McGlinchey himself was to help perpetuate the reputation of the INLA as a ruthlessly violent group by an interview with the *Sunday Tribune* newspaper in which he boasted that he had personally killed about thirty people, and liked to 'get in close' when he was about to take somebody's life. 'I like to get close, to minimise the risk to myself. It's usually just a matter of who gets in first, and getting in close you put your man down first.'

Like any paramilitary group involved in the 'armed struggle' in Ireland, the INLA set about establishing sources of supply for arms and explosives. The leader and founder of the INLA, Seamus Costello, was anxious from the start to ensure that his new group had sufficient materiel for its campaign. Costello, born in 1939, came from Bray, County Wicklow, and joined the republican movement at age sixteen. Within a year, he was taking part in the IRA's Border Campaign, commanding an Active Service Unit (ASU) in South Derry. His activities included destroying bridges and the burning of Magherafelt courthouse. In 1957 he was arrested in Glencree, County Wicklow, on suspicion of subversive activities, and sentenced to six months. On release he was interned at the Curragh.

An intense man and a deep thinker on political issues, he was on the left of the movement and was active in local politics. He was elected to Bray Urban District Council in 1967. When the Provisionals split away, Costello stayed with the Officials, but opposed the 1972 cease-fire and was dismissed from the Official IRA and also from its political wing, Official Sinn Féin. He went on to found the INLA and its political counterpart, the IRSP, in December 1974. In the first year or so of its existence, the INLA managed to secure a quantity of gelignite, stolen from a commercial company in the Irish Republic and smuggled into Northern Ireland, for use in bombing operations there. This was believed to have been supplied by Jim Kerr, who worked in mining. He had a long history of republican activity, but had also served with British forces during the Second World War.

Within a couple of years, Costello had an arms pipeline in operation from an unusual quarter – Australia. From 1977 to 1983, it is reckoned that about sixty firearms were smuggled to Ireland in four shipments by an Irishman who had emigrated to Australia. The first three shipments got through, but the fourth was detected in November 1983 at Baldoyle, north Dublin, after Gardaí discovered an incriminating document on Seamus Ruddy, who had returned to Ireland after his release in Greece. The weapons that got through from Australia included Garand M-1s, Ruger Mini-14s and Egyptian Mausers.[5] These were mostly old firearms, but nevertheless serviceable. However, the final shipment consisted of ten modern M-16 rifles and more than 4,000 rounds of ammunition.

The arms cargoes were sent to Ireland through shipping agencies, in containers labelled as something innocuous like 'household goods'. The final arms shipment was traced back to the person who had dispatched it – an Irish immigrant who had moved to Australia in 1968, becoming an Australian citizen in 1973. The man went on trial in Sydney in early 1984, and told the court that the guns were for 'the defence of my own people against an invading army'. He was convicted on gunrunning charges and fined $17,000.

Costello also looked to the US for arms supplies. In the latter part of 1977, the INLA leader was said to be working on a plan to smuggle rifles from New York, and was having meetings with a Dublin man with contacts in the shipping area in the hope of arranging transport.[6] Costello was waiting in his car in Fairview, Dublin, on the morning of 5 October, apparently for a meeting with this contact, when a gunman from the rival Official IRA walked up to the car.

The gunman, Jim Flynn, a native of South Armagh, had been keeping Costello under surveillance for some time – a feud had been in progress between the two groups. Flynn was a mercurial character with a reputation for unpredictability. Although the OIRA had declared a cease-fire five years before, Flynn was prominent in an OIRA group carrying out 'fundraising' robberies for the movement. The group was known within the OIRA as the 'Dirty Dozen', and did not claim responsibility for the robberies it carried out.

As he came face to face with Costello, Flynn produced a sawn-off shotgun and blasted the INLA leader. He then calmly reloaded and shot Costello again. Costello died almost instantly. Incredibly, Flynn did not have an escape route prepared. He jumped on a bus and went to the flat of another OIRA man on the north side of the city.

Some years later, the INLA took revenge. On 4 June 1982, Flynn was shot dead outside a pub in Fairview, not far from the spot where he had shot Costello. A friend of Flynn's told me he suspected that Flynn was set up by somebody in the OIRA who colluded with the INLA. According to an INLA spokesman in 1982, Flynn was killed after he was fingered as the killer of Seamus Costello by former members of the OIRA. The spokesman stated: 'Our action against Flynn took place after we were informed by former members of the Officials that he had murdered Seamus Costello. The ex-Officials who passed on this information are basically Republicans, and they left the Workers Party [successor to Official Sinn Féin] at the time of the [H-Block] hunger strike because they realised that their party did not represent their own political beliefs.'[7] It is not clear what happened to the cache of arms that Costello was trying to bring in to Ireland.

The USA was never a major source of weaponry for the organisation. The INLA was never able to match the IRA in terms of contacts and support infrastructure among Irish-Americans. Many of these would have had no problem supporting the 'armed struggle' of the Provos but would have been wary of the INLA, as it was seen as a Marxist organisation. In the early 1980s, the INLA had two men, Colm Murphy and another man from County Armagh, seeking to buy arms in New York, but they were arrested by the FBI's PIRA Squad (*see* Chapter 8).

It has been reported that in 1981, an INLA faction led by one of the organisation's most ruthless killers, Gerard 'Dr Death' Steenson, smuggled about a dozen assault rifles by ship from the US into Dublin port.[8] Steenson was later to be killed in an internal feud.

Arms trail from the Middle East

In 1977 the INLA established links with what was to become its most important source of arms and explosives – Palestinian elements based in Lebanon and, later, Prague. Jack Holland and Henry McDonald, in their book *INLA, Deadly Divisions*, a very fine study of the paramilitary organisation, have described how, through left-wing sympathisers in West Germany, the INLA established contact with a Palestinian who was studying in that country. He was a member of F-18, the intelligence section of Fatah, part of the Palestine Liberation Organisation (PLO), and he became the key contact man for the arms deliveries. The PLO arms pipeline, operating with the aid of German sympathisers, continued to function until the mid-1980s.[9]

Palestinian forces in Lebanon had plenty of arms in the late 1970s and early 1980s, and appeared happy to sell some of them to the INLA, which was sympathetic to the Palestinian cause. It is understood that the late Rudolf Raabe, a member of the Revolutionary Cells group, played a key role in putting the INLA in touch with the Palestinians.[10] Unlike the IRA which tended to distrust the extreme left, the INLA established contacts on the European continent with members of extremist groups such as the Revolutionary Cells and Action Directe. Such groups were part of what was termed the New Left, which represented a move away from the traditional communist parties towards a more radical ideology that attracted young people alienated from modern, affluent society.

Paris was an important staging post for the arms coming from the Palestinians. Some of the materiel is believed to have come via Switzerland, where the INLA had the help of one of the group's activists, Jim Kerr. He had previously lived in Nenagh, County Tipperary, and was on the run from the Irish authorities. Kerr was suspected by the French of assisting not only the INLA, but the IRA as well. The French believed that Kerr set up his base in Switzerland so as to take advantage of liberal Swiss laws on extradition, and so as to be close to several international borders that would facilitate frequent contact with extreme left-wing groups on the continent, especially in France and Germany.

Paul Barril, one of the French Gendarmerie's counterterrorism experts, believed that Kerr was a friend of two prominent left-wing activists located in France, Henri Curiel and Pierre Goldman.[11] Both came from families who suffered or were endangered because of their Jewish backgrounds. If it is true that Kerr was friendly with the two men, it would suggest that the Irishman was in France quite some time before settling in Switzerland in 1979.

Curiel, who was born in Egypt, was a founder of the Egyptian communist movement and was deported from Egypt in 1950. He devoted much of his life to assisting Third World liberation movements, and was shot dead at his home in Paris in May 1978, by unknown assailants. Goldman, whose parents were involved in the French Resistance during the Second World War, was one of the leaders of the New Left in France. He was involved in a series of armed robberies, and was jailed for life in 1974 for the murder of two women in 1969 – the conviction was overturned in 1976. While in prison, he wrote his memoirs, dealing in particular with his Jewish background.[12] He was shot dead in a Paris street by extreme right-wing elements in September 1979.

According to Barril, Kerr also maintained close links with former members of Curiel's network, and with at least one of the moving forces behind the French terror group Action Directe.

The left-wing activist who turned informer, Bernard Jegat, would later provide information to the French authorities of INLA dealings he had allegedly witnessed, indicating that Kerr was involved in the transfer to the INLA of a consignment of about 15kgs of plastic explosive, handed over in Paris[13], and a consignment of 3,000 9mm cartridges that was moved from Switzerland to France.[14] The British suspected Kerr of being linked to attacks on British targets in West Germany. Because of Kerr's links with INLA members in Paris and his visits to the city, the British communicated their concerns about Kerr to the French security service, Direction du Surveillance Territoire (DST).

Kerr was an unusual figure, with an air of mystery about him. He came from a well-to-do, highly respectable, middle-class family on Ireland's east coast, whose members were involved in business and the professions. As a young man, he was the black sheep of the family. There were reports from French sources that he had fought with the International Brigade in the Spanish Civil War.[15] Sources in Ireland were unable to confirm this. A person who knew Kerr before the Second World War remembered him thus: 'He was a good-looking chap, with an outgoing manner. I always thought he was easily led. He was always looking for excitement.' Kerr was to find plenty of excitement in his life.

He joined the IRA, and was interned at the Curragh in the early 1940s as part of a general round-up of IRA members. The Irish government, led by Eamon de Valera, feared that IRA activities might undermine Ireland's neutrality during the Second World War. Internees could be released if they signed an agreement not to engage in subversive activity, and Kerr signed himself out after a short period. Neighbours remembered him coming home from the internment camp, and then, surprisingly, going off to England to join the Royal Air Force (RAF) in the war against Nazi Germany. It was highly unusual for an IRA man to join the British forces. It is unclear if the RAF knew about his IRA background when they recruited him. Another person who knew Kerr at this period remarked: 'Nothing would ever surprise me about him.' In the RAF, Kerr became a rear gunner on a bomber – a hazardous occupation.

After returning to Ireland from the war he became involved in the IRA again, during the Border Campaign of the 1950s. One of his close friends in republican circles was Seamus Costello. In the 1970s, Kerr was working in mining operations in County Tipperary when Gardaí came to suspect him of stealing explosives for transfer to Costello's fledgling INLA. In

1975 Kerr appeared before the Special Criminal Court in Dublin, charged with possession of explosives. He was given bail of £1,000 – a sizeable figure in those days – but failed to turn up for his trial. In 1976 the court issued a warrant for his arrest.

In late 1979 Kerr was living in Basle, Switzerland, using the pseudonym Anthony Herbert, and also the Irish version of his name, Seamus Mac Charra. By now he was in his sixties. At a time when other men would be preparing for an easy life of retirement, Kerr was living the furtive life of a fugitive, rubbing shoulders with young revolutionaries from extremist groups dedicated to overthrowing the established order. He lived with a young German woman from the Revolutionary Cells group. During his regular visits to Paris to liaise with INLA activists, he also mixed with members of the IRA. He came to the attention of police and intelligence/security agencies in a range of countries, with the British taking a particular interest in his activities on the Continent.

Police and security services in different jurisdictions communicated with each other about Kerr, his movements and suspected activities. The British tipped off the Irish authorities that Kerr was lying low in Basle. The Swiss notified the French security service, the DST, of his presence in their country. Paul Barril of the French Gendarmerie's counterterrorism wing took a particular interest in Kerr, especially in light of his visits to Paris to meet individuals suspected of being involved in subversive activities.

Barril was a macho cop, a Gallic 'James Bond' figure who had been involved in a number of high-profile exploits around the world, leading anti-terrorism operations. Blue-eyed, clean-cut and with film star looks, he was the subject of many admiring articles in the French media. There were pictures of him in a glamorous black uniform, abseiling from a helicopter, diving in frogman gear or doing karate. He was said to be a crack shot. He was photographed posing with the most advanced firearms of that era. Barril also got results. He helped Saudi Arabian forces liberate hostages from the Grand Mosque at Mecca in November 1979. In Djibouti in East Africa, he freed a busload of children who had been kidnapped. In Corsica, he led a raid on a building occupied by nationalists. Now he was turning his attention to Irish paramilitaries.

Barril has written that as part of an investigation into Irish suspects he paid a number of visits to Switzerland to 'activate' the Swiss security services in regard to Kerr, and to personally keep track of the Irishman.[16] At first, it would appear that the Swiss were unwilling to put Kerr under intense surveillance because there was no evidence he had broken any Swiss laws, but they were later to move against him and detain him.

Kerr was suspected by the French of having contact, in Paris in late January 1982, with Bruno Bréguet, a member of the gang headed by the infamous terrorist Carlos 'The Jackal' – Ilich Ramírez Sánchez.[17] Bréguet was a tall, good-looking young Swiss who had dropped out of his science studies in Lugano to seek a life of adventure as a guerrilla fighting for the Palestinian cause. After throwing in his lot with the Popular Front for the Liberation of Palestine, he was arrested at the Israeli port of Haifa in 1970 with explosives. After serving seven years of a fifteen-year sentence, he was released. In February 1982, Bréguet was arrested by police in Paris, along with Magdalena Kopp, another member of Carlos's gang. Kopp, a quiet, serious-minded young woman from southwest Germany, was, in fact, Carlos's wife. They had married in Lebanon in 1979 and in 1986 she would bear him a daughter, Elba Rosa. Kopp had been a member of the Red Army Faction. Bréguet and Kopp were found to be in possession of arms and explosives when arrested. Carlos was outraged when he heard the two had been detained, and launched a ruthless bombing campaign in an effort to secure their release.

Later in the year the French authorities made another swoop that, like the arrests of Bréguet and Kopp, would receive much publicity. Jim Kerr was apparently very alarmed when three Irish activists, associated with the INLA's political wing, the IRSP, and who became known as the Vincennes Three, were arrested in Paris in August 1982. Arms and explosives were found in the apartment occupied by the three. As outlined in more detail below, the materiel belonged to the INLA and had been planted by members of the Gendarmerie in the apartment. According to Barril, ballistics experts discovered that a GP 35 pistol found at Vincennes belonged to the same lot as a similar pistol found in possession of Bréguet when he was arrested. It was also claimed by Barril that plastic explosive weighing 500 grammes discovered in possession of Bréguet was found by British experts to be of a type recovered only twice previously – in March and September 1981, in Derry, in caches associated with the INLA.[18] The implication was that Kerr transferred materiel not only to the INLA, but to Carlos's man

Bréguet as well, or that they shared the same supplier. Following the arrest of the Vincennes Three, Kerr avoided Paris, but paid visits to Brussels where, the French security services believed, he liaised with an arms dealer known as The Belgian concerning the procurement of arms for the Irish 'struggle'.[19] As outlined in Chapter 6, The Belgian was also believed to be a supplier of arms to the IRA, ETA, and other elements, including followers of Carlos.

Kerr was finally arrested in Basle on 6 April 1984, on foot of an Irish extradition warrant. He mounted a legal challenge, saying he was a co-founder of the IRSP, and describing himself as a 'fighter against the British occupation of Northern Ireland'. The Swiss Supreme Court rejected his claim that the extradition of political offenders was forbidden under international law. The court found that while Kerr had political motives, the offence of which he was accused in Ireland could not be regarded as political, as bombings were out of all proportion to the achievement of political aims.

On 31 October, the Swiss federal courts at Lausanne authorised his extradition to Ireland. He was transferred, under escort, from Berne to London on a Swissair flight on 2 November, and then on to Dublin. In February 1985, he received a ten-year sentence at the Special Criminal Court. By the time he emerged from Portlaoise Prison he was quite elderly. His paramilitary activities had come to an end. He died, in his eighties, in the early years of the present century. During research for this book, some relatives declined to talk about him; others pointed out that they had not seen him for many years, and knew little about his activities.

The activist who became an informant

Arms supplies from the Lebanon were disrupted after the Palestinians were forced to withdraw from Beirut in 1982. However, according to authors Jack Holland and Henry McDonald in their study of the INLA, arms continued to flow from Palestinian elements in Prague until at least 1986.[20] It has been estimated that the Palestinian connection provided the INLA with hundreds of CZ pistols and dozens of AK-47 rifles as well as an unknown quantity of other materiel, including hand grenades. But one of the most important items supplied was Soviet-made plastic explosive. This is believed to have been used in the under-car bomb that killed British politician Airey Neave.[21] As often occurs in these booby-trap car-bomb attacks, the victim's legs were blown off, and he died within minutes.

It has been reported that a quantity of this explosive had been stored along with other materiel by the INLA in Germany, where the organisation had a group of supporters among the extreme left who assisted with the channelling of arms and explosives from the Middle East. (An important figure in this support network was the German Marxist Rudolf Raabe, who fled to Ireland in the 1980s, and is believed to have taken part in at least one bank robbery, before his death in 1991.) According to one account, sixteen ounces of explosive were cut from the large block hidden in Germany and smuggled into England in a chocolate box, where it was used in the Neave assassination.[22]

France was to remain an important centre of INLA activity. One of its advantages was that France did not extradite people for politically-related offences. The INLA had a number of left-wing contacts and sympathisers among the French, including Bernard Jegat, who agreed to hide INLA weapons in his apartment, as they were moved along the arms pipeline to Ireland. Jegat was a middle-class, starry-eyed, left-wing idealist. Born in July 1949 in the Val-d'Oise region of France, his first public brush with authority was in 1969, when he refused to do his military service, and ended up in Fresnes prison. He was protesting against the role played by the French military in the Algerian conflict.

In 1972 he came to Paris and worked for a while in a jazz club. He studied at the University of Vincennes, one of his subjects being 'Cinema and the Struggle against Imperialism'. He became an admirer of Che Guevara and made contact with sympathisers and representatives of a range of 'Third World' liberation movements, such as the Polisario Front. On a more mundane level, in 1974 he received a one-month suspended sentence for issuing a dud cheque for about 2,000 Francs. In 1976 he spent some time in Beirut, hoping to receive training in a Palestinian camp. However, the Civil War hotted up so much that he could not even leave the city. He returned to France and, in January 1977, found work as a freelance journalist with Radio Télévision Belge Francophone (RTBF). He was interested in Irish 'liberation movements' and in 1979, through a French journalist who made the introduction, he came to know members of the INLA, and also members of the organisation's political group, the IRSP.

Jegat agreed to a request by the INLA to store arms in his apartment that were being smuggled from the Middle East. Among the arms that he said passed through his hands, between October 1979 and early 1981, were about 250 CZ pistols, Czech-made weapons of 7.65mm calibre.[23] He provided this information after becoming an informant for the authorities. He also told how he handled other materiel, including explosives and sub-machine guns. He was to tell police that the first consignment of arms he hid in his home consisted of five or six 9mm automatic pistols, and four Uzi sub-machine guns. The weapons, like others he went on to store in his home, had had their serial numbers obliterated, making it impossible to trace their origin. Some time after taking his first delivery, his contacts drove a Rover car into the garage below his residence. The Uzis, which had been disassembled, were placed in a special hiding place in the vehicle. On two or three occasions, arms were collected by the INLA people in this manner. Jegat never thought of noting the registration numbers of these vehicles.

Jegat was given the code name Hennessy. The name had romantic French–Irish connotations. It is the name of a superior French cognac that was originally distilled in the eighteenth century by Richard Hennessy, one of the 'Wild Geese', Irish mercenaries who fought in Dillon's Irish Regiment in the French Army.

Jegat would arrange to pick up weapons after receiving a coded message by phone. He would meet his contact in a café, who in turn would pick up the weapons at a nearby location from the person delivering them. Jegat never saw the person who brought the guns to the vicinity of the café. The contact would pass the weapons on to Jegat. For security reasons, Jegat would generally take a taxi home with the arms.

At one stage, according to Jegat, the INLA were investigating the possibility of doing a deal for the procurement of assault rifles from Portuguese army officers. Jegat was asked to check out the cost of hiring a villa in the Lisbon area with a garage attached, but the deal apparently did not go ahead. On another occasion, in the summer of 1980, he was asked to provide a hiding place in Belgium for twenty M-16 rifles which were being sent to Ireland, either directly or via France. He did what was necessary to solve this particular problem. It is probable that the arms were delivered successfully to Ireland.

It all began to go wrong in August 1982, when terrorists set off a bomb in rue de Rosiers, a Jewish district of Paris, killing six people. The authorities issued photofit pictures of suspects, and Jegat thought one picture resembled an Irish activist he had got to know. This was Michael Plunkett, a bearded, burly native of Dún Laoghaire, County Dublin, who had been chairman of the IRSP. Plunkett, who had been a close friend of Seamus Costello, was at the centre of a long-running courtroom controversy in Ireland. A founding member of the IRSP, he was one of a number of men who were charged with the 1977 robbery of a mail train at Sallins, County Kildare. Plunkett was acquitted, but three others were convicted. Two had their convictions overturned on appeal, while the third, Nicky Kelly, received a presidential pardon. He was later to become a Labour party member of Wicklow County Council.

Despite Jegat's suspicions, it later transpired that Plunkett had no connection whatever with the rue de Rosiers atrocity. However, in the meantime, and after days of tortuous soul-searching, Jegat decided to tip off the authorities. For the intense, serious-minded Jegat, it was not simply a question of phoning his local police station. He tried to contact the renowned left-wing intellectual, Régis Debray, who was working as an adviser to President Mitterand, but Debray was away in the US. Debray had been jailed in Bolivia in the 1960s due to his links with the Cuban revolutionary Che Guevara, who was executed by Bolivian security forces.

Jegat talked to another official instead, who put him in touch with a recently-formed elite security group working from the Élysée Palace. The Élysée Cell was President Mitterand's personal anti-terrorist unit. It was set up in 1982, following a series of terrorist outrages in France, and was headed by the dynamic Christian Prouteau, chief of the French Gendarmerie's elite counterterrorism and hostage-rescue unit, the Groupe d'Intervention de la Gendarmerie Nationale (GIGN). Another key member of the cell was Prouteau's GIGN second-in-command, the swashbuckling Paul Barril.

Barril had a particular interest in Irish paramilitaries in France, and had good contacts among the Gardaí. Security co-operation between France and Ireland had been boosted following a bizarre aircraft hijacking in May 1981. An Australian-born former Trappist monk, Laurence James Downey, hijacked an Aer Lingus airliner flying from Dublin to London, and forced the pilot to land at an airport in northern France, Le Touquet. He demanded that Pope John Paul II reveal the Third Secret of Fatima. The GIGN arrested the hijacker and freed the hostages. Later, between September and December 1981, the Irish government sent Garda officers to France to do courses with the GIGN. As a result, friendly contacts developed between officers from the two countries.

It was brought home to the French Gendarmes by their Irish counterparts around this time that Irish paramilitaries were using connections in France to replenish their stocks of war materiel. Barril would receive phone calls from his Garda contacts on developments regarding Irish paramilitaries based in France. The GIGN was to play a key role in following up on Jegat's information.

At the time Bernard Jegat provided the tip-off to the French authorities about Plunkett, he was storing arms in his apartment – ten automatic pistols and a quantity of plastic explosive, as well as other items. Jegat had been asked to mind these some time before. He handed the arms and explosives over to the Gendarmerie.

On 28 August, a raid was carried out on an apartment at rue Diderot in Vincennes, a suburb of Paris, led by Paul Barril. Michael Plunkett and two other Irish republicans were arrested – Stephen King and Mary Reid.[24] A cache of arms was recovered. It later emerged that the materiel had been planted in the flat by law enforcement, and consisted of items that had been recovered at Jegat's home. As a result, the three were released nine months after their arrest, and initiated legal action. The affair caused severe embarrassment for President Francois Mitterrand, barely a year after he took office. In 1995 Paul Barril lost a libel action against the newspaper *Le Monde* over claims that he framed the three Irish people. However, in April 2003, France's highest court cleared Barril of involvement in the planting of arms and explosives in the apartment.

After he broke cover and turned informant, Bernard Jegat gave the authorities an account of the people who had used his services to hide arms and explosives. Having blown the gaffe, Jegat became concerned for his own safety, fearing that somebody might try to kill him. In fact, there was to be no attempt on his life. In April 1984, he again tried to contact Régis Debray, and this time was successful. He asked Debray for help in quickly moving house and also for a licence to carry a gun. He felt he was caught in

a trap. He desperately needed to escape. Debray wrote a memo immediately to President Mitterand outlining Jegat's concerns.[25] Debray described
Jegat to Mitterand as 'very emotional' and 'unstable', but truly 'an idealist of
the left'.

The following year Jegat made lengthy statements to the French internal
security agency, the DST, giving a detailed account of INLA activities in
France, naming names and giving details of INLA links with other extremist groups in Europe. A few years later, the law took its course in relation to
Jegat's possession of illegal firearms, but he was to be treated leniently. In
September 1991, Jegat got a suspended sentence of fifteen months. No
doubt the court took into account the assistance he had given to the
authorities. In the classic phrase, he had 'done the State some service'. Jegat
died of cancer on 13 February 1995, aged only forty-five.

Death in the forest

One of the victims of incessant feuding within the INLA was the organisation's former gunrunner, Seamus Ruddy. After returning to Ireland from
his adventure in Greece, he had remained politically active for a period. In
1981, he was a visitor to the INLA members in the H-Blocks of the Maze
prison, who had joined with IRA members in a hunger strike that was to
claim ten lives. Ruddy was one of the activists appointed to liaise between
the INLA hunger strikers and the movement and prisoners' families.
Those who died included three INLA members – Patsy O'Hara, Kevin
Lynch and Michael Devine. Ruddy made at least one visit in the company
of Gerry Adams, who was Sinn Fein vice-president at the time.

A couple of years later, after coming to the attention of Gardaí in Dublin in
connection with the arms smuggled from Australia, Ruddy decided to move to
France. He had met Cecilia Moore, a young English woman, in Dublin, and
the two of them took up residence in Paris, living at an apartment on the rue de
l'Indre, in the working-class area of the 20th Arrondissement. Ruddy had by
now dropped out of paramilitary activity. He had found work teaching English
in an adult education college. He retained a keen interest in Irish politics, however, and was involved in the production of left-wing magazines focusing on
the Irish question. Ms Moore recalled that he was also trying to introduce a
trade union into the college where he worked.

The couple decided in 1985 to return to live in Ireland. She travelled to Ireland in the summer of that year, and he planned to join her the following September. She was living in the Cork area, and because the local phone system at that time was imperfect, they would communicate by letter. The last item he sent her through the post was a parcel. It contained a French-style T-shirt. 'It had blue and white stripes,' she recalled. She had told him she liked the garment, and he bought it for her. It was a thoughtful present. There was no covering note. It was to be the last time she ever heard from him.

She became worried after a short while when there was no contact. Friends who were expecting to hear from him got in touch, concerned that there had been no word from him. It was the beginning of Moore's long quest to find out what had happened to her partner. It was said in his circle that members of a faction of the INLA headed by the ruthless 'Big John' O'Reilly had gone to Paris to check into gunrunning routes and arms caches. O'Reilly was seeking to procure arms for his followers and apparently decided that Ruddy was the man who could help him. It was said that Ruddy agreed to meet O'Reilly and a couple of the latter's friends in a Montparnasse bar. Ruddy went along by himself. A friend of Ruddy's said later it was surprising that Ruddy failed to get one of his own friends to tag along for 'security'. A few days before, there had been an incident in Paris in which a former political colleague of Ruddy's had been beaten up. This incident alarmed Irish people in Paris who were involved with the IRSP.

Somehow Ruddy ended up, along with the INLA men, in the area of Rouen, Normandy, about fifty miles northwest of Paris. It was said that when Ruddy was unable to assist O'Reilly with his quest for arms, he was tied to a tree in a remote area of a forest and tortured, and finally murdered, his body dumped in a plastic rubbish bin that had been used for storing arms. Ruddy's friends in the movement believed that O'Reilly was personally involved in the killing. O'Reilly was shot dead in an INLA feud in January 1987. The man deemed responsible for that shooting, Gerard Steenson, founder of the breakaway Irish People's Liberation Organisation, was himself shot dead later that year.

The murder of Seamus Ruddy seems particularly senseless. He posed no threat to anybody, and since he had been out of paramilitary activity for some time, it is doubtful if he had much in the way of useful, up-to-date information to impart.

At the time of writing, Ruddy's body has still not been found, much to the distress of his family and Ms Moore. In May 2000, fifteen years after his murder, the French authorities carried out a dig in a forest near Rouen, after elements in the IRSP/INLA began to co-operate in the late 1990s. Garda and Irish government representatives were present for the search. Information received indicated that Ruddy's body had been buried in a shallow grave at the site of a former arms dump. There were extensive excavations. Those on hand to witness the search included Cecilia Moore, who currently lives in Dublin and is an artist. She was hoping against hope that her long quest had come to an end. But there was no trace of human remains. The forest failed to yield up its secrets.

The murder of Seamus Ruddy, who was in his early thirties when he disappeared, was only one of a remarkable number of deaths caused by INLA-linked feuding within the republican 'family'. As indicated above, even the birth of the INLA in 1975 was marked by bloodshed. In 1987 there was a split in the INLA, leading to a vicious feud that resulted in twelve deaths. One faction was the 'mainstream' INLA; the other called itself the Irish People's Liberation Organisation (IPLO). Another feud developed in 1992 between two factions of the IPLO – the IPLO Army Council faction, led by Jimmy Brown, and the IPLO Belfast Brigade faction, led by Sean Macklin. Both men were shot dead before a truce was called. Shortly after the feud ended, the IRA attacked both wings of the IPLO, resulting in the death of one IPLO member and the wounding of a number of others. The IRA–IPLO feud ended in 1992, with the IPLO becoming defunct as a fighting force. Both IPLO factions, in effect, ceased to function.

However, despite internal differences and feuding, the INLA also found the time and resources to prosecute the campaign of violence against the British. On the Continent, the INLA continued to receive assistance from left-wing extremist groups, as illustrated by a 1985 attempt to bomb Chelsea Barracks in London. Two devices were deployed, each containing up to 40lbs of explosives, along with nuts and bolts. They were clearly meant to kill.

It is believed that the explosives included a French explosive called Gelsuirite, which had been provided by Action Directe. The French terror group had stolen a quantity of the explosive in 1984. Action Directe is said to have shared explosives with other terrorist groups, such as the Red Army Faction in

Germany, and the Communist Fighting Cells in Belgium. An INLA member was in regular contact with Action Directe and it is believed that he was provided with the explosives. Police investigations indicated that a group of INLA members travelled in a camper van from Northern Ireland, picked up the explosives and delivered the materiel to London for the bomb attack.[26] In the event, the two bombs were discovered and defused.

A year later, a man from Derry was sentenced to life for the bomb plot. He always protested his innocence, and the INLA said he was not one of their members and had nothing to do with the bombs. He received early release under the Good Friday Agreement.

The Hollywood scriptwriter who turned gunrunner

Bill Norton was a well-established Hollywood scriptwriter who had worked on a string of movies, both for the big screen and for television. Among the fourteen feature films on which Norton had laboured as a screen writer were *Brannigan*, starring John Wayne; *Dirty Tricks*, starring Elliot Gould and Kate Jackson; and *Gator*, starring Burt Reynolds. He had a particular talent for thrillers, with humour as part of the mix. In the old days, he was said to have been a 'buddy' of Ronald Reagan, later to become a US president. It was reported that the two men had got to know each other when Reagan was prominent in the Screen Actors Guild, while Norton was active in the Screen Writers Guild. Bill Norton lived in California, had all the characteristics of a pillar of the community and had no known family links to Ireland. He was no longer in the first flush of youth. He was a most unlikely gunrunner.

Norton is believed to have come into contact with Sean 'Bap' Hughes, a leading member of the INLA, in 1984. In a way, they were strange bedfellows. Norton moved in fashionable, liberal circles on the West Coast, rubbing shoulders with figures from the movie world. Hughes was an unsophisticated tearaway from the working-class Divis Flats complex in Belfast, who had joined the INLA in its early days. Norton, who had an interest in left-wing causes, made a decision that was to have a calamitous effect on his life – he agreed to procure arms for the INLA, reckoning he would be able to buy the arms on the open market in America, with its relaxed gun laws. He didn't do it for profit. It would appear that starry-eyed idealism was the factor that drew him into the murky world of gunrunning. Was he also driven by a sense of danger, of living on the edge? We can only speculate. Certainly, Norton was to become immersed in a real-life drama that had many of the elements of one of his own movie scripts.

When the news broke in the summer of 1986 that Bill Norton and his wife Eleanor (Ellie) were among a group of people, including Sean Hughes, arrested in France with a cache of arms bound for Ireland, there was shock among the couple's friends and acquaintances. In the latter part of the 1980s I talked to people who had known Norton, and a picture emerged of a rather gentle person. I encountered one young Irishman, Steve, who had met Norton in the summer of 1980. Steve had been working in a hotel in Los Angeles for the summer when he made contacts among people interested in left-wing causes in Latin America. A married couple put him in touch with a friend of theirs who was involved in sending medical aid to the fledgling Sandinista regime in Nicaragua. This turned out to be Bill Norton. Steve stayed with Norton and his wife at their home in Santa Barbara, north of Los Angeles. Norton was very clearly on the left, but apparently gave no sign of supporting violent causes in Ireland. Several years later, Steve was stunned when he learned that Norton had been arrested for gunrunning.

It would appear that when Norton shipped a camper from California to Europe with close to forty weapons hidden in a special X-ray-proof compartment in the summer of 1986, the FBI had well and truly penetrated the operation. An informed source said that Norton had already got an arms shipment through to Ireland. According to the source, the weapons were supposed to go to the INLA faction headed by the much-feared John O'Reilly, but when the arms got to Ireland they ended up in the hands of a rival faction. The INLA was frequently beset by internal divisions and feuds, and Norton may not have fully understood the subtleties. He was probably unaware of the alleged O'Reilly connection with the disappearance of Seamus Ruddy.

Norton's second gunrunning operation was to prove his undoing. Police forces and security services in Ireland, France, the Netherlands and Belgium co-operated in monitoring the movements of the gunrunners. The camper van was shipped by sea to the Dutch port of Rotterdam, where police placed it under surveillance. Police followed the van as it was transported on a truck with Irish registration plates through Belgium and France and on to the port of Le Havre, where it was to be shipped on a car ferry crossing to the Irish port of Rosslare. The French authorities made their move before the camper could be loaded onto the ferry. Those detained in the June swoop included Bill and Ellie Norton, Sean Hughes and another INLA man, Belfast-born James McLaughlin. A young woman was detained for a time, but then released without charge. Also detained was a figure associated with the French left-wing terrorist organisation, Action Directe, with which the INLA had a friendly relationship.

Ostensibly, Norton had a valid reason for taking a camper van to Ireland – he had bought a house at Omeath, County Louth, just south of the Border in the Irish Republic. However, a search of the camper van revealed a cache of two sub-machine guns, twelve Armalite rifles, twenty-three other guns and more than 2,000 rounds of ammunition. At their trial in France in August 1987, Norton and Hughes said they had bought the arms to defend Catholic homes in Northern Ireland and to fight British tyranny there.

Gardaí were particularly pleased at the arrest of Sean Hughes. The Belfast man, aged thirty at the time of his trial in France, was wanted in Ireland for questioning in connection with the murder of a Garda in Dublin in 1982. Hughes was jailed by the French court for four years, as were McLaughlin (thirty-nine) and Norton (sixty-two). Norton's wife Ellie got three years, two of which were suspended. The Nortons had to make arrangements for friends in Ireland to look after their twelve-year-old, adopted, Mexican-born daughter Teresa.

It emerged that Norton had bought the arms at the Pomona gun fair in California. It is hard to find the words, the hyperbole, to describe this gun fair, which used to be held several times a year at Pomona and, during its heyday, was the biggest event of its kind in America. I visited the show in 1989 and was truly amazed – I had never seen so many guns and so many gun enthusiasts assembled in one place before. The venue for the fair was the Los Angeles County Fairgrounds, just off the San Bernardino Freeway. Like so many other things in Los Angeles, the fairgrounds are on a mammoth scale. There are several huge halls, each of which, during the three-day gun show, was packed with hundreds of stalls selling anything and everything that a gun buff could desire or fantasise about.

The gun fair was like a fantasy land for grown-up schoolboys. Quite a few of the visitors came in their own self-designed outfits straight from the world of macho make-belief. Some wore military uniforms of no known armies – armies that existed only in their fertile imaginations. The 'uniforms' were assembled from bits and pieces of army surplus clothing – plentiful supplies of which were on sale at the show. Rambo lookalikes or wannabees were ten-a-penny. Other chaps came dressed as cowboys, resplendent in ten-gallon hats, blue jeans, check shirts, high-heeled western boots and stockman's coats. I suspected that many of these 'cowboys' were really computer programmers, or bankers, or accountants, who had never been near a cow in their lives. Nobody batted an eyelid. Nobody seemed self-conscious or embarrassed. That's the way it was at the Pomona gun show.[27]

How exactly Bill Norton's gunrunning activities came to the notice of the FBI is uncertain. His penchant for buying weapons at the Pomona gun fair in such numbers that they could not have been for his own personal use may well have helped to focus the attention of the authorities on him.

While in prison, Norton continued with his scriptwriting work. He was not allowed to have a typewriter in his cell – it was in the days before laptop computers – but he managed to produce two handwritten scripts which his friend, Hollywood producer Mike Wise, arranged to have typed up and circulated.

Ellie Norton was released in December 1987 due to medical problems. Meanwhile, Bill Norton appealed and a French judge reduced his sentence to two years. He was released from prison in Rouen in early 1988, having served a total of nineteen months.

While the jail sentences served by the Nortons were relatively short, the real punishment was that this middle-aged couple found themselves effectively without a country. The Nortons decided not to return to the US, where they felt they could face federal charges of arms smuggling. There was no question of the French giving them long-term asylum and the couple also apparently feared charges if they went on to their holiday home in the Irish Republic. So the Nortons went to a country which they knew well, and which would not extradite them to the US – Nicaragua, which was then under the left-wing regime of the Sandinistas.

In Nicaragua, the couple became well-known among American ex-pats working to support the Sandinistas. Norton had good contacts at a high level in the regime. In the early 1980s he and his wife had visited Managua and had been guests of the Sandinista minister for culture, Father Ernesto Cardenal. Some time after they settled in Nicaragua, I talked by phone to Ellie Norton at her home in Managua. She said she believed the Irish people held at Le Havre were released a month following their own release. Meanwhile Bill was back working at his old profession of movie script-writer. Ms Norton told me, in fact, that her husband had gone to Cuba in connection with a particular film project. 'He is working on a movie script. It's a marvellous project about an old revolutionary from El Salvador, now living in Cuba, called Miguel Marmot, who was put before a firing squad and escaped.' Even though her husband was largely retired, she said he was still interested in working on 'progressive projects'. Subsequently, Bill Norton was reported to be working on a movie script based on the H-Block hunger strike by Irish republican prisoners. The movie was never made. Bill Norton died in Nicaragua in 1992.

It is not surprising that Norton and his friends tried to use France as a conduit for an arms shipment. France had served as a bolthole for members of the INLA who wished to lie low. Norton's gunrunning sidekick Sean Hughes had been on the run in France for some years from the Irish authorities. After release from prison in France in 1988, the Irish authorities made an unsuccessful attempt to have him extradited to Ireland to face trial for murder. Hughes' lawyer arranged for him to be deported to a French protectorate near Madagascar, where he lived for a number of years with a French woman. After the IRA cease-fire in 1994, he slipped back into Ireland, spending some time in his native Belfast. In 1997 he was arrested for armed robbery at Swinford, County Mayo. Detectives were very interested indeed to find that they had in custody the prime suspect for the murder of a Garda colleague. Hughes got eight years for the armed robbery, and detectives reactivated the investigation into the murder of Garda Patrick Reynolds, who was shot dead at Avonbeg Gardens in Tallaght, Dublin, in February 1982. The young policeman had been shot in the back during a fracas. Gardaí had gone to the flats complex to investigate an armed robbery that had occurred a couple of days previously at Askeaton, County Limerick. Before fleeing, one of the occupants of the flat opened fire, and Garda Reynolds, who was only twenty-two, tragically died. Hughes went to live in Paris some time later, in 1982.

Hughes went on trial at the Special Criminal Court in Dublin in 2000 accused of the murder. The court heard how Gardaí travelled to Paris in late 1982 and took part in an informal identification procedure at the Gare St Lazare. The court was told that a Garda identified Hughes as the man who had shot Garda Reynolds. However, three judges at the Special Criminal Court cleared him of the Reynolds murder, and of possessing firearms with intent to endanger life. The judges were not satisfied that Hughes' fingerprints and spectacles, found at the murder scene, proved he was there at the time of the murder.

As for the Pomona gun fair, where Bill Norton bought guns for use in Ireland – it is no more. It was announced in February 2003 that Great Western Shows Incorporated, which had staged the gun fair three times a year at the Los Angeles County Fairgrounds in Pomona, was moving the show to State Fair Park in Dallas, Texas. The beginning of the end of the gun shows at Pomona came in 1999, when Los Angeles County decided to ban the sale of guns and ammunition on County property. Great Western Shows decided to challenge the ruling. There followed a three-year legal battle, during which the California State Supreme Court, in 2002, affirmed the County's ordinance, ruling that cities and counties should not be forced to allow gun sales on their property. Ultimately the County made a financial settlement with Great Western Shows, and the gun fair at Pomona, which attracted about 35,000 patrons to each event, and which was last held in December 1999, passed into history.

The capture of 'Basher' Flynn

After Bill Norton and his INLA friends were arrested on 11 June 1986 in Le Havre, police mounted a surveillance operation on contacts of those who were detained. The operation bore fruit the following month, when French authorities swooped in Paris and arrested a prominent INLA man, Harry 'Basher' Flynn, and three other Irishmen. The police also recovered three rifles, two pistols, seven hand grenades and two silencers.

Belfast-born Flynn had led an eventful life. He had made two escapes from custody in Northern Ireland. In 1975, while being held on armed robbery charges, he escaped with a number of others through a skylight at Crumlin Road courthouse in Belfast. Recaptured, he was being held at

Long Kesh, later known as the Maze prison, when, on 5 May 1976, he and a number of other prisoners tunnelled out of the jail.

He lived rough for three days, reaching the mountains of South Derry. From there, republican sympathisers spirited him across the Border into the Republic. During an INLA feud in December 1981, a gunman shot him at a Dublin pub, wounding him seriously. He subsequently made his way to Paris and was reportedly in the process of concluding a major arms deal with the INLA's PLO contact in Prague when he was arrested. The £70,000 deal was for the supply of 100 light anti-tank weapons, forty-eight AK-47 assault rifles, three 12.5mm machine guns and two 80mm mortars.[28] There were some unavoidable delays in transferring the weapons and Flynn was arrested before delivery could be made. As a result the arms never got through, and it was to be the last of the INLA arms transactions with the PLO contact in Prague.

Flynn, despite being handcuffed, tried to run away while being transferred between police stations, but was caught by a policeman, a fitness fanatic, who ran after him. When Flynn appeared in court in Paris on arms charges in October 1987, he was given five years, with two suspended. The other three Irishmen were treated quite leniently: William 'Boot' Browning got three years, with eighteen months suspended; George Kevin McCann got a three-year suspended sentence; and another man got a one-year suspended sentence. The British failed in an attempt to have Flynn extradited from France. After he finished his sentence, Flynn returned to Dublin. He subsequently took up residence in Majorca, where he managed a popular Irish bar.

A missile and some Semtex

The breakaway IPLO apparently sought at one stage to acquire a surface-to-air missile through extreme-left contacts on the Continent. It was reported that a friend of Jimmy Brown, leader of one of the IPLO factions, met with a Dutch member of the Red Brigades in 1983, with regard to buying a SAM-7 missile for £7,000. However, nothing came of this attempt.[29] The IPLO went on to become involved in small-scale arms procurement efforts on the Continent in the latter part of the 1980s. An IPLO gunrunning operation came to light in Belgium in dramatic fashion on 9 December 1989, when police decided to check out two men in a car in a remote area of Antwerp docks. It was about 3.30 in the morning, and the police were suspicious. The two-man police patrol asked the two men for their identity papers. One of the men opened fire with a gun, wounding one of the policemen in the arm. The two men escaped. One of them later hijacked a truck at gunpoint, forcing the driver to take him across the border to Amsterdam.

When police searched the car, they found four revolvers, 500 rounds of ammunition and an Irish customs stamp. Police believed the men were planning to smuggle the arms to Ireland on board a ship. Two days after the shooting incident, Anthony Kerr (twenty-seven) was arrested in Amsterdam and extradited to Belgium, where a court sentenced him in December 1990 to four-and-a-half years for shooting and wounding the policeman. Another man was given a jail term in his absence for gunrunning and the robbery of a post office. In September 1991, this man was arrested in Amsterdam and in December a judge ordered his extradition to Belgium.

The INLA continued efforts to smuggle guns into Ireland from the Continent, using the car ferries that ply the routes between French and Irish ports. In September 1990, for instance, customs officers at Ringaskiddy port in County Cork discovered eight assault rifles and 1,000 rounds of ammunition in a camper van that had arrived on a ferry from Roscoff, Brittany. Belfast-born Gerry Burns (thirty-four), who had been living in Dublin, got six years on pleading guilty to charges arising out of the affair, when he appeared in the Special Criminal Court the following month. Burns had a conviction from 1984, when he got a three-year suspended sentence for possession of drugs. He was in trouble again in 2001, when he got five years for illegal possession of arms – two sawn-off shotguns, a revolver, 109 shotgun cartridges and five rounds of revolver ammunition.

During the earlier part of the 1990s, the INLA remained in the market for commercial explosives. Two members of the INLA were arrested and later given heavy prison sentences for trying to steal Gelemex explosives and detonators from a quarry near Wells, Somerset, in 1993. The operation was blown through information given to the British security service, MI5, by an informant, Patrick Daly, who had infiltrated the INLA.

According to evidence given in court, Daly was helped by MI5 to set up a new life under a different name at an undisclosed location. The court also heard that the operation was masterminded by the then chief of staff of the INLA, Hugh Torney.

Torney appears to have been particularly interested in supplies of plastic explosive, especially Semtex. In 1994, he is said to have travelled to Stuttgart, Germany, and then to the Czech city of Pilsen, to secure a quantity of Semtex, which is manufactured in the Czech Republic. 'Cueball' Torney, so called because his favourite weapon in prison is said to have been a pool ball inside two socks, was accompanied in Pilsen by two INLA colleagues. One was a German who, like his fellow-countryman Rudolf Raabe, had joined the INLA. The German came to the INLA through Revolutionary Cells circles in Germany. He had spent some time in Ireland, and attended a high-level INLA meeting at a house in the Muirhevnamore housing estate in Dundalk, just south of the Border in County Louth, prior to the trip to the Continent in his quest for explosives. Among those present were Torney and another senior INLA figure, Gino Gallagher.

The tall, taciturn German was taking his life in his hands entering into the inner councils of the INLA for, according to an extraordinary account that emerged in 2001, he was, in fact, an officer of the German intelligence service, the Bundesamt fur Verfassungsschutz (BfV), or Federal Office for the Protection of the Constitution.[30] His mission was to identify explosives smuggling routes and to close them down.

In Pilsen, Torney and his friends met up with another paramilitary, and a quantity of Semtex was procured from a Czech contact. The German's role was to provide a 'safe house' for the explosives in Germany. It was to be in Schwabisch Hall, a small town forty miles northeast of Stuttgart. However, for unexplained reasons, his BfV bosses decided not to provide such a house. Since there was no place available to hide the Semtex, the paramilitary whom the party met in Pilsen decided to smuggle the explosives back to Ireland himself. It is unclear what happened the Semtex – it may have got through safely.

The German agent was said to have been furious. Torney and his INLA colleague were stopped by police at the main railway station in Stuttgart on their way back to Ireland on 10 August. As they were not in possession of explosives, and there was no hard evidence against them, they were freed after questioning and allowed to go on their way. In November 1994, according to the account, the German agent was invited for talks in London by MI5 and asked to take part in a similar operation, but he turned down the offer.

A noticeable characteristic of the INLA is that over the years it has attracted not just revolutionaries, but individuals inclined towards criminality. For instance, it has been widely reported that two major Irish drug traffickers operating on the Continent are former members of the INLA. One of these men, Tommy 'The Zombie' Savage, who had been living in Amsterdam, was jailed for five years in Athens in March 2006, on charges related to an attempt to smuggle four tonnes of cannabis into Greece in 1997. Savage (fifty-five), who had served nine years in Portlaoise prison for armed robbery, insisted he was innocent and pledged to appeal.

The breakaway IPLO funded some of its activities through the drugs trade. During the 1990s, members of the INLA in Dublin forged links with the drugs gang headed by the crime boss John Gilligan. Gilligan, a career criminal, was suspected of giving the order for the assassination in 1996 of investigative journalist Veronica Guerin. He was eventually cleared of the murder, but was jailed in March 2001 for twenty-eight years for drug dealing – later reduced on appeal by eight years. The INLA connection with the Gilligan gang was apparently to prove useful from the point of view of arms procurement. Gilligan's people imported not just huge quantities of cannabis into Ireland, but also firearms, such as Ingram MAC-10 sub-machine guns and assault rifles. Some of these weapons are said to have been 'donated' to the INLA.[31]

The INLA did not immediately follow suit when the Provisional IRA called a cease-fire in 1994. However, under Chief of Staff Hugh Torney, the organisation operated a *de facto* suspension of violence. In May 1995, Torney and three others were arrested in possession of a cache of weapons near Balbriggan, County Dublin. The arms seized, found in a hold-all bag and the false compartment of a van, included two FN FAL rifles, two AK-47 rifles, two US-made M3 sub-machine guns and twenty 9mm Browning pistols.

When the men appeared in the Special Criminal Court, Torney, in effect, declared an unconditional cease-fire. A statement from Torney and the other defendants was read by a lawyer on their behalf. They claimed that they had been able to influence the INLA to declare a cease-fire in July 1994. Another INLA leader, Gino Gallagher, and his followers declared the cease-fire 'illegal' and they expelled Torney, although some senior figures in the INLA backed him. Gallagher took over as chief of staff, but he was dead within eight months, shot in January 1996, allegedly on Torney's orders.

Yet another feud followed. Torney was shot dead by Gallagher's associates in a drive-by shooting in Lurgan the following September. By the time this 1996 feud came to an end, six lives had been lost. One of the victims was nine-year-old Barbara McAlorum, shot dead as she played in her Belfast home. (The real target was probably her older brother Kevin, who was associated with the Torney group. Thirty-one-year-old Kevin McAlorum was to be shot dead in 2004.) Gallagher's people emerged as the victors in the feud, and the organisation called a cease-fire in 1998. Individuals associated with the INLA continued to engage in intermittent violence, but the worst of the bloodletting was over.

It is difficult to estimate how much war materiel the INLA has left in its armoury. Security forces in the Irish Republic and Northern Ireland have made seizures of INLA arms over the years, but it is unclear how much materiel was brought into the country during the years of INLA gunrunning. A further complication is that some materiel was taken by breakaway factions, or seized by the IRA. One could speculate that the INLA has a range of handguns of various makes; some assault rifles, mainly AK-47s, and a small number of sub-machine guns, mainly Uzis and Scorpions. The organisation may have some Semtex explosive, and it would have the capability to produce home-made explosive. Certainly, the arsenal is far smaller than that assembled by the Provisionals.

The INLA, whose jailed members were given early release under the Good Friday Agreement, has given no indication that it plans to decommission its weapons. Nevertheless, at the time of writing, there is no sign of the organisation returning to 'armed struggle'.

CHAPTER 13

Loyalist Bombers and Gunrunners

From a distance it sounded like a large rock being dropped on an old-fashioned corrugated iron roof. The ominous, dull 'boom' came echoing across the city, followed soon after by two more 'booms'. I had heard sounds like this before, in Belfast during the Troubles, and during rock-blasting operations in the Wicklow Mountains of my childhood. Very quickly, people's worst fears were confirmed – bombs had gone off in Dublin city centre. It was 17 May 1974, and one of the worst atrocities of the Troubles had just taken place.

It is the instinct of most citizens to move away from trouble, but a reporter's instinct is to go chasing it. I drove into the city centre and saw the devastation wrought by the bombers. Most of the casualties had been taken away by the time I reached the scenes of slaughter. A total of twenty-six people had died when three car bombs had gone off in the busy streets. The city was in shock. It later emerged that another car bomb had gone off in the border town of Monaghan, killing seven.

On Parnell Street in Dublin's north inner city, where one of the bombs had exploded, crowds of people were gazing in shocked silence at the pub and other buildings that had been wrecked by the blast. I drove on down O'Connell Street, to the sound of ambulance sirens wailing. The city's main thoroughfare was eerily free of traffic jams, as frightened motorists gave the city centre a wide berth. I quickly reached another of the bomb locations, South Leinster Street, beside Trinity College. Cars were wrecked and the street littered with glass. The last casualty, a young woman, was being helped into an ambulance – one of the walking wounded.

I got a glimpse into the sectarian passions that can be aroused by an atrocity like this. A prosperous-looking middle-aged man in a well-cut business suit was observing the destruction. He had the appearance of a well-heeled accountant or a captain of industry. He turned to me. 'Do you know what?' he said. 'We should go up there, clear all those f***ers out and send them back to Scotland where they came from.' In one citizen at least, the bombers had managed to stir up extreme, primitive 'ethnic cleansing' emotions.

Nobody was ever brought to book for the slaughter of thirty-three people, a matter that causes ongoing distress to the families of the victims. There has been much speculation about these well-planned bomb attacks. Where did the loyalists get the explosives? Did they have enough expertise to carry out such an attack off their own bat at this period? Could the culprits have had help from the North's security forces, either rogue elements or senior figures acting unofficially?

An inquiry was carried out into the atrocities by Mr Justice Henry Barron on behalf of an Irish parliamentary committee, the Joint Committee on Justice, Equality, Defence and Women's Rights. In an interim report in December 2003, Judge Barron found that the Dublin and Monaghan bombings were carried out by two groups of loyalist paramilitaries, one based in Belfast and the other in the area around Portadown/Lurgan. Most, though not all of those involved were members of the Ulster Volunteer Force (UVF), the judge found. He believed it was likely that the bombings were conceived and planned in Belfast, with the mid-Ulster element providing operational assistance.

While Judge Barron did not rule out the involvement of individual members of the security forces in Northern Ireland, he stated that this did not mean that the bombings were officially or unofficially State-sanctioned. He found there was no proof of collusion between the perpetrators and the authorities in Northern Ireland. The judge stated: 'The loyalist groups who carried out the bombings in Dublin were capable of doing so without help from any section of the security forces in Northern Ireland, though this does not rule out the involvement of individual RUC, Ulster Defence Regiment (UDR) or British Army members. The Monaghan bombing in particular bears all the hallmarks of a standard loyalist operation and required no assistance.'

The judge found that while the forensic evidence was inconclusive, the consensus was that there were just two possibilities for the make-up of the Dublin bombs:

(1) That they consisted entirely of commercial explosive; or

(2) That they were made from improvised ANFO explosive, with an unknown amount of commercial explosive added to ensure detonation. (ANFO is a home-made explosive based on a combination of Ammonium Nitrate, which usually came from commercial fertilisers, and fuel oil.)

In relation to the first possibility, Judge Barron said the question arose as to whether loyalist groups could have acquired that much commercial explosive. Expert opinion agreed that the UVF and the Ulster Defence Association (UDA) almost never used bombs made entirely from commercial explosive, and certainly not bombs of the size used in the Dublin attack. However, Judge Barron reckoned that it did not seem beyond the bounds of possibility that a large quantity of explosive could have been acquired through sources in Scotland, England or Canada – where seizures of loyalist arms and explosives were made in the months surrounding the bombings. As to the second possibility, the UVF and UDA were known to have used ANFO, though not to the same extent as the Provisional IRA.

The judge focused in particular on the fact that UVF member William 'Billy' Fulton was arrested in Scotland in June 1974, with explosives hidden in his car. The loyalist, who was suspected of involvement in the Monaghan bombing, was jailed for carrying explosives and died in 1989. The discovery of explosives in Fulton's car further suggested to Judge Barron that sources of supply were available to loyalist extremists without the need for assistance from elements of the security forces.[1] According to a source close to the UVF and interviewed by the Barron Inquiry, the UVF at that time were obtaining small amounts of commercial explosive from mining areas in Great Britain. These were used as booster charges for improvised explosives.

Loyalist bomb attacks in the Republic during the Troubles went back as far as 1969. In that year, the UVF, which developed a particular expertise in bomb-making, set about mounting a bomb attack on an electricity station in Ballyshannon, County Donegal. A UVF man, Thomas McDowell, was critically injured when he was hit by a surge of electricity. Gardaí did not know if he was a loyalist or republican bomber, and called a priest who, in good faith, anointed him in accordance with the last rites of the Catholic Church. For a man who reportedly followed the fundamentalist anti-Rome creed of Ian Paisley's Free Presbyterian Church, this must have been the final indignity. McDowell died after three days.

These early bomb attacks were mostly aimed at installations or symbolic targets. As the UVF campaign gathered momentum, ordinary Catholic members of the public were targeted. The Dublin bombings of 1974 marked a vicious escalation in the bombing campaign in the Republic, and were clearly designed to kill as many civilians as possible.

Just a few weeks before the Dublin bomb attacks, in a separate development, there was a seizure of arms and detonators in the southern English port of Southampton. Three men were arrested after customs and police found the consignment, which included a dozen firearms and ammunition, in a container landed by ship on 26 March. The finding of the detonators was a sinister reminder that loyalists were still very much involved in the procurement and importation of the means to carry out bomb attacks. This particular find was associated with the UDA, more particularly a group of UDA supporters in Leeds, one of whom had been on the local city council. An important aspect of the arms cache was its origin. The investigation showed that it had been shipped from Canada, via New York. Canada, with its extensive mining industry, was potentially an important source of explosives and detonators.

The following December, the three UDA men who had been arrested in connection with the find were given heavy jail sentences, ranging from five to ten years, at Winchester Crown Court. In June 1975, a fourth man was jailed for ten years for conspiracy to contravene sections of the Firearms and Explosives Substances Act, and for conspiracy to contravene the Firearms Act. All those jailed had addresses in Leeds or Liverpool.

Canada was to become an important source of arms for the loyalists. But it was also clear that 'mainland' UK, especially Scotland, was another important source of war materiel. Explosives stolen from mines and, possibly, quarries became an important element in the loyalists' campaign of violence. Not all attempts to smuggle explosives from or via Scotland were successful. In 1973, for instance, twenty sticks of gelignite were found hidden in the cistern of a toilet at a railway station in Stranraer, Scotland. It was thought likely that a loyalist was planning to pick up the explosives and smuggle them across on the ferry from Stranraer to Larne, Northern Ireland. One theory was that the explosives were destined for the UVF, which was seen as more adept at bomb-making than the UDA. Also in 1973, fifty sticks of gelignite were seized by police at a house in Drongan, Ayrshire, Scotland. It was believed that these explosives were also destined for the UVF. The traffic continued into the late 1970s and beyond – in 1978, for instance, 263 sticks of gelignite were discovered on a lorry outside Stranraer.

Police investigating the Southampton find passed on information to police in Canada, who mounted their own investigation. On 8 April 1974, Canadian police carried out raids on the Toronto homes of two men. One was from the Richmond Hill area, and the other, an unemployed immigrant, lived at Etobicoke. Arms seized included nine M-1 carbines, thirteen Sten guns, sixty-six Sten gun ammunition clips and 2,000 rounds of ammunition. Found along with the arms were items of UDA literature and mementoes. It was noted that the suspect who lived at Etobicoke had displayed on a wall a framed UDA crest with the familiar loyalist slogan: 'We shall never forsake the blue skies of Ulster, for the grey mists of an Irish Republic.'

The arms and ammunition were all of types used during the Second World War. The M-1 carbines could be bought legally in Canada. Sten guns were supposed to be altered so they could not be fired before a collector could obtain one. It emerged that Scotland Yard had found the fingerprints of the two men on household articles also found in the crates at Southampton. The two men were charged with conspiring to export arms without a permit. They appeared in court the following November and, in an unexpected development, pleaded guilty to the charges.

Looking for guns

At the beginning of the Troubles, loyalist paramilitaries had access to some handguns, and also legally held weapons such as shotguns. They had some obsolete Mauser rifles that had been imported in 1914 by a previous generation of loyalists, and they had access to some weapons stolen from the security forces. Armouries of the largely part-time force, the UDR, became a favourite target. Some thefts were carried out by loyalists who had joined the UDR. Support groups sprang up in 'mainland' UK and some weapons also arrived through these connections. While loyalist paramilitaries were drawn mainly from the working class, with little or no connection to the gentry, it has been claimed that some aristocrats provided funding for weapons.[2]

The arms black market in Britain was tapped, and small quantities of weapons came from extreme right-wing elements. The loyalist paramilitary groups also looked outside the UK to procure arms such as assault rifles and pistols, and also explosives. The Middle East and Eastern Europe were to figure in arms deals. Members of the UVF travelled to Lebanon in 1977 to seek to buy arms and explosives from the right-wing Christian militia, the Phalange, but no arms deal resulted.[3] In the Irish Republic in 1969, the Department of Defence cancelled plans to sell off surplus rifles from Army stocks, for fear that they might end up in the control of the UVF or some related organisation.[4]

Loyalists manufactured their own sub-machine guns (SMGs), using skills developed in the North's engineering industry, which was traditionally dominated by the Protestant community. The loyalists never moved into the area of improvised mortars, which remained a speciality of the Provisionals. For the loyalists, producing their own SMGs had a certain logic. The weapons were cheap and easy to produce, and were not subject to the vagaries and dangers of smuggling and theft as means of procurement.

I well recall an incident in the early 1970s that underlined the advances made by loyalists in producing sub-machine guns. I was working in the Belfast office of the *Irish Press* at the time, and the newspaper's Northern Editor was the colourful Vincent Browne, destined to become one of the best-known journalists in Ireland. Browne got his hands on a home-made loyalist sub-machine gun, but unfortunately was arrested by the Special Branch while in possession of the weapon at Glengall Street, Belfast, on 13 September 1971. We had to alert the office in Dublin to arrange legal representation for him. The intrepid Browne was simply pursuing a story in his own inimitable way, but was charged with illegal possession of a firearm and given bail. Ultimately the authorities recognised that there was no sinister purpose behind his possession of the weapon, and the larger-than-life journalist was allowed to walk free.

In the late 1980s, loyalists were still turning out home-made sub-machine guns. In September 1988, police raided a small engineering works at Ballynahinch, County Down, and discovered thirty Sten-type weapons. In March 1990, a forty-seven-year-old man was convicted of various charges to do with the manufacture of the weapons. A prosecution lawyer claimed in court that the accused man made a statement to police saying that he began making Sten guns for loyalists in 1972. Another loyalist arms factory was uncovered in a police raid in September 1989 on a workshop at Donaghadee, County Down. In October the following year, a former weapons trainer with the Royal Irish Rangers was jailed for six years, after a court heard that he had been assembling SMGs for the UDA. The court was told that parts for the guns had been made covertly by individuals working at Shorts aircraft factory. In April 1995, police raided a house in Holywood, County Down, and found a small but sophisticated plant for the manufacture of Uzi-type SMGs. Police seized parts sufficient to make 100 Uzi-type weapons.

One of the first major trials to do with an alleged loyalist attempt to procure arms outside of Northern Ireland occurred in 1972. In April that year a prominent loyalist was arrested in London on suspicion of involvement in a major arms deal. He was Charles Harding Smith, a founder of the Woodvale Defence Association (WDA), which merged with the UDA. He had the role of arms-buyer for the UDA, which was developing into a mass movement in response to the armed campaign by republicans.

Earlier in the year, Harding Smith had made contact with a Belfast businessman, who put him in touch with an intermediary, who in turn put the paramilitary boss in touch with a Scots arms dealer. The 'dealer' was, in fact, a Special Branch officer. As a result of these contacts, the Belfast businessman and three WDA men had talks in a room at the Hilton Hotel,

London, with the 'dealer' and his colleague – another undercover Special Branch man. The conversation was secretly taped, and the three WDA men were arrested. One of them was a man called John White, later to become prominent in loyalist political circles.

Oddly, Harding Smith had not gone to the hotel, but he went to the Metropolitan Police HQ later that evening to inquire about his three friends who had been detained – and for his pains was promptly arrested himself. When the case went to trial in December, the prosecution claimed that the UDA had a £350,000 fund for the purchase of arms. However, there was insufficient proof to stand up a charge of conspiracy and the case against Harding Smith and his colleagues collapsed. During his turbulent paramilitary career, Harding Smith survived at least two assassination attempts, and died of natural causes after wisely moving to England.

Following his acquittal on the arms charges, Harding Smith's co-accused, John White, went on to become one of the most notorious loyalist killers of the Troubles. He was jailed for life for the murder, in June 1973, of Senator Paddy Wilson of the SDLP and his friend Ms Irene Andrews. Mr Wilson was a friendly, outgoing man whom I remember from the early 1970s as a regular at McGlade's pub, on Donegall Street in central Belfast. The upstairs lounge was a vibrant meeting place for local and international media, and for movers and shakers of all types, many of whom signed their names in the pub's renowned visitors' book. The Senator and Ms Andrews were, in fact, abducted outside the pub. These two entirely innocent individuals had no connection to paramilitary violence. Ms Andrews, a Protestant, was said to have a keen interest in that most harmless of pursuits, ballroom dancing. They were singled out because he was a Catholic, and they were murdered in an horrific, frenzied knife attack. Senator Wilson was stabbed thirty-two times, Ms Andrews, nineteen.[5] Released after fourteen years in prison, White went on to become chairman of the Ulster Democratic Party, the political wing of the UDA. He also became a close associate of the notorious loyalist paramilitary, Johnny 'Mad Dog' Adair.

There were other court cases in England in the early 1970s as the authorities closed in on loyalist attempts to procure arms. Some of these attempts were amateurish and doomed from the start. In April 1973, four supporters of the UDA, with addresses in Northern Ireland, were convicted at the Central Criminal Court in London of trying to induce a gunsmith to provide them with arms for the loyalist cause. The court heard that one of the men approached Mr A, a gunsmith's assistant, in October 1971, seeking rifles 'under the counter'. Special Branch was promptly informed and the suspects were arrested during subsequent attempts to finalise a deal. They were all middle-class men, pillars of society. Three were found guilty of inciting a London gunsmith to provide them with Bren guns, rifles, sub-machine guns and pistols. A fourth man was found guilty of a similar charge in relation to a quantity of rifles and other fire-arms. Judge Waller said he realised that tremendous emotions must have been involved to make men of good character contemplate illegal activity of this kind, and as a result his duty to impose sentences was a painful one. Two of the men got two years; another got twelve months and a fourth, six months. A fifth man was acquitted.

Loyalist paramilitary groups in Northern Ireland had a range of contacts in Scotland who were willing to help with arms procurement. It appears that one of the early supporters of the loyalist cause was Glasgow crime boss Arthur Thompson. Media reports in the years following his death from a heart attack in 1993 claimed that he ran arms to the UDA in the early 1970s, and also became an informant for the British security service MI5.[6] Thompson, infamous crime godfather of the east end of Glasgow, is claimed to have supplied not only arms but counterfeit currency to loyalist paramilitaries. Journalist Reg McKay, in a book about the crime boss, has described how Thompson, who was reputed to have had links with the notorious London villains the Kray twins, smuggled boxes of arms and ammunition to the UDA, hidden under the floors of trucks travelling to Northern Ireland.[7] The arms were said to have been Second World War vintage, or older, including sub-machine guns and .303 rifles. According to McKay, MI5 found out about Thompson's links to the UDA, visited him while he was being held in prison, put pressure on him, and recruited him as an informant.

The writer also told how the IRA, through an informant, found out about Thompson's gunrunning to the loyalists, and sent a gunman to Glasgow to kill him. The would-be assassin was arrested in connection with alleged offences in Ireland before he could attack Thompson. It was also claimed that in the early 1980s the crime boss's son, Arthur Thompson junior, assembled handguns and rifles for transfer to the UDA. The young man, nicknamed 'Fatboy', was shot dead in a gangland feud in Glasgow in 1991.

To provide back-up to the UDA, a UDA Brigade was set up in Scotland, led by a mercurial Edinburgh pub bouncer called Roddy McDonald, who gloried in the title of 'Supreme Commander'. Discretion was not McDonald's strong point. In September 1976, he announced his intention of buying arms – on television. He told an interviewer: 'We will buy arms from anybody, so if there's a good priest who's got any explosives in the chapel, we will definitely buy them. No danger. We will buy anything from anybody if it will help our cause.' In referring to the 'good priest', McDonald was having a go at the Catholic Church. The Church in Scotland had been very embarrassed indeed after an arms find in a presbytery in Glasgow, shortly after an Irish-born priest had moved to Ireland.

About a year after the television interview, an emotionally disturbed young man, Ross Sutherland (eighteen), who was employed in a gun shop, was working out an arms deal with McDonald. What Sutherland did not tell the loyalist boss was that he planned to kill the owner of the gun shop. Sutherland handed over twelve rifles to McDonald and his friends in return for a promise that he would be paid £2,000. Sutherland, however, attracted the unwanted attention of the police by taking a handgun and shooting his employer through the head. He later received a life sentence for murder. During his trial, he complained dolefully that he had been double-crossed by the UDA – he never got the £2,000 he was promised for the guns.

McDonald and a number of his cohorts went on trial at Glasgow High Court in June 1978, charged with soliciting people to hand over weapons for use in terrorism. McDonald got eight years. The following January, twenty-nine UDA men were sentenced for paramilitary activities. Shortly afterwards, the organisation in Belfast took delivery of ten assault rifles and 1,000 rounds of ammunition, which had come from the 'mainland', via Scotland. The arms were seized in an RUC swoop. The UDA subsequently shot dead one of its own members, Artie Bettice, who had been accused of betraying the shipment.

In July 1979, six UDA men received heavy sentences at Perth Crown Court – one getting sixteen years for conspiracy to support a terrorist organisation by procuring and making arms for terrorist purposes.

The UVF also came under pressure from the authorities in Scotland. In June 1979, nine members of the organisation received heavy sentences at the High Court in Glasgow for terrorist activity. During the case, a miner told how he stole thirty sticks of gelignite from a coal pit in East Lothian for the organisation.

In 1981, police in Scotland struck another blow against the UVF, breaking up a ring that was smuggling arms to Northern Ireland. Arms were being sent from Canada, for transfer via Scotland to Northern Ireland. The weapons were coming from a UVF support group in Toronto headed by a Canadian called Bill Taylor, who had begun running arms for the UVF about 1980. The guns were sent by post, enclosed in lead to prevent them being spotted by X-ray security equipment.

The pipeline was disrupted when parcels containing arms were found at Wellington Street Post Office in Glasgow, in April 1981. Nine men were ultimately found guilty. The courts also heard of how an Englishman supplied over sixty-three pounds of the weedkiller sodium chlorate to a UVF member in Glasgow for transfer to Belfast, where it would be used in the manufacture of explosives.

The UVF gunrunner who hated the 'communist' IRA

Bill Taylor, a Canadian citizen, was to become one of the most significant gunrunners in the history of the UVF. After the break-up by police in 1974 of the comparatively modest gunrunning operation that had been organised by two Toronto-based loyalist sympathisers, there was no indication of any significant loyalist gunrunning from Canada up to the end of that decade. Bill Taylor was to change all that.

A gun enthusiast, Taylor regularly visited gun fairs in Canada and the US, and was a member of one of North America's private militias. He became friendly with a number of expatriates from Ulster and became a convert to the loyalist cause, which he saw as a bulwark against the 'communist' IRA. One of these expatriates put him in touch with the UVF, and a number of Belfast UVF men travelled to Canada to investigate arms importation possibilities. One of them, John Bingham, handed over money to Taylor for arms purchases. An arms pipeline was set up, whereby arms were shipped to Northern Ireland, via the UK. After the Glasgow pipeline was disrupted in the early 1980s, the arms were sent via Liverpool, hidden inside hollowed-out tractor engines. Once again, the materiel was covered with lead sheeting to prevent detection by X-ray equipment. Not long after helping to set up the pipeline, Bingham was shot dead at his home in Bally-sillan Crescent, Belfast, by the IRA, who blamed Bingham and the Ballysillan UVF for the murders of a number of Catholics.

In his gunrunning activities, Taylor had help from a number of individuals. One was Albert Watt, who had emigrated from Northern Ireland to Canada at the start of the Troubles. Another was a man of Catholic background who had emigrated from Manchester. He was a former officer in the Canadian military reserve, and was repelled by the IRA's tactic of shooting down soldiers in the streets. Like Taylor, he was a gun enthusiast.

Taylor had developed considerable skills as a gunsmith, and was able to convert semi-automatic weapons, which were available at gun fairs, to fully automatic. According to one estimate, during his gunrunning years Taylor smuggled hundreds of rifles and sub-machine guns and thousands of rounds of ammunition to Ulster.[8] Among the items he supplied were rapid-fire Ingram MAC-10 machine pistols, which the paramilitaries were particularly pleased to get. Powerful Magnum revolvers were also sent – these were very useful assassination tools.

Taylor's secret work for the UVF came to a sudden end when members of the Royal Canadian Mounted Police, accompanied by local police, raided his Toronto home on Christmas Day 1986. Taylor had a tangled love life, and this had proven his downfall. An embittered girlfriend had tipped off the police about his gunrunning activities. She would be identified in subsequent court hearings only as 'Linda'. Police discovered a formidable arsenal of weapons when they searched Taylor's house, on Forty-first Street in the Etobicoke district, and his 'summer residence' at East Sutton, Ontario. The haul included rifles and automatic pistols, five machine guns, sixteen sub-machine guns, ammunition, silencers, two canisters of tear gas and one of mace. It emerged that the weapons had been bought at gun shows in the US and smuggled into Canada.

The investigation extended to the UK, and Trevor Cubbon, director of a Liverpool road haulage firm was arrested. Albert Watt (forty-four), whose home address was in Collingwood, Ontario, and who worked as a Toronto school caretaker, was picked up by police in his native Belfast in January 1987, and sent to Liverpool for further questioning. Cubbon and Watt appeared in court in Liverpool in connection with the plot to smuggle arms, and in December 1987 both men were sent to jail for four years.

Taylor himself, a forty-one-year-old mechanic, was sentenced to three-and-a-half years in prison in January 1990, when he pleaded guilty to fourteen arms-related charges. The court heard that he bought the arms at gun shows in North America, hid them in a dummy car fuel tank, and then took them to his house or to his workplace, a heavy automotive workshop in Etobicoke.

There was further punishment in store for Taylor. After serving his sentence in Canada, he was extradited to the UK in July 1992. The following October he pleaded guilty at Liverpool Crown Court to conspiring to possess firearms with intent to endanger life. He was sentenced to a year in jail. On release he returned home to Canada, his gunrunning days very definitely over. Having spent much of his adult life being fascinated by guns, it was ironic that he was to lose his life by a gun. He was shot dead in 1995 at an apartment in the Toronto area, during a drunken row. Taylor, a divorced father of two, was shot twice in the face, suffering wounds to the eye and mouth. A friend of Taylor's was arrested in a nearby tavern shortly after the shooting, and charged with second-degree murder.

Other loyalist weapons sources

It has been reported that the UVF took delivery of a small consignment of Israeli-made Uzi sub-machine guns from a source in the England in 1983. The details are given in a book by the author Martin Dillon.[9] The author relates a story told to him by a UVF commander, who said that he was approached by a man, who appeared to be English, on behalf of a third party, who promised a consignment of Uzi sub-machine guns in return for the murder of three young Middle Eastern men who were studying in Belfast. The students were not involved in terrorism, but the third party wanted them blown up at their home so as to give the impression that they were making a bomb.

The UVF commander asked that several Uzis be supplied in advance and this was done. The commander asked the loyalist gunman Michael Stone to take on the job of killing the students, but after checking out the assignment, Stone said he would not do it, as it did not feel right. There was speculation that the Israeli intelligence service Mossad might have been behind the approach. Stone was later to win notoriety in

1988, after he staged a solo gun and grenade attack on a republican funeral in Belfast, murdering three people.

In most cases, loyalist attempts to procure small quantities of weaponry on the black market in 'mainland' UK focused on pistols and rifles. However, in the latter part of the 1980s, police uncovered what they believed was a plot to supply fourteen M-72 anti-tank rocket launchers, and shells, to the UDA. In June 1987 there was a sequel to this investigation, when four men were jailed at Bristol Crown Court for trading in stolen anti-tank rockets. Police believed the rockets were to have been sent to Scotland, and would have fallen into the hands of the UDA. Sent to prison were two British Army corporals, who had stolen the weapons from stores at Warminster, and two militaria dealers.

The South African connection

Former arms dealer Douglas Bernhardt does not really want to talk these days about the time he helped to set up a major arms transaction for loyalists from Northern Ireland. He obviously takes the view that it was a long time ago, the affair brought him a lot of trouble, and he has paid his debt. Bernhardt has moved on since his involvement sparked off an international incident. In an email, he told me, 'I'm afraid that I will be unable to help you with your research.' He added graciously, 'Good luck with the work.'

Bernhardt was one of those international arms dealers for whom South Africa opened up opportunities in the late 1970s and early 1980s. The South African State, because of its apartheid policies, became subject to a mandatory United Nations arms embargo in 1977. In order to get around the boycott, the South African State arms company, Armscor, stepped up its own domestic arms production, and also sought to covertly procure weaponry and arms technology from abroad. Some of this procurement or attempted procurement was carried out through international arms dealers, and Bernhardt was one of these.

Bernhardt originally worked in the motor trade in London, importing expensive American cars for sale to clients in Britain and the Arab world. Some of the limousines, destined for jittery, well-heeled customers in some of the more unstable areas of the Middle East, needed to be armour-plated.

It was but a short step from providing armoured limos to supplying other means of self defence – by the early 1980s, Bernhardt was operating as a bona fide international arms dealer. He founded a company called Field Arms Ltd., doing much of his business in the Arab world, especially the Gulf region.

A flamboyant character with a taste for well-tailored suits and expensive cars, Bernhardt ran his company from a suite of offices at Tilney Street, Mayfair, one of the more prestigious addresses in London. He dealt with some of the top arms companies in Britain and recruited a number of reputable former British Army officers as consultants. However, the company went into receivership in 1986, and Berhhardt swapped his home in Sussex for a dwelling in France, close by the border with Switzerland and within commuting distance of Geneva. He continued to work in the international arms trade, and his business with Armscor was the connection that brought him into contact with Ulster loyalists.

Various sources have indicated that the saga began around 1985, when representatives of the UDA and the UVF came together to discuss co-operation on arms procurement. There was liaison with an Ulsterman who had emigrated to South Africa and become involved in the arms business there. He knew Bernhardt well. It is understood that the Ulsterman said he could supply arms, although he was only interested in a big deal, worth a quarter of a million pounds or more. He suggested an alternative – apart from cash, he would also be interested in getting missile parts or plans. He knew that Armscor, which was working to evade the UN arms embargo, would be greatly interested in procuring missiles, missile parts or indeed blueprints.

Later, representatives of a new loyalist group, Ulster Resistance (UR), joined with the other loyalist organisations in the moves to acquire arms. UR had been launched in November 1986 at a mass rally in Belfast, with the aim of taking action 'as and when required' to defeat the Anglo-Irish Agreement, which loyalists saw as giving the Irish government unacceptable influence over Northern Irish affairs. Dr Ian Paisley, leader of the hard-line Democratic Unionist Party, and his deputy, Peter Robinson, were both present at the UR launch. However, these politicians severed their links with the UR when some elements within the organisation became involved in illegal activities.

The loyalists decided to send one of their number to South Africa to check out what might be on offer in the way of military equipment. This was Brian Nelson, the UDA's intelligence co-ordinator. He was a former soldier and there was a secret side to his career – he was an extremely important undercover agent for British military intelligence. In 1985 Nelson walked in off the street and offered his services to the British Army as an informant. He had served in the Black Watch regiment of the army and had already notched up a terrorist conviction. Nevertheless, the military took him on as an agent, being run by the army's Force Research Unit (FRU).

Nelson became a key target of the Stevens inquiry, set up to investigate collusion between elements in the security forces and loyalist paramilitaries. He was eventually to be jailed for ten years in 1992 for terrorist offences, having pleaded guilty to five counts of conspiracy to murder. He was suspected of helping loyalists target the Belfast solicitor Pat Finucane, who was shot dead in his home in front of his family, in February 1989.[10]

Judge Peter Cory, who investigated the Finucane murder, traced the main features of Nelson's undercover career for his report, issued in 2004. In regard to the moves by Nelson to acquire arms in South Africa, the Cory report stated: 'The Army appears to have at least encouraged Nelson in his attempt to purchase arms in South Africa for the UDA. Nelson certainly went to South Africa in 1985 to meet an arms dealer. His expenses were paid by FRU. The Army appears to have been committed to facilitating Nelson's acquisition of weapons, with the intention that they would be intercepted at some point en route to Northern Ireland.

'Whether the transaction was consummated remains an open question, although, in September 1985, Nelson reported to his handlers that the deal fell through due to the inability of the UDA to raise the necessary funds for the purchase. The evidence with regard to the completion of the arms transaction is frail and contradictory. In any event, it is not necessary to go into any great detail with regard to the result. I mention the proposed transaction simply as an indication of the trust that had been reposed in Nelson by FRU.'

According to one report, the South Africans were suspicious of Nelson, and arranged for a former Northern Ireland loyalist, who was working for the security branch of the South African police, to meet him and check him out.[11] The former loyalist, who was called Billy, met Nelson at his hotel. The UDA man told Billy that he had been mugged earlier that day. Billy later confided that he was told by his controller that the 'muggers' were, in fact, black undercover members of the police security branch, who staged the 'robbery' in order to grab tapes and diaries that Nelson had on him, as part of the process of checking him out.[12]

Billy had been associated with the shadowy Tara loyalist paramilitary group founded by William McGrath, later to become notorious as a paedophile.[13] Billy was instructed to keep up the contacts with Nelson. He told how, the following day, Nelson was taken to a gun shop, which was a front for Armscor, and eventually taken to a secret underground store and shown a selection of weapons. According to Billy, after further investigations the South Africans concluded that Nelson was working for the British, and decided to cut off contacts with the UDA.

British military intelligence were aware from the start, through Nelson, that the loyalists were looking for arms from contacts in South Africa. There have been allegations in the nationalist community that when a large consignment of arms was eventually shipped into Northern Ireland, the British must have known about it, and turned a blind eye to the landing of the weapons. However, Billy's story would suggest that Nelson, and indirectly British intelligence, had been cut out of the loop when the arms deal was eventually clinched, with Ulster Resistance, instead, taking the lead role in negotiating the deal.

Following Nelson's visit to South Africa, the loyalists pressed ahead with moves to acquire a significant consignment of arms. After some unsuccessful efforts to steal missiles or missile parts from the Shorts factory in East Belfast to facilitate an arms deal, loyalist bosses decided to raise the money to purchase arms by means of a major robbery. In June 1987 a raid was carried out on a bank in Portadown, County Armagh, which netted a massive sum, more than £300,000. Some of this money may have ended up in the pockets of paramilitaries. However, it is believed that a sum of £150,000 was made available for an arms consignment.

As was later to emerge in evidence during court hearings in France in 1991, the arms deal was set up with the aid of Bernhardt – he put the loyalists in touch with a Lebanese arms dealer called Joseph Fawzi. A deal was set up with Fawzi at a meeting said to have taken place in Cyprus.

One theory is that the arms involved in the deal had been captured by Israel from Palestinian forces and passed on to the Christian militia, the Lebanese Forces (LF), and that Fawzi acquired them from the LF. The thrifty Israelis have a long tradition of making use of captured weaponry if it is in serviceable condition, by either passing it on to friendly forces or selling it on the open market. Two international arms dealers, Sam Cummings of Interarms and California-based Mike Kokin of Sherwood International, each told me in the 1980s of buying materiel captured by the Israelis on the battlefield. In some cases, inspections of weaponry took place on the battlefield itself.

As regards the rumoured LF connection, I asked the militia's representative in Paris during this period about the story and he scoffed at the idea. 'We need weapons ourselves,' said LF man Antoine Basbous. 'We are trying to get weapons, not give them away!' One theory is that Bernhardt set up the deal for arms from Lebanon as a 'sweetener' for the follow-on deal involving the procurement from the loyalists of missile technology from Northern Ireland, for the benefit of South Africa.

The consignment of arms, which was shipped via Liverpool, arrived in Belfast docks in December 1987, hidden in a cargo of ceramic tiles. It is understood that the arms shipment originated in the harbour of Naquora, southern Lebanon.[14] Ironically, the harbour was a familiar landmark for Irish troops serving with UNIFIL, the peacekeeping force in Lebanon, as it is located just north of the UNIFIL base in Naquora.[15]

The shipment of tiles, with the arms hidden beneath them, was picked up by an unsuspecting haulier at Belfast port and taken to a location in Portadown. The arms consignment consisted of 206 Czechoslovak-made VZ58 assault rifles, ninety-four 9mm Browning pistols, more than 30,000 rounds of ammunition, 450 fragmentation grenades and four RPG-7 grenade launchers with sixty-two grenades. The arms were divided between the three paramilitary groups. The UDA's share of the consignment, minus the RPG-7s, was seized on 8 January 1988, when security forces swooped on a convoy of three cars at Portadown. Three senior UDA men were also arrested.

At the trial of the three men in Belfast Crown Court in October 1988, the consignment of UDA weapons seized was described as the biggest haul of loyalist guns ever uncovered by police. It consisted of sixty-one Czech-made assault rifles, thirty Browning pistols, 150 hand grenades and more than 11,000 rounds of ammunition.[16] Davy Payne, a senior north Belfast UDA commander, was jailed for nineteen years, while his two colleagues, James McCullough and Thomas Aiken, were each jailed for fourteen years.

Just over a month after the Portadown swoop, security forces raided outbuildings at a premises on the Upper Crumlin Road in the northern outskirts of Belfast, and seized another sizeable cache of loyalist weapons, this time belonging to the UVF. The haul included fifty-three rifles and pistols, as well as an RPG-7 rocket launcher and twenty-six warheads. Police sources believed that this was part of the shipment financed in cooperation with the UDA and Ulster Resistance. Loyalist paramilitaries suffered a further setback in November 1988, when the RUC uncovered a number of arms caches in various locations in County Armagh, including one haul that was regarded as a very major find. There was speculation that at least some of these arms came from the shipment financed by the three loyalist groups.

While the security forces succeeded in seizing the UDA's share of the arms consignment, and part of the UVF's share, the Ulster Resistance share seems to have survived almost intact. It was reported that Ulster Resistance later came to an agreement with the UDA and the UVF to share its portion of the arms with these organisations.[17] Security forces believed they seized all four of the RPG-7 rocket launchers that were landed, as well as forty-two of the sixty-two rockets that were supplied. The arms delivered from the Middle East were subsequently used in loyalist attacks, including the 1989 attack by loyalist gunman Michael Stone on a republican funeral, which left three people dead.

Meanwhile, efforts continued to meet the Armscor desire for access to missile technology produced at Shorts in Belfast. As part of the deal, it emerged that a technical officer at the South African embassy in Paris arranged for three loyalists to be trained in South Africa in the firing of the RPG-7. The money being offered to the loyalists appears to have been considerable – it was reported that at one stage £1 million was on the table for a complete missile system or a comprehensive blueprint. The South Africans were said to have offered several million pounds for an actual Starstreak, the most advanced missile being produced by Shorts at that time. The South Africans had an urgent requirement for advanced surface-to-air missiles – their army had suffered reverses in the war in Angola, where it was supporting UNITA rebels in the war against Angolan government forces.

The loyalists set about acquiring missile parts for the potentially lucrative deal with the South Africans. There was said to have been a number of thefts of missile-related parts from Shorts. In October 1988, thieves entered an exhibition area at Shorts' Castlereagh works in East Belfast and stole what was described as 'an item of non-operational training equipment'. Then, on 11 April 1989, thieves managed to steal a dummy Blowpipe missile from a Territorial Army base at Newtownards, County Down.

That same month, Noel Little of Ulster Resistance, and two other men from the group, travelled to Paris to discuss a missile deal with the South Africans. By now, law enforcement agencies were aware of the covert activities of Ulster Resistance. For instance, when Davy Payne was arrested in connection with the arms find, he had Noel Little's phone number written on his hand. British authorities tracked the three men on their way to France. From there, agents of France's security agency, the Direction de la Surveillance du Territoire (DST) took up the surveillance. The DST had already secretly photographed Little on a previous trip to Paris, where he met Bernhardt, as well as the Ulsterman based in South Africa who had originally set up the introduction, and South African diplomats.

DST agents, in the guise of hotel workers, swooped as the three loyalists were meeting at the Hilton with Bernhardt and a South African diplomat. The latter, who was covered by diplomatic immunity, was released. The other four were held for questioning at the offices of the DST. It emerged that the loyalists did not have anything in their possession that could be classified as a weapon – they had with them a cutaway model of a Blowpipe missile. Armscor's agents would have been looking for something more sophisticated and substantial, such as design plans and working parts for the more advanced Javelin and Starstreak missiles, which were being manufactured or under development at Shorts at that time. One theory was that the 'dummy' equipment the loyalists brought with them was to demonstrate that they could deliver the 'real' stuff.

The arrest of the Ulstermen, the arms dealer and the diplomat sparked off an international row. Britain expelled three South African diplomats, as did France. British prime minister Margaret Thatcher was furious. It was said she felt betrayed, not only because Armscor had tried to steal British arms technology, but because the South Africans were associating with a terrorist movement operating in the UK.

As part of a damage-limitation exercise, South African defence minister General Magnus Malan set out his country's stance on the issue in his country's parliament on 3 May 1989. In his remarks, he sought to distance South Africa from the loyalist paramilitaries who had been arrested in Paris. He reiterated that he had ordered an investigation inside Armscor regarding the incident. He explained that in order to neutralise an 'immoral' UN boycott, Armscor considered offers of technology. Armscor, like similar organisations in other countries, worked through arms dealers. In the Paris incident, an agreement was reached with such a dealer, and a diplomat was asked to act as a go-between on behalf of Armscor.

General Malan said that Armscor was not in a position to control associates and contacts of international arms dealers. He emphasised that Armscor did not approach any Irish movement or organisation on its own initiative. When the appointment was made with the arms dealer, it was not known that other persons would be present. The investigation had brought to light that state officials were caught up in matters or activities which did not have the authorisation or approval of the government. Nevertheless, General Malan stated that neither Armscor nor the South African Defence Force had delivered weapons to the Ulster Defence Association or any other organisation in Northern Ireland.

In October 1991, the three Northern Ireland men and their arms dealer contact were given suspended sentences after being convicted by a Paris court of arms trafficking and associating with criminals involved in a terrorist enterprise. Noel Little (forty-one), of Markethill, County Armagh, who was described in court as the main instigator, was given three years and fined 50,000 francs. Another man, from County Down, received two years and a 30,000-franc fine. A third defendant, also from County Down, got one year and was fined 20,000 francs. The arms dealer Douglas Bernhardt (forty-three) got four years and the biggest fine, 100,000 francs. Very little has been heard of Ulster Resistance in recent years, and there have been no indications that the group remained in the covert arms procurement business.

The Polish connection

The spooks were watching intently when the Polish freighter tied up at Tilbury docks, London after a voyage from the bleak Baltic port of Gydnia. The MW *Inowroclaw* had set out on its voyage on 19 November 1993, with a cargo of 230 containers. The rust-streaked freighter unloaded some cargo at Tilbury and proceeded on its voyage up the east cost of England, arriving at Teeside on 24 November. Once again, security people were waiting and watching.

Under the glare of arc lights, a crane began unloading containers. It was after midnight when container number 2030255 was lifted onto the quay. Its contents were described as 'ceramic tiles', and the container had been consigned to a respectable, well-established firm in Belfast. Customs officers and agents of the British security service MI5 were present as the container was opened. Inside, hidden among the tiles, was the biggest illegal arms cargo ever seized in Britain.

The cache included 320 AKM rifles (a more advanced version of the AK-47), two tons of high explosive and thousands of detonators, as well as fifty-three 9mm Makarov pistols, 500 hand grenades, and a huge quantity of ammunition – 14,000 rounds for the pistols and 60,000 for the rifles. The UVF admitted that it was the intended recipient of the cargo of Polish-manufactured arms and munitions. The outlawed group conceded in a statement that the arms seizure was a 'logistical setback', but insisted that it 'in no way diminishes our ability, nor our determination, to carry on the war against the IRA'. The organisation pledged that its members would 'scour the world for arms' to defend themselves and their country.

It emerged that the firm to which the container had been consigned knew nothing about any cargo coming from Poland. It had never done business with the State, which had just shaken off communist rule. It appeared that the UVF planned to have the container taken by road to the Scottish port of Stranraer and from there by ferry to the Northern Ireland port of Larne, from whence it would be taken to a secret location somewhere in Belfast. The arms would probably then have been distributed among various hiding places.

The UVF attempt to procure a large quantity of explosives was particularly sinister. The organisation had an atrocious track record in terrorist bombing, and was believed responsible for the Dublin and Monaghan bombings in 1974, which caused heavy loss of life. It was thought that the UVF was seeking to match the effectiveness in bombing terms of the IRA, which had taken delivery of a large quantity of Semtex high explosive from Libya in the 1980s. One theory was that loyalist paramilitaries were striving to build up their arms stockpiles and terrorist capabilities as the Anglo-Irish Peace Process gathered momentum, amid loyalist fears that the process might lead to a British pullout from Northern Ireland.

It emerged that the Polish arms deal was a 'sting' operation set up by the British security service MI5, in co-operation with its Polish counterpart, the State Protection Office (Urzad Ochrony Pantswa – UOP). This revelation was to stir up controversy, with some commentators suggesting it was all merely a ploy to frighten the Irish government about the loyalist threat, and induce it to make concessions in the Peace Process talks. It was pointed out that no UVF members involved in arranging the arms deal had been arrested.

Law enforcement agencies sometimes allow an illicit arms cargo to proceed to its destination so as to arrest as many as possible of the culprits, including those waiting to receive the arms, but that did not happen in this case. Within days of the seizure, a Polish newspaper, *Zycie Warszawy*, was reporting that the arms had, in fact, come from the Interior Ministry armoury. This development helped to fuel controversy over the arms cache. Had the weapons been transferred across Europe just for a photo opportunity? When the arms were found at Teesport and taken away by the authorities, was 'seizure' the proper term to use?

Questions were asked as to how the 'sting' operation came about. At first, the media had the impression that the British swooped on the shipping container following a tip-off to MI5 from the Polish authorities. According to one version of events, an eagle-eyed clerk in a ministry in Warsaw became suspicious about paperwork to do with an export deal and contacted the Polish security agency UOP, whose agents began tracking middlemen from Northern Ireland looking for arms, while tipping off MI5, whose agents travelled to Poland and began working on the case in co-operation with the Poles. Commentators have suggested that the Poles, who had just emerged from communism and who were looking forward to joining the European Union, would have been eager to prove to the British that they could be trusted in security matters.

According to another version, a UVF arms buyer was detected at work in a European capital, possibly Paris, and the British then enlisted the help of the Poles in setting up a 'sting'. Yet another version suggests that the arms buying operation was blown after a 'mole' in the UVF tipped off the British, who in turn enlisted the help of the Poles in setting up the arms buyers.

What appears to be accepted is that the Poles set up a 'front' company in Warsaw called Eloks to lure the arms buyers. The company address coincided with that of an elderly woman pensioner who would have known little about Northern Ireland, and even less about the black market in arms. It is understood that a female UOP agent dealt with the arms buyers. The Poles used a reputable transport company to take the arms cargo to Gydnia for onward transfer to the UK.

So, why was the arms cargo not allowed to proceed to Northern Ireland, in order to grab all those involved in the illegal operation? It has been suggested that the Poles were anxious that the cargo should not reach Northern Ireland, for fear that, through some mishap, Polish arms should end up in the hands of terrorists. The British security authorities would, no doubt, also have been wary of the danger of another major arms consignment falling into the hands of loyalists, in light of the fact that the paramilitaries had already landed a large arms cargo from Lebanon in 1987. On a more positive note, the coffers of the UVF had been greatly diminished as a result of the 'sting'. Estimates varied as to how much the UVF paid for the cargo – some observers reckoned it may have been more than £200,000.

Loyalist arms and the cease-fire

During the 1990s, loyalist gunrunning operations continued to come to light, usually linked to 'mainland' UK. Frank Portinari, who had joined the extreme-right National Front in the 1970s, and who went on to become a UDA figure in London, was jailed for five years in February 1994 at Birmingham Crown Court, after being caught red-handed with a cache of arms destined for the UDA in Belfast. The court heard how he had meetings with an emissary from Belfast at two pubs in Birmingham and then, in a car park, handed over a bag containing seven guns, including revolvers and semi-automatic pistols, and about 240 rounds of ammunition.

Another far-right activist, Terry Blackham, who was prominent in the National Front, was jailed for four years in 1994 for attempting to smuggle sub-machine guns, a grenade launcher and 2,000 rounds of ammunition to the UDA in East Belfast. He was arrested as he tried to board a ferry with the arms cache.

There was a disturbing development in 1994 – the UVF managed to import quantities of the explosive Powergel, stolen from quarries in Britain. Powergel was soon to figure in bombs deployed by loyalists. Militant elements in the UDA were believed to have been responsible for two booby-trap bombs containing Powergel which were planted in December 1996, aimed at killing members of Sinn Féin, the political wing of the IRA.

The incidents happened during a loyalist cease-fire. The Peace Process in Northern Ireland was gathering momentum at the time. The IRA had declared a cease-fire on 31 August 1994, which was followed by a cease-fire in October called by the Combined Loyalist Military Command, representing the UDA, UVF and the Red Hand Commandos.

The use of Powergel in the two bombs gave rise to speculation that the UVF may have shared some of its stocks with the UDA. In March 1997, a bomb containing 12kg of Powergel was planted at the offices of Sinn Féin in Monaghan, just south of the Border in the Irish Republic. This also occurred during the loyalist cease-fire. Security forces believed the UVF was responsible. The bomb did not explode, although it contained all the correct component parts. This prompted speculation that the bomb may have been intended not to explode, but to act as a warning to the republican movement.

Confidence in the loyalist cease-fire had received another jolt when Lindsay Robb, a prominent loyalist and member of the central executive of the Progressive Unionist Party (PUP), linked to the UVF, was arrested in Scotland in July 1995 for gunrunning, after an undercover MI5 investigation that stretched from Falkirk to Liverpool. Earlier in the year, Robb had taken part in Peace Process talks with the British government at Stormont. Robb, from Lurgan, Co Armagh, went on trial in Glasgow and, after an eleven-day hearing, was found guilty of conspiring to smuggle weapons from Liverpool, via Scotland, to the UVF in Northern Ireland. Evidence given in court indicated that there was not a large arms shipment involved – just a handgun and a machine pistol. Nevertheless, Robb was jailed along with five others when they appeared before Edinburgh High Court in December 1995. Some years after getting early release from prison, he was killed in Glasgow by a knife-wielding assailant.[18]

In the UK during the 1990s, there was a black market in deactivated weapons that had been restored to 'live' status, or that came with the kits necessary to restore them. Some of these weapons made their way to Northern Ireland. In 1995 an Uzi sub-machine gun was found in a cache of arms in Northern Ireland, and was believed bound for loyalists. It was traced to a father-and-son team in Derbyshire – William Mitchell Greenwood and his disabled son Mitchell Verne Greenwood. The two men specialised in the supply of deactivated guns along with ready-made kits and instructions to convert them back to live status.

On another occasion, in 2000, police raided the home of a former member of the Royal Irish Rangers (RIR) regiment in County Armagh and recovered arms and explosives. One of the weapons was a deactivated Uzi which, it emerged, had also been supplied by the Greenwoods. The ex-RIR soldier was suspected of having links to the UVF and neo-Nazis. He was jailed in 2001 for nine years.

In March 2004, the Greenwoods were jailed for seven years each for selling more than 4,000 deactivated weapons with conversion kits. Nottingham Crown Court heard that Greenwood senior (seventy-six) and his forty-two-year-old son had sold AK-47 rifles, Uzi sub-machine guns and pistols from a makeshift shop at their farm in the rural village of South Wingfield. Apart from the two cases cited above, it is unclear if other weapons supplied by the Greenwoods ended up in the hands of loyalist paramilitaries.

Emergence of the LVF

Throughout the Peace Process, there have been diehard elements among the loyalist organisations who were unhappy with the move away from violence. In 1996 a dissident UVF gang in the Portadown area of Mid-Ulster began to engage in acts of terrorism without the sanction of the leadership. The group was expelled and formed the nucleus of the breakaway Loyalist Volunteer Force (LVF), under taciturn, bible-reading terror boss Billy Wright, who was later to be assassinated in prison by the INLA.

The LVF began co-operating with a UDA breakaway group, 'C Company', led by a notorious tearaway, the heavily-tattooed Johnny 'Mad Dog' Adair. Both groups were said to be looking to procure arms. It was believed that LVF members took some arms and explosives with them when they defected from the UVF. A bomb planted by the LVF at Dundalk, just south of the Border in the Irish Republic, was composed of one kilo of Powergel, likely to have come from UVF stocks. Only the detonator went off.

According to one report, Johnny Adair sent an emissary on trips to Amsterdam in the 1999–2000 period to pursue an arms deal with a former Official IRA man. The emissary was shown a warehouse containing an arsenal of weapons, including several types of handgun, assault rifles, pistols, rocket launchers and grenades. It is not clear if a deal resulted.[19]

It was reported in 2000 that Johnny Adair had two meetings with a businessman linked to Ulster Resistance, the group that took delivery of part of the consignment of arms brought in from Lebanon in 1987. Adair wanted to acquire the weapons, but was told they were not for sale.[20] In light of suggestions that Ulster Resistance had already given weapons to the UDA and UVF, it is unclear what arms the group retained at this stage. One source suggested that Ulster Resistance would have been reluctant to give any significant quantity of arms to Adair, for fear they might be used as part of a loyalist feud.

There was another media report in 2004 that the LVF had managed to import a shipment of handguns and sub-machine guns. It was said that the guns were taken off a ship in Belfast harbour onto a small fishing boat and then landed near Carrickfergus.[21] According to a subsequent report in 2004, senior figures in the LVF had concluded a deal with Croatian arms dealers at a meeting in Prague for the supply of handguns, semi-automatic firearms and explosives.[22]

The loyalist paramilitary groups were never as adept at importing arms as the Provisional IRA. Nevertheless, the main loyalist groups have enough weaponry to pursue a terrorist campaign for the foreseeable future, if they choose to return to full-scale conflict. Following the decommissioning of IRA weapons in September 2005, focus has turned to persuading loyalist paramilitaries to put their weapons beyond use. The

Independent International Commission on Decommissioning (IICD), headed by General John de Chastelain, has sought to engage with the paramilitary groups still retaining weapons.

The security forces, in or around 1998, compiled estimates of what the loyalists had in their arsenals, after seizures by the security forces were taken into account, and these estimates were passed to the IICD. It was estimated that the loyalists had eighty sub-machine guns, including home-made weapons; more than 600 handguns; more than seventy Czech-made assault rifles that were part of the arms consignment imported in 1987; as well as 185 hand grenades and twenty-seven FN pistols that also formed part of that shipment (*see* Appendix A).

Other research suggests that the UDA has a collection of weapons that includes AK-47 rifles and a range of old bolt-action rifles, as well as sub-machine guns of various types, including home-made models and the Danish-made 9mm Madsen. (This last weapon was seen in July 1987 being carried in the Sandy Row area of Belfast by a UDA gunman; it was also seen in the possession of a member of the UFF, part of the UDA, in South Belfast in August 1996.) The UDA has a range of handguns, including 9mm Browning pistols. In recent years the arsenal also included the RPG-7 rocket launcher. In 1993 masked UDA men posed for photos in Belfast, one of them with what appeared to be an SA-80, the standard assault rifle of the British Army. It was believed in recent years that the UDA had at least one M-60 machine gun, and a quantity of Russian-made hand grenades. There was a report that the UDA may have imported a sizeable consignment of weapons from Eastern Europe in 1993, but this has not been confirmed.

The UVF is believed to possess a range of assault rifles, including AK-47s, Colt Commandos, Armalites and SLRs. Sub-machine guns may include Ingram MAC-10s (sometimes known as a 'Big Mac'), Sterlings and home-made weapons. Other firearms thought to be in the possession of the group include automatic shotguns, 9mm Browning pistols and Magnum .357 revolvers. The organisation may have the RPG-7 rocket launcher, and a quantity of Soviet-designed RPG-5 hand grenades.

At the time of writing, in early 2006, it is difficult to predict how General de Chastelain's commission will fare as it tries to bring about the decommissioning of loyalist weapons. There were hopes that in the light of the

IRA declaration that its war is over, and the decommissioning of its weapons, the loyalists might also be encouraged to put their arms beyond use. There was bloody feuding among loyalist organisations the UVF and the LVF in recent years. Even though the feuding came to an end in 2005, there were fears that the conflict might encourage elements among loyalism to maintain arsenals of weaponry for emergencies. Decommissioning paramilitary arms has never been an easy process.

CHAPTER 14

The Real IRA Looks East

Soon after breaking away from the IRA in late 1997, Michael McKevitt, leader of the dissident Real IRA (RIRA), turned his mind to a project close to his heart – the setting up of a reliable arms pipeline from abroad for his new paramilitary group. The wily McKevitt, a long-time Provo whose involvement in paramilitary activities dated back to the 1970s, had risen to become quartermaster general of the IRA and was fully aware of the challenges involved in smuggling arms from abroad. When they defected in protest at the IRA cease-fire and the involvement of the republican movement in the Peace Process, McKevitt and his people took some war materiel with them. Nevertheless, McKevitt and the senior figures in his private army wanted their own independent source of supply. They found it in the former Yugoslavia.

A flourishing black market in arms is one of the legacies of the conflict that convulsed the federation of states formerly known as Yugoslavia in the 1990s. Arms left over from the conflict, or 'liberated' from Yugoslav Army arsenals during the war, have ended up in private hands.

Arms dealers in Croatia and Bosnia can supply customers with a range of weapons, with few awkward questions asked. Some of the trade is said to involve the Croatian and Albanian mafia. The region, with its long, porous borders, has become one of the most active areas in the world for arms smuggling. Along the Dalmatian coast of Croatia, there are many small ports from where weapons can be smuggled across the Adriatic to Italy. It is not surprising, therefore, that Michael McKevitt turned to this region to source weapons for the RIRA as long ago as 1998, within a year of the group being founded.

A native of Dundalk, County Louth, McKevitt had joined the Provisional IRA in the early 1970s. He was an unsophisticated man but nevertheless a shrewd and very careful operator. During more than a quarter century of paramilitary activity with the Provos, he never went to jail. However, in February 1975, during a feud between the Provisionals and the Official IRA (OIRA), he was shot in both legs by two OIRA gunmen outside his home.

McKevitt married Bernadette Sands, a sister of Bobby Sands, who died in the H-Block hunger strikes of 1981 and who was elected an MP. McKevitt has three children with Ms Sands and two grown-up children from a previous marriage. He formerly worked in a factory, and then ran a T-shirt printing and souvenir shop in a Dundalk shopping centre with Ms Sands. He also worked as a video cameraman, covering weddings.

Senior figures in the IRA recognised McKevitt's organisational abilities early on, and he rose to a senior position in the organisation. As quartermaster general, he oversaw the importation of arms from Libya in the 1980s – the most important gunrunning operation in the Provisional IRA's history.

It is believed that the first contacts with arms dealers in the region of the former Yugoslavia were made by a senior figure in another republican dissident fringe group, the Continuity IRA (CIRA). This man worked in the region during the 1990s. While located there, he made contact with a Croat national who was working as a driver and interpreter. This man was also a part-time arms dealer, and indicated that he could provide a range of weaponry. It is believed that the CIRA and the RIRA linked up to co-operate in the procurement of arms on the Balkan black market.

A senior RIRA man visited the picturesque Croatian port city of Split in 1998, and made contact with the arms dealer who was to be the central figure in the procurement operation. There was a follow-up visit in May 1999, when the RIRA man was accompanied by a woman from Newry and a man from County Armagh. They travelled via France in a van.

Other visits may also have been made. It has been reported that McKevitt himself visited Croatia in 1999.

It is unclear exactly when or how arms were smuggled back to Ireland, but in the latter part of 1999, Garda intelligence learned that a consignment of weapons had been brought in. In October that year, members of the Garda Emergency Response Unit (ERU) raided an improvised underground bunker located in the cellar of a derelict country house at Stamullen, County Meath, about twenty-five miles north of Dublin. The bunker was being used as a paramilitary training camp. Several individuals were arrested, including a fourteen-year-old boy.[1]

Follow-up searches led detectives to a nearby hay barn. There, the detectives found, hidden in pipes below bales of hay, a Soviet-designed RPG-18 anti-tank weapon. The IRA had acquired an anti-tank weapon, the RPG-7, as long ago as 1972. Further deliveries of the RPG-7 were made from Libya in the mid-1980s. But this was the first time an RPG-18 had been found in the possession of paramilitaries in Ireland, North or South. It was public confirmation that the RIRA had established its own arms pipeline from abroad.

Also recovered was an AK-47 of a type different from those delivered from Libya. The RIRA weapon had a folding stock, which meant it could be more easily concealed, while the Libyan-supplied version had a fixed stock. A Czech-manufactured CZ Model 25 sub-machine gun was also found – it also had a folding stock. A significant element in the cache was 6.5kg of TN500, Yugoslav military explosive.

Arms imported from Croatia were also believed to include the RPG-22 rocket launcher, a version of the RPG-18. Also called the Mukha in Russian, this weapon became widely distributed in the developing world. It is a disposable, single-shot anti-tank weapon with a range of about 200 metres, comprising a glass-fibre tube with a 64mm rocket. It was a particularly common weapon in the wars in former Yugoslavia, and I recall it was one of the items recovered on the battlefield that were on display at the Croatian press office in the Intercontinental Hotel, Zagreb, in the early 1990s.

The arms brought in from Croatia, which had already been smuggled from neighbouring Bosnia, were a vital addition to the RIRA arsenal. It is thought likely that when McKevitt and his people broke away from the IRA, they did not take large amounts of war materiel with them. The break occurred at a stormy IRA convention held in Falcarragh, County Donegal, in October 1997. McKevitt and his supporters on the IRA Executive formally resigned, disgusted at the move away from violence. For McKevitt, the 'armed struggle' may have been more attractive than the complexities of the peace process.

Even though the IRA publicly accused the group of stealing arms, no retaliation appears to have been taken against McKevitt or any of his colleagues on foot of the accusation. Traditionally in the IRA, the sentence for misappropriating weapons was death – this was the penalty laid down in the Green Book, the 1970s-era handbook that every IRA Volunteer had to study. However, the IRA did not execute any of the RIRA people for stealing IRA arms – perhaps for fear of alienating some of the IRA rank-and-file who had their doubts about the Peace Process, and who may have had a sneaking regard for the stance taken by McKevitt.

Had the RIRA cleaned out major dumps, it is unlikely the hard men of the IRA would have turned a blind eye. However, it is suspected that McKevitt's group took Semtex high explosives from the IRA arms dumps, as well as detonators that had originated in Tucson, Arizona, smuggled to the IRA in the late 1980s and early 1990s (*see* Chapter 11). It was reported that an RIRA bomb defused in January 1998 was found to contain a Semtex-based detonating cord of the type used by the Provisionals; there were also two detonators, one of which was an Ireco device of the type acquired by the Provos in Arizona.[2]

Rifles and pistols may also have been filched when the RIRA broke away. In 1998 a young member of the RIRA, Rónán Mac Lochlainn, was shot dead by Gardaí during an attempt to rob a security van in County Wicklow. Among the arms being carried by the RIRA gang was a Kalashnikov rifle. There was speculation that this was one of the weapons stolen from the IRA arsenal by the dissidents.

One of the most important things transferred from the Provisionals to the RIRA was technical know-how. Some IRA bomb-makers are believed to have gone over to the RIRA. Dissident republicans believed to be from the RIRA deployed, on a number of occasions, improvised mortars of IRA design. The type used was the most formidable of the IRA-type mortars, the Mark 15 'barrackbuster', or variations of it. However, while the Provisionals would use an array of firing tubes to fire a 'volley' of projectiles, the dissidents seemed to have a preference for 'single projectile' attacks. Such mortar attacks were carried out on the RUC station at Newry Road, Armagh, on 13 September 2000, and on the British Army's Ebrington Barracks in Derry, on 23 January 2001. No casualties resulted from either operation.

When its paramilitary campaign was up and running, the RIRA carried out a series of car-bomb attacks. One such attack, in the Northern Ireland town of Omagh in August 1998, claimed the lives of twenty-nine civilians. The dead included nine children and a woman pregnant with twins. It was the worst single atrocity of the Troubles, and sparked enormous public outrage. It was suspected that an Ireco detonator of the type procured in Arizona and smuggled to the IRA eight or nine years previously was used to set off the bomb.[3] The RIRA was shamed into calling a cease-fire, but gradually went back on the warpath without declaring that its cease-fire was over. Meanwhile, the organisation pressed ahead with its quest for arms and explosives.

The materiel smuggled from Croatia helped to bolster the RIRA campaign. In September 2000, the RIRA used an RPG-22 rocket launcher to attack the MI6 headquarters in Vauxhall, London. The rocket was launched from a public park, Spring Gardens, on the opposite side of the Thames from the MI6 building. No major damage was done and nobody was hurt, but the audacious attack did garner much publicity for the RIRA. The previous March a similar weapon, believed to be an RPG-18, was found abandoned near the Killymeal barracks at Dungannon in County Tyrone, the base of the British Army's 3rd Battalion, Parachute Regiment.

In the summer of 2000, law enforcement agencies concluded that the RIRA was in the process of trying to procure more weapons in the former Yugoslavia. In July of that year, police in Croatia seized an arms cache in a truck parked in a warehouse in the town of Dobranje, about forty miles southeast of Split. The weapons included seven RPG-18-type weapons, as well as AK-47 rifles, a sizeable quantity of ammunition and twenty packs of TM500 explosives, as well as detonating cord and equipment. The explosives came from the same batch, with the code number 8303, as the explosives found hidden at Stamullen, County Meath, the previous year.

It is believed the weapons found at Dobranje had originated in Bosnia Herzegovina, and had been smuggled across the nearby border into

Croatia. Police formed the view that the materiel seized was destined for the RIRA, and that the capture of the cache disrupted an arms pipeline from the Balkans to dissident Irish republicans. A local man, Ante Cubelic, was arrested on suspicion of arms trafficking. Also arrested were brothers Josip and Tomislav Cubelic and Josip Vuletic. More than two years later, in December 2002, a court in Split ordered the release of the four men, ruling that there was insufficient evidence to prove links to an international plot.

In July 2000, during a routine check, Slovenian border police also found a cache of weapons, hidden in a box attached to the chassis of a Croatian truck at Novo Mesto, about forty-four miles east of the capital Ljubliana. Police believed the shipment was destined for Western Europe, and could not rule out the possibility that it was bound for IRA dissidents. The haul included about fifteen rifles, some pistols and ammunition, 150 hand grenades and nine rocket launchers.

In its quest for arms in Croatia, the RIRA may not have relied solely on the original arms supplier introduced to the organisation by the man from the CIRA. In November 2002, Croat police stopped a car driven by Bozo Grgic at Trilj, forty miles north of Split, and found fifty grenades marked 'Property of NATO Forces' in the boot of his car. The following February, a court in Split heard that it was suspected that the grenades were destined for the RIRA. Grgic claimed the grenades had 'fallen off the back of a lorry', but the court did not believe him. He was jailed for eighteen months.

It has been claimed that the CIRA intermediary who helped set up the RIRA arms procurement operation in Croatia was himself swindled out of £50,000 (€63,487) in 2000 by Dutch criminals, when he tried to import a consignment of black-market cigarettes, with arms and ammunition hidden in the cargo. It was reported that the CIRA man had visited Amsterdam in July 2000 to set up the deal. The arms were said to have been meant for the Fermanagh section of the CIRA. The money was handed over, but the shipment never arrived.[4]

The RIRA turns to Saddam

Despite the arms and explosives being smuggled in from the Balkans, the RIRA was still looking around for further sources of supply. The disruption of the arms pipeline from Croatia by the seizure of the arms cache at

Dobranje was a reminder that even the Balkans connection was not perfect so far as arms procurement was concerned. RIRA chief McKevitt would have known at first hand how the capabilities, as well as the morale, of the Provos had been boosted by the major shipments of arms, ammunition and Semtex that had been smuggled into Ireland from Libya in the mid-1980s. As quartermaster general of the IRA, he had supervised the storage of the materiel.

The problem was, Libya's Colonel Gadaffi was no longer in the business of supplying arms to Irish paramilitaries. The USA, traditional source of weapons for the IRA, also posed problems – the FBI was very proactive, and had broken up a series of gunrunning attempts by means of 'sting' operations. The fall of communism in Eastern Europe meant that an Irish republican could no longer stroll into the offices of the State company of Omnipol in Prague, as the IRA's Dáithí Ó Conaill had done in 1971, apparently with few questions asked, and order a consignment of weapons for 'the boys'. Elements in the Palestinian groups who had previously supplied arms to the IRA and the INLA also no longer appeared to be in that business.

It seemed to senior RIRA activists that a friendly rogue state could solve their procurement problems, and perhaps help out with a generous cash donation as well. With Libya out of the equation, an obvious candidate was the Iraqi regime of Saddam Hussein. There was a huge potential advantage to lining up a government as your benefactor – the arms would be supplied free of charge. That had been the arrangement with Libya's Colonel Gadaffi – his reasons for arming the Provos were political, not commercial. Libya had also given money to the Provos.

It was all so very different in the 'private' sector. The average black-market arms dealer usually looks for cash up front, and quotes high prices because of the extra risks involved in an illegal transaction. Having got his hands on the cash, you can never be certain that he will not betray the operation anyway. For a small paramilitary outfit like the RIRA, funds were not always in plentiful supply – cigarette smuggling and armed robberies were among the group's sources of funding. It would be a great help not to have to actually lay out hard-earned cash for guns.

It became clear to the British security service, MI5, that the RIRA was considering an approach to Iraq to seek support. The tip came from David

Rupert, an American businessman who had infiltrated the organisation and who was working for MI5 and the FBI. MI5 agents looked at the website of the RIRA's political group, the 32 County Sovereignty Committee, and saw an item condemning the UK for taking part in the bombing raids on Iraq as part of Operation Desert Fox in December 1998.

MI5 decided to launch a 'sting' operation against the RIRA, and agents of Arab appearance were lined up to take part in 'Operation Samnite'. The strategy adopted was that an agent or agents would initially make contact, posing as journalists, and then 'reveal' that they were really from Iraqi intelligence. Agents posing as Iraqi journalists made contact in 2000 with a north Dublin republican activist allied to the RIRA. They said they wanted to research a series of articles on the RIRA, the organisation that had so audaciously attacked MI6 HQ in London. An agent was given a phone number to call. He rang the number and the call was answered by Michael McKevitt himself. There were several subsequent phone conversations.

On 7 February the first meeting took place. Two of McKevitt's people, Declan Rafferty and Fintan O'Farrell, met with an agent using the name Samir, at a location in Eastern Europe. Rafferty was a fork-lift driver from the Cooley area of County Louth. O'Farrell was a plastering contractor, originally from Cullaville in South Armagh. Rafferty explained that the RIRA suffered from lack of funds and hardware. He believed that with Iraqi help they could defeat the British.

There was a further meeting between Samir and the two Irishmen on 10 March, followed by a meeting in Slovakia on 9 April. This time Michael McDonald came along to the meeting, and Samir was accompanied by a colleague who was introduced as an Iraqi officer who could authorise the supply of weapons to the RIRA. McDonald, who came from the same area of County Louth as Rafferty, had previous experience in gunrunning. As outlined in Chapter 6, he was jailed in France in 1984, after arms believed bound for the IRA were found on his truck at Le Havre. McDonald was still in the haulage business.

Over dinner, McDonald wrote out a list of what his organisation needed. The quantities were sizeable. The RIRA shopping list, written on a napkin, included 200 rocket-propelled grenades, 5,000kg of plastic explosive, 2,000 detonators and 500 handguns. An MI5 agent purported to blow his nose in the tissue, and then put it in his pocket. It would later prove to be a vital piece of evidence. So as to ensure that any subsequent court case was not jeopardised due to entrapment, the security service's own lawyers were reportedly involved at every stage of the 'sting', even to the extent of going along with agents to towns where meetings with the RIRA people took place. It has been claimed that the RIRA men were the first to raise the question of Iraq supplying weapons and money to the organisation.

McDonald appeared anxious for early delivery, and the second-last meeting was held in Austria. A further meeting was arranged at a Middle Eastern restaurant in Piest'any, a spa in western Slovakia, on 5 July. Members of a Slovakian special police unit were on standby near the restaurant. One of the RIRA men again returned to the subject of the equipment they needed, such as high-powered sniper rifles that could penetrate body armour, and wire-guided missiles 'to kill British soldiers'. They wanted the first shipment to be sent in a truck to Belgium or the Netherlands. They also wanted one million dollars, in four instalments. It appears that the conversation was being bugged, and monitored by other MI5 personnel. When the MI5 lawyers reckoned they had enough evidence, a Home Office international arrest warrant was faxed through to the Slovakian authorities.

As the MI5 men and the three RIRA men drove away from the restaurant in a van, armed Slovakian police wearing balaclava helmets blocked the road and took the three stunned Irishmen into custody. It was said that even the MI5 men looked surprised by how quickly the police moved in. The three suspects were extradited to the UK, and went on trial in Woolwich Crown Court where, in May 2002, they admitted conspiring 'unlawfully and maliciously' to cause an explosion in the UK or Republic of Ireland between 18 February and 6 July 2001. O'Farrell (thirty-five), Rafferty (forty-one) and McDonald (forty-four), all with addresses in County Louth, were each sentenced to thirty years.[5] It was a serious setback for the RIRA.

Meanwhile, McKevitt himself became the target of an elaborate 'sting' operation. FBI/MI5 informant David Rupert infiltrated the ranks of the RIRA, and won the confidence of McKevitt, even attending RIRA Army Council meetings at which McKevitt was present. Rupert was a most unlikely 'plant' to infiltrate the RIRA. A Protestant American of German-Mohawk descent, he was an imposing figure, with a height of six feet seven inches. The trucking boss from Chicago, who had also been a professional wrestler, had had a chequered business past. Through one of his girlfriends who had republican sympathies, he visited Ireland in 1992 and spent time in the west of the country. Apparently in an attempt to escape mounting tax and other debts in America, he returned to Ireland in 1995. It was probably at this period that the FBI began using him as a 'plant' to infiltrate Irish republican circles. For a period, he operated a pub by the sea in County Leitrim, the Drowse Inn.

In 1996 he returned to Chicago and, no doubt at the behest of the FBI, began to attend meetings of the Irish Freedom Committee (IFC), a small group of activists who supported the republican cause in Ireland through political activity. On a previous occasion, the FBI had sought to check out the group by infiltrating another 'plant'. It appears the aim of the exercise was to see if members were involved in gunrunning. No such evidence was to emerge. One of the regular members of the group became suspicious of the newcomer, who came from Boston, and at an IFC meeting in an Irish bar in Chicago in November 1991, he frisked the visitor and found he was wired for sound. There was an angry confrontation, and FBI agents listening in on the eavesdropping equipment burst into the bar and escorted their informant from the premises. Rupert, with his charm and persuasiveness, fared better in winning the confidence of IFC members.

Back in Ireland, during the latter part of the 1990s, Rupert met McKevitt more than twenty times, according to testimony he would later give. Rupert, with three bankruptcies and four marriages behind him, was the star witness when McKevitt ultimately appeared before the Special Criminal Court in Dublin. McKevitt was jailed for twenty years in August 2003, after being convicted of directing the activities of a terrorist organisation between 29 August 1999 and 23 October 2000. Ironically, the offence had been introduced in the wake of the Omagh bomb atrocity, the infamous operation that had been carried out by the organisation that McKevitt helped to found. He was the first person to be convicted of the offence, and was also given a six-year concurrent sentence for membership of an illegal organisation.

McKevitt lost an appeal against conviction in December 2005. The three judges of the Court of Criminal Appeal found that fifty-four-year-old McKevitt, of Beech Park, Blackrock, County Louth, was correctly convicted of directing terrorism. The judges found that the Special Criminal Court was entitled to regard the main prosecution witness, David Rupert, as a credible witness. The appeal court heard that Rupert had been paid $1.4 million by the FBI and £400,000 sterling by the British security services.

With the jailing of other senior figures in the RIRA, the organisation appeared to be in disarray by 2005. However, the body that keeps track of paramilitary groups, the Independent Monitoring Commission (IMC), said in its January 2006 report that the RIRA 'continues to develop its equipment and to seek to recruit members and to acquire munitions'.

In June 2006, police made a number of arrests in Northern Ireland in connection with an alleged RIRA attempt to procure arms in France. It was believed that this was another 'sting' operation involving MI5. It was reported that the RIRA had handed over a large sum of money in France to MI5 officers posing as arms dealers. The consignment of weapons was to include AK-47 assault rifles, sniper rifles and pistols with silencers, as well as heavy machine guns, rocket launchers and SAM-7 missiles. If the RIRA had succeeded in procuring such an arsenal it would have greatly boosted their capabilities, giving them the means to shoot down British Army helicopters; to mount rocket attacks on installations, similar to the attack on MI6 HQ in London in 2000; to carry out long-range sniper attacks on police and military personnel; and to attack security forces' vehicles with armour-piercing ammunition.

CHAPTER 15

A Farewell to Arms

In June 1992, a significant meeting took place in Geneva between a British diplomat and a Libyan emissary. For years, there had been much bad blood between the UK and the Libyan regime headed by the mercurial Colonel Muammar Gadaffi. London saw Libya as a pariah state that supported terrorism. But diplomacy is about resolving differences between nations, and so it was that the two envoys met in the gracious surroundings of the United Nations office, the Palais des Nations, set in a well-tended park overlooking Lake Geneva.

The meeting was held in the elegant offices of the United Nations director general in Europe, Antoine Blanca, and in his presence. The UK representative, Edward Chaplin, deputy head of the UK mission to the UN in Geneva, did not have a background in security, but was one of the up-and-coming Arabists in the Foreign and Commonwealth Office, and had long experience in the Middle East. He spoke Arabic fluently, having spent five years in Baghdad as a child in the 1950s, while his father worked for the chemical conglomerate ICI.[1] The Libyan envoy was the highly-experienced Abdul-Ahi Al Obeidi, ambassador to Tunisia and a former foreign minister, who enjoyed the trust of Colonel Gadaffi. The diplomat was accompanied by a team of three officials. Libya was about to lift the veil on one of the most contentious episodes in its recent history – it was about to provide the British with details of assistance given by the Gadaffi regime to the IRA.

Up to five years previously, Gadaffi had been arming the IRA, but he had now turned his back on the organisation. He had clearly become worried about Libya's status as an 'outcast' in the world community. Libyan intelligence agents were suspected of being responsible for the bombing of Pan Am flight 103 at Lockerbie, Scotland, in 1988. In the wake of that atrocity, the United Nations imposed sanctions on Libya over its failure at the time to hand over two suspects. (The two former intelligence agents were later to be given up, and one was convicted at a special court in The Hague.)

Libya had now become anxious to distance itself publicly from terrorism. In an interview with the Egyptian newspaper *Al Ahram* in January 1991, Gadaffi signalled his disenchantment with the IRA, labelling the organisation as 'terrorist', and saying that a distinction had to be drawn between terrorism and 'armed struggle'. He did not define how these distinctions should be made. In May 1992, a UN special envoy was told in Tripoli by Gadaffi that Libya was prepared to answer questions from the British about Libyan support to the IRA. Analysts considered that Gadaffi wanted to improve relations with Britain, and weaken the international consensus behind sanctions. In spy thriller parlance, Gadaffi wanted to come in from the cold.

It had taken some time to set up the Geneva encounter. There were reports that the meeting had been arranged with the aid of Egyptian, Spanish and Algerian intermediaries. The British submitted nineteen questions to the Libyans in advance. For some reason, the Libyans decided not to supply written replies. Al Obeidi had answers already prepared and he dictated them in Arabic. Despite the Foreign Office man's fluency in Arabic, it would appear that Al Obeidi insisted on his comments being translated into English, and they were duly noted down in longhand by Chaplin. The laborious process took about two hours, longer than expected.

Neither side would comment in detail about the information that had been imparted. With the understatement beloved of British diplomats, Chaplin told reporters that he had received 'some information', and that it would be passed on to London.

It is understood that the information provided by the Libyans included a detailed inventory of arms, ammunition and explosives supplied in the four shipments that got safely through to the Provisionals in 1985–86, prior to the capture of the fifth shipment aboard the *Eksund*. According to one report, the Libyans also supplied details of major financial assistance to the IRA, amounting to millions of pounds sterling in US dollars, French francs and German marks, passed in suitcases to senior IRA men. They also passed on the names of up to twenty IRA men trained in special camps in Libya over the previous two decades.[2] Sources in Dublin confirmed to me that the British passed on to the Irish authorities the details of the war materiel which the Libyans said they supplied to the IRA, although it is likely that the Gardaí already had a good idea of what was in the massive arsenal delivered from Tripoli. The British also passed the information to the Northern Ireland police, the Royal Ulster Constabulary (RUC).

The Garda authorities liaised with the RUC on a joint project to assess the extent of the IRA arsenal. The data supplied by Libya was considered in the context of other information, including analysis of the materiel seized aboard the *Eksund*. Both forces had kept careful records of IRA materiel seized over the years, and it was thus possible to draw up estimates of the types and amounts of Libyan-supplied weaponry still outstanding. It was judged that weaponry from the four pre-*Eksund* shipments formed the greater part of the IRA arsenal. Drawing on intelligence and ballistic records, the security forces also drew up estimates of the amounts of weaponry from sources other than Libya thought to be in the possession of the IRA.

The question has to be posed – to what extent did the IRA leadership itself know what was hidden away in the various hides and bunkers? When senior IRA man Michael McKevitt defected from the IRA to form the dissident Real IRA, it was a blow to the Provos. As quartermaster general of the IRA, he knew the locations of all the bigger arms dumps and kept an inventory of weapons. He had overseen the major deliveries of weaponry from Libya in the mid-1980s.

It has been suggested that while the IRA leadership would have known the broad details of the IRA arms inventory, it may not have possessed the kind of minute detail that McKevitt apparently liked to keep to himself. A knowledgeable source told me that McKevitt gave broad details of the major dumps to the IRA leadership when he defected, but did not provide a detailed inventory. He entrusted his own inventory for safe keeping to an elderly man who was not involved in the republican movement. It was suggested that this elderly man was the only person in the latter part of the 1990s who possessed the IRA's own detailed lists of the types and quantities of weaponry the organisation had stashed away – the contents of each major dump, and details of weapons issued to active service units. McKevitt, who was under constant surveillance by Irish Special Branch, went to jail in 2003 for directing terrorism, but because his elderly friend was unknown to the security forces, it was thought unlikely that he would come under scrutiny, or that the inventory would be seized by the authorities.

If this story is correct, one has to wonder about the degree of accuracy of such an inventory, even if it was drawn up by somebody as knowledgeable as McKevitt. In addition to major dumps where the IRA holds sizeable quantities of war materiel in reserve, known as 'army' dumps, there were many smaller 'unit' dumps or 'hides', containing arms for the use of local active service units. One method of setting up a 'hide' was to place the equipment in airtight plastic barrels, which were then buried or otherwise concealed in the countryside.

Some of the weaponry in the smaller dumps might have gone astray as a result of the deaths or jailing of individuals who had hidden the arms. Other weaponry might have deteriorated due to damp storage conditions. In addition, human error could have entered in. IRA members might simply have been unable to pinpoint a location in the remote countryside where an arms cache was hurriedly concealed in the dead of night. In June 2006 a cache of about 10,000 rounds of high velocity ammunition was found on an embankment in a remote wooded area near Cliffony, County Sligo, which was believed by Garda officers to have been hidden by the IRA about twenty years previously and forgotten about. The rounds, believed to have been part of the materiel imported by the IRA from Libya in the 1980s, were hidden in a plastic drainage pipe sealed at both ends with tar. (It is noteworthy that arms that were hidden by members of the old IRA during the Troubles of the 1920s were still occasionally being found in recent years.) The situation may have been complicated even further by regular seizures of weaponry by the security forces.

Despite all these potential complications, the security forces pressed ahead with their estimates. The estimated IRA inventory of weapons from all the various sources included close to 600 AKM rifles (Libyan-supplied), 400 other rifles, rocket launchers, hundreds of handguns, heavy machine guns capable of bringing down helicopters, and more than two tonnes of Semtex explosive. Also on the list were surface-to-air missiles (probably not useable), and even flame-throwers.

Similar estimates were formulated in regard to what was still outstanding in terms of loyalist weaponry. There was a particular focus on the major arms shipment imported from Lebanon for the UDA, UVF and Ulster Resistance in late 1987. The inventory had to take into account the fact that apart from materiel smuggled in from abroad, loyalists had also been producing their own sub-machine guns (see Appendix A for details of the estimated inventories for the IRA and loyalist groups).

As the Peace Process got under way in the latter part of the 1990s, retired Canadian military man General John de Chastelain began his mission to oversee the decommissioning of paramilitary arms, as head of the Independent International Commission on Decommissioning (IICD). To assist him in his work, he was provided by the RUC and the Gardaí with agreed estimates of the weaponry held both by the IRA and by loyalist paramilitaries. Details of these estimates were leaked in 1998 – the leaked data did not include any estimates for the arms held by the smaller republican paramilitary group, the INLA. Neither did the Real IRA (RIRA), which had just begun operating, or the Continuity IRA (CIRA) figure in the estimates as leaked. The process of putting paramilitary arms beyond use proved to be a slow, tedious process. De Chastelain, a wise and careful man, was to win the accolade of the most patient man in Ireland.[3]

For decades there had been efforts behind the scenes to bring about peace in Northern Ireland. The Irish and British governments engaged in secret contacts with republicans in an effort to bring an end to the violence. There were also to be contacts between the governments and the loyalists to secure a loyalist cease-fire.

Many Irish people had become war-weary. There was a significant event on 11 January 1988, when John Hume, leader of the Social Democratic and Labour Party, which rejected paramilitarism and believed in the peaceful way of the ballot box, held a meeting with Gerry Adams, President of Sinn

Féin. This was the first in a series of discussions between the two men that was to continue over a number of years, and was to pave the way towards peace. During the 1990s, there was support for the Peace Process from the administration of US president Bill Clinton, who sent Senator George Mitchell to Ireland to use his considerable skills in building bridges to help find a way forward.

By the early 1990s, it would appear that senior figures in Sinn Féin/IRA were increasingly coming to the private conclusion that the 'armed struggle' of the IRA was not going to result in the British being pushed out of the North. It seemed that while the IRA could not be defeated, it could not win either. Sinn Féin leader Gerry Adams and his allies saw that the movement could make significant advances by taking the political route. They were encouraged in this view by the electoral breakthroughs made by Sinn Féin during the emotive H-Block hunger strikes of the early 1980s. Some commentators took the view that if the IRA stopped killing people, Sinn Féin would prove more attractive to nationalist voters who had a conscientious objection to murder and mayhem.

The efforts for peace bore fruit in 1994, when the IRA declared a cease-fire. When further progress was not to its satisfaction, the IRA reacted with extreme violence. On 9 February 1996, the IRA exploded a massive bomb at Canary Wharf in the Docklands area of London. Two members of the public died in the blast, scores were injured and the cost of the material damage in this area of modern, high-rise office blocks ran into tens of millions of pounds. Further attacks followed, including a bomb attack on 15 June in Manchester, which injured 200. By summer 1997, there had been an improvement in the political climate with the coming to power of Tony Blair's Labour government and, on 19 July, the IRA announced the restoration of its cease-fire. (It has been alleged that early in 1996, before the IRA went back to war, the organisation bought weapons from arms dealers in Estonia, including individuals linked to the Kaitseliit reserve force. The claim was made by an unnamed official in the Russian Federal Security Service (FSB) who was quoted in a Russian newspaper in May 1996. There was no independent corroboration of the allegation. Estonia hotly denied the claim.)

The Good Friday Agreement (GFA), signed in 1998 and ratified by the Irish people in referenda North and South, introduced an elected

Assembly and a semi-autonomous cross-community government, the Executive. It was a model of compromise, an ingeniously-conceived settlement, designed to guarantee the rights of both communities, and to be respectful of their aspirations. It was designed to bring bitterly opposed parties together in new institutions, despite the atmosphere of deep, mutual distrust among the more extreme elements on both sides. It was also meant to bring paramilitarism to an end, to eliminate the cancer of violence in Irish politics. Among the pay-offs for the paramilitary organisations was the early release of prisoners.

One of the constant stumbling blocks in the Peace Process was the question of the decommissioning of paramilitary arms, especially the sizeable arsenal held by the IRA. The constant message from Ulster Unionist leader David Trimble was, 'No Guns, No Government'. Trimble himself was constantly under pressure from hard-liners in his party, who were sceptical of the GFA.

The GFA featured some 'creative ambiguity' on the question of decommissioning. The agreement committed the signatories to 'to use any influence they may have to achieve the decommissioning of all paramilitary arms', but allowed for political progress to be made even in the absence of the much-desired decommissioning.

During the 1990s, the IRA had adopted an attitude of hard-line opposition to the idea of getting rid of its weapons. This was not surprising. It was said in that era that, even if the IRA gave up its weaponry, it could easily re-arm, but this was true only up to a point. While it is comparatively easy to procure arms abroad, smuggling them to Ireland has always posed difficulties, in light of the fact that Ireland is an island. Arms had to be brought in by sea or air. Over the years, as outlined in this book, many major arms cargoes were seized, and a number of republicans went to jail, including Joe Cahill and Martin Ferris, both of whom were arrested aboard gunrunning vessels.

In December 1998, an IRA spokesman told the BBC and RTÉ that there would be no decommissioning until they had achieved their objective of a united Ireland. This statement has to be seen against a background of traditional IRA doctrine, which sees the IRA and its leadership as the lawful government of all Ireland, even though the IRA is an illegal organisation under the laws of the Irish and British governments. Because of this core republican belief, as outlined in the Green Book, the IRA considered that its war was 'morally justified'. It followed that the IRA considered itself justified in procuring, storing and using arms as part of a war, and in retaining arms even while on cease-fire.

An edition of the Green Book that I have seen, and which was possibly published in the late 1970s, states that the IRA are the 'direct representatives of the 1918 Dáil Éireann parliament, and that as such they are the legal government of the Irish Republic, which has the moral right to pass laws for, and to claim jurisdiction over, the whole geographical fragment of Ireland, its maritime territory, air space, mineral resources, means of production, distribution and exchange and all of its people regardless of creed or loyalty'.

The Green Book goes on: 'This belief, this ethical fact, should and must give moral strength to all volunteers, and all members of every branch of the Republican Movement. The Irish Republican Army, its Leadership, is the lawful government of the Irish Republic, all other parliaments or assemblies claiming the right to speak for and to pass laws on behalf of the Irish people are illegal assemblies, puppet governments of a foreign power, and willing tools of an occupying power. Volunteers must firmly believe without doubt and without reservation that as members of the Irish Republican Army, all orders issued by the Army Authority, and all actions directed by the Army Authority, are the legal orders and the lawful actions of the Government of the Irish Republic. This is one of the most important mainstays of the Republican Movement, the firm belief that all operations and actions directed by the Army are in effect the lawful and legal actions of the Government of all the Irish people.'[4]

The hard-line stance taken in the Green Book towards 'illegal assemblies' was softened somewhat by the decision of Sinn Féin in the 1980s to end the policy of absentionism in regard to Dáil Éireann, so as to allow Sinn Féin TDs to take their seats in the Irish parliament. There was a further softening of attitudes when Sinn Féin signed up to the GFA, and the way was cleared for Sinn Féin representatives to enter the Assembly and Executive set up in Northern Ireland under the terms of that agreement.

Nevertheless, there has never been any indication of a change in the IRA's basic tenet that its leadership constitutes the real government of Ireland. This concept might come as a surprise to the millions who live in the

Republic of Ireland and who have an elected government that is regarded by them as entirely legitimate, and that is recognised as a lawful government throughout the world.

The claim that the IRA leadership is the real government of Ireland is not a claim that Sinn Féin normally makes to the electorate, possibly fearing that the voters might not understand, and might see such a belief as preposterous and even offensive and dictatorial, with a whiff of fascism about it. Still, in terms of decommissioning, the IRA clearly saw itself as having the right to retain arms, and in this context, if any arms were to be put beyond use, the IRA insisted on retaining the right to carry out the decommissioning in its own way and in its own time. There would be no question of handing over arms to the authorities, as this would smack of surrender. Nor would the IRA permit any act of decommissioning to be filmed or photographed for public consumption, as this would smack of humiliation.

The decommissioning issue delayed the implementation of the GFA. Unionists were unhappy with the failure of the IRA to get rid of its arms, and they refused to establish the various institutions of devolved government until there was movement on this issue. Some moderate nationalists regretted that the question of decommissioning of arms had become such a sticking point. It was felt that if Sinn Féin could be brought into the democratic process, and if the IRA declared that the war was over, the weapons could be allowed to rust away in their bunkers. In other words, the damp Irish weather and the passage of time could perform the decommissioning.

Nevertheless, Unionists were finally persuaded to enter an Executive with Sinn Féin and, on 2 December 1999, power was finally passed from Westminster to Belfast, as the power-sharing Executive met for the first time. David Trimble, leader of the Ulster Unionist Party, became first minister; Seamus Mallon of the SDLP was named second minister. Sinn Féin's Martin McGuinness became education minister, while his party colleague Bairbre de Brún took the health portfolio.

The continuing lack of movement on the decommissioning of arms caused ongoing unrest among Unionists, and was to be the cause of recurring crises. In early 2000 the Unionists indicated they would resign from the Executive because of their discontent over the issue. On 3 February

2000, Northern Ireland secretary Peter Mandelson, facing up to stern reality, signed an order suspending the Assembly. There was a break in the impasse the following May, when the IRA issued a statement saying it would 'completely and verifiably' put IRA arms 'beyond use'.

As an interim 'confidence-building' measure, the IRA also agreed to allow two independent inspectors to regularly inspect major arms dumps, so they could confirm that the arms were not being moved or used. Maarti Ahtisaari, the former Finnish president, and ANC secretary general Cyril Ramaphosa carried out this sensitive task. It is thought likely that the major dumps to which they paid secret visits were located in the Irish Republic. One of the roles of the IRA's Southern Command was to provide logistical back-up to the organisation, and to store some of its armaments.

In January 2000, the then Garda commissioner, Pat Byrne, said on RTÉ radio that he had to accept that there were still IRA weapons dumps around the State. He pointed out that the Southern Command of the Provos 'has always been seen within the IRA as providing logistical support'.

Peter Robinson, of Ian Paisley's Democratic Unionist Party (DUP), expressed scepticism in the House of Commons, on 16 May 2000, in regard to 'so-called confidence-building measures'. Robinson went on: 'The intelligence services say there are more than twenty major arms dumps and hundreds of arms hides for the more operational weapons. It is envisaged that the IRA will allow people to look at three of them – not necessarily the three largest. Are the logistics of that inspection to be given to the international body? They will certainly not be given to the security forces ...'

Nevertheless, to allow outsiders to view its arms dumps was a big step for the Provisionals. The IRA has traditionally accorded particular importance to ensuring the security of its arms dumps. In the Green Book, General Order No. 11 deals with the seizure of arms and dumps that are under IRA control, and lays down a dire penalty for any volunteer involved in the seizure of IRA arms. The order states: 'Any Volunteer who seizes or is party to the seizure of arms, ammunition or explosives which are being held under Army Control, shall be deemed guilty of treachery. A duly-constituted court martial shall try all cases. Penalty for breach of this order: Death.'

The IRA has shown that it was prepared to kill not only its own volunteers, but civilians who were party to the seizure of arms. In July 1991, the

IRA murdered Tom Oliver, a farmer from the Cooley area of County Louth, after a small cache of arms hidden in a barrel on farmland was seized by Gardaí. It emerged later that the forty-four-year-old father of seven had come across the barrel when a JCB was carrying out drainage work on land that he rented, and reported it to the authorities.

Oliver was subjected to particularly brutal treatment after being kidnapped, as if his abductors wanted to send a message to the community that reporting arms dumps would not be tolerated. The farmer was stripped of his clothes, interrogated, and killed with six shots that blew part of his head away. Oliver's body, dressed in a boiler suit, was dumped on a road north of the Border, and showed signs of horrendous torture when it was recovered. He was so severely beaten that a priest who saw the bloodied corpse believed that concrete blocks had been dropped on every bone in his body. The victim's brother-in-law John O'Hanlon told a reporter: 'I'll never forget, as long as I live, the screams of Bridie [Mrs Oliver] and the children when they went to the morgue.'[5]

The IRA, concerned about a popular backlash, claimed that Oliver had confessed to operating as an informer, but there was widespread scepticism about the allegation, especially among the local people. Thousands of locals turned out for a rally in protest at the murder by the IRA of their neighbour, a kindly, popular man. Civil rights campaigner Father Denis Faul, who had a long record of opposing the abuses of the security forces in Northern Ireland, was applauded when he told the rally: 'The Provisionals are finished here. Give them no recognition, no help in their Provo activities, above all keep your children away from their influence. Tell your children that violence is wrong and that gunmen are evil. The blackmail and intimidation, the gun, will soon come upon your children if you do not make a stand now.'

Following the murder, republicans were shunned and ostracised in Cooley. Nevertheless, the IRA had probably boosted the security of its dumps and discouraged people from reporting arms caches by, in effect, sending out the message – if you compromise our arms dumps, you will end up like Tom Oliver.

On a practical level, the IRA sought to effectively hide and also to conserve weaponry by building underground concrete bunkers for the bigger caches of weapons. To defeat surveillance from the air, they were often built beneath other structures, such as farm buildings. These bunkers could also be used for the manufacture of improvised weaponry, for example mortars. A political source in Dublin told me that the IRA had come up with an ingenious method of preserving weapons in underground bunkers, using modern technology. Arms were oiled and then vacuum-packed in heavy plastic, ensuring that they would not deteriorate even if dampness penetrated the bunkers where they were stored.

A former British Army officer has described the finding of an underground bunker in the County Tyrone countryside as recently as 2001. It was apparently associated with dissident republicans. According to the account given by Colonel Tim Collins, the bunker was extremely sophisticated. It was built a metre below ground, and measured about fourteen metres long and one-and-a-half metres wide. It had been carefully waterproofed, had carpet on the floor and cupboards along both sides. Even electric light had been installed. Access was through a manhole made to look like a drain.[6]

Some sizeable collections of arms were stored in more temporary facilities. For instance, when Garda officers made their first major discovery of Libyan-supplied weapons on a remote beach in Donegal in January 1988, the arms were packed into two oil tanks buried in the sand, one with a capacity of 300 gallons and the other 600 gallons. The hides were found at Five Fingers Strand, near Malin.

It would appear that bunkers or 'hides' were often located in areas where an IRA member or sympathiser could keep a discreet eye, from a distance, on the facility or the general area where it was located, so as to report any activity by police or military, or by outsiders who might report an arms cache to the authorities. A former IRA member explained that it was important to know if a 'hide' had been compromised. If the arms cache had been found by the security forces, you had to assume they would be lying in wait for the IRA to return to the 'hide', he said. 'In the Six Counties, that could mean the SAS lying in ambush, and those boys would shoot first and ask questions afterwards.'

A report in 2004 by the Morris Tribunal, which has been inquiring into the activities of certain Garda officers in County Donegal, gave an insight into the system used by the IRA for hiding explosives. There were two types of 'hide' – a short-term or 'transit' hide for explosives already made up and ready to be primed, and a 'long-term' hide for more permanent storage, for explosive materials that had not yet been mixed.[7]

The IRA move to allow inspection of their bigger arms dumps helped first minister David Trimble to secure his Unionist Party's backing for a return to government. However, the Unionists were unhappy with further progress on the arms issue and, in July 2001, Trimble resigned as first minister over the failure by the IRA to decommission fully.

Two unexpected events abroad then served to put pressure on the IRA, with some commentators regarding these as key factors in getting the IRA to carry out its first act of decommissioning, in October 2001. In August, three Irish republicans carrying false passports were arrested in Bogota, after emerging from the region of Colombia held by FARC insurgents. FARC, often described as 'narco-terrorists', funded their rebellion with the aid of money from the cocaine trade. The White House took a very poor view of the apparent connection between Irish republicans and FARC, and Sinn Féin leaders saw their influence with the Bush administration quickly draining away. The following month, the 9/11 attack on America occurred. After Osama bin Laden's Al Qaeda disciples destroyed the Twin Towers, killing thousands, attitudes hardened in America towards any group associated with armed insurgency. Some observers considered that from then on, far less tolerance would be shown to the IRA and its political representatives, Sinn Féin, in the corridors of power in Washington.

It was against this background that the IRA finally performed its first act of decommissioning, on 23 October 2001. The following month, the Northern Ireland institutions were up and running again. The IRA decommissioning move helped, to some degree, to get Sinn Féin off the hook with the Bush administration. The act of decommissioning was carried out under the supervision of General de Chastelain's Commission.

It was an historic event, as it was the first time that any Irish republican paramilitary group had voluntarily put arms beyond use. As the IRA emerged from the Civil War of 1923 and as hostilities ceased, the organisation's chief of staff at the time, Frank Aiken, sent out the message to 'dump arms'. At the end of the Border Campaign in 1962, when the IRA of that era declared a cease-fire, arms were hidden away rather than given up or destroyed. When the Official IRA declared a cease-fire in 1972, no arms were surrendered or decommissioned – there may still be small quantities of arms in the possession of individuals who were linked to the Officials.

General de Chastelain told how he and his two colleagues from the IICD, Brigadier Tauno Nieminen of Finland and US diplomat Andrew Sens, were brought to a secret location and witnessed weapons, ammunition and explosives being put permanently beyond use. Also present at the decommissioning event was the IRA intermediary with whom they had been dealing, who the General referred to by the usual IRA pseudonym of 'P O'Neill'. A number of IRA members were present to carry out the actual act of decommissioning, possibly by pouring concrete into a bunker. General de Chastelain said that he and his colleagues examined the materiel before it was decommissioned, satisfying themselves that the equipment was serviceable. They took an inventory of the weapons and ammunition being put beyond use, and weighed the explosives. The general had little else to say – the event had taken place in private, at the behest of the IRA.

On 11 April 2002, another IRA act of decommissioning took place. The IICD reported that in this second act of putting weapons beyond use, a 'substantial' amount of weaponry had been decommissioned. Later in April, a British newspaper claimed that the IRA was secretly buying high-velocity rifles in Russia while pretending to be decommissioning. According to the report, senior IRA commanders bought at least twenty powerful, special forces AN-94 rifles, and ammunition, in Moscow in late 2001. The deal was said to have been detected by the Russian security services, which passed details to British military intelligence in London. Cabinet ministers were briefed on the matter, as were Northern Ireland politicians.[8] The claims were angrily rejected by Sinn Féin leader Gerry Adams.

The following October, the Police Service of Northern Ireland (PSNI), successor force to the RUC, raided Sinn Féin offices at the Belfast seat of government, Stormont, as part of an investigation into alleged IRA intelligence-gathering at the heart of government. First minister David Trimble made it clear that Unionists could no longer stay in the power-sharing executive with Sinn Féin after the disclosure that an IRA spy ring was allegedly operating inside Stormont. The controversy resulted in Northern Ireland secretary Dr John Reid announcing the suspension of devolution and the restoration of direct rule.

On 21 October 2003, the IRA carried out a third act of decommissioning, in advance of the Assembly elections the following month. The decommissioning may have given a boost to Sinn Féin at the polls. In the elections, Sinn Féin and Ian Paisley's Democratic Unionist Party (DUP) emerged as the biggest parties in Northern Ireland on the nationalist and unionist sides respectively. This meant that the most hard-line party on each side had now come to the fore.

From the point of view of analysts of IRA weaponry, this latest act of decommissioning was interesting in light of the revelation that 'heavy' weaponry had been decommissioned. There was speculation that the IRA may have destroyed heavy, improvised mortars, in light of guarded comments made by General de Chastelain. The general, as usual, oversaw the act of decommissioning but was restricted in what he could reveal about the materiel put beyond use. The general declared that IRA 'light, medium and heavy weapons' had been decommissioned. He said that explosives, ammunition and explosives materiel had been put beyond use. He was quoted as saying that part of this included fuses, detonators, timing units and power supplies, as well as a variety of firearms, including automatic guns and a variety of heavy artillery.

Some analysts considered that the only weapons that have been deployed by the IRA that would fit the military definition of 'heavy', or that would conform to the description 'heavy artillery', were the heavier improvised mortars built by IRA engineers during the long years of conflict. The IRA may not have stockpiled many of these heavier mortars. If any were, in fact, decommissioned, the act would have had more symbolic than practical significance, as they can easily be manufactured. (It is known that the IRA has, in the past, stockpiled mortars – certainly the lighter types. A raid by Gardaí on an IRA bomb factory in a fourteen-foot by eight-foot underground bunker in County Laois in 1996 yielded a range of materiel, including forty mortar tubes, with sixteen more tubes found in a workshop above ground.)

Over the years, a range of different types of mortars was produced by the IRA, one of the most recent being the heavy device known as the 'barrackbuster' or Mark 15. The device was used in a number of attacks on police and army bases in Northern Ireland during the 1990s. The mortar was used as recently as 1996, in the IRA attack on a British Army base at Osnabrück, Germany.

The IRA had a number of 12.7mm DShK heavy machine guns in its arsenal, and there has been speculation that General de Chastelain may have been referring to this weapon when he talked of 'heavy weapons' being decommissioned. However, some military analysts believed that these machine guns would have come within the terms of the General's definition of 'medium' weapons.

So what other weapons might the IRA have decommissioned on this occasion? In terms of what are normally defined as 'medium' weapons, such as machine guns and RPG-7 rocket launchers and rockets, the IRA had a range of weaponry in recent years that would fit into this category. As regards 'light weapons', the IRA had a significant estimated inventory, including up to 1,000 assault rifles. Significantly, following the third act of decommissioning, General de Chastelain announced that 'explosives and explosives materials' had been put beyond use. Once again, this may have been a reference to the explosive Semtex. And once again, there was speculation that the decommissioning may have taken place by means of concrete being poured into a bunker. There was no indication that explosives were disposed of by being blown up.

In December 2004, a final, major act of IRA decommissioning seemed to be on the cards. British Prime Minister Tony Blair and Taoiseach Bertie Ahern felt they had come close to a deal to restore Northern Ireland's power-sharing institutions. The deal would have seen two traditional opponents, Ian Paisley's DUP and Gerry Adams' Sinn Féin, go into government together. As part of the deal the IRA was supposed to put all of its weapons beyond use, in the presence of General de Chastelain's commission and Protestant and Catholic clergy. However, the deal fell apart when the IRA refused to concede to DUP demands for photographs to be taken of the arms being decommissioned. Republicans saw the DUP demand as an attempt to humiliate them.

Another stumbling block emerged when the Progressive Democrats in the Irish coalition government stated that the IRA had failed to sign up to a 'no criminality' clause. There were still hopes that a deal could be clinched early in 2005, but these hopes were dashed in the aftermath of the £26.5 million robbery at the Northern Bank in Belfast before Christmas 2004. Both the Irish and British governments said the IRA carried out the raid. IRA bosses were accused of planning the massive robbery even as they were purporting to get rid of their arms to further the Peace Process. The IRA denied involvement in the robbery. Sinn Féin chiefs Gerry Adams and Martin McGuinness angrily denied claims that they knew about the plans for the robbery even while they were engaging in talks to restore the North's institutions.

Irish Justice Minister and Progressive Democrats President Michael McDowell, a virulent critic of Sinn Féin /IRA, declared that there could be no place in government on either side of the Border for a party that supported the use or threatened use of violence, possessed firearms or explosives, usurped the policing function in any part of the island, engaged in armed robbery or theft, or engaged in smuggling and counterfeiting.

Then, at the end of January 2005, came the savage murder by republicans of Belfast man Robert McCartney following a pub row. It was not an IRA-authorised murder, but it was generally accepted that members of the IRA were involved. Republicans carried out a clean-up to destroy forensic evidence, and police met with a wall of silence when they sought to interview certain key witnesses. The dead man's five courageous sisters and his partner went on to mount a campaign for justice, which caught the imagination of the world's media, leading to an international backlash against Sinn Féin and the IRA. In another development, in early February, the IRA announced in an angry statement that it was withdrawing a decommissioning offer it had made in late 2004.

In April, Sinn Féin President Gerry Adams called on the IRA to pursue its goal exclusively though politics. The following month, there were further challenges to the sincerity of the IRA's commitment to the Peace Process, with the publication of a report by the Independent Monitoring Commission (IMC), the four-man watchdog panel appointed to provide assessments on the activities of the IRA and other paramilitary groups in Northern Ireland. The IMC found that the IRA remained active, and cited evidence that the IRA continued to smuggle in armaments in defiance of the disarmament goals of the 1998 Belfast Agreement (also known as the Good Friday Agreement).

The report said that in September 2004 the police discovered, in an IRA arms dump, 10,000 rounds of assault rifle ammunition 'of a type not previously found in Northern Ireland and manufactured since the Belfast Agreement.' These bullets 'may have been only part of a larger consignment,' the report said.[9] According to another report, police traced the bullets to a manufacturer in Russia, who forwarded them to an arms dealer in Germany in 2002.[10] The ten boxes of 7.62mm ammunition, suitable for a Kalashnikov rifle, later entered Northern Ireland, and were found by police in a padlocked cupboard in a house in Twinbrook housing estate, West Belfast, on 28 October 2004. A forty-five-year-old woman appeared in court in connection with the find, but was cleared. Police did not establish how the ammunition was smuggled into Northern Ireland.

At the end of July 2005, there was a long-awaited and significant statement from the IRA. The statement said that the IRA had ordered an end to its armed campaign. 'All IRA units have been ordered to dump arms. All Volunteers have been instructed to assist the development of purely political and democratic programmes through exclusively peaceful means. Volunteers must not engage in any other activities whatsoever.' The statement said that the IRA leadership 'has also authorised our representative to engage with the IICD to complete the process to verifiably put its arms beyond use in a way which will further enhance public confidence and to conclude this as quickly as possible'.

A number of commentators expressed the view that the campaign for justice by the sisters and partner of Robert McCartney was one of the factors that helped to accelerate the IRA's decision to declare that the war is over. Despite the IRA's 'farewell to arms' statement, there were still questions being asked by commentators and politicians – was the IRA also willing to give up the criminality and rackets from which it allegedly derived considerable funds?

The IRA destroys its weapons

The final act in the decommissioning of IRA arms took place in September 2005. For some weeks prior to the IRA's fourth and last act of decommissioning, IRA members gathered weaponry from various dumps and 'hides' into a number of more centralised locations. These were the sites to which General de Chastelain and his colleagues would be brought, accompanied by two clergymen witnesses, to observe the final putting beyond use of the materiel.

The clerical witnesses were the Reverend Harold Good of the Methodist Church, and a Catholic priest, Father Alec Reid C.Ss.R., a member of the Redemptorist Order, based at the Clonard monastery in Belfast. Both are highly-respected, experienced clergymen, deeply committed to the Christian message of peace and reconciliation.

Father Reid would later find himself in the midst of a controversy over remarks he made, in the heat of debate, comparing the treatment of Catholics under Stormont to the treatment of Jews by the Nazis. Nevertheless, Father Reid, a native of County Tipperary, had played an important role behind the scenes in trying to bring peace to the North, and in bringing an end to the IRA's campaign of violence.

He had tried, in 1988, to save two British Army corporals who had lost their way and driven into the midst of an IRA funeral in Belfast. The soldiers were overpowered by a crowd, beaten, stripped and then shot dead by the IRA. A picture of Father Reid kneeling in prayer over the bruised, naked body of one of the dead soldiers became one of the most poignant images of the Troubles.

The Reverend Good had ministered in the deprived Dublin of the 1950s, and to black congregations in the US during the civil rights campaigns of the 1960s. At the start of the Troubles he served in the traditionally Protestant Shankill Road area of Belfast, and was also a part-time chaplain at Crumlin Road Prison, ministering to loyalist prisoners. He has recalled that while based later in East Belfast, it was often part of his job to break the news to RUC wives that their husbands had been killed.[11] In the late 1970s he had begun a discreet dialogue with republicans.

The locations where the IRA arms were gathered for decommissioning are understood to have included farm outhouses and warehouse-type buildings. The actual decommissioning was carried out over a number of days, concluding on Saturday, 24 September. Early each morning, an IRA intermediary driving a closed van would collect General de Chastelain, Andrew Sens, Brigadier General Tauno Nieminen and the two clergymen, and transport them to the location where arms were being put beyond use that day.

At each location, the IRA deployed a team of its members, under the command of a senior Provisional, to deal with the decommissioning. Extra helpers were available as required. Much preparatory work was done in advance of the arrival of de Chastelain and his colleagues. Weapons were tagged with reference numbers, and laid out in orderly fashion, in order to facilitate the taking of an inventory by the IICD. De Chastelain personally removed vital parts from weapons, but the final act of decommissioning was left to the IRA members themselves.

Obviously, the IRA wanted to dispel any notion that they had 'surrendered' arms, or had suffered 'defeat'. The actual method of decommissioning was not disclosed. There was speculation that arms were placed in a trench, and a corrosive substance poured over them, followed by the pouring of cement. Since the agreed decommissioning process does not allow for weapons to be forensically examined before they are put beyond use, one could speculate that the IRA used the opportunity to dispose of weapons that had been used in murders, punishment attacks and other crimes.

After coming away from the location, the IICD members would work until late at night, writing up inventories of the items they had witnessed being decommissioned.

Types of weaponry and explosives decommissioned

For supporters of the peace process, it was encouraging to note that Semtex explosive was decommissioned. The powerful Libyan-supplied explosive, still in six-by-four-inch brown sealed packets, was one of the most valuable items in the Provo arsenal. It was used in mortars, car bombs and other devices, and facilitated the strategy of targeting economic and political targets on the UK 'mainland'.

Among the infantry weapons decommissioned was a sizeable number of Romanian-manufactured AKM assault rifles supplied by Libya. It is understood that other rifles put beyond use included Armalites, which were probably smuggled from the US in the 1970s. As regards other weaponry, it is known that pistols and revolvers were decommissioned, and from a previous era, at least one Sten gun and one Bren gun.

De Chastelain and his colleagues used weighing scales to weigh ammunition and calculate the numbers of rounds. It is believed that hundreds of thousands of rounds were put beyond use. The scales would also have been used to weigh explosives. At a press conference, de Chastelain said there was 'a lot of ammunition', mostly still in the manufacturers' boxes, but a lot also loose, either in belts or in individual rounds of a wide variety of sizes. In explanatory notes accompanying the 1998 estimated inventory given to de Chastelain, the security forces stated that approximately 1.5 million rounds of ammunition were imported in the four Libyan shipments that got through to the IRA. The document stated: 'While substantial quantities of ammunition have been recovered in various jurisdictions, it is impossible to quantify what amount has been expended both operationally and in training.'

During his press conference, General de Chastelain confirmed that surface-to-air missiles (SAMs) were destroyed. It can be assumed that these were the SA-7B 'Grail' missiles (often referred to as SAM-7s) supplied by Libya in the 1980s. The Provisionals never realised their ambition to use a SAM to bring down a British Army helicopter, although they did hit helicopters by other means – heavy machine guns (HMGs), such as the US-made M60 and the Soviet-designed 12.7mm DShK ('Dooshka'), were among the weapons deployed by the Provisionals in an anti-aircraft role. It was suspected that the IRA may have fired a SAM-7 missile at a British Army helicopter from south of the Border in 1988, but without scoring a hit. In April 1999 two spent SAM-7 battery packs were found in isolated countryside near Pomeroy, County Tyrone, suggesting that the IRA had been test-ing the weapon.

General de Chastelain revealed that other support weapons put beyond use included RPG-7 rocket launchers and the grenades for these launchers, as well as heavy machine guns. The latter were likely to have included Libyan-supplied 12.7mm DShK HMGs. Among the more unusual weap-ons decommissioned were a number of flame-throwers, again supplied by Libya. These were believed to be Eastern Bloc manportable LPO-50 light infantry flame-throwers.

In his remarks to the press, de Chastelain referred to mortars being decommissioned. It was generally assumed that this was a reference to improvised mortars. While the IRA did try to procure conventional mili-tary mortars on occasion, it was thought that the only type of mortar in the arsenal of the IRA was the 'home-made' variety. The IRA had built up considerable experience in the production of such home-made mortars over the years. (Indeed, it was suspected that the three Irish republicans arrested after visiting the FARC-held region of Colombia in August 2001 had been involved in a programme to teach FARC insurgents how to manufacture such mortars. This was denied by the three men.) De Chastelain indicated that other improvised weapons were also put beyond use, as well as items such as timer power units (TPUs), used in the construction of bombs. 'Explosive substances' were decommissioned – this could be a reference to the raw materials used in the manufacture of 'home-made' explosives.

Because of the long delay in getting to the final stages of IRA decommissioning, General de Chastelain asked the security forces to update the estimates of paramilitary weapons that had been supplied to him in the late 1990s. In September 2004 he received an updated estimated inventory of IRA arms. The updated estimates were used by de Chastelain and his IICD colleagues as a yardstick by which to judge the final IRA act of decommissioning. De Chastelain declared that the large amounts of weaponry put beyond use were consistent with the British and Irish security forces' estimates of what the PIRA had hidden in its arms dumps. He and his colleagues were satisfied that the PIRA had put all its arms beyond use.

De Chastelain and his IICD colleagues are precluded from disclosing inventories of arms put beyond use until all the paramilitary organisations have decommissioned their arms. Inevitably, there were those who questioned if the IRA had really totally disarmed, with the Reverend Ian Paisley and his DUP expressing particular scepticism. Some journalists reported that the IRA had held back some handguns for defensive purposes or for reasons of 'internal security' – claims that were denied by republicans.

General de Chastelain and his IICD colleagues remained convinced that the IRA had totally decommissioned, and this belief was shared by the clergymen witnesses. Nevertheless, de Chastelain did concede that they had no way of knowing for certain that the IRA had not retained some arms. But it was their understanding from the discussions they had with the IRA, and based on what they had seen, that the organisation was sincere when it said it had decommissioned all its arms.

De Chastelain also suggested that there might be arms that had been lost due to the person who hid them having died. It could be that, in a number of years' time, somebody could stumble across a field and find some arms belonging to the IRA. That person could then say that when the Commission members had reported they had got everything, they were wrong. De Chastelain posed a rhetorical question: 'Is that possible? Of course it is.' In November, during a meeting in Edinburgh of the British–Irish Parliamentary Body, I asked Northern Secretary Peter Hain if he thought the IRA had secretly retained some arms. He made it clear that he accepted the verdict of the IICD.

The debate as to whether or not the IRA had fully disarmed was given a new lease of life in early 2006. Differences arose on the arms issue between the de Chastelain Commission and the watchdog group, the IMC. In its report issued on 1 February 2006, the IMC concluded that while most indicators suggested that the IRA was evolving in a 'positive direction', they had received reports that 'not all PIRA's weapons and ammunition were handed over for decommissioning in September'. De Chastelain's IICD, in a report issued about the same time, stood over its conclusion the previous September that the IRA had decommissioned all its arms.

The IICD said that security sources in Northern Ireland had informed it in December of intelligence that the IRA had retained weapons. The IICD did not identify these sources, but it was thought likely that they were the PSNI and MI5. The IICD made its own inquiries, discussing the intelligence findings with the Garda Síochána. The IICD stated: 'Intelligence available to the Garda at the time of decommissioning last year indicated that extensive efforts had been made by the IRA to locate and gather weapons which, in turn, were put beyond use in the process overseen by us. Further, the Garda informed us that what they regard as reliable sources in relation to the IRA and its weaponry, have produced no intelligence suggesting any arms have been retained.'

The IICD also spoke to the IRA representative with whom it had dealt on decommissioning. The IRA intermediary reiterated that all the arms that had been dumped following the July 2005 order to all IRA units to dump arms, had been collected and put beyond use in September under the supervision of the IICD. He assured the IICD that no IRA arms had been retained or placed in long-term hides. The IICD added: 'We conclude that in the absence of evidence to the contrary, our 26 September assessment regarding IRA weapons remains correct.'

In a worrying development, the IMC report suggested that the reports it had received indicated that there was a range of different kinds of weapons and ammunition outstanding, and that the materiel 'goes beyond what might possibly have been expected to have missed decommissioning, such as a limited number of handguns kept for personal protection or some items the whereabouts of which was no longer known'. The report went on: 'We recognise that if these reports were confirmed the key question would be how much the PIRA leadership knew about these weapons. These same reports do not cast doubt on the declared intention of the PIRA leadership to eschew terrorism. For our part, we are clear that this latter is their strategic intent.'

The British and Irish governments, as they renewed efforts in early 2006 to revive the North's political institutions, and to persuade Ian Paisley's DUP to assist in restoring devolution, seized on the more optimistic aspects of the IMC report. For its part, the Irish Government, on the weapons issue, appeared to show preference for the findings of the IICD rather than those of the IMC, regarding the IICD as the body specifically set up to deal with decommissioning. An Irish Government source remarked at the time that the security forces themselves in the North were divided on the arms issue, with some elements going along with the IICD verdict, as indeed did the Garda Síochána.

The IMC's ninth report, issued in April 2006, gave a more optimistic view of the situation regarding IRA arms. The IMC recalled that they had referred in their previous report to having received reports that not all the IRA's weapons and ammunition had been handed over for decommissioning in September 2005. 'We did not say three months ago that the PIRA leadership had in any way given instructions to retain arms. Indeed, our present assessment is that such of the arms as were reported to us as having been retained, would have been withheld under local control despite the instructions of the leadership. We note that, as reported by the IICD, the leadership claimed only to have decommissioned all the arms "under its control". The relevant points are that the amount of unsurrendered material was not significant in comparison to what was decommissioned and that these reports do not cast doubt on the declared intention of the PIRA leadership to eschew terrorism and to follow the political path.'

De Chastelain focuses on the loyalists

Apart from the issue of IRA arms, the IICD also had to deal with the outstanding issue of loyalist arms. In the wake of IRA decommissioning in September 2005, the commission held a number of meetings with the Ulster Political Research Group (UPRG), a group linked to the UDA. A UDA representative took part in some of the meetings. In its report dated 19 January 2006, the IICD hinted that the UDA would consider decommissioning in return for economic aid for loyalist areas. The report stated: 'While these [meetings] have not led to firm decommissioning proposals, we are advised that the UDA is prepared to address the issue of arms in the context of a satisfactory consideration by the British government of its community's economic concerns.'

According to the report, the UVF had not resumed formal contact with the Commission, but de Chastelain and his colleagues were hoping to reopen the channel in the coming months.

There were reports in late 2005 that the Loyalist Volunteer Force (LVF) might disband. This small, ruthless group was the first paramilitary organisation to decommission some weapons, some would say opportunistically, under the supervision of the IICD, in December 1998. The IICD report commented: 'While the LVF has not resumed formal contact with us, it has authorised informal discussions with an intermediary and we have held a number of meetings with him. We are aware of recent media reports in which the LVF has signalled its intention to stand down its activities. While we have no indication how such a stand down would involve the disposals of LVF arms, we have emphasised that their decommissioning must take place under our supervision. We are led to understand that the LVF wishes to received community-related assurances from the British government before any action on its arms proceeds.'

Epilogue

In writing the history of gunrunning and the Irish Troubles, one has to bear in mind the human tragedies that resulted from the manner in which the imported weapons were used. Many were killed with firearms and explosives smuggled in from abroad. Both communities suffered. Many families on both sides of the divide have been left in mourning. Everybody who died in the conflict was somebody's son or daughter, somebody's husband or wife, somebody's father or mother, somebody's partner or loved one.

On a personal level, I was stunned when a friend phoned me in the middle of the night in September 2001 to convey some awful news. Martin O'Hagan, a journalist colleague on the *Sunday World* in Northern Ireland, had been shot dead by loyalists in Lurgan, County Armagh, as he walked home from the pub with his wife Marie. I had spoken to him on the phone only a short time previously. He called me to see if I had a phone number for the wife of one of the Colombia Three. In fact, I didn't.

He was his usual cheerful self – outgoing, lively and full of enthusiasm. Two days later he was dead. It was believed that members of the Loyalist Volunteer Force were responsible. Martin had angered the group by exposing how they operated a drugs distribution network while at the same time carrying out murderous sectarian attacks on

Catholics. Martin, who hated sectarianism and whose widow Marie is a Protestant, was the first working journalist to be killed in Northern Ireland since the outbreak of the Troubles in 1969. It was not the first time loyalists had shot a journalist – in 1984 Jim Campbell was shot and seriously wounded in another loyalist assassination attempt. He still has a bullet lodged in his body.

Attending Martin's funeral, I saw at first hand the devastation wrought on his family by that senseless, callous murder. So many people had hoped that with the signing of the Good Friday Agreement in 1998, the killing would be over for good. But still murders were happening, although thankfully on a smaller scale than during the years of full-scale conflict. We watched Marty being laid to rest on a gloomy afternoon in a rain-swept cemetery near Lurgan. It was a grim reminder that, despite the Peace Process, some of the gunmen had still not gone away.

The turmoil in Northern Ireland sucked many young people into paramilitary activity on both sides who, in other circumstances, might have been law-abiding citizens. Marty himself had been a member of the Official IRA in his youth, before abandoning paramilitary activity and taking the path of peace. He told me that in the early years of the Troubles he smuggled guns into the North from the South, hidden in a car. It would have been interesting to talk to him in more detail about those activities during research for this book, but it was not to be.

Marty was just one of many victims of loyalist paramilitary killers. A notable 1999 study, *Northern Ireland's Troubles – The Human Costs*,[1] showed that loyalist paramilitaries made an horrific contribution to the death toll during the decades of conflict. The study by Marie-Therese Fay, Mike Morrissey and Marie Smyth, found that loyalists killed 983 people – including 735 Catholics. (By comparison, deaths attributed to the British Army totalled 318, while fifty-three deaths were attributed to the RUC.) In some cases, Catholics were abducted and tortured by loyalist paramilitaries before being killed, the aim clearly being to spread terror among the Catholic population. Many Catholics who had no links to paramilitary activity were murdered, simply because of their religion.

The study stated that almost half of the total figure for Catholic deaths could be attributed to loyalist paramilitaries. The latter, of course, were also responsible for a sizeable number of Protestant fatalities, inflicting almost a fifth of these deaths. The authors of the study remark that 'a significant source of deaths within each community has been the paramilitaries that claim to defend them'.

Of all the paramilitary groups, the Provisional IRA was the most effective procurer of arms, and the imported weapons helped it to become a highly efficient killing machine. In line with the strategy outlined in their internal handbook, the Green Book, the IRA set out to kill as many of the 'enemy' as possible, and by the time the organisation called off attacks on the security forces it had amassed a considerable tally in terms of deaths inflicted. No quarter was given to what might be termed prisoners of war, and there is no reference in the Green Book to the Geneva Convention on the treatment of prisoners. Any British soldier or Northern Ireland policeman who fell into the hands of the IRA was killed. 'Sending the Brits home in coffins,' was the way that one republican described the IRA campaign to me.

But it was not just men and women in uniform who died – the Provos also killed hundreds of civilians. Indeed the IRA emerged as the biggest single source of deaths during the conflict. The study cited above found that out of 3,601 deaths over the years of the conflict, close on half were caused by the IRA – a total of 1,684 deaths. The Provos suffered 355 casualties, which meant that they managed to kill at least five people for every death they suffered themselves. As the journalist Fintan O'Toole put it, the IRA 'dominated the killing game'.[2]

The figures also brought home the extent of the casualties resulting from paramilitary feuding. O'Toole, commenting in a newspaper column on the statistics, wrote: 'The largest number of republican paramilitaries killed in the conflict were murdered, not by the RUC or the British Army, or the loyalist terror gangs, but by their own comrades. The INLA and the IRA have been responsible for the deaths of 164 of their own members. The Army, RUC, UDR and loyalist paramilitaries killed 161. It is striking, for example, that even in a largely Catholic area like west Belfast, more republican paramilitaries were killed by their own side (forty-two) than by the British Army, UDR, RUC and loyalists (forty-one) put together.'[3]

The study showed that republican paramilitaries caused the deaths of 713 civilians, most of whom were killed by the IRA. Civilians were killed in a variety of ways – for instance, through being caught up in bombs planted in public places. Young people were among the victims – the study showed that the IRA killed seventy-three children under the age of eighteen.[4] The IRA were firm believers in the use of capital punishment, and various categories of civilians were considered 'legitimate targets' and marked down for death, such as those who carried out building or repair work on security force installations.

Young men accused of criminal activity were also killed, even though, in any normal society, their alleged offences would not have been regarded as in any way deserving of the death penalty.[5] In addition, there were non-combatants who were assassinated by the IRA, apparently because of their views or background.[6] Leaving out members of the British Army or those killed in Britain or on the Continent, whose religious affiliations were generally not reported, the study found that the IRA killed 745 Protestants and 381 Catholics.

The latter figure for Catholic deaths inflicted by the Provos is significant, as it means that, on the 1999 figures, the IRA killed more than a quarter of the 1,543 Catholics who died in the conflict. Members of the IRA usually saw themselves as defenders of the nationalist community. It was a view shared by their supporters abroad, and was one of the motivating factors behind the flow of arms into Ireland during the years of the Troubles. Nevertheless, the organisation was responsible for a sizeable death toll among Catholics. The authors of the study found that this could be partially explained by the republican bombing campaign, particularly in city centres, where casualties were more random. By comparison with the IRA's tally of 381 Catholic deaths, the British Army, the RUC and the UDR killed 316 Catholics between them. One of the great ironies of the Troubles is that the IRA killed more Catholics than the North's security forces put together.[7]

APPENDIX A: ESTIMATES OF ARMS HOLDINGS BY PARAMILITARY GROUPS

In the latter part of the 1990s, as the peace progress got under way and as the decommissioning of paramilitary weapons became an issue, the Garda Síochána and the RUC drew up estimates of the arms being held by republican and loyalist paramilitary organisations.[1] This information was given to the Independent International Commission on Decommissioning. The author's interpretation of that data is given in this appendix.

As the tables show, much of the weaponry estimated to have been held by the IRA was delivered in the four Libyan shipments that got through to the organisation in 1986–87, before the fifth shipment, aboard the *Eksund*, was seized by the French.

Obviously, these estimates relate to the period before decommissioning started – there were three acts of decommissioning of IRA war materiel, in October 2001, April 2002 and October 2003, before the fourth and final act in September 2005. Neither do the estimates take into account seizures of weapons that occurred after 1998, materiel stolen by those who broke away from the IRA to set up the Real IRA (RIRA), or deliveries of new weaponry from Florida in 1999.

The estimates of IRA arms were updated in 2004 and given to General John de Chastelain's IICD, which used these updated figures as a yardstick by which to assess the final IRA act of decommissioning in September 2005.

PIRA ARMS

Table One

PIRA weaponry – estimates of types and quantities of weapons delivered to the IRA from Libya in four shipments, 1986–87, prior to seizure of fifth shipment on board the *Eksund*. (estimates valid as of 1998):

Designation	Role	Amounts supplied	Amounts recovered by security forces	Amounts outstanding
N/A	9mm pistols	50	32	18
Webley	Revolvers	130	62	68
AKM	Assault rifles	1200	612	588
N/A	Hand grenades	275	160	115
GPMG	Machine guns	40	30	10
DSHK	Heavy machine guns	26	9	17
RPG-7	Rocket-propelled grenade launchers	33	22	11
RPG-7	Grenades for above	130	84	46
SAM-7B	Surface-to-air missiles	10	1	9
Probably LPO-50	Light infantry flame-throwers	10	3	7

Table Two

Other Libyan-supplied items believed outstanding from the pre-*Eksund* shipments (estimates valid as of 1998):

Designation	Role	Amounts Outstanding
N/A	Electric detonators	711
N/A	Plain detonators	493
Semtex	Explosive	2,635kg

Note: The security forces noted, in notes accompanying the estimates applicable as of 1998, that approximately 1.5 million rounds of ammunition were imported into Ireland in the four Libyan-supplied arms shipments that got through in the 1980s. However, the compilers of the estimates stated that while substantial quantities of ammunition had been recovered, it was impossible to estimate the quantities expended in operations and in training.

Table Three

Other weaponry in possession of the PIRA from non-Libyan shipments was believed to include the following (estimates valid as of 1998):

Role	Amounts Outstanding
Handguns	460+
Rifles	c.400
Sub-machine guns	40
Shotguns	31
.50 inch heavy machine guns	3

From the above figures, it would appear that, around the time of the 1998 Belfast Agreement, IRA arms included the following:

Table Four

Estimated PIRA arms from all sources (1998 estimates):

Type	Amount
Rifles	c.1,000
Handguns	c.600

Note: Although not mentioned in the estimates drawn up by security forces, the PIRA had another significant weapon in its arsenal – the Barrett sniping rifle. In 1998 it was thought likely that the IRA had at least one such weapon available.

Updating the inventory – possible differences between 1998 and 2004 estimates of IRA weaponry

The security forces in Northern Ireland and in the Irish Republic were called upon to update the estimated inventory of IRA weapons originally drawn up in the late 1990s. An updated estimated inventory was provided to General John de Chastelain and the IICD in 2004. The original estimates of IRA weaponry provided to the IICD were leaked in 1998, and the tables in this appendix are based on that data. It is unclear how the 2004 estimates differ from the 1998 estimates. Comments by General de Chastelain at his press conference on 26 September 2005, following the final act of IRA decommissioning, indicate that the format in the 2004 inventory was different from the 1998 version, with the security forces estimating the number of a particular type of weapon in a wide range of figures, between X and Y, rather than giving a single 'ballpark' figure as before. Details of the 2004 estimates have not been confirmed, at the time of writing. The IICD has stated that the IRA arms decommissioned tallied with the estimates. However, the IICD has always maintained the most scrupulous confidentiality in these matters. As a result question marks are likely to remain for some time about the quantities of materiel put out of use in the four acts of decommissioning.

The security forces are likely to have taken a number of factors into account in updating the estimates:

- Materiel stolen by dissidents:

  When the Real IRA (RIRA) broke away from the IRA in 1997/98, some materiel was taken from IRA stocks. The IRA itself has stated that materiel was stolen by the dissidents. The then quartermaster general of the IRA, Michael McKevitt, led the breakaway RIRA group and he would have had the best knowledge of the Provisionals' arms dumps, their contents and location. One could speculate that the McKevitt group only took small quantities of materiel. Had McKevitt's people cleared out major dumps, it is likely that the IRA would have retaliated with force, in line with guidelines in the Green Book, which lays down the death penalty for any volunteer who misappropriates weaponry.

  It is believed that Semtex formed part of the materiel taken by the RIRA, as well as some AKM rifles. However, arms discovered in RIRA dumps have not included large quantities of Provo materiel. Moreover, the RIRA went to considerable lengths to establish new sources of arms supply in eastern Europe, indicating that the organisation was not in possession of large amounts of ex-IRA weaponry.

- Arms imports from Florida in 1999:

  The security forces, in updating the estimated IRA inventory, would have taken into account arms smuggled into Ireland from Florida in 1999. This gunrunning operation, taking place as it did after the signing of the Good Friday Agreement, was particularly controversial as it raised questions about the commitment of the republican movement to the Peace Process and to decommissioning. According to some media reports, considerable numbers of firearms were smuggled into Ireland from Florida at this period – the figure of 200 has been mentioned. In fact, the actual figure may be much smaller. In June 2000, when three Irishmen were convicted on arms trafficking charges in a Florida court, evidence given during the hearing indicated that 118 weapons were ordered by the smugglers, and eighty-six purchased. Of these, fifty-seven were seized and twenty-nine never located. These twenty-nine weapons may have reached Ireland. It has been reported that three guns allegedly from the Florida batch were seized when members of an IRA vigilante gang were arrested in Cork. Another of the Florida-originated weapons was used, according to media reports, in the murder of republican dissident Joe O'Connor in 2000.

- Seizures of arms by security forces:

In revising the estimates, security forces would have taken account of arms seized since the estimates were originally compiled. Among a number of small seizures was the capture, in January 1999, of two .50 Browning heavy machine guns and a .30 Browning general-purpose machine gun. The weapons were found in an arms dump in County Monaghan.

- Natural wastage:

The security forces may have taken into account the 'natural wastage' factor in revising the estimates. Much of the IRA's materiel came into the country up to twenty years ago, or even further back. There is a reasonable chance that some of it was mislaid or lost. In his 26 September 2005 press conference, General de Chastelain remarked that some arms may have been lost 'in terms of an individual who was given responsibility having died and the location never having been found'.

Conclusion

It is reasonable to speculate that the above factors should not radically alter the 1998 estimates. It is also possible, of course, that the security forces concluded that their estimates at that time were in some cases inaccurate.

IRA improvised weaponry and home-made explosives (HME)

The Provisional IRA was not totally reliant on conventional weapons smuggled in from abroad or acquired through other means. The organisation developed considerable expertise over the years in 'do-it-yourself' weaponry and explosives. Provo engineers designed and built improvised weapons, such as home-made mortars – crude, throwaway, easily-assembled, short-range weapons that were often inaccurate but could cause devastating damage when the operators got lucky. The advantage from a guerrilla point of view was that they could be designed to be fired by a timing device, command wire or radio-control device. This allowed the operator to distance himself from the firing scene, once the mortars were placed in position, allowing a more secure getaway. The mortar tubes would be fixed on a flat-bed truck or a tractor trailer, or even inside a van with the roof cut out and the space camouflaged with painted cardboard. In later mortar designs, the IRA would usually deploy a range of tubes – up to as many as eighteen – each fixed at a slightly different angle in order to achieve a range of 'hits'.

The IRA also manufactured home-made explosive from fertiliser and other materials, for use in a variety of devices. These included mortar bombs, landmines and car bombs; devices designed to destroy buildings or other installations, anti-personnel devices and anti-armour devices. There were different types of home-made explosives – they became known by names such as 'Anfo' (fertilizer and diesel oil mix) and 'Annie' (a mixture of nitrobenzene and ammonium nitrate). Home-made weapons designed to be thrown included the nail bomb, an anti-personnel device. In the latter part of the 1980s, the IRA began to deploy the Improvised Anti-Armour Grenade (IAAG), also known as a drogue bomb, featuring a warhead with Semtex high-explosive, also designed to be thrown at a vehicle or dropped from overhead. One British military expert has recalled how another improvised weapon, the Mark 15 'coffee jar grenade', became the IRA's frequent weapon of choice for ambushing patrols or hitting static locations in the early 1990s.[2]

The IRA's General Headquarters had an Engineering Department, believed by the British to have been organised loosely on the basis of two sub-sections. There was a heavy engineering section, responsible for the design and building of weapons such as mortars and anti-armour projectiles, while an electronics section was responsible for producing devices such as timer mechanisms and radio-control components, designed to set off explosive devices.[3]

The first improvised mortar to be deployed by the IRA was fired at a security forces target in May 1972. It was a crude device, dubbed by the British Army a 'Mark 1'. The bomb consisted of a 50mm copper pipe filled with ten ounces of plastic explosive. The firing tube was a steel pipe. Propulsion was by means of a .303 cartridge.

The Provisionals went on to develop a range of other mortars over the years. The Mark 10 mortar, which made its debut in 1979, featured a steel firing tube and a bomb usually made from an oxy-acetylene gas cylinder and with an 18kg warhead of home-made explosive. The range was about 200 metres. An attack with bombs fired from nine Mark 10 mortar tubes on 28 February 1985 led to the greatest single loss of police lives during the Troubles, when nine RUC personnel were killed after one of the projectiles penetrated the roof of the canteen at Newry RUC station. The Mark 10 mortar, fired from a Transit van, was also used in the attack on the offices of British prime minister John Major at Downing Street, in February 1991.

As the security forces took measures to defend their installations against mortar attacks, the IRA went on to build bigger, more lethal devices. The arrival of Semtex explosive from Libya in the latter part of the 1980s enabled the IRA mortar designers to deploy more lethally powerful warheads. In late 1992, the IRA began to deploy its most powerful mortar to date – the Mark 15 'barrack-buster'. This was designed to fire a one-metre-long bomb made from a gas cylinder with more than 70kg of explosives. The range was more than 250 metres.

In the meantime, in the late 1980s, the IRA developed a Mark 12 mortar that was designed to be fired horizontally, rather than in the traditional high arc, towards the target. The Mark 12 was designed particularly with a view to hitting a moving vehicle.

Among other weapons developed by the IRA that could be used against vehicles, was an improvised projected grenade (IPG). The grenade, which made its debut in the mid-1980s, contained high explosive, and was designed to be fired from a launcher and to explode on impact. The IPG was succeeded by the more advanced projected recoilless improvised grenade (PRIG), which was first used in anger in May 1991, when it was fired at an RUC vehicle. It has been described as a home-made version of the Russian rocket-propelled grenade, the RPG-7.[4]

There were reports in the mid-1990s that the IRA was working on the development of a new mortar, dubbed the Mark 17, but few details emerged. It is assumed that any such projects, if still in development, would have been abandoned following the IRA's declaration in 2005 that its war was over.

Loyalist arms

A significant proportion of loyalist weaponry was believed to consist of arms smuggled into Northern Ireland in 1987 in one shipment for the UVF, UDA and Ulster Resistance. Table Five outlines the estimated amounts delivered, together with the amounts recovered, according to figures compiled by security forces.

Table Five

Loyalist arms shipment, 1987 (estimates valid as of 1998):

Designation	Role	Estimated contents of 1987 shipment	Amounts recovered by security forces	Amounts outstanding
FN	9mm pistol	94	67	27
VZ58	7.62 assault rifle	206	132	74
RPG-7	Rocket launcher	4	4	0
RPG-7	Rockets for above	62	42	20
RGD	Grenade	536	351	185

Table Six

Other arms reported to be 'ballistically outstanding' in possession of loyalist paramilitaries (estimates valid as of 1998; there may be some overlap between Tables Five and Six):

Role	Amounts ballistically outstanding
Handguns	674
Rifles	34
Sub-machine guns, including home-made	80
Shotguns	33

APPENDIX B: REPUBLICAN/NATIONALIST ARMS PROCUREMENT

Explanatory note: Tables in Appendices B and C cover arms procurement operations, confirmed and unconfirmed, successful and unsuccessful, and also arms deals or procurement operations that were reportedly being negotiated or worked on and later abandoned, from the late 1960s to present day. Obviously there were successful gunrunning operations that never came to light and that do not figure in the tables. One has to bear this in mind when examining the considerable number of arms cargoes that were intercepted by the authorities. Some entries feature in more than one table. In the tables, the entry 'Origin' indicates the country from which the weaponry was smuggled, rather than country of manufacture. Weights of materiel seized are presented in the tables in line with the weights as reported in the media at the time or as supplied by authorities – whether in terms of tons, tonnes, pounds or kilogrammes.

Table One
Saor Éire

War materiel: types and quantities	Origin	Date	Status	Comments
9mm Star pistols .38 hand guns	UK	Latter part of 1960s	Successful	Used by this small paramilitary group to carry out bank robberies in the Irish Republic and Northern Ireland in the late 1960s and early 1970s.
Handguns	Europe	Late 1960s	Unconfirmed	During research for this book, a former member of Saor Éire said that guns were imported from the Continent. There is no independent confirmation for this claim.

Table Two
Pre-split IRA

War materiel: types and quantities	Origin	Date	Status	Comments
60 x M-1 rifles/carbines Handguns M3 sub-machine guns 60,000 rounds of ammunition	USA	1969	Successful	Arms left over from the Border Campaign, supplied by George Harrison and smuggled to Ireland. Arms went to the element that was later to form the PIRA; some may have gone to the element that formed the OIRA (see also OIRA and PIRA Tables).
N/A	UK	1969	Alleged gun-running attempt	Eamonn Smullen, later to go with Official Sinn Féin, was arrested in 1969 after it was alleged that he had tried to incite a Huddersfield gun dealer to transfer arms.
Handguns (reportedly)	N/A	October1969	Successful, according to testimony by head of Irish Special Branch.	Arms said to have been smuggled through Dublin Airport with the aid of Jock Haughey, and handed over to IRA chief Cathal Goulding. It has been claimed that other shipments may also have been brought in at this period.

Table Three
Official IRA

War materiel: types and quantities	Origin	Date	Status	Comments
M-1 rifles Pistols	USA	1969	Possibly successful	Arms left over from the Border Campaign, supplied by George Harrison and smuggled to Ireland. Arms went to the element that was later to form the PIRA; some may have gone to the element that formed the OIRA.
70 x rifles 10 x Walther pistols 2 x machine guns 41,600 x rounds	USSR	1972	Unconfirmed	According to KGB files, arms were delivered by Moscow to the OIRA; the cache was said to have been left submerged in the sea for collection. OIRA chief Cathal Goulding denied receiving arms. There is no confirmation that the arms actually entered into service with the OIRA.
Seized in ship at Dublin port: 17 x rifles, including Armalites, Winchesters & Springfields 29,000 x rounds 60lbs gunpowder Seized in follow-up search in Toronto: 5 x Sten sub-machine guns 11 x handguns 10,000 x rounds	Canada	1973	Arms intercepted & seized (it is unclear if these arms were for the OIRA or the PIRA)	Gardaí seized arms in Dublin port on a ship that arrived from Canada. An Irish emigrant living in Canada was arrested after he flew into Dublin Airport. In a follow-up search, another cache of arms was found in a house at Scarborough, Toronto. There was a report that these arms were bound for the OIRA, but the PIRA cannot be ruled out as the intended recipient (see also PIRA Table).

Table Four

Covert arms procurement attempts that were to be funded with money which, a parliamentary inquiry found, was improperly diverted from an Irish state fund for the 'relief of distress' in Northern Ireland

War materiel: types and quantities	Origin	Date	Status	Comments
Types of arms under negotiation are believed to have included: Rifles Sub-machine guns Pistols Machine guns	UK	Nov 1969	Operation aborted	Jock Haughey and Belfast republican John Kelly tried to set up a deal in London with an arms dealer, suspected of being 'set-up' by British intelligence. No arms were delivered.
M-1 rifles Machine pistols Pistols Ammunition	USA	Dec 1969	Operation abandoned – may have been revived later	Republicans John Kelly and Sean Keenan set up an arms deal in New York with the help of local sympathisers. The deal was cancelled on instructions from Irish Army intelligence officer Captain James Kelly and Minister Neil Blaney. A source claimed that the deal was later revived and that arms were delivered to the IRA.
400 x sub-machine guns 25 x heavy machine guns c.400 x pistols c.250,000 x rounds of ammunition 40 x bulletproof vests	Austria/West Germany	1970	Operation aborted	A Dáil inquiry found that the arms were bought with funds improperly diverted from a fund for the relief of distress in Northern Ireland. All the defendants were acquitted. The transaction led to the famed Arms Trial (see also PIRA Table).

Table Five

Other miscellaneous arms procurement

War materiel: types and quantities	Origin	Date	Status	Comments
N/A	UK	1969	Alleged attempt to procure arms	Two Belfast men were held for six months in Brixton Prison, London, after being charged in connection with an alleged arms deal. It was claimed the men were trying to procure arms for a defence committee in the Short Strand area of Belfast. Charges were dropped and the men released.
Rifles Revolvers Bren guns Ammunition	UK	1970	Partly successful?	A number of men, including an arms dealer, were jailed in 1970–71 in London over this attempt to procure arms. Some arms were seized; evidence indicated that other arms got through to Belfast. The court heard the arms were for defence committees. There was no mention of an IRA connection in press reports of court proceedings.

Table Six

Provisional IRA

War materiel: types and quantities	Origin	Date	Status	Comments
60 x M-1 rifles/carbines Handguns Sub-machine guns 60,000 rounds of ammunition	USA	1969	Successful	Arms smuggled by the George Harrison network to the pre-split IRA. Most of these weapons probably ended up with the Provisionals; some may have gone to the OIRA.
Possibly more than 2,000 firearms, including Armalites, sub-machine guns, pistols, M-60 machine guns, and ammunition	USA	1970–79	Successful	The George Harrison network in the US was one of the main sources of arms for the IRA in the 1970s.
400 x sub-machine guns 25 x heavy machine guns c.400 x pistols c.250,000 rounds of ammunition 40 x bulletproof vests	Austria/ West Germany	1970	Unsuccessful	The deal that gave rise to the Arms Trial. Although Captain James Kelly bought these arms for the defence of Northern nationalists, rather than for the IRA, the emerging PIRA would almost certainly have taken them over had they been imported and sent to Northern Ireland. The arms never reached Ireland; only bulletproof vests were delivered.
N/A	USA	c.1970	Reportedly successful	A source claimed that an arms deal in New York originally negotiated by John Kelly and Sean Keenan (see above) subsequently bore fruit, and that arms were delivered to Ireland.
50 x revolvers	Spain	c.1970	Unconfirmed	Arms were donated to the IRA by the Basque group ETA, according to former IRA activist Maria McGuire, in her book To Take Arms.
20 x rifles	USA	c.1970	Successful	A Noraid activist and an arms dealer, both from Yonkers, were jailed in 1975 over this operation. A court in Manhattan heard that twenty rifles had been bought, twelve of which were later seized in Ireland.
N/A	Mexico/USA	Early 1970s	Alleged gun-running attempt	Five men, who became known as the Fort Worth Five, were jailed in Texas in 1972, after refusing to testify before a Grand Jury investigating an alleged attempt to run guns from Mexico, via New York, to Ireland. There is no evidence that the men were involved in any such operation.
360+ rifles, including: Armalites Lee-Enfields Springfields M-1 carbines 100,000+ rounds of ammunition	USA	1970–73	Successful	According to US authorities, these arms were smuggled to Northern Ireland by a group of IRA sympathisers in Philadelphia. About half the weapons were said to have been recovered in Northern Ireland. Two Noraid members were convicted on conspiracy charges.

War materiel: types and quantities	Origin	Date	Status	Comments
4.5 tons of small arms: 40 x carbines 20 x rifles 6 x machine pistols 9,680 x rounds 500 x fragmentation grenades 4 x anti-tank rocket launchers 200 x rocket-propelled grenades 520 x detonators	Czechoslo-vakia	1971	Arms intercepted	This operation was organised by senior IRA figure Daithí ÓConaill. The arms were bought from Omnipol in Czechoslovakia, and were seized at Schiphol Airport in the Netherlands. The operation had been infiltrated by British intelligence.
7 x rifles, including 3 x Armalites 37 x hand grenades Ammunition	USA	1971	Arms intercepted	The weapons were smuggled in six suit-cases from New York on the QE2, and found at Cobh. An arms dealer and a Noraid activist were charged.
11 x M-1 carbines 19 x Lee Enfield .303 rifles 4 x AR-180 Armalite rifles 22 x FN semi-automatic rifles	USA	1971–72	Unclear	An Irish activist and a Manhattan gun dealer were prosecuted by the BATF regarding the purchase of arms in New York. It is unclear if the arms were actu-ally delivered to Ireland.
Unknown quantity of RPG-7 rocket launchers Rockets for above	Libya	1972	Successful	Arms said to have been flown into Shan-non Airport by two mercenaries on board a small aircraft, and then smuggled out of the airport.
2 x rifles 3 x pistols 350 x rounds	USA	1972	Arms intercepted	Arms were found in a trunk at Heathrow Airport, London, en route to Ireland. San Francisco resident Charles Malone was later convicted. There was also a probe into an alleged arms conspiracy in Butte, Montana.
N/A	Czecho-slovakia	1972	Reported attempt at deal; unsuccessful	Arms dealer Gunther Leinhauser report-edly tried to buy arms for the IRA from Omnipol, Prague, but the firm refused to do business with him. It may have been part of a British intelligence 'sting' operation.
Seized in ship at Dublin port: 17 x rifles, including Armalites, Winchesters & Springfields 29,000 x rounds 60lbs gunpowder Seized in follow-up search in Toronto: 5 x Sten sub-machine guns 11 x handguns 10,000 x rounds	Canada	1973	Arms inter-cepted & seized	Gardaí seized arms in Dublin port on a ship that had arrived from Canada. An Irish emigrant living in Canada was arrested after he flew into Dublin Airport. In a follow-up search, another cache of arms was found in a house at Scarbor-ough, Toronto. There was a report that these arms might have been bound for the OIRA but, in light of the OIRA's ceasefire, the PIRA cannot be ruled out as the intended recipient.

War materiel: types and quantities	Origin	Date	Status	Comments
Five tonnes of arms: 247 x AKM rifles 243 x revolvers 24,000 x rounds 97 x anti-tank mines 500 x grenades 300kg gelignite 48lbs high explosive	Libya	1973	Arms intercepted	This arms cargo, being transported on the *Claudia*, was seized by the Irish Navy off the Waterford coast. Senior IRA figure Joe Cahill and others were arrested. British intelligence had been tipped off.
175 x Armalite rifles 20,000 x rounds	USA	1974	Some arms seized	A group known as the Baltimore Four were indicted after a cache of seventy rifles was seized in a truck. It is unclear what happened to the other weapons referred to in the indictment.
15 x FN rifles 1 x .50 machine gun barrel	Canada	1974	Arms intercepted	A number of men were jailed in Canada after these weapons were seized while being smuggled across the border into the US. One of those jailed was a Michigan Noraid activist.
Assault rifles Handguns Ammunition	USA	1974–76	Reportedly successful	Over a two-year period arms were smuggled to Ireland in coffins by Boston underworld figure Patrick Nee, according to an account in his book, *A Criminal and an Irishman*.
1,000 M-1 carbines Ammunition	Belgium	1976	Alleged attempt to procure weapons	A Sinn Féin man was jailed at the Old Bailey in 1977 after the court heard evidence from mercenary John Banks of an alleged attempt to procure arms, which were supposed to have been stored in Belgium. Banks denied defence allegations that he had acted as an agent provocateur. Two other men were also jailed.
218 firearms, including: Rifles Handguns	USA	1970s	Probably successful	These arms were bought from a gun shop in New Hampshire; a report of an investigation in 1975 indicated that a number of the weapons had turned up in Ireland.
29 x AK-47 rifles 29 x sub-machine guns 108 x hand grenades 11,000 x rounds of SLR ammunition 36kgs 9mm ammunition 7 x RPG-7 rocket launchers Mortars 1 x light machine gun Explosives: 168 x 1lb sticks of trinitrotoluene 264lbs TNT 428lbs plastic explosive	Lebanon	1977	Arms intercepted	These arms are believed to have been supplied by PLO elements in Lebanon. They were loaded in Cyprus and seized on board a ship in Antwerp. Seamus McCollum was later jailed by a Dublin court.

War materiel: types and quantities	Origin	Date	Status	Comments
6 x M-60 machine guns 50 x M-16 rifles?	USA	1977	Successful	The M-60s were stolen from the US armoury and acquired by George Harrison, and then smuggled to Ireland. It is likely that fifty M-16 rifles also acquired were also sent to Ireland.
Explosives and bomb-making equipment; details unavailable	South Africa	1978	Explosives intercepted	Materiel was found in baggage unloaded in Dublin port from a cargo ship that had sailed from Capetown.
150 x firearms, including: 2 x M-60 machine guns 15 x M-16 rifles M-14 rifles 1 x AK-47 60,000 x rounds	USA	1979	Arms intercepted	This major arms cargo was seized at Dublin port. It had been organised by the Harrison network.
350 x MAC-10 sub-machine guns 12 x AK-47 rifles	USA	1981	Unsuccessful	The FBI foiled this gunrunning attempt in a 'sting' operation. The accused men were acquitted, but it led to the break-up of the Harrison network.
N/A	Continental Europe	1982–83	Outcome unknown	According to Sean Callaghan in his book *The Informer*, an IRA group assembled a shipment of arms and explosives from Middle Eastern sources. This was stored near Milan, Italy, for transfer to Ireland. According to another writer, James Adams, in his book *The Financing of Terror*, an IRA arms-buying group that was operating on the Continent at this period was defrauded by arms dealers and failed to procure any arms.[1]
51 x rifles (including 25 x Armalite AR-15s, and HK91s) 55 x blasting caps Remote control devices	USA	1982	Arms intercepted	These arms were seized at Newark port, New Jersey, leading to the break-up of the gunrunning group headed by Gabriel Megahey.
5 x FIM-43 'Redeye' surface-to-air missiles	USA	1982	Unsuccessful	Gabriel Megahey and Gerry McGeough were jailed following this FBI 'sting' operation in New Orleans and New York.
Explosive material: 430 metres of detonating cord	France	1982	Intercepted (Unclear if destined for IRA or INLA)	A French republican sympathiser was arrested at Cherbourg port after detonating cord was found hidden in his car.
Reportedly explosives and sub-machine guns	USA	1983	Successful, according to a republican source	According to a republican source, this arms shipment, including explosives and sub-machine guns, was smuggled via France to Ireland. No independent confirmation is available.
25 x handguns 12,000 x rounds 2 x hand grenades 22lbs explosive 200 x detonators 500 yards detonator wire	Belgium?	1983	Arms intercepted	French authorities seized this cargo in a truck at Le Havre. The driver, Michael Christopher McDonald, was jailed. The arms may have come from a source in Belgium.

War materiel: types and quantities	Origin	Date	Status	Comments
Explosives	USA	1983	Unsuccessful	The FBI arrested an Irishman over an alleged attempt to buy explosives in Wyoming. It may have been related to the IRA, but there is no confirmation of this.
30 x rifles 25 x handguns 10 x blocks of C-4 explosive 2,500 x rounds of ammunition 15 x electrical detonators	USA	Earlier part of 1980s	Reportedly successful	Patrick Nee, the Boston underworld figure who figured in the *Valhalla* operation (*see* next entry below) told the author that another shipment of arms had got through to Ireland prior to the interception of the *Valhalla/Marita Ann* shipment. In his book, *A Criminal and an Irishman*, he gave details of the arms supplied, hidden in a vehicle shipped from Newark, New Jersey, to Ireland via Le Havre.
Unknown	USA	Early 1980s	Reportedly successful	Kevin Weeks, an associate of Boston crime boss James 'Whitey' Bolger, claims in his autobiography *Brutal* (written with Phyllis Karas), that he and Bulger were involved in procuring and smuggling consignments of arms to Ireland in the two years prior to the *Valhalla* shipment. It would appear that these were small consignments.
Seven tonnes of arms: 91 x rifles (mainly Armalites) 8 x sub-machine guns 13 x shotguns 51 x handguns hand grenades 70,000 x rounds 3 x heavy machine guns 1,000 x rounds (armour-piercing)	USA	1984	Arms intercepted	This arms cargo was assembled with the aid of people linked to Boston crime boss Whitey Bulger. Transported on the *Valhalla* and offloaded onto the trawler *Marita Ann*, it was seized by the Irish Navy off the County Kerry coast.
Reportedly: 50+ x G3 rifles 1 x MG3 machine gun 4 x sub-machine guns 2 x cannons	Norway	1984–86	Successful	These arms were stolen from the Norwegian Army in 1984, and possibly acquired by the IRA through a Belgian source. Some were seized by Irish authorities.
Firearms – details unavailable	USA	1985	Unsuccessful	The FBI foiled this attempt to buy arms in Colorado, and an Irishman was deported. It may have been related to the IRA, but there is no confirmation of this.
Sniper rifle – details unavailable	USA	1985	Weapon intercepted	This rifle was found beneath a panel in a cargo aircraft at Dublin Airport, following a flight from New York.
7 x revolvers 4 x pistols 550 x rounds 1 x Barrett M82 sniper rifle 200 x .50-calibre rounds	USA	1986	Arms intercepted	The Barrett sniper rifle and other guns were found in packages at a Dublin postal sorting office.

War materiel: types and quantities	Origin	Date	Status	Comments
40 x firearms, including: 13 x FN FAL rifles 1 x AK-47 rifle 70,000 rounds Also: 2 x hand grenades 4 x drums of nitrobenzene	Origin uncertain	1986	Arms seized	These arms were found in a container in Amsterdam. Two prominent IRA men, Brendan McFarlane and Gerry Kelly, were arrested.
100 x M-16 rifles 5,000 x rounds 1 x FIM-43 'Redeye' surface-to-air missile	USA	1986	Unsuccessful	This FBI 'sting' operation in Boston led to several men being jailed.
1200 x AKM rifles 130 x Webley revolvers 50 x 9mm pistols 390 x hand grenades 26 x DSHK heavy machine guns 40 x GPMG machine guns 33 x RPG-7 rocket launchers 130 x RPG-7 rockets 10 x SAM-7B surface-to-air missiles 10 x LPO-50 flame throwers 711 x electric detonators 493 x plain detonators 2658kg Semtex explosive	Libya	1986–87	Successful	Four shipments of arms provided by Libya were landed in County Wicklow by skipper Adrian Hopkins. These were the most significant deliveries of arms to the IRA during the period of the Troubles.
1,000 x AKM rifles 10 x 12.7mm heavy machine guns 9mm M-12 machine guns 600 x F-1 hand grenades 50 tonnes of ammunition RPG-7 rocket launchers RPG-7 rockets Mortars 20 x SAM-7 surface-to-air missiles 2,000kg Semtex explosive Detonators & fuses	Libya	1987	Arms intercepted	This was the final shipment of arms from Libya, seized by French customs aboard the *Eksund*.
Bomb-related technology and components	USA	c.1978–88	Successful	US defence scientist Richard C Johnson was alleged to have assisted the IRA in developing bomb techniques.
Improvised SAM systems	USA	1988–89	Unsuccessful	The FBI broke up this attempt to develop and transfer to Ireland improvised SAM (surface-to-air missile) systems.
50–100 x rifles, including Armalites and M-16s	USA	1988	Unsuccessful	The FBI foiled this plot to buy arms in Alabama for the IRA; two men were jailed.

War materiel: types and quantities	Origin	Date	Status	Comments
380 gallons of nitroben-zene, packed into 30 drums.	Netherlands	1988	Bomb mate-rial intercepted	Irish police seized this consignment of nitrobenzene, intended for making bombs, at Kells, County Meath. The truck driver was jailed.
.308 Ruger rifle	USA	1988	Weapon intercepted	This sniper rifle was intercepted at a Dublin postal sorting office. An Irish cus-toms officer was later jailed.
Radio transmitters related to bomb detonation	Netherlands	1988	Devices intercepted	This equipment was intercepted at a Dublin postal sorting office.
Bomb-making materiel: Quantity of sodium chlorate Mercury-tilt switches	France?	1989	Bomb mate-rial intercepted	Belfast man Leonard Hardy was arrested at Rosslare harbour coming off a ferry from France, in possession of this mate-riel. He was later jailed.
Barrett 'Light Fifty' sniping rifle	USA	1989	Possibly successful	FBI agents uncovered evidence that IRA man Martin Quigley may have sent a sniper rifle, apparently a Barrett 'Light Fifty', procured in the US in summer 1989, to Ireland.
Stinger surface-to-air missile Barrett sniper rifles	USA	1989–90	Unsuccessful	Kevin McKinley, Seamus Moley and Joe McColgan were jailed after this Florida-based attempt to procure a Stinger mis-sile. McKinley was also alleged to have sought Barrett sniper rifles.
Ireco detonators: 2,500 x electrical detonators 400 x fuse detonators	Tucson, Ari-zona, USA	1989–93	Mostly successful	Detonators procured in Tucson were smuggled to Ireland, via New York and Canada. Kevin McKinley, Seamus Moley and a third man were later jailed (see below).
140 x Detonators	USA	1993	Intercepted	A package containing these detonators was intercepted in the Irish Republic after being mailed from Yonkers, New York. They were believed to be part of a batch acquired in Tucson, Arizona (see above).
2 x Barrett 90 sniper rifles	USA	1995	Reportedly successful	These rifles were smuggled to Ireland, according to Toby Harnden in his book Bandit Country.
N/A	Estonia	1996	Alleged arms deal	According to allegations quoted in a Moscow newspaper, the IRA bought weapons from arms dealers in Estonia in early 1996.
3 x handguns 500 x rounds of ammunition	Florida, USA	1997	Intercepted	A Derry-born woman was sentenced to six months' house arrest after guns and ammunition were found at a Dublin postal sorting office.
Mainly handguns? 118 ordered; 86 purchased; 57 seized; 29 not found – presumed delivered to Ireland	Florida, USA	1999	Partly successful	Four Irish people were jailed following this operation. A leading figure in the operation was Belfast IRA man Conor Claxton. Some guns were seized; others got through.

War materiel: types and quantities	Origin	Date	Status	Comments
Ammunition for assault rifles	N/A	After 1998	Successful	The Independent Monitoring Commission (IMC) reported that the PSNI found, in 2004 in a PIRA arms dump, about 10,000 rounds of ammunition for assault rifles – ammunition that had been manufactured after the Good Friday Agreement of 1998. Police believed the bullets may have been part of a bigger arms consignment.
c.20 x AN-94 rifles Ammunition	Russia	2001	Alleged delivery	A quantity of rifles was bought by IRA men in Moscow, according to a report in the *Sunday Telegraph*. The report was denied by Sinn Féin leader Gerry Adams.

Table Seven
INLA and factions

War materiel: types and quantities	Origin	Date	Status	Comments
20 x rifles	USA	1977	Outcome Unknown	INLA chief Seamus Costello was believed to be trying to arrange shipping for a consignment of about twenty rifles from the US when he was shot dead.
A series of shipments, reportedly amounting to hundreds of firearms, including rifles, sub-machine guns and pistols, as well as ammunition, hand grenades and explosives	Lebanon/ Czecho-slovakia	1977 to mid-1980s	Successful	Arms were reportedly supplied by elements in the PLO, firstly from Lebanon and later from Prague[2] (details of some individual shipments are outlined below).
Estimated 60 x assault rifles, including: Ruger Mini-14 Garand M-1 Springfield M1A Mauser G98 Simonov	Australia	1977–82	Successful	An INLA sympathiser in Australia, an Irish-born immigrant, is believed to have sent these weapons to Ireland in three shipments as freight.[3]
c.12 x AK-47 rifles Soviet-made explosives	Lebanon	1978	Successful	These were reportedly smuggled to Ireland by INLA gunrunner Seamus Ruddy.[4]
AK-47 rifles 36 x hand grenades Explosives	Lebanon	1979	Intercepted	INLA gunrunner Seamus Ruddy and colleagues were arrested by Greek border police en route to Ireland.
250 x 7.62mm CZ automatic pistols	Lebanon?	1979–81	Successful	INLA sympathiser Bernard Jegat told police he stored guns at his home in Paris. The arms were being smuggled to Ireland.
20 x M-16 rifles	Belgium	1980	Probably successful	INLA sympathiser Bernard Jegat told police how he arranged a hiding place in Belgium for twenty rifles, to be delivered to Ireland. It is presumed the operation was successful.

War materiel: types and quantities	Origin	Date	Status	Comments
c.12 x rifles	USA	1981	Reportedly successful	Arms were reportedly smuggled through Dublin port by the late Gerard Steenson.[5]
20 x M-16 rifles	USA	1982	Unsuccessful	Two men from Northern Ireland were arrested in a 'sting' operation by the FBI PIRA Squad in New York, and later jailed.
Explosive material: 430 metres of detonating cord	France	1982	Intercepted (Unclear if destined for IRA or INLA)	As outlined in the Provisional IRA Table, a Frenchman was arrested at Cherbourg port for trying to smuggle detonating cord to Ireland.
10 x M-16 rifles 4,000+ x rounds	Australia	1983	Intercepted	The fourth shipment sent from Australia by an Irish immigrant and INLA sympathiser was seized in Dublin. The man was later arrested.
Gelsuirite explosives	France	1985	Successful	Explosives were reportedly supplied to the INLA by extremist group Action Directe, and then smuggled to London for an attempt to bomb Chelsea Barracks.
Consignment thought to consist of: Armalite rifles Handguns Ammunition	USA	c.1985	Reportedly successful	An arms consignment was delivered successfully to Ireland by Hollywood scriptwriter Bill Norton, according to a source (see below).
c.40 firearms, including: 12 x AR-15 rifles 24 x handguns 2 x machine guns 2,200 x rounds Silencers	USA	1986	Arms intercepted	This arms cargo was seized in a camper van at Le Havre. Bill Norton and others were arrested.
3 x rifles 2 x pistols 7 x hand grenades 2 x silencers	France	1986	Arms intercepted	Arms were seized when Harry 'Basher' Flynn was arrested in Paris with three others. It is presumed the arms were meant for transfer to Ireland. Details are unavailable as to the origin of the weapons, prior to their seizure in France.
4 x revolvers 500 x rounds	European continent	1989	Arms intercepted	Police in Antwerp, Belgium, seized this shipment. Two IPLO men were suspected of planning to smuggle the arms on a ship to Ireland.
8 x assault rifles Ammunition	France?	1990	Arms intercepted	Arms were found in a camper van which had arrived on a ferry from Roscoff by Irish customs officers. A Belfast man was jailed for six years.
Gelemex explosives Detonators	UK	1993	Unsuccessful	Two INLA men were arrested after attempting to steal explosives from a quarry near Wells, Somerset. The operation was blown by an MI5 informant within the INLA.
Semtex explosive	Czech Republic	1994	Reported procurement	The INLA reportedly procured Semtex in the Czech city of Pilsen, according to a report in *The Times*. An undercover German security operation failed to seize the Semtex.[6]

Table Eight
Real IRA (RIRA) and Continuity IRA (CIRA)

War materiel: types and quantities	Origin	Date	Status	Comments
RPG-18 anti-tank weapons RPG-22 anti-tank weapons AK-47 rifles CZ Model 25 sub-machine guns Ammunition TN500 military explosive (quantities unavailable)	Former Yugoslavia	c.1998–99	Successful	These arms are believed to have originated in Bosnia, to have been smuggled into Croatia and taken from there to Ireland, by the RIRA.
7 x RPG-18-type anti-tank weapons AK-47 rifles 20 x packs of TM500 explosive Detonating cord & equipment	Former Yugoslavia	2000	Arms seized	An arms cache was found by police in a warehouse at Dobranje, Croatia, believed destined for the RIRA. Local men were arrested but later cleared.
15 x rifles Pistols Ammunition 150 x hand grenades 9 x rocket launchers	Former Yugoslavia	2000	Arms intercepted (RIRA link unconfirmed)	This arms cache was seized by border police in Slovenia. There was speculation that it may have been bound for IRA dissidents.
N/A	Netherlands	2000	Reported unsuccessful attempt	A CIRA arms trafficker paid Dutch criminals in Amsterdam for a consignment of arms, ammunition and black-market cigarettes, but the shipment never arrived, according to a story in the *Sunday Times*.
War materiel requested included: 500 x handguns 200 x rocket propelled grenades 2,000 x detonators 5000kg plastic explosive	Gunrunners thought source was to be Iraq	2001	Unsuccessful – MI5 'sting'	Three RIRA members received long jail sentences in the UK after an MI5 'sting' operation. The RIRA men thought they were dealing with Iraqi representatives.
50 x grenades	Former Yugoslavia	2002	Grenades seized	Police found these grenades in a car at Trilj, north of Split, Croatia. They were believed destined for the RIRA. A local man was jailed.
Arms reportedly were to include: AK-47 assault rifles Sniper rifles Pistols Support equipment: Heavy machine guns Rocket launchers SAM-7 surface to air missiles	France	2006	Unsuccessful; MI5 'sting' operation?	Police in Northern Ireland arrested a number of individuals in June 2006. It was reported that the arrests followed an attempt by the RIRA to buy arms in France. A large sum of money was said to have been handed over. The indications were that this may have been an MI5 'sting' operation.

APPENDIX C: LOYALIST ARMS PROCUREMENT

(*See* Explanatory note, Appendix B.)

Table One

War materiel: types and quantities	Origin	Date	Outcome	Comments
Quantities of gelignite	UK	Late 1960s, early 1970s	Successful	It is believed that gelignite stolen from coal mines was smuggled into Northern Ireland in the early years of the Troubles for the use of the UVF in bomb attacks.
Rifles Sub-machine guns	UK (Scotland)	Early 1970s	Reportedly successful	According to media reports, Glasgow crime boss Arthur Thompson smuggled arms to the UDA in the early years of the Troubles.
20 x sticks of gelignite	UK (Scotland)	1973	Explosives seized	It is believed that explosives, found in a toilet cistern at a railway station in Stranraer, Scotland, were due to be smuggled on a ferry to Northern Ireland, and were most likely destined for the UVF.
50 x sticks of gelignite	UK (Scotland)	1973	Explosives seized	Police found this gelignite at a house in Ayrshire, Scotland. It was believed that the explosives were en route to the UVF.
Explosives	UK (Scotland)	1974	Explosives seized	UVF man William Fulton was arrested in Scotland with explosives in his car. It was presumed that the explosives were bound for Northern Ireland.
12 x firearms Detonators	Canada	1974	Arms intercepted	Arms and detonators smuggled by ship from Canada, destined for the UDA, were seized at Southampton. The find was significant because of the inclusion of detonators. It also exposed an arms pipeline from Canada, where explosives are widely used in mining.

War materiel: types and quantities	Origin	Date	Outcome	Comments
9 x M-1 carbines 13 x Sten sub-machine guns 66 x Sten gun ammunition clips 2,000 x rounds	Canada	1974	Arms seized	Two Canadian loyalists were arrested in Toronto and charged with conspiring to send arms to the UDA. The arms were seized in the aftermath of an arms haul in Southampton (see above).
30 x sticks of gelignite	UK (Scotland)	Late 1970s	Probably successful	During a court case in Glasgow in 1979, a miner told how he stole thirty sticks of gelignite from a coal pit in East Lothian for the UVF.
10 x assault rifles 1,000 x rounds	UK via Scotland	1979	Arms intercepted	This UDA arms consignment was seized by the RUC shortly after delivery to Belfast.
Rifles Handguns	UK (Scotland)	Early 1980s	Reportedly successful	Arthur Thompson Junior, son of Glasgow crime boss Arthur Thompson, assembled rifles and handguns and transferred them to the UDA, according to Reg McKay in his book *The Last Godfather*.
Bomb materiel: 63lbs of sodium chlorate	UK	1981	Intercepted	A man was arrested by police at Euston railway station, London, after a quantity of the weedkiller sodium chlorate was handed over to a Scottish loyalist. Police believed it was destined for the UVF for use in home-made explosives.
Uzi sub-machine guns	UK?	1983	Reportedly successful	A UVF source was quoted by Martin Dillon in his book *Stone Cold* as saying a number of Uzi sub-machine guns were provided by a mystery man who wanted three Middle-Eastern students killed.
Possibly hundreds of firearms, including: rifles, sub-machine guns, pistols and ammunition. Among types supplied were Colt Commando rifles, Ingram MAC-10 sub-machine guns and Smith & Wesson .357 Magnum revolvers.	Canada	1980–86	Successful	A group of Canada-based loyalists headed by Bill Taylor sent arms to the UVF, hidden in freight shipped via the UK over several years. Other operations by this group were unsuccessful (see below).
14 x M72 rocket launchers Shells for launchers	UK	1987	Arms seized	Two British Army corporals and two militaria dealers were jailed in the UK after a plot was uncovered to send anti-tank weapons, stolen from the British Army, to the UDA.

War materiel: types and quantities	Origin	Date	Outcome	Comments
206 x 7.62mm VZ58 rifles 94 x Browning 9mm pistols 536 X RDG grenades 4 x RPG-7 rocket launchers 62 x rocket-propelled grenades 30,000+ x rounds	Lebanon	1987	Successful	Arms were smuggled into Belfast docks in December 1987 for the UDA, UVF and UR. The cargo was landed successfully, but much of it was later seized by security forces. The shipment was arranged by a South African-linked arms dealer, but is believed to have been shipped from the harbour of Naquora, southern Lebanon.
320 x AKM rifles 53 x 9mm Makarov pistols 500 x hand grenades 14,000 x rounds for pistols 60,000 x rounds for rifles 2 tons of high explosive Thousands of detonators	Poland	1993	Arms intercepted	This arms consignment for the UVF was seized at Teeside, UK, after being shipped from a Polish port. Believed to be an MI5 'sting' operation, the arms came from the Polish state arsenal.
7 x handguns 240 x rounds	UK	1993	Arms intercepted	These arms were intercepted in Birmingham. A London-based UDA man was jailed.
Sub-machine guns Grenade launcher 2,000 x rounds	UK	1994	Arms intercepted	This shipment, believed bound for the UDA, was intercepted at the ferry.
Powergel explosive	UK	1994	Successful	A quantity of Powergel explosive is believed to have been smuggled by the UVF from 'mainland' UK into Northern Ireland.
1 x machine gun 1 x semi-automatic pistol Ammunition	UK	1995	Arms siezed	High-profile loyalist Lindsay Robb, a member of the political wing of the UVF, was jailed along with five others at Edinburgh on arms charges. Robb always protested his innocence.
Handguns Sub-machine guns	N/A	2004	Reportedly successful	According to a media report, the LVF imported a consignment of handguns and sub-machine guns. It was said that the guns were taken off a ship in Belfast harbour by a small fishing boat and then landed near Carrickfergus.
Handguns Other firearms Explosives	Former Yugoslavia	2004	Reported arms deal	According to a media report, LVF members did a deal with Croatian arms dealers for an arms consignment, at a meeting in Prague.

BIBLIOGRAPHY

Adams, James, *The Financing of Terror*, New English Library, London, 1988.

Adams, James, *The New Spies*, Pimlico, London, 1995.

Adams, James, *Trading in Death*, Hutchinson, London, 1990.

Alexander, Y & O'Day, A, *Terrorism in Ireland*, Croom Helm, Kent, UK, 1984.

Anderson, Brendan, *Joe Cahill*, O'Brien Press, Dublin, 2002.

Andrew, Christopher & Mitrokhin, V, *The Mitrokhin Archive*, Penguin, London, 2000.

Anonymous, *Fianna Fáil and the IRA Connection*, Dublin, 1970s.

Arnold, Bruce, *Haughey, His Life And Unlucky Deeds*, HarperCollins, London, 1994.

Barrett, JJ, *Martin Ferris, Man of Kerry*, Brandon, Dingle, County Kerry, 2005.

Barril, Paul, *Guerres secrètes à l'Élysée*, Albin Michel, Paris, 1996.

Barril, Paul, *Missions très spéciales*, Presses de la cité, Paris, 1984.

Beau, Jean-Michel, *L'Honneur d'un Gendarme*, Sand, France, 1989.

Bew, Paul & Gillespie, G, *Northern Ireland*, Gill & MacMillan, Dublin, 1993.

Bloch, J & Fitzgerald, P, *British Intelligence & Covert Action*, Brandon, Dingle, 1983.

Boland, Kevin, *Up Dev!*, Dublin.

Bowyer Bell, J, *The Secret Army, The IRA 1916–1979*, Poolbeg Press, Dublin 1979.

Brady, Seamus, *Arms and the Men*, Dublin, 1971.

Brogan, Patrick & Zarca, Albert, *Deadly Business*, Michael Joseph, London, 1984.

Clarke, Liam & Johnston, K., *Martin McGuinness*, Mainstream, Edinburgh, 2001.

Collins, Stephen, *The Power Game*, O'Brien Press, Dublin, 2001.

Collins, Tim, *Rules of Engagement, A Life in Conflict*, Headline, London, 2005.

Coogan, Tim Pat, *The IRA*, Pall Mall Press, London 1970.

Coogan, Tim Pat, *The Troubles*, Arrow Books, London, 1996.

Cusack, Jim & McDonald, Henry, *UVF*, Poolbeg, Dublin, 1997.

Davies, Nicholas, *Ten-Thirty-Three*, Mainstream, Edinburgh, 1999.

De Bréadún, Deaglán, *The Far Side of Revenge*, The Collins Press, Cork, 2001.

Derogy, Jacques & Pontaut, Jean-Marie, *Enquête sur trois secrets d'Etat*, Laffont, Paris, 1986.

Devine, TM, & McMillan, JF, *Celebrating Columba*, John Donald, Edinburgh, 1999.

Dillon, Martin, *25 Years of Terror*, Bantam, London 1999.

Dillon, Martin, *Stone Cold, The True Story of Michael Stone and the Milltown Massacre*, Hutchinson, London, 1992.

Dillon, Martin, *The Dirty War*, Arrow Books, London, 1991.

Dillon, Martin, *The Trigger Men*, Mainstream, Edinburgh, 2004.

Dillon, Martin, *Killer in Clowntown*, Arrow Books, London, 1992.

Dorrill, Stephen, *MI6*, Fourth Estate, London, 2000.

Dwyer, T Ryle, *Haughey's Forty Years of Controversy*, Mercier Press, Cork, 2005.

Dwyer, T Ryle, *Nice Fellow*, Mercier Press, Cork 2001.

Dwyer, T Ryle, *Short Fellow*, Marino Books, Dublin, 1999.

Ellis Owen, Arwell, *The Anglo-Irish Agreement*, University of Wales Press, Cardiff, 1994.

English, Richard, *Armed Struggle*, Pan Books, London, 2003.

Faligot, Roger, *Nous avons tué Mountbatten*, Jean Picollec, Paris, 1981.

Faulkner, Pádraig, *As I Saw It*, Wolfhound Press, Dublin 2005.

Fay, M, Morrissey, M & Smyth, M, *Northern Ireland's Troubles*, Pluto, London, 1999.

Flynn, S & Yeates, P, *Smack*, Gill and Macmillan, Dublin, 1985.

Geraghty, Tony, *The Irish War*, HarperCollins, London, 1998.

Harnden, Toby, *Bandit Country*, Hodder & Stoughton, London 1999.

Hennessey, Thomas, *Northern Ireland: The Origins of the Troubles*, Gill & Macmillan, Dublin, 2005.

Hogg, Ian, & Adam, Rob, *Jane's Guns Recognition Guide*, HarperCollins, Glasgow, 1996.

Hogg, Ian V, *Infantry Support Weapons*, Greenhill Books, London, 2002.

Holland, Jack, *The American Connection*, Poolbeg Press, Dublin, 1989.

Holland, Jack & McDonald, Henry, *INLA, Deadly Divisions*, Torc, Dublin, 1994.

Holland, Jack & Phoenix, Susan, *Phoenix, Policing The Shadows*, Coronet, London, 1997.

Insight Team, *Sunday Times, Ulster*, Penguin, UK, 1972.

Kelly, James, *Orders for the Captain?*, Dublin, 1971.

Kelly, James, *The Thimbleriggers*, James Kelly, Dublin, 1999.

Larkin, Paul, *A Very British Jihad*, Beyond the Pale, Belfast, 2004.

Lehr, Dick & O'Neill, Gerard, *Black Mass*, Public Affairs, Oxford, 2000.

Lister, David & Jordan, Hugh, *Mad Dog*, Mainstream, Edinburgh, 2003.

Loftus, John & McIntyre, Emily, *Valhalla's Wake*, Atlantic Monthly Press, New York, 1989.

McDonald, Henry & Cusack, Jim, *UDA*, Penguin, Dublin, 2004.

McGuire, Maria, *To Take Arms*, Macmillan, London 1973.

McKay, Reg, *The Last Godfather*, Black & White Publishing, Edinburgh, 2004.

Mac Stiofáin, Seán, *Memoirs of a Revolutionary*, Gordon Cremonesi, London, 1975.

Matera, Dary, *FBI's Ten Most Wanted*, HarperTorch, New York, 2003.

Ménage, Gilles, *L'Oeil du Pouvoir*, Fayard, Paris, 1999.

Mills, Michael, *Hurler on the Ditch*, Currach Press, Dublin, 2005.

Mockler, Anthony, *The New Mercenaries*, Sidgwick & Jackson, London, 1985.

Moloney, Ed, *A Secret History of the IRA*, Penguin Allen Lane, London, 2002.

Mooney, John, *Gangster*, Cutting Edge, Edinburgh, 2001.

Mooney, John & O'Toole, Michael, *Black Operations*, Maverick, County Meath, 2003.

Nee, Patrick, Farrell, Richard & Blythe, Michael, *A Criminal and an Irishman*, Steerforth Press, Hanover, New Hampshire, 2006.

O'Brien, Brendan, *The Long War*, O'Brien Press, Dublin, 1993.

O'Brien, Justin, *The Arms Trial*, Gill & Macmillan, Dublin, 2000.

O'Brien, Justin, *The Modern Prince*, Merlin, 2002.

O'Callaghan, Sean, *The Informer*, Corgi, London, 1999.

O'Clery, Conor, *Daring Diplomacy*, Roberts Rinehart, Colorado, 1997.

O'Donovan, Donal, *Dreamers of Dreams*, Kilbride Books, County Wicklow, 1984.

Ó Dochartaigh, Niall, *From Civil Rights to Armalites*, Palgrave Macmillan, UK, 2005.

O'Mahony, TP, *Jack Lynch*, Blackwater Press, Dublin, 1991.

O'Reilly, Dermot (Editor), *Accepting the Challenge, The Memoirs of Michael Flannery*, Cló Saoirse – Irish Freedom Press, Dublin, 2001.

Porch, Douglas, *The French Secret Services*, Oxford University Press, Oxford, 1997.

Robinson, Jeffrey, *The Sink*, Constable & Robinson, London, 2003.

Rowan, Brian, *The Armed Peace*, Mainstream, Edinburgh, 2004.

Seale, P & McConville, M, *The Hilton Assignment*, Fontana, London, 1974.

Sharrock, David & Devenport, Mark, *Man of War, Man of Peace*, Macmillan, 1997.

Smith, Steve, *3-2-1 Bomb Gone*, Sutton Publishing, Stroud, Gloucestershire, 2006.

Stephan, Enno, *Spies in Ireland*, Four Square, London, 1965.

Taylor, Peter, *Brits*, Bloomsbury, London, 2001.

Taylor, Peter, *Loyalists*, Bloomsbury, London, 2000.

Taylor, Peter, *Provos*, Bloomsbury, London, 1997.

Urban, Mark, *Big Boys' Rules*, Faber & Faber, London, 1992.

Walsh, Liz, *The Final Beat*, Gill & Macmillan, Dublin, 2001.

Weeks, Kevin & Karas, Phyllis, *Brutal, The Untold Story Of My Life Inside Whitey Bulger's Irish Mob*, Regan Books, New York, 2006.

West, Nigel, *The Secret War for the Falklands*, Little Brown, London 1997.

Williams, Paul, *Crime Lords*, Merlin, Dublin, 2003.

ENDNOTES

Introduction

1   Collusion was not universal. It would appear that the majority of the members of the Northern Ireland security forces did their duty according to the book, having regard to the large numbers of loyalist paramilitaries jailed for murder and other offences.
2   Robin Eames, *Chains to be Broken: A Personal Reflection on Northern Ireland and its People*, Blackstaff Press, Belfast, 1993, pp. 16–17; cited in Richard English, *Armed Struggle, A History of the IRA*, Pan Books, London, 2004, p.374.
3   Organisational Structure of the PIRA: The supreme authority of the IRA is the General Army Convention (GAC), which meets only rarely. According to the IRA Constitution, the GAC is to meet once every two years unless a majority deem it better for military reasons to postpone a meeting. Delegates to the GAC include IRA members selected by various units within the organisation, from Active Service Unit (ASU) upwards, as well as the members of the Army Council.

   One of the roles of the GAC is to select a twelve-member Army Executive. The Executive meets at least once every six months. One of the roles of the executive is to select the members of the seven-person Army Council. Members of the Council always include the chief of staff, the adjutant general and the quartermaster general. When the GAC is not in session, the Army Council is the supreme authority of the IRA.

   The General Headquarters (GHQ) Staff implements Army Council decisions, and acts as the link between the Council and the Northern and Southern commands. The Northern Command covers Northern Ireland as well as the Republic's border counties – Donegal, Leitrim, Cavan, Monaghan and Louth: a total of eleven counties. The Southern Command, which covers twenty-one counties, has a much smaller number of personnel, spread lightly around the Republic.

   The operational arm consisted of cells known as Active Service Units (ASUs). These usually consisted of five to eight members, although sometimes more. Occasionally, special teams were assembled by the Army Council/GHQ Staff for particular operations.
4   John Cooney, 'The Irish Republican Brotherhood in Scotland', in TM Devine and JF McMillan (editors), *Celebrating Columba, Irish-Scottish Connections 597–1997*, John Donald, Edinburgh, 1999.

Chapter 1: Saor Éire and the Haughey Connection

1   Liam Ó Ruairc, 'A Little Known Republican Military Group: Saor Éire', *The Blanket*, 13 January 2005.
2   Ken Whelan and Eugene Masterson, *Bertie Ahern, Taoiseach and Peacemaker*, Blackwater Press, Dublin, 1998, pp. 9–10.

3   Interview in Dublin, July 2004.

4   Peter Berry was a legendary secretary of the Department of Justice, one of the most powerful civil servants in the history of the State. He joined the Department in 1927, and the first justice minister he served, Kevin O'Higgins, was assassinated later that year. Berry, born in County Kerry, had a particular role in dealing with subversives, and was effective head of the State's security apparatus for thirty-six years. He had an encyclopaedic knowledge of individuals and groups that were considered a threat to state security. In the latter part of his career, he served as secretary of the Justice Department for ten years. He played a key role in thwarting the attempt to import arms in 1970, the affair that gave rise to the Arms Trial later that year. He was the State's chief witness in the trial, which resulted in Charles
and others being acquitted. By the time of his retirement he had notched up forty-four years of service in the Department. He died of a heart attack in 1978, aged sixty-nine.

5   Ó Ruairc, *op. cit.*

6   *Ibid.*

7   Walsh was given a paramilitary funeral in Dublin. As the cortege halted outside the GPO on O'Connell Street, an associate of Walsh's, the Dublin criminal Christy 'Bronco' Dunne, fired a shot in the air. He was arrested, but in February 1971 was acquitted in regard to the shooting incident. However, he assaulted District Justice Robert Ó hUadhaigh and got six months in Portlaoise Prison.

8   See the first episode of the four-part TV series *Haughey*, made by Mint Productions and broadcast on RTÉ 1, 13 June 2005.

9   On the setting up of the Free State, the Free State leader Michael Collins ordered arms to be sent covertly to Northern Ireland for the defence of Northern nationalists. The man who smuggled a consignment of Lee Enfield .303 rifles and ammunition across the border from County Donegal to County Tyrone, hidden in an oil tanker, was Sean Haughey. (See Tim Pat Coogan, *Michael Collins*, Arrow Books, London, 1991, pp. 350, 351. See also T Ryle Dwyer, *Short Fellow*, Marino Books, Dublin, 1995, pp. 13–14.) Ironically, the smuggling operation foreshadowed the gunrunning controversy that was to engulf his son Charlie about a half-century later. One source whom I interviewed believed that Sean Haughey's wife Sarah McWilliams assisted in this operation. She was a member of Cumann na mBan.

10 See Vincent Browne, 'The Good, the Bad and TV Psychobabble – Public Disservice Broadcasting', *Village* magazine, 17–23 June 2005.

11 See the story by Dick Walsh, 'Abortive London Arms Deal', *Irish Times*, 10 February 1971. This is quite an extraordinary account, clearly based on 'inside' information. Much of the detail of the visit by Jock Haughey and The Intermediary to London is based on this account.

Chapter 2: The Gun Dealer and the Arms Crisis

1   Albert Luykx had been living in Ireland since 1948. Born in 1917, he was a Flemish nationalist, a member of the Dutch-speaking community which opposed what it saw as the overlordship in Belgium of the French-speaking Walloon community. At the outbreak of the Second World War he was a member of a Flemish political party, the Flemish National Union (FNU). He has described himself as coming from a background that was strongly Catholic and anti-Communist. He was aged twenty-three and working in his father's sawmill when the Germans overran Belgium. Many Flemings were sympathetic to the Germans, looking to them to redress the wrongs which they felt they were suffering at the hands of

the French-speaking elite. Luykx was one of thousands sentenced to death in Belgium after the war for alleged collaboration with the Germans – a charge he always vehemently denied. Many of those accused of collaboration were Flemish.

In February 1971 Luykx issued a detailed statement refuting remarks made about him in the Dáil by Dr John O'Connell, a Labour Deputy. Luykx said he had objected to the excessively pro-German policies of the FNU, and was expelled in 1943. He said he helped many Belgians avoid being sent to Germany for forced labour by using the name of his father's sawmills to arrange work permits for them. His brother, a priest, was in the resistance, and asked him to assist a boy who had been arrested by the Belgian police in possession of a revolver and handed over to the Germans. He went to the Germans to plead for the boy, and worked out a deal whereby the boy signed a paper agreeing to work voluntarily in Germany, in return for the gun charges being dropped. However, after the war, the boy returned to Belgium and said Luykx had informed on him. Luykx was arrested as was his brother the priest, but the latter was released.

Luykx was given a death sentence, but it was not confirmed by the government and, after a successful appeal, it was commuted to twenty years in prison. In August 1948, after three-and-a-half years, he escaped from Beverloo detention camp and hid out in Antwerp. A priest brought him to the Netherlands, where he went into hiding. With the aid of another priest, he managed to get a Dutch passport under the fictitious name of Frans Faes. With the aid of that passport he made his way to Ireland in October 1948. He presented himself to the Aliens Office in Dublin Castle, told his story, and was granted a residency permit in the name of Albert A Luykx, alias Frans Faes. A stateless person, in 1954 he applied for Irish citizenship and was granted it. Four of his six children were born in Ireland, and all were educated and brought up in Ireland.

In July 1968 the Belgian authorities decided that the verdict against Luykx had expired, but he was still forbidden to enter Belgium. However, by 1970 this restriction had been lifted, and he was permitted to enter the country of his birth. This facilitated his travels on the Continent in connection with Captain Kelly's arms-buying operation, which included visits to Belgium.

2   In later years, former chief of staff of the Provisional IRA Seán Mac Stíofáin would tell an RTÉ interviewer that a unit of the IRA was standing by to take the guns if they came into Dublin port on 25 March 1970. 'Certainly, the IRA was going to take the guns for itself.' See Michael Mills, *Hurler on the Ditch*, Currach Press, Dublin, 2005, p.69. In his biography, *Memoirs of a Revolutionary*, Cremonisi, 1975, Mac Stíofáin tells a different story (p.140). He states that the weapons were meant not for the IRA, but for the Belfast Defence Committees, and gives the impression that he knew little about the proposed importation. According to Mac Stíofáin, early in 1970 they were informed that the arms would be arriving within weeks. He had no other information, except that the consignment 'would consist of various types of weapons suitable for defensive action ...'

3   The Irish Defence Forces' Intelligence Section was organised at this period on the basis of a Security Sub-Section headed by a lieutenant-colonel, with a commandant as staff officer; a Combat Intelligence Sub-Section, headed by a lieutenant-colonel; and a Press and Publicity Department, headed by a captain. Few details have ever emerged about the activities of the Security Section, which had the role of monitoring the activities of subversives. Among its least publicised roles, Army intelligence had the task of liaising with other intelligence/security agencies, including the US Central Intelligence Agency (CIA). In the mid-1990s I interviewed a former CIA man, Cleveland Cram, who was an expert on Irish affairs and who knew Colonel Hefferon well. Cram, who joined the agency in its early days in 1950, and who had studied Irish politics at Harvard, said that in the post-war years the then taoiseach,

Éamon de Valera, was willing to allow Army intelligence to liaise with the CIA, but did not want the agency to be based on Irish soil. The compromise, which some might say was typical of Dev's hair-splitting ingenuity, was that the CIA would liaise with Irish military intelligence from its London station. Cram, who had spent a couple of spells in London, recalled with pleasure his annual trips to Dublin up to the 1960s. He would stay in the Gresham Hotel, and then make his way to the Army intelligence building near the Phoenix Park for a meeting with the director. The last director of intelligence with whom he liaised was Colonel Hefferon. I got the impression that these were quite relaxed meetings. The main CIA focus at the time would have been on the Soviet Union, and in terms of Soviet communist subversion there would have been little of interest to the Americans occurring in the Ireland of that time. Dublin was not exactly the Casablanca of the espionage world – it was something of a backwater. Cram also had the role of liaising with MI5 and MI6. He died in January 1999, aged eighty-one.

4   Seán Mac Stíofáin, *Memoirs of a Revolutionary*, Gordon Cremonesi, London, 1975, p.147.
5   John Hunter, 'Death of the Englishman who led the Provisionals', *The Observer*, 20 May 2001.
6   Seán Mac Stíofáin, *op. cit.*, p.148.
7   Hunter, *op. cit.*
8   See book by the historian Thomas Hennessey, *Northern Ireland: The Origins of the Troubles*, Gill & Macmillan, Dublin, 2005.
9   See Captain Kelly's remarks at the PAC inquiry, as reported in the *Irish Times*, 11 February 1971.
10 Captain James Kelly, *The Thimbleriggers*, James Kelly, Dublin, 1999, pp. 21–24.
11 According to a former member of the pre-split IRA, whom I interviewed in 2006, the arms deal negotiated by Kelly and Keenan in New York was to bear fruit subsequently, and an arms consignment was delivered to Ireland. The source said that Kelly and Keenan would not necessarily have known about it at the time, but he was adamant that the arms came through. He said that there was fundraising in America to pay for the consignment.
12 The question arises – was British intelligence being kept informed of Irish Special Branch investigations into the attempt to procure arms, through its own mole in the Gardaí? It emerged in late 1972 that British intelligence had an important source in C3, the Garda Crime and Security Branch, when an MI6 agent and a Garda were arrested in Dublin. It is unclear when the collaboration between the two began. (See also Chapter 4.)
13 Seamus Brady, *Arms and the Men*, Dublin, 1971, p.126.
14 Berry Papers, *Magill*, June 1980.
15 *Nouvel Observateur*, 25 January 1996.
16 *This Week*, 8 May 1970.
17 Vincent Browne, The Arms Crisis 1970, *Magill*, May 1980.
18 TP O'Mahony, *Jack Lynch, A Biography*, Blackwater Press, Dublin, 1991, p.162.
19 Deaglán de Bréadún, 'Arms Crisis Guns May Have Ended Up In The Philippines', *Irish Times*, 2 January 2003.
20 Statement of Desmond O'Malley TD, 9 May 2001. Mr O'Malley was refuting claims made in a 'Prime Time' programme on RTÉ television about the editing of witness statements for the Arms Trial.
21 Pádraig Faulkner, *As I Saw It*, Wolfhound Press, Dublin, 2005, pp. 93–94.
22 Justin O'Brien, *The Arms Trial*, Gill & Macmillan, Dublin, 2000, p.211.
23 Tim Pat Coogan, *Michael Collins*, Arrow Books, London, 1991, p.247.
24 Deaglán de Bréadún, 'Row with Arms Dealer over State Monies Revealed', *Irish Times*, 2 January 2003.

25 John Cooney, 'Government Tries to Get Back £20,000 Used In 1970 Arms Deal', *Irish Times*, 26 May 1977.

26 De Bréadún, *op. cit.*

27 In retirement, Haughey once again became a major figure of controversy after it was revealed that he had received sizeable money payments from wealthy friends. In August 1997 the McCracken Tribunal published its report, and found it was 'quite unacceptable that a member of Dáil Éireann, and in particular a cabinet minister and taoiseach, should be supported in his personal lifestyle by gifts made to him personally'. Further investigations were carried out by the Moriarty Tribunal, adding to the controversy and the aura of scandal surrounding Haughey. On the other hand, there are many who worked closely with Haughey who have retained a positive attitude towards the man they called 'The Boss', preferring to remember his extraordinary ability as a minister, and his achievements in government. The former taoiseach always had the ability to inspire loyalty and affection among his supporters, as well as revulsion among his opponents.

Chapter 3: The IRA and the Harrison Network

1 Róisín McAliskey was held in custody for almost fifteen months in 1997–98 in the UK, in connection with a German extradition request over her alleged role in a mortar bomb attack on a British Army base at Osnabruck, Germany, in 1996. British home secretary Jack Straw decided to halt her extradition on health grounds. She was released, and the UK authorities decided not to pursue a prosecution against her due to lack of evidence.

2 George Harrison's friend and fellow US-based republican, Michael Flannery, a founder of Noraid, has recalled in his memoirs how he and his friends were hoping that the United States would keep its promise not to enter the Second World War. 'England did not stop trying by every means to enlist our [America's] aid as Hitler seemed to have the upper hand. Luck was in Britain's favour, as Japan raided Pearl Harbour. The result was that the United States did enter the war.' See Dermot O'Reilly (Editor), *Accepting the Challenge, The Memoirs of Michael Flannery*, Cló Saoirse – Irish Freedom Press, Dublin, 2001, p.124.

3 Sean Russell made an unexpected return to the newspaper headlines when mystery activists cut the head off his statue in Fairview Park, Dublin, in December 2004. Members of an unnamed 'anti-fascist' group claimed that they attacked the memorial to the former chief of staff of the IRA, erected in 1950, in protest over his 'collaboration' with the German Nazis during the Second World War. The group said in a statement: 'As Europe prepares to commemorate the liberation of the Auschwitz death camp sixty years ago, citizens of this State can no longer tolerate the shameful presence of a memorial to the Nazi collaborator Sean Russell in a public park in our nation's capital city.' The statement added: 'In order to atone for this obscenity at the heart of Dublin, Volunteers in defence of Irish democracy have acted to permanently remove this symbol of Republican treachery from the city's landscape.'

4 Ed Moloney, *A Secret History of the IRA*, Allen Lane, London, 2002, pp. 114–5.

5 Peter Taylor, *Provos*, Bloomsbury, London, 1997, p.108.

6 Jack Holland, *The American Connection*, Poolbeg Press, Dublin, 1989, pp. 85–86.

7 The year before Kingsmill, there was another massacre of Protestants. Republican gunmen, believed to be from the IRA, burst into Tullyvallen Orange Hall in South Armagh in September 1975, and opened fire. Five members of the Orange Lodge died. The victims were at prayer when they were attacked.

8   Robert Fisk, 'Counter-insurgency Forces' Previous Visits Recalled', *The Times*, 8 January 1976.
9   Joyce Wadler, 'Unbowed and Unashamed of his IRA Role', *New York Times*, 16 March 2000.
10 Bernard Weintraub, 'IRA Aid Unit in the Bronx Linked to Flow of Arms', *New York Times*, 16 December 1975. See also Patrick Nee, Richard Farrell & Michael Blythe, *A Criminal and an Irishman*, Steerforth Press, Hanover, New Hampshire, 2006, pp. 152–3.
11 In the Dáil the following day, 20 October 1971, justice minister Des O'Malley, taking into account the Cobh arms seizure, gave an outline of the arms that had been seized by the Gardaí from illegal organisations from August 1969 to date. The total figures were: sixteen machine guns, forty-nine rifles, fifty-six pistols, four shotguns, 23,265 rounds of ammunition, 559½lbs of gelignite, forty-nine grenades, 129 detonators and twenty coils of fuse. The minister went on to say: 'I think these figures are a great credit to the Garda Síochána because the amount of weapons, ammunition and explosives and so on that have been seized is very considerable by any standards and absolutely gives the lie to this line that is sold in Northern Ireland and sold to British newspapers and to British public opinion about our allegedly allowing the Twenty-six Counties to be used as a base or an armoury for the Six Counties.'
12 Gladstone and his wife also sought $4 million in compensation, and phone chats with President Reagan and animal-loving actress Doris Day. Other demands included a meeting with Governor Mario Cuomo and a range of TV stars. They finally settled for an emotional reunion with two of the dogs they used to own, and being allowed to pet them. The animals, including a husky called Brian, had been hastily borrowed from their new owners. News stories about the incident recalled Larry's previous IRA gunrunning conviction.
13 Michael McKinley, 'The International Dimensions of Terrorism in Ireland', in Y Alexander & A O'Day, *Terrorism in Ireland*, Croom Helm, Kent, UK, 1984, pp. 20–21.
14 Weintraub, *op. cit.*
15 Ellis Henican, 'The Truth About Harry', *Newsday*, 17 March 1999.
16 Fógraí Bháis – Harry Hillick, *An Phoblacht*, 10 November 2005.
17 *Newsweek*, 1 December 1975.
18 Ed Blanche, 'British Army and IRA Wage Hi-Tech War', *Associated Press*, 8 April 1984.
19 Niall O'Dowd, 'US Customs probe for IRA "undercover agent"', *Irish Press*, 10 August 1984.

Chapter 4: The Spooks and the Arms Deal in Prague

1   Maria McGuire, *To Take Arms*, Macmillan, London, 1973.
2   In Italy during the Second World War, Major Donald Gurrey served with the British Army Counter Intelligence Branch, known as GSI (b), at Allied Force Headquarters. Part of his role was to deal with German agents who crossed the lines into Allied-held territory, and also to track down 'stay-behind' agents equipped with radio transmitters. The British sought to 'turn' agents who had been captured, to get them to work against their former masters. Gurrey was operating against the German military intelligence service, the Abwehr, and also the Sicherheitsdienst, the intelligence service of the SS, whose agents were mounting sabotage operations. After the war, Gurrey joined MI6. After three years service in Berlin, he went on to serve in France (1949–50). At the height of the Cold War he was based in Warsaw (1954–57), before moving on to Singapore (1957–59). He served in the Dominican Republic in the Caribbean (1960–62) during a turbulent period in that country's history – the state's brutal dictator, Rafael Trujillo, was assassinated in 1961.

3 Maria McGuire, *op. cit.*
4 Nigel West, *The Secret War for the Falklands,* Little Brown, London, 1997, p.169.
5 Patrick Seale and Maureen McConville, *The Hilton Assignment*, Fontana, London, 1974.
6 Nigel West, *op. cit.,* p.169.
7 See story by Antony Terry, Mark Ottaway, *Sunday Times*, 24 October 1971.
8 Maria McGuire, *op. cit.,* p.75.
9 Maria McGuire, *op. cit.*
10 Seán Mac Stíofáin, *Memoirs of a Revolutionary*, Gordon Cremonesi, London, 1975, pp. 308–9.
11 Colin Smith, *Carlos, Portrait of a Terrorist*, Sphere Books Ltd., London, 1976.
12 Christopher Andrew & Vasili Mitrokhin, *The Mitrokhin Archive*, Penguin, London, 2000.
13 *Times*, 30 April 1981, p.7.
14 Sam Dowling came from a remarkable Dublin family. His brother, the late Jack Dowling, was a member of the IRA in the 1930s, but went on to join the Irish defence forces during the Second World War, known as the 'Emergency' in Ireland, rising to the rank of captain. Said Sam Dowling: 'Jack was in the IRA and he and others were going to be interned. They were given the option of joining the Free State Army or being interned, and some of them joined the Free State Army. He was one of them.' Jack became a prominent TV producer with the State broadcasting service RTÉ, and in the late 1960s was at the centre of a controversy over the running of the station. He and two other producers, Lelia Doolan and Bob Quinn, resigned from RTÉ, alleging that commercial considerations were influencing some progammes, especially the consumer show *Home Truths*, of which Dowling was producer.
15 'Training the IRA', *This Week*, 10 February 1972.
16 Michael McKinley, Dimensions of The International Terrorism in Ireland, in Y Alexander & A O'Day, *Terrorism in Ireland*, Croom Helm, Kent, UK, 1984, pp. 20–21.
17 Seán Mac Stíofáin, *op. cit.*, p.355.
18 *The Times*, 21 April 1975.
19 *The Times*, 1 April 1974.
20 *The Times*, 15 December 1977.

Chapter 5: The Infiltration of the *Claudia* Operation

1 Nigel West, *The Secret War for the Falklands*, Little Brown, London, 1997, p.160.
2 As indicated in the notes for Chapter 4, a book with this title was written about the affair. See Patrick Seale and Maureen McConville, *The Hilton Assignment*, Fontana, London, 1974.
3 Seale & McConville, *Ibid.*
4 *Observer*, 17 June 1973.
5 British television news report on ITN, News at Ten, 29 November 1973.
6 *Observer*, 17 June 1973.
7 Brendan Anderson, *Joe Cahill, A Life In the IRA* , O'Brien Press, Dublin, 2002, p.271.
8 James Adams, *Trading in Death*, Hutchinson, London, 1990, pp. 13–14.
9 Anderson, *op. cit.*, Chapter 11.
10 *Ibid.*, Chapter 11.
11 Sean O'Callaghan, *The Informer*, Corgi, London, 1999, Chapter 5.
12 'West German was middleman in IRA arms deal', *The Times*, 3 April 1973.
13 Anderson, *op. cit.*,Chapter 11.
14 *Ibid.*

15 *Irish Independent,* 5 April 1973.

16 Adams, *op. cit.,* pp. 14–15.

17 Lorna Siggins, 'A priceless vessel sails into history', *Irish Times*, 3 March 2001.

18 Other details of materiel seized on the *Claudia*:
    Rifles:
        7.62 AKM rifles
        with folding butt: 198
        with timber butt: 49
        Total: 247
    Rifle-related equipment:
        Bayonets & scabbards: 246
        Magazines: 850
    Rifle accessories:
        Pouches, magazines: 200
        Rifle covers (canvas): 200
        Slings: 200
        Oil cans: 200
    Revolvers:
        Smith & Wesson revolvers
        .38 long barrel: 162
        .38 short barrel: 21
        Webley Mk 4 .38: 52
        Colt Police Special .38: 6
        Enfield .38: 2
        Total: 243
    Explosive materiel:
        Primers: 20
        Cordtex 500 ft coils: 2
        Safety fuse No 11 Mk 2 coils: 35
        Igniter safety fuse percussion: 20
    Mines:
        TM46 anti-tank mines: 97

19 See article headlined, 'Minister Never Knew Extent of Libya Weapons Consignments', *Irish Independent*, 2 January 2004.

20 West, *op. cit.,* pp. 175–6.

21 In retirement, Donald Gurrey wrote a book about his wartime experiences in Italy as a British Army counter-intelligence officer. *Across the Lines, Axis Intelligence and Sabotage Operations, 1943–1945* was published in 1994 by Parapress, Tunbridge Wells. Gurrey lived in Dorking, Surrey, and died in his eighty-sixth year, in October 2005.

22 Divall's airline received a baptism of fire in the strife-torn Congo of the early 1960s. In Divall's own words, he was 'involved behind the scenes' in the Congo during the secession of Katanga. With the aid of finance provided by certain individuals in the major Belgian mining concern Union Miniere, Divall was delivering arms originating in Belgium to the forces of Moise Tshombe, who became President of the mineral-rich breakaway state. The secession had led to civil war in the Congo with Tshombe recruiting mercenaries to bolster up his forces in the fighting against UN troops, which included an Irish contingent.
    Divall's next known adventure was in the Biafran conflict of the late 1960s, flying 'anything that had to be carried' into the breakaway state that was locked in a bloody civil war

with federal Nigerian forces. Divall flew both arms and relief supplies into the embattled enclave, that had been set up by the Ibo people who considered they had been persecuted and discriminated against by the federal authorities in Lagos. The relief supplies were flown in at the behest of various Catholic missionaries and relief organisations. Divall was not supposed to carry military supplies on these particular flights but, unknown to the missionaries and relief workers involved, the Biafrans would get him to use any spare capacity to ferry in war materiel as well. Divall recalled coming into contact at this period with the Irish Holy Ghost Fathers, who were very close to the Ibos, and who founded Africa Concern to help the famine victims in Biafra. (The organisation was the forerunner of today's non-denominational developing world relief group, Concern.) Divall recalled meeting the late Father Michael Doheny, the deeply dedicated Holy Ghost Father active in Africa Concern, who was working on the famine relief effort at the time. He flew supplies for another Catholic missionary, Father Peters. Divall was operating two Constellations at the time. One of his regular runs was from Libreville, Gabon, into the Biafran airstrip at Uli.

Biafra collapsed, but Divall nevertheless was to find that his gunrunning skills remained in high demand in other conflicts in sub-Saharan Africa during the 1970s. In the early years of the decade his air transport company, which operated a couple of Dakotas based in Kampala, Uganda, was flying relief supplies on behalf of the Rome-based Verona Fathers to a camp for Sudanese civil war refugees in northern Uganda. Divall admitted to me that, unknown to the Verona Fathers, he was also running guns during these flights at the behest of the high-ranking army officer (later to be President) Idi Amin, whom he got to know personally. Amin belonged to the Kakwa tribe, whose people inhabited not only Uganda but southern Sudan as well. Amin thus had sympathy with the south Sudanese insurgents who were at loggerheads with the Arab-dominated regime in Khartoum. Divall told me how on the flights north to the refugee camp he would make a 'detour' or 'get lost along the way' and land secretly at a Ugandan military air base at Gula where the army had a big arms dump. He would take military supplies on board and then 'stray' across the border into Sudan where he would land at a clandestine bush air strip operated by the German-born mercenary Rolf Steiner.

The Angolan conflict of the mid-1970s provided Divall with another lucrative market for his gunrunning skills. He was operating another small air transport company, which was registered in the Caribbean island of Grenada. He ran guns on behalf of the CIA to the Unita rebels, who were fighting the new MPLA government which had taken power following the departure of the Portuguese. Divall told me how he would pick up arms in different places for transfer to Unita. One location was Rundu, situated in the Caprivi Strip in northern Namibia. Another location was Grootfontein, further south in Namibia. Other arms consignments came via the Zambian capital Lusaka, or Kinshasa in Zaire. Divall said they would run the weapons into Angola using jungle strips where they could land without being shot down. Divall had flown planes himself in operations prior to Angola, but did not do so during his involvement with Unita, which lasted from 1975 up to March 1976.

23 See article in *The Guardian*, 28 October 1976.
24 See biography of arms dealer Sam Cummings: Patrick Brogan and Albert Zarca, *Deadly Business*, Michael Joseph, London, 1984, Chapter 19; also, Seymour Hersh, 'The Qaddafi Connection', *New York Times*, 14 June 1981.
25 See Joe Humphreys, 'IRA Aimed for "Full Strength" Assault on Loyalists', *Irish Times*, 29 December 2005.
26 Brogan and Zarca, *op. cit.*, p.107.

Chapter 6: The Liverpudlian, the Greek Cypriots and Arms from Lebanon

1   See article by Niall Kiely, 'IRA guns: how they closed the Cyprus route', *Hibernia*, July 1978.
2   See Tim Pat Coogan, *The IRA*, Pall Mall, London, 1970, pp. 282–3; also, J Bowyer Bell, *The Secret Army*, Sphere, London, 1970, pp. 333–4.
3   Author's interview with Rauf Denktash, 1995.
4   Interview with Dr Garret FitzGerald, cited in Alexander, Y & O'Day, A, *Terrorism in Ireland*, Croom Helm, Kent, UK, 1984.
5   James Adams, *The Financing of Terror*, New English Library, London, 1988, p.182.
6   Gilles Ménage, *L'Oeil de Pouvoir, Les affaires de l'Etat, 1981–1986*, Fayard, Paris, 1999, Chapter 6.
7   Ménage, *op. cit.*
8   Capitaine Barril, *Missions très spéciales*, Presses de la Cité, Paris, 1984, Annexe 1.
9   Denis Staunton, 'Stasi's IRA files suggest CIA link', *Irish Times*, 29 June 1996.
10 *Ibid.*
11 Jim Cusack, 'Powerful US sniping rifle used in IRA killings', *Irish Times*, 25 November 1992.

Chapter 7: The FBI Man and the Mayo Gunrunner

1   While US customs undoubtedly deserved the respect accorded to the service by Lou Stephens, it has been alleged (*see* Chapter 8) that there was a leak of information from an individual in customs to the IRA following an arms seizure at Newark port in 1982.
2   Ed Moloney, *A Secret History of the IRA*, Penguin Allen Lane, London 2002, Appendix 5.
3   Robbie Mac Gabhann, *Volunteer Eamonn O'Doherty*, An Phoblacht, 11 November 1999.
4   Moloney, *op. cit.*, p.16.
5   Conor O'Clery, *Daring Diplomacy*, Roberts Rinehart, Colorado, USA, 1997, p.177.
6   Attorney Michael Kennedy represented Michael Flannery; Frank Durkan was George Harrison's attorney; William Mogulescu and Lawrence Vogelman defended Thomas Falvey; while Daniel Gormley was represented by David Lewis. Attorney David Kirby represented the prosecution.
7   Trancript of Flannery trial, quoted in Dermot O'Reilly (Editor), *Accepting the Challenge, The Memoirs of Michael Flannery*, Cló Saoirse – Irish Freedom Press, Dublin, 2001.

Chapter 8: A Quest for Missiles

1   Martin Dillon, *25 Years of Terror, The IRA's War against the British*, Bantam Books, 1994, Chapter 13.
2   See United States Court of Appeals for the Second Circuit, Nos. 83-1313, 83-1315, 83-1317, 83-1318; 743 F.2d 59; 1984.
3   *Ibid.*
4   CBS News, 'Before Your Eyes: Don't Take My Daddy', 24 August 1998.
5   United States Court of Appeal, Second Circuit; Nos 416, 417, Dockets 83-1287, 83-1294; Argued, 16 Nov 1983; Decided, 14 Feb 1984.
6   Ed Moloney, *A Secret History of the IRA*, Penguin Allen Lane, London, 2002, pp. 313–4.
7   Carol Coulter, 'Barrett believes immigration will be key issue', *Irish Times*, 7 June 2004.

8   Kevin Cullen, 'Man vows US return despite forced repatriation to Ireland', *Boston Globe*, 1 May 1994.
9   FBI Law Enforcement Bulletin, 1987.

Chapter 9: The Curse of the *Valhalla*

1   According to the authorised biography of the County Kerry republican Martin Ferris, the rendezvous point was 178 miles west of the Blaskets, at a point 52□30' north and 14□10' west. See JJ Barrett, *Martin Ferris, Man of Kerry*, Brandon, Dingle, County Kerry, 2005, p.138.
2   Peter Gelzinis, 'Running with Whitey the Rat; Ex-crony's Shocking Tales of Betrayal', *Boston Herald*, 13 February 2005.
3   Patrick Nee, Richard Farrell & Michael Blythe, *A Criminal and an Irishman*, Steerforth Press, Hanover, New Hampshire, 2006, p.152.
4   Nee, *op. cit.*, p.145.
5   *Ibid.*
6   Nee, *op. cit.*, pp. 157-160.
7   Kevin Weeks & Phyllis Karas, *Brutal, The Untold Story Of My Life Inside Whitey Bulger's Irish Mob*, Regan Books, New Yorik, 2006, pp. 114–5.
8   See Civil Action court papers, in US District Court, District of Massachusetts, Estate of John L McIntyre v United States of America and others (including James Bulger and Stephen Flemmi), filed 8 March 2001, Paragraph 251.
9   Jeffrey Robinson, *The Sink*, Constable & Robinson, London, 2003, p.109.
10 Nee, *op. cit.*, p.183.
11 United States v Joseph P Murray Jr, Robert Andersen Jr, and Patrick Nee, aka Patrick Mullen; Criminal No 86-118-T. Statement of Facts in Support of Guilty Pleas to Information no 1 (Arms Offenses.) Submitted by US Attorney Frank L. McNamara Junior and Assistant US Attorney, Gary Crossen to United States District Court, District of Massachusetts.
12 John Loftus & Emily McIntyre, *Valhalla's Wake, The IRA, MI6, and the Assassination of a Young American*, The Atlantic Monthly Press, New York, 1989, p.52.
13 Civil Action court papers, in US District Court, District of Massachusetts, Estate of John L McIntyre v United States of America and others (including James Bulger and Stephen Flemmi), filed 8 March 2001.
14 *Ibid.*
15 Elizabeth W Crowley, 'Mob Victim's Family Upset; Might Sue Government', *The Patriot Ledger*, 17 January 2000.
16 Shelly Murphy, 'FBI role in man's slaying probed', *Boston Globe*, 11 October 1999.
17 Sean O'Callaghan, *The Informer*, Corgi, London, 1999, Chapter 15.
18 Kevin Cullen, 'Bulger hurt IRA effort, sources say; "Whitey" allegedly sank gunrunning bid', *Boston Globe*, 14 June 1997.
19 Nee, *op. cit.*, pp. 205–7.
20 One of Steve Flemmi's victims was twenty-six-year-old Deborah Hussey, daughter of a long-time girlfriend, Marion Hussey. Deborah's remains were found alongside those of John McIntyre's. Flemmi told investigators that he was angry when Marion threw him out of their home, after finding out that he had molested Deborah when she was a teenager. Flemmi said he took Deborah shopping 'for a new coat', but brought her to a house in South Boston where Whitey Bulger strangled her, in early 1985. According to testimony that would later be given in court by Kevin Weeks, Flemmi believed that Deborah was still alive after being strangled by Bulger so he (Flemmi) wrapped a rope around her neck and twisted it with the

aid of a stick to finish her off. Flemmi then pulled her teeth out with a pliers in case her body might be identified.

Flemmi admitted he had another woman, Debra Davis, killed because she was about to leave him for another man. The mobster feared that she knew too much about his criminal activities and the fact that he was an FBI informant. Flemmi told the authorities he lured Debra (twenty-six) to a location in South Boston in late 1981, where Bulger strangled her. Flemmi picked up a further life sentence in late 2004 for his role in yet another murder, that of businessman Roger Wheeler, who was shot dead in 1981 in Tulsa.

21 Stephen Flemmi was giving evidence in the legal case taken by the family of John McIntyre against the federal government and the FBI which opened at the US District Court in Boston in June 2006. The family were seeking $50 million in damages.

22 Weeks & Karas, *op. cit.*, pp. 157–8.

23 See Minority Staff of the Permanent Subcommittee on Investigations, United States Senate, *Report on Correspondent Banking, Case History No. 8, Swiss American Bank, Swiss American National Bank*, 5 February 2001.

24 John Fitzgerald had used a complex web of banking transactions to 'launder' the money. The report by Minority Staff of the Permanent Subcommittee on Investigations, United States Senate, *Report on Correspondent Banking, Case History No. 8, Swiss American Bank, Swiss American National Bank*, 5 February 2001, found that he started by setting up a company registered in the Caribbean island of St Lucia. The corporation was called Halcyon Days Investments Ltd, and Fitzgerald opened an account in that company's name at the Canadian Imperial Bank of Commerce in St Lucia. Between January and March 1985, Fitzgerald and other members of the drug organisation deposited $3 million into the account. In May 1985, the account was closed and all of the funds (in excess of $3 million) were transferred to a bank in the Cayman Islands through a cheque issued to the bank. The total in the account subsequently grew to $5 million. In the autumn of 1985, the $5 million in funds were wire-transferred through a series of other accounts and finally on to the SAB and SANB. The funds grew to $7 million.

Fitzgerald was ultimately arrested. He was indicted in May 1993 for racketeering, conspiracy and money laundering. The following August he pleaded guilty to the charges. As part of his arrangement with the US authorities, he forfeited all of the proceeds of illicit activities that had been salted away in the accounts at SAB and SANB. Then everything began to get even more complicated. Fitzgerald died before the US government could get its hands on the money, for which a forfeiture order was issued. Talks between US officials and the Antiguan authorities dragged on for two years. Finally, in November 1995, an Antiguan official informed the US that nearly one year before, about $5 million of the Fitzgerald funds had been transferred from the Swiss Antiguan Bank Group to the Antiguan government. The money had been used to pay 'pending debts' and was thus no longer available. The remaining $2 million had been retained by the bank. It was unclear whether the funds were retained as a set-off against outstanding Antiguan loans or whether they were retained to cover expenses incurred by the bank.

The US State Department sent a senior official, Jon Winer, to Antigua to see if he could collect the cash. Winer was, at the time, deputy assistant secretary for international law enforcement affairs. He was told by the Antiguan government that records of the relevant bank accounts were not available because they had been destroyed in a hurricane.

25 Nee, *op. cit.*, p.5.

26 JJ Barrett, *Martin Ferris, Man of Kerry*, Brandon, Dingle, County Kerry, 2005, Chapter 9.

27 Interview with the author, early 1980s. Billy McKee, one of the founders of the Provisional IRA, led a thirty-two-day hunger strike at Crumlin Road prison, Belfast, in 1972. The strike

resulted in the authorities giving special category status to paramilitary prisoners. Concessions included prisoners being allowed to wear their own clothes, and being housed in a separate wing, away from 'ordinary' criminals.

28 Brian Rohan, 'Twelve Years On, An Informer's Sting Endures: Sean O'Callaghan's Release Revisits Pain on a Boston Family', *Irish Voice*, 18 February 1997.

29 John Loftus & Emily McIntyre, *Valhalla's Wake, The IRA, MI6, and the Assassination of a Young American*, The Atlantic Monthly Press, New York, 1989.

Chapter 10: The *Eksund* and the Spy in the Sky

1 It has been suggested that the French received a tip-off about the Libyan gunrunning operation from the Americans. According to a working paper 'Intimate Relations' (p.6) by Charles Grant, published by the London-based Centre for European Reform, British and French intelligence agencies sometimes worked very closely together. This was a tradition which, according to some, stretched back to the Second World War, when the British Special Operations Executive supported the French Resistance. The report states: 'In the 1980s, the French services helped the British to intercept boats that were running Libyan guns to the IRA – even though the initial tip-off had come from the Americans.'

2 *Libération*, 27 November 1987.

3 Gabriel Cleary, from Friarstown in Tallaght, County Dublin, was one of a number of men arrested at an underground IRA bomb factory at Clonaslee, County Laois, in 1996. He was jailed for twenty years at the Special Criminal Court in Dublin in February 1998.

Chapter 11: High-Tech Operators of the IRA

1 United States Court of Appeal for the First Circuit, US v Richard Clark Johnson, No. 90-2010; US v Martin Quigley, No. 90-2011; US v Christina Leigh Reid, No. 90-2012.

2 Elizabeth Neuffer, 'Little-known Espionage Law Cloaks Wiretaps in Secrecy', *Boston Globe*, 23 July 1989.

3 Seán Mac Stíofáin, *Memoirs of a Revolutionary*, Gordon Cremonesi, London, 1975, pp. 301–2.

4 Toby Harnden, *'Bandit Country'*, Hodder & Stoughton, London 1999, p.256.

5 'Canadian spy agency helped in arrests of IRA suspects', *Toronto Star*, 19 January 1990.

6 In a document, No. CR 92-587-TUC-JMR, presented to the US District Court, District of Arizona, the prosecution claimed that detonators of the name brand and type purchased in Tucson were recovered in Northern Ireland, England and the Republic of Ireland in the period 1991–93. The document stated: 'January 1991 was the first time that these brand and type of detonators had been used by the IRA in Northern Ireland.' Starting in February 1992, detonators of this type began to be recovered in IRA devices in England. According to the document, in March 1992 officials in the Irish Republic discovered a weapons cache that contained eighteen detonators, as well as other munitions and weapons – six were fuse detonators and twelve were electric detonators. On August 25 1993, a package containing 140 electric detonators was recovered in the Republic of Ireland. The package had been mailed on July 29 1993, from Yonkers, New York.

7 Sean O'Driscoll, 'Clinton Accused of Meddling In IRA Gunrunning Case', *Irish Voice*, 13 January 2004.

Chapter 12: Arms and the INLA

1 Capitaine Barril, *Guerres secrètes à l'Élysée*, Presses de la Cité, Paris, 1984, p.177.
2 Jack Holland & Henry McDonald, *INLA, Deadly Divisions*, Torc, Dublin, 1994, p.130.
3 See statement made by Bernard Jegat to Jean-Marc Fay, Commissaire de Police, and Jean-Patrick Borgniet, Inspecteur Principal, Police Judiciaire officers based in Paris, 22 January 1985. Statement reproduced in Appendices to Gilles Ménage, *L'Oeil de Pouvoir, Les Affaires de l'Etat*, Fayard, Paris, 1999, pp. 843–4.
4 Holland & McDonald, *op. cit.*, p.144.
5 *Ibid.*, p.253.
6 *Ibid.*, p.112.
7 Interview, *Starry Plough*, June/July 1982.
8 Holland & McDonald, *op. cit.*, pp. 195, 210.
9 *Ibid.*, p.130
10 *Ibid.*
11 Barril, *op. cit.*, p.157.
12 Pierre Goldman, *Souvenirs obscurs d'un juif polonais né en France,* Seuil, Paris, 1975.
13 Gilles Ménage, *L'Oeil de Pouvoir, Les Affaires de l'Etat*, Fayard, Paris, 1999, pp. 622–3.
14 *Ibid.*, p.626.
15 *Ibid.*, p.643. See also Jacques Derogy & Jean-Marie Pontaut, *Enquête sur trois secrets d'Etat*, Laffont, Paris, 1986, p.65, and Capitaine Barril, *Missions très spéciales*, Presses de la Cité, Paris, 1984, p.177.
16 Barril, *op. cit.*, p.178.
17 *Ibid*, p.177.
18 *Ibid*, pp. 177–8.
19 Ménage, *op. cit.*, p.643.
20 Holland & McDonald, *op. cit.,* Chapter 11.
21 *Ibid.*
22 'A worldwide web of terrorism', *The Times*, 8 January 2001.
23 Statement by Bernard Jegat to the Police Judiciare, 16 January 1984, reproduced in Gilles Ménage, *L'Oeil de Pouvoir, Les affaires de l'Etat, 1981–1986*, Fayard, Paris, 1999, p.835.
24 Mary Reid was married for a time to Cathal Óg Goulding, son of Cathal Goulding who was chief of staff of the Official IRA. She returned to live in Ireland in 1987. She later became a college lecturer in Derry, and was found dead on a beach at Inishowen, County Donegal, on 29 January 2003.
25 See: 'Note de Régis Debray au president de la Republique apres sa recontre avec Bernard Jegat le 19 avril 1984', reproduced in Ménage, *op. cit.*, pp. 828–9.
26 Stewart Tendler, 'French Link In Chelsea Bombing', *The Times*, 26 Nov 1986.
27 When I visited the fair you could buy guns and ammunition there of almost any vintage or calibre, together with almost every conceivable type of accessory. There was everything to be had – ranging from collector's items dating back to the US Civil War to the latest version of the latest assault rifle; from the tiniest hand gun to the most sophisticated anti-terrorist rapid-fire weapon; from crude 'Saturday Night Specials' to heavy machine guns. Apart from guns there were all kinds of other items of interest to the Rambo type, the survivalist, the mercenary, the big game hunter and to those who simply fantasised about being any or all of these things. It would be wrong to give the impression that this was an all-male affair. Many of the gun buffs had brought wives or girlfriends along, and some of the stalls had women working behind the counters.

Traders came from all over America to the gun show. Most were probably small-time operatives who ran gun shops in their home towns. Some of these traders had a very definite right-wing aura about them, like the trader who put up the sign 'Genuine Reloaders Only – No Wimps'. Some big international arms dealers, who also happened to be in the retail business, were represented also – Mike Kokin's Sherwood International had a large stall selling, among other things, military surplus that had been bought from Israel. Kokin was one of those dealers who would buy war materiel captured by Israel on the battlefield.

When I visited the fair, feelings were running high among the gun buffs. State legislators in California and federal legislators in Washington were engaged in one of their periodic attempts to tighten controls on the importation and sale of deadly weapons. These anti-gun moves had brought the lobbyists, the campaigners and the protestors out in force at the Pomona gun show. Members of such groups as the National Rifle Association, the Second Amendment Foundation and the Gun Owners Action Committee were giving out leaflets and canvassing support for their particular point of view.

Maybe the heightened atmosphere of protest, the feeling that gun buffs were being got at, led to my run-in with one particular trader. He was a dealer in heavy machine guns from Kentucky, a man with a lot of anger simmering inside. He became suspicious when I showed an undue curiosity in his wares. He quizzed me as to who I was and where I came from. And when I told him I was a journalist, I could almost physically feel the anger welling up inside him. He told me he suspected I was one of those 'liberal, cock-suckin' commies' who were trying to bring in gun control and to interfere with the rights of people like himself. He said guys like me ran the risk of getting 'beat up' in the car park. The gun trader had some burly friends hanging around his stall who looked like they might well be prepared to help out in this regard. To cut a long story short, I did some quick talking and managed to placate him. When I had calmed him down, he began talking to me in a rather more reasonable way. He emphasised that people like himself were very law-abiding, and should not be the target of gun control law reforms just because a few nuts used guns to massacre innocent people. The Kentucky arms trader sought to convey that gun traders and people who attended events like the Pomona gun fair were good, law-abiding citizens – pillars of society.

28 Holland & McDonald, *op. cit.*, p.251.
29 Jack Holland & Susan Phoenix, *Phoenix, Policing the Shadow, The Secret War Against Terrorism in Northern Ireland*, Coronet Books, London, 1997, p.178.
30 Ian Cobain & Allan Hall, 'A Spy in the INLA', *The Times*, 8 January 2001.
31 John Mooney, *Gangster*, Cutting Edge, Edinburgh, 2001, pp. 73–74.

Chapter 13: Loyalist Bombers and Gunrunners

1 Nevertheless, suspicions persisted in some quarters that individual RUC, UDR or British Army members might have been involved. While hard evidence may be lacking in this regard, suspicions persisted in 2005, due partly to the witholding by the British Government of some information from the inquiry on security grounds. In his report, Judge Barron remarked: 'Correspondence with the Northern Ireland Office undoubtedly produced some useful information; but its value was reduced by the reluctance to make original documents available and the refusal to supply other information on security grounds. While the Inquiry fully understands the position taken by the British Government on these matters, it must be said that the scope of this report is limited as a result.'

Following another inquiry into pre-1974 incidents, which included bomb attacks in Dublin in 1972 and 1973, Judge Barron reported that he had received no co-operation from the British Government, sparking off much criticism of the British stance on the matter. Sean Ardagh TD, Chairman of the Joint Committee on Justice, Equality, Defence and Women's Rights, said in February 2005: 'They [the British Government] have a moral responsibility as well as a responsibility to justice to co-operate with us. We will continue in every way to pursue them and continue to attack their position.' However, in February 2006, there were indications that the British authorities may be willing to co-operate with inquiries into the Dublin and Monaghan bombings. The sole member of a commission investigating the bombings, the prominent Irish barrister Patrick McEntee SC, informed the Irish Government that a number of entities indicated a willingness to meet with the commission to discuss certain matters relevant to its terms of reference.

2   Martin Dillon, *The Trigger men*, Mainstream, Edinburgh, 2004, p.117.

3   Jim Cusack & Henry McDonald, *UVF*, Poolbeg, Dublin, 1997, pp. 195–6.

4   Captain James Kelly, *The Thimbleriggers, The Dublin Arms Trials of 1970*, James Kelly, Dublin, 1999, p.14. According to Captain Kelly, another reason for cancelling the sale of the arms was the consideration that they should be held in reserve in case it became necessary 'to distribute them to a defenceless minority in Northern Ireland at some future date'.

5   The murders were claimed by the Ulster Freedom Fighters, who said the two were killed in retaliation for the murder by the IRA of a 'retarded boy'. This was apparently a reference to the abduction and murder by members of the Official IRA of a sixteen-year-old Protestant, David Walker, who was found shot dead in the Lower Falls area on 21 June 1973.

6   See Reg McKay and David Leslie, 'Arthur Sold Weapons to Terrorists and Passed Info Back to Spy Masters', *News of the World*, 15 June 2003; also Reg McKay, 'The Last Godfather: Big Tex: The MI5 Informant and UDA Gun-Runner', *Daily Record*, 3 November 2004.

7   Reg McKay, *The Last Godfather, The Life and Times of Arthur Thompson*, Black and White Publishing, Edinburgh, 2004, Chapter 10.

8   Cusack & McDonald, *op. cit.*, p.211.

9   Martin Dillon, *Stone Cold, The True Story of Michael Stone and the Milltown Massacre*, Hutchinson, London, 1992, p.68.

10 Judge Peter Cory comments in his report *Cory Collusion Inquiry – Patrick Finucane*, 1 April 2004: 'There is every reason to believe that Nelson would have been aware of the plot to murder Patrick Finucane and that he may have had some involvement in it. I note that William Stobie, an SB [Special Branch] agent, told a journalist that Nelson was present at a meeting where the details of the assassination were discussed.'

11 'Brian Nelson's visit to Durban', *Belfast Telegraph*, 15 April 1996.

12 *Ibid.*

13 The Tara loyalist paramilitary group was founded in 1966 by William McGrath, and promoted a quasi-religious, anti-Catholic ideology. McGrath, a homosexual, was housemaster of Kincora Boys Home in Belfast. In the early 1980s, he and two other staff members at the home were convicted of gross indecency against boys in their care.

14 See Cusack & McDonald, *op. cit.*; also Peter Taylor, *Loyalists*, Bloomsbury, London, 2000.

15 Naquora is situated in what used to be the Israeli-controlled area (ICA) during the period when part of South Lebanon was occupied by Israeli troops, supported by a local militia, the South Lebanon Army (SLA). It was widely believed that Naquora harbour was used for smuggling operations that had received the blessing of the SLA, which maintained a fortified base just beside the port. According to some reports that appeared in Arabic-language publications in Beirut, Israeli-supplied war materiel was covertly shipped from Naquora to a harbour further up the coast for the forces of General Michel Aoun during the period of the Lebanese civil war. Aoun, a Christian soldier-politician, headed one of two rival

governments in Lebanon from 1988 to 1990, and during that period his army engaged in grim artillery duels with Syrian forces in Beirut.

16 The rifles were described in media reports as AK-47s, but were almost certainly CZ58 weapons. These look externally like AK-47s, but are quite distinct, having a different internal operating system.

17 Jack Holland & Susan Phoenix, *Phoenix, Policing the Shadows, The Secret War Against Terrorism in Northern Ireland*, Coronet Books, London, 1997, p.237.

18 Lindsay Robb, who received a ten-year sentence, maintained his innocence and launched an unsuccessful appeal. In 1997 he was transferred to Maghaberry Prison in Northern Ireland, later joining the wing occupied by members of the hard-line Loyalist Volunteer Force (LVF), which had broken away from the UVF. In January 1999, he became the first LVF prisoner to be freed under the terms of the Good Friday Agreement. He had served just four years of his ten-year term. He returned to live in Scotland, and in January 2006 was stabbed to death as he sat in his Ford Fiesta car in a busy street in the Ruchazie area in the east end of Glasgow.

19 David Lister & Hugh Jordan, *Mad Dog*, Mainstream, Edinburgh, 2003, pp. 221–2.

20 Vincent Kearney, 'Adair "tried to buy arms" ahead of bloody Belfast loyalist feud', *Sunday Times*, 17 September 2000.

21 'Cops Missed LVF Arms', *Sunday Life*, 18 April 2004.

22 Stephen Breen, 'LVF arms deal with Croats "secured"', *Sunday Life*, 26 September 2004.

Chapter 14: The Real IRA Looks East

1 One of the six men jailed in connection with the Stamullen training camp at the Special Criminal Court in May 2001 was Martin Conlon. The thirty-one-year-old man, from Railway Street, Armagh, was in charge of the training session, and he got four years. He was released in 2004 and in November the following year he was murdered. Conlon was confronted by two masked, armed men at a friend's flat in Armagh, incapacitated with a stun gun and driven away in his own Volkswagen Passat car. About a half-hour later, he was dumped by the side of the road, dying from gunshot wounds to the head. Although the killing had all the hallmarks of a paramilitary murder, no organisation claimed responsibility. In the immediate aftermath, there was a mystery as to the motives behind the murder. There was speculation about an internal paramilitary dispute, and speculation also that he might have been killed because of some aspect of his private life.

2 Toby Harnden and Patrick Bishop, *Daily Telegraph*, 'Former munitions chief confirmed head of Real IRA', *Vancouver Sun*, 19 August 1998.

3 Thomas Harding, 'Real IRA leader is finally brought to justice after three decades of terror', *Daily Telegraph*, 7 August 2003.

4 Maeve Sheehan, 'IRA Dissidents Lose £50,000 in Arms Swindle', *Sunday Times*, 24 December 2000.

5 In July 2005 the sentences were reduced by two years following an appeal.

Chapter 15: A Farewell to Arms

1 While serving as first secretary at the British Embassy in Tehran in 1987, Edward Chaplin was abducted and beaten by Revolutionary Guards and held for twenty-four hours, apparently in retaliation for the arrest in Manchester of an Iranian diplomat for alleged shoplifting. He went on to head the Middle East and North Africa Department of the Foreign and

Commonwealth Office, and in April 2004 was appointed UK Ambassador to Iraq, the first British envoy in Iraq since the 1991 Gulf War.

2   James Adams, 'Libyans Name 20 of the IRA's Top Terrorists', *Sunday Times*, 21 June 1992.

3   General John de Chastelain had a distinguished career in the military and in the diplomatic service, and an interesting, cosmopolitan family background. He served as Canada's chief of the defence staff and as Canadian ambassador to the USA. He was born a British subject in 1937, in Romania. His father, Alfred Gardyne de Chastelain, a Scottish oil engineer, was working at the time in Bucharest for British Petroleum. His mother, Marion Elizabeth (Walsh) de Chastelain, was American. During the Second World War, both parents worked 'underground' for the British. De Chastelain senior was a member of the Special Operations Executive, which was involved in sabotage and subversion behind enemy lines. He was held prisoner for a period in Romania by the pro-Axis regime. Marion de Chastelain worked in New York for Sir William Stephenson, a Canadian with the codename 'Intrepid' who ran British intelligence operations in the city. One of her roles was to control a woman agent called Cynthia who infiltrated the pro-Vichy French Embassy in Washington. The intelligence background of General de Chastelain's parents was a matter of public record, and apparently caused no difficulties between the General and the IRA in the decommissioning process.

4   This belief has caused difficulty for Sinn Féin spokespersons in public debate in recent years. There are IRA actions which have caused particular embarrassment to the movement – including the murder of Detective Garda Jerry McCabe, who was shot dead in an unprovoked attack during an IRA robbery attempt at Adare, County Limerick, in 1996. A number of IRA men were jailed for manslaughter following the murder. Yet, because the robbery was sanctioned by the IRA, Republicans cannot condemn such a killing as a crime. The compromise is to say it was 'wrong'. Likewise, the abduction and murder in 1972 of mother of ten Jean McConville, after she reportedly comforted a dying British soldier, is not condemned as a crime, because it was sanctioned by the IRA. Again, the more neutral term 'wrong' is used. Republicans were able to condemn as a crime the murder of Robert McCartney at a Belfast pub in January 2005. Although it was generally acknowledged that the victim was beaten and stabbed to death by members of the IRA after he tried to take to safety a friend who had been seriously injured in an attack by republicans, the murder was not officially sanctioned by the IRA. Thus, it was not just 'wrong', but also a 'crime'.

5   Cal McCrystal, 'The Vale of Tears', *The Independent*, 6 October 1991.

6   Tim Collins, *Rules of Engagement, A Life in Conflict*, Headline, London, 2005, p.81.

7   Judge Morris in his 2004 report of the Tribunal of Inquiry, dealing with explosives 'finds' in Donegal, commented: 'It made little sense for a terrorist organisation to place munitions into the farm outbuildings of an "unsympathetic" farmer who might discover them in the ordinary course of his or her business. It also made sense for them to place their hides away from the public gaze so that their operatives could come and go as they pleased without the obvious danger of detection. A hide by the side of a main road would not make much sense, in that context. In remote areas there would usually be some 'sympathiser' in the vicinity of a hide to note, and report, unusual activity. This was not invariably the case. Useful evidence on the activities of the "Provisional IRA" was given by Chief Superintendent Tom Monahan. He dealt in particular detail with the use made by the "Provisional IRA" of transit hides, which were short-term places for the storing of munitions.

'As to the kind of places that might be used, he said: "It would be some place that would be convenient probably to a roadway, it would be dry, it would be secure but it would still be off the beaten path as such. And some place again that would be under some level of control by the IRA or some of their people. And it would be a very short-term situation with a bomb made up maybe. It may be in a vehicle that would be parked in a shed or it may be in a beer keg, or prior to that you had milk churns, which were very commonly used back in the seventies and eighties, and you might have a number of these made up with the explosives material all *in situ*, ready to be primed and a timing device attached to it. So they would be very short-term hides. If the materials hadn't been mixed it would be a long-term hide, in my view. If they were mixed and ready for priming, with a timing device and a detonator, that would be a transit hide. The actual mixing of the home-made explosives (HME) took some time and it took space because of the quantities involved. You would have to mix it almost akin to mixing cement with a shovel or else using a small cement mixer to get the ingredients properly mixed. So if they weren't put together, if the homemade explosive wasn't mixed with either fuel oil, which is the ammonium nitrate fuel oil ingredient, or with sugar, or with nitrobenzene, there were three or four ingredients that were utilised by the IRA. If they weren't in some container to be used to convey the bomb, it was normal they'd be either in a vehicle or in a beer keg, a creamery can or something of that nature. Sometimes very large bombs were found to fill a whole tractor-trailer maybe of four or five drums, oil drums maybe. But if they weren't, if the HME wasn't made up and contained in some container like that then it would take some considerable time to get that process ready."'

8   David Bamber, 'IRA Rearms With Russian Special Forces Super-Rifle', *Sunday Telegraph*, 21 April 2002.
9   In light of the very large stocks of ammunition supplied by Libya to the IRA, much of which survived in arms dumps, it is difficult to understand why these additional stocks of ammunition, manufactured after the 1998 Good Friday Agreement, were smuggled into Northern Ireland.
10 Jonathan McCambridge, 'IMC briefed about Provos' deadly cache', *Belfast Telegraph*, 10 October 2005.
11 John O'Farrell, 'Profile: Reverend Harold Good', *Slugger O'Toole* website, 3 October 2005.

Epilogue

1   M Fay, M Morrissey & M Smyth, *Northern Ireland's Trouble – The Human Costs*, Pluto, London, 1999.
2   Fintan O'Toole, 'IRA must face up to the grotesque reality', *Irish Times*, 16 April 1999.
3   *Ibid.*
4   In October 2004, the IRA admitted that it had killed a fifteen-year-old boy, Bernard Teggart, almost thirty years before, and apologised for the incident. The boy, who was said to have a mental age of eight, was abducted in 1973 by the IRA from the De La Salle Brothers' Training Centre in West Belfast, where he was a resident. He was later found with his hands and feet bound and with gunshot wounds to his head. A piece of paper with the word 'tout' was pinned to his chest. It was alleged that the boy had witnessed IRA men hijacking a beer lorry, and had blurted out: 'I'm going to tell on youse.' Two men were later arrested in connection with the hijack. There is no indication that the boy had actually informed on the men. The boy's father, Daniel Teggart (forty-four), had been shot dead by the British Army two years before, on the night that internment without trial was introduced in Northern Ireland.
5   John McClory (seventeen) and Brian McKinney (twenty-two) were abducted and killed in 1978, and their bodies secretly buried, after it was alleged they stole IRA weapons to carry out a robbery.

6   High profile examples include English-born businessmen Jeffrey Agate and James Nicholson, killed in Northern Ireland in 1977 during an IRA lurch to the left – apparently because they were members of the 'employer class'; Reverend Robert Bradford, a Methodist minister and Unionist MP, shot dead in 1981; Edgar Graham, a Unionist Party activist and university lecturer, shot dead in 1983; and Ian Gow, a Conservative MP killed in a booby trap bomb attack in 1990.
7   O'Toole, *op. cit.*

Appendix A: Estimates of arms held by paramilitary groups in Ireland

1   The security forces' estimates were first published in *Magill* magazine, June 1998. See also Sean Boyne, 'Decommissioning signals end of Provisional IRA's armed struggle', *Jane's Intelligence Review*, 1 November 2005.
2   Steve Smith, *3-2-1 Bomb Gone*, Sutton Publishing, Stroud, Gloucestershire, 2006, p.148.
3   Smith, *Ibid.*, pp. 132–3.
4   Tony Geraghty, *The Irish War*, HarperCollins, London, 2000, p.197.

Appendix B: Republican/Nationalist Arms Procurement

1   James Adams, *The Financing of Terror*, New English Library, London, 1988, p.182.
2   See Jack Holland & Henry McDonald, *INLA, Deadly Divisions*, Torc, Dublin, 1994.
3   *Ibid.*
4   *Ibid.*
5   *Ibid.*
6   Ian Cobain & Allan Hall, 'A Spy in the INLA', *The Times*, 8 January 2001.

INDEX

Ulster Defence Association (UDA), 282, 352-5,
  357-60, 364-9, 374-5, 377-8, 371, 377, 395,
  415, 427, 441-3
Ulster Defence Regiment (UDR), 15, 21, 148,
  352, 355, 418-9
Ulster Democratic Party, 358
Ulster Freedom Fighters (UFF), 462
Ulster Political Research Group (UPRG), 415
Ulster Resistance (IR), 365, 367, 369-71, 377,
  395, 427
Ulster Unionist Party, 317, 397, 399, 403-4
Ulster Volunteer Force, 25, 135, 228, 352-6,
  360-3, 365, 369, 372-9, 395, 415, 427,
  441-3
Ulster Workers' Council, 282
UOP, Polish security service, 373

Valhalla, the, 236, 239-53, 256-67
Vincennes Three, 178, 331-2, 336
Vuletic, Josip, 385

Wallace, Agnes Jane, 324
Waller, judge, 359
Walsh, Liam, 30, 33, 38, 61-2
Watt, Albert, 362
Webster, judge, 192-3
Weeks, Kevin, 240, 243, 258-62,
Weis, judge, 106-7
Westmacott, capt Herbert Richard, 224
Weston, Galen, 94
Whelan, Donal (Duck), 154
White, Harry, 28
White, Jeffrey, 110
White, John, 358
Williams, Tom, 147
Wilson, Ed, 157, 167
Wilson, North Carolina, 113, 118
Wilson, sen Paddy, 358
Winslow, chief inspector, 126
Winslow ('John White'), John, 191, 196, 198,
  225
Winter, Howard (Howie), 259
Winterbottom, Lord, 159
Wolfe Tone Society, 123
Woodvale Defence Association (WDA), 357
Workers Party, 122, 133-4, 136-7, 326
Wright, Billy, 376

Yugoslavia, 24, 145, 380